Professional ASP.NET 3.5 AJAX

Professional
ASP.NET 3.5 AJAX

Professional

ASP.NET 3.5 AJAX

Bill Evjen
Matt Gibbs
Dan Wahlin
Dave Reed

WILEY

Wiley Publishing, Inc.

Professional ASP.NET 3.5 AJAX

Published by
Wiley Publishing, Inc.
10475 Crosspoint Boulevard
Indianapolis, IN 46256
www.wiley.com

Copyright © 2009 by Wiley Publishing, Inc., Indianapolis, Indiana

Published simultaneously in Canada

ISBN: 978-0-470-39217-1

Manufactured in the United States of America

10 9 8 7 6 5 4 3 2 1

Library of Congress Cataloging-in-Publication Data is available from the publisher.

For general information on our other products and services please contact our Customer Care Department within the United States at (877) 762-2974, outside the United States at (317) 572-3993 or fax (317) 572-4002.

Wiley also publishes its books in a variety of electronic formats. Some content that appears in print may not be available in electronic books.

To my lovely wife, Tuija.
— Bill Evjen

I dedicate this book to my family for their continued support. They've witnessed demos of features still under development and my time away from home to work on and support the platform. Heather, Josh, Kelley, and Adam know more than they probably want to know about Web development.
— Matt Gibbs

I'd like to thank my wife, Heedy, and two boys, Danny and Jeffery, for their patience, love, and support while I was working on this book.
— Dan Wahlin

Dedicated to my dear daughter, Sky, who never ceases to amaze me.
— Dave Reed

About the Authors

Bill Evjen is an active proponent of .NET technologies and community-based learning initiatives for .NET. He has been actively involved with .NET since the first bits were released in 2000. In the same year, Bill founded the St. Louis .NET User Group (www.stlnet.org), one of the world's first such groups. Bill is also the founder and former executive director of the International .NET Association (www.ineta.org), which represents more than 500,000 members worldwide.

Based in St. Louis, Missouri, Bill is an acclaimed author and speaker on ASP.NET and XML Web services. He has authored or coauthored more than 15 books including *Professional ASP.NET 3.5, Professional C# 2008, Professional VB 2008, ASP.NET Professional Secrets, XML Web Services for ASP.NET,* and *Web Services Enhancements: Understanding the WSE for Enterprise Applications* (all published by Wiley). In addition to writing, Bill is a speaker at numerous conferences, including DevConnections, VSLive, and TechEd. Along with these items, Bill works closely with Microsoft as a Microsoft regional director and an MVP.

Bill is Global Head of Platform Architecture for Lipper (www.lipperweb.com), a wholly owned subsidiary of Thomson Reuters, the international news and financial services company. He graduated from Western Washington University in Bellingham, Washington, with a Russian language degree. When he isn't tinkering on the computer, he can usually be found at his summer house in Toivakka, Finland. You can reach Bill at evjen@yahoo.com.

Matt Gibbs is currently the group manager of the .NET Development Platform team in Shanghai. Matt has been working on Microsoft development technologies since joining the IIS 4 team to work on "classic" ASP in 1997. He has coauthored several books on ASP and ASP.NET and enjoys traveling to meet new people and share information on development.

Dan Wahlin (Microsoft Most Valuable Professional for Connected Systems) is a .NET development instructor and architecture consultant at Interface Technical Training (www.interfacett.com). Dan founded the XML for ASP.NET Developers Web site (www.xmlforasp.net), which focuses on using ASP.NET, Silverlight, AJAX, and XML Web services in Microsoft's .NET platform. He's also on the INETA Speaker's Bureau and speaks at several conferences. Dan has authored/coauthored numerous books over the years on .NET technologies with his latest being *Professional ASP.NET 3.5 AJAX* and *Professional Silverlight 2 for ASP.NET Developers*. Dan also writes for several online technical newsletters, blogs at http://weblogs.asp.net/dwahlin, and updates what he's up to from time to time at www.twitter.com/danwahlin. When he's not working with technology, he enjoys sports and writing and recording music to relax a little: http://weblogs.asp.net/dwahlin/archive/tags/Music/default.aspx.

Dave Reed is a developer on the ASP.NET team, and has worked on ASP.NET AJAX since the first beta version in 2006. Before that, Dave was a senior web developer for a banking technology company for four years, and worked on large, highly dynamic ASP.NET Web sites. He has a bachelor's degree in computer science from California State University, Northridge. Dave is a speaker at the occasional Microsoft conference, such as the insiders summit. Dave has always been passionate about programming and considers it a hobby as well as a career. He maintains a popular blog on advanced .NET and ASP.NET topics at http://weblogs.asp.net/infinitiesloop, where he enjoys spending time helping the community with general .NET and ASP.NET questions. His most popular article is on ASP.NET ViewState and is typically one of the first Internet search results for the term ViewState. When he is not working, Dave enjoys spending time with his family and his baby girl, Sky. He enjoys gaming in his spare time to relax a little, and can often be found on Xbox Live playing Halo 3 with the gamer tag InfinitiesLoop.

About the Technical Editor

Robert Fayman has been developing and maintaining applications for the past 10 years. Although his programming language of choice is C#, he often spends more time maintaining code written in classic ASP and PHP. In his spare time, he spends many hours researching the newest technologies trying to find more tools that he can add to his toolbox. When he is not behind the computer, he enjoys spending time with his wife, two sons, dog, and cat.

Credits

Acquisitions Editor
Katie Mohr

Development Editor
Kelly Talbot

Technical Editor
Robert Fayman

Production Editor
Kathleen Wisor

Copy Editor
Foxxe Editorial Services

Editorial Manager
Mary Beth Wakefield

Production Manager
Tim Tate

Vice President and Executive Group Publisher
Richard Swadley

Vice President and Executive Publisher
Barry Pruett

Associate Publisher
Jim Minatel

Project Coordinator, Cover
Lynsey Stanford

Compositor
Craig Woods, Happenstance Type-O-Rama

Proofreader
Nancy Hanger, Windhaven

Indexer
Robert Swanson

Acknowledgments

Thanks to Katie Mohr and Jim Minatel for the opportunity to get on a great book with a great team. This book really came together with the help and assistance of Kelly Talbot and Sydney Jones. Thanks to our technical editor Bob Fayman as well.

Special thanks goes to my family for putting up with my writing time away from playing and the family. Thank you Tuija, Sofia, Henri, and Kalle "Donut Head."

— *Bill Evjen*

First, I have to acknowledge the support of my family and their tolerance for my working on this book in the middle of other family activities. Kelly Talbot has helped marshal me through this particularly hectic round of updates and additions. And, of course, thanks to the very talented people on the ASP.NET, both past and present. I have learned a lot from this hard-working and enthusiastic team.

— *Matt Gibbs*

I'd like to thank my wife Heedy and two boys, Danny and Jeffery, for putting up with the long hours I spend in the office studying new technologies and writing books and articles. I love them and sincerely appreciate their patience with me. I'm extremely lucky to have such a great family.

I'd also like to thank my Mom and Dad, Danny and Elaine, for bringing me up in such a positive, caring environment where succeeding in life was always encouraged. I love both of you and am forever in debt for the years of service you've given and the many life lessons you've taught me.

— *Dan Wahlin*

Thank you Mom and Dad, for finally giving in and buying me that first computer. Your love and unrelenting support has made everything leading up to this book possible. Thank you to all of my wonderful family, especially my wife, Marianne. Thank you Scott Guthrie and Matt Gibbs for giving me a chance to prove myself, and to all the members of the ASP.NET team who each inspire me to improve myself in new and different ways.

— *Dave Reed*

Contents

Contents

Contents

Contents

Contents

Contents

Introduction

ASP.NET revolutionized Web application development. The platform handles many of the complexities of creating Web applications. Now ASP.NET AJAX takes the development platform even further. The lines between rich client applications and traditionally less interactive browser-based applications are being further blurred with the use of this technology.

The ASP.NET AJAX Library brings object-oriented programming to JavaScript development for modern browsers, and the ASP.NET AJAX Extensions makes it easy to write rich Web applications that communicate with the Web server asynchronously. Again, the complexities are made easy by using ASP.NET.

The new server controls that are part of ASP.NET AJAX make it simple to designate parts of the page to be updated automatically without making the user pause and wait while the data is refreshed. You can have partial page updates without writing a single line of code. Other new controls let you alert the user that background work is happening and designate regular intervals at which updates occur. In addition, the ASP.NET AJAX Control Toolkit makes it easy to make your user interface really come to life with animations, modal dialogs, transition effects, and more.

Ajax is definitely the hot buzzword in the Web application world at the moment. Ajax is an acronym for Asynchronous JavaScript and XML and, in Web application development, it signifies the capability to build applications that make use of the XMLHttpRequest object.

The creation and the inclusion of the XMLHttpRequest object in JavaScript and the fact that most upper-level browsers support the use of this object led to creation of the Ajax model. Ajax applications, although they have been around for a few years, gained greater popularity after Google released a number of notable, Ajax-enabled applications such as Google Maps and Google Suggest. These applications demonstrated the value of Ajax.

Shortly thereafter, Microsoft released a beta for a new toolkit that enabled developers to incorporate Ajax features in their Web applications. This toolkit, code-named Atlas and later renamed ASP.NET AJAX, makes it extremely simple to start using Ajax features in applications today.

Prior to Visual Studio 2008, the ASP.NET AJAX product used to be a separate application that developers were required to install on their machine and the Web server that they were working with. This release gained in popularity quite rapidly and has now been made a part of the Visual Studio 2008 offering. Not only is it a part of the Visual Studio 2008 IDE, the ASP.NET AJAX product is also baked into the .NET Framework 3.5. This means that in order to use ASP.NET AJAX, developers are not going to need to install anything if they are working with ASP.NET 3.5.

Overall, Microsoft has fully integrated the entire ASP.NET AJAX experience in that developers can easily use Visual Studio and its visual designers to work with your Ajax-enabled pages and even have the full debugging story that they would want to have with their applications. Using Visual Studio 2008, developers are now able to debug straight into the JavaScript that they are using in the pages.

In addition, it is important to note that Microsoft focused a lot of attention on cross-platform compatibility with ASP.NET AJAX. Developers will find that the Ajax-enabled applications that they build upon the .NET Framework 3.5 are able to work within all the major up-level browsers out there (e.g., FireFox and Opera).

Who This Book Is For

This book is aimed at experienced ASP.NET developers looking to add AJAX to their applications, and experienced Web developers who want to move to using ASP.NET and AJAX together.

In this book, I assume that you already have an understanding of how ASP.NET works. For an in-depth discussion of ASP.NET, I recommend *Professional ASP.NET 3.5* by Bill Evjen, et al. (Wrox, 2008). The focus here is on how you can extend ASP.NET applications to update portions of the page asynchronously and to add richer UI elements to a page. ASP.NET AJAX makes it easy to enrich your existing application or to design a new application to provide a better experience for users. The differences among modern browsers have been abstracted, allowing you to write to a common set of APIs and trust that the user will get the correct behavior whether they are using Internet Explorer, Firefox, or Safari.

If you know how to author ASP.NET pages, you can easily start using the Microsoft AJAX library to manipulate the browser's Document Object Model and communicate with the server to update the user's view of data without forcing them to wait for the entire page to be refreshed.

What This Book Covers

This book covers ASP.NET 3.5 AJAX. It does not cover ASP.NET 3.5, on which ASP.NET AJAX is built. The examples lead you from the core of what is included in the ASP.NET AJAX Library through the core controls you would first start using. You build on that using the core JavaScript library and the ASP.NET AJAX Toolkit before covering debugging, deployment, and custom control development.

The ASP.NET 3.5 release includes the Microsoft AJAX Library as well as the server controls that can be used in ASP.NET pages to extend applications, making them more rich and interactive. It does so by leveraging the ASP.NET AJAX Library, which is JavaScript that runs in the browser. The server controls and JavaScript Library work together to let you update HTML with data obtained asynchronously from the server. The ASP.NET application services are exposed to JavaScript classes in the ASP.NET AJAX Library, making authentication and personalization accessible from the browser.

Chapter 1 introduces you to ASP.NET AJAX. This book discusses the need for AJAX Libraries and explains how ASP.NET AJAX compares to other AJAX Libraries. You will see how ASP.NET AJAX is composed of client and server pieces and that you can use the client library with any server platform you choose. In Chapter 2, the focus is on the most popular and easily applied feature of ASP.NET, the UpdatePanel control. This control allows you to automatically update portions of a page asynchronously, without subjecting the user to a visible pause while the page refreshes. Chapters 3 and 4 give you some key information about working with JavaScript and how the ASP.NET AJAX Library makes development with JavaScript easier. The book then works through several key features, including control of script resources and working with the ScriptManager control in Chapter 5, the new ASP.NET 3.5 ability to work with the back button in Chapter 6, and the ASP.NET AJAX Toolkit in Chapter 7 and all it has to offer for creating rich user interfaces. The next chapter, Chapter 8, looks at how to use ASP.NET's application services (such as the Membership and Role management systems) with ASP.NET AJAX. Chapter 9 looks at networking objects. Chapter 10 looks at working with animations in ASP.NET AJAX. Chapter 11 shows you how to develop custom AJAX controls. Chapters 12, 13, and 14 show the reader how to incorporate Ajax in some other ASP.NET core features such as Web Parts, localization, and state management. Chapter 15 looks at what is required to test and debug Ajax applications, and finally, Chapter 16 explores how to deploy ASP.NET AJAX applications.

What You Need to Use This Book

ASP.NET AJAX 3.5 builds on top of ASP.NET, so you will need to have version 3.5 of the .NET Framework installed. There are two separate types of download for the .NET Framework. The redistributable package is required for application to run and needs to be on development, test, and server machines. The SDK (Software Development Kit) is a set of tools for use in developing applications. Both are available from `http://msdn.microsoft.com/en-us/netframework/cc378097.aspx`.

The examples use Visual Web Developer. The free Express version is available at `www.microsoft.com/express`.

Conventions

To help you get the most from the text and keep track of what's happening, we've used a number of conventions throughout the book.

> **Boxes like this one hold important, not-to-be forgotten information that is directly relevant to the surrounding text.**

Notes, tips, hints, tricks, and asides to the current discussion are offset and placed in italics like this.

As for styles in the text:

- ❑ We *highlight* new terms and important words when we introduce them.
- ❑ We show keyboard strokes like this: Ctrl+A.
- ❑ We show file names, URLs, and code within the text like this: `persistence.properties`.
- ❑ We present code in two different ways:

```
We use a monofont type with no highlighting for most code examples.
```

```
We use gray highlighting to emphasize code that's particularly important in the
present context.
```

Source Code

As you work through the examples in this book, you may choose either to type in all the code manually or to use the source code files that accompany the book. All of the source code used in this book is available for download at `www.wrox.com`. Once at the site, simply locate the book's title (either by using the Search box or by using one of the title lists) and click the Download Code link on the book's detail page to obtain all the source code for the book.

Because many books have similar titles, you may find it easiest to search by ISBN; this book's ISBN is 978-0-470-39217-1.

Once you download the code, just decompress it with your favorite compression tool. Alternately, you can go to the main Wrox code download page at `www.wrox.com/dynamic/books/download.aspx` to see the code available for this book and all other Wrox books.

Errata

We make every effort to ensure that there are no errors in the text or in the code. However, no one is perfect, and mistakes do occur. If you find an error in one of our books, such as a spelling mistake or faulty piece of code, we would be very grateful for your feedback. By sending in errata you may save another reader hours of frustration and at the same time you will be helping us provide even higher-quality information.

To find the errata page for this book, go to www.wrox.com and locate the title using the Search box or one of the title lists. Then, on the book details page, click the Book Errata link. On this page you can view all errata that has been submitted for this book and posted by Wrox editors. A complete book list, including links to each book's errata is also available at www.wrox.com/misc-pages/booklist.shtml.

If you don't spot "your" error on the Book Errata page, go to www.wrox.com/contact/techsupport .shtml and complete the form there to send us the error you have found. We'll check the information and, if appropriate, post a message to the book's errata page and fix the problem in subsequent editions of the book.

p2p.wrox.com

For author and peer discussion, join the P2P forums at http://p2p.wrox.com. The forums are a Web-based system for you to post messages relating to Wrox books and related technologies and interact with other readers and technology users. The forums offer a subscription feature to e-mail you topics of interest of your choosing when new posts are made to the forums. Wrox authors, editors, other industry experts, and your fellow readers are present on these forums.

At http://p2p.wrox.com you will find a number of different forums that will help you not only as you read this book but also as you develop your own applications. To join the forums, just follow these steps:

1. Go to p2p.wrox.com and click the Register link.

2. Read the terms of use and click Agree.

3. Complete the required information to join as well as any optional information you wish to provide, and click Submit.

4. You will receive an e-mail with information describing how to verify your account and complete the joining process.

   You can read messages in the forums without joining P2P, but in order to post your own messages, you must join.

Once you join, you can post new messages and respond to messages other users post. You can read messages at any time on the Web. If you would like to have new messages from a particular forum e-mailed to you, click the Subscribe to this forum icon by the forum name in the forum listing.

For more information about how to use the Wrox P2P, be sure to read the P2P FAQs for answers to questions about how the forum software works as well as many common questions specific to P2P and Wrox books. To read the FAQs, click the FAQ link on any P2P page.

1

Overview of AJAX

AJAX has definitely been the hot buzzword in the Web application world for the last few years. AJAX is an acronym for Asynchronous JavaScript and XML and, in Web application development, it signifies the capability to build applications that make use of the XMLHttpRequest object.

The creation and inclusion of the XMLHttpRequest object in JavaScript and the fact that most upper-level browsers support it led to the creation of the AJAX model. AJAX applications, although they have been around for a few years, gained popularity after Google released a number of notable, AJAX-enabled applications such as Google Maps and Google Suggest. These applications demonstrated to the world the real value of AJAX, and every developer that saw these applications in action immediately went out to do research in how these applications were built.

AJAX is now an out-of-the-box feature of ASP.NET 3.5, and every ASP.NET application that you build is AJAX-enabled by default. This means that you don't have to create a separate AJAX project for your Web applications as the standard projects in Visual Studio for Web application development will already be enabled to use ASP.NET AJAX. This is one of the main new features of ASP.NET 3.5 because of the power that AJAX brings to your applications. The AJAX capability has become so popular since the release of ASP.NET 3.5 that most ASP.NET applications built today make use of at least some features provided by this technology.

Why AJAX Applications Are Needed

Web applications were in a rather stagnant state for many years. The first "Web" applications were nothing more than text and some images, all represented in basic HTML tags. However, this wasn't what people wanted; they wanted more — more interactivity, a more integrated workflow, more responsiveness, and an overall richer experience.

When building applications, even today, you have to make some specific decisions that really end up dictating the capabilities and reach of your application. Probably one of the more important decisions is the choice of building the application as a "thin" client or a "thick" client.

A thick client application is a term used for applications that are either MFC (in the C++ world) or Windows Forms applications. These types of applications also provide the container along with all the container contents and workflows. A thick client application is typically a compiled executable that end users can run in the confines of their own environment, usually without any dependencies elsewhere (for example, from an upstream server).

A thin client application is the term generally used for Web applications. These types of applications are typically viewed in a browser, and your application can provide end user workflows as long as it is contained within this well-known container. A thin client application is one whose processing and rendering are controlled at a single point (the upstream server), and the results of the view are sent down as HTML to a browser to be viewed by the client.

Typically, a Web application is something that requires the end user to have Internet access in order to work with the application. On the other hand, a thick client application was once generally considered a self-contained application that worked entirely locally on the client's machine. However, in the last few years, this perception has changed as thick clients have evolved into what are termed "smart clients" and now make use of the Internet to display data and to provide workflows.

Web applications have historically been less rich and responsive than desktop applications. End users don't necessarily understand the details of how an application works, but they know that interacting with a Web site in the browser is distinctly different from using an application installed locally. Web applications are accessible from just about any browser, just about anywhere, but what these browsers present is limited by what you can do with markup and script code running in the browser.

There are definitely pros and cons in working with either type of application. The thick client application style is touted as more fluid and more responsive to an end user's actions. Thick client applications require that users perform an installation on their machine but let developers leverage the advanced mouse and graphics capabilities of the operating system that would be extremely difficult to implement in a Web browser, and also take advantage of the user's machine for tasks such as offline storage.

Conversely, the main complaint about Web applications for many years has been that every action by an end user typically takes numerous seconds and results in a jerky page refresh.

Conversely, Web applications can be updated just by changing what is running on the server, and site visitors get the latest version of that application instantaneously. However, it is much more difficult to update a desktop application, because you would have to get users to perform yet another installation or else ensure that the application has been coded to include a clever system for doing updates automatically.

Web applications are said to use a zero-deployment model, but desktop applications use a heavy deployment and configuration model. The choice is often characterized as a tradeoff between rich and reach: Desktop applications generally offer a richer user experience than what could be offered in the browser, but with a Web application you are able to reach users anywhere on any OS with almost no extra effort. Furthermore, many companies have restrictive policies in place regarding what software can be installed on employees' machines, and they often don't allow employees to have administrative access that is required to install new applications, so Web applications are the only viable option in many situations.

AJAX is the first real leap of a technology to bridge this historic wall between thick and thin. AJAX, though still working through the browser, focuses on bringing richness to Web applications by allowing for extremely interactive workflows that usually were only found in the thick client camp.

Bringing Richness to Web Applications

Years ago, having a Web presence was a distinguishing factor for companies. That is no longer the case. Now just having a Web presence is no longer enough. Companies are distinguishing themselves further through Web applications that react intuitively to customer actions and anticipate user input. This book shows you how ASP.NET AJAX addresses specific Web development challenges and paves the way for taking your Web site to another level of user experience.

The fundamental set of technologies used in the AJAX model that enable the next generation of Web applications is not entirely new. You will find that many people point to Google, Flickr, and several other services as prime examples of leveraging AJAX and its underlying technologies in unique ways. The applications have some unique features, but in reality, the underlying technologies have been around and in use for nearly a decade. Look at how Microsoft Exchange Server provided rich access to e-mail from a Web browser in the Outlook Web Access application, and the concept of ubiquitous access from a browser while leveraging a common set of browser features for a rich user experience has been around for years. In this case, users get a remarkably full-featured application with no local installation and are able to access e-mail from virtually any machine.

While the AJAX acronym is nice, it doesn't do much to explain what is actually happening. Instead of building a Web application to be just a series of page views and postbacks, developers are using JavaScript to communicate asynchronously with the Web server and update parts of the page dynamically. This means that the Web page can dynamically adapt its appearance as the user interacts with it, and it can even post or fetch data to or from the Web server in the background. Gone are the days of the ugly post-back, which clears the user's screen and breaks his concentration! Instead, you need to post back now only if you want to change to a different Web page.

> *Even that rule can be bent. Some applications are pushing this boundary and completely changing the user's view, just as though they navigated to a new page, but they do so through an asynchronous post and by changing the page content without actually navigating to a new URL.*

The AJAX acronym refers to XML as the data format being exchanged between client and server, but in reality, applications are being built that retrieve simple pieces of text, XML, and JSON (JavaScript Object Notation) (which is discussed in more detail in Chapter 4). Part of the AJAX appeal is not even covered by the acronym alone: In addition, to communicating with the server without blocking, developers are leveraging Dynamic HTML (DHTML) and Cascading Style Sheets (CSS) to create truly amazing user interfaces. JavaScript code running on the client communicates asynchronously with the server and then uses DHTML to dynamically modify the page, which supports rich animations, transitions, and updates to the content while the user continues interacting with the page. In many cases, end users will sometimes forget they are using a Web application!

Just remember that AJAX is not a single holistic entity but instead is a novel and creative way of using a combination of technologies such as the XMLHttpRequest object, HTML, XHTML, CSS, DOM, XML, JSON, XSLT, and JavaScript. You might be thinking of the difficulties of piecing this all together to get the Web applications you want to build. Be ready to be wowed, however, as the focus of this book is on showing you how to use the built-in technologies provided by ASP.NET 3.5 to give you this power in an easy to use manner.

Who Benefits from AJAX?

AJAX offers benefits to both end users and developers. For end users, it reduces the "rich or reach" conflict; for developers, it helps in overcoming the constraints raised by HTTP such as the dreaded page postback.

Why End Users Want AJAX Applications

Users tend to view desktop applications as a commitment. They install a program, usually from a disk pulled from a costly shrink-wrapped box. The program consumes hard disk space as well as a position in the program menu. The user may need to update the program periodically or perform an upgrade later on to get new features. If the program is proactive about updating itself, the user is confronted regularly with dialogs about accepting patches or downloads. In exchange for this investment of time, money, and energy, the user is repaid with an application that is able to leverage the operating system and machine resources. It is a rich application. It has local storage capabilities, offers quick response times, and can present a compelling and intuitive graphical user interface.

More and more applications are becoming accessible from the Web browser, where the full resources of the hardware and OS are not available, but the user commitment of a desktop application is not required. Over the years, interacting with a Web application has meant a predictable pattern for users. They click a link in the page, and the browser flashes while the user waits until the page is repainted (the dreaded page postback). This cycle is repeated over and over. The user looks at what is presented on the page, interacts with it, and clicks somewhere on the page. The browser then produces an audible click for feedback and begins to postback to the server. The screen of the Web browser flashes blank and some icon spins or flashes while the user waits for a new version of the page to be returned from the server. Many times, the new version of the page is almost exactly the same as the previous version, with only part of the page being updated. And then the cycle begins all over again. This has a sluggish feeling even when the user has a high-speed network connection and is simply unacceptable for some types of applications.

The AJAX set of technologies has changed what users expect from Web applications. JavaScript code running in the browser works to exchange data with the Web server asynchronously. There is no click sound and the browser does not flash. The request to the server is non-blocking, which means the user is able to continue viewing the page and interacting with it. The script gets the updated data from the server and modifies the page dynamically, using the DHTML coding methodology. The user is able to continue looking at the page while parts of it are updated in the background. AJAX is used to provide a more responsive experience, making Web applications behave more like desktop installations. JavaScript is used to provide a richer experience with support for drag-and-drop, modal dialogs, and seemingly instantaneous updates to various parts of the page based on user inputs.

A big part of successfully leveraging AJAX technologies is in the perceived performance increase. Users appreciate Web applications that anticipate their actions. If you also use JavaScript code in the background to pre-fetch images and data that may be needed, users can get a speedy response without the usual pause that accompanies their actions. Nobody wants to wait for data exchanges between client and server; studies have shown that a time lag between user input and subsequent UI changes can significantly reduce their productivity and give them the frustrating feeling that they are fighting the application. Users want Web applications to behave like desktop installations but without the overhead associated with an installation. As more applications employ smart caching, anticipate user actions, and provide richer UIs, the difference between Web and desktop applications is definitely becoming blurred. Expectations for Web applications are rising. The end user has now seen that it is possible to avoid the commitment of installing a desktop application and still have a rich and responsive experience.

Why Developers Want AJAX

Often, the first question to arise when starting a new development project is what type of application it will be. Should it be a desktop application or a Web application? This is a key decision because it has historically dictated a lot about the nature of the application and the development problem space. Many developers are now choosing to build Web applications by default unless something about the application dictates that it must be a desktop install. If it must run offline or if it requires a user interface that is too complex to achieve in HTML, targeting the Web browser may be ruled out, and developers are forced to write a standalone application.

Developers have a difficult job writing modern Web applications due to the inherent World Wide Web functionality constraints imposed by the use of the Hypertext Transfer Protocol (HTTP) and the way that browsers use it. HTTP is a stateless protocol. The Web browser requests a page, possibly carrying some sort of state (a querystring or form input parameters), and the Web server processes the request and sends a response that includes HTML-rendered content. The Web server can only react to the information supplied in the current request and does not know any additional information from the request itself, such as any details about the path the user took to get to the current view.

When the response is rendered, the connection may be broken and the server will not have any information to preserve for the next request. From the server's perspective, it is simply listening for requests to come in from any browser anywhere and then reacting. The browser issues a request to the page and receives an HTML page in response. It uses the HTML it receives to render the user interface. The user interacts with the page, and, in response, the browser clears the screen and submits a new request to the server, carrying some information about user input or actions. Again, a complete HTML page is returned. The browser then presents the new version of HTML. Fundamentally, the HTTP protocol is stateless. The server gets a request and responds to it. The request carries limited information about the ongoing conversation that is happening between client and server. This can definitely be a problem.

AJAX makes this much better. AJAX breaks this pattern by updating portions of the page separately, via partial page rendering. Figure 1-1 shows a typical non-AJAX series of browser and server interactions (requests and responses). Each request results in full-page rendering. In response, the browser updates the user's entire view with the HTML that is returned.

The sequence presented here in Figure 1-1 is typical of the type of Web application that we have been living with for many years now. It has a request and response cycle that is abrupt and rather noticeable to the end user. Let it be said that, with the introduction of AJAX technologies, these types of applications are changing quickly to the new model this technology provides.

On the other hand, Figure 1-2 shows how AJAX is employed to improve the user's experience.

In this case, a request is made for the initial page rendering. From there, asynchronous requests to the server are made. An asynchronous request is a background request to send or receive data in an entirely nonvisual manner (meaning that there won't be any resulting page flickering). They are asynchronous because the user interface is not frozen during this time, and users can continue interacting with the page while the data transfer is taking place. These calls get just an incremental update for the page instead of getting an entirely new page.

JavaScript running on the client reacts to the new data and updates various portions of the page as desired. The number of requests to the server may be no different, or in some cases, there may actually be more calls to the server, but the users' perception is that the application feels more responsive. End users are not forced to pause, even if it is only a slight pause, and wait for the server while staring at a blank browser screen. This model, while chatty in some regards, provides the fluidity you are looking for in your Web applications.

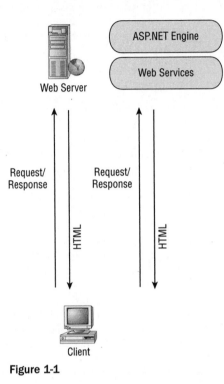

Figure 1-1

AJAX applications make use of the XMLHttpRequest object as an initiator and caller of the underlying data needed by the application to make the necessary changes. These requests are routed through a serialization process before being transmitted across the wire. In most cases, the output is some type of XML (such as SOAP) or JSON (for those who want an especially a tight format). The response from the server is then deserialized and provided to the JavaScript on the page, which then interacts with DHTML to render the parts of the page, outside of the normal postback process.

Technologies of AJAX

Almost a decade ago, the Microsoft Exchange Server team created an ActiveX control called XMLHttpRequest that could be instantiated from JavaScript and used to communicate with the server. Using the XMLHttpRequest object, you could send information to the server and get data back without clearing the screen and painting a completely new HTML page. JavaScript code could then manipulate the HTML dynamically on the client, avoiding the annoying flash and the wait that users associate with Web browsing. This functionality was not limited to Internet Explorer for long. Soon, other browsers included XMLHttpRequest objects as well. Developers could now write richer applications with their reach extending across various operating systems.

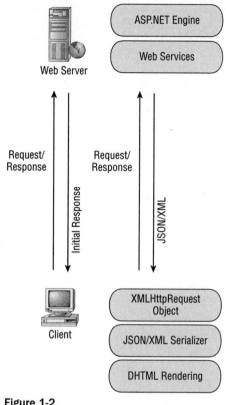

Figure 1-2

The browsers that can make use of this object include the following:

- ❑ Internet Explorer 5.0 and above (currently in version 8.0)
- ❑ Safari 3.1
- ❑ Firefox 3
- ❑ Opera 8+
- ❑ Netscape 9

The browsers also created an advanced Document Object Model (DOM) to represent the browser, the window, the page, and the HTML elements it contained. The DOM exposed events and responded to input, allowing the page to be manipulated with script. Dynamic HTML (DHTML) opened the door to writing rich interfaces hosted within the Web browser. Developers started writing hundreds and even thousands of lines of JavaScript code to make rich and compelling applications that would not require any client installation and could be accessed from any browser anywhere. Web applications began to move to a whole new level of richness. Without AJAX libraries, you would be faced with writing lots and lots of JavaScript code and debugging the sometimes subtle variations in different browsers to reach this new level of richness.

JavaScript Libraries and AJAX

Developers have had access to AJAX technologies for years, and many have been leveraging AJAX to push the limits of what can be done in the Web browser. But what is really making AJAX more compelling now are the comprehensive script libraries and integration with server technologies that make it easier to write rich Web applications and avoid the need to become an expert on the different versions of JavaScript. A JavaScript library is referenced within the HTML of a page by using the <script> tag:

```
<html>
    <head>
        <script src="http://www.someSite.com/someScript.js"
          type="text/javascript">
        </script>
    </head>
. . .
```

The script is downloaded and cached by the browser. Other pages within the application can reference the same URL for script, and the browser will not even bother to go back to the server to get it. The functionality of that script file is available for use from within the page rendered to the browser. A script library sent to the browser and then leveraged for writing a richer UI and a more responsive application is at the heart of all AJAX libraries.

The Initiator Component

To initiate calls to the back end server, you need JavaScript on the client to invoke the XMLHttpRequest object, which takes charge of making these out-of-bound calls. This component works to send data back and forth asynchronously. This core capability is browser-independent and allows for requests and responses to occur without interrupting the end user experience.

The JavaScript Component

AJAX technologies take advantage of the common support for JavaScript found in modern browsers. Because there is a standard that is supported across the various browsers, you can write scripts knowing that they will run. This wasn't always the case.

In the mid-1990s, Netscape and Microsoft (along with others) collaborated on a standard for a scripting language that they would support in their Web browsers. The standard is called EcmaScript. Microsoft's implementation is called JScript, but the language is generally referred to as JavaScript, as it was called in Netscape. (It has nothing to do with Java, but someone must have thought the association was useful for marketing purposes.) JavaScript program snippets are sent down to the browser along with the HTML, and they run inside the user's browser to affect how the page is processed on the client.

JavaScript is not compiled; it is interpreted. There is no static type-checking as you get in C++ and C#. You can declare a variable without needing to specify a type, and the type to which the variable refers can change at any time. This makes it easy to start programming in JavaScript, but there is inevitably a certain amount of danger in allowing the data type of a variable to change dynamically at runtime. In the following snippet, notice that the variable can reference any type without difficulty:

```
var something = 1;
something = true;
something = "a string";
```

JavaScript is a dynamic language. Types can actually be extended during program execution by other code. This means that you can write code that creates types on the fly. Because there is no enforcement of type safety, your code can receive these types as parameters or return values without any problem. This provides a great degree of flexibility and coding power.

The fundamental types in JavaScript are strings, numbers, Booleans, and functions. There is also support for objects and arrays, which are collections of the fundamental types. Some additional objects that are considered essential for many programming tasks are included in JavaScript. This includes support for regular expressions and date and time operations.

You can use the plus operator on strings in JavaScript to concatenate them:

```
var theEnd = "THE END.";
var result = "Beginning, " + "middle, and " + theEnd;
```

In this example, the result variable is now the string: `"Beginning, middle, and THE END"`.

JavaScript interpreters use the IEEE floating-point standard for storing numbers. Ignoring the gory details, you can assume that for most programming tasks you won't have any trouble.

The Boolean type in JavaScript is about what you would expect it to be but maybe not exactly so. The Boolean represents whether or not an expression is true, but it uses the C-style convention using integer values 0 and 1.

Variables can exist in JavaScript without having a value, and a variable may simply be undefined, which can produce unexpected results. In this snippet of JavaScript, three variables are declared, and all of these comparisons are designed to return a true value.

```
<script type="text/javascript">
    var one = 1;
    var zero = 0;
    var undefinedVar;

    if(one) {
        alert("1 is true");
    }

    if(!zero) {
        alert("0 is false");
    }

    if(!undefinedVar) {

        // this test tells us that "undefinedVar" either contains 0,
        // or is really undefined: both of which equate to false
        alert("undefinedVar is false");
    }

    if(one != zero) {
        alert("one and zero are not the same");
    }
</script>
```

You can check specifically to see if a variable has been defined like this:

```
if( typeof(undefinedVar ) == "undefined" ) {
    alert("undefinedVar is undefined");
}
```

Variables can also have a null value, which is not the same thing as being undefined, because a null value does constitute a value.

Functions are also real types in JavaScript. They can accept arguments and return values. Functions can be passed to other functions and can be created dynamically by other script code.

Here are two equivalent definitions for a function called Add() that will take two variables and return the result of applying the plus operator. Notice that this did not state that it takes two numbers. Remember, JavaScript variables do not have a defined type, so I could just as easily pass two strings and concatenate them with my Add() function.

```
<script type="text/javascript">
    function Add(x, y) {
        return x + y;
    }

    var AddAgain = function(x, y) { return x + y; }
</script>
```

Once either of these styles is used to create a function, it can be called from that scope and any nested scope to perform the addition. There is no advantage to one of these forms over the other. You can simply choose to use the syntax that you prefer.

```
<script type="text/javascript">
    var result = Add(36, 24);
    alert(result);   //displays 60

    var stringResult = Add("Hello ", "there.");
    alert(stringResult); //displays "Hello there."
</script>
```

Objects and arrays are just collections of other types. Array types do not require that the values they hold be named. Instead, you can access them by index. The values held in an object are referenced by field or property names. Objects can also hold functions (which can be accessor functions to give public visibility to local variables), which lets you create data structures that represent entities in JavaScript code. Missing from this sort of object-oriented programming is a concept of type inheritance. Although, there are things like the Microsoft AJAX Library, which provides a set of classes and recommended patterns for achieving inheritance in JavaScript, making it more natural to switch between JavaScript and other high-level languages. The following code example includes a definition for an Album object that holds and returns the artist and album title. An array is then used to store information about several albums.

```
<script type="text/javascript">
    // define an object named Album - note that this object is typeless
    Album = function(title, artist) {
        var _title = title;
        var _artist = artist;
```

```
        this.get_title = function() { return _title; }
        this.get_artist = function() { return _artist; }
    }

    // create object instances by calling the constructor
    var albumA = new Album("Rift", "Phish");
    var albumB = new Album("A Picture of Nectar", "Phish");

    // create an array to hold the instances (also typeless)
    var albumArray = new Array();

    albumArray[0] = albumA;
    albumArray[1] = albumB;

    // iterate over the array to show the album titles
    for(var i = 0; i < albumArray.length; i++) {
        alert((albumArray[i]).get_title()); // call get_title accessor
    }
</script>
```

The Web Services Component

The fundamental concept of Web services is powerful and continues to evolve and advance. The original Simple Object Access Protocol (SOAP) standard is the use of the HTTP protocol to pass XML-formatted data to the server from a client and receive XML-formatted results in return. This can be from within a Web browser using the XMLHttpRequest object or directly from a desktop application or another server. Before Web services became widely adopted, it was not uncommon for developers to programmatically request a page as an HTML document and extract the desired data from it, a technique known as screen-scraping. This causes all sorts of frustrations as sites are continually updated and the screen-scraping clients must try to keep up by modifying their parsing code to adapt to the new HTML that the target site is rendering.

This resulted in frustration, because sites that presented data using HTML visual pages were prone to modifying those pages, and this would break the screen-scraping program, which expected to see the data in the original format. Web services were created as a nonvisual way to transfer data over the Web, and they are the natural way to isolate remote method calls from the presentation layer. Now, instead of screen-scraping, you are able to call a Web service and have XML-formatted data returned that is easily consumed by a program.

By passing plain-text data formatted as XML and by eliminating the visual elements, data passed in Web services is much easier to parse than HTML. Moreover, since XML can contain an embedded schema, code can inspect the schema and use it to determine the structure and types used in the data. You can extend the schema passed with the data being returned without worrying that consuming applications will be broken, and therefore XML readers can be somewhat tolerant of modifications that would have certainly caused a screen-scraper a great deal of grief!

The schema for data can be extended without requiring all consumers to be updated. Consumers can easily get the parts of the XML document they wish to process and disregard the rest. This has progressed beyond simple XML formats. Unlike previous implementations of Web services, you can now define Web service contracts to be built to employ arbitrary encoding and utilize any one of a number of wire protocols. What drives the Web service concept is the ability to access data easily from various applications in a loosely coupled way, and the new Microsoft Windows Communication Foundation (WCF) takes this concept to a completely new level, allowing the contract to specify wire protocols, deployment strategies, and logging infrastructure, along with providing support for transactions.

ASP.NET AJAX provides a set of JavaScript proxy objects to access some new Web services built into ASP .NET. Profile information, membership services, and role management can be easily accessed from the client. Developers don't need to create their own infrastructure to support these fundamental application services but can include a few lines of code to take advantage of server resources from JavaScript code running in the browser, thereby dramatically extending the reach of ASP.NET to include both the client and the server. Moreover, because the JavaScript libraries are designed to be easy to use by developers already familiar with server-side .NET programming, all of this extra functionality comes in a friendly package that is easy to leverage.

The Dynamic HTML Component

Dynamic HTML is not a freestanding technology. It is the use of a set of technologies in a specific way. HTML is returned to the browser following a Web server request. The browser then renders the page, and the user is able to view it. The browser also exposes the DOM that represents the structure of the HTML being displayed. The DOM can be accessed from JavaScript embedded in, or referenced by, the page. The appearance of the HTML is affected by applying Cascading Style Sheets (CSS), which control colors, fonts, position, visibility, and more. You can bind JavaScript code to events that the browser will raise when users perform certain actions, such as hovering over a particular element or entering text in a textbox. The JavaScript code can update text or manipulate the CSS settings for elements within the page. It can also communicate with the server to expand the dynamic nature of the page even further. The user will see a dynamically changing user interface that responds to his actions in real time, which will greatly enhance his overall experience, thereby increasing his productivity and satisfaction with the application. This one piece of the pie is the one that changes the underlying page without the page refresh.

All these pieces together, in the end, provide you the tools that you need to build state-of-the-art applications for today's Web world.

AJAX Libraries

ASP.NET AJAX is the focus of this book. ASP.NET AJAX is an AJAX library that provides you with the tools and components that you need to tie all the varying aforementioned technologies together. Although this book is about ASP.NET AJAX in particular, there are many third-party AJAX libraries that can be used with ASP.NET, although not all of them were specifically designed for it.

Some of these AJAX libraries are mainly focused on providing JavaScript libraries for use from within the browser to make manipulation of the browser DOM easier. Others include some level of server functionality for use within ASP.NET pages (where server controls will render on the client side).

This section briefly highlights some of what these libraries offer. The ASP.NET AJAX Framework can coexist with script and controls from other libraries, although given the dynamic nature of the JavaScript language, it is possible to extend types so that they conflict with each other. Mixing and matching libraries might work just fine for many uses, but you might find conflicts in other cases. So if you decide to move forward on this route, make sure that you are aware of the potential problems. Some of the available libraries include the following:

❑ **Ajax.NET Professional**: Michael Schwartz developed Ajax.NET Professional as a tool primarily used to simplify the data transport mechanism that enables a client JavaScript routine to communicate with a server program. The server code is simple to use. You merely need to register the control in your page and decorate some code-behind methods with attributes to designate which ones can be called from the client. Then you can leverage the script library to make the calls and pass data. This is intended for developers who are well versed in DHTML, and there are not many prebuilt visual controls. This is a lightweight solution with very little overhead in terms of bytes transferred and processing cycles needed on the client and server. The source code is available, and the package is free (www.ajaxpro.info).

❑ **Anthem.NET**: Anthem.NET is a SourceForge project where users are able to download the sources to the project. It targets ASP.NET 1.1 and ASP.NET 2.0. It has a set of server controls that use their underlying JavaScript library to communicate with the server. They provide the ability to access the state of controls on the page during an asynchronous callback. At the time of writing, the Anthem.NET Web page (http://anthem-dot-net.sourceforge.net) points out that the Anthem.NET user needs to be an experienced ASP.NET developer to get the most out of it. However, this is generally easier to use than Ajax.NET Professional, especially for developers who are not well versed in DHTML. This project is similar to ASP.NET AJAX in many ways but is not as comprehensive.

❑ **DoJo**: The DoJo toolkit can be found at www.dojotoolkit.com. It is a client-side library for AJAX development without ties to any server technology. DoJo has a type system for JavaScript and a function for binding script to events from JavaScript objects or DHTML elements. One of its strengths is rich support for dynamic script loading. You can specify dependencies and ordering in the way that scripts are retrieved and processed.

❑ **Prototype**: The Prototype script library is available at www.prototypejs.org. It does not target any server technology for integration. It has a type system for scripting in a more object-oriented way, along with some shortcut syntaxes for dealing with JavaScript arrays as well as accessing and manipulating HTML elements on the page. Prototype provides networking functionality and a method for automatically updating an HTML element with the results of an HTTP request when given a URL. The Prototype library also has functions for associating script objects and methods with DOM objects and events. The library is focused on simplifying tasks that can be cumbersome and tedious. It does not provide much help for producing a richer user interface but puts forth the building blocks for an improved Web-scripting experience.

❑ **Script.aculo.us**: The Script.aculo.us library can be found at the Web site of the same name, http://script.aculo.us. Their tagline is "it's about the user interface, baby!" which accurately describes their focus. http://script.aculo.us is built on top of the Prototype script library and picks up where it stops. It includes functionality for adding drag-and-drop support to an application. It has a lot of effects code for fading, shrinking, moving, and otherwise animating DOM elements. http://script.aculo.us also has a slider control and a library for manipulating lists of elements.

❑ **Rico**: The Rico library also builds on top of the Prototype script library. It has support for adding drag-and-drop behavior to browser DOM elements. It also has some controls to bind JavaScript objects to DOM elements for manipulating data. Rico has constructs for revealing and hiding portions of a page using an accordion style. It also has animation, sizing, and fading effects prebuilt for easier use. These UI helpers are available at www.openrico.org.

Although there are many options out there for ASP.NET developers, you will find that the toolkit defined in this book is the most integrated with ASP.NET and will be one of the more robust options in your arsenal.

Creating a Simple Web Page with AJAX

Although this book focuses on the power of using AJAX with ASP.NET 3.5 and the AJAX capabilities this framework brings to AJAX development, it is also interesting to see how you could build a simple AJAX-enabled HTML page without the use of any of the aforementioned frameworks.

To show this in action, create an ASP.NET solution within Visual Studio 2008. The first step you can take is to build the Web service that will return a value to be loaded up through the AJAX process. The code (in C#) of the Web service is presented here in Listing 1-1.

Listing 1-1: The Web service to communicate with the AJAX-enabled Web page

```
using System.Web.Services;

/// <summary>
/// Summary description for WebService
/// </summary>
[WebService(Namespace = "http://tempuri.org/")]
[WebServiceBinding(ConformsTo = WsiProfiles.BasicProfile1_1)]
public class WebService : System.Web.Services.WebService {

    [WebMethod]
    public string HelloWorld() {
        return "Hello Ajax World!";
    }
}
```

This is a simple C# Web service and as you can see from the single WebMethod, it only returns a string with no required parameters on the input. The AJAX page that you create for this example works with this Web service, and calls the Web service using the HTTP-GET protocol. By default, ASP.NET disallows HTTP-GET and you have to enable this capability in the web.config file in order for this example to work. Listing 1-2 shows the additions you need to make to this file.

Listing 1-2: Changing the web.config file in order to allow HTTP-GET

```
<system.web>
    <webServices>
        <protocols>
            <add name="HttpGet" />
        </protocols>
    </webServices>
</system.web>
```

Including the <add> element within the <protocols> element enables the HTTP-GET protocol so that your Web page will be able to make the AJAX calls to it. Finally, the HTML page that will make the AJAX call is represented here in Listing 1-3.

Listing 1-3: The HTML page that will make the AJAX calls to the Web service

```
<html xmlns="http://www.w3.org/1999/xhtml">
<head runat="server">
    <title>Basic Ajax Page</title>

    <script type="text/javascript" language="javascript">
        function InitiationFunction()
        {
         var xmlHttp;

         try
         {
             // Try this for non-Microsoft browsers
             xmlHttp = new XMLHttpRequest();
         }
         catch (e)
         {
             // These are utilized for Microsoft IE browsers
             try
             {
                 xmlHttp=new ActiveXObject("Msxml2.XMLHTTP");
             }
             catch (e)
             {
                 try
                 {
                     xmlHttp=new ActiveXObject("Microsoft.XMLHTTP");
                 }
                 catch (e)
                 {
                     alert("Your browser does not support AJAX!");
                     return false;
                 }
             }
         }

    xmlHttp.onreadystatechange = function()
    {
      if(xmlHttp.readyState == 4 && xmlHttp.status == 200)
      {
        response  = xmlHttp.responseXML;
        document.forms[0].statement.value =
            response.getElementsByTagName("string")[0].firstChild.nodeValue;
      }
    }

    xmlHttp.open("GET","/BasicAjax/WebService.asmx/HelloWorld?",true);
    xmlHttp.send(null);
    }
    </script>

</head>
<body>
```

Continued

15

Listing 1-3: The HTML page that will make the AJAX calls to the Web service *(continued)*

```
<form>
  <div>
      Statement from server:
      <input type="text" name="statement" />
      <br />
      <br />
      <input id="Button1" type="button" value="Button"
       onclick="InitiationFunction()" />
  </div>
  </form>
</body>
</html>
```

From this bit of code, you can see that the HTML page creates an instance of the XMLHttpRequest object. From there, a JavaScript function is assigned to the onreadystatechange attribute. Whenever the state of the XMLHttpRequest instance changes, the function is invoked. Since, for this example, you are interested only in changing the page after the page is actually loaded, you are able to specify when the actual function is utilized by checking the readystate attribute of the XMLHttpRequest object.

```
if(xmlHttp.readyState == 4 && xmlHttp.status == 200)
{

}
```

In this case, the readystate is checked to see if it equals a value of 4 and if the request status is equal to 200, a normal request was received. If the status attribute is equal to something other than 200, a server-side error most likely occurred. A readystate value of 4 means that the page is loaded. The possible values of the readystate attribute include 0, 1, 2, 3, and 4. A value of 0 (which is the default value) means that the object is uninitialized. A value of 1 means that the open() method was called successfully, a value of 2 means that the request was sent but that no response was yet received, a value of 3 means that the message is being received, and a value of 4 (again) means that the response is fully loaded.

The open() method called by the XMLHttpRequest object is quite simple, as it is an HTTP-GET request made to the specific URL of your service.

When you run this page and click the button found on the page, you are presented with results illustrated in Figure 1-3.

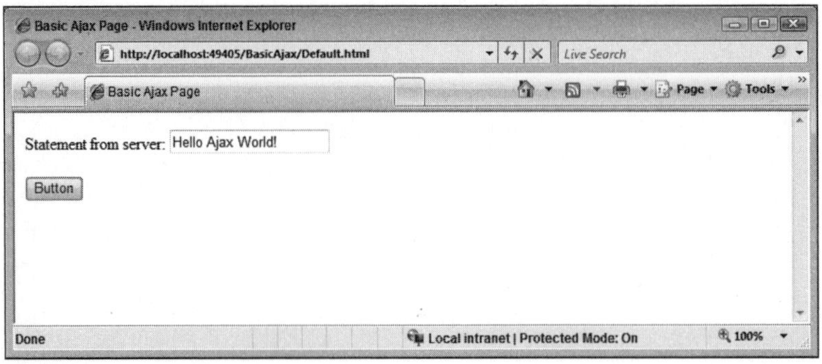

Figure 1-3

The Power of AJAX

Without the advanced use of JavaScript running in the browser, Web applications have their logic running on the server. This means many page refreshes for potentially small updates to the user's view. With AJAX, much of the logic surrounding user interactions can be moved to the client. This presents its own set of challenges. Some examples of using AJAX include streaming large datasets, managed entirely in JavaScript, to the browser. While JavaScript is a powerful language, the debugging facilities and options for error handling are very limited. Putting complex application logic on the client can take a lot of time, effort, and patience. AJAX as a whole allows you to naturally migrate some parts of the application processing to the client, while leveraging partial page rendering to let the server actually control some aspects of the page view.

Some Web sites make an application run entirely from a single page request, where JavaScript and AJAX will do a great deal of work. This presents some tough challenges. Users generally expect that the Back button will take them to the state of the application they were just viewing, but with AJAX applications, this is not necessarily the case. The client may be sending some information to the server for persistent state management (perhaps in server memory or a database), but this requires extra code and special attention to error handling and recovery.

The richest, most maintainable applications seem to be those that balance client and server resources to provide quick response times, easy access to server resources, and a minimum of blocking operations while new page views are fetched.

ASP.NET AJAX itself provides a mix of client and server programming features. The Microsoft AJAX library is aimed at client development. It provides a type system for an object-oriented approach to JavaScript development. It makes it easy to register code to respond to events. It provides useful functions to simplify common tasks like finding elements on the page, attaching event handlers, and accessing the server. The server features include functionality for managing JavaScript code to be sent to the client, declaring regions of the page to be updated asynchronously, creating timers for continuous updates, and accessing ASP.NET services such as user profile data and authentication.

Summary

The Web has evolved over the last decade from providing a static presence to being the default choice for developers writing applications. With Web applications, you get reach without having to deal with the deployment and servicing issues that accompany desktop applications. But the bar continues to move higher for Web applications as users come to expect more. AJAX technologies are driving Web applications to rival rich desktop apps. You can use the results of asynchronous communication with the Web server to update portions of the page without forcing the user to stop his or her work and wait for the page to post back and be repainted. Dynamic HTML allows you to create a rich GUI with transitions and animations leveraging CSS for colors, fonts, positioning, and more.

ASP.NET AJAX includes the Microsoft AJAX library, which makes writing browser-based JavaScript easier and simplifies many common client programming tasks. It is easy to attach code to DOM events, write JavaScript in an object-oriented way, and access the server for persistent storage, authentication, and updated data.

ASP.NET AJAX also includes extensions to version 2.0 of the .NET Framework that can greatly improve your Web application. There is built-in support for returning data in the JSON format that is easily consumed by JavaScript in the browser.

In this book, you will see how the client and server features of ASP.NET AJAX make it easier to push the limits of what you can do with a Web application! You learn how to update portions of a page asynchronously and how to manage the scripts that are used in the browser. You will find out how to use the networking facilities, with a dive into accessing ASP.NET services such as authentication and profile storage. You will get a closer look at the JavaScript language and how the Microsoft AJAX library builds on the language to simplify programming tasks. You will also see what ASP.NET AJAX offers for adding a richer UI to Web applications and look at how to debug and test Web applications.

2

ASP.NET 3.5 and AJAX

AJAX is simply so powerful that most Web applications you build today will make some use of it. In addition to new applications, development teams are now looking back at applications built in the pre-AJAX world and looking at how to incorporate the technology to bring their applications inline.

AJAX arrived on the scene with such a splash that Microsoft was quite quick to adapt ASP.NET to handle it. Shortly after the mainstream introduction of AJAX, Microsoft released a beta for a new toolkit that enabled developers to incorporate AJAX features in their Web applications. This toolkit, code-named *Atlas* and later renamed ASP.NET AJAX, made it extremely simple to start using AJAX features in your ASP.NET 2.0 applications.

The ASP.NET AJAX toolkit was not part of the default .NET Framework 2.0 install. If you are using the .NET Framework 2.0, it is an extra component that you must download from the Internet. If you are using ASP.NET 3.5, you don't have to worry about installing the ASP.NET AJAX toolkit, as everything you need is already in place for you by default. Now, when building ASP.NET 3.5 applications using Visual Studio 2008, your applications are AJAX-enabled by default.

ASP.NET 3.5 Brings a Lot to the Table

Prior to Visual Studio 2008, the ASP.NET AJAX product was a separate installation that you were required to install on your machine and the Web server that you were working with. This release gained in popularity quite rapidly and is now a part of the Visual Studio 2008 offering. Not only is it a part of the Visual Studio 2008 IDE but the ASP.NET AJAX product is also baked into the .NET Framework 3.5. This means that to use ASP.NET AJAX, you don't need to install anything if you are working with ASP.NET 3.5.

> *If you are using an ASP.NET version that is prior to the ASP.NET 3.5 release, then you need to visit* www.asp.net/AJAX *to get the components required to work with AJAX.*

ASP.NET AJAX is now just part of the ASP.NET Framework. When you create a new Web application, you do not have to create a separate type of ASP.NET application. Instead, all ASP.NET applications that you create are now AJAX-enabled.

If you have already worked with ASP.NET AJAX prior to this 3.5 release, you will find that there is really nothing new to learn. The entire technology is seamlessly integrated into the overall development experience.

To sum up what AJAX is all about in relation to ASP.NET in a simple phrase, it would be "an improved experience for the end user through partial page updates and a better user interface." At the core of the ASP.NET AJAX offering is the UpdatePanel control (introduced in this chapter), which provides the capability to have portions of a page update asynchronously. The other half of the equation is richer user interface (UI) elements: controls that leverage the browser features better or extenders that enhance the functionality of other controls.

Overall, Microsoft has fully integrated the entire ASP.NET AJAX experience so you can easily use Visual Studio 2008 and its visual designers to work with your AJAX-enabled pages and even have the full debugging story that you would want to have with your applications. Using Visual Studio 2008, you are now able to debug the JavaScript that you are using in the pages.

In addition, it is important to note that Microsoft focused a lot of attention on cross-platform compatibility with ASP.NET AJAX. You will find that the AJAX-enabled applications that you build upon the .NET Framework 3.5 can work within all the major up-level browsers out there (e.g., Firefox and Opera).

Client-Side Technologies

There really are two parts of the ASP.NET AJAX story. The first is a client-side framework and a set of services that are completely on the client-side. The other part of the story is a server-side framework. Remember that the client-side of ASP.NET AJAX is all about the client communicating asynchronous requests to the server side of the offering.

For this reason, Microsoft offers a Client Script Library, which is a JavaScript library that takes care of the required communications. The Client Script Library is presented in Figure 2-1.

The Client Script Library provides a JavaScript, object-oriented interface that is reasonably consistent with aspects of the .NET Framework. Because browser compatibility components are built in, any work that you build in this layer or (in most cases) work that you let ASP.NET AJAX perform for you here will function with a multitude of different browsers. Also, several components support a rich UI infrastructure that produces many things that would take some serious time to build yourself.

The interesting thing about the client-side technologies that are provided by ASP.NET AJAX is that they are completely independent of ASP.NET. In fact, any developer can freely download the Microsoft AJAX Library (again from www.asp.net/AJAX) and use it with other Web technologies such as PHP (found at www.php.net) and Java Server Pages (also known as JSP). With that said, really the entire Web story is a lot more complete with the server-side technologies that are provided with ASP.NET AJAX.

Server-Side Technologies

As an ASP.NET developer, you will most likely be spending most of your time on the server-side aspect of ASP.NET AJAX. Remember that ASP.NET AJAX is all about the client-side technologies talking back to the server-side technologies. You can actually perform quite a bit on the server-side of ASP.NET AJAX.

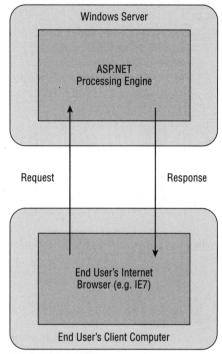

Figure 2-1

The server-side framework knows how to deal with client requests (e.g., putting responses in the correct format). The server-side framework also takes care of the marshaling of objects back and forth between JavaScript objects and the .NET objects that you are using in your server-side code. Figure 2-2 illustrates the server-side framework provided by ASP.NET AJAX.

When you have the .NET Framework 3.5, you have the ASP.NET AJAX Server Extensions on top of the core ASP.NET 2.0 Framework, the Windows Communication Foundation, as well as ASP.NET-based Web services (.asmx).

Developing with ASP.NET AJAX

There are a couple of types of Web developers out there. There are the Web developers who are used to working with ASP.NET and who have experience working with server-side controls and manipulating these controls on the server side. Then there are developers who concentrate on the client side and work with DHTML and JavaScript to manipulate and control the page and its behaviors.

With that said, it is important to realize that ASP.NET AJAX was designed for both types of developers. If you want to work more on the server side of ASP.NET AJAX, you can use the new ScriptManager control and the new UpdatePanel control to AJAX-enable your current ASP.NET applications with little work on your part. All this work can be done using the same programming models that you are quite familiar with in ASP.NET.

Both the ScriptManager and the UpdatePanel controls are discussed later in this chapter.

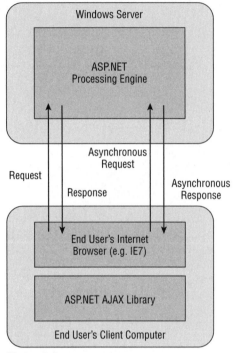

Figure 2-2

You can also use the Client Script Library directly and gain greater control over what is happening on the client's machine. This book will make use of both throughout. Next, this chapter looks at building a simple Web application that makes use of AJAX.

ASP.NET AJAX Applications

The next step is to build a basic sample utilizing this new framework. First, create a new ASP.NET Web Site application using the New Web Site dialog. Name the project **AjaxWebSite**. You will notice (as shown here in Figure 2-3) that there is not a separate type of ASP.NET project for building an ASP.NET AJAX application because every ASP.NET application that you now build is AJAX-enabled.

After you create the application, you will be presented with what is now a standard Web site project. However, you may notice some additional settings in the `web.config` file that are new to ASP.NET 3.5. At the top of the `web.config` file, there are new configuration sections that are registered that deal with AJAX. This section of `web.config` is presented in Listing 2-1.

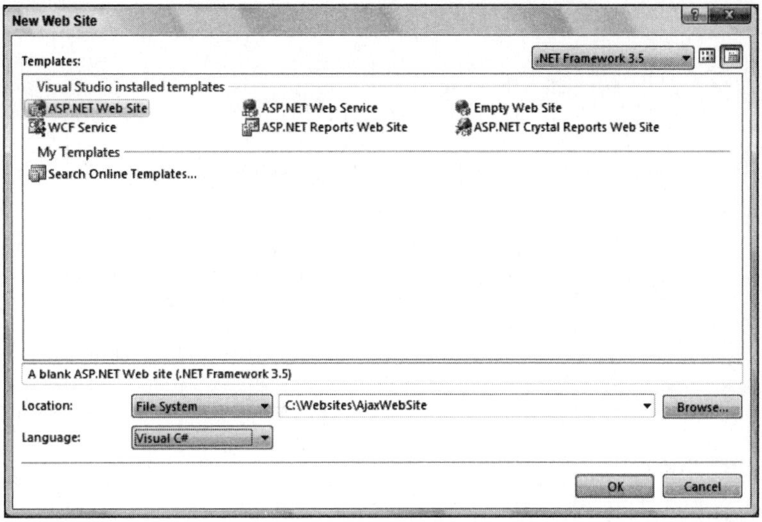

Figure 2-3

Listing 2-1: The <configSections> element for an ASP.NET 3.5 application

```xml
<?xml version="1.0"?>

<configuration>
  <configSections>
    <sectionGroup name="system.web.extensions"
     type="System.Web.Configuration.SystemWebExtensionsSectionGroup,
       System.Web.Extensions, Version=3.5.0.0, Culture=neutral,
       PublicKeyToken=31BF3856AD364E35">
      <sectionGroup name="scripting"
       type="System.Web.Configuration.ScriptingSectionGroup,
          System.Web.Extensions, Version=3.5.0.0, Culture=neutral,
          PublicKeyToken=31BF3856AD364E35">
        <section name="scriptResourceHandler"
         type="System.Web.Configuration.ScriptingScriptResourceHandlerSection,
            System.Web.Extensions, Version=3.5.0.0, Culture=neutral,
            PublicKeyToken=31BF3856AD364E35" requirePermission="false"
          allowDefinition="MachineToApplication"/>
          <sectionGroup name="webServices"
           type="System.Web.Configuration.ScriptingWebServicesSectionGroup,
              System.Web.Extensions, Version=3.5.0.0, Culture=neutral,
              PublicKeyToken=31BF3856AD364E35">
            <section name="jsonSerialization"
             type="System.Web.Configuration.ScriptingJsonSerializationSection,
                System.Web.Extensions, Version=3.5.0.0, Culture=neutral,
                PublicKeyToken=31BF3856AD364E35" requirePermission="false"
              allowDefinition="Everywhere" />
            <section name="profileService"
             type="System.Web.Configuration.ScriptingProfileServiceSection,
```

Continued

23

Listing 2-1: The <configSections> element for an ASP.NET 3.5 application *(continued)*

```
                    System.Web.Extensions, Version=3.5.0.0, Culture=neutral,
                    PublicKeyToken=31BF3856AD364E35" requirePermission="false"
                allowDefinition="MachineToApplication" />
              <section name="authenticationService"
              type="System.Web.Configuration.
                        ScriptingAuthenticationServiceSection,
                 System.Web.Extensions, Version=3.5.0.0, Culture=neutral,
                  PublicKeyToken=31BF3856AD364E35" requirePermission="false"
              allowDefinition="MachineToApplication" />
              <section name="roleService"
               type="System.Web.Configuration.ScriptingRoleServiceSection,
                  System.Web.Extensions, Version=3.5.0.0, Culture=neutral,
                   PublicKeyToken=31BF3856AD364E35" requirePermission="false"
                 allowDefinition="MachineToApplication" />
           </sectionGroup>
        </sectionGroup>
      </sectionGroup>
   </configSections>

   <!-- Configuration removed for clarity -->

   </configuration>
```

In addition to the <configSections> element now a part of the web.config, you will also find a new <system.webServer> section. This section is for ASP.NET AJAX applications that are running within the confines of IIS 7.0. This section of configuration code is presented here in Listing 2-2.

Listing 2-2: The <system.webServer> section for AJAX and IIS 7.0

```
<system.webServer>
   <validation validateIntegratedModeConfiguration="false"/>
   <modules>
      <remove name="ScriptModule" />
      <add name="ScriptModule" preCondition="managedHandler"
          type="System.Web.Handlers.ScriptModule, System.Web.Extensions,
          Version=3.5.0.0, Culture=neutral, PublicKeyToken=31BF3856AD364E35"/>
   </modules>
   <handlers>
      <remove name="WebServiceHandlerFactory-Integrated"/>
      <remove name="ScriptHandlerFactory" />
      <remove name="ScriptHandlerFactoryAppServices" />
      <remove name="ScriptResource" />
      <add name="ScriptHandlerFactory" verb="*" path="*.asmx"
       preCondition="integratedMode"
       type="System.Web.Script.Services.ScriptHandlerFactory,
             System.Web.Extensions, Version=3.5.0.0, Culture=neutral,
             PublicKeyToken=31BF3856AD364E35"/>
      <add name="ScriptHandlerFactoryAppServices" verb="*"
       path="*_AppService.axd" preCondition="integratedMode"
       type="System.Web.Script.Services.ScriptHandlerFactory,
```

Listing 2-2: The <system.webServer> section for AJAX and IIS 7.0 *(continued)*

```
                System.Web.Extensions, Version=3.5.0.0, Culture=neutral,
                PublicKeyToken=31BF3856AD364E35"/>
        <add name="ScriptResource" preCondition="integratedMode" verb="GET,HEAD"
          path="ScriptResource.axd" type="System.Web.Handlers.ScriptResourceHandler,
                    System.Web.Extensions, Version=3.5.0.0, Culture=neutral,
                        PublicKeyToken=31BF3856AD364E35" />
    </handlers></system.webServer>
```

With these aspects of the `web.config` file in place (as provided by the ASP.NET Web Site project type), the next step is to build a simple ASP.NET page that does not yet make use of AJAX.

Building a Simple ASP.NET Page without AJAX

The first step is to build a simple page that does not yet make use of the AJAX capabilities offered by ASP.NET 3.5. Your page needs only a Label control and Button server control. The code for the page is presented in Listing 2-3.

Listing 2-3: A simple ASP.NET 3.5 page that does not use AJAX

```
<%@ Page Language="C#" %>

<script runat="server">
    protected void Button1_Click(object sender, EventArgs e)
    {
        Label1.Text = DateTime.Now.ToString();
    }
</script>

<html xmlns="http://www.w3.org/1999/xhtml">
<head runat="server">
    <title>My Normal ASP.NET Page</title>
</head>
<body>
    <form id="form1" runat="server">
    <div>
        <asp:Label ID="Label1" runat="server"></asp:Label>
        <br />
        <br />
        <asp:Button ID="Button1" runat="server" Text="Click to get machine time"
            onclick="Button1_Click" />
    </div>
    </form>
</body>
</html>
```

When you pull this page up in the browser, it contains only a single button. When the button is clicked, the Label control that is on the page is populated with the time from the server machine. Before the button is clicked, the page's code is similar to the code presented in Listing 2-4.

Listing 2-4: The page output for a page that is not using AJAX

```
<!DOCTYPE html PUBLIC "-//W3C//DTD XHTML 1.0 Transitional//EN"
 "http://www.w3.org/TR/xhtml1/DTD/xhtml1-transitional.dtd">

<html xmlns="http://www.w3.org/1999/xhtml">
<head><title>
 My Normal ASP.NET Page
</title></head>
<body>
    <form name="form1" method="post" action="Default.aspx" id="form1">
<div>
<input type="hidden" name="__VIEWSTATE" id="__VIEWSTATE"
 value="/wEPDwULLTE4OTg4OTc0MjVkZIgwrMMmvqXJHfogxzgZ92wTUORS" />
</div>
    <div>
        <span id="Label1"></span>
        <br />
        <br />
        <input type="submit" name="Button1" value="Click to get machine time"
         id="Button1" />
    </div>
<div>

 <input type="hidden" name="__EVENTVALIDATION" id="__EVENTVALIDATION"
  value="/wEWAgLFpoapCAKM54rGBkhUDe2q/7eVsROfd9QCMK6CwiI7" />
</div></form>
</body>
</html>
```

There is not much in this code. There is a little ViewState and a typical form that will be posted back to the `Default.aspx` page. When the end user clicks the button on the page, a full post back to the server occurs and the entire page is reprocessed and returned to the client's browser. Really, the only change made to the page is that the `<span id="Lable1"></span>` element is populated with a value, but in this case, the entire page is returned. This return is presented here in Listing 2-5.

Listing 2-5: The returned code from the button click event

```
<html xmlns="http://www.w3.org/1999/xhtml">
<head id="Head1"><title>
 My Normal ASP.NET Page
</title></head>
<body>
    <form name="form1" method="post" action="Default.aspx" id="form1">
<div>
<input type="hidden" name="__VIEWSTATE" id="__VIEWSTATE"
 value="/wEPDwUKLTE2MjY5MTY1NQ9kFgICAw9kFgICAQ8PFgIeBFRleHQFEzcvMy8yMDA
      4IDU6MzM6NDAgQU1kZGSDYMwC9k0QFgaZvlblIaJEWMQxIA==" />
</div>

    <div>
        <span id="Label1">7/3/2008 5:33:40 AM</span>
```

Listing 2-5: The returned code from the button click event *(continued)*

```
            <br />
            <br />
            <input type="submit" name="Button1" value="Click to get machine time"

              id="Button1" />
        </div>

    <div>

      <input type="hidden" name="__EVENTVALIDATION" id="__EVENTVALIDATION"
      value="/wEWAgLFsJKtCwKM54rGBmLn3/qARdTOYYDTaj6+5D8E4bEQ" />
    </div></form>
    </body>
    </html>
```

From this, you can see that the entire page was returned back to the client. This process causes the entire page in the browser to disappear and reload (causing the flash). All this work and data moving across the wire only to deal with a small bit of content actually changing on the page.

Next, this chapter reviews building a simple ASP.NET page that makes use of the built-in ASP.NET AJAX capabilities.

Building a Simple ASP.NET Page Using AJAX

After seeing the first example on a simple page that didn't deal with AJAX in any manner, the next step is to build upon that page from Listing 2-3 and add the built-in AJAX capabilities to it. For this example, you will be adding some additional controls. Two of the controls to add are typical ASP.NET server controls — another Label and Button server control. In addition to these controls, you are going to have to add some ASP.NET AJAX controls.

One new thing you will find in the Visual Studio 2008 toolbox is a new section titled AJAX Extensions. This section includes the new AJAX focused controls that are provided as part of ASP.NET 3.5. This new section is shown in Figure 2-4.

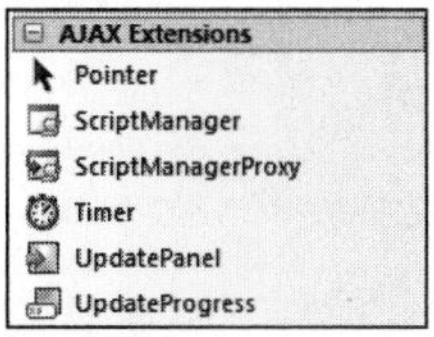

Figure 2-4

From the AJAX Extensions group in the Visual Studio 2008 toolbox, add a ScriptManager server control to the top of your ASP.NET page and include the second Label and Button control inside an UpdatePanel control. The UpdatePanel control is a template server control; you can include any number of items within it (just as other templated ASP.NET server controls). When you have your page set up, the design view should look something like Figure 2-5.

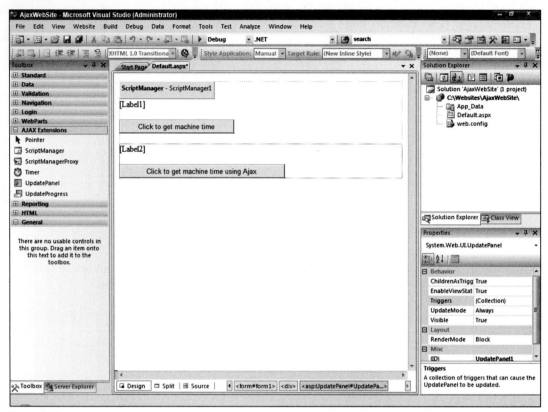

Figure 2-5

When you have this all together on the design view of the ASP.NET page you are working with, the code for this page should be similar to what is presented in Listing 2-6.

Listing 2-6: A simple ASP.NET AJAX page

```
<%@ Page Language="C#" %>

<script runat="server">
    protected void Button1_Click(object sender, EventArgs e)
    {
        Label1.Text = DateTime.Now.ToString();
    }

    protected void Button2_Click(object sender, EventArgs e)
    {
        Label2.Text = DateTime.Now.ToString();
    }
</script>

<html xmlns="http://www.w3.org/1999/xhtml">
<head runat="server">
```

Listing 2-6: A simple ASP.NET AJAX page *(continued)*

```
        <title>My ASP.NET AJAX Page</title>
    </head>
    <body>
        <form id="form1" runat="server">
        <div>
            <asp:ScriptManager ID="ScriptManager1" runat="server">
            </asp:ScriptManager>
            <asp:Label ID="Label1" runat="server"></asp:Label>
            <br />
            <br />
            <asp:Button ID="Button1" runat="server" Text="Click to get machine time"
                onclick="Button1_Click" />
            <br />
            <br />
            <asp:UpdatePanel ID="UpdatePanel1" runat="server">
                <ContentTemplate>
                    <asp:Label ID="Label2" runat="server" Text=""></asp:Label>
                    <br />
                    <br />
                    <asp:Button ID="Button2" runat="server"
                     Text="Click to get machine time using AJAX"
                     onclick="Button2_Click" />
                </ContentTemplate>
            </asp:UpdatePanel>
        </div>
        </form>
    </body>
</html>
```

When this page is pulled up in the browser, it has two buttons. The first button causes a complete page postback and updates the current time in the Label1 server control.

Clicking on the second button causes an AJAX asynchronous postback. Clicking this second button updates the current server time in the Label2 server control. When you click the AJAX button, the time in Label1 will not change at all, as it is outside of the UpdatePanel. A screenshot of the end result is presented in Figure 2-6.

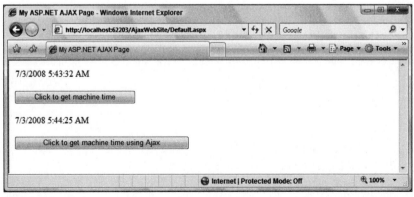

Figure 2-6

Though you might think the code needed for the initial layout of the page will be quite similar (if not the same) as the example that didn't use AJAX, when you first pull up this page from Listing 2-6, the code of the page is actually quite different from the page that was built not using AJAX. Listing 2-7 shows the page results that you will see.

Listing 2-7: The page output for a page that is using AJAX

```
<html xmlns="http://www.w3.org/1999/xhtml">
<head><title>
My ASP.NET AJAX Page
</title></head>
<body>
    <form name="form1" method="post" action="Default.aspx" id="form1">
<div>
<input type="hidden" name="__EVENTTARGET" id="__EVENTTARGET" value="" />
<input type="hidden" name="__EVENTARGUMENT" id="__EVENTARGUMENT" value="" />
<input type="hidden" name="__VIEWSTATE" id="__VIEWSTATE"
 value="/wEPDwULLTE4NzE5NTc5MzRkZDRIzHpPZg4GaO9Hox9A/RnOflkm" />
</div>

<script type="text/javascript">
//<![CDATA[
var theForm = document.forms['form1'];
if (!theForm) {
    theForm = document.form1;
}
function __doPostBack(eventTarget, eventArgument) {
    if (!theForm.onsubmit || (theForm.onsubmit() != false)) {
        theForm.__EVENTTARGET.value = eventTarget;
        theForm.__EVENTARGUMENT.value = eventArgument;
        theForm.submit();
    }
}
//]]>
</script>

<script src="/AJAXWebSite/WebResource.axd?d=o84znEj-
 n4cYi0Wg0pFXCg2&amp;t=633285028458684000" type="text/javascript"></script>

<script src="/AJAXWebSite/ScriptResource.axd?
 d=FETsh5584DXpx8XqIhEM50YSKyR2GkoMoAqraYEDU5_
 gi1SUmL2Gt7rQTRBAw561SojJRQe0OjVI8SiYDjmpYmFP0
 CO8wBFGhtKKJwm2MeE1&amp;t=633285035850304000" type="text/javascript"></script>
<script type="text/javascript">
//<![CDATA[
if (typeof(Sys) === 'undefined') throw new Error('ASP.NET AJAX client-side
  framework failed to load.');
//]]>
</script>

<script src="/AJAXWebSite/ScriptResource.axd?
 d=FETsh5584DXpx8XqIhEM50YSKyR2GkoMoAqraYEDU5_
```

Listing 2-7: The page output for a page that is using AJAX *(continued)*

```
gi1SUmL2Gt7rQTRBAw5617AYfmRViCoO21Z3XwZ33TGiC
 t92e_UOqfrP30mdEYnJYs09ulU1xBLj8TjXOLR1k0&amp;t=633285035850304000"
 type="text/javascript"></script>
     <div>
         <script type="text/javascript">
//<![CDATA[
Sys.WebForms.PageRequestManager._initialize('ScriptManager1',
         document.getElementById('form1'));
Sys.WebForms.PageRequestManager.getInstance()._updateControls(['tUpdatePanel1'],
         [], [], 90);
//]]>
</script>
         <span id="Label1"></span>
         <br />
         <br />
         <input type="submit" name="Button1" value="Click to get machine time"
          id="Button1" />
         <br />
         <br />
         <div id="UpdatePanel1">

                 <span id="Label2"></span>
                 <br />
                 <br />
                 <input type="submit" name="Button2" value="Click to get machine
                  time using AJAX" id="Button2" />
</div>
     </div>
<div>

 <input type="hidden" name="__EVENTVALIDATION" id="__EVENTVALIDATION"
         value="/wEWAwLktbDGDgKM54rGBgK7q7GGCMYnNq57VIqmVD2sRDQqfnOsgWQK" />
</div>

<script type="text/javascript">
//<![CDATA[
Sys.Application.initialize();
//]]>
</script>
</form>
</body>
</html>
```

From this page result, if you click Button1 and perform the full-page postback, you get this entire bit of code back in a response — even though you are interested in updating only a small portion of the page! Again, the reason for this is because it is not using any AJAX capabilities at all. However, if you click Button2 — the button specifically put in place to work with the underlying AJAX capabilities of the page — you send the request that is shown in Listing 2-8 to the back-end server.

Listing 2-8: The asynchronous request from the ASP.NET AJAX page

```
POST /AJAXWebSite/Default.aspx HTTP/1.1
Accept: */*
Accept-Language: en-US
Referer: http://localhost.:62203/AJAXWebSite/Default.aspx
x-microsoftAJAX: Delta=true
Content-Type: application/x-www-form-urlencoded; charset=utf-8
Cache-Control: no-cache
UA-CPU: x86
Accept-Encoding: gzip, deflate
User-Agent: Mozilla/4.0 (compatible; MSIE 7.0; Windows NT 6.0; SLCC1; .NET CLR 2.0.
        50727;
Media Center PC 5.0; .NET CLR 1.1.4322; .NET CLR 3.5.21022; .NET CLR 3.0.04506)
Host: localhost.:62203
Content-Length: 334
Proxy-Connection: Keep-Alive
Pragma: no-cache

ScriptManager1=UpdatePanel1%7CButton2&__EVENTTARGET=&__EVENTARGUMENT=&__VIEWSTATE=%
2FwEPDwULLTE4NzE5NTc5MzQPZBYCAgQPZBYCAgMPDxYCHgRUZXh0BRQxMS8zLzIwMDcgMjoxNzo1NSBQTW
RkZHZxUyYQG0M25t8U7vLbHRJuKlcS&__EVENTVALIDATION=%2FwEWAwKCxdk9AoznisYGArursYYI1844
hk7V466AsW31G5yIZ73%2Bc6o%3D&Button2=Click%20to%20get%20machine%20time%20using%20Aj
ax
```

The response that comes back in return from this request is presented here in Listing 2-9:

Listing 2-9: The asynchronous response from the ASP.NET AJAX page

```
HTTP/1.1 200 OK
Server: ASP.NET Development Server/9.0.0.0
Date: Thu, 03 Jul 2008 10:44:25 GMT
X-AspNet-Version: 2.0.50727
Cache-Control: private
Content-Type: text/plain; charset=utf-8
Content-Length: 796
Connection: Close

239|updatePanel|UpdatePanel1|
                <span id="Label2">07/3/2008 5:44:25 AM</span>
                <br />
                <br />
                <input type="submit" name="Button2" value="Click to get machine
                time using AJAX" id="Button2" />

|172|hiddenField|__VIEWSTATE|/wEPDwULLTE4NzE5NTc5MzQPZBYCAgQPZBYEAgMPDxYCHgRUZXh0BR
QxMS8zLzIwMDcgMjoxNzo1NSBQTWRkAgcPZBYCZg9kFgICAQ8PFgIfAAUUMTEvMy8yMDA3IDI6MTc6NTggU
E1kZGQ4ipZIg91+XSI/dqxFueSUwcrXGw==|56|hiddenField|__EVENTVALIDATION|/wEWAwKCz4mbCA
K7q7GGCAKM54rGBj8b4/mkKNKhV59qX9SdCzqU3AiM|0|asyncPostBackControlIDs|||0|postBackCo
ntrolIDs|||13|updatePanelIDs||tUpdatePanel1|0|childUpdatePanelIDs|||12|panelsToRefr
eshIDs||UpdatePanel1|2|asyncPostBackTimeout||90|12|formAction||Default.aspx|22|page
Title||My ASP.NET AJAX Page|
```

To view the requests and responses in a similar manner to what is presented in Listing 2-9, you can use any HTTP sniffer. I recommend Fiddler found at www.fiddlertool.com.

From Listing 2-9 here, you can see that the response is much smaller than an entire Web page! Also notice that this output includes the HTTP header as well. In fact, the main part of the response is only the code that is contained within the UpdatePanel server control and nothing more. The items at the bottom deal with the ViewState of the page (as it has now changed) and some other small page changes.

When not using AJAX and a postback is occurring, the entire page is reloaded into the browser. In this case, there is a visible flicker of the browser as the previous rendering is removed and the new rendering is displayed. The user usually notices this interruption, and this can interfere with their train of thought when working with your application.

This is quite different from the smooth responsiveness users are accustomed to when working with desktop applications and the jarring nature of these types of Web applications can be disconcerting or annoying to end users. This click-pause-flicker pattern is what the UpdatePanel control helps you overcome. A Web application can now be almost as responsive as a thick client Windows application! The small delays required for passing data between the client and the server are still there, but they are much easier to tolerate now. In many cases, the user may not even notice these delays, because you can distribute the updates so they do not all occur at once.

When you have the smaller responses for the page that perform the page changes that you are really looking for (and nothing more), you will find that the pages are quite a bit better overall. First off, the performance of the page is going to be considerably better (even more so for larger pages) as you are only updating the sections of the pages that need to change and you are not continually moving repetitive code around to be transmitted on the wire and then in turn, interpreted by processing engines.

Probably the most important benefit is for the end users who are now working with the UI of an application that has quite a bit more fluidity to it. The application will feel more responsive to the end user.

ASP.NET AJAX's Server-Side Controls

The AJAX Extensions section in the Visual Studio 2008 toolbox, provides few controls for your use. Those controls that are there are focused on allowing you to AJAX-enable your ASP.NET applications. They are enabling controls. If you are looking for more specific server controls that take advantage of the new AJAX model, then look at the ASP.NET AJAX Control Toolkit — a separate download that is covered in Chapter 6.

The ASP.NET AJAX server controls that come with ASP.NET 3.5 are laid out in the following table.

ASP.NET AJAX Server Control	Description
ScriptManager	A component control that manages the marshalling of messages to the AJAX-enabled server for the parts of the page requiring partial updates. To work, every ASP.NET page requires a ScriptManager control. It is important to note that you can have only a single ScriptManager control on a page.

Continued

(continued)

ASP.NET AJAX Server Control	Description
ScriptManagerProxy	A component control that acts as a ScriptManager control for a content page. The ScriptManagerProxy control, which sits on the content page (or subpage), works in conjunction with a required ScriptManager control that resides on the master page.
Timer	The Timer control executes client-side events at specific intervals and allows specific parts of your page to update or refresh at these moments.
UpdatePanel	A container control that allows you to define specific areas of the page that are enabled to work with the ScriptManager. These areas can then, in turn, make the partial page postbacks and update themselves outside the normal ASP.NET page postback process.
UpdateProgress	A control that allows you to display a visual element to the end user to show that a partial-page postback is occurring to the part of the page making the update. This is an ideal control to use when you have long-running AJAX updates.

The next few sections of this chapter look at these new controls and how to use them within your ASP.NET pages.

The ScriptManager Control

Probably the most important control in your ASP.NET AJAX arsenal is the ScriptManager server control, which works with the page to allow for partial page rendering. You use a single ScriptManager control on each page that you want to use the AJAX capabilities provided by ASP.NET 3.5. When placed in conjunction with the UpdatePanel server control, AJAX-enabling your ASP.NET applications can be as simple as adding two server controls to the page and then you are ready to go!

The ScriptManager control takes care of managing the JavaScript libraries that are utilized on your page as well as marshaling the messages back and forth between the server and the client for the partial page rendering process. The marshaling of the messages can be done using either SOAP or JSON through the ScriptManager control. By default, JSON is being used.

If you place only a single ScriptManager control on your ASP.NET page, it takes care of loading the JavaScript libraries needed by ASP.NET AJAX. The page for this is presented in Listing 2-10.

Listing 2-10: An ASP.NET page that includes only the ScriptManager control

```
<%@ Page Language="C#" %>

<html xmlns="http://www.w3.org/1999/xhtml">
<head runat="server">
    <title>The ScriptManager Control</title>
</head>
<body>
    <form id="form1" runat="server">
```

Listing 2-10: An ASP.NET page that includes only the ScriptManager control *(continued)*

```
    <div>
        <asp:ScriptManager ID="ScriptManager1" runat="server">
        </asp:ScriptManager>
    </div>
    </form>
</body>
</html>
```

From Listing 2-10, you can see that this control is like all other ASP.NET controls and needs only an `ID` and a `runat` attribute to do its work. The page output from this bit of ASP.NET code is presented in Listing 2-11.

Listing 2-11: The page output from the ScriptManager control

```
<html xmlns="http://www.w3.org/1999/xhtml">
<head><title>
 The ScriptManager Control
</title></head>
<body>
    <form name="form1" method="post" action="Default2.aspx" id="form1">
<div>
<input type="hidden" name="__EVENTTARGET" id="__EVENTTARGET" value="" />
<input type="hidden" name="__EVENTARGUMENT" id="__EVENTARGUMENT" value="" />
<input type="hidden" name="__VIEWSTATE" id="__VIEWSTATE"
 value="/wEPDwULLTEzNjQ0OTQ1MDdkZO9dCw2QaeC4D8AwACTbOkD1OX4h" />
</div>

<script type="text/javascript">
//<![CDATA[
var theForm = document.forms['form1'];
if (!theForm) {
    theForm = document.form1;
}
function __doPostBack(eventTarget, eventArgument) {
    if (!theForm.onsubmit || (theForm.onsubmit() != false)) {
        theForm.__EVENTTARGET.value = eventTarget;
        theForm.__EVENTARGUMENT.value = eventArgument;
        theForm.submit();
    }
}
//]]>
</script>

<script src="/AJAXWebSite/WebResource.axd?d=o84znEj-
 n4cYi0Wg0pFXCg2&amp;t=633285028458684000" type="text/javascript"></script>

<script src="/AJAXWebSite/ScriptResource.axd?d=
 FETsh5584DXpx8XqIhEM50YSKyR2GkoMoAqraYEDU5_gi1SUmL2Gt7rQTRBAw561SojJR
 Qe0OjVI8SiYDjmpYmFP0CO8wBFGhtKKJwm2MeE1&amp;t=633285035850304000"
 type="text/javascript"></script>
```

Continued

Listing 2-11: The page output from the ScriptManager control *(continued)*

```
<script type="text/javascript">
//<![CDATA[
if (typeof(Sys) === 'undefined') throw new Error('ASP.NET AJAX client-side
 framework failed to load.');
//]]>
</script>

<script src="/AJAXWebSite/ScriptResource.axd?d=FETsh5584DXpx8XqIhEM50YSKyR2GkoMo
 AqraYEDU5_gi1SUmL2Gt7rQTRBAw5617AYfmRViCoO21Z3XwZ33TGiCt92e_UOqfrP30mdEYnJYs09ul
 U1xBLj8TjXOLR1k0&amp;t=633285035850304000" type="text/javascript"></script>
    <div>
        <script type="text/javascript">
//<![CDATA[
Sys.WebForms.PageRequestManager._initialize('ScriptManager1',
 document.getElementById('form1'));
Sys.WebForms.PageRequestManager.getInstance()._updateControls([], [], [], 90);
//]]>
</script>
    </div>

<script type="text/javascript">
//<![CDATA[
Sys.Application.initialize();
//]]>
</script>

</form>
</body>
</html>
```

The page output shows that a number of JavaScript libraries are loaded with the page. You will also notice that the script sources are dynamically registered and available through the HTTP handler provided through the `ScriptResource.axd` handler.

If you are interested in seeing the contents of the JavaScript libraries, you can use the `src` attribute's URL in the address bar of your browser and you will be prompted to download the JavaScript file that is referenced. You will be prompted to save the `ScriptResource.axd` file, but you can rename it to make use of a `.txt` or `.js` extension if you wish.

An interesting point about the ScriptManager is that it deals with the scripts that are sent to the client by taking the extra step to compress them.

The ScriptManagerProxy Control

The ScriptManagerProxy control was actually introduced to work specifically with the master page capability that ASP.NET offers. As with the ScriptManager control in the previous section, you need a single ScriptManager control on each page that is going to be working with ASP.NET AJAX. However, with that said, the big question is what do you do when you are utilizing master pages. Do you need to put the ScriptManager control on the master page and how does this work with the content pages that use the master page?

When you create a new master page from the Add New Item dialog, in addition to an option for a Master Page, there is also an option to add an AJAX Master Page. This option creates the page shown in Listing 2-12.

Listing 2-12: The AJAX Master Page

```
<%@ Master Language="C#" %>

<script runat="server">

</script>

<html xmlns="http://www.w3.org/1999/xhtml">
<head runat="server">
    <title>Untitled Page</title>
    <asp:ContentPlaceHolder id="head" runat="server">
    </asp:ContentPlaceHolder>
</head>
<body>
    <form id="form1" runat="server">
    <div>
        <asp:ScriptManager ID="ScriptManager1" runat="server" />
        <asp:ContentPlaceHolder id="ContentPlaceHolder1" runat="server">

        </asp:ContentPlaceHolder>
    </div>
    </form>
</body>
</html>
```

This code shows that there is indeed a ScriptManager control on the page and that this control will be added to each and every content page that uses this master page. You do not have to do anything special to a content page to use the ASP.NET AJAX capabilities provided by the master page. Instead, you can create a content page that is no different from any other content page that you might be used to creating.

However, if you are going to want to modify the ScriptManager control that is on the master page in any way, then you have to add a ScriptManagerProxy control to the content page, as shown in Listing 2-13.

Listing 2-13: Adding to the ScriptManager control from the content page

```
<%@ Page Language="C#" MasterPageFile="~/AJAXMaster.master" %>

<asp:Content ID="Content1" ContentPlaceHolderID="head" Runat="Server">
</asp:Content>
<asp:Content ID="Content2" ContentPlaceHolderID="ContentPlaceHolder1"
 Runat="Server">
 <asp:ScriptManagerProxy ID="ScriptManagerProxy1" runat="server">
    <Scripts>
        <asp:ScriptReference Path="myOtherScript.js" />
    </Scripts>
 </asp:ScriptManagerProxy>
</asp:Content>
```

In this case, the content page adds to the ScriptManager control that is on the master page by interjecting a script reference from the content page. If you use a ScriptManagerProxy control on a content page and there does not happen to be a ScriptManager control on the master page, you will get an error.

The UpdatePanel Control

The UpdatePanel server control is an AJAX-specific control that is new in ASP.NET 3.5. The UpdatePanel control is the control that you are likely to use the most when dealing with AJAX. This control preserves the postback model and allows you to perform a partial page render.

The UpdatePanel control is a container control, which means that it does not actually have UI-specific items associated with it. It allows you to mark page regions as eligible to be refreshed independently. It is a way to trigger a partial page postback and update only the portion of the page that the UpdatePanel specifies.

When a control within the UpdatePanel control triggers a postback, the UpdatePanel intervenes to initiate the postback asynchronously and update just that portion of the page. The term asynchronously means that end users do not have to stop and wait for the result from the server. Rather, they are able to continue servicing the page with other JavaScript code and can interact with other controls while waiting for the response from the server.

When the application makes the call to the server, the application provides the name of a JavaScript callback function that is called when the response has been received. That callback function receives the results and updates various page controls accordingly.

The <ContentTemplate> and <Triggers> Element

There are a couple of ways to deal with the controls on the page that initiate the asynchronous page postbacks. The first is by far the simplest and is shown in Listing 2-14.

Listing 2-14: Putting the triggers inside the UpdatePanel control

```
<%@ Page Language="C#" %>

<script runat="server">
    protected void Button1_Click(object sender, EventArgs e)
    {
        Label1.Text = "This button was clicked on " + DateTime.Now.ToString();
    }
</script>
<html xmlns="http://www.w3.org/1999/xhtml">
<head runat="server">
    <title>UpdatePanel Control</title>
</head>
<body>
    <form id="form1" runat="server">
    <div>
        <asp:ScriptManager ID="ScriptManager1" runat="server">
        </asp:ScriptManager>
        <asp:UpdatePanel ID="UpdatePanel1" runat="server">
            <ContentTemplate>
                <asp:Label ID="Label1" runat="server"></asp:Label>
```

Listing 2-14: Putting the triggers inside the UpdatePanel control *(continued)*

```
                <br />
                <br />
                <asp:Button ID="Button1" runat="server"
                 Text="Click to initiate async request"
                 OnClick="Button1_Click" />
            </ContentTemplate>
        </asp:UpdatePanel>
    </div>
    </form>
</body>
</html>
```

In this case, the Label and Button server controls are contained within the UpdatePanel server control. The `<asp:UpdatePanel>` element has two possible sub-elements: `<ContentTemplate>` and the `<Triggers>` elements. Any content that needs to be changed with the asynchronous page postbacks should be contained within the `<ContentTemplate>` section of the UpdatePanel control.

By default, any type of control trigger (something that would normally trigger a page postback) that is contained within the `<ContentTemplate>` section instead causes the asynchronous page postback. That means, in the case of Listing 2-14, the button on the page will trigger an asynchronous page postback instead of a full-page postback. Each click on the button changes the time displayed in the Label control.

This highlights a key point about the UpdatePanel control: When using the UpdatePanel, the code for the page executes just as though it were a regular postback. You can see from the code listing that there was not any code on the page that did anything specific for partial page updates. The code never made reference to the UpdatePanel control, and yet only part of the page changed. The UpdatePanel gathers the rendering from controls within the UpdatePanel and abandons most of the rest of the output. It also returns the updated hidden fields with things like ViewState that need to reflect the new state of the page.

Listing 2-14 demonstrates one of the big issues with this model: When the asynchronous postback occurs, you are not only sending the date/time value for the Label control, but you are also sending back the entire code for the button that is on the page. This occurs within the UpdatePanel control when any of the child controls contained within would normally trigger a postback. This is because the default value for the `UpdateMode` property of the UpdatePanel control is set to `Always`, and the default value of the `ChildrenAsTriggers` property is set to `true`. When using the default UpdatePanel control in this manner, your postbacks will appear as something similar to what is presented here.

```
265|updatePanel|UpdatePanel1|
    <span id="Label1">This button was clicked on 07/3/2008 5:44:25 AM</span>
    <br />
    <br />
    <input type="submit" name="Button1" value="Click to initiate async request"
     id="Button1" />
            |164|hiddenField|__VIEWSTATE|/wEPDwUKLTU2NzQ4MzIwMw9kFgICBA9kFgICAw9kFg
            JmD2QWAgIBDw8WAh4EVGV4dAUxVGhpcyBidXR0b24gd2FzIGNsaWNrZWQgb24gMTEvMT
            gvMjAwNyAxMToONToyMSBBTWRkZKJIG4WhyQvUwPCX4PxI5FEUFtC|48|hiddenField|
            __EVENTVALIDATION|/wEWAgL43YXdBwKM54rGBlI52OYVl/McOV61BYd/3wSj+RkD|0|
            asyncPostBackControlIDs|||0|postBackControlIDs|||13|updatePanelIDs||
            tUpdatePanel1|0|childUpdatePanelIDs|||12|panelsToRefreshIDs||UpdatePane
            l1|2|asyncPostBackTimeout||90|22|formAction||SimpleUpdatePanel.aspx|11|
            pageTitle||UpdatePanel|
```

This bit of code which constitutes the response that is sent back to the client via the asynchronous postback shows that the entire section contained within the UpdatePanel control is reissued. You can slim down your pages by including only the portions of the page that are actually updating. If you take the button outside of the `<ContentTemplate>` section of the UpdatePanel control, then you have to include a `<Triggers>` section within the control.

The reason for this is that, while the content that you want to change with the asynchronous postback is all contained within the `<ContentTemplate>` section, you have to tie up a page event to cause the postback to occur. This is how the `<Triggers>` section of the UpdatePanel control is used. You use this section of the control to specify the various triggers that initiate an asynchronous page postback. Using the `<Triggers>` element within the UpdatePanel control, you can rewrite Listing 2-14 as shown in Listing 2-15.

Listing 2-15: Using a trigger to cause the asynchronous page postback

```
<%@ Page Language="C#" %>

<script runat="server">

    protected void Button1_Click(object sender, EventArgs e)
    {
        Label1.Text = "This button was clicked on " + DateTime.Now.ToString();
    }
</script>
<html xmlns="http://www.w3.org/1999/xhtml">
<head runat="server">
    <title>UpdatePanel</title>
</head>
<body>
    <form id="form1" runat="server">
    <div>
        <asp:ScriptManager ID="ScriptManager1" runat="server">
        </asp:ScriptManager>
        <asp:UpdatePanel ID="UpdatePanel1" runat="server">
            <ContentTemplate>
                <asp:Label ID="Label1" runat="server"></asp:Label>
            </ContentTemplate>
            <Triggers>
                <asp:AsyncPostBackTrigger ControlID="Button1" EventName="Click" />
            </Triggers>
        </asp:UpdatePanel>
        <br />
        <br />
        <asp:Button ID="Button1" runat="server"
         Text="Click to initiate async request"
         OnClick="Button1_Click" />
    </div>
    </form>
</body>
</html>
```

In this case, the Button control and the HTML elements are outside the `<ContentTemplate>` section of the UpdatePanel control and therefore will not be sent back to the client for each asynchronous page postback. The only item contained in the `<ContentTemplate>` section is the only item on the page that needs to change with the postbacks — the Label control. Tying this all together is the `<Triggers>` section.

The `<Triggers>` section can contain two possible controls: AsyncPostBackTrigger and PostBackTrigger. In this case, the AsyncPostBackTrigger is used. The PostBackTrigger control causes a full page postback, whereas the AsyncPostBackTrigger control causes only an asynchronous page postback (obviously as described by the names of the controls).

As you can see from the example in Listing 2-15, which uses the AsyncPostBackTrigger element, only two attributes are used to tie the Button control to the trigger for the asynchronous postback: the `ControlID` and the `EventName` attributes. The control you want to act as the initiator of the asynchronous page postback is put as the value of the `ControlID` attribute (the control's name as specified by the control's ID attribute). The `EventName` attribute's value is the name of the event for the control that is specified in the `ControlID` that you want to be called in the asynchronous request from the client. In this case, the Button control's `Click()` event is called and this is the event that changes the value of the control that resides within the `<ContentTemplate>` section of the UpdatePanel control.

Running this page and clicking on the button gives you a smaller asynchronous response back to the client.

```
108|updatePanel|UpdatePanel1|
   <span id="Label1">This button was clicked on 11/18/2008 11:58:56 AM</span>
        |164|hiddenField|__VIEWSTATE|/wEPDwUKMjA2NjQ2MDYzNw9kFgICBA9kFgICAw9kFg
        JmD2QWAgIBDw8WAh4EVGV4dAUxVGhpcyBidXR0b24gd2FzIGNsaWNrZWQgb24gMTEvMTEgv
        MjAwNyAxMTo1ODo1NiBBTWRkZZJA9uj9wwRaasgTrZo85rVvLnoi|48|hiddenField|
        __EVENTVALIDATION|/wEWAgKK3YDTDAKM54rGBqrbjV4/u4ks3aKsn7Xz8xNFE8G/|7|
        asyncPostBackControlIDs||Button1|0|postBackControlIDs|||13|
        updatePanelIDs||tUpdatePanel1|0|childUpdatePanelIDs|||12|
        panelsToRefreshIDs||UpdatePanel1|2|asyncPostBackTimeout||
        90|22|formAction||SimpleUpdatePanel.aspx|11|pageTitle||
        UpdatePanel|
```

Although not considerably smaller than the previous example, it is smaller and the size similarity is really due to the size of the page used in this example (pages that are more voluminous would show more dramatic improvements). Pages with heavy content associated with them can show some dramatic size reductions, depending on how you structure your pages with the UpdatePanel control.

The UpdateMode and ChildrenAsTriggers Properties

Two important properties of the UpdatePanel control that you will find include the `UpdateMode` and `ChildrenAsTriggers` properties. The `UpdateMode` property is of the type `UpdatePanelUpdateMode`. The two possible values of this property are `Always` and `Conditional`. The default mode of `Always` means that the UpdatePanel will be refreshed anytime a child control initiates a postback. You saw this in action in the previous examples.

This behavior corresponds to the `ChildrenAsTriggers` property's default value of `true`. When an UpdatePanel is triggered to refresh, and if the control is using the default settings, the child control's postback will trigger an update. One interesting point is that if you set `ChildrenAsTriggers` to a value of `false` without changing the `UpdateMode` value to `Conditional`, you will then get the error shown in Figure 2-7.

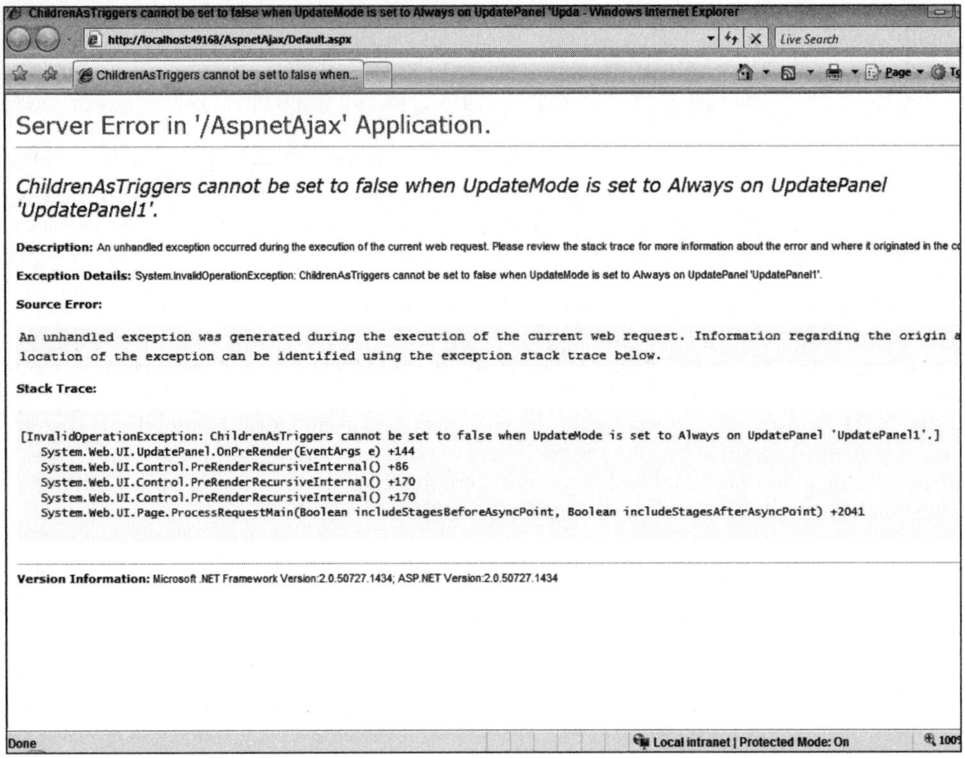

Figure 2-7

The following table summarizes the results of possible combinations of UpdateMode and ChildrenAsTriggers properties.

UpdateMode	ChildrenAsTriggers	Result
Always	False	This combination is a set of illegal parameters and will result in an exception.
Always	True	In this combination, the UpdatePanel control will refresh either if the entire page refreshes or if a child control contained within the control initiates a postback.
Conditional	False	With these two settings, the UpdatePanel control will refresh if the entire page refreshes or if another control outside the UpdatePanel control triggers a postback. With this combination, none of the nested child controls within the UpdatePanel control will be able to initiate a postback.
Conditional	True	Using this combination, the UpdatePanel control refreshes if the entire page refreshes or when a child control within the UpdatePanel controls performs a postback or when a trigger control outside the panel initiates a refresh.

As stated, you cannot set `ChildrenAsTriggers` to `false` while the `UpdateMode` is set to `Always`. The two property settings are contradictory to each other, as you would be asking the UpdatePanel control to refresh based on the child controls while simultaneously saying that the child controls should not trigger updates. In order for the `false` setting to work, the `UpdateMode` property needs to be set to the only other possible setting of `Conditional`.

When the `UpdateMode` property is set to a value of `Conditional` and the `ChildrenAsTriggers` property is set to a value of `false`, the UpdatePanel control will not refresh unless the entire page is updated or when a control outside the UpdatePanel is defined as the trigger and initiates a postback. Listing 2-16 illustrates this behavior.

Listing 2-16: Using the UpdateMode and ChildrenAsTriggers properties

```
<%@ Page Language="C#" %>

<script runat="server">
    protected override void OnLoad(EventArgs e)
    {
        base.OnLoad(e);
        string theTime = DateTime.Now.ToLongTimeString();

        for (int i = 0; i < 3; i++)
        {
            theTime += "<br />" + theTime;
        }

        time1.Text = theTime;
        time2.Text = theTime;
    }

    protected void Button3_Click(object sender, EventArgs e)
    {
        Response.Write("You performed a complete page postback on " +
            DateTime.Now);
    }
</script>

<html xmlns="http://www.w3.org/1999/xhtml">
<head id="Head1" runat="server">
    <title>UpdatePanel Triggers</title>
</head>
<body>
    <form id="form1" runat="server">
    <div>
        <asp:ScriptManager ID="ScriptManager1" runat="server">
        </asp:ScriptManager>
        <asp:Button ID="Button1" runat="server" Text="Update the top UpdatePanel"
            Width="350px" />
        <br />
        <br />
        <asp:Button ID="Button2" runat="server"
```

Continued

Listing 2-16: Using the UpdateMode and ChildrenAsTriggers properties *(continued)*

```
                Text="Update the bottom UpdatePanel"
                Width="350px" />
        <br />
        <br />
        <asp:Button ID="Button3" runat="server" onclick="Button3_Click"
            Text="Perform a complete page postback" Width="350px" />
        <br />
        <br />
        <asp:UpdatePanel ID="UpdatePanel1" runat="server" UpdateMode="Conditional">
            <Triggers>
                <asp:AsyncPostBackTrigger ControlID="Button1" EventName="Click" />
            </Triggers>
            <ContentTemplate>
                <div style="border-style: solid; background-color: gray;">
                    <asp:Label runat="server" ID="time1"></asp:Label><br />
                    <br />
                </div>
                <br />
            </ContentTemplate>
        </asp:UpdatePanel>
        <asp:UpdatePanel ID="UpdatePanel2" runat="server" UpdateMode="Conditional"
            ChildrenAsTriggers="false">
            <Triggers>
                <asp:AsyncPostBackTrigger ControlID="Button2" EventName="Click" />
            </Triggers>
            <ContentTemplate>
                <div style="border-style: solid; background-color: gray;">
                    <asp:Label runat="server" ID="time2"></asp:Label><br />
                </div>
                <br />
            </ContentTemplate>
        </asp:UpdatePanel>
    </div>
    </form>
</body>
</html>
```

This example contains two UpdatePanel controls, each with a Label control that displays the time retrieved from the server (or machine you are working with for your development). The three buttons at the top of the page are outside of the UpdatePanel controls themselves. Running this page, you would get results that are similar to those in Figure 2-8.

Looking back at the code for this page, The UpdateMode property of both UpdatePanel controls is set to a value of Conditional. This example also sets the ChildrenAsTriggers property to false on only the last of the UpdatePanel controls, but in reality it is completely unnecessary in this example as there are not any child controls that cause a postback, so the setting does not affect the behavior.

There is also a button on the page (Button3) that does a complete page postback and in this case, if clicked, it updates the contents of both UpdatePanel controls.

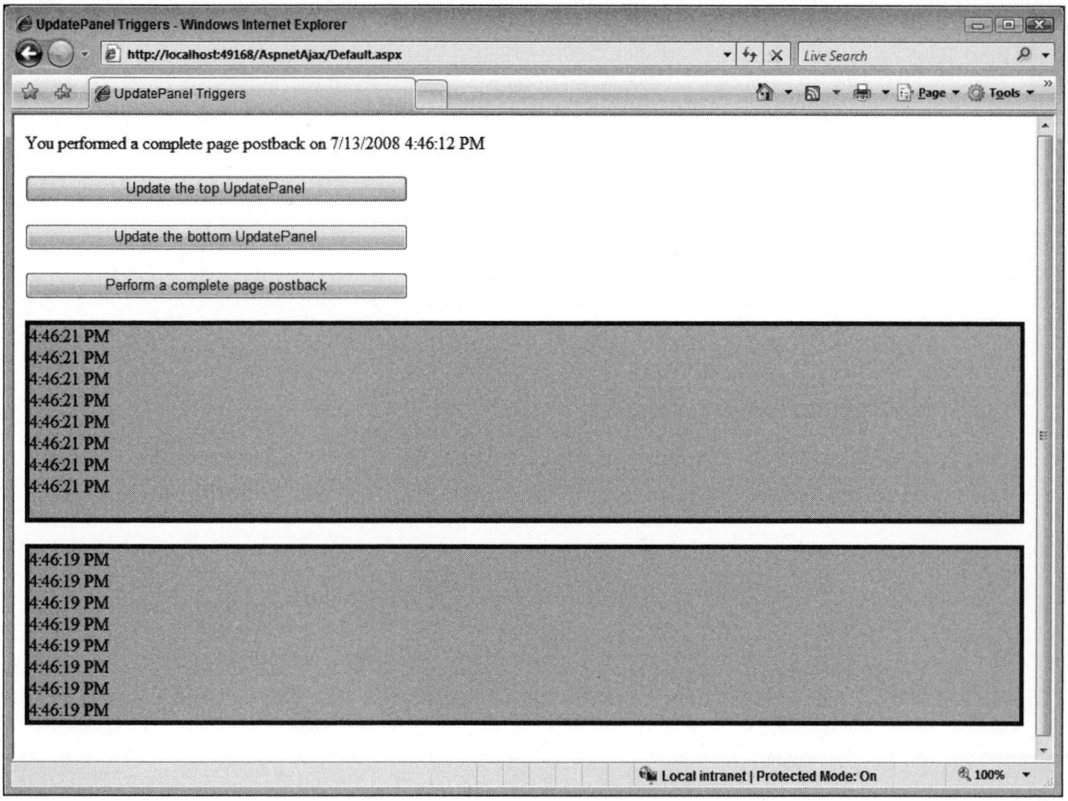

Figure 2-8

Usually, update calls made using the UpdatePanel are done asynchronously. However, in some cases you will want to have a full-page postback occur instead. You can make exceptions to the partial page update behavior by defining a PostBackTrigger within the UpdatePanel control. For this behavior requirement, the event name does not need to be defined. Instead, you just provide a value of the ControlID property as is illustrated here in this partial code example.

```
<Triggers>
    <asp:PostBackTrigger ControlID="Button2" />
</Triggers>
```

Building Triggers Using Visual Studio 2008

If you like to work on the design surface of Visual Studio when building your ASP.NET pages, you will find that there is good support for building your ASP.NET AJAX pages, including the creation of triggers in the UpdatePanel control. To see this in action, place a single UpdatePanel server control on your page and view the control details in the Properties dialog within Visual Studio. The Triggers item in the list has a button next to it that allows you to modify the items associated with it. This is illustrated in Figure 2-9.

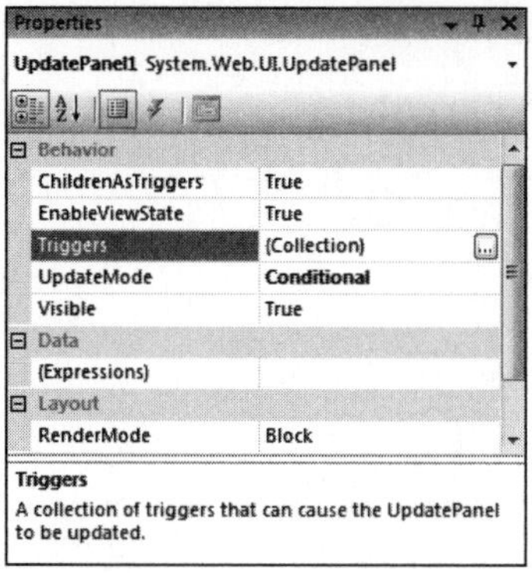

Figure 2-9

Clicking on the button in the Properties dialog launches the UpdatePanelTrigger Collection Editor, as shown in Figure 2-10. This editor allows you to add any number of triggers and to associate them to a control and a control event very easily. Figure 2-10 assumes you have a button on the page to work with.

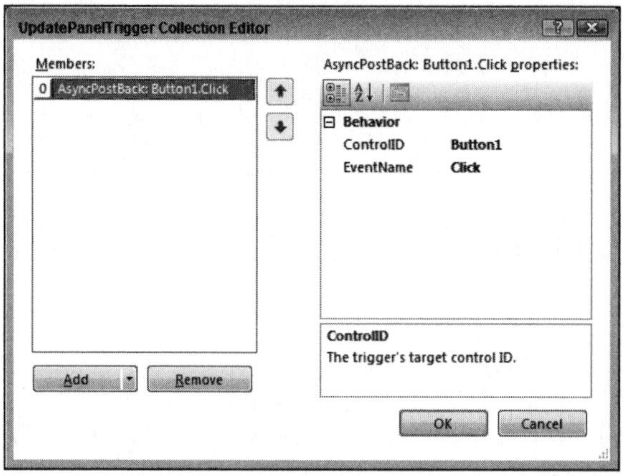

Figure 2-10

Clicking the OK button here adds the trigger to the <Triggers> section of your UpdatePanel control.

Invoking Updates from the Server Using the Update() Method

So far, the examples have all been about controlling partial-page updates from within the browser by allowing the UpdatePanel to work with control triggers such as a button click event. It is important to understand that while you can easily work with the UpdatePanel control in this manner to perform the asynchronous page updates your application requires, it is also just as easy to access the update behaviors for your page through programmatic interaction with the UpdatePanel control itself.

The UpdatePanel control provides an Update() method that allows a region of the page to be refreshed programmatically from server-side code. During a partial page update, remember that the page runs normally and the UpdatePanel controls are just updating without the user seeing a full page postback. Any condition during the page execution can be a reason to update a portion of the page programmatically. Listing 2-17 illustrates an example of this in action.

Listing 2-17: Programmatically triggering updates using the Update() method

```
<%@ Page Language="C#" %>

<script runat="server">
    protected override void OnLoad(EventArgs e)
    {
        var tempTime = Session["LastTime"];

        if (tempTime != null)
        {
            DateTime lastTime = (DateTime)tempTime;

            if (DateTime.Now > lastTime.AddSeconds(4))
            {
                UpdatePanel2.Update();
                Session["lastTime"] = DateTime.Now;
            }
        }
        else
        {
            Session["lastTime"] = DateTime.Now;
        }

        base.OnLoad(e);
        string theTime = DateTime.Now.ToLongTimeString();

        for (int i = 0; i < 3; i++)
        {
            theTime += "<br />" + theTime;
        }

        time1.Text = theTime;
        time2.Text = theTime;
    }

</script>

<html xmlns="http://www.w3.org/1999/xhtml">
<head id="Head1" runat="server">
    <title>Programmatically triggering using the Update method</title>
</head>
<body>
    <form id="form1" runat="server">
    <div>
        <asp:ScriptManager ID="ScriptManager1" runat="server">
        </asp:ScriptManager>
        <asp:Button ID="Button1" runat="server" Text="Update Conditionally" />
        <br />
        <asp:UpdatePanel ID="UpdatePanel1" runat="server" UpdateMode="Conditional">
            <Triggers>
                <asp:AsyncPostBackTrigger ControlID="Button1" EventName="Click" />
            </Triggers>
            <ContentTemplate>
```

Continued

47

Listing 2-17: Programmatically triggering updates using the Update() method *(continued)*

```
                <div style="border-style: solid; background-color: gray;">
                    <asp:Label runat="server" ID="time1"></asp:Label><br />
                    <br />
                </div>
                <br />
            </ContentTemplate>
        </asp:UpdatePanel>
        <asp:UpdatePanel ID="UpdatePanel2" runat="server" UpdateMode="Conditional">
            <ContentTemplate>
                <div style="border-style: solid; background-color: gray;">
                    <asp:Label runat="server" ID="time2"></asp:Label><br />
                </div>
                <br />
            </ContentTemplate>
        </asp:UpdatePanel>
    </div>
    </form>
</body>
</html>
```

In Listing 2-17, the page code updating the time is changed to conditionally call the Update() method of the UpdatePanel control of the second UpdatePanel at the same time the first UpdatePanel is being refreshed. The current time is stored in the Session object on each call. When the page executes, the current time is checked against the time stored previously in Session. If this difference in time is more than four seconds, then the Update() method is invoked. The refreshed view of that portion of the page is then also updated when the call completes and the first UpdatePanel is updated. Running this page will give you results similar to those in Figure 2-11.

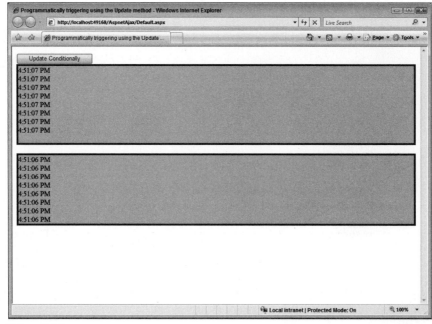

Figure 2-11

The RenderMode Property

Although the UpdatePanel does not have a visible rendering of its own, it wraps the rendering of the content placed in the ContentTemplate section in an HTML element. The default behavior is to use a <div> element as the wrapper, but the RenderMode property of the UpdatePanel control allows you to switch to use a <span> element instead. Setting the RenderMode to a value of Block results in the rendering being placed inside a <div> element. Setting RenderMode to Inline indicates that a <span> element should be used.

The UpdatePanel Control's Place within the ASP.NET Page Lifecycle

The ASP.NET page execution lifecycle is not altered by the partial rendering feature provided by ASP.NET AJAX. The ScriptManager control participates in the lifecycle to facilitate the partial page updates. It coordinates gathering the renderings from the UpdatePanels that need to be refreshed during an asynchronous post and carrying the hidden fields necessary to make the following post function correctly.

Controls that modify the ViewState on the page, even if they are not in the UpdatePanel being affected, do not have to take any special action to ensure the change is available in subsequent requests. Event validation, cross-page posting, and ASP.NET's ability to maintain the scroll position all continue to work when using a UpdatePanel control on your page.

When using the UpdatePanel control, it is vital to remember that the page lifecycle is the same as it has always been. It is nice that no special pains are required to start taking advantage of partial-page updates, but do not forget that the overhead on the server is the same and that the traffic between browser and server can still be significant. For example, if you have a GridView or other data control on the page that is making use of ViewState to avoid trips to the database, that ViewState will be carried with each request even when the data is not being updated. As this ViewState baggage can slow down partial page updates, you should carefully consider which controls need to have ViewState enabled, and disable it on controls that don't need it.

There are several ways to determine whether your code is executing in the context of a partial-page update. To find information about the current state, the control author can walk up the control tree to determine whether the controls are contained within an UpdatePanel and query the IsInPartialRendering property. This property reveals whether the UpdatePanel is rendering back to the browser with asynchronous updates in order to take custom actions if desired. The ScriptManager control can let you know if the page is executing as the result of an UpdatePanel initiated asynchronous post. To accomplish this, check the IsInAsyncPostBack property to make the determination:

```
if (ScriptManager1.IsInAsyncPostBack)
{

}
```

The Timer Control

One common task when working with asynchronous postbacks from your ASP.NET pages is that you might want these asynchronous postbacks to occur at specific intervals. To accomplish this, you use the Timer control available to you from the AJAX Extensions part of the toolbox. A simple example to demonstrate how this control works involves putting some timestamps on your page and setting postbacks to occur at specific timed intervals. This example is illustrated in Listing 2-18.

Listing 2-18: Using the Timer control

```
<%@ Page Language="C#" %>

<script runat="server">
    protected void Page_Load(object sender, EventArgs e)
    {
        if (!Page.IsPostBack) {
            Label1.Text = DateTime.Now.ToString();
        }
    }

    protected void Timer1_Tick(object sender, EventArgs e)
    {
        Label1.Text = DateTime.Now.ToString();
    }
</script>
<html xmlns="http://www.w3.org/1999/xhtml">
<head runat="server">
    <title>Timer Example</title>
</head>
<body>
    <form id="form1" runat="server">
    <div>
        <asp:ScriptManager ID="ScriptManager1" runat="server" />
        <asp:UpdatePanel ID="UpdatePanel1" runat="server">
            <ContentTemplate>
                <asp:Label ID="Label1" runat="server" Text="Label"></asp:Label>
                <asp:Timer ID="Timer1" runat="server" OnTick="Timer1_Tick"
                Interval="10000">
                </asp:Timer>
            </ContentTemplate>
        </asp:UpdatePanel>
    </div>
    </form>
</body>
</html>
```

In this case, there are only three visible controls on the page. The first is the ScriptManager control followed by a Label and the Timer control. When this page loads for the first time, the Label control is populated with the `DateTime` value through the invocation of the `Page_Load` event handler. After this initial load of the `DateTime` value to the Label control, the Timer control takes care of changing this value.

The `OnTick` attribute from the Timer control enables you to accomplish this task. It points to the event that is triggered when the time span specified in the `Interval` attribute is reached.

The `Interval` attribute is set to `10000`, which is 10,000 milliseconds (remember that there are 1,000 milliseconds to every second). This means, that every 10 seconds an asynchronous postback is performed and the `Timer1_Tick()` function is called.

When you run this page, the time changes on the page every 10 seconds.

The UpdateProgress Control

The final server control in the AJAX Extensions section of Visual Studio 2008 is the UpdateProgress control. Some asynchronous postbacks take time to execute because of the size of the response or because of the computing time required to get a result together to send back to the client. The UpdateProgress control allows you to provide a visual signifier to the clients to show that indeed work is being done and they will get results soon (and that the browser simply didn't just lock up).

Listing 2-19 shows a textual implementation of the UpdateProgress control.

Listing 2-19: Using the UpdateProgess control to show a text message to the client

```
<%@ Page Language="C#" %>

<script runat="server">

    protected void Button1_Click(object sender, EventArgs e)
    {
        System.Threading.Thread.Sleep(10000);
        Label1.Text = "This button was clicked on " + DateTime.Now.ToString();
    }
</script>
<html xmlns="http://www.w3.org/1999/xhtml">
<head runat="server">
    <title>UpdatePanel</title>
</head>
<body>
    <form id="form1" runat="server">
    <div>
        <asp:ScriptManager ID="ScriptManager1" runat="server">
        </asp:ScriptManager>
        <asp:UpdateProgress ID="UpdateProgress1" runat="server">
            <ProgressTemplate>
                An update is occurring...
            </ProgressTemplate>
        </asp:UpdateProgress>
        <asp:UpdatePanel ID="UpdatePanel1" runat="server" UpdateMode="Conditional">
            <ContentTemplate>
                <asp:Label ID="Label1" runat="server"></asp:Label>
            </ContentTemplate>
            <Triggers>
                <asp:AsyncPostBackTrigger ControlID="Button1" EventName="Click" />
            </Triggers>
        </asp:UpdatePanel>
        <br />
        <br />
        <asp:Button ID="Button1" runat="server"
         Text="Click to initiate async request"
         OnClick="Button1_Click" />
    </div>
    </form>
</body>
</html>
```

To add some delay to the response (in order to simulate a long-running computer process) the `Thread.Sleep()` method is called. From here, you add an UpdateProgess control to the part of the page where you want the update message to be presented. In this case, the UpdateProgress control was added above the UpdatePanel server control. This control does not go inside the UpdatePanel control; instead, it sits outside of the control. However, like the UpdatePanel control, the UpdateProgress control is a template control.

The UpdateProgress control has only a single sub-element: the `<ProgressTemplate>` element. Whatever you place in this section of the control will appear when the UpdateProgress control is triggered. In this case, the only item present in this section of the control is some text. When you run this page, you get the update shown in Figure 2-12.

The text will appear immediately in this case and will not disappear until the asynchronous postback has finished. The items you put in the `<ProgressTemplate>` section is actually contained in the page, but its display is turned off through Cascading Style Sheets (CSS).

```
<div id="UpdateProgress1" style="display:none;">
    An update is occurring...
</div>
```

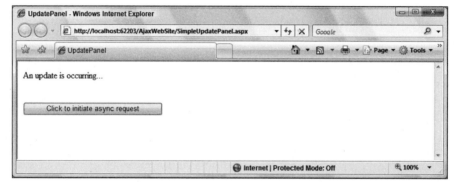

Figure 2-12

Controlling When the Message Appears

Right now, the UpdateProgress appears as soon as the button is clicked. However, some of your processes might not take that long and you might not always want a progress notification going out to the client. The UpdateProgress control includes a `DisplayAfter` attribute, which allows you to control when the progress update message appears. The use of the `DisplayAfter` attribute is shown in Listing 2-20.

Listing 2-20: Using the DisplayAfter attribute

```
<asp:UpdateProgress ID="UpdateProgress1" runat="server" DisplayAfter="5000">
    <ProgressTemplate>
        An update is occurring...
    </ProgressTemplate>
</asp:UpdateProgress>
```

The value of the `DisplayAfter` property is a number that represents the number of milliseconds that the UpdateProgress control will wait until it displays what is contained within the `<ProgressTemplate>` section. The code in Listing 2-20 specifies that the text found in the `<ProgressTemplate>` section will not be displayed for 5,000 milliseconds (5 seconds).

Adding an Image to the `<ProcessTemplate>`

The previous examples, which make use of the UpdateProgress control, use this control with text, but you can put anything you want within this template control. For instance, you can put a spinning wheel image that will show the end user that the request is being processed. The use of the image is shown in Listing 2-21.

Listing 2-21: Using an image in the `<ProcessTemplate>` section

```
<asp:UpdateProgress ID="UpdateProgress1" runat="server" DisplayAfter="5000">
    <ProgressTemplate>
        <asp:Image ID="Image1" runat="server" ImageUrl="~/spinningwheel.gif" />
    </ProgressTemplate>
</asp:UpdateProgress>
```

Just as the in the text approach, the code for the image is already placed on the client's page instance and is just turned off via CSS:

```
<div id="UpdateProgress1" style="display:none;">
    <img id="Image1" src="spinningwheel.gif" style="border-width:0px;" />
</div>
```

Displaying Behaviors of the Progress Indicators

The `DynamicLayout` property of the UpdateProgress control is one that you might not change that often. The default behavior of this property is not to allocate any space for the contents of the UpdateProgress control. Figure 2-13 presents a page when no update is being made.

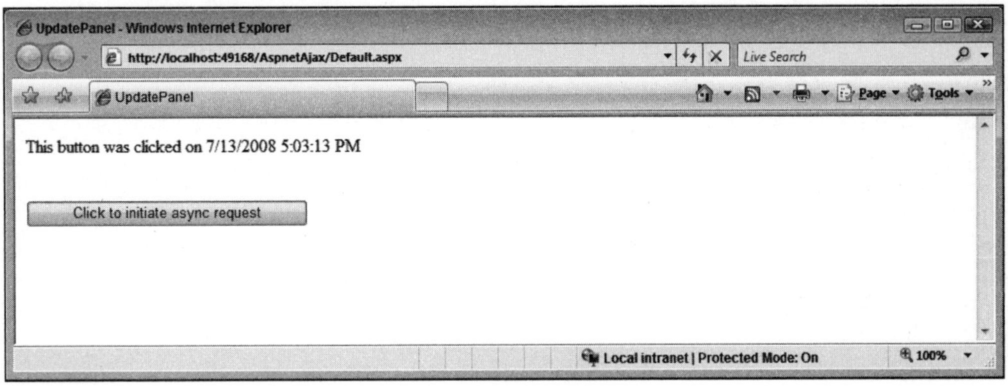

Figure 2-13

Notice that no space is provided for the `Progress.gif` image. Instead, room is made for this indicator only when it is needed. One result of this setting is that the rest of the page is shifted down slightly to make room for the indicators that you end up using. This can be disconcerting to users to see the page layout change and shift for a short time period. To preallocate the space required for the progress indicator and avoid a shift in the layout, you will want to set the `DynamicLayout` property to `false` as presented here:

```
<asp:UpdateProgress ID="UpdateProgress1" runat="server" DynamicLayout="false"  >
```

This produces a page with the results illustrated in Figure 2-14.

The layout options really depend on the nature of your application. One point to understand is that the UpdateProgress control will display its indicator for every asynchronous postback that occurs on the page unless you assign it specifically to a single UpdatePanel, using the `AssociatedUpdatePanelID` property:

```
<asp:UpdateProgress ID="UpdateProgress1" runat="server"
AssociatedUpdatePanelID="UpdatePanel1" >
```

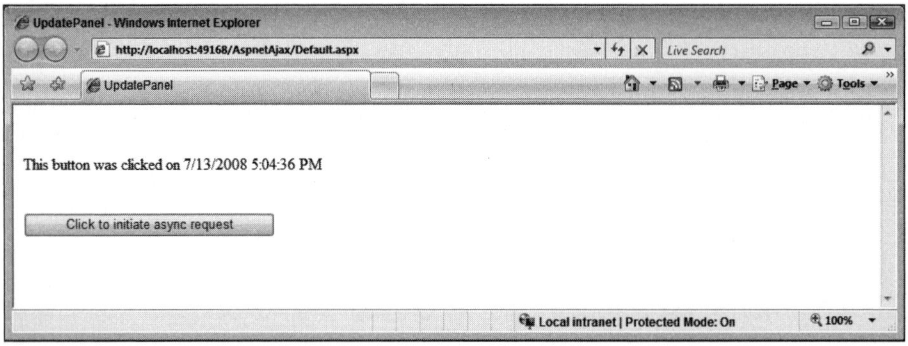

Figure 2-14

One common approach is to use a CSS class with the UpdateProgress control that manipulates its positioning so that the `<ProgressTemplate>` contents are displayed as a layer right over the top of the UpdatePanel being affected. The following is an example set of styles that, when associated with a `<div>` element for an UpdateProgress, produces a small square on the screen to contain whatever images or other information you want to display while an update is occurring.

```
<style type="text/css">
.progress
{
    border:solid;
    background-color: white;
    position: absolute;
    top: 180px;
    left: 180px;
    width: 60px;
    height: 60px;
    padding-left:40px;
    padding-top:40px;
    z-index:1
}
</style>
```

Using Multiple UpdatePanel Controls

So far, this chapter has showed you how to work with a single UpdatePanel control, but it is important to realize that you can have multiple UpdatePanel controls on a single page. This, in the end, will give you the ability to control the output to specific regions of the page when you want.

An example of using more than a single UpdatePanel control is presented in Listing 2-22.

Listing 2-22: Using more than one UpdatePanel control

```
<%@ Page Language="C#" %>

<script runat="server">
    protected void Button1_Click(object sender, EventArgs e)
    {
        Label1.Text = "Label1 was populated on " + DateTime.Now;
        Label2.Text = "Label2 was populated on " + DateTime.Now;
    }
</script>
<html xmlns="http://www.w3.org/1999/xhtml">
<head runat="server">
    <title>Multiple UpdatePanel Controls</title>
</head>
<body>
    <form id="form1" runat="server">
    <div>
        <asp:ScriptManager ID="ScriptManager1" runat="server">
        </asp:ScriptManager>
        <asp:UpdatePanel ID="UpdatePanel1" runat="server">
            <ContentTemplate>
                <asp:Label ID="Label1" runat="server"></asp:Label>
            </ContentTemplate>
            <Triggers>
                <asp:AsyncPostBackTrigger ControlID="Button1" EventName="Click" />
            </Triggers>
        </asp:UpdatePanel>
        <asp:UpdatePanel ID="UpdatePanel2" runat="server">
            <ContentTemplate>
                <asp:Label ID="Label2" runat="server"></asp:Label>
            </ContentTemplate>
        </asp:UpdatePanel>
        <br />
        <br />
        <asp:Button ID="Button1" runat="server"
         Text="Click to initiate async request"
         OnClick="Button1_Click" />
    </div>
    </form>
</body>
</html>
```

This is an interesting page. There are two UpdatePanel controls on the page: UpdatePanel1 and UpdatePanel2. Each of these areas contain a single Label control that can take a date/time value from a server response.

The UpdatePanel1 control has an associated trigger: the Button control on the page. When this button is clicked, the Button1_Click() event triggers and does its job. If you run this page, both of the UpdatePanel controls are updated according to the Button1_Click() event. This is illustrated in Figure 2-15.

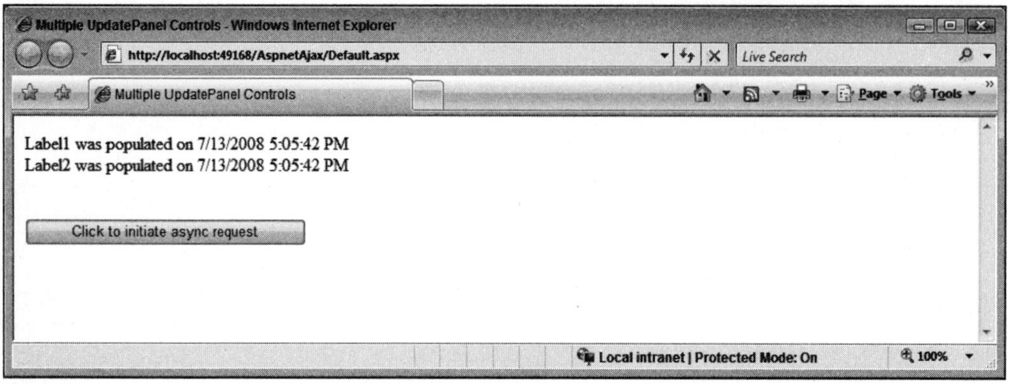

Figure 2-15

Both UpdatePanel sections were updated with the button click event because, by default, all UpdatePanel controls on a single page update with *each* asynchronous postback that occurs. This means that the postback that occurred with the Button1 button control also causes a postback to occur with the UpdatePanel2 control.

You can actually control this behavior through the UpdatePanel's UpdateMode property. The UpdateMode property can take two possible enumerations — Always and Conditional. If you do not set this property, it uses the value of Always, meaning that each UpdatePanel control always updates with each asynchronous request.

The other option is to set the property to Conditional. This means that the UpdatePanel updates only if one of the trigger conditions is met. For an example of this, change the UpdatePanel controls on the page so that they are now using an UpdateMode of Conditional, as shown in Listing 2-23.

Listing 2-23: Using more than one UpdatePanel control

```
<%@ Page Language="C#" %>

<script runat="server">
    protected void Button1_Click(object sender, EventArgs e)
    {
        Label1.Text = "Label1 was populated on " + DateTime.Now;
        Label2.Text = "Label2 was populated on " + DateTime.Now;
    }
```

Listing 2-23: Using more than one UpdatePanel control *(continued)*

```
</script>
<html xmlns="http://www.w3.org/1999/xhtml">
<head runat="server">
    <title>Multiple UpdatePanel Controls</title>
</head>
<body>
    <form id="form1" runat="server">
    <div>
        <asp:ScriptManager ID="ScriptManager1" runat="server">
        </asp:ScriptManager>
        <asp:UpdatePanel ID="UpdatePanel1" runat="server" UpdateMode="Conditional">
            <ContentTemplate>
                <asp:Label ID="Label1" runat="server"></asp:Label>
            </ContentTemplate>
            <Triggers>
                <asp:AsyncPostBackTrigger ControlID="Button1" EventName="Click" />
            </Triggers>
        </asp:UpdatePanel>
        <asp:UpdatePanel ID="UpdatePanel2" runat="server" UpdateMode="Conditional">
            <ContentTemplate>
                <asp:Label ID="Label2" runat="server"></asp:Label>
            </ContentTemplate>
        </asp:UpdatePanel>
        <br />
        <br />
        <asp:Button ID="Button1" runat="server"
         Text="Click to initiate async request"
         OnClick="Button1_Click" />
    </div>
    </form>
</body>
</html>
```

Now that both of the UpdatePanel controls are set to have an `UpdateMode` of `Conditional`, when running this page, you will see the results presented in Figure 2-16.

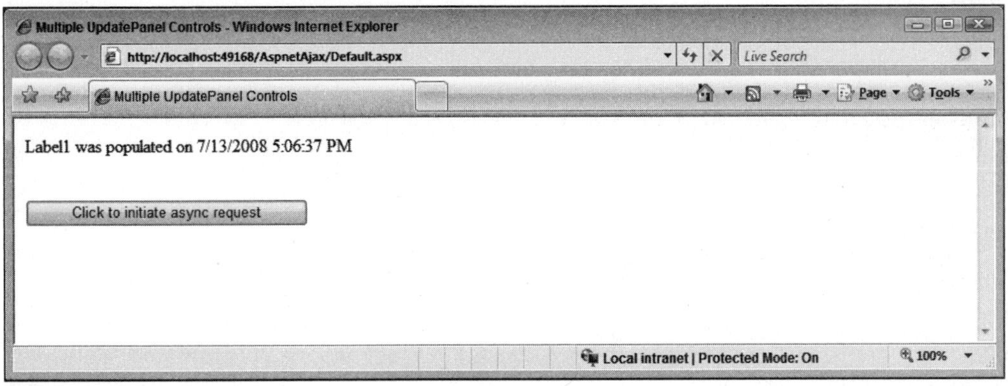

Figure 2-16

In this case, only the right Label control, Label1, was updated with the asynchronous request even though the `Button1_Click()` event tries to change the values of both Label1 and Label2. The reason for this is that the UpdatePanel2 control had no trigger that was met.

The Client-Side Page Request Lifecycle

ASP.NET developers have been working with the ASP.NET page lifecycle since the first days of ASP. NET 1.0. An ASP.NET developer knows that they are able to interact with the page and its rendering at one of many specific moments in the page request or response lifecycles. For instance, working with page as it is being loaded is as simple as using the `Page_Load()` event within your page's code-behind.

```
protected void Page_Load(object sender, EventArgs e)
{
    // Perform desired actions here
}
```

As with the series of server-side interactions with the page lifecycle, you are also able to interact with the page lifecycle on the client side through a series of page lifecycle events. This is an important feature, and even using DOM today within the browser, you are able to currently work with the page's invocation of the `window.onload()` and `window.onunload()` events using JavaScript. However, you are able to work with these two events only when the ASP.NET page does a complete and full page postback. This means that the asynchronous postbacks, or partial-page postbacks, that ASP.NET AJAX performs would be unable to work with such events.

Interacting with the client-side page events is a matter of using the `PageRequestManager` class provided with ASP.NET AJAX. The `PageRequestManager` class is the glue between the ScriptManager control on the page and the control that needs to make use of the partial-page updating. The lifecycle provided by the `PageRequestManager` object for asynchronous page requests includes five events detailed here:

❑   `initializeRequest()`

❑   `beginRequest()`

❑   `pageLoading()`

❑   `pageLoaded()`

❑   `endRequest()`

To get at an instance of the `PageRequestManager`, you are going to have to call the `getInstance()` method on the client through JavaScript. An example of this in action is presented here in Listing 2-24.

Listing 2-24: Using PageRequestManager

```
<%@ Page Language="C#" %>

<script runat="server">
    protected override void OnLoad(EventArgs e)
    {
        if (Session["count"] == null)
```

Listing 2-24: Using PageRequestManager *(continued)*

```
        {
            Session["count"] = 1;
        }
        else
        {
            Session["count"] = ((int)Session["count"]) + 1;
        }

        System.Threading.Thread.Sleep(1000);
        theCount.Text = "count = " + Session["count"];
    }
</script>

<html xmlns="http://www.w3.org/1999/xhtml">
<head runat="server">
    <title>Using PageRequestManager</title>
</head>
<body>
    <form id="form1" runat="server">
    <div>
        <asp:ScriptManager ID="ScriptManager1" runat="server">
        </asp:ScriptManager>

        <script type="text/javascript">
            var initializeCount = 0;
            var beginCount = 0;
            var loadingCount = 0;
            var loadedCount = 0;
            var endCount = 0;

            var prm = Sys.WebForms.PageRequestManager.getInstance();
            prm.add_initializeRequest(initializeRequest);
            prm.add_beginRequest(beginRequest);
            prm.add_pageLoading(pageLoading);
            prm.add_pageLoaded(pageLoaded);
            prm.add_endRequest(endRequest);

            function initializeRequest(sender, initializeRequestEventArgs) {
                initializeCount = initializeCount + 1;
            }

            function beginRequest(sender, beginRequestEventArgs) {
                beginCount = beginCount + 1;
            }

            function pageLoading(sender, pageLoadingEventArgs) {
                loadingCount = loadingCount + 1;
            }

            function pageLoaded(sender, pageLoadedEventArgs) {
                loadedCount = loadedCount + 1;
            }
```

Continued

59

Listing 2-24: Using PageRequestManager *(continued)*

```
                    function endRequest(sender, endRequestEventArgs) {

                        endCount = endCount + 1;
                    }

                    function showCounts() {
                        var message = "initialized = " + initializeCount +
                                "\r\nbegin = " + beginCount +
                                "\r\nloading = " + loadingCount +
                                "\r\nloaded = " + loadedCount +
                                "\r\nend = " + endCount;
                        alert(message);
                    }
                </script>

                <div style="border-style: solid">
                    <asp:UpdatePanel runat="server">
                        <ContentTemplate>
                            <br />
                             <asp:Label runat="server" ID="theCount"></asp:Label>
                            <br />
                            <asp:Button runat="server" Text="Refresh" ID="RefreshButton" />
                            <br /><br />
                        </ContentTemplate>
                    </asp:UpdatePanel>
                </div>
                <br />
                <input type="button" onclick="showCounts()" value="Show Counts" />
            </div>
        </form>
    </body>
</html>
```

When the page is first retrieved, the pageLoaded() event is fired. As the message in Figure 2-17 shows, the pageLoaded() event occurs for all requests, synchronous and asynchronous. When the request for the partial page request initiates by clicking the button in the UpdatePanel, the initializeRequest alert will be shown. This event does not occur for the full postback triggered by the button outside the UpdatePanel. It is part of the asynchronous lifecycle implemented by the PageRequestManager.

After the page is first run, it shows one page execution and one pageLoaded. As shown in Figure 2-17, the other counts are zero. If you click the Refresh button and wait, all of the counts are incremented by one. However, if you click the button several times quickly, the counts begin to change out of synch with each other. You will notice that the page execution count you get corresponds to the count of the pageLoaded counter. This count is one ahead of the beginRequest, loadingPage, and endRequest counters. However, the initializedRequest counter is now much higher. As I clicked the button faster than the request could be initiated, the previous start would be canceled in favor of the newer request. At that point, the multiple starts are essentially seen as simultaneous, and only one is advanced to the beginRequest event.

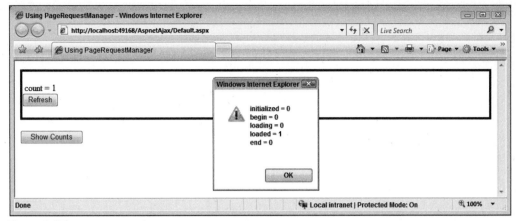

Figure 2-17

The potentially confusing thing about the series of events is that they do not fire all of the time. Requests can be canceled or preempted by another request. The page from Listing 2-24 sets up counters that are incremented for each time the event handlers are invoked. It also increments a counter on the server for every time the page executes. The count is then displayed inside an UpdatePanel control. The page sleeps briefly so that a request can be initiated while another is pending. There is also a button for displaying the current counter values.

Canceling a Request

The `initializeRequest()` event alerts you to the fact that a request is about to begin and gives you access to the element responsible for initiating the request. You can examine the state of things and explicitly cancel the request here before it even begins based on other factors. For example, you can query the `PageRequestManager` object and see if an asynchronous postback is already underway as presented here in Listing 2-25.

Listing 2-25: Checking to see if an asynchronous postback is occurring

```
function initializeRequest(sender, initializeRequestEventArgs) {
    var prm = Sys.WebForms.PageRequestManager.getInstance();

    if(prm.get_isInAsyncPostBack() === true) {
        initializeRequestEventArgs.set_cancel(true);
        alert("canceling event from " +
            initializeRequestEventArgs.get_postBackElement().id);
    }

    initializeCount = initializeCount + 1;
}
```

That would prevent the new request from starting, but you also might want to abort a request after it has started. Suppose that you included a Cancel button in your page:

```
<input type="button" onclick="cancelRequest()" value="Cancel Request" />
```

In the `onClick()` handler, you could then abort a request that is already underway but not yet completed:

```
function cancelRequest() {
    var prm = Sys.WebForms.PageRequestManager.getInstance();

    if(prm.get_isInAsyncPostBack() === true) {
        prm.abortPostBack();
    }
}
```

You can see in Figure 2-18 that the count of calls to the different event handlers can get out of synch. The number of times the page executed is no longer the same as the number of times the page was loaded. Requests were canceled after the page execution was already started. The `endRequest()` event is still called for every `beginRequest()` event invoked. And once the `pageLoading()` event started, the load finished and the `pageLoaded()` event was called.

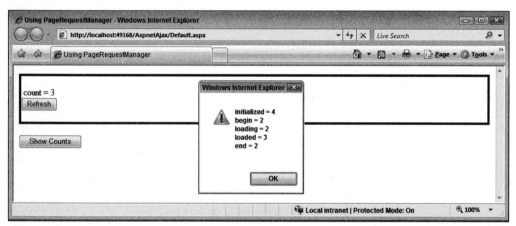

Figure 2-18

You can count on getting an `endRequest()` event if the `beginRequest()` event is invoked, even if the request is canceled. However, as you have seen, you cannot expect each event for every request initialized. Other factors that skew the lifecycle come into play.

Detecting Errors

Not to sound pessimistic, but just when you think everything is going great, inevitably something goes wrong. The `EndRequestEventArgs` includes an error property to allow you to detect and react to errors that have occurred during asynchronous requests. The default behavior is to display an error, but you may want to change this to save some user state and navigate to your own error page or to provide a recovery path unique to your application.

To demonstrate, the following code example in Listing 2-26 simply throws a `NotImplementedException` for postbacks to the server:

Listing 2-26: Throwing an exception

```
<script runat="server">
    protected override void OnLoad(EventArgs e) {
        if(IsPostBack) {
            throw new NotImplementedException("Something terrible has happened!");
        }
    }
</script>
```

The `endRequest()` handler then displays the error description and sets the `errorHandled` property so the `PageRequestManager` will not react to it any further:

```
function endRequest(sender, endRequestEventArgs) {
    var theError = endRequestEventArgs.get_error();
    if(theError !== null) {
        alert(theError.description);
        endRequestEventArgs.set_errorHandled(true);
    }
}
```

The `EndRequestEventHandler` also exposes a property to indicate whether the request was aborted while it was being processed:

```
function endRequest(sender, endRequestEventArgs) {
    if(endRequestEventArgs.get_aborted()) {
        alert("Request was aborted");
    }
}
```

Working with Updates

Part of the complexity of partial page updates comes in establishing and maintaining relationships between elements on the page as the page evolves and as parts of the page are updated independently from one another. Of course, in real applications, you will have event handlers attached to DHTML Document Object Model (DOM) elements within an UpdatePanel that affect other parts of the page. When an asynchronous postback occurs, the event hookup will be lost and must be reestablished.

As updates occur, how do you effectively pull items out of the update and use these values elsewhere on the page? Listing 2-27 provides an example of how to accomplish this task.

Listing 2-27: Using data from the updates that occur

```
<%@ Page Language="C#" %>

<script runat="server">
    protected override void OnLoad(EventArgs e)
    {
        string text = DateTime.Now.ToLongTimeString();
        theTime.Text = text;
        theTime2.Text = text;
    }
</script>

<html xmlns="http://www.w3.org/1999/xhtml">
<head runat="server">
    <title>Managing Updates</title>
</head>
<body>
    <form id="form1" runat="server">
    <div>
        <asp:ScriptManager ID="ScriptManager1" runat="server">
        </asp:ScriptManager>

        <script type="text/javascript">
        var prm = Sys.WebForms.PageRequestManager.getInstance();
        prm.add_pageLoaded(pageLoaded);

        function pageLoaded(sender, pageLoadedEventArgs)
        {
            var panelsCreated = pageLoadedEventArgs.get_panelsCreated();
            for(var i = 0; i < panelsCreated.length; i++) {
                if(panelsCreated[i].id === "panel1") {
                    hookupPanelOne();
                }
            }

            var panelsUpdated = pageLoadedEventArgs.get_panelsUpdated();
            for(var i = 0; i < panelsUpdated.length; i++) {
                if(panelsUpdated[i].id === "panel1") {
                    hookupPanelOne();
                }
            }
        }

        function hookupPanelOne()
        {
            $get('<%= theDuplicate.ClientID %>').innerHTML =
            $get('<%= theTime.ClientID %>').innerHTML;
        }
        </script>

        <asp:UpdatePanel runat="server" ID="panel1" UpdateMode="Conditional">
            <ContentTemplate>
                Panel One
```

Listing 2-27: Using data from the updates that occur *(continued)*

```
                    <asp:Label runat="server" ID="theTime"></asp:Label><br />
                    <asp:Button runat="server" Text="Refresh" ID="RefreshButton" />
                    <br /><br />
                </ContentTemplate>
            </asp:UpdatePanel>
        </div>
        <br />
        <div style="border-style: solid">
            <asp:UpdatePanel runat="server" ID="panel2" UpdateMode="Conditional">
                <ContentTemplate>
                    Panel Two
                    <asp:Label runat="server" ID="theTime2"></asp:Label><br />
                    <asp:Button runat="server" Text="Refresh" ID="RefreshButton2" />
                    <br /><br />
                </ContentTemplate>
            </asp:UpdatePanel>
            <br />
        </div>
        The Time from Panel One is:
        <asp:Label runat="server" ID="theDuplicate" /><br />
        </form>
    </body>
    </html>
```

If the dependency were as simple as getting one string and copying it as this example is trying to accomplish here, it would not merit any extra work. In this case, you could just copy it over in a pageLoaded() event handler and be done with it.

In a more realistic example, the dependencies would probably be more labor intensive. Instead of blindly doing the work each time any part of the page is updated, you would want to do the work only when necessary. In this case, that would be just when panel1 was changing. Instead of putting the code directly in the pageLoaded() event handler, it goes in a separate function:

```
function hookupPanelOne() {
    $get('<%= theDuplicate.ClientID %>').innerHTML =
    $get('<%= theTime.ClientID %>').innerHTML;
}
```

The $get syntax is a shortcut for locating the item in the browser's DOM. To tell when the hookupPanelOne() function needs to be called, this bit of code examines which UpdatePanel controls are being created and which are being updated in the pageLoaded() event handler. The PageLoadedEventArgs provides property accessors that return arrays of the newly created and updated UpdatePanel controls.

```
function pageLoaded(sender, pageLoadedEventArgs) {
    var panelsCreated = pageLoadedEventArgs.get_panelsCreated();
    for(var i = 0; i < panelsCreated.length; i++) {
        if(panelsCreated[i].id === "panel1") {
            hookupPanelOne();
        }
    }
```

```
        var panelsUpdated = pageLoadedEventArgs.get_panelsUpdated();
        for(var i = 0; i < panelsUpdated.length; i++) {
            if(panelsUpdated[i].id === "panel1") {
                hookupPanelOne();
            }
        }
    }
}
```

Yes, this looks like a lot of overhead for a simple example, but if you had cascading dependencies or were making additional Web Service calls as the result of an UpdatePanel control being refreshed, you could save extra work for the browser and the server by updating the dependency only when it's necessary. Putting it all together results in the page shown in Figure 2-19. The panels can update independently, and the Duplicate span is changed as a function of updates to the first panel only.

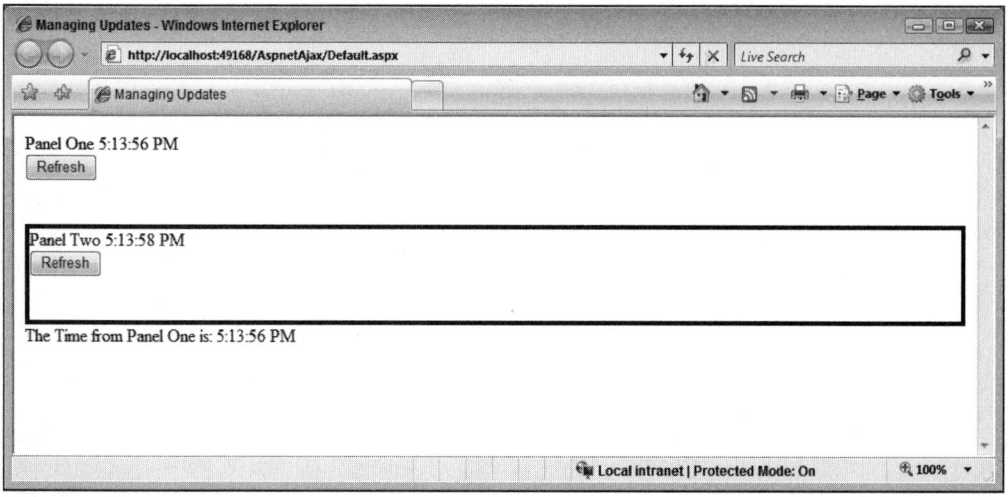

Figure 2-19

Summary

ASP.NET AJAX is an outstanding technology that will fundamentally change the approach to Web application development. No longer do you need to completely tear down a page and rebuild it for each and every request. Instead, you are able to rebuild the pages slowly in sections as the end user requests them. The line between the thin-client world and the thick-client world just got a lot more opaque.

ASP.NET AJAX includes the Microsoft AJAX Library that makes writing browser-based JavaScript easier and simplifies many common client programming tasks. It is easy to attach code to DOM events, write JavaScript in an object-oriented way, and access the server for persistent storage, authentication, and updated data.

ASP.NET AJAX also includes extensions to version 2.0 of the .NET Framework that can greatly improve your Web application. There is built-in support for returning data in the JSON format that is easily consumed by JavaScript in the browser.

The UpdatePanel is a simple and flexible control for adding partial page updates to an ASP.NET application. You can take an existing application and identify parts of a page that can be updated independently, bypassing the click-pause-flash pattern that annoys users in Web applications. The ViewState and other hidden fields are updated automatically as part of the ScriptManager's coordination of UpdatePanel controls on the page.

The default behavior is to have every action that would have triggered a postback from a child control of the UpdatePanel cause a partial page update. The children controls are treated as triggers; thus, the `ChildrenAsTriggers` property is `true` by default. You can also configure triggers to be events on controls elsewhere on the page.

The `PageRequestManager` provides a whole lifecycle of events in the browser that allows you to control how asynchronous requests occur. You can cancel requests before they start, abort them while they are in flight, and react to any errors that happen while they are being processed.

As soon as you start initiating asynchronous requests, the need may arise to cancel requests before they start, or abort them before they complete. The `PageRequestManager` provides events that give you fine-grained control over the asynchronous requests. Moreover, when errors occur during the page request, you can detect them and react accordingly.

The UpdateProgress control makes it easy to let the end user know that an asynchronous request is being processed. Without it, a long-running request can leave users feeling that their actions are being ignored. You can have an UpdateProgress control associated with each UpdatePanel or a single UpdateProgress associated with multiple UpdatePanels.

You can easily update parts of the page out of band, based on the user clicking a button, and you can also update parts of the page automatically. The Timer control makes it simple to define an interval to have parts of the page refreshed without user intervention.

The UpdatePanel and `PageRequestManager` work together with the help of the ScriptManager to provide a platform for developing a more responsive and intuitive user experience. The extensibility points make it easy to integrate partial page rendering into existing complex applications.

3

JavaScript for the ASP.NET Developer

As an ASP.NET developer, you are used to writing code using a high-level language such as C# or Visual Basic. The main development tool for .NET developers, Visual Studio, provides Intellisense that makes coding in these languages easier. Also using Visual Studio, you will find that there is rich support for debugging the code, and you get warnings and errors about many things during compilation. Visual Studio will even background-compile your code and give you updated warnings as you go to help you find problems without needing to perform an explicit compilation. The .NET Framework provides a comprehensive set of class libraries that can be used from any .NET-compatible language and helps to simplify complex programming tasks. With that said, many developers who are focused on the Web realize that writing JavaScript is an entirely different world in this regard.

This chapter introduces you to JavaScript with a bias toward the ASP.NET developer. You will see how JavaScript development is different from what you are used to with .NET languages. In addition, you will see how the browser gets JavaScript. This chapter introduces the basics of the language and explains the closure and prototype aspects of JavaScript coding, along with some techniques to apply for writing faster and more efficient JavaScript. If you look at the code of the Microsoft AJAX Library, you will see that the Microsoft ASP.NET team also uses these tactics in their JavaScript development efforts. If you are already familiar with JavaScript, you may want to skip the early sections of this chapter, where there is a core introduction of JavaScript, and instead look at some approaches for improving JavaScript code found later in the chapter.

> *This chapter is not meant to be an exhaustive treatment of JavaScript. There are comprehensive books and online tutorials that can take you through the language step by step and highlight differences among the minor version releases from Microsoft, Netscape, and Mozilla. I recommend* Professional JavaScript for Web Developers *by Nicholas C. Zakas (2005), or* The JavaScript Bible *by Danny Goodman and Michael Morrison (2007), both from Wiley Publishing. The goal here is to highlight the key facts and interesting aspects of the language that may be unfamiliar to someone coming from C# or Visual Basic and help you to skip some of the pitfalls that hinder development efforts or slow down JavaScript code.*

Using JavaScript on the Client

The JavaScript language can be used independently of the browser. There are JavaScript interpreters for managing operating system components, interacting with COM objects, and automating server administration tasks. To use JavaScript in the browser, you should be aware of a few considerations.

First, you need to manage getting the script to the browser for a page effectively. As the amount of JavaScript you use grows, you will want to make use of the browser's ability to cache scripts for performance reasons. You also need to be aware of how the user's interaction with a page while background operations are performed affects the user's perception of the page's performance. In some conditions, you want your users to know that they are waiting for an action to be performed so they don't become frustrated, and in other cases, you want to ensure that the page is responsive while something happens transparently in the background. In addition, JavaScript resources can be embedded directly in a DLL and do not have to be deployed as text files on disk, as you might be accustomed to doing.

Getting JavaScript to the Browser

Before diving into the fundamentals of the language, you should understand how JavaScript code gets to the browser as part of a Web application. The HTML script tag is used to separate the script code from the markup, so the browser will be able to distinguish the difference. Listing 3-1 shows the two possible methods for including JavaScript in a page.

In the first example, the script code is included directly in the page within an HTML script element. The second example (the last line) defines the script code in a separate file and uses the `src` attribute of the script element in the page to provide the URL that the browser should use to retrieve the code.

Listing 3-1: Two methods for getting JavaScript in your ASP.NET page

```
<script type="text/javascript">
   alert("Hello World");
</script>

<script type="text/javascript" src="scripts/code.js" ></script>
```

It used to be common to include `language="javascript"` in the script tag as well, but the language attribute has been deprecated in the latest HTML standards, although it is still accepted by most browsers at the present time. Multiple script tags can be included in the HTML source, so you can have many different sections of script code in a single page. Any code that is not defined within a JavaScript function is executed immediately when the page loads. The W3C standard includes the `defer` attribute to instruct the browser that it need not delay rendering of the HTML while the script is downloaded or parsed. This can be useful when you know that a particular piece of script code will not need to run until after the page has been completely rendered. Be aware, however, that users will start interacting with the page as soon as it is rendered. Users do not like waiting for page loads, and they certainly are not watching the animated browser icon to see if the browser is still busy loading part of the page that they cannot see. Therefore, the `defer` attribute is not commonly used.

If you use `defer` and the user performs actions in a partially rendered page, the code that tries to execute something from a deferred script before it is has finished loading will generate errors for the user. This is baffling to users, and the only recovery action is to load the page again. The error message they get is usually something vague about a function or variable being undefined. They do not have any way to know that the undefined something may not have loaded yet, so they may even repeat the same process and get the same error. The safest approach is to include script references earlier in the page whenever possible and avoid using deferred loading. This will make it more likely that the browser has your script code when the user starts interacting with the page. Of course, even this is not a guarantee.

To protect yourself from errors caused by early user interaction with a page, you can include a top-level piece of code to disable elements that might depend on load order. This way, you can avoid triggering the use of code that is still being fetched. For example, you can disable a Submit button in an HTML form to prevent the user from clicking it and needing some associated validation scripts before they are available.

Using .NET to Include Your Client-Side Scripts

ASP.NET uses the `Page.ClientScript` property to register and place JavaScript functions on your ASP.NET pages. Three of these methods are reviewed here. More methods and properties than just these three are available through the `ClientScript` object (which references an instance of `System.Web.UI.ClientScriptManager`), but these are the more useful ones. You can find the rest in the SDK documentation.

The `Page.RegisterStartupScript` *and the* `Page.RegisterClientScriptBlock` *methods from the .NET Framework 1.0/1.1 are now considered obsolete. Both of these possibilities for registering scripts required a key/script set of parameters. Because two separate methods were involved, there was an extreme possibility that some key name collisions would occur. The* `Page.ClientScript` *property is meant to bring all the script registrations under one umbrella, making your code less error prone.*

Using Page.ClientScript.RegisterClientScriptBlock

The `RegisterClientScriptBlock` method allows you to place a JavaScript function at the top of the page. This means that the script is in place for the startup of the page in the browser. Its use is illustrated in Listing 3-2.

Listing 3-2: Using the RegisterClientScriptBlock method

```
<%@ Page Language="C#" %>

<script runat="server">
    protected void Page_Load(object sender, EventArgs e)
    {
      string myScript = @"function AlertHello() { alert('Hello ASP.NET'); }";
      Page.ClientScript.RegisterClientScriptBlock(this.GetType(),
        "MyScript", myScript, true);
    }
</script>
```

From this example, you can see that you create the JavaScript function `AlertHello()` as a string called `myScript`. Then using the `Page.ClientScript.RegisterClientScriptBlock` method, you program the script to be placed on the page. The two possible constructions of the `RegisterClientScriptBlock` method are the following:

❑   RegisterClientScriptBlock (*type, key, script*)

❑   RegisterClientScriptBlock (*type, key, script, script tag specification*)

In the example from Listing 3-2, you are specifying the type as this.GetType(), the key, the script to include, and then a Boolean value setting of true so that .NET places the script on the ASP.NET page with <script> tags automatically. When running the page, you can view the source code for the page to see the results:

```
<html xmlns="http://www.w3.org/1999/xhtml">
<head><title>
    Adding JavaScript
</title></head>
<body>
    <form method="post" action="JavaScriptPage.aspx" id="form1">
<div>
<input type="hidden" name="__VIEWSTATE"
 value="/wEPDwUKMTY3NzE5MjIyMGRkiyYSRMg+bcXi9DiawYlbxndiTDo=" />
</div>


<script type="text/javascript">
<!--
function AlertHello() { alert('Hello ASP.NET'); }// -->
</script>

    <div>
        <input type="submit" name="Button1" value="Button" onclick="AlertHello();"
          id="Button1" />
    </div>
    </form>
</body>
</html>
```

This code shows that the script specified was indeed included on the ASP.NET page before the page code. Not only were the <script> tags included, the proper comment tags were added around the script (so older browsers will not break).

Using Page.ClientScript.RegisterStartupScript

The RegisterStartupScript method is not too much different from the RegisterClientScriptBlock method. The big difference is that the RegisterStartupScript places the script at the bottom of the ASP.NET page instead of at the top. In fact, the RegisterStartupScript method even takes the same constructors as the RegisterClientScriptBlock method:

❑   RegisterStartupScript (*type, key, script*)

❑   RegisterStartupScript (type, key, script, script tag specification)

So what difference does it make where the script is registered on the page? A lot, actually!

If you have a bit of JavaScript that is working with one of the controls on your page, in most cases you want to use the RegisterStartupScript method instead of RegisterClientScriptBlock. For example, you'd use the following code to create a page that includes a simple <asp:TextBox> control that contains a default value of Hello ASP.NET:

```
<asp:TextBox ID="TextBox1" Runat="server">Hello ASP.NET</asp:TextBox>
```

Then use the `RegisterClientScriptBlock` method to place a script on the page that utilizes the value in the `TextBox1` control, as illustrated in Listing 3-3.

Listing 3-3: Improperly using the RegisterClientScriptBlock method

```
protected void Page_Load(object sender, EventArgs e)
{
    string myScript = @"alert(document.forms[0]['TextBox1'].value);";
    Page.ClientScript.RegisterClientScriptBlock(this.GetType(),
        "MyScript", myScript, true);
}
```

Running this page (depending on which version of IE you are using for this example) gives you a JavaScript error, as shown in Figure 3-1.

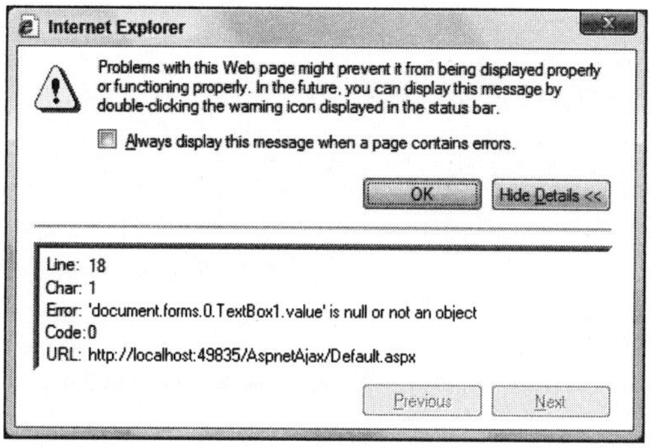

Figure 3-1

This error occurs because the JavaScript function fired before the text box was even placed on the screen. Therefore, the JavaScript function did not find TextBox1, and that caused an error to be thrown by the page. Now try the `RegisterStartupScript` method shown in Listing 3-4.

Listing 3-4: Using the RegisterStartupScript method

```
protected void Page_Load(object sender, EventArgs e)
{
    string myScript = @"alert(document.forms[0]['TextBox1'].value);";
    Page.ClientScript.RegisterStartupScript(this.GetType(),
        "MyScript", myScript, true);
}
```

This approach puts the JavaScript function at the bottom of the ASP.NET page, so when the JavaScript actually starts, it finds the TextBox1 element and works as planned. The result is shown in Figure 3-2.

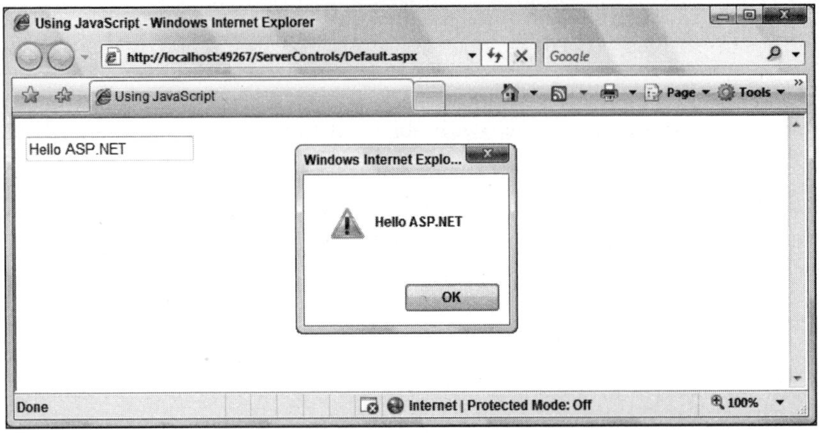

Figure 3-2

Using Page.ClientScript.RegisterClientScriptInclude

The final method is `RegisterClientScriptInclude`. Many developers place their JavaScript inside a `.js` file, which is considered a best practice because it makes it very easy to make global JavaScript changes to the application. You can register the script files on your ASP.NET pages by using the `RegisterClientScriptInclude` method illustrated in Listing 3-5.

Listing 3-5: Using the RegisterClientScriptInclude method

```
string myScript = "myJavaScriptCode.js";
Page.ClientScript.RegisterClientScriptInclude("myKey", myScript);
```

This creates the following construction on the ASP.NET page:

```
<script src="myJavaScriptCode.js" type="text/javascript"></script>
```

Perceived Performance

If you allow users to interact with a page before all the script code has been downloaded, the page appears to them to be ready to use. By temporarily disabling the page postback, you can ensure safety and allow users to enter their data on the page while the scripts continue loading in the background.

In addition to the perceived performance advantage, some applications temporarily disable elements of the form that cause a postback in order to avoid a complication with a security feature of ASP.NET. Some controls can be registered for validation, and ASP.NET will round-trip the set of valid values set for that control. The possible values are hashed (a cryptographic signature is calculated on them and later validated after postback) and round-tripped along with the values so that the server can detect any attempt by malicious code to submit something other than the valid list of values. Because the set of authentic values has to be collected while the page is being rendered and may not be fully assembled until after the form has been fully rendered, the hashed data is included after the closing form element.

When a specific Web form is fairly large or complex, the set of validation values can also be large, so it is possible for the user to interact with the form and submit it before the browser receives the validation data. The browser would then be unable to submit the set of valid values back to the server, and the user will see an error when the page is posted back on the server and the validation values are missing. Therefore, to prevent this scenario, you can disable the postback until you are sure that the browser has received all of the validation values.

In Listing 3-6, the Submit button is disabled initially in the HTML markup. The script element contains a function to enable the Submit button along with a line of script for attaching the function to the window's `onload` event. Thus, the button will be disabled initially and then enabled after the whole page has been loaded.

Listing 3-6: Disabling the Submit button until the entire page is loaded

```
<%@ Page Language="C#" %>

<html xmlns="http://www.w3.org/1999/xhtml">
<head runat="server">
    <title>Example</title>
</head>
<body>
    <form id="form1" runat="server">

    <script type="text/javascript">
        function enableSubmit()
        {
            var elt = document.getElementById('submitButton');
            alert("Enabling form now");
            elt.disabled = false;
        }

        window.onload = enableSubmit;
    </script>

    <div>
        <input type="submit" id="submitButton" value="Submit"
         disabled="disabled" />
    </div>
    </form>
</body>
</html>
```

When you run this example, you get the following results as illustrated here in Figure 3-3. This example is before the button is enabled again.

Notice that this example only disabled the Submit button. Your first inclination might be to disable the entire form and have everything in it disabled, but that would not be portable to all the browsers. In a real application with several elements that might cause a postback, you would have to disable all of them initially and then enable them during the `onload()` event.

Figure 3-3

There is not a limit to the number of script tags allowed on a page, but browsers typically open only one or two channels back to the server for scripts and images, so it appears as though the page is loading slowly. You can improve the perceived performance of page loading by using several script tags to contain your JavaScript code so that the browser can download multiple scripts simultaneously. Although this may not complete the overall load any faster, allowing the user to start interacting with the page earlier makes it seem to be loading faster to the user.

Script Resources

One of the longstanding difficulties with the deployment of Web applications to Web servers is ensuring that the right versions of all the miscellaneous files are deployed. Ever since ASP.NET 2.0, you have been able to include JavaScript code as a text resource embedded in the compiled DLL for an application. This allows you to create a Web server control that includes the script files internally and can be deployed with only configuration entries and a single DLL. This ensures that the correct script files will always be sent to the user and will not have to be maintained in a folder on the server. ASP.NET will then field requests for those script resources via its built-in Web Resource handler.

If you view the source for just about any .aspx page, you will see references to WebResource.axd followed by a set of querystring parameters used to retrieve the appropriate embedded resource. At first glance, it looks like a bunch of garbage, but if you extract one of those URL querystrings from a typical page's source and paste it into your browser's address window to request it separately, the proper resource is returned to you. An example of this is shown here:

```
http://www.mysite.com/WebResource.axd?d=3843647524 -- -
HJKAeoedaslathlmhueeuyr&amp;t=111205042031232968
```

The Web Resource handler is used for more than just JavaScript files; it can also be used for image files. Since the first version of ASP.NET did not have this functionality, some developers modified the standard ASP.NET JavaScript files themselves to obtain certain types of custom behaviors. To maintain functionality for those customizations when upgrading to the next release, ASP.NET checks for the existence of those external script files in an application and uses them instead of the ones provided by Microsoft in `System.Web.dll`. However, this `WebResource.axd` mechanism can still be used by your own Web controls, regardless of whether it is used for the standard ASP.NET scripts used by all pages.

> **Switching back and forth between languages can be a challenge. Visual Basic is not case sensitive, but C# is. Like C#, JavaScript is also case sensitive. The .NET Framework Design Guidelines advocate variable and API naming conventions that are different from JavaScript's. The convention in .NET development is to use camel-casing for member variables, with leading underscores for privates. Pascal casing is used for public members.**
>
> **Although, when writing JavaScript, camel-casing is employed for public members. Developers have come to rely on these conventions, so it pays to be attentive to these details although it can be confusing at first, especially if you are switching languages often.**

Variable Types in JavaScript

When working with any programming language, you as a developer need to be concerned with the data types that you are working with. C# is a strongly typed language. This means that whenever you are going to work with a specific data point, you first need to cast the object you are working with to a specific data type. For example, to work with a string in C#, you are going to have to use something like the following bit of code:

```
string myString = "Hello World!";
```

JavaScript, on the other hand, is often characterized as having no data types. Everything in JavaScript is just an object. This is basically a true statement; however, some primitive types can be assigned to variables, and the variables can pick up those types (this is similar to variants for those of you with COM experience). Numbers, strings, Booleans, and functions are the primitive types in JavaScript. They are the building blocks for all objects in JavaScript. Even the higher order "types" that are pre-defined, such as arrays and regular expressions, are just collections of the basic types.

Listing 3-7 declares a few variables, assigns them integer values, and then displays true or false after treating them as Boolean values. The key thing to note is that JavaScript follows the C-style convention of treating 0 as false and everything else as true. When the page is run, the result is to display true for one, false for zero, and true for negative one.

Listing 3-7: Working with Booleans in JavaScript

```html
<html xmlns="http://www.w3.org/1999/xhtml">
<head runat="server">
    <title>Booleans</title>

    <script type="text/javascript">
        var myOne = 1;
        var myZero = 0;
        var myNegativeOne = -1;

        if(myOne) {
            alert(true);
        }

        if(!myZero) {
            alert(false);
        }

        if(myNegativeOne) {
            alert(true);
        }
    </script>

</head>
<body>
    <form id="form1" runat="server">
    <div>
    </div>
    </form>
</body>
</html>
```

To the .NET developer, this set of basic types is pretty straightforward. Strings, numbers, and Booleans are fundamental to all programming tasks, so having them as basic types seems natural. However, you cannot anchor a variable to specific data types when they are declared in JavaScript, so you have to use greater care when writing code. You will not get an error if you assign a string to a number variable, since the variable is not locked down to holding only numbers. Still, this can generate an odd error at runtime when you try to access that variable as a number. This is a common problem of all typeless interpreted languages.

Without the ability to tie variables to specific types, you lack static type safety. The language is not compiled; it is interpreted. Types can be created at runtime and dynamically altered during script execution. In other languages, you must declare a type for a variable, and if the variable refers to an object of a different type, you get a compilation error. Another option in C++ and .NET languages is to coerce variables carefully from one type to another. This is not the case in JavaScript. There is only one type of variable declaration, and no type specifier is permitted. Any variable can refer to any kind of object at any time. In Listing 3-8, a single variable is declared and then assigned to the fundamental types used in the previous example. This example uses the typeof operator to show that the type reference changes while the script is being executed.

Listing 3-8: Changing type references at runtime

```html
<html xmlns="http://www.w3.org/1999/xhtml">
<head runat="server">
    <title>Working with types</title>

<script type="text/javascript">
    var variable;
    alert(typeof(variable));//refers to something undefined;

    variable = 1;// refers to a number
    alert(typeof(variable));

    variable = true; //refers to a Boolean
    alert(typeof(variable));

    variable = "This is my string."; //refers to a string

    alert(typeof(variable));
</script>

</head>
<body>
    <form id="form1" runat="server">
    <div>
    </div>
    </form>
</body>
</html>
```

Running this example, you will get four alert boxes (message boxes). The first returns the type of the variable object based upon the declaration of the following:

```
var variable;
```

Since nothing is assigned to this object in this statement, there is actually no type associated with it, and you will therefore, get an alert as is shown here in Figure 3-4.

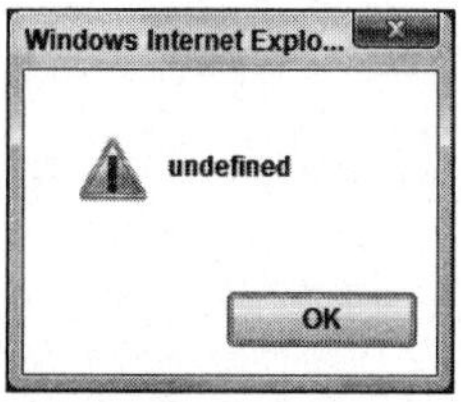

Figure 3-4

The next three alerts also display the type that the variable object is set at. The type is actually inferred from the value that is assigned to the object at the time. An assignment of 1 means that the object should be treated as a number and an assignment of a string means that the variable object is automatically treated as a string object. Based upon the assignments, you will see the rest of the alerts as presented here in Figure 3-5.

Figure 3-5

To show how this works in greater detail, take a look at the example in Listing 3-9.

Listing 3-9: Adding two numbers together

```
<script type="text/javascript">
    var variable1 = 3;
    var variable2 = 5;
    var result;

    result = variable1 + variable2;

    alert(typeof(result));
    alert(result);
</script>
```

In this example, three objects are created. The first two, `variable1` and `variable2` are assigned numbers as values. This also means that these objects are of type number upon assignment. The third object declared is the `result` object and upon assignment, this object is in an undefined state. Then, the `result` object is populated with the `variable1` and `variable2` objects added together with the `result = variable1 + variable2;` statement.

This produces the alerts illustrated in Figure 3-6.

Figure 3-6

Though, consider the following change to the code from Listing 3-9. The change of code is here in Listing 3-10 and changes the 3 and 5 values to strings of "3" and "5".

Listing 3-10: Adding two strings together

```
<script type="text/javascript">
    var variable1 = "3";
    var variable2 = "5";
    var result;

    result = variable1 + variable2;

    alert(typeof(result));
    alert(result);
</script>
```

This instead results in the alerts presented here in Figure 3-7.

Figure 3-7

JavaScript does not consider this to be an error, because this is how it was designed to work (but this particular code snippet may not be a wise way to write your code, of course). Any variable can point to any object at any time. At first glance, this lack of type checking may not seem important, but it is a key element to the power that JavaScript can bring to your code. It is also central to some of the complications you will encounter when programming with JavaScript.

The Microsoft AJAX Library takes advantage of the extensible nature of JavaScript to extend its functionality to provide a more familiar object-oriented approach to development, even when using a type-less language, by layering some additional standard type treatment onto the language.

Microsoft could not modify the underlying typeless nature of the language, but they were able to provide a better way of using it that allows you to represent types in some ways that help to mitigate the underlying limitations.

In addition to the basic building block types, two other types are central to programming in JavaScript. Anything that is not a number, Boolean, or string is either a function or an object. A function in JavaScript is a first-class type. It can be passed as an argument to another object. A function can receive arbitrary arguments to act on for execution. A function can return primitive types, or it can even return a new function. Listing 3-11 presents an example that is admittedly not very useful in the real world but illustrates this point.

The `CreateFunction()` function actually creates and returns one of two new functions that are stored and then invoked by calling `CreateFunction()`. By calling `CreateFunction()` you produce a function to double or triple numbers. In reality, you would just use the built-in math libraries for this sort of thing.

Listing 3-11: Working with functions

```html
<html xmlns="http://www.w3.org/1999/xhtml">
<head>
    <title>Code Test Page</title>
</head>
<body>

    <script type="text/javascript">
        function CreateFunction(s) {
            if (s ===2) {
                return function (s) { return s*2; }
            }
            else if( s=== 3) {
                return function(s) { return s*3; }
            }
        }

        var DoubleIt = CreateFunction(2);
        var TripleIt = CreateFunction(3);

        alert(DoubleIt(2));
        alert(TripleIt(4));

        alert(typeof(CreateFunction));
        alert(typeof(DoubleIt));
    </script>

</body>
</html>
```

Language Anomalies

Despite using a familiar syntax with keywords you probably recognize, there are a couple of things about JavaScript that can catch you by surprise. The way objects are compared for equality is probably different than you expect. Moreover, the JavaScript language has the notion of objects being null or undefined. If you do not recognize these unique characteristics of JavaScript, you can get yourself into trouble and spend a lot of time debugging to find the source of the problem.

What Is Equality?

If you are just getting started with JavaScript and coming from a compiled language like C# or Visual Basic, be prepared for a whole new kind of debugging challenge! Not only is JavaScript typeless; it doesn't use a compiler! Remember it is interpreted. The only way to detect syntax errors, even simple ones, such as improper case, is to run the code. In addition, you must exercise every possible code path just to do what a compiler would do for you. This is one example of the huge benefit you can get from using the Microsoft ASP.NET AJAX Client Script Library: There is a large amount of fully debugged code ready for you to use in your own applications!

One thing to note is that JavaScript shares its treatment of Boolean values with the C programming language. JavaScript and C need a double equal sign for a logical test, and they use a single equal sign for an assignment. This can become painfully apparent when you find a missing equal sign in a comparison test. JavaScript programmers quickly find that assignment is not equality, except in the eyes of the script. Listing 3-12 attempts to test the value of the year variable but instead mistakenly includes only one equal sign instead of the required two. This means that this example is actually assigning a new value to the year variable, and the value of this assignment is nonzero, so when treated as a Boolean, the assignment evaluates to a value of true.

Listing 3-12: Mistakenly assigning values to the year variable

```html
<html xmlns="http://www.w3.org/1999/xhtml">
<head>
    <title>Assignment Is True</title>

    <script type="text/javascript">
        var year = 1970;

        if(year = 1968) {
          alert("This is true");
        }
        else {
          alert("This is false");
        }
    </script>

</head>
<body>
    <form id="form1" runat="server">
    <div>

    </div>
    </form>
</body>
</html>
```

You might be telling yourself that this is a silly mistake that you aren't likely to make yourself. If you are a C# programmer, you may be lulled into a false sense of security because the compiler catches these errors for you, but these kinds of errors are still common in the real world.

In addition, there is more to this comparison-testing subject in JavaScript. Even if you never accidentally use a single equals character instead of two, you might still not be safe from problems with equality checks. You may intend to test for equality, but JavaScript's type coercion can still prove to be a problem. Listing 3-13 shows an example of how mistakes of this nature are quite possible.

Listing 3-13: More mistakes with JavaScript

```html
<html xmlns="http://www.w3.org/1999/xhtml">
<head>
    <title>Equality</title>
```

Continued

Listing 3-13: More mistakes with JavaScript *(continued)*

```
<script type="text/javascript">
    var album;

    if(album == null){
     alert("album is null");
    }

    if ((album != true) && (album != false)) {
     alert("album is not true or false");
    }

    if(!album) {
     alert("but !album is true");
    }

    if (5 == "5") {
     alert("number 5 equals string 5");
    }

    if ((0 == false) && (1 == true) && (!0) && (1)) {
     alert("0 is false and 1 is true");
    }

    if (('true' != 1) && ('false' != false)) {
     alert("but 1 is not 'true' and false is not 'false'");
    }

    if ('undefined' == typeof(album)) {
     alert("the album type is undefined");
    }
</script>

</head>
<body>
    <form id="form1" runat="server">
    <div>
    </div>
    </form>
</body>
</html>
```

Consider the code from this listing. In this example, the album variable is defined and then checked with the equality operator against a value of null. In this example, it equates to a value of true. The album variable has not been assigned yet and when evaluated against null it is seen as equivalent.

```
var album;

if(album == null){
    alert("album is null");
}
```

The next check shows that the variable is not true or false when checked explicitly. After that, the album variable is treated as a Boolean, and by definition, a Boolean cannot be both not true and not false. It has to be one or the other, so it is coerced into one automatically, and JavaScript will treat it as false (the "!" not operator forces it to be treated as a Boolean even though we already determined that it is not a Boolean). Is your head starting to spin?

Other types will be coerced automatically for comparison as well. The next equality check shows the string 5 being compared to the number 5 and evaluating to a value of true. The number is coerced to a string for comparison purposes, similarly to the .ToString() method in .NET.

In JavaScript, a Boolean's true and false values are treated as one and zero, respectively. Zero is false, and a the one value is interpreted as true. However, the strings are not converted to equivalent Booleans, which hardly seems to make sense anymore.

The last comparison shows that JavaScript also has the concept of variables being undefined. Because nothing has been assigned to the album variable. At this moment, its type is undefined.

Null, Undefined, or Something Else

When working with JavaScript, the subtle difference between something being undefined or null can easily turn into a problem within your code. One approach is to take advantage of JavaScript's type coercion with a double negative. Instead of checking explicitly for undefined or null, you can apply the inverse operator twice:

```
if (!!something)
{

}
```

This approach can be extended to equality comparisons to avoid some of the confusion in the previous example in Listing 3-13. The string value of "5" is not really equivalent to a number value of 5 because the types are actually quite different, and in many cases you simply do not want them to be treated as equal.

JavaScript originally had the equality and inequality operators that were in earlier examples. Later in JavaScript's history, the strict equality and strict inequality operators were introduced. Instead of using two equal signs, you use three. This syntax results in a comparison performed without coercing types, so the types must be equal, and the values must be equal.

In Listing 3-14, this example duplicates the previous code listing but changes to using the strict equality and inequality operators. The results are more intuitive and generally different from the previous set of comparisons.

Listing 3-14: Using strict equality and inequality operators

```
<html xmlns="http://www.w3.org/1999/xhtml">
<head>
    <title>Inequality</title>

    <script type="text/javascript">
        var album;

        if(album !== null){
```

Continued

Listing 3-14: Using strict equality and inequality operators *(continued)*

```
            alert ("album  is not null");
        }

        if ('undefined' === typeof(album)) {
            alert("the album type is undefined");
        }

        if ((album !== true) && (album !== false)) {
            alert("album is not true or false");
        }

        if (5 !== "5") {
            alert("the number 5 is not equal to the string");
        }

        if ((0 !== false) && (1 !== true)) {
            alert("false is not 0 and true is not 1");
        }
    </script>

</head>
<body>
    <form id="form1" runat="server">
    <div>
    </div>
    </form>
</body>
</html>
```

In this example, notice that the undefined album variable is not strictly equivalent to a value of null. It is actually 'undefined', which means it does not have a type at that current moment in time. In addition, while it is undefined, it is neither true nor false as it was before with the standard equality operators. The number 5 is no longer considered equivalent to the string data type. Moreover, 0 and 1 are not really the same as true and false. Null is a value, not a type, and if you assign a null to a variable, it will take on the object type, which is not the same as having a type of undefined.

I recommend using the strict equality operators as your default for performing comparisons. You should use the original equality comparisons only when you specifically want the types to be coerced as part of the comparison. This will save you hours of frustration in the end.

Scoping Variables

Not only can variables in JavaScript be used to refer to any type of object at any time, they can actually be used without being declared at all. This can be a source of problems that are hard to identify because it will not be considered an error if you mistype a variable name. Rather, JavaScript will just assume that you are introducing a new variable.

A variable's scope is the context of code where that variable can be accessed. Whenever a variable is defined, it is assigned a scope for access based on where it is in the code. It is available to all inner scopes; loops, function calls, and further nested control structures. Basically, it is available from the point it is first defined until the scope in which it was defined exits.

A variable is never available at a higher scope. If you declare a variable for use within function MyFunction(), for example, that variable and its value are not available to the caller but are available to any functions that MyFunction() calls. In fact, the variable is available to any functions called by functions that MyFunction() calls. This means there is no concept of local variables that are not visible outside your function (only those you call, and the functions they call, can see them).

JavaScript allows you to use a variable without declaring it (where it will be implicitly declared), but it changes the scope for that variable from what you would typically expect. An undeclared variable is automatically assigned a global scope. In many cases, this is not a problem. A variable used within a function may not be accessed from a containing scope, so no other code is affected. However, some variable names may be reused. In addition, without requiring explicit declaration, the outside scope can be affected unintentionally. This can result in problems that are hard to debug, since they depend on the scope in which variables are used in addition to where the problem occurs.

Illustrated here in Listing 3-15, two values are assigned to two variables, one of which is defined and one of which is not. The same thing is also done inside a nested function call. This function is able to modify both the declared and undeclared variables from the parent scope. When the function returns, the caller is able to use the variable that was used without declaration inside the function. The other variable is scoped to the function and is no longer available after the function returns.

Listing 3-15: Working with variable scope

```html
<html xmlns="http://www.w3.org/1999/xhtml">
<head>
    <title>Scope</title>

    <script type="text/javascript">

        // Use of a global variable without declaration
        someUndeclaredVariable = "some undeclared variable";

        // Global variable declaration

        var someDeclaredVariable = "some declared variable";

        function someFunction() {
            // Variable declared local to the function
            var nestedDeclared = "a nested declared variable";

            // Undeclared variable used in function becomes global in scope
            nestedUndeclared = "a nested undeclared variable";

            // Update the global variables
            someUndeclaredVariable = "modified undeclared variable";
            someDeclaredVariable = "modified declared variable";
        }

        someFunction();
```

Continued

Listing 3-15: Working with variable scope *(continued)*

```
                // Check the existence and values of the variables
                if(!!someUndeclaredVariable) {
                    document.write("someUndeclaredVariable = " + someUndeclaredVariable +
                        "<br />");
                }

                if(!!someDeclaredVariable) {
                    document.write("someDeclaredVariable = " + someDeclaredVariable +
                        "<br />");
                }

                if(!!nestedUndeclared) {
                    document.write("nestedUndeclared = " + nestedUndeclared + "<br />");
                }

                if(!!nestedDeclared) {
                    document.write("nestedDeclared =" + nestedDeclared + "<br />");
                }

        </script>

    </head>
    <body>
        <form id="form1" runat="server">
        <div>
        </div>
        </form>
    </body>
</html>
```

Figure 3-8 shows the output of running the page from within both Microsoft's Internet Explorer and Mozilla's Firefox. Although there are attempts to access and write each of the four variables, only the two used in the global scope and the one used in a nested scope without declaration are available. The undeclared variables are automatically elevated to a global scope. The declared variable is limited to the scope in which it is defined. In a simple example like this, it appears straightforward, but in real-world, complex development tasks, the scoping of undefined variables can easily lead to problems that are hard to isolate and fix.

In Figure 3-8, notice the small yellow exclamation point icon in the lower-left corner of Internet Explorer. This is an indication of an error on the page. When it is double-clicked, a dialog will appear that explains that there is a script error on the page. In fact, you can instruct Internet Explorer to treat this as an error. That way instead of getting an exclamation point in the corner, a dialog box alerts you that the undeclared variable was used.

The details view of the error says that script code on the page is attempting to use an undeclared variable. In Firefox, the Tools menu has an option for launching a JavaScript console for working with script on the page. The Firefox console shows additional warnings when running in strict mode. To access the configuration settings, enter about:config in the address bar of the browser and press Enter.

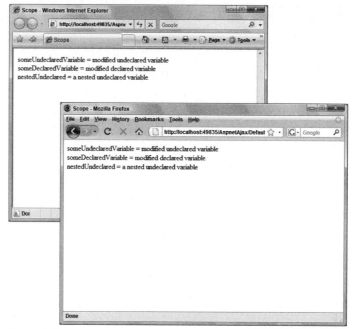

Figure 3-8

When you use this command, a long list of available configuration settings is displayed. Any setting that has been changed from the default value will be in bold text, while the rest are in regular text. Scroll down until you see `javascript.options.script` and double-click on that line in particular. This action will toggle the value to true from its default value of false.

Any use of undeclared variables will then be flagged in the JavaScript console as a warning. The browser window itself will not show an error, but the JavaScript console will show the warning when it is made visible by selecting it in the Tools menu (by selecting Tools ⇨ Error Console). Internet Explorer and Firefox both provide ways to find any undeclared variables you have used because of the problems that arise when coding that way. Always declare variables to limit their scope and avoid modifying data unintentionally. Figure 3-9 shows the configuration screen for Mozilla Firefox and the JavaScript console, with a warning visible for using an undeclared variable.

Sometimes you want to test to see whether a variable is in scope without causing an error. You do this by testing for it as a member of the window class. If an object exists, it will be coerced to true in a Boolean test; if false, it does not exist:

```
if(window.nestedDeclared)
{
    document.write("nestedDeclared =" + nestedDeclared + "<br />");
}
else
{
    document.write("nestedDeclared is not in scope");
}
```

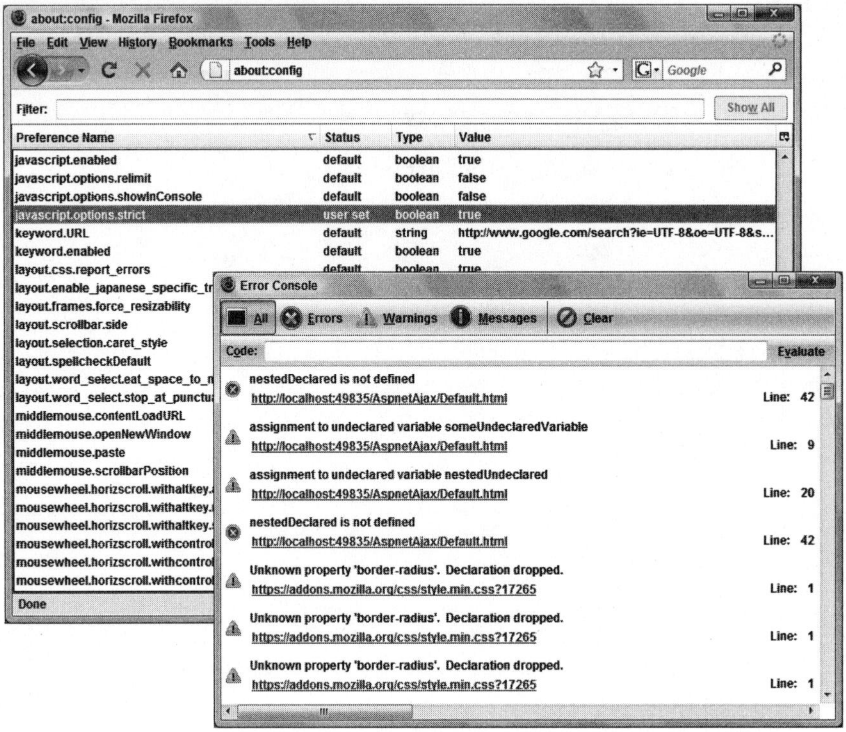

Figure 3-9

Using Prototypes

The function type in JavaScript allows you to define custom types. JavaScript does not support static type checking, so you can be creative in creating and using custom types on the fly. The object-oriented programming paradigm has made programming at a higher level the standard for many developers and is more appropriate than procedural programming for most tasks. JavaScript does not support inheritance as other object-oriented languages do, but functions can be used to model data types. As a dynamic language, JavaScript opens the door for some interesting type definitions that can make the code look more familiar to C# and Visual Basic developers.

Listing 3-16 includes a simple definition of an `album` object in C#. There are string variables for storing the title and artist for the album. For this class, there is also a constructor that takes the artist and title and stores them in the local variables.

Listing 3-16: A C# example of an Album object

```
using System;

public class Album
{
```

Listing 3-16: A C# example of an Album object *(continued)*

```csharp
    private string _title = String.Empty;
    private string _artist = String.Empty;

    public Album(string title, string artist)
    {
      this._title = title;
      this._artist = artist;
    }
  }
```

You can model the same object in JavaScript using a function. Listing 3-17 has a JavaScript function with two arguments: `title` and `artist`. This is just like the constructor in C# presented in Listing 3-16. The JavaScript function takes the two arguments and assigns them to the local variables declared inside the function.

Listing 3-17: A complex type as a JavaScript function

```html
<script type="text/javascript">

   function Album(title, artist)
   {
       this._title = title;
       this._artist = artist;
   }

   var album1 = new Album("The Colour and the Shape", "Foo Fighters");
   var album2 = new Album("Rocket to Russia", "Ramones");

</script>
```

The album type can be extended to include a property that provides a string representation with both the title and artist. In C#, this would mean adding a new property to the class and recompiling it. In JavaScript, a type can even be modified while the script is still running. The `prototype` property of an object represents the type itself (which should not be confused with a C programming language prototype, which is only used to give a function a signature).

When using the prototype to extend a type, the change applies to all instances of the object. Listing 3-18 adds the `Listing` property to the `Album` type using the prototype.

Listing 3-18: Adding the Listing property to the Album type

```html
<script type="text/javascript">

   function Album(title, artist)
   {
       this._title = title;
       this._artist = artist;
   }
```

Continued

Listing 3-18: Adding the Listing property to the Album type *(continued)*

```
var album1 = new Album("The Colour and the Shape", "Foo Fighters");
var album2 = new Album("Rocket to Russia", "Ramones");


function listing()
{
    return this._artist + ": " + this._title;
}

Album.prototype.Listing = listing;

alert(album1.Listing());
alert(album2.Listing());

</script>
```

Running this example will produce the results shown in Figure 3-10.

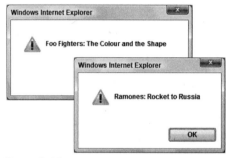

Figure 3-10

The prototype object represents the object type itself; think of it as a type definition. Any instance of the object inherits all of its prototype information. All of the objects of that type that have already been created get the updated abilities of the base type immediately. Of course, a new function can be added to the object definition so that all instances of the object created in the future will receive the functionality without your having to modify the prototype directly.

The disadvantage is that each instance gets a copy that way. Using the prototype of an object to extend its functionality is a natural way to model static methods and properties in C# and C++. Modifying the prototype in JavaScript is like modifying the basetype in a .NET type without requiring derived types to be aware of the change.

The prototype object of JavaScript even allows built-in types (such as String) to be modified. When you add functionality to the intrinsic objects provided by the scripting engine, you begin to appreciate the power and flexibility of a dynamic language. You are not forced to subclass the type and switch all of your code to use some new derived type to add something that you need.

In .NET code, you could do this by recompiling, when you have access to the original class sources, but in JavaScript you can modify a type without access to the sources. Listing 3-19 adds the `StrangeCaseIt()` method to the built-in JavaScript String type. Notice that the string is declared and assigned before the new function is created. The `StrangeCaseIt()` function is then added to the `String` instance using its prototype. Now all strings, including the one that already exists in the code, have access to this new functionality but have not had to pay any overhead associated with carrying the information about the new method along.

Listing 3-19: Modifying types

```
<html xmlns="http://www.w3.org/1999/xhtml">
<head>
    <title>Modifying types</title>

    <script type="text/javascript">

        var sample = "SomeThing";

        function StrangeCaseIt() {
            var returnVal = "";

            for(var i = 0; i < this.length; i++) {
                if(this.substr(i, 1).toUpperCase() == this.substr(i, 1))
                {
                    returnVal += this.substr(i, 1).toLowerCase();
                }
                else
                {
                    returnVal += this.substr(i, 1).toUpperCase();
                }
            }
            return returnVal;
        }

        String.prototype.StrangeCaseIt = StrangeCaseIt;

        var result = sample.StrangeCaseIt();

        document.write(sample + "<br />");
        document.write(result + "<br />");

    </script>

</head>
<body>
    <form id="form1" runat="server">
    <div>
    </div>
    </form>
</body>
</html>
```

The code from this listing produces the results illustrated in Figure 3-11.

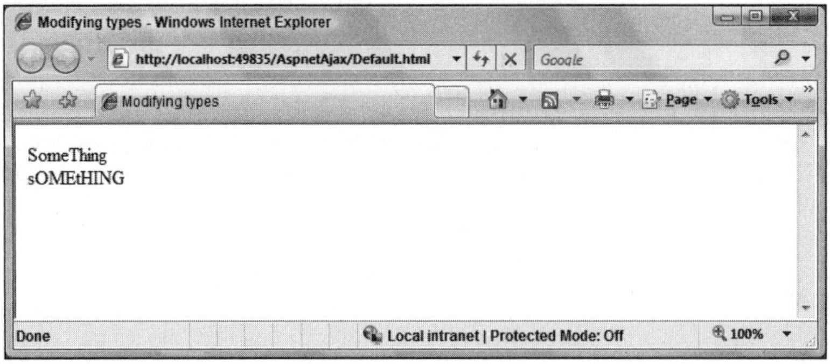

Figure 3-11

The Microsoft AJAX Library makes heavy use of the prototype object to extend functionality and provide a more natural programming environment for the .NET developer. Chapter 7 of this book goes into more detail about this extended functionality and how a familiar object-oriented approach is made available with ASP.NET AJAX. For now, just note that this type system functionality is provided by leveraging the prototype feature of JavaScript.

When using the prototype object, the use of the `this` reference can be confusing. The `this` reference refers to the object currently in scope at the time the code runs. Remember, the prototype applies to the type itself and all instances of it. It is a specific reference meant to eliminate global members from being included in an object you are extending.

When creating object extensions using the prototype, omitting the `this` reference to use object variables is interpreted as an error. You must specify that the reference is for another variable in the object scope. Think of the prototype extensions as operating in isolation from the rest of the code. You do not want your program to be affected by the scope in which the object runs, so you have to be specific about every reference you make. This has to do with the fact that JavaScript uses lexical scoping, not dynamic scoping. Instead of allowing you to reference anything in scope for a prototype extension when the function is called, the object must exist when the function is defined. Always use the `this` operator to refer to object variables because anything that is not part of the object definition could be different when the code executes next and could lead to problems.

Close on Closures

When discussing the prototype object, it is necessary to consider JavaScript closures. The prototype is used to extend the definition of an object, regardless of what other scope is in effect. The prototype is available as a characteristic of the type, regardless of whether you have an instance of the object. The prototype is independent from the state during which it was created. Closures, on the other hand, are used to leverage the scope in play at the time the closure is created. A closure refers to the way you can define an inner function to take advantage of the state of the outer function's context and make it visible externally so it can execute after the outer function has returned. The behavior of the closure can depend on the state and scope that existed when the closure was created. Scoping behavior is the same in JavaScript as it is in C# and Visual Basic, with one notable exception (as shown in Figure 3-1 at the beginning of the chapter): Using a variable without declaring it gives it a global scope.

If you search for information on closures, you are bound to find some hard-to-follow, overly complex scientific explanations. Concrete specific examples are generally better at explaining closures than formal definitions. The prototype can reference properties and functions using the `this` operator, but the lexical scoping means that any outside variables that happen to exist do not come into play. It is typically an error when you try to use transient state information in a prototype extension. The various instances of the object type being extended should not leverage any other scope that happens to be in existence, unless it is deliberate access to global information. A closure function captures the state of its scope at the time it is created.

Scoping is much easier to see through an example. Listing 3-20 contains a function that creates another function. The function created just squares the variable according to the scope that was in effect when the closure was created. The code loops from 0 to 10, calling the function creator and storing the results. Then another loop goes through the stored functions and invokes each one.

Listing 3-20: Scoping in JavaScript

```html
<html xmlns="http://www.w3.org/1999/xhtml">
<head>
    <title>Scoping in JavaScript</title>

    <script type="text/javascript">
        function CreateFunction(num) {
            var NewFunction = function() {
                document.write(num + " squared = " + num*num + "<br />");
            }
            return NewFunction;
        }

        var functions = new Array();

        for(var i = 0; i < 10; i++) {
            functions[i] = CreateFunction(i);
        }

        for(var j = 0; j < 10; j++) {
            functions[j]();
        }
    </script>

</head>
<body>
    <form id="form1" runat="server">
    <div>
    </div>
    </form>
</body>
</html>
```

When the functions are created, they carry with them the scope that existed at that time. It does not matter that the variable used when creating the function has subsequently changed or even gone out of scope. The function reflects the closure of the scope in effect at the time it was created. The num variable no longer exists once the function-creating method returns, but the state of the transient variable is captured and used when the new function is invoked. Figure 3-12 shows the results of calling the functions to output their values.

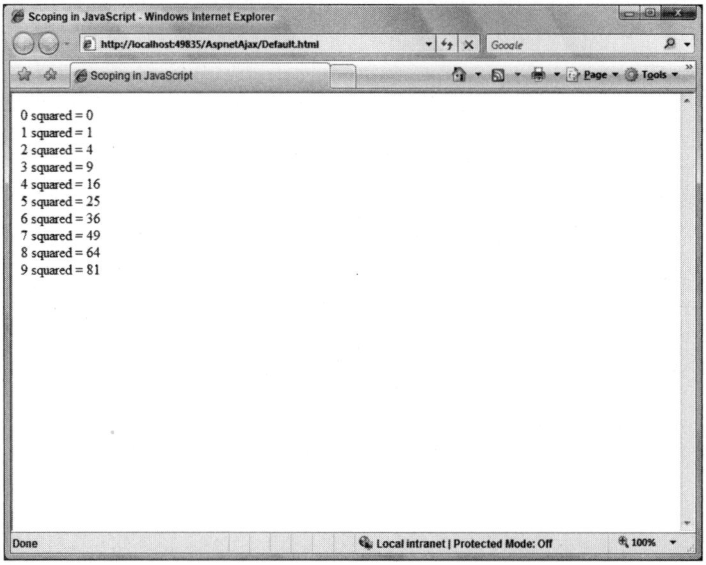

Figure 3-12

In the previous example, the scope of the variable being used was limited to the function that was creating new functions. The variable is declared as a function argument and is no longer available after the function returns. However, the closure that is created captures the state of that variable in that scope, and the function created is able to use it later when it is invoked.

Listing 3-21 modifies the example slightly to show how the scope is captured in a closure. A variable in the global scope is referenced from within the function being created. The variable is declared before the loop that is creating functions, and the variable is incremented during each pass. When the created functions are called, the scope that existed at the time of creation, not the value in play at that time is used. Although the value for the variable was different while each closure was created, just as in the previous example, the scope was different and thus the function is different.

Listing 3-21: Scoping in JavaScript

```
<html xmlns="http://www.w3.org/1999/xhtml">
<head>
    <title>Scoping in JavaScript</title>

    <script type="text/javascript">
        function CreateFunction(num) {
         var NewFunction = function() {
          document.write( num + " squared = " + num*num +
                          " and globalNum= " + globalNum + "<br />");
         }
         return NewFunction;
        }


        var globalNum = 0;
```

Listing 3-21: Scoping in JavaScript *(continued)*

```
            var functions = new Array();

            for(var i = 0; i < 10; i++) {

                globalNum = globalNum + 2;
                functions[i] = CreateFunction(i);
            }

            for(var j = 0; j < 10; j++) {
                functions[j]();
            }
        </script>

    </head>
    <body>
        <form id="form1" runat="server">
        <div>
        </div>
        </form>
    </body>
</html>
```

Every function that was created shows the current value of the global variable based on the captured scope. The variable was global when the closure was created, and the value at the time is immaterial. The scope is captured and the value of the variable when the closure function is actually called is used. Since it is in the global scope, the current value of the variable is still in effect when the individual functions stored in the collection of functions are called. They all show the same value for the global variable as it is now, despite that the value was different when each function was created, as you can see in Figure 3-13.

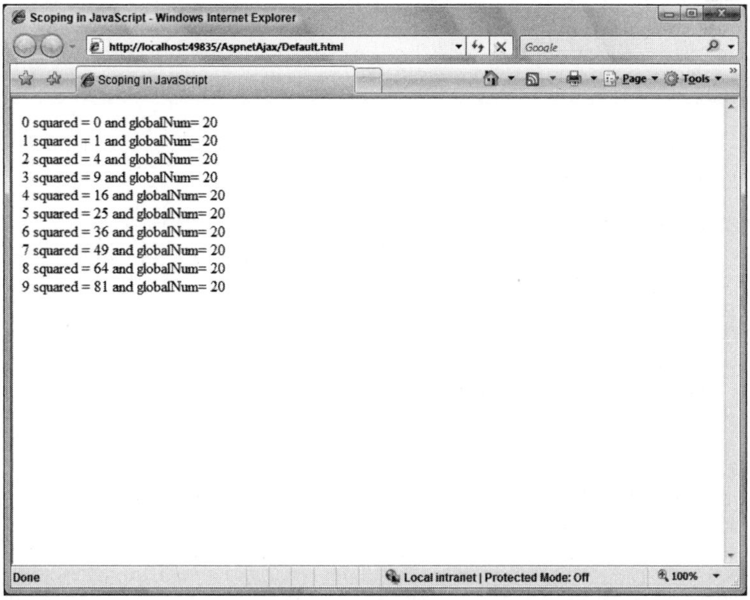

Figure 3-13

Garbage Collection

JavaScript is a garbage-collected language. When an object goes out of scope and there are no longer references to it, the system can free it and reclaim the memory and resources. This is one of the language features of C# and Visual Basic that makes them easy to use. C++ programmers are used to painstakingly allocating and freeing memory and objects by hand. Managing your own memory can be tedious, and mistakes can be devastating. JavaScript tracks which variables refer to what, and when there are no lingering references to an object, it is freed.

DOM Elements

Ultimately, what makes JavaScript useful in the browser is that it is able to access the Document Object Model (DOM). You can attach JavaScript functions to browser events and dynamically modify the HTML elements, CSS, and behavior of the page. Thus, JavaScript can take static pages and make them rich and interactive. Earlier in Listing 3-6, code is attached to the `onload()` event of the browser's window element.

As browsers evolved, they developed different DOMs. The World Wide Web consortium established a standard meant to provide isolation from the differences. In reality, there are still some challenges in writing code that will work on all of the major browsers, but the Microsoft AJAX Library provides some abstractions that make it easier to write code compatible with many popular browsers.

Avoiding Memory Leaks

Closures, garbage collection, and access to the DOM come together in a way that can manifest itself as a memory leak in the browser. It is easy to end up with circular references that involve a DOM element. The garbage collector in Internet Explorer sees this as a persistent reference and fails to recognize that the object can be freed. Even when a new page is loaded, the resource is still held, although the element does not exist anymore. Over time, the amount of memory consumed by the browser will creep up until the process is restarted.

A common way to create circular references is to attach a JavaScript function to the event of an HTML element. If the event handler code then references a property of the element, you have a circular reference. The Microsoft AJAX Library provides constructs for binding events that also clean up the circular references.

To avoid memory leaks, many developers attach Javascript functions to the unload event of the window. This event fires when the user is through with the page and is moving on. In the event handler, the user will loop through DOM and set the event handlers to null to break the circular references. Listing 3-22 is an example of attaching an event handler to a DOM element that creates a circular reference by accessing the source element.

Listing 3-22: Breaking circular references

```
<html xmlns="http://www.w3.org/1999/xhtml">
<head>
    <title>Circular Reference</title>

    <script type="text/javascript">
```

Listing 3-22: Breaking circular references *(continued)*

```
        function eventHandler() {
            var tb = document.getElementById("tb");
            if(!!tb) {
                tb.value = "Something else";
            }
        }

    </script>

</head>
<body>
    <form id="form1" runat="server">
    <div>
        <input type="text" id="tb" onclick="eventHandler()" />
    </div>
    </form>
</body>
</html>
```

Evaluating eval()

In a compiled language like C# and Visual Basic, it is difficult to create and use code dynamically. The .NET Framework provides the CodeDOM (code document object model) classes for defining functionality and then producing the equivalent code, but this is not typically employed during code execution, because of its difficulty. JavaScript is dynamic in that it allows types to be created and modified on the fly. Furthermore, it natively supports the ability in the eval() function to have any arbitrary script executed. It functions just as if it were a predefined piece of code. This means that you can easily write code that uses runtime values during code execution to create new code that is then executed. Essentially, you can create and execute code on the fly based on other input and variables.

Variable assignments can be based on any runtime condition and used elsewhere in JavaScript code. Listing 3-23 assigns some names to variables and then creates a string which is a piece of code that aggregates the values into a single variable and then displays that variable. Note that the values are pulled together into a piece of code that will use them all. This is distinctly different from having a piece of code that combines strings. The variables happen to be strings, but the eval statement is simply executing a piece of code passed to it as a string.

Listing 3-23: Using eval()

```
<html xmlns="http://www.w3.org/1999/xhtml">
<head>
    <title>Using eval</title>

    <script type="text/javascript">
        var aName = "Sofia";
        var anotherName = "Henri";
        var yetAnotherName = "Kalle";
```

Continued

Listing 3-23: Using eval() *(continued)*

```
            var stopAlready = "and Tuija";

            var someCode = "var names = '" + aName + ", " + anotherName + ", " +
                yetAnotherName + ", " + stopAlready + "'";
            var moreCode = "eval(someCode); alert(names);";

            function showNames() {
                eval(moreCode);
            }

            showNames ();
        </script>

    </head>
    <body>
        <form id="form1" runat="server">
        <div>
        </div>
        </form>
    </body>
    </html>
```

Running this code will display your list of names in an alert, as illustrated in Figure 3-14.

Figure 3-14

Of course, just gathering some strings and displaying them can be accomplished without the use of the eval() function. However, if you find yourself iterating over a collection in code where you are writing repetitive code in a pattern, consider whether eval() might make the code easier to read and maintain. The eval() function is a powerful way to execute any arbitrary JavaScript code on the fly. In this example, the call to showNames() results in performing an eval() on the moreCode variable, which in turn evaluates the variables and displays the values. It is a convoluted way to get the job done, but the point is that you can compose code based on dynamic values.

The eval() function does not come without tradeoffs. Code executed with eval() is generally slower than code run directly. Having code that runs other code is a level of indirection that comes at a price. Numerous articles and blog posts advocate never using eval() at all. Not only is performance a concern, but security comes into play as well. It is very tempting to use eval() to operate on user input, but user input cannot be trusted. In the confines of the browser sandbox, much of what a user might try to do would not reveal anything interesting, but treating user input as trusted code and executing it can open all sorts of unforeseen security concerns. Generally, you should never use eval() on user input.

One common use of `eval()` is to access fields of an object. Instead of calling `eval("something." + someField)`, you can usually switch to using `something["someField"]`. This is generally more intuitive for others to read, easier to maintain, and faster in the browser.

Handling Exceptions

JavaScript supports a familiar type of exception handling for C# developers. Code can throw an exception. If located inside a `try` block, a corresponding `catch` block can handle the exception. After that, a `finally` block will execute to take care of any necessary cleanup or global recovery approach. The `try-catch-finally` pattern is important in being able to write robust code that can recover from error conditions.

The Java runtime environment (not JavaScript) requires that code declare up front any type of exception that it may want to catch. When the code is compiled, the types of exceptions that may be thrown are checked. You must explicitly catch all of the possible exception types. Unlike the Java runtime environment, the .NET Framework does not require you to declare what type of exception a method may throw. You can catch the base-exception type and then deal with more specific exception types as you see fit. You can even define custom exception types derived from existing types for greater specialization. In JavaScript, there are no static checks on types of exceptions. You simply catch the exception, which has a base type of object, and react as you see fit. It is not uncommon to have exception-handling code that looks at the details of the exception thrown to determine what the course of action should be. In many situations, throwing a basic `Exception` object using a string constructor is adequate for signaling what recovery action is necessary. This choice is entirely a runtime determination.

Listing 3-24 shows a set of `try-catch-finally` blocks. The runtime overhead and complexity associated with exception-handling semantics in other languages is not the same in JavaScript. If your preference is to use exceptions as part of flow control, you need not worry about a significant impact on performance.

Listing 3-24: Working with exceptions

```html
<html xmlns="http://www.w3.org/1999/xhtml">
<head>
    <title>Exceptions</title>

    <script type="text/javascript">
        try {
            var now = new Date().getTime();
            if ((now % 2) === 0) {
                throw "even ticks";
            }
            else {
                throw "odd ticks";
            }
        }
        catch (ex) {
            if(ex === "even ticks") {
                document.write("an even exception occurred <br />");
            }
            else if (ex === "odd ticks") {
```

Continued

Listing 3-24: Working with exceptions *(continued)*

```
                document.write("an odd exception occured <br />");
            }
            else {
                alert(ex);
                document.write("a mathematical anomaly occured");
            }
        }
        finally {
            document.write("all done");
        }
    </script>

</head>
<body>
    <form id="form1" runat="server">
    <div>
    </div>
    </form>
</body>
</html>
```

Getting Parts of a String

Switching back and forth between languages can have its pitfalls. There may be something slightly different between the two that continues to trip you up. Accessing parts of a string is a common programming task and one that may trip you up as you go back and forth from JavaScript to C# or Visual Basic.

The substr() function for extracting part of a string is used in C and C++, while the Substring() method is supported in C# and Visual Basic. They are both available in JavaScript. They all operate on 0-based strings. If you are also using Visual Basic, which is 1-based, this may be an initial obstacle.

Both substr() and Substring() have versions that accept a single argument and return the remainder of the string starting at that index. The two argument versions behave slightly differently. The substr() function takes a start index and the number of characters to extract. The Substring() function takes a start index and an end index. In isolation, this seems straightforward, but you will undoubtedly be coding in something other than JavaScript part of the time and may find yourself scratching your head trying to remember which language supports which version. JavaScript has them both. Listing 3-25 utilizes both functions.

Listing 3-25: Utilizing both substr() and substring()

```
<html xmlns="http://www.w3.org/1999/xhtml">
<head>
    <title>Substrings</title>

    <script type="text/javascript">
        var aString = "0123456789";
```

Listing 3-25: Utilizing both substr() and substring() *(continued)*

```
        document.write(aString.substr(2) + "<br />");
        document.write(aString.substring(2) + "<br />");
        document.write(aString.substr(2, 5) + "<br />");
        document.write(aString.substring(2, 5) + "<br />");
    </script>

</head>
<body>
    <form id="form1" runat="server">
    <div>
    </div>
    </form>
</body>
</html>
```

The result of running Listing 3-25, where both versions are called with identical arguments, is shown in Figure 3-15.

Better JavaScript

As you leverage JavaScript more in creating richer Web applications, a few practices may help you produce more robust and faster pages. For all of the advantages JavaScript brings, it also has some drawbacks that become apparent the more predominant a part of the page it becomes. The amount of script in a page can easily surpass the amount of HTML. Performance can start to lag.

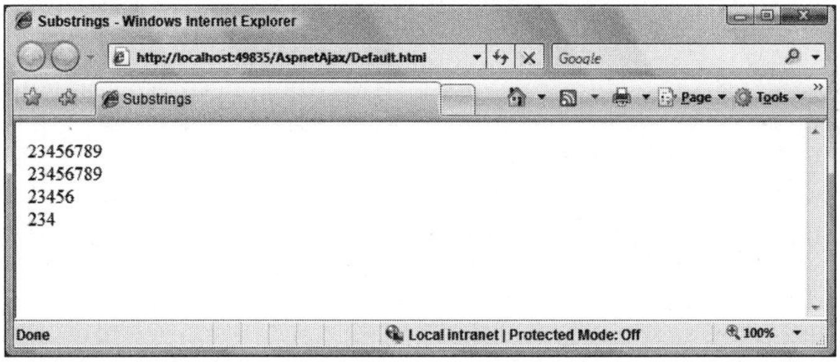

Figure 3-15

Reducing Script

With bigger quantities of script being used in the page, the size of the script itself can become an issue. IIS supports compressing responses, but it is not turned on by default. Text compresses very well, which greatly reduces the number of bytes sent to the client. To enable compression in IIS, access the Internet Services Manager plug-in for the Microsoft Management Console. You can do this by entering `inetmgr` in the run dialog in the start menu. Right-click the Web Sites folder and select Properties. Options for enabling static and dynamic content are on the Services tab. There is CPU cost associated with compression, so you may want to enable it only for static content if the dynamic content is not cacheable (since the static content is always cacheable, it can be compressed once and not repeatedly).

Another technique for reducing the size of the script is variable substitution. You see this referred to as script compression. The approach is to replace variable names with short versions. When writing code, it is nice to have meaningful names, but because the script engine does not care about this, smaller names also work fine. Tools are available that take script and do this replacement for you. However, it can make debugging difficult, because the variable names and even function names can be replaced with short, meaningless versions. It may seem like reducing the size of the script does not buy you much, and for a single page load, the difference will be small. However, when you look at the effect it can have on the server, there is a big benefit. Smaller scripts can be returned faster. The connections and threads used to service the request are freed up sooner, so a single server can scale to accommodate more simultaneous users.

Using Cache Variables

In a compiled language, the code generator can do some tricks to make the executing code faster. A variable referenced repeatedly in a function may have its pointer stored in a register for easy and fast access throughout the function. In JavaScript, variable resolution is late bound. Each time a variable is used, the scope chain is searched to find the object. This can be time-consuming. Rather than building up strings while storing them in a DOM element, it's better to build them up in a local variable and then do a single assignment to the DOM element. When looping through arrays, you can actually improve performance by initializing a variable with the length of the array and checking against that instead of accessing the length property each time.

`for(var i=0, var l = someArray.length; i < l; i++)` is faster than

`for(var i=0; i < someArray.length; i++)`.

The kind of speedup you might see from this sort of optimization is not nearly as dramatic as what you can get with caching of function pointers. JavaScript function lookups are expensive, and scope resolution and lookups to access functions on DOM elements are even more expensive. One way to think of it is that reducing the number of dots in your code improves the performance. Listing 3-26 has two versions of the same method, inspired by the blog from the Internet Explorer team. While there is nothing technically wrong with the first version, the second will be much faster for any reasonably large collection.

Listing 3-26: Looking at performance

```
<script type="text/javascript">

    function UpdateValues() {
        var elt = document.getElementById("something");

        for(var i = 0; i < myArray.length; i++) {
            elt.appendChild(myArray[i]);
        }
    }

    function UpdateValuesCaching() {
        var eltFunc = document.getElementById("something").appendChild;

        for(var i = 0, var l = myArray.length; i < l; i++) {
```

Listing 3-26: Looking at performance *(continued)*

```
            eltFunc(myArray[i]);
        }
    }

    </script>
```

The second version caches a reference to the `appendChild()` function and then invokes it directly. This saves the overhead of repeatedly resolving the function name to the actual function call. When multiple scopes and namespaces are involved, the performance advantage is increased.

Summary

This chapter provided a brief introduction to JavaScript. You saw how script is included in a page and explored techniques for minimizing the overhead associated with loading script. JavaScript is a dynamic language that allows types to be modified on the fly using the prototype. You can also create closures with functions that capture a given scope for even greater flexibility.

Not only does JavaScript have support for the fundamental types of string, number, and Boolean, but it also treats functions as first-class types as well as objects. The late binding nature of JavaScript means that you can improve performance by caching aggressively. In addition, you have seen that JavaScript can be confusing with support for null as well as undefined types. The equality operators and strict equality operators can complicate things further, so being explicit about what you are after will eliminate frustration in the end.

Understanding the ASP.NET AJAX Client Library

It is true that many of the application improvements that result from using AJAX occur because you are doing more in the JavaScript language in the browser. This does include the asynchronous communications with the server, preloading images and data, manipulation of the browser DOM, and more. What these improvements in the model all have in common is an increased use of JavaScript on your pages is needed to accomplish these tasks.

ASP.NET AJAX, as built into ASP.NET 3.5, provides some key features that make including and working with JavaScript easier overall. By employing some similar patterns, Microsoft has really gone the extra mile in making working with JavaScript feel similar to working with C# and Visual Basic. This chapter looks at the type system provided by the Microsoft AJAX Library that makes it easier to employ familiar OOP (object-oriented programming) patterns in your JavaScript development. This chapter also reviews a set of JavaScript classes that provide core functionality similar to the base class libraries found in the .NET Framework.

The AJAX Library brings concepts from the .NET Framework to JavaScript running in the browser, making the server and client coding models a bit more consistent. However, because JavaScript is inherently quite different from C# or Visual Basic, and because you cannot leverage the .NET Framework on the user's computer, you should not expect a high degree of compatibility and consistency here. The AJAX Library has also added a client-side page lifecycle, similar in concept to the ASP.NET server-side page lifecycle. This addition makes it easy to participate in the processing of the page, work with partial page rendering, and provide event handlers for user actions.

It is important to point out here that with ASP.NET AJAX, you get many of the application advantages without writing a lot of JavaScript yourself. In Chapter 2, for example, you saw how to use server controls that automatically generate JavaScript for you to enable partial page rendering. In Chapter 6 of this book, you will see a set of controls from the AJAX Control Toolkit that provide some interesting UI features that leverage the Microsoft AJAX Library and do not require you to write a lot of JavaScript. Microsoft has done a great deal of work for you. When you want to write your own controls, add custom event handlers, or start doing more in the browser, however, you will likely need to write custom JavaScript code. The ASP.NET AJAX Client Library and some recommended coding patterns make you more productive in that work.

The Browser Page Lifecycle

One of the first things to understand about the ASP.NET AJAX Library is that it establishes a page life-cycle for JavaScript code running in the browser. It is not as complex as the server page lifecycle, but it is central to interacting with some of the more complex features. This lifecycle gives you some easy "hooks" that you need to tap into in order to do the processing you want to do at the right time.

Although the JavaScript event mechanism is simpler than that provided by the .NET Framework, it is sufficient for your needs. Listing 4-1 shows a very basic page built with ASP.NET. This page simply pops up a box with the word *Hello*, but it shows a basic starting point. To use the Microsoft AJAX Library and initiate the client-side lifecycle in the browser, there is a ScriptManager control on the page. This takes care of rendering the references to the scripts that make up the library, which the browser will have to request when the page loads.

Listing 4-1: Working with the pageLoad() and pageUnload() functions

```
<%@ Page Language="C#" %>

<html xmlns="http://www.w3.org/1999/xhtml">
<head runat="server">
    <title>Simple Hello</title>

    <script type="text/javascript">
        function pageLoad(sender, args) {
            alert("Hello");
        }

        function pageUnload(sender, args) {
            alert("Goodbye");
        }
    </script>

</head>
<body>
    <form id="form1" runat="server">
    <div>
        <asp:ScriptManager ID="ScriptManager1" runat="server">
        </asp:ScriptManager>
    </div>
    </form>
</body>
</html>
```

The `pageLoad()` and `pageUnload()` functions are the primary points where you will interact with the browser page lifecycle. The `pageLoad()` function is automatically called after the page is initially retrieved from the Web server and some script processing has occurred. In turn, the `pageUnload()`

function is then called whenever a subsequent request is initiated (for postback, partial page rendering, shutting down the browser instance, or even when navigating to a different application).

When the page from Listing 4-1 is run, you will first be presented with the alert dialog box with the text *Hello* right when the page is first pulled up in the browser. Then if you shut down the browser instance, you will then be presented with the second alert stating *Goodbye*.

When the page is loaded again, even during partial rendering, the `pageLoad()` function will again be triggered. Chapter 11 of this book discusses building custom controls and shows additional details of the page lifecycle beyond those presented here.

Using the Type System

The JavaScript language has a familiar syntax if you are used to C#, Java, or C++. However, as you saw in Chapter 3, JavaScript does not have built-in support for most object-oriented programming (OOP) concepts. This is not a problem by itself, but as you switch back and forth between C# or Visual Basic and JavaScript, you may find that you miss the familiar OOP constructs you are used to in the richer languages.

When using JavaScript, there is no support for inheritance of types and no standard way of declaring interface definitions or enumerations. What's a developer to do? In the past, it meant that you adopted your own conventions in writing JavaScript. This becomes problematic as more people with unique approaches are added to a project, because there can be inconsistencies that make maintenance and new development more difficult. ASP.NET AJAX provides the ability to leverage OOP constructs when writing JavaScript. You will see many small code examples that demonstrate a set of recommended standard patterns and show how the Microsoft AJAX Library functions are used.

The AJAX Library brings classic OOP concepts to JavaScript. It adds namespace support for grouping functionality. It also provides helpful debugging facilities, a schema for providing type information, and a means for localizing string and image resources.

Part of the ASP.NET team's motivation for creating the AJAX Library and these patterns for development was to make JavaScript coding more like the C# coding that developers are used to. The ASP.NET team, in putting together ASP.NET AJAX, has tried to find the right balance between leveraging the features of a dynamic language and adopting a rigid approach more suitable to development with a statically typed language.

Declaring Namespaces

In the .NET Framework, like functionalities are grouped into namespaces. Graphics classes are under the `System.Graphics` namespace, while ASP.NET Framework classes are under the `System.Web` namespace. The use of namespaces is central to providing an organized and structured way for finding and accessing functionality. Namespaces are nothing more than prefixes used in front of class and type names, but through the use of standard conventions, namespaces are used to organize sets of similar functionality and are then typically housed in a single DLL. Your application declares which assemblies are referenced at compile time and this establishes which namespaces are available for use during development and which assemblies are required at runtime. The AJAX Library also supports the concept of namespaces. It uses namespaces for its own objects and provides you with the ability to do the same.

The AJAX Library synthesizes namespaces by creating objects with those names. Class definitions can be organized logically in just the same way that you would organize them using C# or Visual Basic. You can group functionality naturally into separate namespaces and use them as independent resources. If you create separate files for different namespaces, you can even load them conditionally the same way the Common Language Runtime loads just the assemblies it needs for an application and does so on demand. This achieves a benefit similar to what happens in .NET Framework applications where the overhead associated with using some functionality in a namespace is not incurred unless the feature is used. It is a pay-for-play model. An application does not need to send the script associated with a namespace if the functionality is not used in that page.

For an example of working with namespaces, Listing 4-2 demonstrates the basics of namespace support. The `Wrox.AspAjax.Samples` namespace is created via the `Type.registerNamespace()` function. Notice that you do not have to first create the `Wrox` and `Wrox.AspAjax` namespaces in order to register the `Samples` namespace under them. You can specify the whole namespace, and the AJAX Library will automatically create any levels of the hierarchy that do not exist already on your behalf.

Listing 4-2: Registering namespaces

```
<%@ Page Language="C#" %>

<html xmlns="http://www.w3.org/1999/xhtml">
<head runat="server">
    <title>ASP.NET AJAX Namespaces</title>

    <script type="text/javascript">

        function pageLoad(sender, args) {
            Type.registerNamespace('Wrox.AspAjax.Samples');

            alert(Type.isNamespace(Wrox.AspAjax)); //displays 'true'
            alert(Type.isNamespace(Wrox.AspAjax.Samples.Album)); //displays 'false'

            var namespaces = Type.getRootNamespaces();

            for(var i = 0, length = namespaces.length; i < length; i++) {
                alert(namespaces[i].getName()); //displays 'Sys' and 'Wrox'
            }
        }

    </script>

</head>
<body>
    <form id="form1" runat="server">
    <div>
        <asp:ScriptManager ID="ScriptManager1" runat="server">
        </asp:ScriptManager>
    </div>
    </form>
</body>
</html>
```

In this example, the call to `Type.registerNamespace()` creates three different objects: `Wrox`, `AspAjax`, and `Samples`. The `Wrox` object contains the `AspAjax` object, which in turn contains the `Samples` object. The objects all carry some metadata so the type system can identify them as namespaces and use them to hold any other objects that are added to the namespace.

The `Type.isNamespace()` function returns a Boolean. The code did not create an `Album` namespace, so for that check, it returns a value of false in the alert dialog. The set of global namespaces is retrieved by calling the `Type.getRootnamespaces()` function. Looping through the returned array and calling `getName()` on each reveals that, in addition to the new `Wrox` namespace, there is also a `Sys` namespace. This namespace contains the AJAX Library functionality.

Although doing so is not technically required, it's a good idea to use namespaces to organize your own code, even if just to avoid cluttering up the global namespace. Because JavaScript is an interpreted language, the operation of resolving names is expensive. Every time you call a function, the JavaScript engine has to figure out where the code lives. Resolving variables also involves searching the current scope and containing scopes until the reference is resolved. The more global objects you have, the more expensive it is for the script engine to access them. Namespace objects also allow navigating to classes in the hierarchy more readily than would happen in a flat global arrangement. Thus, namespaces offer a performance benefit as well as provide a programmer convenient way of grouping functionality. Namespaces by themselves, however, are not much use until you create classes that will provide useful functionality in them.

When you are working with scope, it is important to remember that it is pertinent when you are resolving namespaces and variable namespaces. Listing 4-3 demonstrates scope in JavaScript.

Listing 4-3: Working with scope in JavaScript

```
<%@ Page Language="C#" %>

<html xmlns="http://www.w3.org/1999/xhtml">
<head runat="server">
    <title>Scope</title>

    <script type="text/javascript">

        var x = 38;
        var y = 38;

        function doSomething(x) {
            x = x + x;
            y = y + y;

            alert("doSomething() called. Now x = " + x + " and y = " + y);

            return x;
        }

        function pageLoad(sender, args) {
            alert("Before calling doSomething(), x = " + x + " and y = " + y);

            doSomething(x);
```

Continued

Listing 4-3: Working with scope in JavaScript *(continued)*

```
                    alert("Back in pageLoad() after doSomething().\n"  +
                        "x still equals " + x + " but y now equals " + y);
            }

        </script>

    </head>
    <body>
        <form id="form1" runat="server">
        <div>
            <asp:ScriptManager ID="ScriptManager1" runat="server">
            </asp:ScriptManager>
        </div>
        </form>
    </body>
    </html>
```

In this example, the code uses global variable x and passes it to a function called doSomething(), where x is doubled. After the function returns, the value of x is the same as before the call within the pageLoad() function. The change to x is scoped to the function. The call to the function is performed by passing a value, not a reference. The return value of the function is not assigned back to the global x variable.

You can fix this by changing the pageLoad() function to do this with the doSomething() method:

```
x = doSomething(x);
```

Creating Classes

One thing you are most likely going to want to do is create classes when working with JavaScript. JavaScript functions are used to represent class objects in the type system. The AJAX Library follows the pattern of declaring a function as the class constructor. JavaScript allows you to modify the prototype of the function directly, which is how the AJAX Library creates class members. The class must then be registered so that it can participate in the semantics of the type system.

Listing 4-4 shows how to create a complex type, the Album type, in the Wrox.AspAjax.Samples namespace.

Listing 4-4: Creating classes or complex types in JavaScript

```
<%@ Page Language="C#" %>

<html xmlns="http://www.w3.org/1999/xhtml">
<head runat="server">
    <title>Classes</title>

    <script type="text/javascript">

        function pageLoad(sender, args) {
            Type.registerNamespace('Wrox.AspAjax.Samples.Album');
```

Listing 4-4: Creating classes or complex types in JavaScript *(continued)*

```
            Wrox.AspAjax.Samples.Album = function(title, artist) {
                this._title = title;
                this._artist = artist;
            }

            Wrox.AspAjax.Samples.Album.prototype = {
                get_title: function () {
                    return this._title;
                },
                get_artist: function() {
                    return this._artist;
                }
            }

            Wrox.AspAjax.Samples.Album.registerClass
                        ('Wrox.AspAjax.Samples.Album');
            var anAlbum =
                new Wrox.AspAjax.Samples.Album("Lost Highway", "Bon Jovi");

            alert(anAlbum.get_title());
        }

    </script>

</head>
<body>
    <form id="form1" runat="server">
    <div>
        <asp:ScriptManager ID="ScriptManager1" runat="server">
        </asp:ScriptManager>
    </div>
    </form>
</body>
</html>
```

This example, when run, creates a complex Album type and alerts you to the album's title by calling the get_Title() method of the class. This method returns the title property. Running this page produces an alert that says "Lost Highway."

For this to work, you first need to create a constructor. The constructor takes two parameters and assigns them to local variables. The object prototype is modified to declare two property accessors.

Notice that the local members are accessed with a prefix of this. The script engine can then scope the lookup to the type and avoid searching any containing scopes. If you do not use this to indicate that the reference is local to the type, you end up creating objects in the global scope and seeing errors that can be confusing and time-consuming to track down.

The call to registerClass() looks a little odd, as it is on the type being registered. The prototype of the base type in JavaScript has been modified to add type-system support. Once the type is registered, an instance of it can be created and its members called.

The `registerClass()` function actually has three possible parameters: The first one is for the name of the type, the second is for the base type being extended, and the last is for specifying any interfaces that the class implements. Instances of using these classes are provided in later examples in this chapter.

JavaScript treats parameters as optional. This can be convenient. Instead of needing to define a bunch of different methods with different names in order to accommodate different combinations of parameters, you can write just one that knows how to process all of the optional inputs. Because the language treats all parameters as optional, however, you need to explicitly check that the inputs are valid for what you are doing. The caller can invoke the function with whatever set of parameters it wants to pass.

Although JavaScript allows types to be dynamically modified, and ASP.NET AJAX uses this to add the type system functionality into existing objects, it is not the approach recommended for mainstream development. Instead of modifying a type directly, you can inherit from it and extend it in new members by overriding existing ones.

In Listing 4-5, the `Album` type is extended by the `TributeAlbum` class, and adds one more piece of information: the artist being honored.

Listing 4-5: Inheritance of types

```
<%@ Page Language="C#" %>

<html xmlns="http://www.w3.org/1999/xhtml">
<head runat="server">
    <title>Classes</title>

    <script type="text/javascript">

        function pageLoad(sender, args) {
            Type.registerNamespace('Wrox.AspAjax.Samples.Album');

            Wrox.AspAjax.Samples.Album = function(title, artist) {
                this._title = title;
                this._artist = artist;
            }

            Wrox.AspAjax.Samples.Album.prototype = {
                get_title: function () {
                    return this._title;
                },
                get_artist: function() {
                    return this._artist;
                }
            }

            Wrox.AspAjax.Samples.Album.registerClass('Wrox.AspAjax.Samples.Album');

            Wrox.AspAjax.Samples.TributeAlbum =
              function(title, artist, tributeArtist) {
                Wrox.AspAjax.Samples.TributeAlbum.initializeBase(this,
                    [title, artist]);
                this._tributeArtist = tributeArtist;
```

Listing 4-5: Inheritance of types *(continued)*

```
        }

        Wrox.AspAjax.Samples.TributeAlbum.prototype = {
            get_tributeArtist: function() {
                return this._tributeArtist;
            },
            set_tributeArtist: function(tributeArtist) {
                this._tributeArtist = tributeArtist;
            }
        }

        Wrox.AspAjax.Samples.TributeAlbum.registerClass(
            'Wrox.AspAjax.Samples.TributeAlbum',
            Wrox.AspAjax.Samples.Album);

        var anotherAlbum =
            new Wrox.AspAjax.Samples.TributeAlbum("We're a Happy Family",
                "Various Artists", "Ramones");

        alert(anotherAlbum.get_title());
        alert(anotherAlbum.get_tributeArtist());
    }

    </script>

</head>
<body>
    <form id="form1" runat="server">
    <div>
        <asp:ScriptManager ID="ScriptManager1" runat="server">
        </asp:ScriptManager>
    </div>
    </form>
</body>
</html>
```

When this page is run, you get two alerts, one that states the album ("We're a Happy Family") and another that states the name of the tribute band ("Ramones").

The constructor must explicitly call `initializeBase()` and pass itself, using the `this` keyword, along with an array of the arguments to pass to the constructor of the base type. The AJAX Library allows you to employ object-oriented principles, but doing so requires that you follow some coding patterns like this. Without the call to `initializeBase()`, when you try to call something on the base type, you get an error. In Microsoft's Internet Explorer, the message reads:

```
Object doesn't support this property or method
```

This is not the most helpful message! In Mozilla's Firefox, it fails silently, but if you have the JavaScript console open, an error message is displayed that more explicitly identifies the actual problem:

```
anotherAlbum.get_title is not a function.
```

Chapter 15 provides more details about debugging.

The call to `initializeBase()` takes care of producing the final type with inheritance semantics in place. The base class constructor is called with the arguments provided.

The type system of the AJAX Library also provides some reflection functions that let you explore the relationship between objects. Listing 4-6 demonstrates calls to `inheritsFrom()` and `isInstanceOfType()` using the `Album` and `TributeAlbum` types. This is simply a copy of the page from the previous listing with these lines added at the end of the `pageLoad()` function. Again, you see that these methods are available automatically as part of using ASP.NET AJAX. The AJAX Library has modified the underlying JavaScript type so that any class you register can use this functionality. Listing 4-6 shows the use of these functions.

Listing 4-6: Using some reflection functions

```
if(Wrox.AspAjax.Samples.TributeAlbum.isInstanceOfType(anAlbum) == false) {
    alert("anAlbum is not a TributeAlbum");
}

if (Wrox.AspAjax.Samples.TributeAlbum.isInstanceOfType(anotherAlbum) == true) {
    alert("anotherAlbum is a TributeAlbum");
}

if (Wrox.AspAjax.Samples.TributeAlbum.inheritsFrom(Wrox.AspAjax.Samples.Album)
    == true ) {
    alert("TributeAlbum inherits from Album");
}

if (Wrox.AspAjax.Samples.Album.inheritsFrom(Wrox.AspAjax.Samples.TributeAlbum)
    == true) {
    alert("Album does not inherit from TributeAlbum");
}
```

For this to work, you are going to have to add the instantiation of the `anAlbum` object:

```
var anAlbum = new Wrox.AspAjax.Samples.Album("Lost Highway", "Bon Jovi");
```

At first glance, the type references in Listing 4-6 look long. JavaScript does not have the equivalent of the `using` statement that makes namespaces available to code without being explicit. With a compiled language, the cost of the lookup can be paid when the binary is created and symbolic references are created.

In an interpreted language like JavaScript, you can speed up the lookup by providing a shortcut for the long type name by providing aliases that reference the fully qualified name. When you create global object aliases, you defeat the purpose of the namespace containers. Each subsequent lookup can get a little more expensive for every item in the checked scope. The ideal time to create aliases is when something is going to be referenced frequently and you can alias it temporarily, when it will soon go out of scope and the alias will be cleaned up.

If the code in Listing 4-6 were going to be run frequently, or if it contained many more calls to the types, it would probably be worth caching a reference to the type thus avoiding the repeated lookups.

Creating a local alias is easy; just declare a variable and assign the type to it. Listing 4-7 demonstrates creating and using aliases for the `Album` and `TributeAlbum` types.

Listing 4-7: Creating aliases for specific types

```
var tributeAlbum = Wrox.AspAjax.Samples.TributeAlbum;
var album = Wrox.AspAjax.Samples.Album;

if(tributeAlbum.isInstanceOfType(anAlbum) == false) {
    alert("anAlbum is not a TributeAlbum");
}

if (tributeAlbum.isInstanceOfType(anotherAlbum) == true) {
    alert("anotherAlbum is a TributeAlbum");
}

if (tributeAlbum.inheritsFrom(album) == true) {
    alert("TributeAlbum inherits from Album");
}

if (album.inheritsFrom(tributeAlbum) == false) {
    alert("Album does not inherit from TributeAlbum");
}
```

The AJAX library provides a method for explicitly calling a base method implementation. This is often used when a derived type wants to take the result from the base type and modify it before returning it to the caller. It is not limited to calling into the base type from a derived type's implementation. You can also call a base method for an object. In a language like C++, you can cast an object to its base type to access a specific method implementation. Likewise, this pattern in JavaScript lets you access the base method even though JavaScript cannot support the casting semantic for this purpose.

Looking at Listing 4-8, the `TributeAlbum` class adds an override for the `get_artist()` method. It calls the base implementation and then prepends it with the string `TRIBUTE:` before returning it. This is again a slight modification to the previous example, which makes use of the `Album` and `TributeAlbum` types.

Listing 4-8: Altering the base get_artist() method

```
Wrox.AspAjax.Samples.TributeAlbum.prototype = {
    get_tributeArtist: function() {
        return this._tributeArtist;
    },
    set_tributeArtist: function(tributeArtist) {
        this._tributeArtist = tributeArtist;
    },

    get_artist: function() {
        return ("TRIBUTE: " +
            Wrox.AspAjax.Samples.TributeAlbum.callBaseMethod(this, "get_artist"));
    }
}
```

When running this with the previous examples, you won't see a change in the alerts. To see a change from the code changes made in Listing 4-8, throw up a new alert that calls the `get_artist()` method of the `TributeAlbum` type:

```
alert(anotherAlbum.get_artist());
```

When doing this, you get the response:

```
TRIBUTE: Various Artists
```

It is important to note that there are also several auxiliary functions for inspecting the types you create with the AJAX Library. You may not use them much in your application development, but it is interesting to see what you can do with the dynamic environment of JavaScript. The `Type.parse()` function takes the name of a type, resolves it, and creates an instance of it. The `Type.isClass()` function checks that an object has been registered with the type system. You can traverse and inspect object inheritance chains using the `getName()` and `getBaseType()` methods.

Listing 4-9 illustrates checking that the object is an instance of a type registered with the ASP.NET AJAX type system and then gets the name of the base type from which it derives.

Listing 4-9: Checking an object is an instance of a type registered with the type system

```
var typeString = "Wrox.AspAjax.Samples.TributeAlbum";
var typeCheck = Type.parse(typeString);

alert(Type.isClass(typeCheck));

if(Type.isClass(typeCheck)) {
    alert(typeCheck.getBaseType().getName());
}
```

In this case, the `TributeAlbum` object is parsed using `Type.parse()`. From there, an alert is thrown with a statement from the `isClass()` method. In this case, it states `true`, meaning that `TributeAlbum` is indeed a class. From there, another alert is displayed stating the name of the base type: `Wrox.AspAjax.Samples`.

Using Interfaces

Interfaces are a convenient way to define standard behaviors that other types can implement. Although JavaScript has no built-in support for interfaces, Microsoft has developed a way to mimic interfaces in JavaScript. As in .NET, an interface is a contract that states that the implementer of the interface must provide all of the functionality specified in the interface. The interface itself is only a specification and has no functionality of its own. When a type declares that it implements an interface, you are assured of the set of features it offers. Types can use interfaces to establish contracts for behavior that can then be enforced at runtime.

Creating interface definitions follows the same pattern as creating classes shown in earlier examples. The function name is the name of the interface. The prototype of the function is modified to add the interface members. The convention used in defining interface members is to throw `Error.notImplemented` for each member, so any class that implements the interface then needs to override the interface members to provide real implementations or the exception is thrown. Enforcing that the class actually overrides every member is the sort of thing that would be caught during compilation with a .NET Framework language, but JavaScript has to detect these problems at runtime.

Listing 4-10 defines the `IProvideTrackInfo` interface with methods for getting the track count and the track listing. The `registerInterface()` method is available on the type itself, just as the class methods were.

Listing 4-10: Working with interfaces

```
<%@ Page Language="C#" %>

<html xmlns="http://www.w3.org/1999/xhtml">
<head runat="server">
    <title>Interfaces</title>

    <script type="text/javascript">

        function pageLoad(sender, args) {

            Type.registerNamespace('Wrox.AspAjax.Samples');

            Wrox.AspAjax.Samples.IProvideTrackInfo = function() {
                throw Error.notImplemented();
            }

            Wrox.AspAjax.Samples.IProvideTrackInfo.prototype = {
                get_trackCount: function() {
                    throw Error.notImplemented();
                },
                get_tracks: function() {
                    throw Error.notImplemented();
                }
            }

            Wrox.AspAjax.Samples.IProvideTrackInfo.registerInterface(
                'Wrox.AspAjax.Samples.IProvideTrackInfo');

        }

    </script>

</head>
<body>
    <form id="form1" runat="server">
    <div>
        <asp:ScriptManager ID="ScriptManager1" runat="server">
        </asp:ScriptManager>
    </div>
    </form>
</body>
</html>
```

Obviously, when overriding the methods in a class that implements the interface, you would not want to call the base method and trigger the error!

Given a type, you can call getInterfaces() to retrieve the complete set of interfaces that it implements. You can also check for a specific interface implementation by using the implementsInterface() method on the type. In addition, you might need to check whether a type is itself an interface with isInterface(). These are all operators on types, but there is also the isImplementedBy() function, which takes an object instance and ascertains whether it is of a type that implements the interface.

For most development tasks, you just define and use interfaces without using the methods for examining which objects implement what interfaces. However, for more involved scenarios, the advanced functionality is useful. Listing 4-11 shows the use of these methods on the IProvideTrackInfo interface. First, for this example, the Album class is modified to implement the interface.

Listing 4-11: Working with the IProvideTrackInfo interface

```
<%@ Page Language="C#" %>

<html xmlns="http://www.w3.org/1999/xhtml">
<head runat="server">
    <title>Interfaces</title>

    <script type="text/javascript">

        function pageLoad(sender, args) {

            Type.registerNamespace('Wrox.AspAjax.Samples');

            Wrox.AspAjax.Samples.IProvideTrackInfo = function() {
                throw Error.notImplemented();
            }

            Wrox.AspAjax.Samples.IProvideTrackInfo.prototype = {
                get_trackCount: function() {
                    throw Error.notImplemented();
                },
                get_tracks: function() {
                    throw Error.notImplemented();
                }
            }

            Wrox.AspAjax.Samples.IProvideTrackInfo.registerInterface(
                'Wrox.AspAjax.Samples.IProvideTrackInfo');

            Wrox.AspAjax.Samples.Album = function(title, artist) {
                this._title = title;
                this._artist = artist;

                this._trackCount = 0;
                this._tracks = null;
            }
```

Listing 4-11: Working with the IProvideTrackInfo interface *(continued)*

```
Wrox.AspAjax.Samples.Album.prototype = {
    get_title: function() {
        return this._title;
    },
    get_artist: function() {
        return this._artist;
    },
    get_trackCount: function() {
        return _trackCount;
    },

    get_tracks: function() {
        return _tracks;
    },
    set_tracks: function(tracks) {
        if(typeof(tracks) !== 'undefined' && tracks !== null) {
            _trackCount = tracks.length;
            _tracks = tracks;
        }
    }
}

Wrox.AspAjax.Samples.Album.registerClass('Wrox.AspAjax.Samples.Album',
    null, Wrox.AspAjax.Samples.IProvideTrackInfo);

var album = new Wrox.AspAjax.Samples.Album('Lost Highway', 'Bon Jovi');
var tracks = new Array(12);
tracks[0] = 'Lost Highway';
tracks[1] = 'Summertime';
tracks[2] = 'You Want To Make A Memory';
tracks[3] = "Whole Lot Of Leavin'";
tracks[4] = 'We Got It Going On';
tracks[5] = 'Any Other Day';
tracks[6] = 'Seat Next To You';
tracks[7] = "Everybody's Broken";
tracks[8] = "Till We Ain't Strangers Anymore";
tracks[9] = 'The Last Night';
tracks[10] = 'One Step Closer';
tracks[11] = 'I Love This Town';

album.set_tracks(tracks);

alert(Wrox.AspAjax.Samples.Album.implementsInterface(
    Wrox.AspAjax.Samples.IProvideTrackInfo) === true);
alert(Wrox.AspAjax.Samples.IProvideTrackInfo.isImplementedBy(album)
    === true);
alert(Type.isInterface(Wrox.AspAjax.Samples.IProvideTrackInfo)
    === true);

    }

</script>
```

Continued

Listing 4-11: Working with the IProvideTrackInfo interface *(continued)*

```
    </head>
    <body>
        <form id="form1" runat="server">
        <div>
            <asp:ScriptManager ID="ScriptManager1" runat="server">
            </asp:ScriptManager>
        </div>
        </form>
    </body>
    </html>
```

Defining Enums and Flags

So far in this chapter, you have seen the Microsoft AJAX Library conventions for using namespaces, creating classes, and declaring interfaces as well as how to implement them. The last AJAX Library language feature I will cover is enumerations. The ASP.NET AJAX type system provides for defining enumerations and a specialized version of them used as combinable flags.

Enums let you establish a set of possible values. When using an enum, you know that it has to take on one of those values. Enum values are considered mutually exclusive. Colors are a typical example of an enum. If something is brown, it is not also green. Sure, you could argue that something could be yellow and blue and thus green, but enums take a single value. If the item is green, it is just green and nothing else from that enumeration.

For an example of working with enums, Listing 4-12 defines an enum for music genres. This listing allows you to assign an album, for example, to the Blues or Industrial category, but you cannot make it both Rock and Classical. Although it is possible to suggest something is of genre Classic Rock, but that is the point: an enum, by definition, can have only one value.

Listing 4-12: Working with enumerations

```
    <%@ Page Language="C#" Debug="true" %>

    <html xmlns="http://www.w3.org/1999/xhtml">
    <head runat="server">
        <title>Enumerations</title>

        <script type="text/javascript">

            function pageLoad(sender, args) {

                Type.registerNamespace('Wrox.AspAjax.Samples');

                Wrox.AspAjax.Samples.MusicGenre = function() {
                    throw Error.invalidOperation();
                }

                Wrox.AspAjax.Samples.MusicGenre.prototype = {
```

Listing 4-12: Working with enumerations *(continued)*

```
                    Blues:        1,
                    Classical:    2,
                    Electronic:   3,
                    Folk:         4,
                    Industrial:   5,
                    Jazz:         6,
                    NewAge:       7,
                    HipHop:       8,
                    Rock:         9,
                    WorldFusion:  10
            }

        Wrox.AspAjax.Samples.MusicGenre.registerEnum(
            'Wrox.AspAjax.Samples.MusicGenre');

        var genre = Wrox.AspAjax.Samples.MusicGenre.Industrial;
        alert(Wrox.AspAjax.Samples.MusicGenre.toString(genre));
            // This displays 'Industrial'

        alert(genre === Wrox.AspAjax.Samples.MusicGenre.Industrial);
            // This displays 'true'
        genre = 22; //assign an invalid value
        alert(Wrox.AspAjax.Samples.MusicGenre.toString(genre));
            // This displays an error in debug mode


        }

    </script>

</head>
<body>
    <form id="form1" runat="server">
    <div>
        <asp:ScriptManager ID="ScriptManager1" runat="server">
        </asp:ScriptManager>
    </div>
    </form>
</body>
</html>
```

At the end of Listing 4-12, the `genre` object is assigned an integer that is not part of the enum. The AJAX Library does not see the assignment of an integer to a variable but can check when the value is treated as an enum when calling `toString()` on it.

Normally, the invalid value is just displayed as an empty string, but Microsoft has added a terrific new feature to help you diagnose problems in JavaScript code: When you enable debugging by setting `debug="true"` in the compilation section of your `web.config` file (which is the typical setting on developer's computers), more detailed information is produced. Figure 4-1 shows the dialog that Internet Explorer displays for this error when running in debug mode.

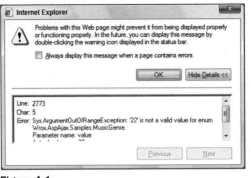

Figure 4-1

Firefox also shows the error in the JavaScript console, if you have selected the option to show it from the Tools menu. The error message from Firefox is shown in Figure 4-2.

Figure 4-2

Flags are a specialized type of enum. In fact, they are so similar that ASP.NET AJAX does not define a separate type for flags. You create and register a flags type the same way you create an enum, but the call to registerClass() takes an additional parameter for indicating that the enum registration should be treated the same way as flag registration. However, when you define the enum as supporting flags, the behavior is distinctly different.

When an enum is declared as supporting flags, the values assigned to it are tracked as individual entries instead of as a single distinct value. If you use the logical OR operator (|) to combine enum values, what you end up with is the single enum value that is the sum of the parts.

```
genre = Wrox.ASPAJAX.Samples.MusicGenre.Blues |
    Wrox.ASPAJAX.Samples.MusicGenre.Classical;

alert(Wrox.ASPAJAX.Samples.MusicGenre.toString(genre));
```

Combining `Blues`, which has an enum value of 1, and `Classical`, which has an enum value of 2, results in a variable with a value of 3. The enum for `MusicGenre` treats that as `Electronic` (the enum for a value of 3) and a `toString()` call displays the same. It would be hard-pressed to come up with an example of music that is `Electronic`, `Classical`, and `Blues` all at the same time!

The combined value is still within the allowable range of values for the `MusicGenre` enum, so no error is encountered. However, since enums are ultimately supposed to designate a single value, you do get an error when defining a value that exceeds the defined range. If you decide that something is `Electronic` and `Rock`, the combination results in an error. Three plus nine is greater than the `WorldFusion` top value of 10. When `debug` is set to a value of `true`, any attempt to display the value results in an error.

In Listing 4-13 defines some music categories for which multiple values make sense. Music does not necessarily need to be assigned to just one of these personal categories. There is music that you might like to listen to while running and driving but that is too distracting for coding time. Then there is holiday music that you might listen to while hosting a party, but it would not provide motivation for running an extra mile or two.

Listing 4-13: Working with flags

```
<%@ Page Language="C#" Debug="true" %>

<html xmlns="http://www.w3.org/1999/xhtml">
<head runat="server">
    <title>ASP.NET AJAX Flags</title>

    <script type="text/javascript">

        function pageLoad(sender, args) {

            Type.registerNamespace('Wrox.AspAjax.Samples');
                Wrox.AspAjax.Samples.MyCategory = function() {
                    throw Error.invalidOperation();
                }

            Wrox.AspAjax.Samples.MyCategory.prototype = {
                Running: 1,
                Driving: 2,
                Dinner: 4,
                Holiday: 8,
                Entertaining: 16,
                Coding: 32
            }

            Wrox.AspAjax.Samples.MyCategory.registerEnum(
                'Wrox.AspAjax.Samples.MyCategory', true);

            var category = Wrox.AspAjax.Samples.MyCategory.Running |
                Wrox.AspAjax.Samples.MyCategory.Driving |
                Wrox.AspAjax.Samples.MyCategory.Coding;

            alert(Wrox.AspAjax.Samples.MyCategory.toString(category));
```

Continued

Listing 4-13: Working with flags *(continued)*

```
var myCategory = Wrox.AspAjax.Samples.MyCategory;

if(category & myCategory.Running)
    alert("Running")
if(category & myCategory.Driving)
    alert("Driving");
if(category & myCategory.Dinner)
    alert("Dinner");
if(category & myCategory.Holiday)
    alert("Holiday");
if(category & myCategory.Entertaining)
    alert("Entertaining")
if(category & myCategory.Coding)
    alert("Coding");

}

</script>

</head>
<body>
    <form id="form1" runat="server">
    <div>
        <asp:ScriptManager ID="ScriptManager1" runat="server">
        </asp:ScriptManager>
    </div>
    </form>
</body>
</html>
```

The `toString()` call on the flag reveals that the AJAX Library has tracked the set of combined flags. No longer is the result treated as a single value. Instead, the set of values are displayed through alerts (in the following order): `Running`, `Driving`, and `Coding`. Notice that the individual values for flag elements follow the pattern of doubling. This enables the combination semantics in the same way that flags operate at the bit level.

Base Class Library

The AJAX Library takes a familiar set of features from the base class library of the .NET Framework and brings it to JavaScript in the browser for you to use in building your applications. It is by no means an equivalent set of functionality as what the base class library offers, but it does go a long way toward simplifying your JavaScript coding tasks.

The String Class

Basic support for removing whitespace is added to JavaScript strings with new methods. The `trim()` method performs the equivalent of `trimStart()` and `trimEnd()`. The instance of the string is not modified by the trim calls. Instead, a copy of the string is returned with the requested change. Listing 4-14 demonstrates using the `trim()`, `trimStart()`, and `trimEnd()` functions.

Listing 4-14: Working with the String class

```
<%@ Page Language="C#" %>

<html xmlns="http://www.w3.org/1999/xhtml">
<head runat="server">
    <title>Using Trim Functions</title>

    <script type="text/javascript">

        function pageLoad(sender, args) {

            var one = ' leading whitespace';
            var two = 'trailing whitespace ';
            var three = ' leading and trailing whitespace ';

            alert('.' + one.trimStart() + '.');
            alert(one);  //the original string is not modified
            alert('.' + two.trimEnd() + '.');
            alert('.' + three.trim() + '.');

        }

    </script>

</head>
<body>
    <form id="form1" runat="server">
    <div>
        <asp:ScriptManager ID="ScriptManager1" runat="server">
        </asp:ScriptManager>
    </div>
    </form>
</body>
</html>
```

The trim methods are just shortcuts to what you can do with a regular expression. However, they do provide a certain familiarity. This holds true of the `beginsWith()` and `endsWith()` methods, too. You could write the functionality easily yourself but having method names that are clear and easy to use makes the transition in and out of JavaScript easier.

Dates and Numbers

The complexities of formatting really come into play when dealing with dates and numbers. The ASP.NET AJAX Library adds `format()` and `localeFormat()` methods to the string, date, and number objects. The format and methods are key for effectively controlling output. Instead of concatenating pieces of text with variables, you can call `String.format()` to have variables put into placeholders of a single string. The placeholders in the string are a pair of curly braces containing a variable number and optional format string. The number indicates which of the parameters following the string will be used. A variety of format strings like those available in the .NET Framework allow you to easily control how numbers are represented.

The `localeFormat()` goes further by respecting culture-specific settings in formatting dates and numbers. You can establish the culture that the user prefers and know that your data is being formatted and displayed correctly in the browser.

Listing 4-15 illustrates some examples of string formatting.

Listing 4-15: Working with dates

```
<%@ Page Language="C#" %>
<%@ Import Namespace="System.Threading"%>
<%@ Import Namespace="System.Globalization"%>

<script runat="server">

    protected void Page_Load(object sender, EventArgs e)
    {
        Thread.CurrentThread.CurrentCulture =
            CultureInfo.CreateSpecificCulture("fi-FI");
    }

</script>

<html xmlns="http://www.w3.org/1999/xhtml">
<head runat="server">
    <title>Dates and time</title>

    <script type="text/javascript">

        function pageLoad(sender, args) {

            var d = new Date();
            var message =
                String.localeFormat("{0}\n{1}\n{2}\n{3}\n{4}\n{5}\n{6}\n{7}",
                d.format("d"),
                d.format("D"),
                d.format("t"),
                d.format("T"),
                d.format("F"),
                d.format("M"),
                d.format("s"),
                d.format("Y") );
            alert(message);

        }

    </script>

</head>
<body>
    <form id="form1" runat="server">
    <div>
        <asp:ScriptManager ID="ScriptManager1" runat="server"
        EnableScriptGlobalization="true">
```

Listing 4-15: Working with dates *(continued)*

```
        </asp:ScriptManager>
    </div>
    </form>
</body>
</html>
```

The result of using the various date formats is shown in the pop-up window in Figure 4-3.

Figure 4-3

Arrays

The `Array` type is used heavily in JavaScript coding. It can be treated as a stack and as a queue, and it allows for sparse arrays. Many basic data structures can use the `Array` as the underlying building storage mechanism. The AJAX Library adds a set of static functions to the `Array` type that improve its usability and make it more familiar. During a preview release of the AJAX Extensions, the additional functionality was added to the `Array` prototype. After careful consideration, this approach was changed in order to avoid incompatibilities with other JavaScript libraries.

If you are already used to the JavaScript `Array` methods, you may recognize that the new methods are wrappers to use the method names from the .NET Framework base class library. You also get the benefit of some very detailed analysis into the performance characteristics of working with arrays. For example, adding a single element to an array is best accomplished by using an indexer with assignment rather than calling `Push()`. The AJAX Library provides the `Array.add()` method to expose a less awkward method.

```
array[array.length] = something; //is more efficient than
array.Push(something);
```

Listing 4-16 demonstrates using the additional `Array` methods to work with an Array. The `add()`, `contains()`, and `clear()` methods do what you would expect, but the static methods on the `Array` type take a little getting used to. The `parse()` method takes a string that looks like an array listing and parses it for the individual elements. However, the `forEach()` method is most interesting. You pass the array and a callback method, and the `forEach()` method is then automatically called for each element of the array. In this case, you need to pass a reference to a function that simply displays the element of the array using the built-in alert method.

Listing 4-16: Working with arrays

```
<%@ Page Language="C#" Debug="true" %>

<html xmlns="http://www.w3.org/1999/xhtml">
<head runat="server">
    <title>Arrays</title>

    <script type="text/javascript">

        function pageLoad(sender, args) {

            var array = new Array();
            Array.add(array, "Lost Highway");
            Array.add(array, "Have a Nice Day");

            if(Array.contains(array, "Lost Highway")) {
                Array.clear(array);
            }
            array = Array.parse("['Lost Highway', 'Slippery When Wet']");

            var items = ["New Jersey", "Cross Road", "One Wild Night"];
            Array.addRange(array, items);
            Array.insert(array, 1, "Have a Nice Day");

            for(var i = 0; i < array.length; i++) {
                alert(array[i]);
            }

            Array.forEach(array, arrayMethod);

        }

        function arrayMethod(element, index, array) {
            alert(element);
        }

    </script>

</head>
<body>
    <form id="form1" runat="server">
    <div>
        <asp:ScriptManager ID="ScriptManager1" runat="server">
        </asp:ScriptManager>
    </div>
    </form>
</body>
</html>
```

The debate around extending the Array prototype centers on problems that can be encountered when iterating over the members of the type as you cannot extend the type as you are iterating through it. Providing this functionality as static methods avoids those problems. The type can also be used as an associative array, but the generally accepted pattern is to use the object itself for creating associative arrays. For compatibility, arrays are better suited for collections of objects or numeric index associations.

Listing 4-17 illustrates using an object as an associative array.

Listing 4-17: Working with associative arrays

```
<%@ Page Language="C#" Debug="true" %>

<html xmlns="http://www.w3.org/1999/xhtml">
<head runat="server">
    <title>Arrays</title>

    <script type="text/javascript">

        function pageLoad(sender, args) {

            var releaseDates = new Object();
            releaseDates["Lost Highway"] = new Date("June 19, 2007");
            releaseDates["Have a Nice Day"] = new Date("September 20, 2005");
            releaseDates["Slippery When Wet"] = new Date("August 1, 1986");
            releaseDates["Cross Road"] = new Date("October 18, 1994");

            for(var property in releaseDates) {
                alert(property + " was released " + releaseDates[property]);
            }

        }

    </script>

</head>
<body>
    <form id="form1" runat="server">
    <div>
        <asp:ScriptManager ID="ScriptManager1" runat="server">
        </asp:ScriptManager>
    </div>
    </form>
</body>
</html>
```

Arrays in JavaScript have methods similar to those presented through the .NET Framework's `Array` type. Some possible methods are presented here.

The `add()` method allows you to add a single item to the array:

```
var albums = ['Lost Highway', 'Cross Road'];
Array.add(albums, 'Have a Nice Day');

for(var i = 0; i<albums.length; i++)
{
    alert(albums[i]);
}
```

The addRange() method allows you to add ranges of items to the array:

```
var albums1 = ['Lost Highway', 'Cross Road'];
var albums2 = ['Have a Nice Day', 'Slippery When Wet'];
Array.addRange(albums1, albums2);

for(var i = 0; i<albums1.length; i++)
{
    alert(albums1[i]);
}
```

In this case, everything is added to the albums1 instance and running this code, results in four alerts from albums1 — one for each album.

You will also find a clear() method. This will do what it says — clear out your array object.

```
var albums = ['Lost Highway', 'Cross Road'];
Array.add(albums, 'Have a Nice Day');

for(var i = 0; i<albums.length; i++)
{
    alert(albums[i]);
}

Array.clear(albums);

alert(albums.length);
```

In this case, the first set of three alerts shows the name of each album found in the collection. The fourth alert, comes after the array is cleared using the clear() method and therefore shows a length value of 0.

The clone() method copies the values of your array to another array instance. This means that if you change the value in the array you copied from, the copy still retains its original values. An example of using the clone() method is presented here:

```
var albums = ['Lost Highway', 'Cross Road'];
var albumsCopy = Array.clone(albums);

albums[1] = "DELETED";

alert(albums[0] + "\n" + albums[1]);
alert(albumsCopy[0] + "\n" + albumsCopy[1]);
```

This produces a set of alerts as shown in Figure 4-4.

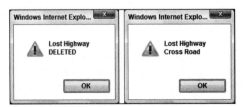

Figure 4-4

The contains() method returns a Boolean value that specifies whether the item you were looking for was found in the array:

```
var albums = ['Lost Highway', 'Cross Road'];

alert(Array.contains(albums, "Lost Highway"));
alert(Array.contains(albums, "Lost"));
```

In this case, the first alert is true because the item Lost Highway will be found, but the word Lost returns false because partial matches are not allowed.

The push() and pop() methods allow you to enqueue and dequeue items on the stack:

```
var anArray = [];
anArray.push(1);
anArray.push(2);
anArray.push(3);

alert(anArray.pop());
alert(anArray.pop());
alert(anArray.pop());
```

In this case, items are put onto the stack of the array in the order of 1, 2, 3 and then they are dequeued from the stack in the opposite order of 3, 2, and 1.

Just as you can add items to the array, you can remove items using the Array.remove() and Array.removeAt() methods.

Booleans

Booleans are true/false or 0/1 values, also known as a bit. You will find a Boolean type within the ASP.NET AJAX Framework that allows you to use true or false string values instead of the standard 0 or 1 values for Booleans. To accomplish this task, you will need to use the parse() method on the Boolean type.

```
var myBoolean = "true";
alert(Boolean.parse(myBoolean));
```

Supporting IntelliSense

Most people agree that one of the best features of Visual Studio is IntelliSense. Having contextual information about class members during development makes the process more efficient. It eliminates a lot of the need to jump back and forth between coding and documentation. Not only does IntelliSense give you information about what members are available, but it also provides abbreviated help about parameters and return values.

A big part of the IntelliSense feature is driven by the use of reflection by Visual Studio over the managed types referenced by the project. However, this does not work very well with a dynamic language like JavaScript. Even though, ASP.NET has worked out a way to provide IntelliSense with the JavaScript that you type.

You will only find this feature with the ASP.NET 3.5 release and when using Visual Studio 2008. When you start typing, you will immediately see IntelliSense for the JavaScript that you are working with. This is illustrated here in Figure 4-5.

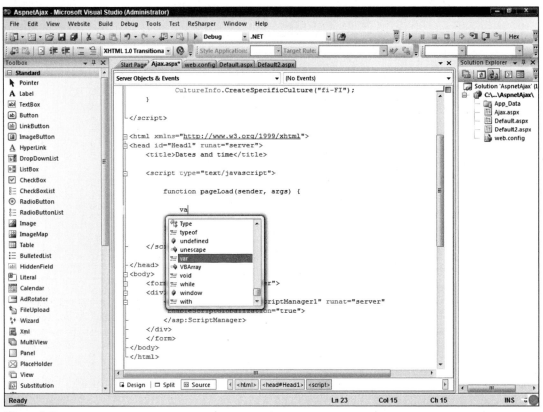

Figure 4-5

IntelliSense with JavaScript simply works in Visual Studio, which uses inference when figuring out what to display. For instance, if you are working with a <div> tag through JavaScript, Visual Studio's IntelliSense will figure out through inference that it is an HTML element and provide you with the proper methods and properties in the IntelliSense drop-down.

For instance, suppose that you have the following code snippet in your <body> section:

```
<form id="form1" runat="server">
    <div>
        <div id="label1">abc</div>
        <asp:ScriptManager ID="ScriptManager1" runat="server">
        </asp:ScriptManager>
    </div>
</form>
```

Here you can see that you have a `<div>` element called `label1` with an initial value of `abc`. Through, typing in Visual Studio 2008, you will see that VS knows that this is an HTML element and will provide you with the appropriate list of options. This is illustrated in Figure 4-6.

Figure 4-6

Visual Studio even takes the extra steps of working with and understanding the files that are imported into your files and providing the IntelliSense options that these files might expose to the code you are working with. For example, suppose that you have a simple JavaScript file with a function to change passed in text to uppercase. You might want to keep this function in a separate JavaScript file. This `.js` file is illustrated in Listing 4-18.

Listing 4-18: A separate .js file

```javascript
function uppercaseItems(passInString)
{
    var returnValue = passInString.toString().toUpperCase();

    return returnValue;
}
```

Now that this function, `uppercaseItems()` is in a separate `.js` file. Include this file in your ASP.NET page as such:

```
<script src="MyFunctions.js" type="text/javascript"></script>
```

When you include this and you and you are working with items, you will have the `uppercaseItems()` method at your disposal as illustrated here in Figure 4-7.

Figure 4-7

You can also provide XML doc comments that then are presented in the IntelliSense. XML doc comments provide information about JavaScript code to let you know how to use it. The first item typically included is a summary statement, as shown in Listing 4-19. The `Album` object can proclaim to developers that it intends to be a repository for information about an album. This may seem obvious in this discussion, but as the number of classes grows and the use of intuitive names decreases, the need for an IntelliSense aid is more apparent.

Listing 4-19 repeats the `Album` class code from Listing 4-4 and includes XML doc comments. For each function, there is a summary statement. If a function takes parameters, they are described in `param` entries, and finally there is information about the return type.

Listing 4-19: Providing documentation to your JavaScript

```
<%@ Page Language="C#" Debug="true" %>

<html xmlns="http://www.w3.org/1999/xhtml">
<head runat="server">
    <title>XML Documentation</title>

    <script type="text/javascript">

        function pageLoad(sender, args) {

            Type.registerNamespace('Wrox.AspAjax.Samples');

            Wrox.AspAjax.Samples.Album = function(title, artist) {

                /// <summary>Use this method to create a new Album.</summary>
```

Listing 4-19: Providing documentation to your JavaScript *(continued)*

```
                    /// <param name="title" type="String" optional="false"
                    ///  mayBeNull="false">The album title.</param>
                    /// <param name="artist" type="String" optional="false"
                    ///  mayBeNull="false">The album artist.</param>
                    /// <returns type="Album">An Album object.</returns>
                    this._title = title;
                    this._artist = artist;
                }

                Wrox.AspAjax.Samples.Album.prototype = {
                    get_title: function() {

                    /// <summary>Album title accessor.</summary>
                    /// <returns  type="String">Album title.</returns>
                        return this._title;
                    },
                    get_artist: function() {

                    /// <summary>Album artist accessor.</summary>
                    /// <returns type="String">Album artist.</returns>.
                        return this._artist;
                    }
                }

                Wrox.AspAjax.Samples.Album.registerClass
                        ('Wrox.AspAjax.Samples.Album');
                var anAlbum = new Wrox.AspAjax.Samples.Album("Have a Nice Day",
                    "Bon Jovi");
                alert(anAlbum.get_title());

            }

        </script>

    </head>
    <body>
        <form id="form1" runat="server">
        <div>
            <asp:ScriptManager ID="ScriptManager1" runat="server">
            </asp:ScriptManager>
        </div>
        </form>
    </body>
    </html>
```

The parameter doc comments indicate whether, including the parameter in the function call is optional and whether nulls are allowed. XML doc comments added to enums provide information about the individual fields. The album genre enum with comments is shown in Listing 4-20.

Listing 4-20: XML documentation for enumerations

```
Wrox.AspAjax.Samples.MusicGenre = function() {
    /// <summary>Classifies types of music into a distinct genre.</summary>
    /// <field name="Blues" type="Number" integer="true" static="true" />
    /// <field name="Classical" type="Number" integer="true" static="true" />
    /// <field name="Electronic" type="Number" integer="true" static="true" />
    /// <field name="Folk" type="Number" integer="true" static="true" />
    /// <field name="Industrial" type="Number" integer="true" static="true" />
    /// <field name="Jazz" type="Number" integer="true" static="true" />
    /// <field name="NewAge" type="Number" integer="true" static="true" />
    /// <field name="HipHop" type="Number" integer="true" static="true" />
    /// <field name="Rock" type="Number" integer="true" static="true" />
    /// <field name="WorldFusion" type="Number" integer="true" static="true" />
    throw Error.invalidOperation();
}

Wrox.AspAjax.Samples.MusicGenre.prototype = {
    Blues: 1,
    Classical: 2,
    Electronic: 3,
    Folk: 4,
    Industrial: 5,
    Jazz: 6,
    NewAge: 7,
    HipHop: 8,
    Rock: 9,
    WorldFusion: 10
}

Wrox.AspAjax.Samples.MusicGenre.registerEnum('Wrox.ASPAJAX.Samples.MusicGenre');
```

For enumerations, the information looks somewhat redundant, but for Visual Studio to consistently pick up and display the correct IntelliSense information, the comments should be complete. Another use of the XML doc comments is to include example usage. This can be helpful in providing the developer a quick sample without requiring him or her to switch to the more complete documentation. It is especially useful when working with complex functions for which some contextual information is needed to understand usage; seeing it used in one code snippet is often as helpful as many paragraphs of help information. Listing 4-21 is an example directly from the Error object of the ASP.NET AJAX Library. The popStackFrame() function merits an example to aid in its use.

Listing 4-21: Commenting a function

```
Error.prototype.popStackFrame = function() {
    /// <summary>
    /// Updates the fileName and lineNumber fields based on the next frame in the
    /// stack trace. Call this method whenever an instance of Error is returned
    /// from a function. This makes the fileName and lineNumber reported in the
    /// FireFox console point to the location where the exception was thrown, not
    /// the location where the instance of Error was created.
    /// </summary>
```

Listing 4-21: Commenting a function *(continued)*

```
/// <example>
/// function checkParam(param, expectedType) {
///      if (!expectedType.isInstanceOfType(param)) {
///          var e = new Error("invalid type");
///          e.popStackFrame();
///          return e;
///      }
/// }
/// </example>
```

Returning back to the `uppercaseItems()` function presented in Listing 4-18, you can now add documentation to this method. This is presented here in Listing 4-22.

Listing 4-22: Adding documentation to the uppercaseItems() function

```
function uppercaseItems(passInString)
{
    /// <summary>This method simply uppercases a passed-in string</summary>
    /// <param name="passInString">This is the string you pass in</param>
    /// <returns>A string in uppercase</returns>
    var returnValue = passInString.toString().toUpperCase();

    return returnValue;
}
```

However, now when you find the function reference through IntelliSense, you will see the comments as presented in Figure 4-8.

Also, after selecting the function and working to pass in the correct parameter, you are presented with the following assistance through IntelliSense as illustrated in Figure 4-9.

Errors and Debugging

Chapter 15 provides detailed information about testing and debugging ASP.NET AJAX applications, but this chapter on the AJAX Library would not be complete without a basic introduction to the debugging facilities. Debugging JavaScript can be quite challenging because of its dynamic interpreted nature. One of the reasons it is so difficult to debug is due to the fact that without being able to precompile JavaScript code, you often end up finding mistakes through runtime failures and errors. Further, runtime errors are not always helpful at assisting you identify the problem, although the extra debug mode messages are helpful.

It is important to note that Visual Studio 2008 now provides the ability to debug your JavaScript code directly in Visual Studio 2008. This allows you to step through your JavaScript code in the same manner as you step through your C# or Visual Basic code. Again, Chapter 15 covers this feature in more detail.

This next section shows you how to create your own debug trace window.

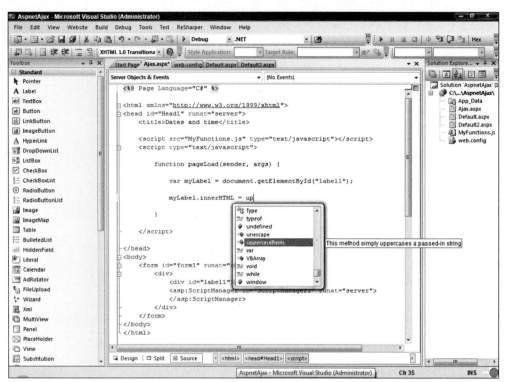

Figure 4-8

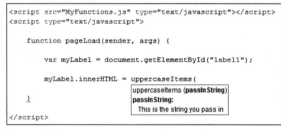

Figure 4-9

The Debug Trace Console

The Debug class makes tracking down issues easier. One of the facilities it supports is providing trace information from your code. You should always provide release and debug versions of your scripts, and your debug versions can include extra trace information. The output can go to Visual Studio, the Firefox console, or directly into a text area on your page. (Again, detailed information and examples will be covered in Chapter 15.) Listing 4-23 shows that if you include a TextArea element in your page with an ID value of TraceConsole, the Debug class puts trace information there.

Listing 4-23: Creating a trace window

```
<%@ Page Language="C#" Debug="true" %>

<html xmlns="http://www.w3.org/1999/xhtml">
<head runat="server">
    <title>Trace information</title>

    <script type="text/javascript">

        function pageLoad(sender, args) {

            Sys.Debug.trace("Trace information is sent to the TraceConsole");
            Sys.Debug.trace("This message was sent on " + Date());

        }

    </script>

</head>
<body>
    <form id="form1" runat="server">
    <div>
        <asp:ScriptManager ID="ScriptManager1" runat="server">
        </asp:ScriptManager>

        <textarea id="TraceConsole" cols="512" rows="10"
         style="width:100%;border:solid black 1px"></textarea>

    </div>
    </form>
</body>
</html>
```

The results are shown in Figure 4-10. Notice that Internet Explorer and Firefox do not format the date string exactly the same, but in both the debug output utilizes the TraceConsole.

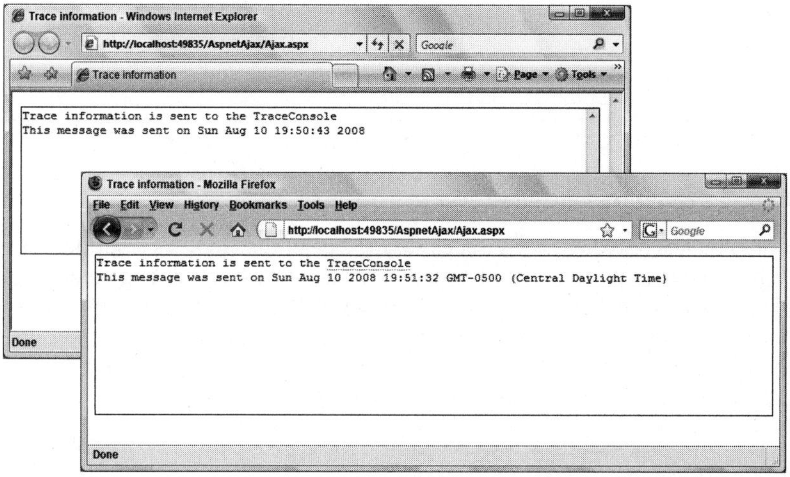

Figure 4-10

Creating Errors

The ASP.NET AJAX Library provides an `Error` object for dealing with errors in a standard way across applications. The static create method of the `Error` object allows you to create a custom error by passing in a message and a JSON-formatted error info object. It also includes static methods for creating a set of standard errors that correspond to frequently used exceptions in the .NET Framework.

```
var e = Error.create("custom error", { name: "My Error"});
throw(e);
```

You may find that you do not need custom errors, but you can still take advantage of the built-in error types. The common exceptions to throw are listed here with their major arguments.

- ❑ `Error.argument (paramName, message)`
- ❑ `Error.argumentNull (paramName, message)`
- ❑ `Error.argumentOutOfRange (paramName, actualValue, message)`
- ❑ `Error.argumentType (paramName, actualType, expectedType, message)`
- ❑ `Error.argumentUndefined (paramName, message)`
- ❑ `Error.invalidOperation (message)`
- ❑ `Error.notImplemented (message)`
- ❑ `Error.parameterCount (message)`

These error functions extend the native JavaScript object and work with it to provide additional debugging information. In Listing 4-24, an `argumentNull` error is created and thrown. First, it is caught, and the `Debug.traceDump()` method is called on it to examine the details of the error. Then it is thrown again without being caught. The error information is then bubbled up to the user, as you would normally expect. The trace output and browser dialog are shown in Figure 4-11.

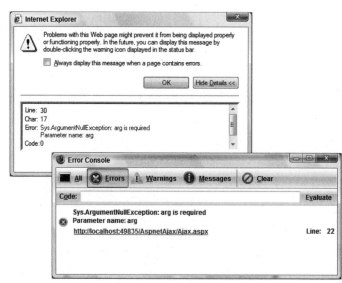

Figure 4-11

Listing 4-24: Throwing exceptions

```
<%@ Page Language="C#" Debug="true" %>

<html xmlns="http://www.w3.org/1999/xhtml">
<head runat="server">
    <title>Trace information</title>

    <script type="text/javascript">

        function pageLoad(sender, args) {

            Sys.Debug.trace("Trace information is sent to the TraceConsole");

            try {
                throwError(null);
            }

            catch(e) {
                Sys.Debug.traceDump(e, "the error");
            }

            throwError(null);

        }

        function throwError(arg) {
            if(arg === null) {
                var e = Error.argumentNull("arg", "arg is required");
                e.popStackFrame();
                throw(e);
            }
        }

    </script>

</head>
<body>
    <form id="form1" runat="server">
    <div>
        <asp:ScriptManager ID="ScriptManager1" runat="server">
        </asp:ScriptManager>

        <textarea id="TraceConsole" cols="512" rows="10"
         style="width:100%;border:solid black 1px"></textarea>

    </div>
    </form>
</body>
</html>
```

Figure 4-12 shows the `TraceConsole` and a pop-up dialog offering the user the opportunity to debug.

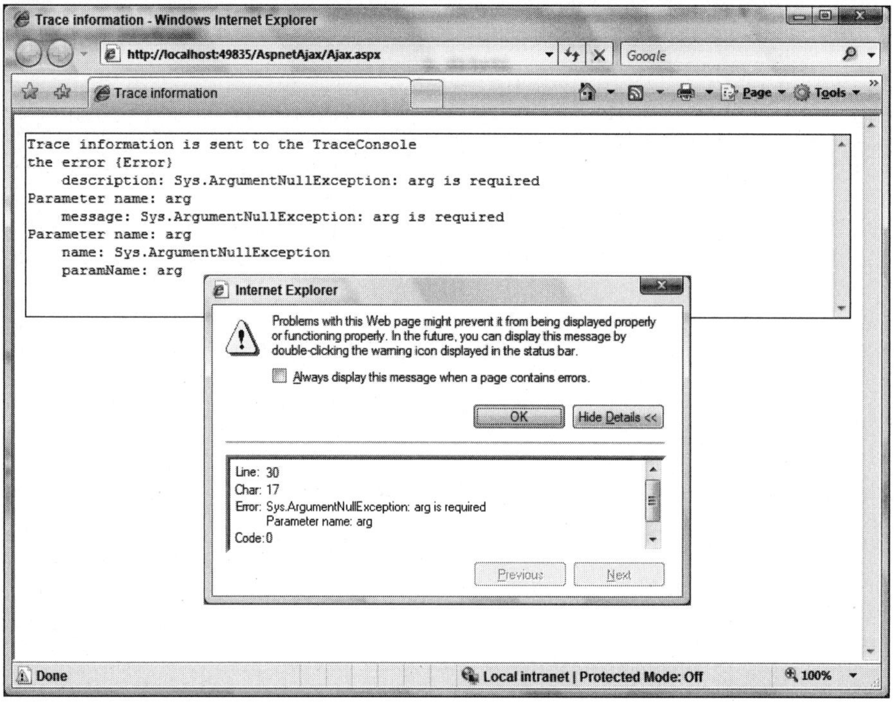

Figure 4-12

Validate Params

JavaScript does not have the access modifiers used in compiled languages. You cannot declare that something is private or protected. The only way that code is made inaccessible is for it to go out of scope during execution. This can lead to some clumsy coding. You may want something to be a private implementation detail, but JavaScript does not provide a clean way to do this. The ASP.NET AJAX Library does not provide a way to simulate access modifiers for JavaScript either. It does; however, borrow a pattern from the .NET Coding Guidelines: Members that the developer considers private are prefixed with an underscore.

Typically, since they are supposed to be private, you would probably not explore those methods, but the _validateParams() method deserves mention. This method is included on the Function object and is called dozens of times from the AJAX Library in the debug scripts. The calls reflect the information from the XML doc comments. The debug version of the AJAX Library methods checks for required parameters, checks the type of parameters, and validates where null arguments are not allowed.

Even if you are not seeing functional problems as you develop an application, the best practice is to enable the debug mode temporarily before deployment and do some testing. Do not leave debugging enabled during deployment, though. The parameter validation and debug information take a heavy toll on performance.

When an error is encountered during a call to _validateParams(), an exception is thrown and you can then break into the debugger and find the source of the error. This can be very helpful in getting to the root of a problem or in finding subtle errors before deployment.

The Browser Object

ASP.NET has extensive information about various browsers. It provides a whole system for analyzing headers sent in by a browser and producing a complex Browser object that you can use from the page to tailor the application for the user. The control adapter architecture is based on this configuration system being able to specify where custom renderings should be used for particular browsers.

The AJAX Library specifies some basic browser definitions and determines which one is being used. JavaScript code can then easily check the browser object and draw conclusions about any unique requirements of the browser.

Listing 4-25 displays the information currently stored in the Browser object. It also shows how you can use an indexer to set custom properties on the Browser object. Remember that you can do this for any object in JavaScript. This is a case where extensibility is easy and intuitive.

Listing 4-25: Working with the Browser object

```
<%@ Page Language="C#" Debug="true" %>

<html xmlns="http://www.w3.org/1999/xhtml">
<head runat="server">
    <title>Browser object</title>

    <script type="text/javascript">

        function pageLoad(sender, args) {

            Sys.Debug.trace("name = " + Sys.Browser.name);
            Sys.Debug.trace("version = " + Sys.Browser.version.toString());
            Sys.Debug.trace("hasDebuggerStatement = " +
                Sys.Browser.hasDebuggerStatement.toString());

            if(Sys.Browser.agent === Sys.Browser.InternetExplorer) {
                Sys.Debug.trace("agent = Sys.Browser.InternetExplorer");
            }
            else if(Sys.Browser.agent === Sys.Browser.Firefox) {
                Sys.Debug.trace("agent = Sys.Browser.Firefox");
            }
            else if(Sys.Browser.agent === Sys.Browser.Safari) {
                Sys.Debug.trace("agent = Sys.Browser.Safari");
            }
            else if(Sys.Browser.agent === Sys.Browser.Opera) {
                Sys.Debug.trace("agent = Sys.Browser.Opera");
            }

            Sys.Browser.agent["supportsAudio"] = true;
            Sys.Debug.trace(String.format("{0} supportsAudio = {1}",
                Sys.Browser.name,
                Sys.Browser.agent["supportsAudio"].toString()));

        }
```

Continued

145

Listing 4-25: Working with the Browser object *(continued)*

```
            function someMethod(argument) {
                if(argument === null) {
                    alert("null");
                }
            }


        </script>

    </head>
    <body>
        <form id="form1" runat="server">
        <div>
            <asp:ScriptManager ID="ScriptManager1" runat="server">
            </asp:ScriptManager>

            <textarea id="TraceConsole" cols="512" rows="10"
             style="width:100%;border:solid black 1px"></textarea>

        </div>
        </form>
    </body>
</html>
```

The different values returned by the `Sys.Browser` properties are shown in Figure 4-13.

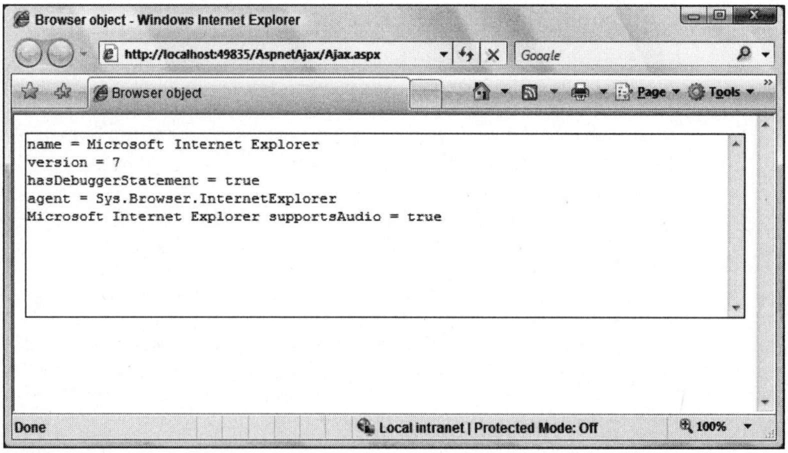

Figure 4-13

The Sys Namespace

You have already seen some use of the Sys namespace through examples in this chapter such as the previous Sys.Browser example. The Sys namespace is the root namespace within ASP.NET AJAX and a lot of classes and interfaces there are available for use within your JavaScript code.

Microsoft has extended upon the JavaScript library to provide you with the extra items that you are most likely going to want to work with when coding your ASP.NET AJAX pages. These extensions are similar to what you are used to in working with the .NET Framework.

The following table details the available objects found in the Sys namespace.

Object in Sys namespace	Description
Sys.Application	Manages client components that are registered with the application
Sys.ApplicationLoadEventArgs	Holds event arguments for the load event of the Application class
Sys.CancelEventArgs	Provides a means to cancel events
Sys.Component	Provides the base class for the Control and Behavior classes, and for any other object whose lifetime should be managed by Microsoft ASP.NET AJAX
Sys.CultureInfo	Like the CultureInfo object in the .NET Framework, this holds culture related settings
Sys.Debug	Provides tracing and debugging information
Sys.EventArgs	Allows for passing of event argument information
Sys.EventHandlerList	Provides a collection of client events for a component
Sys.IContainer	An interface that provides a common interface for all components that can contain other components
Sys.IDisposable	An interface that allows you to close, reset, or release resources
Sys.INotifyDisposing	An interface that provides notifications of disposing events
Sys.INotifyPropertyChange	An interface that provides notification of property changes
Sys.PropertyChangedEventArgs	Used by the propertyChanged event to signify which property changed
Sys.Res	Provides static, culture-neutral exception messages that are used by the Microsoft AJAX Library framework
Sys.StringBuilder	Provides the ability to perform string concatenation
Sys Exceptions	Raises an Error Object; these are exceptions raised by ASP.NET AJAX

Besides the root `Sys` namespace. You will also find `Sys.Net`, `Sys.Serialization`, `Sys.Services`, `Sys.WebForms`, and `Sys.UI`.

❑   `Sys.Net` allows you to make Web service calls, work with the `WebRequest` object, work with Web service errors, and provides you with XMLHttp support.

❑   `Sys.Serialization` helps you take care of the serialization and deserialization of JSON formatted data.

❑   `Sys.Services` allows you to work with the ASP.NET services such as the ASP.NET membership and role management systems that were introduced with ASP.NET 2.0.

❑   `Sys.WebForms` lets you deal with the loading and unloading of ASP.NET pages. Finally, `Sys.UI` allows you to deal with things occurring with the page's UI, such as where the mouse is located on the page, how to deal with keys being pressed, or dealing with the DOM.

Summary

The ASP.NET AJAX Library brings familiar aspects of programming with the .NET Framework to JavaScript. You can create namespaces to group functionality. The AJAX Library provides a framework for using object-oriented development patterns from JavaScript. You can define interfaces and classes that implement them. You can extend types and call on the base implementation. The ASP.NET AJAX Library provides a set of exceptions in the `Error` class that work with the JavaScript `Error` object and provide a natural way to find and report problems. There is also debug support with verbose error messages to help you find bugs.

The AJAX Library also includes information about the browser object so that you can reliably customize your actions for the user's environment. It also provides classes that assist in debugging. When running with debugging enabled, the ASP.NET AJAX Library validates parameters passed to the framework classes and helps you avoid errors.

The ASP.NET AJAX Library helps you to write JavaScript code in a familiar and intuitive way. Transitioning between Visual Basic or C# and JavaScript is easier. You get a set of base class libraries that function in the browser the same way you see them work on the server. You get help working with strings and data that perform with high performance. The ASP.NET AJAX Library also aids you in localizing your output for the application user.

Fundamentally, the ASP.NET AJAX Library is focused on making JavaScript programming easier. You can take advantage of ASP.NET on the server and leverage JavaScript in the browser. Although the languages you are using on client and server are different, you get a familiar set of functionality that makes the transition back and forth easier.

Using the ScriptManager

AJAX development centers on using more JavaScript than traditional Web applications. With increased use of JavaScript comes the need for better ways to manage, reference, localize (that is, provide different script versions for specific language and culture combinations), and transmit script code to the client browser. The ASP.NET ScriptManager is at the center of ASP.NET AJAX functionality. The ScriptManager is the key component that coordinates the use of JavaScript for the Microsoft AJAX Library. Custom controls also use it to take advantage of script compression and reliable loading, as well as for automatic access to localized and debug versions of scripts.

In this chapter, you see what the ScriptManager does and how you can control it. You see how to use the ScriptManager to include your scripts, and how to use the Microsoft AJAX Library scripts. You also learn how to take advantage of the ScriptManager for accessing scripts embedded in a .dll, combining multiple scripts into one script, and how it functions to retrieve localized script resources.

The Ubiquitous ScriptManager

A ScriptManager is required on every page that you want to use the Microsoft AJAX Library. When the ScriptManager is included in the page, the Microsoft AJAX Library scripts are rendered to the browser. This enables support for using the ASP.NET AJAX Client Library, and by default enables support for partial page rendering. Listing 5-1 (Bare.aspx) is a page with a barebones ScriptManager that does nothing more than render the Microsoft AJAX Library files to the browser.

Listing 5-1: Including the ScriptManager (Bare.aspx)

```
<!DOCTYPE html PUBLIC "-//W3C//DTD XHTML 1.0 Transitional//EN"
  "http://www.w3.org/TR/xhtml1/DTD/xhtml1-transitional.dtd"><html
xmlns="http://www.w3.org/1999/xhtml">
<head runat="server">
    <title>ASP.NET AJAX ScriptManager</title>
</head>
```

Continued

Listing 5-1: Including the ScriptManager (Bare.aspx) *(continued)*

```
<body>
    <form id="form1" runat="server">
    <asp:ScriptManager ID="ScriptManager1" runat="server" />
    <div>
    </div>
    </form>
</body>
</html>
```

Upon running this page and viewing the rendered HTML source, notice how the rendering changes when the ScriptManager is added to the page. You get five new script elements in the HTML sent to the browser.

The following HTML and JavaScript is part of what is sent to the browser when `Bare.aspx` is requested. You can see that querystring parameters in the script references are long. They include time stamp elements and unique hash identifiers for script that is registered dynamically. If you copy the path from the `src` attribute of the `script` element and paste it into your browser's address bar, you get the actual script resources returned from the server.

```
<script type="text/javascript">
//<![CDATA[
var theForm = document.forms['form1'];
if (!theForm) {
    theForm = document.form1;
}
function __doPostBack(eventTarget, eventArgument) {
    if (!theForm.onsubmit || (theForm.onsubmit() != false)) {
        theForm.__EVENTTARGET.value = eventTarget;
        theForm.__EVENTARGUMENT.value = eventArgument;
        theForm.submit();
    }
}
//]]>
</script>

<script src="/chapter05/WebResource.axd?d=6kIHBZsykATBSq3fbEmsYQ2&amp;t=
632968784944906146" type="text/javascript"></script>


<script src="/chapter05/ScriptResource.axd?d=9x_HPpGK-eN7tqV0Ff_J6PdW6
RyjdfhhTabpkRyiakKJ_a_q_nueOi1SMgVHCnyemAE_Wi1zmQc6dppn1_ShJ3RT853s6OS8dnx
NpQibyXs1&amp;t=633054056223442000" type="text/javascript"></script>

<script src="/chapter05/ScriptResource.axd?d=9x_HPpGK-eN7tqV0Ff_J6PdW6
RyjdfhhTabpkRyiakKJ_a_q_nueOi1SMgVHCnyemAE_Wi1zmQc6dppn1_ShJ_clCUeTRolYBVlv
TyhBCrs1&amp;t=633054056223442000" type="text/javascript"></script>
```

The first script is rendered inline in the HTML without a callback to the server. There is no `src` attribute on the `script` element. It is the method for initiating a postback. The second is a script reference for the approximately 500 lines of JavaScript included in most ASP.NET pages. Certain ASP.NET features, such as callbacks, validation, and focus management, require this script, and it is included automatically if any of those features are used on the page.

The next script reference is for the Microsoft AJAX Library. This is the JavaScript that supports the client-side type system and base class libraries you saw in Chapter 4. The script is an embedded resource in the `System.Web.Extensions.dll`, extracted by the HTTP request to the `ScriptResource.axd` handler. The code can be used with other server technologies, as it is focused on enriched client-side development. There are debug and release versions of the script files, discussed later in this chapter.

The fourth script reference is for the MicrosoftWebForms Library. This script provides support for the UpdatePanel and the lifecycle of events associated with using partial page rendering.

The other two script entries are rendered inline in the page. You can see this in the following code, which is again part of the page output from requesting `Bare.aspx` from Listing 5-1. The first is for the PageRequestManager that handles partial page updates. The second piece of script performs the primary startup of the client page lifecycle by initializing the application object.

```
<script type="text/javascript">
//<![CDATA[
Sys.WebForms.PageRequestManager._initialize('ScriptManager1', document.
getElementById('form1'));
Sys.WebForms.PageRequestManager.getInstance()._updateControls([], [], [], 90);
//]]>
</script>

<script type="text/javascript">
//<![CDATA[-
Sys.Application.initialize();
//]]>
</script>
```

You have seen that including the ScriptManager in the page results in rendering the scripts necessary to use the client-side Microsoft AJAX Library and to take advantage of partial page rendering as well. It also renders the scripts necessary for initiating the lifecycle of JavaScript events.

Adding Script References

The ScriptManager element can contain a scripts collection for adding scripts to the page. The way you would typically include a separate file of JavaScript in a page would be to use the HTML script element. You set the `type` attribute to `"text/javascript"` and the `src` attribute to the path of the JavaScript file, as shown in the following code:

```
<script type="text/javascript" src="script.js"></script>
```

Instead of writing the script element directly, the script can be added to the set of scripts that the ScriptManager controls using a ScriptReference element. By including it this way, you are assured that it will be loaded at a point when the Microsoft AJAX Library is available, and that it is only loaded once in the page even if controls on the page also require it and attempt to register it automatically. This is shown in Listing 5-2 (`ScriptReference.aspx`).

Listing 5-2: Referencing a Script

```
<!DOCTYPE html PUBLIC "-//W3C//DTD XHTML 1.1//EN"
"http://www.w3.org/TR/xhtml11/DTD/xhtml11.dtd">
<html xmlns="http://www.w3.org/1999/xhtml">
<head runat="server">
 <title>ScriptManager</title>
</head>
<body>
    <form id="form1" runat="server">
    <asp:ScriptManager runat="server" ID="ScriptManager1">

    <Scripts>
        <asp:ScriptReference Path="sample.js" />
    </Scripts>
    </asp:ScriptManager>
<div>
</div>
</form>
</body>
</html>
```

The Notify Callback

If you look at the end of one of the Microsoft AJAX library scripts, you will notice a call to the `Sys.Application.notifyScriptLoaded` method. If a script does not have this call, a JavaScript error is encountered during partial page updates when asynchronous updates are happening and new scripts are being loaded, as shown in Figure 5-1.

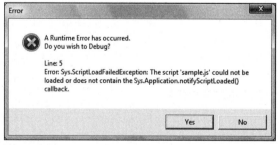

Figure 5-1

A call to `Sys.Application.notifyScriptLoaded` is required so that the ScriptManager can provide the client lifecycle reliably on various browsers. It is crucial during partial page updates, since controls in the new rendering may have never been on the page before, and therefore might register script references that weren't there before. Since the page has already initially loaded, these scripts must be loaded dynamically. Just like regular script elements, the dynamically loaded scripts might depend on each other, so they must be loaded synchronously and in order. However, not all browsers provide a way of detecting when a script has loaded, so this call is required to let ScriptManager know it is okay to begin loading the next script. Listing 5-3 (`Sample.js`) shows the recommended way of calling the required notification function when the Microsoft AJAX Library is present and still function reliably when used separately. Note that if your script is an embedded resource, the callback is added automatically.

Listing 5-3: The script load notification callback

```
// filesystem based script resource

function identityFunction(arg) {
    return arg;
}
```

```
if(typeof(Sys) !== 'undefined') Sys.Application.notifyScriptLoaded();
```

Rather than directly making the call, first check that the Sys namespace is defined. The script can then be included in a page where the Microsoft AJAX Library is not being used without causing an error.

Setting the ScriptMode

ScriptManager and ScriptReferences both allow you to set the ScriptMode. The default value of this enum is Auto. The other possible values are Release, Debug, and Inherit. The ScriptMode determines whether release or debug versions of the scripts are used. When set to Auto, the determination is primarily the result of server settings. Debug scripts are used when debug is set to true in the compilation section of the web.config file, or when the debug page directive is set to true. The deployment setting in the configuration file trumps all of the other settings. When retail is set to true, all other debug settings are treated as false and you won't get debug versions of the scripts.

ASP.NET AJAX includes release and debug versions of the scripts, but for ScriptReferences that refer to files on disk, the ScriptManager does not assume that you have provided debug versions of the script, so the path given is used regardless of the server's debug setting. The Auto setting for ScriptMode is almost identical to the Inherits value, except for this behavior. Inherits will take the value directly from the ScriptManager. The ScriptManager doesn't look to configuration or page settings when the ScriptMode is set directly to Release or Debug.

The pattern you use to provide debug versions of scripts is to add .debug to the filename before the .js suffix. The name the ScriptManager assumes for the debug version of Sample.js is Sample .debug.js. The filenames are not validated, so specifying the debug version of a script file that doesn't exist results in an error like the one shown in Figure 5-2. Again, this error is only produced when script loading is validated during asynchronous postbacks, not during the initial loading of the page.

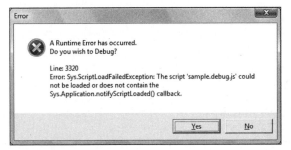

Figure 5-2

153

The choice of using .debug in the script name is arbitrary, but it does allow automation in finding the right version of scripts on disk, as well as when they are embedded as resources in a .dll. You won't have to keep swapping files during development and deployment. You can set the Debug mode you want and get the right version for the scripts you want to debug. For file-based script resources, you toggle between the release and debug versions by setting the ScriptMode attribute to Debug directly on the ScriptReference.

Embedding Script Resources

There are some advantages to embedding JavaScript files as resources in a .dll and deploying them that way. You don't have to wonder whether someone has modified the scripts on the server. You can maintain a set of release and debug scripts in a single location and use the ScriptManager to dynamically switch between versions. If you have server controls that depend on the script, you can be sure that your controls and script are updated as one. And once deployed, you have version information on the scripts, allowing for easier maintenance and servicing.

One key difference exists in how the ScriptManager treats scripts retrieved from the file system compared with those embedded as a resource in a .dll. When the path to a script is used, the ScriptManager references the script directly. The script itself is not modified (no extra calls are injected). When a script is retrieved as an embedded resource, however, the ScriptManager provides a callback to the ScriptResource handler, which injects the call to Sys.Application.notify-ScriptLoaded for you automatically. This allows you to start using embedded scripts that you already have with ASP.NET AJAX without having to rebuild the .dlls.

In Visual Studio, you first create a class library project. You can do this from your existing Web application by right-clicking the Solution name in the Solution Explorer window. From the Add New Project dialog, you can add a new project by selecting the Class Library template. (See Figure 5-3.) Alternatively, you can choose to create a new Project from the File menu. In the dialog where you select the Class Library template you can also choose to add this project to the current Visual Studio Solution by selecting Add to solution in the Solution drop-down.

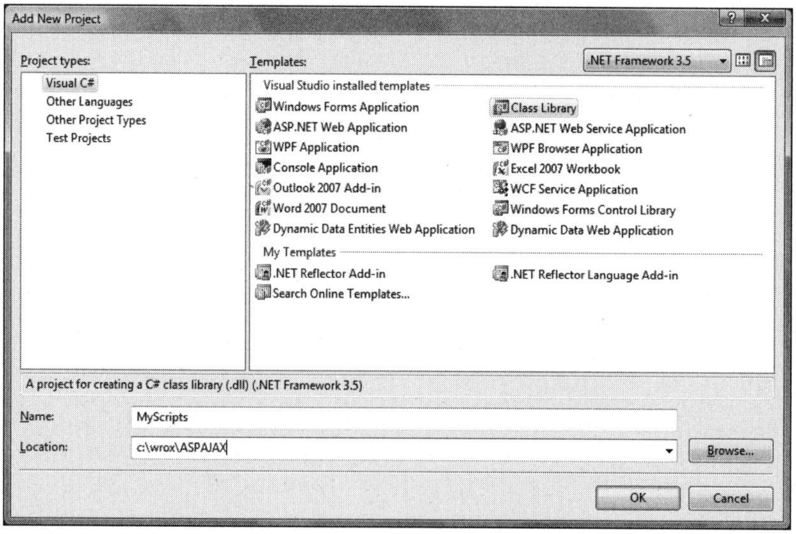

Figure 5-3

You create the script files as you normally would, by adding JavaScript files to the project. Remember that using the naming convention of adding .debug into the filename for the debug version of a script enables automatic switching between release and debug versions at runtime. To embed the scripts into the resulting .dll, you set the Build Action in the Properties pane for the script file to Embedded Resource, as shown in Figure 5-4.

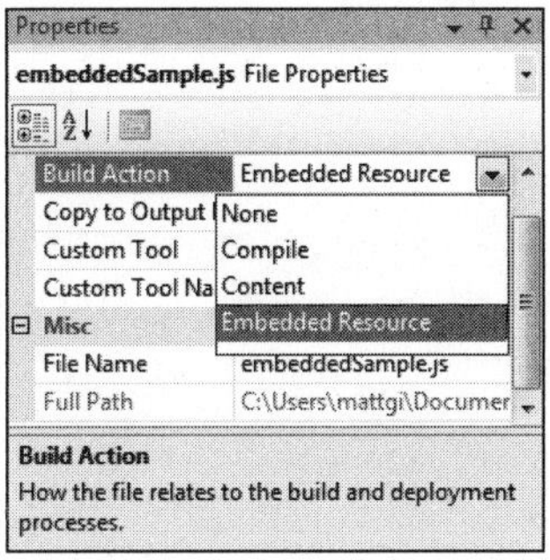

Figure 5-4

In this example, I have added embeddedSample.js with a function called doubleArg that just returns double what it is passed. Listing 5-4 (embeddedSample.debug.js) includes some error checking. For some functions, you want to do parameter validation in release scripts, but for many situations, you just want the extra checks only during development and testing. In general, because your end users will be downloading and executing the release version of the script, it is better to do what is faster and smaller in release mode, whereas in Debug mode you can perform larger, slower validation routines to catch errors during development. You might also log information that would be useful while debugging.

Listing 5-4: Debug mode error checking (embeddedSample.debug.js)

```
function doubleArg(arg) {
    if(typeof(arg) === 'undefined') {
        throw Error.argumentUndefined('arg');
    }
    if(arg === null) {
        throw Error.argumentNull('arg');
    }
    if((arg % 0) === 0) {
        throw Error.argumentOutOfRange('arg', arg);
    }

    return 2*arg;
}
```

To be able to add a ScriptReference for the embeddedSample script, you need to define the WebResource for the project. The WebResource attribute is in the System.Web.UI namespace. The attribute is used in the code of your project to include the script into the compiled .dll. The project needs a compile-time reference to the System.Web assembly to compile. Right-click the References entry of the Solution Explorer in Visual Studio and select Add Reference. Figure 5-5 shows the dialog where you can select System.Web.

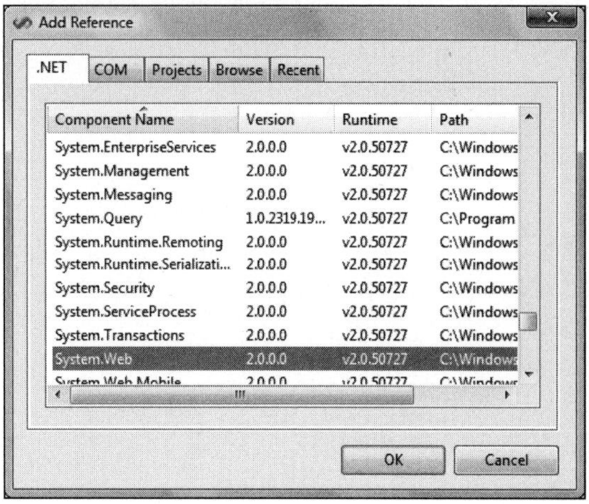

Figure 5-5

The `WebResource` is added to the `AssemblyInfo.cs` file, which is in the Properties directory of the class library project. The `WebResource` attribute tells ASP.NET the names and types of resources available from assemblies in your Web project. In this case, there are two resources, and both of them are JavaScript files to be embedded in the assembly:

```
[assembly: WebResource("MyScripts.embeddedSample.js", "application/x-javascript")]
[assembly: WebResource("MyScripts.embeddedSample.debug.js", "application/x-
javascript")]
```

If you create the class library as a project within your Web project solution in Visual Studio, you can modify the properties of the project to have the resource assembly copied into the `bin` directory of your Web application. If it is a separate solution, you need to explicitly set the output location or copy the `.dll` into your application manually.

To declare the dependency on the separate project, right-click on the Web Project in the Solution Explorer and select the Add Reference option. From there, you can select the project with the embedded resources. Also, you have to select the script file in the Solution Explorer of Visual Studio, and in the Property Grid set the Build Action to the Embedded Resource value. This is the same place where you can choose to copy the output to a specific location when the `.dll` is compiled.

Now you have a `.dll` with script resources embedded and can include them in your page with a ScriptReference. Listing 5-5 (`EmbeddedReference.aspx`) is a page that includes the script and calls to the `doubleArg` function with valid and invalid parameters.

Listing 5-5: Referencing embedded scripts

```
<%@ Page Language="C#" %>

<!DOCTYPE html PUBLIC "-//W3C//DTD XHTML 1.1//EN"
"http://www.w3.org/TR/xhtml11/DTD/xhtml11.dtd">
<html xmlns="http://www.w3.org/1999/xhtml">
```

Listing 5-5: Referencing embedded scripts *(continued)*

```
<head runat="server">
 <title>ScriptManager</title>

</head>
<body>
    <form id="form1" runat="server">

    <asp:ScriptManager runat="server" ID="ScriptManager1" >
    <Scripts>
        <asp:ScriptReference Name="MyScripts.embeddedSample.js"
Assembly="MyScripts" />
    </Scripts>
    </asp:ScriptManager>
</div>
</form>
</body>
</html>

<script type="text/javascript">
function pageLoad() {
    alert(doubleArg(3));
    alert(doubleArg());
}
</script>
```

When debugging is not enabled for the page, the browser displays the number 6 and NaN. The second call to the function does not include an argument, and the release script just tries to double it and returns the "Not a Number" JavaScript value. When using the debug version of the script, however, you get the benefit of running the debug version of the script, and a better error message is displayed, explaining that the argument cannot be undefined.

You saw when using the path attribute of a ScriptReference to load a script from a file that the ScriptManager does not switch automatically between debug and release versions of the script. And when using the name and assembly attributes to specify loading of an embedded script, it will pick up the right version based on the server setting. If you do not provide a debug version of the script, the ScriptManager will notice this and fall back to the release version. It is not an error to skip inclusion of debug script resources.

You can include all three attributes — Name, Assembly, and Path — in a single ScriptReference element and get a slightly different behavior still. The path will be used to retrieve the script from disk, but the determination of whether or not a debug version of the script is available is made by looking at the embedded resources. If you have a debug embedded resource and choose to get the script from disk, it is an error to try and retrieve the debug version if it does not exist on disk. The ScriptManager will not fallback from the file system to the embedded resource.

The main benefit to specifying Name, Assembly, and Path, is that the script at the path you specify replaces the resource based script. Any control on the page that requests the resource based script will automatically use the path you specify instead. You can actually use this technique to load the framework scripts from disk, too. This gives you a way to easily modify resource based scripts without having to recompile the assembly they live in, which is especially useful if the assembly is not your own.

Script Localization

The .NET Framework has good support for providing and using localized resources in .NET applications. This is a feature that has been lacking in JavaScript. ASP.NET AJAX makes it possible to provide localized string resources and have the correct language used automatically at runtime.

It follows the same principle as the previous example of embedded script resources but extends it to automatically generate a string resource class. The following JavaScript function uses the `shortText` and `longText` properties of the `Res` class.

```
function LocalizedMessage() {
    alert(Wrox.ASPAJAX.Samples.LocalizedMessage.Res.shortText);
    alert(Wrox.ASPAJAX.Samples.LocalizedMessage.Res.longText);
}
```

But you haven't defined the `Res` class. Instead, the `ScriptResource` attribute is used along with the `WebResource` attribute to instruct the ScriptManager to create the class. The `WebResource` attribute is still required to specify the resource name and its type. Then the `ScriptResource` attribute is added with the name of the script resource, along with the name of the string resources to use and the name of the class to create in JavaScript for use in the browser. Figure 5-6 shows adding a resource file to the project. The `WebResource` and `ScriptResource` attributes are added to the `AssemblyInfo.cs` class of the project as shown in the following:

```
[assembly: WebResource("MyScripts.LocalizedMessage.js", "application/x-
javascript")]
[assembly: ScriptResource("MyScripts.LocalizedMessage.js",
    "MyScripts.LocalizedMessage",
    "Wrox.ASPAJAX.Samples.LocalizedMessage.Res")]
```

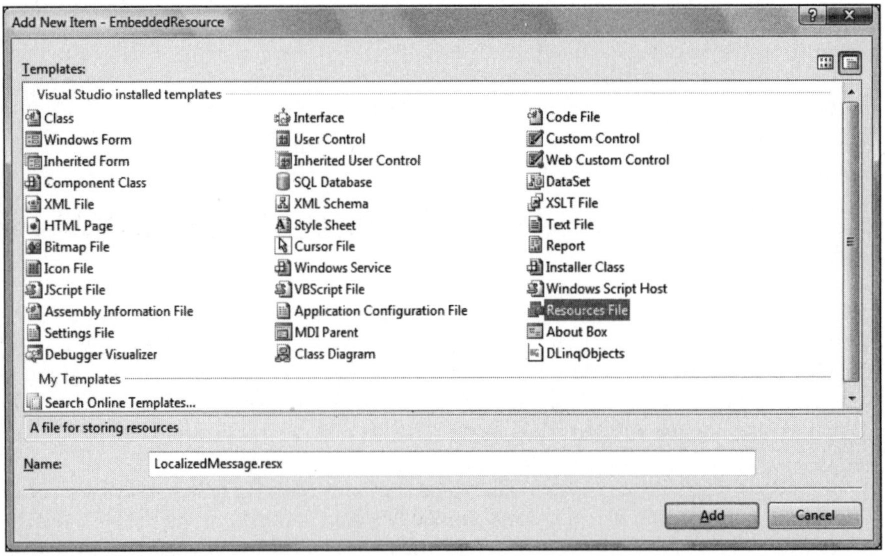

Figure 5-6

The name of the `.resx` files you create is key, as it is used to determine the culture of the resources contained in that file. You can define `shortText` and `longText` keys in the `LocalizedMessage.resx` file and then create a `LocalizedMessage.fr-FR.resx` file to house French translations of the messages. In this case, `fr` means the French language, and `FR` means the French culture. In some cases, a given language can have several culture variations, for example, American English versus British English. Figure 5-7 shows the French resource file. As you can see, it really is just a set of name-value pairs being established for cultures that will be accessed in the application.

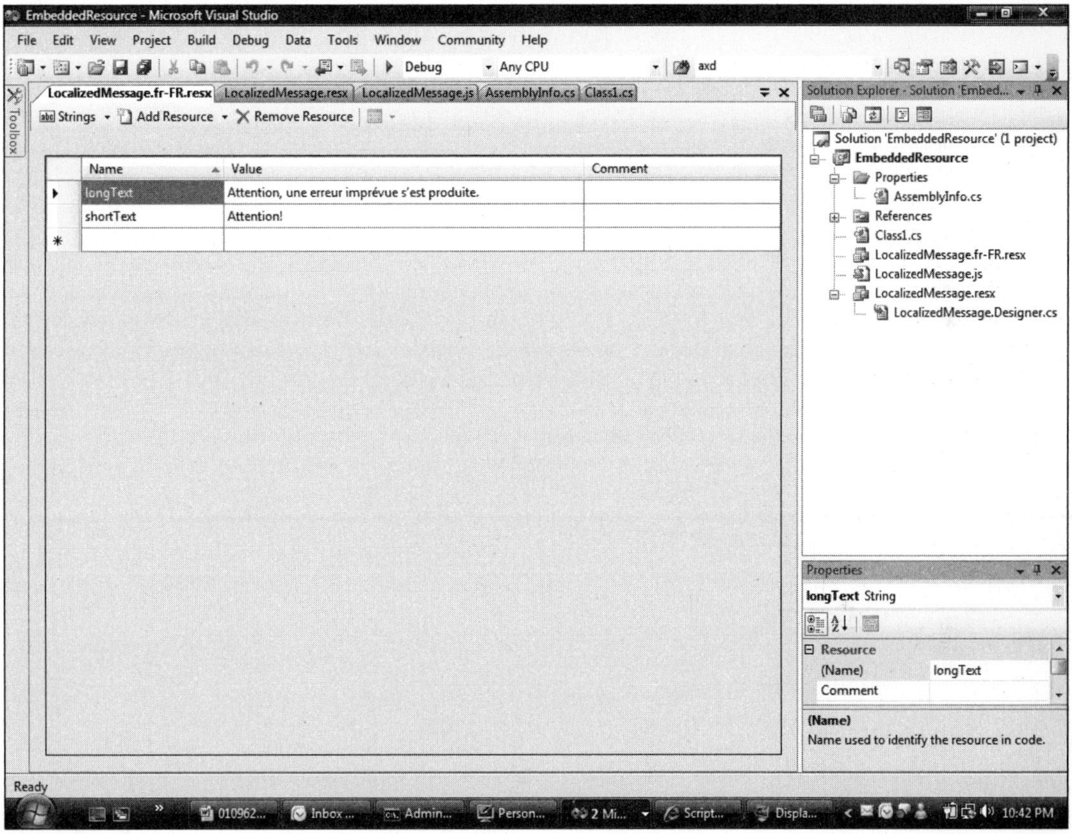

Figure 5-7

To use localized resources, you do not have to provide versions for every possible culture known to the .NET Framework. A request for a culture that does not have localized versions of the strings will fall back to the default strings instead. To enable localization on the ScriptManager, you must set the `EnableLocalization` property to `true`. It is `false` by default.

Another default setting of ASP.NET needs to be changed to make effective use of the localization feature. The ScriptManager will provide the localized resources in the culture setting under which the page is running. By default, this does not reflect the user's language setting in the browser. The browser will send with each Web request to the server an ordered list of language preferences. By setting the `UICulture` to `Auto`, ASP.NET will take the top entry from the list of languages and use that culture to execute the request. Note that it does not try subsequent entries in the list if the first one is not a valid culture on the server. Listing 5-6 (`LocalizedResource.aspx`) is a page that sets the culture, enables localization, includes the ScriptReference for the localized file, and calls the `localizedMessage` function, which uses the resources.

Listing 5-6: Enabling localization (LocalizedResource.aspx)

```
<%@ Page Language="C#" UICulture="Auto" %>
<!DOCTYPE html PUBLIC "-//W3C//DTD XHTML 1.1//EN"
"http://www.w3.org/TR/xhtml11/DTD/xhtml11.dtd">
<html xmlns="http://www.w3.org/1999/xhtml">
<head runat="server">
    <title>ScriptManager</title>
</head>
<body>
    <form id="form1" runat="server">

    <asp:ScriptManager runat="server" ID="ScriptManager1"
EnableScriptLocalization="true">
    <Scripts>
        <asp:ScriptReference Assembly="MyScripts"
Name="MyScripts.LocalizedMessage.js" />
    </Scripts>
    </asp:ScriptManager>
<div>
</div>
</form>
</body>

<script type="text/javascript">
function pageLoad() {
    LocalizedMessage();
}
</script>
</html>
```

Now, if the language preference in the browser is English, the page will display Attention messages in English. The Options dialog of your browser allows you to add, remove, and reorder your language preference. Figure 5-8 shows adding French to the list of preferred languages. Remember that ASP.NET will only try the topmost item from the preferred languages list. When French is the most preferred language, the `UICulture` for the thread processing the server request is switched to French, and the ScriptManager selects the French resource strings.

Script Globalization

Script localization allows you to provide for specific translations of text for use in JavaScript in the browser. Script globalization is the ability to format and parse data using a specific culture. For example, it is customary in U.S. English for dates to be formatted as month, followed by the day and then the year (8/21/1993), but in many other cultures, the day of the month is presented first

(21/8/1993). The ScriptManager will populate a `CultureInfo` object, with the data from the culture being used to process the page on the server when `EnableScriptGlobalization` is set to `true`. It is `false` by default. For script localization, you change the Page `UICulture` property to `Auto`, but for globalization you use the `Culture` property. `UICulture` is for language choice, while `Culture` is for date and number parsing and formatting.

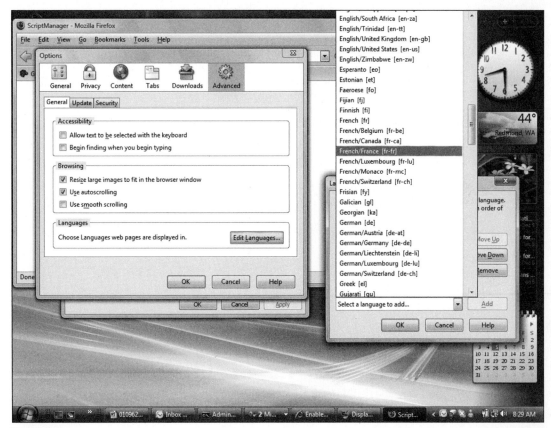

Figure 5-8

Listing 5-7 (`Globalization.aspx`) shows the string formatting functions using `String.localeFormat`. This version of the formatting API will respect the current culture setting in the browser. With globalization, you can get language-specific formatting in the browser without needing to provide localized resource files in your application.

Listing 5-7: Enabling script globalization (Globalization.aspx)

```
<%@Page Language="C#" Culture="Auto" %>

<!DOCTYPE html PUBLIC "-//W3C//DTD XHTML 1.1//EN"
"http://www.w3.org/TR/xhtml11/DTD/xhtml11.dtd">
<html xmlns="http://www.w3.org/1999/xhtml">
```

Continued

Listing 5-7: Enabling script globalization (Globalization.aspx) *(continued)*

```
<head runat="server">
    <title>EnableGlobalization</title>
</head>
<body>
    <form id="form1" runat="server">

        <asp:ScriptManager runat="server" ID="ScriptManager1"
EnableScriptGlobalization="true" >
        </asp:ScriptManager>
<div>
    <input type="text" id="textbox" value="something"/>
</div>
</form>
</body>
<script type="text/javascript">
function pageLoad(sender, args) {
    var d = new Date();
    var message = String.format("With {0} culture date formats
are:\n{1}\n{2}\n{3}\n{4}\n{5}\n{6}\n{7}\n{8}",

        Sys.CultureInfo.CurrentCulture.name,
        d.localeFormat("d"),
        d.localeFormat("D"),
        d.localeFormat("t"),
        d.localeFormat("T"),
        d.localeFormat("F"),
        d.localeFormat("M"),
        d.localeFormat("s"),
        d.localeFormat("Y") );
    alert(message);
}
</script>
</html>
```

Service References

Much of the emphasis of richer application development centers on leveraging Web services through asynchronous communications with the server. ASP.NET AJAX makes this easy. You can declare references to Web services within the ScriptManager in much the same way that the previous examples do for scripts. Suppose you want to mark the time that some event occurred on the client. You might provide a Web service like the one in Listing 5-8 (Servertime.asmx) so that you are not relying on the local time of the user's machine, which may not be accurate.

Listing 5-8: Sample Web service (Servertime.asmx)

```
<%@ WebService Language="C#" Class="Wrox.ASPAJAX.Samples.TimeOfDay" %>

using System;
using System.Web;
using System.Web.Script.Services;
```

Listing 5-8: Sample Web service (Servertime.asmx) *(continued)*

```
using System.Web.Services;
using System.Web.Services.Protocols;

namespace Wrox.ASPAJAX.Samples
{

    [ScriptService]
    [WebService(Namespace = "http://tempuri.org/")]
    [WebServiceBinding(ConformsTo = WsiProfiles.BasicProfile1_1)]
    public class TimeOfDay : System.Web.Services.WebService
    {
        [WebMethod]
        public string TheTime()
        {
            return DateTime.Now.ToString();
        }
    }
}
```

By including the `ScriptService` attribute on the class declaration, you declare to ASP.NET that it should provide a JavaScript proxy class for use in calling the Web service. If you navigate directly to the `.asmx` file that contains the Web service, ASP.NET provides a page that allows you to invoke the methods directly from the browser without writing any code. In a similar vein, if you navigate to the `.asmx` file in the browser and append `/js` to the URL, ASP.NET returns dynamically generated JavaScript code that creates a proxy object that can be used to invoke the method directly from script.

The ScriptManager will generate a script element for the proxy code associated with each `ScriptReference` it contains, automatically adding the `/js` suffix to retrieve the JavaScript proxy object for that service. You can optionally set the `InlineScript` property to `true` to have the proxy code rendered directly in the page. Listing 5-9 (`ServiceReference.aspx`) includes a `ScriptReference` to the `TimeOfDay` Web service. The `pageLoad` function first sets the timeout to 1000 milliseconds from the default value, where there is no client timeout. The code then invokes the Web service providing the names of callback functions to invoke for success or failure.

Web browsers limit the number of simultaneous connections they make back to the server, typically to two. So, if you have a lot of ScriptReference elements in a page, you may want to consider having some select ones rendered inline to avoid contention for multiple concurrent requests to download the proxies. However, the tradeoff is that inline scripts are not cached by the browser and bloat the size of the page. Large, frequently used scripts should be external references to take advantage of browser caching. The frequency of returning versus new visitors is also a factor, because caching benefits returning visitors (less is downloaded the second visit), whereas making the proxies inline benefits new visitors (fewer files for the browser to download).

Listing 5-9: Calling a Web service (ServiceReference.aspx)

```
<!DOCTYPE html PUBLIC "-//W3C//DTD XHTML 1.1//EN" "http://www.w3.org/TR/xhtml11/
DTD/xhtml11.dtd">
<html xmlns="http://www.w3.org/1999/xhtml">
<head runat="server">
```
Continued

Listing 5-9: Calling a Web service (ServiceReference.aspx) *(continued)*

```
    <title>ASP.NET AJAX Service Reference</title>
</head>
<body>
  <form id="form1" runat="server">

    <asp:ScriptManager runat="server" ID="ScriptManager1">
    <Services>
    <asp:ServiceReference Path="ServerTime.asmx" />
    </Services>
    </asp:ScriptManager>
  <div>
  </div>
  </form>
</body>

<script type="text/javascript">
function pageLoad() {
 Wrox.ASPAJAX.Samples.TimeOfDay.set_timeout(1000);
 Wrox.ASPAJAX.Samples.TimeOfDay.TheTime(success, failed, "arbitrary info for the
callback")
}

function success(result, userContext) {
 alert(result + " " + userContext);
}

function failed(result) {
    var message = String.format("statusCode={0}\r\nexceptionType
={1}\r\ntimedOut={2}\r\nmessage={3}\r\nstackTrace={4}",
    result.get_statusCode(),
    result.get_exceptionType(),
    result.get_timedOut(),
    result.get_message(),
    result.get_stackTrace());
    alert(message);
}
</script>
</html>
```

The third argument passed to the proxy for invoking the Web service is called the `userContext`. It is not sent to the server but is passed to the completion callback function. This allows you to carry extra data to your callback that is not involved in the Web service call without consuming resources to roundtrip it to the server.

Even code that runs correctly almost all of the time can encounter something unexpected. Listing 5-10 (`ThrowError.asmx`) demonstrates this by throwing an exception to the Web service code from Listing 5-8. If an error is encountered and an exception thrown, or if the timeout is exceeded, the error callback is called instead of the success completion function.

Listing 5-10: Throwing an exception from a Web service (ThrowError.asmx)

```
<%@ WebService Language="C#" Class="ThrowError" %>

using System;
using System.Web;
using System.Web.Services;
using System.Web.Services.Protocols;

[WebService(Namespace = "http://tempuri.org/")]
[WebServiceBinding(ConformsTo = WsiProfiles.BasicProfile1_1)]
public class ThrowError  : System.Web.Services.WebService {

 [WebMethod]
 public string TheTime(){

      throw new Exception("failed miserably");
 }
}
```

The object passed to the error handler provides a JavaScript call stack when an exception is thrown. It also carries any exception message, what the HTTP status code was, and whether or not the error was caused by a timeout. The result of throwing this exception is shown in Figure 5-9.

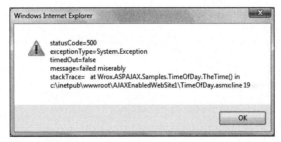

Figure 5-9

ASP.NET Application Services

ASP.NET AJAX provides a client framework that simplifies JavaScript development, but as you have seen, it also provides server-focused solutions for easily accessing Web services and localizing script resources. In addition, ASP.NET AJAX makes it easy to leverage the user authentication, roles, and profile management features of ASP.NET.

Authentication and role services allow you to remotely check user credentials in JavaScript against a central user repository. ASP.NET provides a default database and authentication scheme that you can use. The profile service allows you to store and retrieve data for each authenticated user on the server. ASP.NET AJAX makes this information available from JavaScript running in the browser.

Authentication Service

ASP.NET Forms Authentication allows you to store user credentials in a database or other back end without creating individual Windows accounts for every user. ASP.NET AJAX makes it possible to authenticate users against the server storage directly from JavaScript in the browser.

First, Forms Authentication must be enabled for the application that requires credentials using the `authentication` section under `system.web` in the application configuration file. The following configuration data from a `web.config` file shows setting the `authentication mode` to `Forms` and defining that cookies should be used to store the authentication ticket. ASP.NET supports carrying the authentication ticket in the URL of requests, but when authenticating from JavaScript, cookies must be used.

```
<authentication mode="Forms">
  <forms cookieless="UseCookies" />
</authentication>
<authorization>
  <deny users="?" />
  <allow users="*" />
</authorization>
```

That configuration will enable Forms Authentication using cookies. The `deny` element uses the question mark to indicate that the anonymous user is not allowed. The `allow` element uses the asterisk to allow all authenticated users.

That is enough to get Forms Authentication going for a Web request, but accessing it from JavaScript also requires explicitly setting it in the `system.web.extensions` configuration section. This is shown in the following configuration entry from an ASP.NET AJAX application.

```
<system.web.extensions>
    <scripting>
        <webServices>
            <authenticationService enabled="true" />
        </webServices>
    </scripting>
</system.web.extensions>
```

By default, ASP.NET will create a database using Microsoft SQL Express for development. You can use the `aspnet_regsql` tool to populate your existing database with the tables and schema for using the default authentication providers.

With the configuration in place, you can call login and logout against the ASP.NET Authentication Service from JavaScript. The login method requires a username and password. You can also specify that the authentication cookie be persisted beyond when the browser is closed, any custom data that should be available in the callback, and the `redirectUrl` to use upon successful login. Of course, you can provide callback functions for success and failure.

Listing 5-11 (`Login.aspx`) includes code for logging a user in and out in the click handler of a button. The logout function has fewer parameters: the `redirectUrl` to use (use `null` for the current page), completion callbacks for logout, and a failed attempt to logout, and the `userContext` object to pass to the callbacks. The `userContext` is not sent to the server and then returned to the client. Instead, the AJAX infrastructure sets up the call to the server, puts the custom data aside, and passes it to the completion function when the call to the server is complete.

Listing 5-11: Accessing the authentication service (Login.aspx)

```
<!DOCTYPE html PUBLIC "-//W3C//DTD XHTML 1.0 Transitional//EN" "http://www.w3.org/
TR/xhtml1/DTD/xhtml1-transitional.dtd">
<html xmlns="http://www.w3.org/1999/xhtml" >
<head id="Head1" runat="server">
 <title>ASP.NET AJAX Login</title>
</head>
<body>
<form id="form1" runat="server">
<asp:ScriptManager runat="server" ID="ScriptManager1" >
</asp:ScriptManager>
<div>Username: <input type="text" name="username" /></div>
<div>Password: <input type="password" name="password"></div>
<div>
    <input type="button" id="loginButton" value="Login"/><br />
    <input type="button" id="logoutButton" value="Logout" />
</div>

<div id="Results"></div>
 </form>
</body>
<script type="text/javascript">

function pageLoad() {
    document.getElementById('loginButton').attachEvent('onclick', login);
    $addHandler($get('logoutButton'), 'click', logout);
}

function login() {
    var u = $get('username').value;
    var p = $get('password').value;
    var isPersistent = false;
    var customInfo = null;
    var redirectUrl = null;
    Sys.Services.AuthenticationService.login(u, p, isPersistent, customInfo,
redirectUrl, loginCompleted, loginFailed);
}

function loginCompleted(result, context, methodName) {
    if(result) {
        alert("Successfuly logged in.");
    }
    else {
        alert("Failed to login.");
    }
}

function loginFailed(error, context, methodName) {
    alert(error.get_message());
}
function logout() {
    Sys.Services.AuthenticationService.logout('Default.aspx');
}
</script>
</html>
```

When using the built-in Authentication Service, it is enabled through configuration, as you've seen. But you have the flexibility to customize the membership feature beyond what is provided natively by ASP. NET. The `AuthenticationService` element of the ScriptManager allows you to set the path of the service to a custom Web service: `<AuthenticationService path="authenticate.asmx" />`. You can write your own service with the Login and Logout method signatures required and use it to validate credentials against any custom middle tier or back-end data store that you want. Listing 5-12 is an example of a service with the appropriate method signatures so that the JavaScript `AuthenticationService` classes will successfully call the custom implementation.

Listing 5-12: A customized authentication service

```csharp
<%@ WebService Language="C#" Class="Wrox.ASPAJAX.Samples.Authenticate" %>
using System.Web;
using System.Web.Security;
using System.Web.Services;
using System.Web.Script.Services;

namespace Wrox.ASPAJAX.Samples
{

    [ScriptService]
    [WebService(Namespace = "http://tempuri.org/")]
    [WebServiceBinding(ConformsTo = WsiProfiles.BasicProfile1_1)]
    public class Authenticate : System.Web.Services.WebService
    {
        [WebMethod]

        public bool Login(string userName, string password)
        {
            //storing passwords in code is a BAD security practice
            if (userName == "Matt" && password == "MyPassword!")
            {
                FormsAuthentication.SetAuthCookie(userName, false);
                return true;
            }
            return false;
        }

        [WebMethod]

        public void Logout()
        {
            FormsAuthentication.SignOut();
        }
    }
}
```

Role Service

The ASP.NET role management feature allows you to assign roles to user accounts. For example, some users may have the "premium member" role, or the "administrator" role. The capabilities of the site available to the user can depend on what roles they are a member of. Role data for the currently authenticated user can be made available from JavaScript using the built-in role service that ASP.NET AJAX provides.

To enable the role management feature, you use the `roleManager` section inside `system.web`. This is shown in the following example section from a `web.config` file.

```
<system.web>
    <roleManager enabled="true" />
</system.web>
```

The role service for access from JavaScript must be enabled separately. This is so that you have to opt in to the ability to retrieve role information from the client. Only the roles for the currently authenticated user can ever be retrieved, but it is still a good idea only to enable client access to them if you need it.

To enable the Role service, you use the `roleService` section inside the `system.web.extensions` section, as shown here.

```
<system.web.extensions>
    <scripting>
        <webServices>
            <roleService enabled="true" />
        </webServices>
    </scripting>
</system.web.extensions>
```

The role service allows you to retrieve the current user's list of roles using the `load` function. This initiates a request to the server, which completes asynchronously. That operation will either succeed or fail, so the load function also takes success and failure callback parameters. After roles have been successfully loaded, you can use the `isUserInRole` method to test for the membership of the user in a particular role, or you can use the `get_roles` property to access the list directly. Listing 5-13 (`Role.aspx`) shows a simple page that loads the roles, displays them, and tests for the PremiumMember role.

Listing 5-13: Accessing the role service (Role.aspx)

```
<!DOCTYPE html PUBLIC "-//W3C//DTD XHTML 1.0 Transitional//EN" "http://www.w3.org/
TR/xhtml1/DTD/xhtml1-transitional.dtd">
<html xmlns="http://www.w3.org/1999/xhtml">
<head id="Head1" runat="server">
    <title>ASP.NET AJAX Role Service</title>
    <script type="text/javascript">
    function pageLoad() {
        Sys.Services.RoleService.load(loadCompleted, loadFailed);
    }

    function loadCompleted() {
        var roles = Sys.Services.RoleService.get_roles();
        var isPremium = Sys.Services.RoleService.isUserInRole("PremiumMember");
        var rolesSpan = $get('roles');
        rolesSpan.innerHTML = roles.join(',') + " Premium Member? " + isPremium;
    }

    function loadFailed(error, context, methodName) {
        alert(error.get_message());
    }
    </script>
```

Continued

Listing 5-13: Accessing the role service (Role.aspx) *(continued)*

```
    </head>
    <body>
        <form id="form1" runat="server">
        <asp:ScriptManager runat="server" ID="ScriptManager1">
        </asp:ScriptManager>
        <div>
            Your roles: <span id="roles"></span>
        </div>
        </form>
    </body>
    </html>
```

Loading roles from the server takes time to complete because the server must issue a request to the Role service asynchronously. If you would rather the roles be available immediately when the page loads, you can configure ScriptManager to emit them with the page rendering, eliminating the need to load them asynchronously later. To load roles automatically, you set the LoadRoles property of the RoleService element of the ScriptManager to true.

```
    <asp:ScriptManager runat="server" ID="ScriptManager1">
        <RoleServices LoadRoles="true" />
    </asp:ScriptManager>
```

Even if you automatically load roles, you might still have a need to load them asynchronously later on. For example, if you use the ASP.NET AJAX authentication service to log a different user in, the roles will be incorrect until they are loaded again. You might also be performing asynchronous operations that cause changes to the roles on the server, which would also require a refresh.

Profile Service

The ASP.NET profile feature allows you to automatically store and retrieve data for each user of a Web application. It can even be enabled for anonymous users that have not been authenticated. ASP.NET will issue a unique identifier to the user to be able to retrieve the profile data on subsequent requests. The service must be enabled for ASP.NET and additionally for JavaScript access from the browser. In your application's web.config file, you use the profile section inside system.web to enable profile management. This is shown in the following example section from a web.config file.

```
    <system.web>
        <anonymousIdentification enabled="true"/>
        <profile>
            <properties>
                <add name="favoriteArtist" type="System.String"/>
                <add name="favoriteAlbum" type="System.String"/>
            </properties>
        </profile>
    </system.web>
```

There are no default properties tracked for personalization. They must be defined inside the properties element of the profile configuration section. I have defined favoriteArtist and favoriteAlbum string properties. Because space is consumed in the database to track the personalization data for each user, it is disabled by default for anonymous users. Once it is enabled with the anonymousIdentification element, every unique visitor to the Web application will be issued a unique identifier, and an entry will be created for them in the database.

The profile service must be enabled separately for direct client access. This is so that you have to opt in to the ability to retrieve and update personalization data remotely. Without requiring users to be authenticated, it is possible for spoof requests to be sent to the application and modify the data.

The system.web.extensions section has a profileService section where it is enabled. You also define what profile properties should be readable and which should be writable through the service, which may not be the same as those available through directly accessing the profile management APIs on the server. In other words, when accessed directly from the server, all properties are accessible, but you can limit the access further for JavaScript access. The following configuration element from the <system.web.extensions> section of the web.config file sets up both properties for read and write access.

```
<system.web.extensions>
    <scripting>
        <webServices>
            <profileService enabled="true"
                readAccessProperties="favoriteArtist,favoriteAlbum"
                writeAccessProperties="favoriteArtist,favoriteAlbum" />
        </webServices>
    </scripting>
</system.web.extensions>
```

Now JavaScript code in a page can directly store and retrieve user personalization data. In Listing 5-14 (Profile.aspx), several items are populated in the user profile from code running on the server. Once the data is stored in the profile, it will be available automatically in subsequent requests. In the ProfileService element of the ScriptManager, the LoadProperties attribute can be set to a comma-delimited list of Profile properties that should be prepopulated in the JavaScript sent to the browser, similar to the role service LoadRoles feature. This is useful for profile information used often, and you want to avoid having to call back to the server later to retrieve it. This code tells it to load the favoriteArtist property but not favoriteAlbum.

> ASP.NET allows you to plug in your own provider so you can easily customize where the data is stored. For these examples, I am using a custom Profile data provider that just stores the data in memory temporarily rather than setting up a database.

There are two buttons on the page. One is the showArtist button and the other is showAlbum. The click handler for the showArtist button accesses the profile property directly and displays it. Because the album information was not prepopulated, the showAlbum handler has to perform a callback to get the data. It sets up success- and failure-completion functions to be called when the callback is complete. The success callback updates the album to a new value. After a postback, the showAlbum handler will retrieve the new value from the profile service.

Listing 5-14: Accessing the profile service (Profile.aspx)

```
<%@ Page Language="C#"%>

<!DOCTYPE html PUBLIC "-//W3C//DTD XHTML 1.1//EN"
```

Continued

Listing 5-14: Accessing the profile service (Profile.aspx) *(continued)*

```
"http://www.w3.org/TR/xhtml11/DTD/xhtml11.dtd">
<html xmlns="http://www.w3.org/1999/xhtml">
<head runat="server">
<title>Profile Service</title>
</head>

<script runat="server" language="c#">
void Page_Load() {
    if(!this.IsPostBack) {
        Profile.favoriteArtist = "Phish";
        Profile.favoriteAlbum = "Rift";
    }
}
</script>
<body>
 <form id="form1" runat="server">
 <asp:ScriptManager runat="server" ID="ScriptManager1" >

 <ProfileService LoadProperties="favoriteAlbum" />
 </asp:ScriptManager>
 <div>
 <input type="button" value="Get Artist" id="showArtist" /><br />
 <input type="button" value="Get Album" id="showAlbum" /></div>
 </form>
</body>
<script type="text/javascript">

function pageLoad() {
    $addHandler($get('showArtist'), 'click', displayArtist);
    $addHandler($get('showAlbum'), 'click', displayAlbum);
}

function displayArtist() {
    var p = Sys.Services.ProfileService;
    p.load(["favoriteArtist"], loadCompleted, loadFailed);
}

function loadCompleted(count) {
    alert(Sys.Services.ProfileService.properties.favoriteArtist);
}

function loadFailed() {
    alert('load failed');
}

function displayAlbum() {
    alert(Sys.Services.ProfileService.properties.favoriteAlbum);
    Sys.Services.ProfileService.properties.favoriteAlbum = "Round Room";
    Sys.Services.ProfileService.save(["favoriteAlbum"]);
}
</script>
</html>
```

The Profile Service example makes use of basic string properties, but you can also easily use more complex types. ASP.NET AJAX uses JSON (JavaScript Object Notation) serialization to move data back and forth between client and server. If you define an `Album` type with properties for `AlbumName` and `Artist`, the Profile Service will automatically manage the type in .NET code on the server and in JavaScript in the browser. Listing 5-15 (`Album.cs`) is such a type.

Listing 5-15: Using custom types (Album.cs)

```
using System;
using System.Web;
using System.Web.UI;

namespace Wrox.ASPAJAX.Samples {

public class Album {
    private string _artist = String.Empty;
    private string _name = String.Empty;

    public Album() {
    }

    public Album(string artist, string name) {
        _artist = artist;
        _name = name;
    }

    public string Artist {
        get {
            return _artist;
        }
        set {
            _artist = value;
        }
    }

    public string AlbumName {
        get {
            return _name;
        }
        set {
            _name = value;
        }
    }
}
}
```

Adding this type to the `Profile` section of `web.config` makes the type available for inclusion in the `LoadProperties` attribute of the `ProfileService` element of ScriptManager. The Profile Service will then serialize the type as a JSON object both when reading and writing the property. Instead of setting each property individually, as shown here:

```
Sys.Services.ProfileService.properties.nextAlbumToBuy.Artist = 'Phish';
Sys.Services.ProfileService.properties.nextAlbumToBuy.AlbumName = 'Round Room';
```

You can assign it as a JSON object and know that the Profile Service will be able to serialize it and send it to the server for deserialization:

```
Sys.Services.ProfileService.properties.nextAlbumToBuy = { Arist: 'Phish',
AlbumName: 'Round Room' };
```

One thing that caught me off guard in building this sample was the behavior of the success callback for saving Profile properties. Notice that the `save` and `load` methods of the `Sys.Services.ProfileService` class take an array of properties. This allows you to save and load multiple profile properties in one call. The success callback will be called even when there is a problem updating all of the Profile properties. The success callback has an argument that is the count of the number of properties that were successfully updated. If there are problems updating some, or even all, of the properties included, the success callback will be called unless there is some fundamental problem with the service call itself.

Error Handling

Inevitably something happens and an exception is thrown. It might be a timeout accessing a remote service or an offline database in the middle tier. You may not have accounted correctly for all of the edge cases that can occur when processing user input. Adding asynchronous callbacks to more of the ASP.NET application provides additional challenges in handling errors in a user-friendly way.

Allowing Custom Errors

If your user encounters an error with your ASP.NET application, you may be taking advantage of ASP.NET custom errors to redirect the user. You can provide a page with a look and feel consistent with the rest of the site that provides something more user-friendly than a developer-focused error message. At the same time, you might log some information using tracing functionality so that you are aware of the frequency with which users are encountering errors. Then you can follow up to try and improve the experience and prevent the error from occurring in the future.

With asynchronous postbacks and partial rendering, an exception can go back to the script that initiated the callback, and the default behavior is to throw a JavaScript exception. This happens even if you have custom errors enabled for your application. Part of the reason that the default behavior is not to follow redirects is the potential to navigate away from a page where a user has invested time updating a state in stages without navigating between pages. Your objective is to keep the user's data on his page while showing him an error. When redirected to an error page, the user's reaction is to hit the Back button. This can put the browser in a state before it begins interacting with the page, thereby losing the user's data. The AJAX History feature, described in Chapter 6, includes methods for putting interim stages in the browser's history, but not automatically.

When an error occurs in this condition, you don't want the user to be redirected to a custom error page. Instead, you can provide an `endRequest` event handler and alert the user to the error without redirecting the user to an error page. Then you can return the user to the view he or she had before the error occurred to continue working with the application. The following JavaScript code demonstrates handling the `endRequest` event and checking for error conditions.

```
function pageLoad() {
    Sys.WebForms.PageRequestManager.getInstance().add_endRequest(endRequestHandler);
```

```
    }

function endRequestHandler(sender, arg) {
    if (arg.get_error() !== null) {
        //alert user of problem and continue
        arg.set_errorHandled(true);
    }
}
```

If your application doesn't need to recover from error conditions in this way, you can set the allowCustomErrorsRedirect property of the ScriptManager to true to continue following the custom error handling that would occur when not using partial page rendering.

```
<asp:ScriptManager runat="server" ID="ScriptManager1"
AllowCustomErrorsRedirect="true" >
```

Handling Errors during Asynchronous Postbacks

ASP.NET AJAX allows you to trap an error that occurs during asynchronous postback processing. You can provide a static error message so that the user's browser doesn't receive a .NET exception, or you can provide an error handler that will run on the server and do something more to recover from the error condition.

The ScriptManager has an AsyncPostBackErrorMessage property that can be used instead of the actual exception message that would normally be displayed.

```
<asp:ScriptManager runat="server" ID="ScriptManager1"
AsyncPostBackErrorMessage="Please try again tomorrow." >
```

The following code shows handling the error event before it is sent to the client. It doesn't simulate an error but shows how to set up your own code to run when an error occurs. The exact nature of how to recover gracefully is up to you, although I should admit that it is not always feasible to do so. Sometimes, trying to recover from a problem puts the user in a position of repeating the action even though server resources are not available to process the request. Staging an infinite loop for the user is not an optimal application experience. Just remember to spend a reasonable amount of time testing error conditions to minimize the chance of unexpected behavior that may upset users.

```
<%@ Page Language="C#" %>
<!DOCTYPE html PUBLIC "-//W3C//DTD XHTML 1.0 Strict//EN"
"http://www.w3.org/TR/xhtml1/DTD/xhtml1-strict.dtd">
<script runat="server">
private void OnAsyncPostBackError(object sender, AsyncPostBackErrorEventArgs e) {
    ScriptManager.AsyncPostBackErrorMessage = "Please call me at home. Something
erroneous has occurred.";
}
</script>

<html xmlns="http://www.w3.org/1999/xhtml" xml:lang="en" lang="en">
<head id="Head1" runat="server">
  <title>Error Handling</title>
</head>
<body>
```

```
      <form id="Form1" runat="server">
      <asp:ScriptManager runat="server" ID="ScriptManager"
EnablePartialRendering="true" OnAsyncPostBackError="OnAsyncPostBackError">
      </asp:ScriptManager>
      </form>
</body>
</html>
```

Asynchronous Timeout

The ScriptManager allows you to customize how long to wait in the browser before considering the request orphaned and timing out. By default, the client will wait for the server to close the connection before assuming that the request has been abandoned. To specify a new default timeout for all requests, you use the `AsyncPostBackTimeout` property. The unit of measurement is seconds.

```
<asp:ScriptManager runat="server" ID="ScriptManager"
    EnablePartialRendering="true" AsyncPostBackTimeout="60" >
```

Customizing the Location of Scripts

You've seen how you can provide Release and Debug versions of JavaScript files on disk, and the ScriptManager will automatically reference the correct version. And you've seen how to embed scripts in a `.dll` for easier servicing. ASP.NET AJAX also allows you to further customize script reference behavior.

Setting the Script Path

You may want to put the common scripts for nested applications in a single location to allow the browser to cache a single copy for multiple directories. Typically, ASP.NET AJAX returns relative path references for embedded script resources, so the browser can end up caching multiple copies of a script for different applications within the same domain. The ScriptManager's `ScriptPath` property allows you to define a path to use in lieu of the normal discovery process. This allows you to put the scripts in a single location and have all references in the domain refer to that location. This also has a performance benefit, because it is faster to load a static JavaScript file from disk than to extract it from an assembly through the `ScriptResource.axd` handler.

At first, this may not seem like much, but when you consider that, even compressed, the amount of script to enable ASP.NET AJAX scenarios is more than 10K, allowing each user to get just one copy instead of one for each subdomain or nested application can really add up. The perceived performance for the user in eliminating excess calls can be significant.

The following code demonstrates setting the `ScriptPath` to a central location for greater caching. Of course, this will not bypass browser security restrictions regarding isolating domain references, but for nested directories, it can increase perceived performance significantly.

```
<asp:ScriptManager runat="server" ID="ScriptManager"
    ScriptPath="~/CommonScripts" >
</asp:ScriptManager>
```

I didn't say overall performance is better, but perceived performance can be improved. Here's the explanation: There are two aspects to the user experience associated with loading script. The first is how long it takes to retrieve the script from the server. The browser is good about caching script, so I tend to discount this overhead. Once the browser has the script for an application, it doesn't need to retrieve it for each subsequent request. The second aspect of performance is how long it takes to load and process the script. The ASP.NET team has done comparisons of the prototype and closure models for JavaScript development. The prototype model yields the best overall loading performance across various browsers. Although the processing time can ultimately be the bottleneck in loading script, avoiding unnecessary script retrieval can help an application feel more responsive for the user.

Resolving Script References

In addition to setting a static location for scripts, you can provide a handler to determine the location of scripts to use at runtime. The ScriptManager has an event called ResolveScriptReference that triggers for each script and allows you to customize the behavior. For many situations, using the ResolveScriptReference event may not be necessary, but when you find that something about a script needs to be modified without replacing the .dll in which it resides, this event can be a lifesaver.

ScriptManager Proxy

All of the examples in this chapter have been freestanding pages. There hasn't been a master page involved in the layout. But, of course, master pages are often the centerpiece of real-world site designs. To use ASP.NET partial rendering features, you need a ScriptManager control on the page, but there can be only one. So, if you have a master page where there is a ScriptManager control, and you want to override or customize some settings in a content page, you cannot simply add another ScriptManager. Instead, ASP.NET provides the ScriptManagerProxy control.

The ScriptManagerProxy control allows a content page to interact with the primary ScriptManager control from the master page and to set values unique to the content page being requested. The ScriptManagerProxy supports all of the same settings you have seen for the ScriptManager, except that it is used in a content page to reference the ScriptManager control that exists on the master page. Using the proxy without a ScriptManager control to reference in the master will result in an error.

Script Compression

One of the concerns about leveraging JavaScript in the browser more for AJAX scenarios is the increased volume of script being sent to the client. The ScriptManager compresses scripts so that the data sent from server to browser is smaller. In addition, the ASP.NET AJAX scripts are distinctly different in the release and debug versions. Besides just skipping the extra parameter validation and error information, the release version of the scripts employs a process for removing extraneous comments and unnecessary whitespace. Tabs, newlines, and extra spaces are removed to make the size of the script as small as possible before it is compressed and sent to the client. In fact, the scripts are analyzed to reduce variable names to single letters for internal use to minimize the overall script size.

Moving Script References

Normally, script references are rendered as script elements at the top of the form. ScriptManager allows you to move script references to the bottom of the form by setting the `LoadScriptsBeforeUI` property to `false`.

```
<asp:ScriptManager runat="server" ID="ScriptManager"
    LoadScriptsBeforeUI="false">
</asp:ScriptManager>
```

This may improve the perceived performance of your page, since the main part loads first, and then scripts begin loading. However, the server must still process the requests, and the page still appears in the loading state while the scripts load. Also, doing this requires special care to be sure that there is no inline script in your page that depends on any of the scripts. For example, a client-side `onclick` event handler may fire after the main part of the page is visible but before any scripts have loaded. Depending on what the handler is doing, it is easy to accidentally depend on something in one of the scripts, resulting in a JavaScript error only if the user is fast enough to trigger it, which can be a very difficult problem to track down. Still, it can be a very effective performance enhancement if done properly, especially if used in addition to script combining.

Script Combining

Script compression allows you to reduce the size of scripts sent to the client, but it doesn't reduce the number of separate scripts an ASP.NET AJAX page may be using. Besides the framework scripts `MicrosoftAjax.js` (the core framework) and `MicrosoftAjaxWebForms.js` (for partial rendering), there may be additional script references specified in the ScriptManager. ASP.NET AJAX compatible controls and components on the page may each require additional scripts that are embedded in their respective assemblies, adding even further to the number of scripts the page requires. A page can easily require a dozen or more scripts, even if there are no script references declared.

Script references are rendered as `<script>` elements at the top of the form. Each reference is processed by the browser, which issues a request to the server. Requests involve overhead to process, and involve network latency. If there are a dozen script references, there will be a dozen requests to the server, each with its own overhead and network latency. Script references are typically cached on the client thereafter, but if many of your users are first-time visitors that do not have a saturated cache, that may not be of much help.

It may not seem so bad. If the browser requested all 12 scripts simultaneously, they could load in parallel. However, that is not how the browser does it. Since one script may depend on another, the browser must load them in sequential order. Also, since scripts may contain calls to `document.write`, browsers load them each synchronously. Even if the browser could load them in parallel, it is limited to just two active connections to a single domain at a time.

All of this means that the user must wait for scripts to download and execute before the page even becomes visible, which can cause the page to feel slow to load. ScriptManager allows you to reduce the number of scripts your page requires by giving you the ability to combine scripts from different sources into one automatically. To do so, simply declare the script references inside the `CompositeScript` element:

```
<asp:ScriptManager runat="server" ID="ScriptManager1">
    <CompositeScript>
```

```
        <Scripts>
            <asp:ScriptReference Name="MicrosoftAjax.js" />
            <asp:ScriptReference Name="MicrosoftAjaxWebForms.js" />
        </Scripts>
    </CompositeScript>
</asp:ScriptManager>
```

If your page uses an UpdatePanel, it requires at least these two scripts. This combines them into one. In this case, the scripts are resources built into the framework, but you can also specify your own embedded scripts and path-based scripts, or any combination of these.

```
<asp:ScriptManager runat="server" ID="ScriptManager1">
    <CompositeScript>
        <Scripts>
            <asp:ScriptReference Name="MicrosoftAjax.js" />
            <asp:ScriptReference Name="MicrosoftAjaxWebForms.js" />
            <asp:ScriptReference Name="MyEmbeddedScript.js" Assembly="MyAssembly" />
            <asp:ScriptReference Path="~/PathBasedScript.js"  />
            <asp:ScriptReference Name="ComponentEmbeddedScript.js"
                Assembly="ComponentAssembly" Path="ExtractedComponentScript.js" />
        </Scripts>
    </CompositeScript>
</asp:ScriptManager>
```

MyEmbeddedScript.js is an embedded resource in the MyAssembly assembly, PathBasedScript.js is a static script file in the root of the Web application, and ComponentEmbeddedScript.js is an embedded resource in a referenced assembly from a third-party component that has been extracted and put on disk for customization. All of these script references work as they normally do, but they are all combined into a single script on the server and rendered as a single reference to the ScriptResource.axd handler.

Determining Which Scripts to Combine

You might wonder why all scripts for a given page aren't just automatically combined by the framework, all the time. During development, the ASP.NET AJAX team considered an automatic combining option. At first, that seems like a good idea. With very little effort, you could quickly and easily reduce your page's script count. However, the team quickly realized that it's actually possible for combining scripts to *hurt* the overall performance of your site. Each combination of scripts forms a unique script, separately cached by the browser. It requires careful consideration of the scripts you are using and how users typically navigate through your site to get the maximum benefit out of script combining.

Consider the following example. Your site consists of two pages: Page 1 and Page 2. Page 1 uses scripts A, B, and C. Page 2 uses scripts C and D. If on Page 1 you combined scripts A, B, and C, and on Page 2 you combined C and D, then upon navigating to Page 2, the user will actually be downloading script C for the second time! The individual performance of each page is better on its own than it is with no combining. However, without combining, the user would only have had to download script D when going to Page 2, so the actual performance of Page 2 is slower with full script combining. More bandwidth is used, as well.

What can you do to improve performance of each page and of the site in general? As you can see, it depends largely on the usage pattern of your site. You could combine only A and B on Page 1. Then, users would get two scripts on Page 1 — the combined A and B, and separately, C. When navigating to Page 2, they'd only need to download script D. This reduces redundant bandwidth downloading script C, but Page 1 still has two scripts, and if someone navigates directly to Page 2, there are also two scripts. So things are better than without any script combining, but perhaps there is room for improvement.

There is no golden rule with script combining, just some general guidelines you can follow:

❑ Think of your pages as groups of functionality. If there's a certain set of pages that users are likely to visit together in one session (such as a search results page and a detail page), and they all require about the same scripts, it may be best to use a combination of scripts common to all pages in that set. For example, combine scripts A, B, C and D on both Page 1 and 2. Whatever page the user hits first, they "front load" all the scripts they are likely to use in this session. Upon navigating to another page in the group, there are zero scripts to download.

❑ Avoid combinations that are different but contain a common script, as it will cause the common script to be downloaded separately with each combination.

❑ Keep script combinations in a particular order. If there are two combinations that contain the same scripts but in a different order, they each have different URLs, and so are cached separately.

Combining Scripts Manually

Just like normal ScriptReferences, the `CompositeScript` element of the ScriptManager supports the `Path` attribute. By specifying scripts within a `CompositeScript` element and specifying the path to a static script file, you are substituting all scripts in the combination for the static script.

```
<asp:ScriptManager runat="server" ID="ScriptManager1">
    <CompositeScript Path="~/Scripts/CombinedScript.js">
        <Scripts>
            <asp:ScriptReference Name="MicrosoftAjax.js" />
            <asp:ScriptReference Name="MicrosoftAjaxWebForms.js" />
            <asp:ScriptReference Name="MyEmbeddedScript.js" Assembly="MyAssembly"
/>
            <asp:ScriptReference Path="~/PathBasedScript.js" />
            <asp:ScriptReference Name="ComponentEmbeddedScript.js"
                Assembly="ComponentAssembly" Path="ExtractedComponentScript.js" />
        </Scripts>
    </CompositeScript>
</asp:ScriptManager>
```

In this example, all the script references are combined into the `CombinedScript.js` in the Scripts directory, a task that you must do yourself rather than allowing ScriptManager to do automatically. This really maximizes the performance of your page! Not only are all the scripts combined into one, they are loaded statically from disk, which involves less overhead than retrieving it from the `ScriptResource.axd` handler. It also reduces the size of the rendered HTML, since multiple script elements are now one, and its URL is just a short path. Automatically combined scripts result in a long URL, because information about each of the scripts is encoded within it.

Of course, this feature requires that you combine the scripts yourself. The simplest way to do that is — you guessed it — use script combining! Simply specify your script references, view the page in the browser, look at the HTML source, paste the `ScriptResource.axd` URL into the browser's address bar, and you have your combined script.

The Script Reference Profiler

It's not always obvious what scripts your page requires because you may be using a number of third-party components that register scripts automatically with the ScriptManager. Viewing the HTML source of your page doesn't help much, since those scripts are likely embedded resources, and so are served through a `ScriptResource.axd` URL, which doesn't give any clues as to which script it is for. Conceivably, you could use the `ResolveScriptReference` event of the ScriptManager to determine all the scripts required by your page. But thankfully, a tool already exists: the Script Reference Profiler. Just put the Script Reference Profiler control on your page, and it lists exactly the scripts that have been registered. Then all you need to do is copy and paste the list into the `CompositeScript` reference. You can download the tool from `codeplex.com/aspnet/Release/ProjectReleases .aspx?ReleaseId=13356`.

Compatibility

Those who have written custom controls for ASP.NET 2.0 may look at the ScriptManager in ASP.NET 3.5 and wonder why many of the APIs are the same as what already exists on the ClientScriptManager object. The ASP.NET 2.0 ClientScriptManager was written to support postbacks and callbacks where the burden of partial page updates was left to the control developer. The ScriptManager focuses on enabling partial page rendering for controls natively. To allow the ScriptManager to effectively update parts of the page, custom controls need to use its methods for registering script so that partial page updates will correctly manage the script with the browser.

Controls can typically be updated to work with partial rendering by simply exchanging the calls to the ClientScriptManager for calls to the new ScriptManager control. For example, the ASP.NET validator controls registered JavaScript with the ClientScriptManager and would fail to execute correctly during partial page updates but work correctly after being updated to call the equivalent ScriptManager controls.

The ScriptManager methods for script registration are static and have the same signature as those on the ClientScriptManager, except for their first parameter. The first parameter is a control, and is meant to be set to the control that is registering the resource or the page if it is page code doing the registration. This allows ScriptManager to determine which controls on a page require which resources.

Summary

The ScriptManager is the centerpiece of ASP.NET AJAX functionality. It controls the switching between release and debug versions of scripts. You saw how to create embedded script resources and register them with the ScriptManager to get automatic switching between versions.

The ScriptManager lets you specify Web service references and produces JavaScript proxies for easily calling them from the browser. JSON serialization is used to efficiently move data between client and server without some of the overhead associated with XML formatting.

The ScriptManager also provides access to the Authentication, Role, and Profile features of ASP.NET. This allows you more control over when and how you secure your application and leverage personalization data.

Script combining is a powerful feature that allows you to maximize the performance of script loading, if used properly, by reducing the number of scripts the user must download.

To participate in partial rendering with the UpdatePanel, controls need to use the script registration APIs on the ScriptManager. The ScriptManager can then control when and how the script is available in the browser to allow partial updates to happen and avoid reloading script unnecessarily.

6

Controlling the Back Button

AJAX applications make asynchronous, out-of-band calls to the server, and typically update the page dynamically based on the data returned. The result is a seamless incremental update to the page without fully reloading it. However, while this mechanism enables some wonderful applications, it completely bypasses one of the browser features users are most familiar with — navigation history. Because the update to the page is done in the background and the page is not actually reloaded, the user is technically always on the same page. But if large changes are made to the page, they may not feel like it is the same page, and so would probably expect that clicking their browser's back button would take them to the previous state. Unfortunately, they are going to end up on whatever page they were on before first loading that page, which could even be another Web site.

It may seem that the back button is basically broken in AJAX applications, unless care is taken to restore it to normal operation. But actually, an AJAX application gains greater control over the navigation history than is possible with a traditional application! Using the tools you will learn about in this chapter, you will see how to take control over when the browser creates history points, making it possible to choose exactly which operations should get them, and which should not.

The Document Fragment Indicator

Browsers don't only create navigation history points when a page loads. For years they have supported *fragment indicators*. You may have used this feature before. Most commonly it is used to allow for links on a document to point to different sections of it. For example, a long listing of products on a product listing page might include a "back to top" link after each product, which returns the user back to the top of the document when clicking on it. These types of links use anchor tags whose href value uses the # symbol, known as a fragment indicator. It tells the browser to jump the scroll position to the portion of the page with that name.

```
<a name="top"></a>
...
<a href="#here">Back to Top</a>
```

The great thing about this browser feature is that it creates a navigation history point even though the page isn't actually changed. This makes it the perfect candidate for adding logical navigation points to an AJAX-enabled page.

Sample Application

In this section you look at an application that does not useASP.NET AJAX to see how it behaves with regard to browser history points and some of the problems they cause. Listing 6-1 (`AlbumSearch.aspx`), included in the sample code for this chapter, along with Listing 6-2 (`AlbumSearch.aspx.cs`), is a Web page that allows the user to search for a Phish album by name by typing in a search box and clicking the search button. Search results are displayed in a `ListView` control, and there are buttons for sorting the results by Title or Release Date.

Listing 6-1: AlbumSearch.aspx

```
<%@ Page Language="C#" CodeFile="AlbumSearch.aspx.cs" Inherits="AlbumSearch" %>
<!DOCTYPE html PUBLIC "-//W3C//DTD XHTML 1.0 Transitional//EN" "http://www.w3.org/
    TR/xhtml1/DTD/xhtml1-transitional.dtd">
<html xmlns="http://www.w3.org/1999/xhtml">
<head runat="server">
    <title>Phish Album Search</title>
</head>
<body>
    <form id="form1" runat="server">
    <asp:TextBox id="txtSearch" runat="server" />
    <asp:Button ID="cmdSearch" runat="server" Text="Search" />

    <asp:ListView ID="AlbumList" runat="server">
        <LayoutTemplate>
            <p>
            Sort Order:
            [<asp:LinkButton ID="SortByTitle" runat="server"
                CommandName="Sort" CommandArgument="Title"
                Text="Title" /> |
            <asp:LinkButton ID="SortByDate" runat="server"
                CommandName="Sort" CommandArgument="ReleaseDate"
                Text="Release Date" />]
            </p>
            <div id="itemPlaceholder" runat="server"></div>
        </LayoutTemplate>
        <ItemTemplate>
            <div style="font-weight:bold">
                <%# Eval("Title") %>
            </div>
            <div style="font-style:italic">
                Released
                <%# Eval("ReleaseDate", "{0:MMM dd, yyyy}") %>
            </div>
        </ItemTemplate>
        <ItemSeparatorTemplate>
            <hr />
```

Listing 6-1: AlbumSearch.aspx *(continued)*

```
            </ItemSeparatorTemplate>
        </asp:ListView>
        </form>
    </body>
    </html>
```

A textbox and button serve as the search area. A ListView control displays the search results, and contains two LinkButton controls for sorting by Title or Release Date. The code-behind in Listing 6-2 (AlbumSearch.aspx.cs) shows how it is wired all together.

Listing 6-2: AlbumSearch.aspx.cs

```csharp
using System;
using System.Linq;
using System.Web.UI;
using Wrox.ASPAJAX.Samples;

public partial class AlbumSearch : System.Web.UI.Page
{
    protected override void OnInit(EventArgs e) {
        cmdSearch.Click += cmdSearch_Click;
        AlbumList.Sorting += AlbumList_Sorting;
        base.OnInit(e);
    }

    private void AlbumList_Sorting(object sender, System.Web.UI.WebControls.
        ListViewSortEventArgs e) {
        AlbumList.DataSource = FindAlbums(ViewState["CurrentTerm"] as string,
        e.SortExpression);
        AlbumList.DataBind();
    }

    private void cmdSearch_Click(object sender, EventArgs e) {
        string term;
        ViewState["CurrentTerm"] = term = txtSearch.Text;
        AlbumList.DataSource = FindAlbums(term, "");
        AlbumList.DataBind();
    }

    protected override void Render(HtmlTextWriter writer) {
        string term = ViewState["CurrentTerm"] as string;
        if (!String.IsNullOrEmpty(term)) {
            Page.Title = "Phish Album Search - \"" + Server.HtmlEncode(term) +
    "\"";
        }
        else {
            Page.Title = "Phish Album Search";
        }
        base.Render(writer);
```

Continued

Listing 6-2: AlbumSearch.aspx.cs *(continued)*

```
    }

    private object FindAlbums(string searchTerm, string orderBy) {
        return from album in Album.PhishAlbums
                where album.Title.IndexOf(searchTerm,
 StringComparison.OrdinalIgnoreCase) != -1
                orderby orderBy == "Title" ? (object)album.Title :
 (object)album.ReleaseDate
                    select album;
    }
}
```

Note that both searching and sorting causes a full page refresh, as it posts back to the server. Figure 6-1 shows the results after performing the following sequence.

1. Search for "blue."

2. Sort by Release Date.

3. Search for "live."

4. Sort by Release Date.

5. Sort by Title.

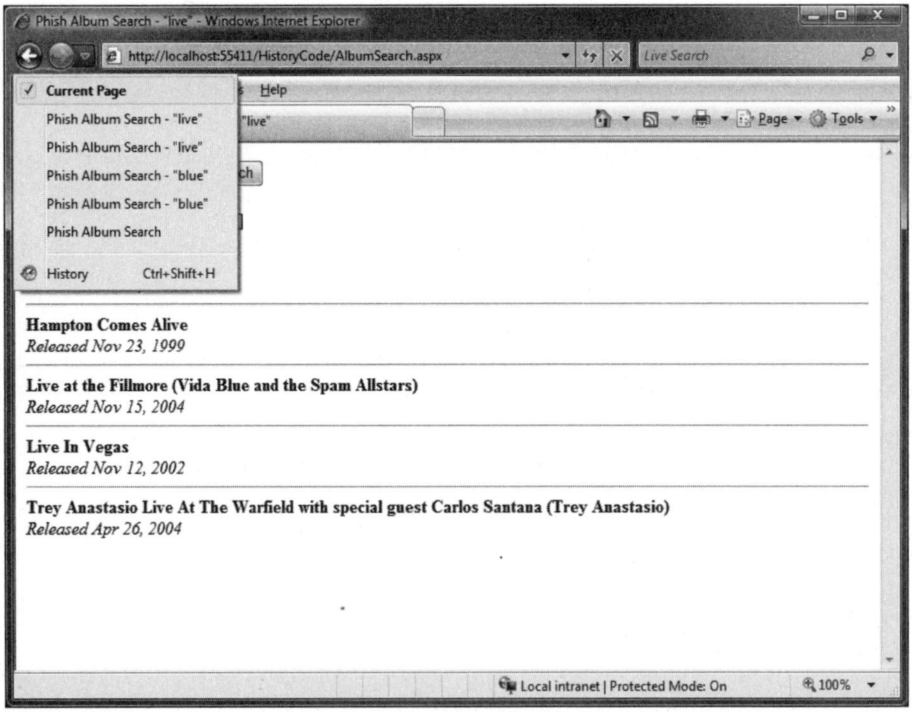

Figure 6-1

The back button menu shown in Figure 6-1 displays all of the history points the browser created while performing these steps. Notice that the page title includes the search term, and that each one is listed twice. This is because after each search the results are sorted, resulting in another postback with the same search term. Also, clicking back doesn't do what you want it to do here. For the purpose of this Web page, you want the back and forward buttons to jump between different searches, not including any sorting the user has performed between searches. But currently, clicking back will merely change the sort order back to Release Date. You have to click back a second time to get back to the search results for "live."

There is yet another problem with this Web page. Because each of these operations is a postback, the browser displays a scary warning dialog stating that it must resubmit the data to the server if the user attempts to refresh the page. Figure 6-2 shows what this dialog looks like in Internet Explorer. Other browsers have similar dialogs.

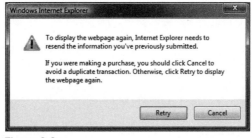

Figure 6-2

Enabling Partial Updates

You can easily get rid of this warning dialog by using AJAX techniques to update the page. That way, the page isn't actually reloading, so the browser can refresh the page without warning the user. The simplest way to do that of course is to wrap the search box and ListView in an UpdatePanel control, as in Listing 6-3 (`AlbumSearchUpdatePanel.aspx`). The code-behind for this page (`AlbumSearchUpdatePanel.aspx.cs`) is the same as in Listing 6-2 since no logic has changed, except the class name is `AlbumSearchUpdatePanel`.

Listing 6-3: AlbumSearchUpdatePanel.aspx

```
<%@ Page Language="C#" CodeFile="AlbumSearchUpdatePanel.aspx.cs"
    Inherits="AlbumSearchUpdatePanel" %>
<!DOCTYPE html PUBLIC "-//W3C//DTD XHTML 1.0 Transitional//EN"
    "http://www.w3.org/TR/xhtml1/DTD/xhtml1-transitional.dtd">
<html xmlns="http://www.w3.org/1999/xhtml">
<head runat="server">
    <title>Phish Album Search</title>
</head>
<body>
    <form id="form1" runat="server">
    <asp:ScriptManager ID="ScriptManager1" runat="server" />
```

Continued

Listing 6-3: AlbumSearchUpdatePanel.aspx *(continued)*

```
<asp:UpdatePanel ID="UpdatePanel1" runat="server">
    <ContentTemplate>
        <asp:TextBox id="txtSearch" runat="server" />
        <asp:Button ID="cmdSearch" runat="server" Text="Search" />
        <asp:ListView ID="AlbumList" runat="server">
            <LayoutTemplate>
                <p>
                Sort Order:
                [<asp:LinkButton ID="SortByTitle" runat="server"
                    CommandName="Sort" CommandArgument="Title"
                    Text="Title" /> |
                <asp:LinkButton ID="SortByDate" runat="server"
                    CommandName="Sort" CommandArgument="ReleaseDate"
                    Text="Release Date" />]
                </p>
                <div id="itemPlaceholder" runat="server"></div>
            </LayoutTemplate>
            <ItemTemplate>
                <div style="font-weight:bold">
                    <%# Eval("Title") %>
                </div>
                <div style="font-style:italic">
                    Released
                    <%# Eval("ReleaseDate", "{0:MMM dd, yyyy}") %>
                </div>
            </ItemTemplate>
            <ItemSeparatorTemplate>
                <hr />
            </ItemSeparatorTemplate>
        </asp:ListView>
    </ContentTemplate>
</asp:UpdatePanel>
    </form>
</body>
</html>
```

The Web page now seems more responsive thanks to the incremental updates and lack of a full-page refresh, and now you can refresh the page without that pesky dialog. However, refreshing the page returns it to its original state, with no search term selected. And now the back button support in the application is even worse; now nothing creates history points! Note the disabled back button in Figure 6-3.

Adding History Support

Now that you have seen the AJAX enabled application, you are ready to see how start controlling the navigation history. History support is built into the framework, but it is disabled by default because it performs some initialization on the page that would be unnecessary if you weren't using the feature. For example, it requires a hidden IFRAME to work on some browsers, which is created for you automatically. To enable history support, set the EnableHistory property on the ScriptManager.

```
<asp:ScriptManager id="ScriptManager1" runat="server" EnableHistory="true" />
```

Figure 6-3

When using history there are two tasks you are mainly concerned with: creating history points and handling navigation events. To create a history point, you associate a value with it by calling the AddHistoryPoint method on the ScriptManager.

```
ScriptManager1.AddHistoryPoint(key, value, title);
```

The value is important because you use it to restore state when a navigation event occurs. History maintains values as a list of key-value pairs, so it is possible for multiple components on a page to maintain history points without interfering with one another, if they use different keys. In addition to the key and value, you can optionally associate a title with the history point, which will appear as the page title in the browser's history.

When the user uses one of the history points you have added, the ScriptManager raises a Navigate event. The event receives a HistoryEventArgs instance, which contains the key-value collection at that point in history. Here, you retrieve the same value you added when calling AddHistoryPoint, which you can use to restore the state of the application as appropriate.

```
ScriptManager1.Navigate +=
    new EventHandler<HistoryEventArgs>(ScriptManager1_Navigate);

private void ScriptManager1_Navigate(object sender, HistoryEventArgs e)
{
    string value = e.State["key"];
}
```

It is important to know that when adding history points from the server-side, navigation events are handled by performing a postback. Later you will see how to add history points purely on the client, which does not necessarily require a postback to process. Because navigation events are a form of asynchronous postback, it's important that you do not add a history point while navigating. Clicking the back button should "consume" a history point, not create a new one! Depending on your scenario, you may or may not know whether an event that is occurring was caused by a normal user operation or a navigation event. Thankfully, when in doubt you can always check the IsNavigating property.

```
if (!ScriptManager1.IsNavigating) {
    // add history point
}
```

That's all there is to it. Adding history points and handling the navigation event is all you have to do. Listing 6-4 (AlbumSearchHistory.aspx) is the markup for the history enabled album search page. The differences from the previous version are highlighted.

Listing 6-4: AlbumSearchHistory.aspx

```
<%@ Page Language="C#" CodeFile="AlbumSearchHistory.aspx.cs"
    Inherits="AlbumSearchHistory" %>
<!DOCTYPE html PUBLIC "-//W3C//DTD XHTML 1.0 Transitional//EN"
    "http://www.w3.org/TR/xhtml1/DTD/xhtml1-transitional.dtd">
<html xmlns="http://www.w3.org/1999/xhtml">
<head runat="server">
    <title>Phish Album Search</title>
</head>
<body>
    <form id="form1" runat="server">
    <asp:ScriptManager ID="ScriptManager1" runat="server"
        EnableHistory="true" />
    <asp:UpdatePanel ID="UpdatePanel1" runat="server">
        <ContentTemplate>
        <asp:TextBox id="txtSearch" runat="server" />
        <asp:Button ID="cmdSearch" runat="server" Text="Search" />
        <asp:ListView ID="AlbumList" runat="server">
            <LayoutTemplate>
                <p>
                Sort Order:
                [<asp:LinkButton ID="SortByTitle" runat="server"
                    CommandName="Sort" CommandArgument="Title"
                    Text="Title" /> |
                <asp:LinkButton ID="SortByDate" runat="server"
                    CommandName="Sort" CommandArgument="ReleaseDate"
                    Text="Release Date" />]
                </p>
                <div id="itemPlaceholder" runat="server"></div>
            </LayoutTemplate>
            <ItemTemplate>
                <div style="font-weight:bold">
                    <%# Eval("Title") %>
                </div>
                <div style="font-style:italic">
                    Released
```

Listing 6-4: AlbumSearchHistory.aspx *(continued)*

```
                    <%# Eval("ReleaseDate", "{0:MMM dd, yyyy}") %>
                </div>
            </ItemTemplate>
            <ItemSeparatorTemplate>
                <hr />
            </ItemSeparatorTemplate>
        </asp:ListView>
        </ContentTemplate>
    </asp:UpdatePanel>
    </form>
</body>
</html>
```

Listing 6-5 (`AlbumSearchHistory.aspx.cs`) is the history-enabled code-behind and highlights the differences from the previous version.

Listing 6-5: AlbumSearchHistory.aspx.cs

```csharp
using System;
using System.Linq;
using System.Web.UI;
using Wrox.ASPAJAX.Samples;

public partial class AlbumSearchHistory : System.Web.UI.Page
{
    protected override void OnInit(EventArgs e) {
        cmdSearch.Click += cmdSearch_Click;
        AlbumList.Sorting += AlbumList_Sorting;
        ScriptManager1.Navigate +=
            new EventHandler<HistoryEventArgs>(ScriptManager1_Navigate);
        base.OnInit(e);
    }

    private void ScriptManager1_Navigate(object sender, HistoryEventArgs e) {
        string term = e.State["term"];
        if (!String.IsNullOrEmpty(term)) {
            // restore the search results
            ViewState["CurrentTerm"] = txtSearch.Text = term;
            AlbumList.DataSource = FindAlbums(term, "");
            AlbumList.DataBind();
        }
        else {
            // navigated to the original state,
            // restore page with no results
            ViewState["CurrentTerm"] = txtSearch.Text = "";
            AlbumList.DataSource = null;
            AlbumList.DataBind();
        }
    }
```

Continued

191

Listing 6-5: AlbumSearchHistory.aspx.cs *(continued)*

```
private void AlbumList_Sorting(object sender,
    System.Web.UI.WebControls.ListViewSortEventArgs e) {
    AlbumList.DataSource = FindAlbums(ViewState["CurrentTerm"] as string,
    e.SortExpression);
    AlbumList.DataBind();
}

private void cmdSearch_Click(object sender, EventArgs e) {
    string term;
    ViewState["CurrentTerm"] = term = txtSearch.Text;
    AlbumList.DataSource = FindAlbums(term, "");
    AlbumList.DataBind();

    ScriptManager1.AddHistoryPoint("term", term,
        "Phish Album Search - \"" + Server.HtmlEncode(term) + "\"");
}

protected override void Render(HtmlTextWriter writer) {
    string term = ViewState["CurrentTerm"] as string;
    if (!String.IsNullOrEmpty(term)) {
        Page.Title = "Phish Album Search - \"" +
        Server.HtmlEncode(term) + "\"";
    }
    else {
        Page.Title = "Phish Album Search";
    }
    base.Render(writer);
}

private object FindAlbums(string searchTerm, string orderBy) {
    return from album in Album.PhishAlbums
            where album.Title.IndexOf(searchTerm,
                StringComparison.OrdinalIgnoreCase) != -1
            orderby orderBy == "Title" ? (object)album.Title :
                (object)album.ReleaseDate
            select album;
}
}
```

The `cmdSearch_Click` event fires when the user searches for an album. That is the only time history points to be added for this Web page. Notice that a history point is not added when the user sorts the results in the `AlbumList_Sorting` event.

The `ScriptManager1_Navigate` event handler is responsible for restoring the page state to what it should be based on the information added to the history point the user is navigating to. The search term is stored in history state, so we need to rerun the search term. But that is not all that needs to be done. When the user clicks back, the page performs an asynchronous postback. Only the changes you perform in the `Navigate` event cause changes in the page's resulting state. You are in complete control over the new state of the form. You should of course try to restore the state to what it actually was when the history point was added, but that may sometimes mean more than you imagine. For example, in this Web page besides rerunning the search term, the value of the Search TextBox must be reset to that term. Otherwise, the results are updated, but the TextBox still holds the same value! That might mean displaying the results for "blue" but seeing "live" in the textbox.

So when setting history points, be sure to take note of all the things on the page that the user might change, and be sure to store what state information makes sense in the history point. Not everything will be worth the effort of saving, so it is a judgment call only you can make for your particular page. For example, the state of a dynamically expanding TreeView or Menu control that may just happen to be on the side of the page may not be worth storing. Try to find the minimum set of data required.

Figure 6-4 shows the results of running the history-enabled album search application, performing the same sequence of searches used in the original search.

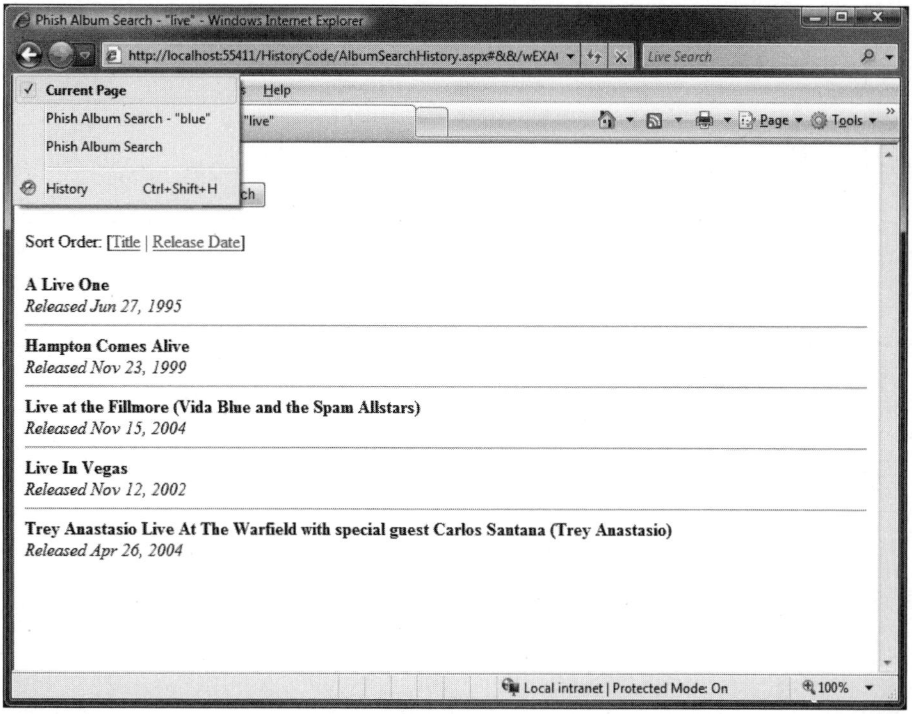

Figure 6-4

Compare the back button menu with that in Figure 6-1. Now there are no longer any duplicate entries! Clicking back and forward navigates through search terms, regardless of any sorting operations done between them.

Also interesting to note, the "click" sound you normally hear when navigating across pages in Internet Explorer doesn't occur when performing asynchronous postbacks, but it does when a navigation point has been added. You should hear the click sound when clicking the search button, but not when sorting, which adds further feedback to the user that they have performed an operation that the page considers a navigation event.

Remember the refresh button problem? In the original application, refreshing caused the browser to display a scary dialog. (Refer to Figure 6-2.) When including AJAX support, the dialog went away but refreshing reset the state of the page. In the history-enabled version, as an added bonus, refreshing the page does exactly what you would expect! It works because AJAX history state is stored in the document fragment, which is part of the URL as shown in Figure 6-5. Since it is part of the URL, it survives refreshes, and the state it represents is pushed through to the ScriptManager's `navigate` event.

Figure 6-5

State Encoding

By default, history points added from the server side are encoded or encrypted (depending on whether ViewState for the page is encrypted). This causes the data in the fragment indicator to look rather messy, as in Figure 6-5. This is the default behavior to protect the data from tampering by the user, since it is in plain sight on the URL, and is inevitably processed on the server. However, regardless of whether the data can be tampered with, you should treat history state as if it were user input. Don't trust it. Always validate that the data makes sense and is in the range of acceptable values for your application.

To turn encoding off, you set the `EnableSecureHistoryState` property `false`.

```
<asp:ScriptManager ID="ScriptManager1" runat="server"
    EnableHistory="true" EnableSecureHistoryState="false" />
```

Now the history state will be easily readable on the URL. For example, if you add two history points, you might see something like `http://localhost/Default.aspx#&&key1=value1&key2=value2`. The nice thing about this is it provides a clue about what loading the URL will do, and it gives advanced users a way to "hack" the URL. For example, if you're on a product listing page and see `product=widgets` in the URL, you know you could probably just change it to `product=wedges`, to see wedges instead. While you certainly shouldn't rely on that kind of navigation as a primary means of navigating your site, it gives your site an organized feel. Just be sure to expect garbage values and handle them accordingly!

Managing History Client-Side

So far you have seen how to add history points and handle the navigation event only from server-side code. When history points are used in combination with an UpdatePanel control, they provide an extremely easy way to manage history. But wrapping content in an UpdatePanel is not the only way to write an ASP.NET AJAX page. When an UpdatePanel refreshes, although the page does not fully reload, the entire page is still being posted back to the server. This is necessary for UpdatePanel to integrate seamlessly with the server-side page model. But often it is more efficient to incrementally update the page content in the more traditional AJAX style, by calling a Web service or other end point to fetch data, and to rebuild HTML on the client-side based on that data. Such a mechanism does not rely on ASP.NET postbacks, and so the ScriptManager's server-side APIs for managing history are not available. Thankfully, ASP.NET AJAX History supports a purely client-side approach as well.

Client-Side Updates

Using the client-side history APIs is just as easy as using them server-side. To illustrate, Listing 6-6 (AlbumSearchClient.aspx) shows the original album search application converted to work using client-side techniques.

Listing 6-6: AlbumSearchClient.aspx

```csharp
<%@ Page Language="C#" %>
<!DOCTYPE html PUBLIC "-//W3C//DTD XHTML 1.0 Transitional//EN" "http://www.w3.org/
    TR/xhtml1/DTD/xhtml1-transitional.dtd">
<html xmlns="http://www.w3.org/1999/xhtml">
<head runat="server">
    <title>Phish Album Search</title>
    <script type="text/javascript">
    var Albums = [
        { title: "A Live One", date: "1995/06/27" },
        { title: "Hampton Comes Alive", date: "1999/11/23" },
        { title: "Live In Vegas", date: "2002/11/12" },
        { title: "Vida Blue", date: "2002/06/25" },
        { title: "The Illustrated Band (Vida Blue)", date: "2003/10/14" }
    ];

    function executeSearch() {
        var term = $get('txtSearch').value.toLowerCase();
        var results = [];
        for (var i = 0; i < Albums.length; i++) {
            var album = Albums[i];
            if (album.title.toLowerCase().indexOf(term) !== -1) {
                results.push(album);
            }
        }
        printResults(results);
        document.title = 'Phish Album Search - "' + term + '"';
    }

    function printResults(results) {
        var list = $get('albumList');
        list.innerHTML = "";

        var sb = new Sys.StringBuilder();
        for (var i = 0; i < results.length; i++) {
            var album = results[i];
            if (!sb.isEmpty()) {
                sb.append("<hr/>");
            }
```

Continued

Listing 6-6: AlbumSearchClient.aspx *(continued)*

```
                sb.append("<div style='font-weight:bold'>");
                sb.append(album.title);
                sb.append("</div><div style='font-style:italic'>Released ");
                sb.append(new Date(album.date).format("MMM dd, yyyy"));
                sb.append("</div>");
            }
            list.innerHTML = sb.toString();
        }
    </script>
</head>
<body>
    <form id="form1" runat="server">
    <asp:ScriptManager ID="ScriptManager1" runat="server" />

    <input type="text" id="txtSearch" />
    <input type="button" value="Search" onclick="executeSearch()" />

    <div id="albumList">
    </div>
    </form>
</body>
</html>
```

Rather than use a ListView control on the server to render data that came from the server, this code builds the HTML dynamically on the client based on data retrieved only on the client side, via the `printResults()` function. For simplicity, the data is declared inline on the page in the `Albums` global array. Normally, this data would be retrieved by other means, such as by calling a Web service. The `executeSearch()` function filters the `Albums` array based on the occurrence of the search term in the album titles. Also for simplicity, sort functionality is missing, but could easily be added. Figure 6-6 shows the page running after performing a search.

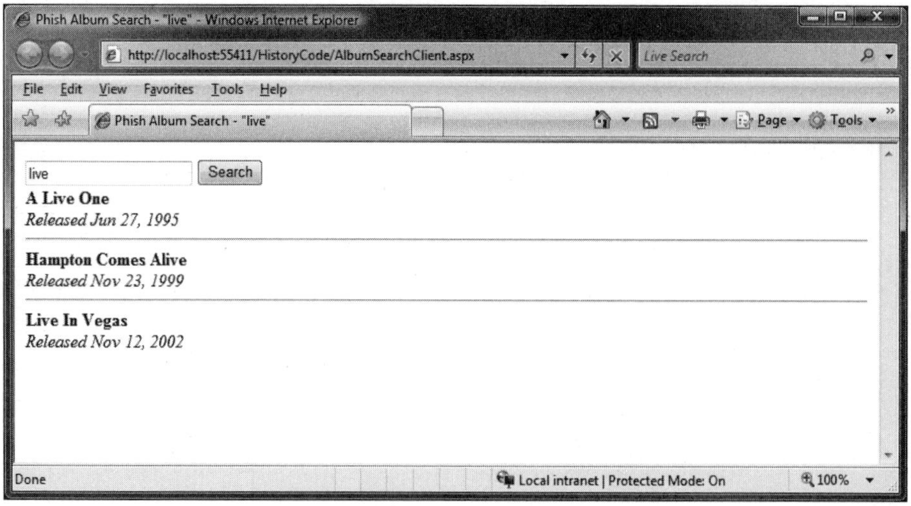

Figure 6-6

Notice the back button is disabled, as expected based on what the code is doing. Similar to the UpdatePanel based solution, there is no page reloading here, so the browser does not create any history points.

Adding History Support

Adding history support is just a matter of calling the equivalent client-side APIs on the `Sys.Application` client class instead of the ScriptManager. Listing 6-7 (`AlbumSearchClientHistory.aspx`) shows the necessary changes.

Listing 6-7: AlbumSearchClientHistory.aspx

```
<%@ Page Language="C#" %>
<!DOCTYPE html PUBLIC "-//W3C//DTD XHTML 1.0 Transitional//EN" "http://www.w3.org/
    TR/xhtml1/DTD/xhtml1-transitional.dtd">
<html xmlns="http://www.w3.org/1999/xhtml">
<head runat="server">
    <title>Phish Album Search</title>
    <script type="text/javascript">
    var Albums = [
        { title: "A Live One", date: "1995/06/27" },
        { title: "Hampton Comes Alive", date: "1999/11/23" },
        { title: "Live In Vegas", date: "2002/11/12" },
        { title: "Vida Blue", date: "2002/06/25" },
        { title: "The Illustrated Band (Vida Blue)", date: "2003/10/14" }
    ];

    function onSearch() {
        var term = $get('txtSearch').value.toLowerCase();
        var title = 'Phish Album Search - "' + term + '"';
        Sys.Application.addHistoryPoint({ term: term }, title);
    }

    function executeSearch() {
        var term = $get('txtSearch').value.toLowerCase();
        var results = [];
        for (var i = 0; i < Albums.length; i++) {
            var album = Albums[i];
            if (album.title.toLowerCase().indexOf(term) !== -1) {
                results.push(album);
            }
        }
        printResults(results);
        var title = 'Phish Album Search - "' + term + '"';
        document.title = title;
    }

    function printResults(results) {
        var list = $get('albumList');
        list.innerHTML = "";

        var sb = new Sys.StringBuilder();
```

Continued

Listing 6-7: AlbumSearchClientHistory.aspx *(continued)*

```
                for (var i = 0; i < results.length; i++) {
                    var album = results[i];
                    if (!sb.isEmpty()) {
                        sb.append("<hr/>");
                    }
                    sb.append("<div style='font-weight:bold'>");
                    sb.append(album.title);
                    sb.append("</div><div style='font-style:italic'>Released ");
                    sb.append(new Date(album.date).format("MMM dd, yyyy"));
                    sb.append("</div>");
                }
                list.innerHTML = sb.toString();
            }

            function onNavigate(sender, args) {
                $get('txtSearch').value = (args.get_state().term || "");
                executeSearch();
            }
        </script>
    </head>
    <body>
        <form id="form1" runat="server">
        <asp:ScriptManager ID="ScriptManager1" runat="server"
            EnableHistory="true" ClientNavigateHandler="onNavigate" />

        <input type="text" id="txtSearch" />
        <input type="button" value="Search" onclick="onSearch()" />

        <div id="albumList">
        </div>
        </form>
    </body>
</html>
```

First, you set the `EnableHistory` property of the ScriptManager to `true`, just like for server-side support. Even though you are using history points only client-side, you must still enable it. Actually, it is possible to use client-side history without enabling it on the ScriptManager, and in fact, without a ScriptManager or even ASP.NET, but doing so requires setting up an IFRAME in Internet Explorer. Using the document fragment for history management in a manner that works across all browsers is tricky business, and this just happens to be one of the requirements for it to work in Internet Explorer. ScriptManager does this for you automatically. If you are still interested in doing it manually, you can attempt to use history to see a very detailed error message explaining the requirements, as in Figure 6-7.

Next, you set the ScriptManager `ClientNavigateHandler` property. This is a shortcut to declaring an event handler for the client-side `Sys.Application.navigate` event, equivalent to the server-side `ScriptManager.Navigate` event. You may also hook into in the usual client-side way, but be sure to do it with inline code inside of the `<form>` element. Putting it in the `<head>` element fails because the `Sys.Application` class has not been created yet at that point, and putting it inside the `pageLoad` function is too late, as a navigate event occurs before the `Sys.Application.load` event occurs if the user refreshes the page or links to your page with the document fragment already set:

```
Sys.Application.add_navigate(onNavigate);
```

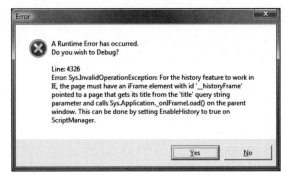

Figure 6-7

To add a history point, call the `Sys.Application.addHistoryPoint` method:

```
Sys.Application.addHistoryPoint({ term: term }, title);
```

The first argument accepts a JavaScript object that serves as a dictionary of key-value pairs. The `{ }` block is a short-hand way of creating such an object in JavaScript. The second argument is the optional title of the history point.

Unlike the server-side, when adding a history point client-side, the navigate event is immediately fired. So rather than the search button executing the search and then adding the history point, it adds only the history point. That causes the `ClientNavigateHandler` to execute, which executes the search. If the search button directly executes the search, the search is performed twice: once when the search is executed and again when the navigate event fires as a result of adding the history point.

```
function onSearch() {
    var term = $get('txtSearch').value.toLowerCase();
    var title = 'Phish Album Search - "' + term + '"';
    Sys.Application.addHistoryPoint({ term: term }, title);
}
```

And again, just like the server-side navigate event handler, the client-side navigate event handler is responsible for restoring the state of the page at the time the history point was added.

```
function onNavigate(sender, args) {
    $get('txtSearch').value = (args.get_state().term || "");
    executeSearch();
}
```

The `args` parameter is of type `Sys.HistoryEventArgs`, which has a `state` property. The state is the name-value pair object containing all the history point data, so the `term` field is used to retrieve the value. However, it is possible for there to be no term, such as when the user clicks back all the way to when they first loaded the page and hadn't performed a search yet. In JavaScript, the term would be `undefined`. In that case, an empty string should be the search term. Using the or-operator `||` with an empty string ensures the value is an empty string in that case. Figure 6-8 shows the result after searching for "blue" and "live."

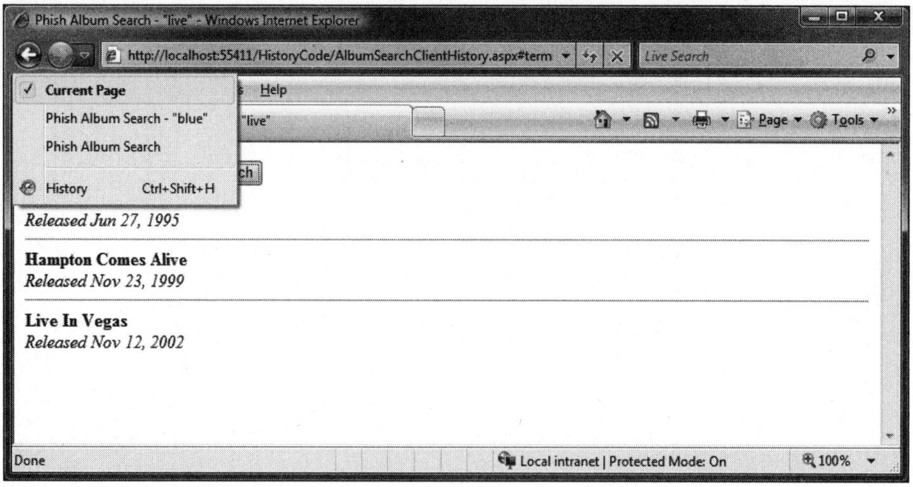

Figure 6-8

Deep Linking

Another fortunate side effect of adding history support to your pages is that it enables users to bookmark the page at a particular state and return to it later. For example, in the album search application, after performing a search for "blue," the user may bookmark the page or copy and paste the URL to share with others. Since the search term is encoded on the URL, the search is automatically restored to "blue" when the user returns.

Summary

While AJAX applications can tremendously improve the user experience, they don't naturally integrate with the browser navigation history feature. However, even normal Web applications suffer from poor integration with navigation history. Enabling navigation history support on an ASP.NET AJAX page not only restores the functionality a non-AJAX page would have but can improve on it.

ASP.NET AJAX supports easily creating navigation history points programmatically from the server side or client side. Server-side history points integrates well with pages that use the UpdatePanel control, while client-side history points can be used no matter how partial updates are done, even if the server-side technology is not ASP.NET.

ASP.NET AJAX history enabled pages not only provide logical navigation points for the user, but they can handle refreshes by the user, and can naturally be bookmarked or "deep linked" so that users can return to a particular state of the AJAX page.

7

The ASP.NET AJAX Toolkit

With the installation of the .NET Framework 3.5 and through using Visual Studio 2008, you will find a few controls available that allow you to build ASP.NET applications with AJAX capabilities. The .NET Framework 3.5 is the framework that takes your applications to the next level. There is so much that you can accomplish with this framework, including adding specific AJAX capabilities to your user and custom server controls. Every little tweak you make to your application in adding AJAX enhancements will make your application seem more fluid and responsive to the end user.

You might be wondering where the big new AJAX-enabled server controls are for this edition of Visual Studio 2008 if this is indeed a new world for building controls. The reason you do not see a new section of AJAX server controls is that Microsoft's work in this space has been treated as an open-source project instead of just blending it into Visual Studio 2008 as a whole.

Developers at Microsoft and in the community have been working on a series of AJAX-capable server controls that you can use in your ASP.NET applications. These controls are collectively called the ASP.NET AJAX Control Toolkit. If you go to www.asp.net/ajax, you will find a link to the Control Toolkit for downloading. When you choose to download the Control Toolkit, you are directed to the ASP.NET AJAX Control Toolkit's page on CodePlex at www.codeplex.com/ Release/ProjectReleases.aspx?ReleaseId=16488. This page is presented in Figure 7-1.

As you have seen so far, ASP.NET AJAX is the foundation on which to build richer Web applications that leverage the browser more fully but it does not have the rich UI elements that really blur the distinction between Web and desktop applications. With the Microsoft AJAX Library, you can apply familiar object-oriented design concepts and use the scripts across a variety of modern browsers. The ASP.NET AJAX Extensions (a series of out-of-bound releases from the ASP.NET team to add extra functionality to the ASP.NET offering) include several powerful ASP.NET controls that make it easy to add AJAX functionality to an existing application or build better user experiences into a new application. The AJAX Toolkit was developed to provide some rich ASP.NET AJAX controls that you can use to make your Web applications really come to life. The Toolkit makes it easy to push the user interface of an application beyond what users expect from a Web application.

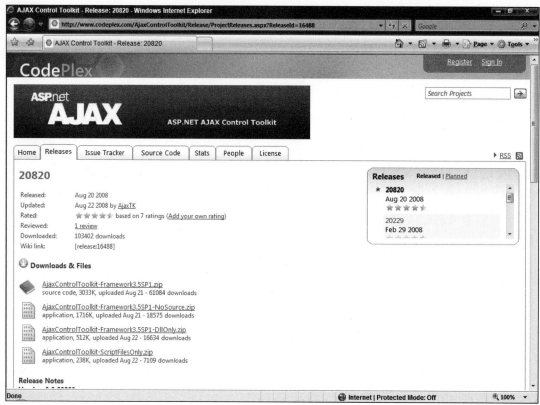

Figure 7-1

The Toolkit is a shared source project with code contributions from developers from Microsoft and elsewhere. Most developers who download the AJAX Extensions should also download the Toolkit for the additional set of controls it contains. The CodePlex project mentioned in this chapter allows you to download a compiled DLL with the controls and extenders, or you can download the source code and project files and compile it yourself. Either way, make sure that you add the DLL to your toolbox in Visual Studio, as described shortly.

The Toolkit contains some new controls that have AJAX functionality and many control extenders. The control extenders attach to another control to enhance or "extend" the control's functionality. When you install the Toolkit, it creates a sample Web application that includes examples that show how to use the controls. Because the controls cover such a wide variety of application-development areas, they are presented here in three categories: page layout controls, user interface effects, and pop-ups. Within each category, the controls are listed alphabetically; the control names are self-explanatory, so you will find it easy to locate the information you need when using this chapter for later reference.

Also, note that the Toolkit project is ongoing and will continue to evolve as developers contribute to it. This chapter is up to date as of the time of this writing, but I expect that more controls will be added to the Toolkit regularly.

Downloading and Installing

Since the ASP.NET AJAX Control Toolkit is not part of the default installation of Visual Studio 2008, you have to set the controls up yourself. At the Control Toolkit's site on CodePlex, there are a couple of options available to you.

First, you can download a Control Toolkit that is specifically targeted at Visual Studio 2008. On the CodePlex page for this project, there are two ways to do this. The ASP.NET AJAX Control Toolkit can be downloaded as source code or as a compiled DLL.

The source control option allows you to take the code for the controls and ASP.NET AJAX Extenders and change the behavior of the controls or extenders yourself. The DLL option is a single Visual Studio installer file and a sample application.

There are a couple of parts to the installation. One part provides a series of new controls that are built with AJAX capabilities in mind. Another part is a series of control extenders (extensions upon preexisting controls). You will also find some new template additions for your Visual Studio 2008.

To get set up, download the .zip file from the CodePlex site and unzip it where you want on your machine. The following sections show you how to work with the various parts of the Control Toolkit.

New Visual Studio Templates

Included in the download is a .vsi file (Visual Studio Installer) called AjaxControlExtender.vsi. This installer installs four new Visual Studio projects for your future use. The installer options are presented in Figure 7-2.

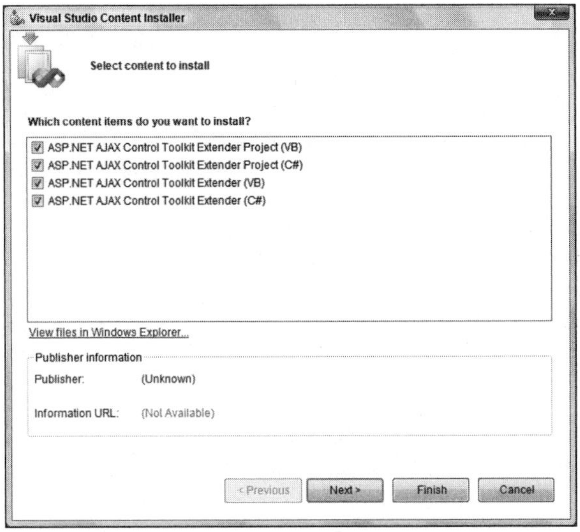

Figure 7-2

After installing these options, you have access to the new project types they provide, as illustrated here in Figure 7-3.

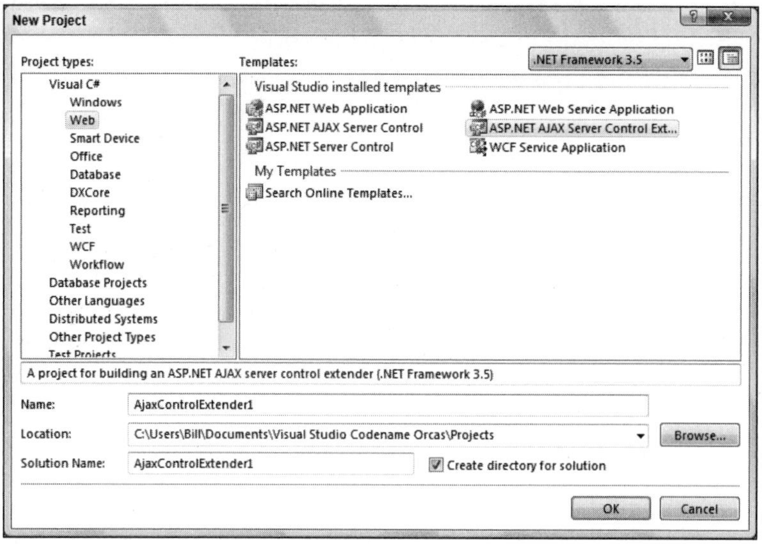

Figure 7-3

Adding the New Controls to the VS2008 Toolbox

In addition to new project types, you also have the ability to add the new controls that are available to your Visual Studio 2008 toolbox. To accomplish this task, right-click in the toolbox and select Add Tab from the provided menu. Name the tab as you wish; for this example the tab was named AJAX Controls.

With the new tab in your toolbox, right-click on the tab and select Choose Items from the provided menu. This action is illustrated in Figure 7-4.

Figure 7-4

Selecting Choose Items from the menu gives you the Choose Toolbox Items dialog. From there, select the AjaxControlToolkit.dll file from the sample application's Bin folder. Remember that the SampleWebSite is a component that was downloaded and unzipped as part of the Control Toolkit. Once you find the DLL and click on the Open button, the Choose Toolbox Items dialog changes to include the controls that are contained within this DLL. The controls are highlighted in the dialog and are already selected for you, as shown in Figure 7-5.

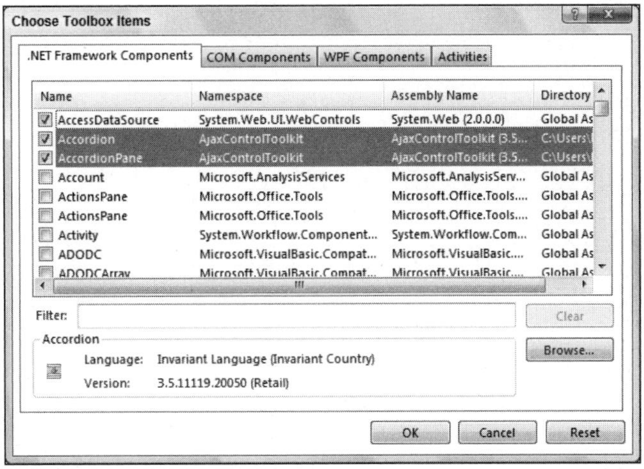

Figure 7-5

From here, click the OK button and the ASP.NET AJAX Control Toolkit's new controls will be added to your Visual Studio toolbox. The end result is presented in Figure 7-6.

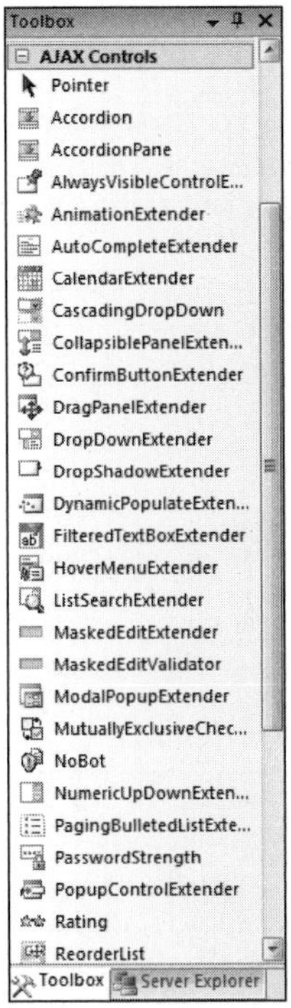

Figure 7-6

The ASP.NET AJAX Controls

The number of controls and extenders available from the Control Toolkit is large. There are more than 35 controls and extenders at your disposal. This section will look at these new items and how to use them in your ASP.NET applications.

When you add an ASP.NET AJAX server control to your page, one thing you will notice is that a lot of DLLs are added to your solution in the language folders within the Bin folder. You will need to have the `AjaxControlToolkit.dll` with the language DLLs when you reference it. An example of what you will find is presented in Figure 7-7.

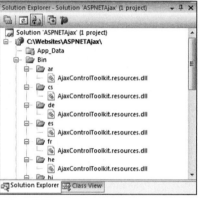

Figure 7-7

If you look at one of the DLLs with Lutz Roeder's .NET Reflector tool (`www.red-gate.com/products/reflector`), you will notice that it is focused on the client-side localization required by many applications. The `AjaxControlToolkit.resources.dll` for the Russian language within Reflector is shown in Figure 7-8.

Besides adding the localization DLLs to your project, the ASP.NET AJAX control is added the same way that any other custom server control would be in ASP.NET. Listing 7-1 shows what your ASP.NET page would look like after adding a single ASP.NET AJAX control to your page.

Listing 7-1: Changes to the ASP.NET page after adding an ASP.NET AJAX control

```
<%@ Page Language="C#" AutoEventWireup="true"
    CodeFile="Default.aspx.cs" Inherits="_Default" %>

<%@ Register Assembly="AjaxControlToolkit"
    Namespace="AjaxControlToolkit" TagPrefix="cc1" %>

<!DOCTYPE html PUBLIC "-//W3C//DTD XHTML 1.0 Transitional//EN"
  "http://www.w3.org/TR/xhtml1/DTD/xhtml1-transitional.dtd">

<html xmlns="http://www.w3.org/1999/xhtml">
```

Listing 7-1: Changes to the ASP.NET page after adding an ASP.NET AJAX control *(continued)*

```
<head runat="server">
    <title>First Page</title>
</head>
<body>
    <form id="form1" runat="server">
    <div>
        <cc1:AlwaysVisibleControlExtender
          ID="AlwaysVisibleControlExtender1" runat="server">
        </cc1:AlwaysVisibleControlExtender>
    </div>
    </form>
</body>
</html>
```

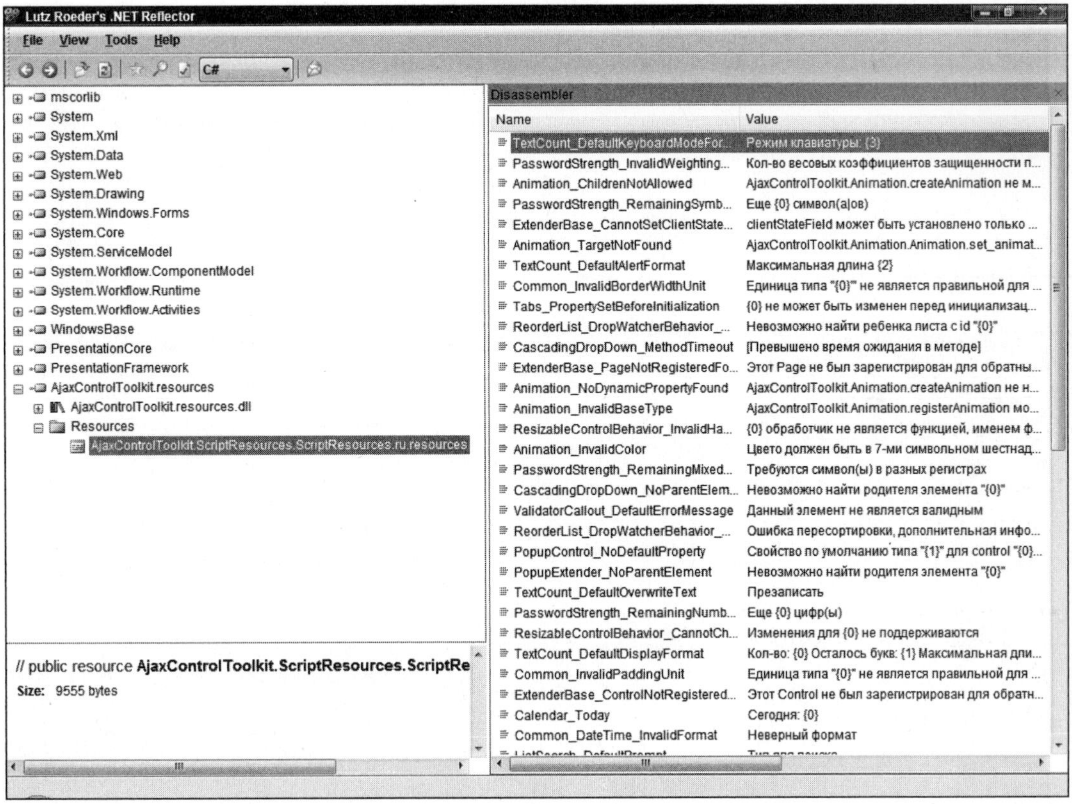

Figure 7-8

In this example, you can see that the ASP.NET AJAX control is registered on the page using the @Register directive. This directive points to the AjaxControlToolkit assembly and gives all controls that use this assembly reference a tag prefix of cc1, which is why you see the AlwaysVisibleControlExtender control prefixed with <cc1:[control name]>.

ASP.NET AJAX Control Toolkit Extenders

The first set of items that we will look at includes the new extenders that are part of the ASP.NET AJAX Control Toolkit. Extenders are basically controls that reach out and extend other controls. For instance, you can add a RequiredFieldValidator server control to a page and associate it to a TextBox control and the TextBox control will be extended. Instead of working as it normally would, just accepting text, it now has a new behavior. If nothing is entered into the control, the control will trigger an event in the RequiredFieldValidator control, whose client-side behavior is controlled by JavaScript.

What you will see with the ASP.NET AJAX Control Toolkit's extenders is that they pretty much accomplish the same thing. The controls extend the behavior of the ASP.NET server controls with additional JavaScript on the client as well as some server-side communications.

The ASP.NET AJAX extender controls are built using the ASP.NET AJAX extensions framework. The next few pages will now focus on using these new extenders within your ASP.NET applications.

AlwaysVisibleControlExtender

When presenting information in the browser, you may want to keep a piece of information fixed in the user's view. Screen space is a limited commodity, and there are cases where something should always be available without ever having to scroll. The AlwaysVisibleControlExtender lets you designate any ASP.NET control as having this characteristic. You specify a position for the control using the AlwaysVisibleControlExtender, and while the user scrolls the page to view other information, the control you designate is always kept in view. It seems to move around as the user scrolls the screen or resizes the window, so that it stays in the same relative position in the viewable portion of the browser window.

The AlwaysVisibleControlExtender has only six properties. An example of using this control is presented here in Listing 7-2.

Listing 7-2: Using the AlwaysVisibleControlExtender

```
<%@ Page Language="C#" %>

<%@ Register Assembly="AjaxControlToolkit" Namespace="AjaxControlToolkit"
    TagPrefix="cc1" %>

<html xmlns="http://www.w3.org/1999/xhtml">
<head runat="server">
    <title>AlwaysVisibleControlExtender</title>
</head>
<body>
    <form id="form1" runat="server">
    <div>
        <asp:ScriptManager ID="ScriptManager1" runat="server">
        </asp:ScriptManager>
        <asp:Label runat="server" ID="todaysQuote" BorderStyle="solid"
         Style="text-align: right; border-spacing: 10px">
            Section to always show!</asp:Label>
```

Listing 7-2: Using the AlwaysVisibleControlExtender *(continued)*

```
        <cc1:AlwaysVisibleControlExtender ID="AlwaysVisibleControlExtender1"
          runat="server" TargetControlID="todaysQuote" VerticalSide="Top"
          VerticalOffset="10" HorizontalSide="Right"
          HorizontalOffset="10" ScrollEffectDuration="1.0">
        </cc1:AlwaysVisibleControlExtender>
        <br />
      </div>
      <div style="width: 400px; text-align: left">
        Lorem ipsum dolor sit amet, consectetuer adipiscing elit.
        Etiam nulla nisi, rutrum eu, iaculis ac, placerat vitae, enim.
        Aliquam non augue. Vestibulum ante ipsum primis
        in faucibus orci luctus et ultrices posuere cubilia Curae;
        Mauris sollicitudin molestie
        felis. Pellentesque a orci at eros tincidunt tempor.
        Curabitur ultricies nunc vel
        tellus. Pellentesque ullamcorper ultrices velit.
        Sed tristique elementum leo. Curabitur
        mi mauris, lobortis a, malesuada at, blandit tincidunt, magna.
        Praesent in nulla.
        Quisque a nibh vel lacus pellentesque adipiscing.... more
      </div>
      </form>
  </body>
  </html>
```

In this case, a text that requires the end user to scroll the page in their browser instance is presented. For this example, I am using the Lorem Ipsum example text found at www.lipsum.com. The AlwaysVisibleControlExtender control is present, and its presence requires that you also have a ScriptManager control on the page as well (this is the same requirement for all ASP.NET AJAX controls).

The AlwaysVisibleControlExtender1 control extends the todaysQuote Label control through the use of the TargetControlID attribute. In this case, the value of the TargetControlID attribute points to the todaysQuote control.

Listing 7-2 shows setting all six to nondefault values. TargetControlID is set to the Label control as discussed. Then, following the recommendation of the Toolkit developers, the Label has been given a position using CSS to minimize flashing as it is repositioned during scrolling. The VerticalSide is set to Top (the options are Top, Middle, and Bottom). The VerticalOffset default is 0 but is set to 10px for some spacing. The HorizontalSide is set to Right (the options are Left, Right, and Center), and again the HorizontalOffset is adjusted up. Finally, the ScrollEffectDuration is set to one second. This controls the duration of the animation effect when the control is repositioned during scrolling.

The result of the code from Listing 7-2 is presented in Figure 7-9.

You can see the effect of the AlwaysVisibleControlExtender in Figure 7-9. The text "Section to always show!" is kept in view in the upper right, while the other text is allowed to scroll.

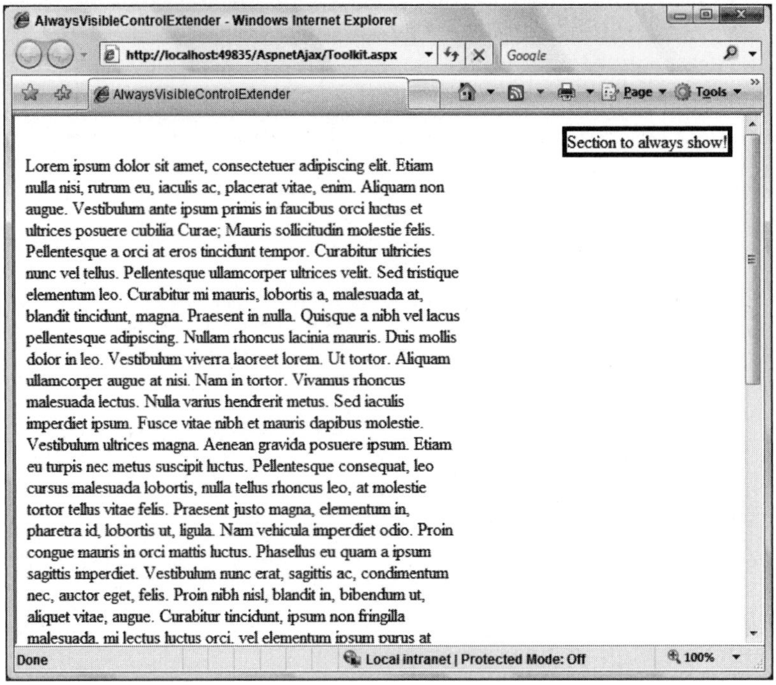

Figure 7-9

AnimationExtender

The AnimationExtender server control provides a tremendous number of capabilities. It allows you to program fluid animations to the controls that you put on the page. There is a lot that you can do with this control (much more than what can be shown in this chapter).

This control allows you to program elements that can move around the page based upon specific end user triggers (such as a button click). You will find that there are specific events you can use to program your animations, as listed here:

- ❑ `OnClick`
- ❑ `OnHoverOver`
- ❑ `OnHoverOut`
- ❑ `OnLoad`
- ❑ `OnMouseOver`
- ❑ `OnMouseOut`

Creating animations is not as straightforward as many would like, as there is little Visual Studio support (such as wizards or even IntelliSense). For an example of creating your first animation, Listing 7-3 shows how you can fade an element in and out of the page based upon an end user action.

Listing 7-3: Using the AnimationExtender to fade a background color

```
<%@ Page Language="C#" %>

<%@ Register Assembly="AjaxControlToolkit" Namespace="AjaxControlToolkit"
    TagPrefix="cc1" %>

<html xmlns="http://www.w3.org/1999/xhtml">
<head runat="server">
    <title>AnimationExtender</title>
</head>
<body>
    <form id="form1" runat="server">
    <div>
        <asp:ScriptManager ID="ScriptManager1" runat="server" />
        <cc1:AnimationExtender ID="AnimationExtender1" runat="server"
            TargetControlID="Panel1">
            <Animations>
                <OnClick>
                    <Sequence>
                        <Color PropertyKey="background" StartValue="#999966"
                            EndValue="#FFFFFF" Duration="5.0" />
                    </Sequence>
                </OnClick>
            </Animations>
        </cc1:AnimationExtender>
        <asp:Panel ID="Panel1" runat="server" BorderColor="Black"
            BorderWidth="3px" Font-Bold="True" Width="600px">
            Lorem ipsum dolor sit amet, consectetuer adipiscing elit.
            Donec accumsan lorem. Ut consectetuer tempus metus. Aenean tincidunt
            venenatis tellus. Suspendisse molestie cursus ipsum. Curabitur ut
            lectus. Nulla ac dolor nec elit convallis vulputate. Nullam pharetra
            pulvinar nunc. Duis orci. Phasellus a tortor at nunc mattis congue.
            Vestibulum porta tellus eu orci. Suspendisse quis massa. Maecenas
            varius, erat non ullamcorper nonummy, mauris erat eleifend odio, ut
            gravida nisl neque a ipsum. Vivamus facilisis. Cras viverra. Curabitur
            ut augue eget dolor semper posuere. Aenean at magna eu eros tempor
            pharetra. Aenean mauris.
        </asp:Panel>
    </div>
    </form>
</body>
</html>
```

If you pull up the page from Listing 7-3, you will see that it uses a single AnimationExtender control that is working off the Panel1 control. This connection is made using the `TargetControlID` property.

As stated, typing the code that is contained within the AnimationExtender control is not enabled by IntelliSense, so you are going to have to look up the animations that you are going to want to create through the documentation. In the case of the previous example, the `<OnClick>` element is utilized to define a sequence of events that need to occur when the control is clicked. For this example, there is only one animation defined within the `<Sequence>` element — a color change to the background of the element. Here, the `<Color>` element states that the background CSS property will need to start at the color #999966 and change completely to color #FFFFFF within 5 seconds (defined using the `Duration` property).

211

If you pull up this page and click the Panel element, you see the color change from the described start color to the end color over a 5-second interval.

AutoCompleteExtender

The AutoCompleteExtender control provides you the ability to help the end user find what they might be looking for when they have to type in search terms within a TextBox control. Like the product Google Suggest (shown here in Figure 7-10), once you start typing characters in the textbox, you get results from a data store that matches what you have typed so far.

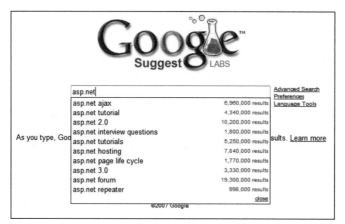

Figure 7-10

To establish something similar for yourself, create a new page that contains only a ScriptManager control, an AutoCompleteExtender control, and a TextBox control. The ASP.NET portion of the page should appear as presented in Listing 7-4.

Listing 7-4: The ASP.NET page

```
<%@ Page Language="C#" AutoEventWireup="true" CodeFile="AutoComplete.aspx.cs"
    Inherits="AutoComplete" %>

<%@ Register Assembly="AjaxControlToolkit" Namespace="AjaxControlToolkit"
    TagPrefix="cc1" %>

<html xmlns="http://www.w3.org/1999/xhtml">
<head runat="server">
    <title>AutoComplete</title>
</head>
<body>
    <form id="form1" runat="server">
    <div>
        <asp:ScriptManager ID="ScriptManager1" runat="server">
        </asp:ScriptManager>
        <cc1:AutoCompleteExtender ID="AutoCompleteExtender1" runat="server"
```

Listing 7-4: The ASP.NET page *(continued)*

```
                TargetControlID="TextBox1" ServiceMethod="GetCompletionList"
                UseContextKey="True">
            </cc1:AutoCompleteExtender>
            <asp:TextBox ID="TextBox1" runat="server"></asp:TextBox>
        </div>
        </form>
    </body>
    </html>
```

Again, like the other ASP.NET AJAX controls, you extend the TextBox control using the `TargetControlID` property. When you first add these controls to the page, you will not have the `ServiceMethod` property defined in the AutoCompleteExtender control. Using Visual Studio 2008, you can make the framework for a service method and tie the extender control to this method all from the design surface. Expanding the TextBox control's smart tag, select the Add AutoComplete page method option from the provided menu. What you will see is presented in Figure 7-11.

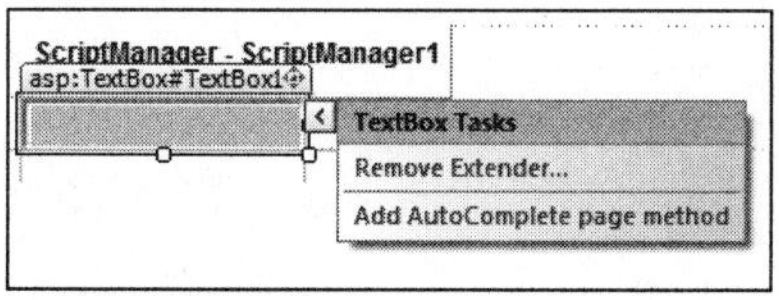

Figure 7-11

This action creates a service method in the code behind for your page. Listing 7-4 shows the steps necessary to complete this method to call the company names from the Northwind database.

The following example makes use of the `Northwind.mdf` *SQL Server Express Database file. To get this database, search for "Northwind and pubs Sample Databases for SQL Server 2000." You can find this link at* www.microsoft.com/downloads/details.aspx?familyid=06616212-0356-46a0-8da2-eebc53a68034&displaylang=en. *Once installed, you will find the* Northwind.mdf *file in the* C:\ SQL Server 2000 Sample Databases *directory. To add this database to your ASP.NET application, create an* App_Data *folder within your project (if it isn't already there) and right-click on the folder and select Add Existing Item. From the provided dialog box, you are then able to browse to the location of the* Northwind.mdf *file that you just installed. If you are having trouble getting permissions to work with the database, make a data connection to the file from the Visual Studio Server Explorer by right-clicking on the Data Connections node and selecting Add New Connection from the provided menu. You will be asked to be made the appropriate user of the database. Then VS will make the appropriate changes on your behalf for this to occur.*

Listing 7-5: The code-behind that sets up the service method for auto-complete

```
using System.Collections.Generic;
using System.Data;
using System.Data.SqlClient;

public partial class AutoComplete : System.Web.UI.Page
{
```
Continued

Listing 7-5: The code-behind that sets up the service method for auto-complete *(continued)*

```
[System.Web.Services.WebMethodAttribute(),
 System.Web.Script.Services.ScriptMethodAttribute()]
public static string[] GetCompletionList(string prefixText, int count,
    string contextKey)
{
    SqlConnection conn;
    SqlCommand cmd;
    string cmdString =
        "Select CompanyName from Customers WHERE CompanyName LIKE '" +
        prefixText + "%'";
    conn = new
        SqlConnection(@"Data Source=.\SQLEXPRESS;
        AttachDbFilename=|DataDirectory|\NORTHWND.MDF;
        Integrated Security=True;User Instance=True");
    // Put this string on one line in your code
    cmd = new SqlCommand(cmdString, conn);
    conn.Open();

    SqlDataReader myReader;
    List<string> returnData = new List<string>();

    myReader = cmd.ExecuteReader(CommandBehavior.CloseConnection);

    while (myReader.Read())
    {
        returnData.Add(myReader["CompanyName"].ToString());
    }

    return returnData.ToArray();
    }
}
```

When you run this page and type the characters `alf` into the textbox, the `GetCompletionList()` method is called passing in these characters. These characters are retrievable through the `prefixText` parameter (you can also use the `count` parameter, whose default value is 10). The Northwind database is called by using the `prefixText` value, and this is what is returned back to the TextBox1 control. In the end, you get a drop-down list of the items that match the first three characters entered in the textbox. This is illustrated here in Figure 7-12.

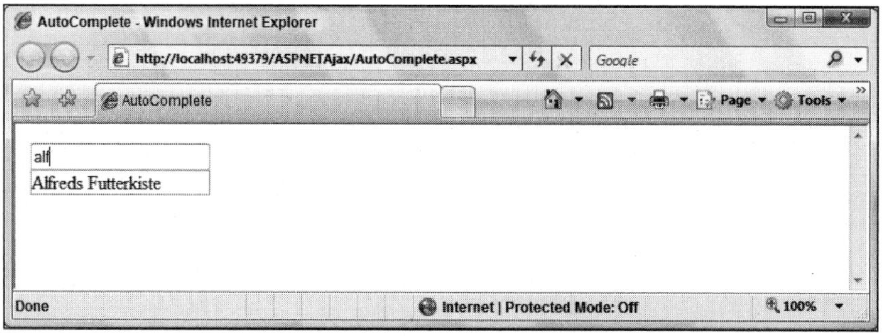

Figure 7-12

It is good to know that the results after they are called the first time are cached. This caching is controlled via the `EnableCaching` property (it is defaulted to `true`). You can also change the style of the drop-down auto-complete list. You can configure the style, change how many elements appear, and alter many more points of this feature. Note that you are not required to call a method that is exposed on the same page as the control as the example in this book demonstrates, but you can call another server-side method on another page or a Web method.

CalendarExtender

Selecting a date is a common requirement of many applications. The CalendarExtender attaches to a textbox and pops up a calendar for selecting a date. By default, the calendar is shown when the textbox gets focus, but if you set the `PopupButtonID` to the ID of another control, the calendar becomes visible when that control is clicked.

The CalendarExtender control allows you to make it simple for your end users to select a date within a form. If there is one point in the form that slows form submission up, it is selecting dates and trying to figure out the format of the date the form requires.

The quickest way to select a date in a form is to get a calendar that can be navigated and allow a date to be selected quickly. The selection then is translated to a textual date format in the textbox. The CalendarExtender is very easy to use and has just a few key properties. The `TargetControlID` points to the textbox that gets the selected date. The `Format` property specifies the string format for the date input of the textbox in case you want to make any changes to the format. The CalendarExtender control gives you all the client-side code required for this kind of action. Listing 7-6 shows you an example of providing a Calendar control off your TextBox controls.

Listing 7-6: Using a Calendar control from a TextBox control

```
<%@ Page Language="C#" %>

<%@ Register Assembly="AjaxControlToolkit" Namespace="AjaxControlToolkit"
    TagPrefix="cc1" %>

<html xmlns="http://www.w3.org/1999/xhtml">
<head runat="server">
    <title>CalendarExtender</title>
</head>
<body>
    <form id="form1" runat="server">
    <div>
        <asp:ScriptManager ID="ScriptManager1" runat="server">
        </asp:ScriptManager>
        <cc1:CalendarExtender ID="CalendarExtender1" runat="server"
         TargetControlID="TextBox1">
        </cc1:CalendarExtender>
        <asp:TextBox ID="TextBox1" runat="server"></asp:TextBox>
    </div>
    </form>
</body>
</html>
```

When you run this page, the result will be a single textbox on the page and the textbox will appear no different from any other textbox. However, when the end user clicks inside of the textbox, a calendar will then appear directly below the textbox as shown in Figure 7-13.

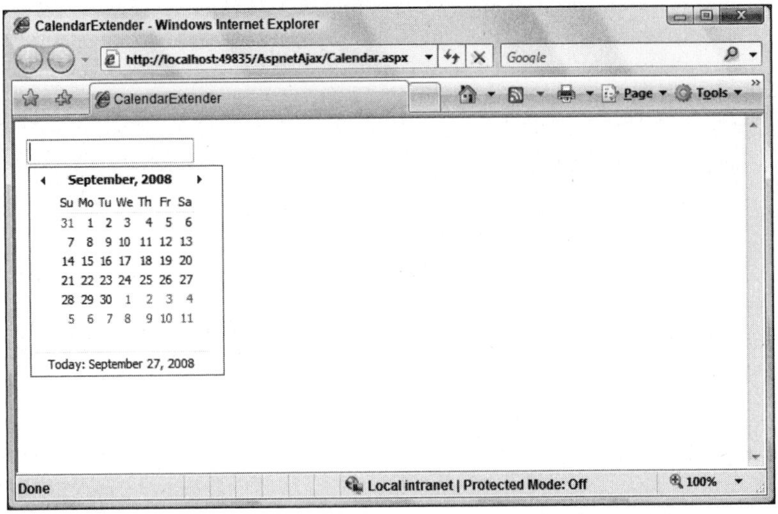

Figure 7-13

Then, when the end user selects a date from the calendar, the date is placed as text within the textbox as illustrated in Figure 7-14.

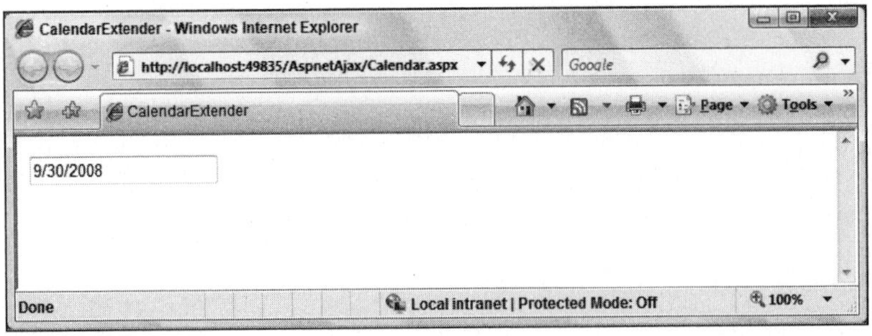

Figure 7-14

Some of the properties exposed from this control are `FirstDayOfWeek` and `PopupPosition` (which include the options `Left`, `Right`, `BottomLeft`, `BottomRight`, `TopLeft`, and `TopRight`). You can also change how the calendar is initiated on the client. Some sites like to have a calendar button next to the textbox and only pop-up the calendar option when the end user clicks on this button. If this is something that you like to do on your pages, then you are going to want to make use of the `PopupButtonID` property, which should point to the ID of the image or button that you are using.

CollapsiblePanelExtender

The CollapsiblePanelExtender server control allows you to collapse one control into another. When working with two Panel server controls, you can provide a nice means to control any real estate issues that you might be experiencing on your ASP.NET page.

The CollapsiblePanelExtender is similar to the Accordion control (presented later in this chapter) but does not target multiple content areas. An ASP.NET Panel control is shown or hidden from view based on the user's interaction with a given control. This allows you to hide something the user does not always need to see. The `TargetControlID` is shown when the `ExpandControlID` is clicked or hidden when the `CollapseControlID` is clicked. Alternatively, it can be shown or hidden based on a mouse hover if the `AutoCollapse` and `AutoExpand` properties are set to `true`.

Listing 7-7 demonstrates the use of a CollapsiblePanelExtender to set the panel size to `0` when it is collapsed and to `300` pixels when it is expanded. Another panel is used as the selector for expanding and collapsing the panel. In addition, a label is included that is designated as the `TextLabelID`. The value of the Label control is changed between the `ExpandedText` and `CollapsedText` values based on the current state.

Listing 7-7: Using the CollapsiblePanelExtender with two Panel controls

```
<%@ Page Language="C#" %>

<%@ Register Assembly="AjaxControlToolkit" Namespace="AjaxControlToolkit"
TagPrefix="cc1" %>

<html xmlns="http://www.w3.org/1999/xhtml">
<head id="Head1" runat="server">
    <title>CollapsiblePanelExtender</title>
</head>
<body>
    <form id="form1" runat="server">
    <div>
        <asp:ScriptManager ID="ScriptManager1" runat="server">
        </asp:ScriptManager>
        <asp:Panel ID="Panel1" runat="server" BackColor="#000066"
         ForeColor="White">
            <asp:Label ID="Label2" runat="server"
             Text="This is my title"></asp:Label>
            <asp:Label ID="Label1" runat="server"></asp:Label>
        </asp:Panel>
        <asp:Panel ID="Panel2" runat="server" Style="overflow: hidden;" Height="0">
            Lorem ipsum dolor sit amet, consectetuer adipiscing elit.
            Donec accumsan lorem. Ut consectetuer tempus metus. Aenean tincidunt
            venenatis tellus. Suspendisse molestie cursus ipsum. Curabitur ut
            lectus. Nulla ac dolor nec elit convallis vulputate.
            Nullam pharetra pulvinar nunc. Duis orci. Phasellus a tortor at nunc
            mattis congue. Vestibulum porta tellus eu orci. Suspendisse quis massa.
            Maecenas varius, erat non ullamcorper nonummy, mauris erat eleifend
            odio, ut gravida nisl neque a ipsum. Vivamus facilisis. Cras viverra.
            Curabitur ut augue eget dolor semper posuere. Aenean at
```

Continued

Listing 7-7: Using the CollapsiblePanelExtender with two Panel controls *(continued)*

```
            magna eu eros tempor pharetra. Aenean mauris.
        </asp:Panel>
        <cc1:CollapsiblePanelExtender ID="CollapsiblePanelExtender1" runat="server"
         TargetControlID="Panel2" Collapsed="true" ExpandControlID="Panel1"
         CollapseControlID="Panel1"
         CollapsedSize="1"
         ExpandedSize="300" CollapsedText="[Click to expand]"
         ExpandedText="[Click to collapse]" TextLabelID="Label1"
         SuppressPostBack="true">
        </cc1:CollapsiblePanelExtender>
    </div>
    </form>
</body>
</html>
```

In this case, when the page is pulled up for the first time, you will only see the contents of Panel1 — the title panel. By default, you would usually see both controls, but since the Collapsed property is set to true in the CollapsiblePanelExtender control, you will only see Panel1. Clicking on the Label1 control within the Panel control will then expose out the contents of Panel2. In fact, the contents will slide out from the Panel1 control. Tying these two controls together to do this action is accomplished through the use of the CollapsiblePanelExtender control. This control's TargetControlID is assigned to the second Panel control — Panel2, as this is the control that needs to expand onto the page. The ExpandControlID property is the control that initiates the expansion.

Once expanded, it is when the end user clicks on the Panel1 will the contents disappear by sliding back into Panel1. This is accomplished by assigning the CollapseControlID property to Panel1.

ConfirmButtonExtender and ModalPopupExtender

The ConfirmButtonExtender is slick. I believe slick is the technical term. Usually before allowing your end users to delete data via a browser application, you want to confirm that they really want to do such actions. The ConfirmButtonExtender allows you to question the end user's action and reconfirm that they want the action to occur.

In order to work with this control, you set the TargetControlID to a Button control or a control that is derived from a button. When the button is clicked, the value of the ConfirmText property is shown, along with OK and Cancel buttons. If the user clicks the OK button, the button fires normally. If not, the button click is canceled. Listing 7-8 is a page that updates a label with the time on the server each time the button is clicked but only if the ConfirmButtonExtender allows the submission to occur.

Listing 7-8: Using the ConfirmButtonExtender control to reconfirm a user action

```
<%@ Page Language="C#" %>

<%@ Register Assembly="AjaxControlToolkit" Namespace="AjaxControlToolkit"
    TagPrefix="cc1" %>

<script runat="server">
```

**Listing 7-8: Using the ConfirmButtonExtender control to reconfirm a
user action** *(continued)*

```
        protected void Page_Load(object sender, EventArgs e)
        {
            Label1.Text = DateTime.Now.ToLongTimeString();
        }

    </script>

    <html xmlns="http://www.w3.org/1999/xhtml">
    <head id="Head1" runat="server">
        <title>ConfirmButtonExtender</title>
    </head>
    <body>
        <form id="form1" runat="server">
        <div>
            <asp:ScriptManager ID="ScriptManager1" runat="server">
            </asp:ScriptManager>
            <asp:Label ID="Label1" runat="server"></asp:Label><br />
            <cc1:ConfirmButtonExtender ID="ConfirmButtonExtender1" runat="server"
             TargetControlID="Button1"
             ConfirmText="Are you sure you wanted to click this button?">
            </cc1:ConfirmButtonExtender>
            <asp:Button ID="Button1" runat="server" Text="Button" />
        </div>
        </form>
    </body>
    </html>
```

In this case, the ConfirmButtonExtender extends the Button1 server control and adds a confirmation
dialog using the text defined with the ConfirmText property. This dialog is shown in Figure 7-15.

Figure 7-15

If the end user clicks the OK button in this instance, the page functions normally as if the dialog never
appeared. However, if the Cancel button is clicked, by default the dialog disappears and the form isn't
submitted (it will be as if the button was not clicked at all). In this case, you can also capture the Cancel
button being clicked and perform a client-side operation through the OnClientClick() event, giving it
the value of a client-side JavaScript function.

Instead of using the browsers modal dialogs, you can create your own to use as the confirmation
form. To accomplish this task, you need to use the new ModalPopupExtender server control. The
ModalPopupExtender control points to another control to use for the confirmation.

219

The ModalPopupExtender prevents the user from interacting with the underlying page until a modal dialog has been addressed by the user. It is very similar to the HoverMenuExtender, except that the user must work with the control designated by the PopupControlID before he or she can proceed. It has properties for specifying the OkControlID and the CancelControlID, along with OnOkScript and OnCancelScript properties that will run based on the user's selection. Listing 7-9 shows how to make use of this control.

Listing 7-9: Using the ModalPopupExtender control to create your own confirmation form

```
<%@ Page Language="C#" %>

<%@ Register Assembly="AjaxControlToolkit" Namespace="AjaxControlToolkit"
 TagPrefix="cc1" %>

<html xmlns="http://www.w3.org/1999/xhtml">
<head runat="server">
    <title>ConfirmButtonExtender</title>
</head>
<body>
    <form id="form1" runat="server">
    <div>
        <asp:ScriptManager ID="ScriptManager1" runat="server">
        </asp:ScriptManager>
        <cc1:ConfirmButtonExtender ID="ConfirmButtonExtender1" runat="server"
         TargetControlID="Button1"
         DisplayModalPopupID="ModalPopupExtender1">
        </cc1:ConfirmButtonExtender>
        <cc1:ModalPopupExtender ID="ModalPopupExtender1" runat="server"
            CancelControlID="ButtonNo" OkControlID="ButtonYes"
            PopupControlID="Panel1"
            TargetControlID="Button1">
        </cc1:ModalPopupExtender>
        <asp:Button ID="Button1" runat="server" Text="Button" />
        <asp:Panel ID="Panel1" runat="server"
         style="display:none; background-color:White; width:200;
         border-width:2px; border-color:Black; border-style:solid; padding:20px;">
         Are you sure you wanted to click this button?<br />
         <asp:Button ID="ButtonYes" runat="server" Text="Yes" />
         <asp:Button ID="ButtonNo" runat="server" Text="No" />
        </asp:Panel>
    </div>
    </form>
</body>
</html>
```

In this example, the ConfirmButtonExtender still points to the Button1 control on the page, meaning that when the button is clicked, the ConfirmButtonExtender takes action. Instead of using the ConfirmText property, the DisplayModalPopupID property is used. In this case, it points to the ModalPopupExtender1 control — another extender control.

The ModalPopupExtender control, in turn, references the Panel1 control on the page through the use of the PopupControlID property. The contents of this Panel control are used for the confirmation on the button click. For this to work, the ModalPopupExtender control has to have a value for the OkControlID and the CancelControlID properties. In this case, these two properties point to the two Button controls that are contained in the Panel control. If you run this page, you get the results presented in Figure 7-16.

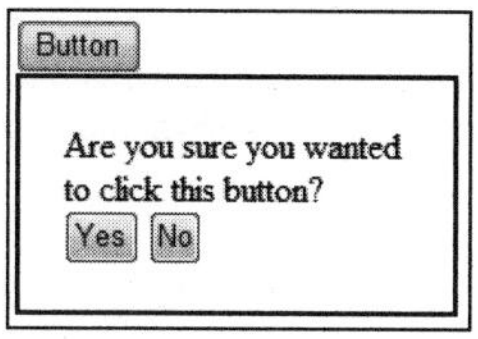

Figure 7-16

DragPanelExtender

The DragPanelExtender allows you to allow the end user to move an element in defined area around the page as desired. The end user actually has the ability to drag and drop the element anywhere on the browser page.

To enable this feature, you have to do a few things. The first suggestion is to create a `<div>` area on the page that is large enough for you to drag the item around in. From there, you are going to need a control that will be used as the drag handle and another control that will follow the drag handle around. In the example in Listing 7-10, the Label control is used as the drag handle, while the Panel2 control is the content that is dragged around the screen.

Listing 7-10: Dragging a Panel control around the page

```
<%@ Page Language="C#" %>

<%@ Register Assembly="AjaxControlToolkit" Namespace="AjaxControlToolkit"
    TagPrefix="cc1" %>

<html xmlns="http://www.w3.org/1999/xhtml">
<head runat="server">
    <title>DragPanel control</title>
</head>
<body>
    <form id="form1" runat="server">
    <div>
        <asp:ScriptManager ID="ScriptManager1" runat="server">
        </asp:ScriptManager>
        <div style="height: 600px;">
            <cc1:DragPanelExtender ID="DragPanelExtender1" runat="server"
             DragHandleID="Label1" TargetControlID="Panel1">
            </cc1:DragPanelExtender>
            <asp:Panel ID="Panel1" runat="server" Width="450px">
                <asp:Label ID="Label1" runat="server"
                 Text="Drag this Label control to move the control"
```

Continued

221

Listing 7-10: Dragging a Panel control around the page *(continued)*

```
                    BackColor="DarkBlue" ForeColor="White"></asp:Label>
                    <asp:Panel ID="Panel2" runat="server" Width="450px">
        Lorem ipsum dolor sit amet, consectetuer adipiscing elit.
        Donec accumsan lorem. Ut consectetuer tempus metus. Aenean tincidunt
        venenatis tellus. Suspendisse molestie cursus ipsum. Curabitur ut
        lectus. Nulla ac dolor nec elit convallis vulputate. Nullam pharetra
        pulvinar nunc. Duis orci. Phasellus a tortor at nunc mattis congue.
        Vestibulum porta tellus eu orci. Suspendisse quis massa. Maecenas
        varius, erat non ullamcorper nonummy, mauris erat eleifend odio, ut
        gravida nisl neque a ipsum. Vivamus facilisis. Cras viverra. Curabitur
        ut augue eget dolor semper posuere. Aenean at magna eu eros tempor
        pharetra. Aenean mauris.
                    </asp:Panel>
                </asp:Panel>
            </div>
        </div>
        </form>
    </body>
    </html>
```

In this case, a `<div>` element with a height of 600 pixels is created. Within this defined area, a DragPanelExtender control is used and targets the `Panel1` control through the use of the `TargetControlID` property being assigned to this control.

Within the Panel1 control are two other server controls — a Label and another Panel control. The Label control is assigned to be the drag handle using the `DragHandleID` property of the DragPanelExtender control. With this little bit of code in place, you are able to drag the `Panel1` control around on your browser window. Figure 7-17 shows the Label control being held and used as a handle to drag around the Panel control.

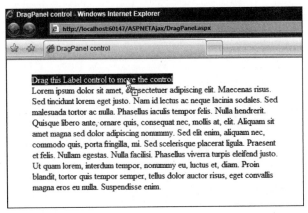

Figure 7-17

DropDownExtender

The DropDownExtender control allows you to take any control and provide a drop-down list of other options below it for selection. It provides a different framework than a typical DropDownList control as it allows for an extreme level of customization. Listing 7-11 shows how you can even use an image as the initiator of drop-down list of options.

Listing 7-11: Using an Image control as an initiator of a drop-down list

```
<%@ Page Language="C#" %>

<%@ Register Assembly="AjaxControlToolkit" Namespace="AjaxControlToolkit"
    TagPrefix="cc1" %>

<script runat="server">
    protected void Page_Load(object sender, EventArgs e)
    {
        Image1.ImageUrl = "Images/Creek.jpg";
    }

    protected void Option_Click(object sender, EventArgs e)
    {
        Image1.ImageUrl = "Images/" + ((LinkButton)sender).Text + ".jpg";
    }
</script>
<html xmlns="http://www.w3.org/1999/xhtml">
<head runat="server">
    <title>DropDownExtender Control</title>
</head>
<body>
    <form id="form1" runat="server">
    <div>
        <asp:ScriptManager ID="ScriptManager1" runat="server">
        </asp:ScriptManager>
        <asp:UpdatePanel ID="UpdatePanel1" runat="server">
            <ContentTemplate>
                <cc1:DropDownExtender ID="DropDownExtender1" runat="server"
                 DropDownControlID="Panel1" TargetControlID="Image1">
                </cc1:DropDownExtender>
                <asp:Image ID="Image1" runat="server">
                </asp:Image>
            <asp:Panel ID="Panel1" runat="server" Height="50px" Width="125px">
                <asp:LinkButton ID="Option1" runat="server"
                 OnClick="Option_Click">Creek</asp:LinkButton>
                <asp:LinkButton ID="Option2" runat="server"
                 OnClick="Option_Click">Dock</asp:LinkButton>
                <asp:LinkButton ID="Option3" runat="server"
                 OnClick="Option_Click">Garden</asp:LinkButton>
            </asp:Panel>
            </ContentTemplate>
        </asp:UpdatePanel>
    </div>
    </form>
</body>
</html>
```

In this case, a DropDownExtender control is tied to an Image control that on the `Page_Load()` event displays a specific image. The DropDownExtender control has two specific properties that need to be set. The first is the `TargetControlID` property that defines the control that becomes the initiator of the drop-down list. The second property that is important to understand is the `DropDownControlID` property that defines the element on the page that will be used for the drop-down items that appear below the control. In this case, it is a Panel control with three LinkButton controls.

Each of the LinkButton controls designates a specific image that should appear on the page; selecting one of the options changes the image to the selected choice through the `Option_Click()` method. Running this page gives you the results illustrated in Figure 7-18.

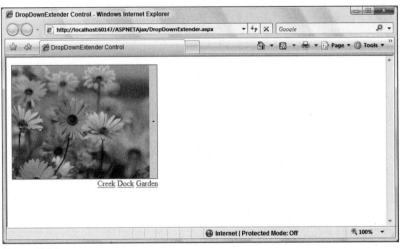

Figure 7-18

DropShadowExtender

The DropShadowExtender allows you to add a DropShadow effect to an ASP.NET Panel or image on the page. You set the `TargetControlID` and can then control the `Width`, `Opacity`, and whether or not the corners should be `Rounded`. If the panel can be moved or resized, you can also set the `TrackPosition` property to `true` to indicate that JavaScript should run to track the panel and update the DropShadow as needed.

The first thought for an example is an image (as shown here in Listing 7-12), but you can use it for any control that you wish.

Listing 7-12: Using the DropShadowExtender with an Image control

```
<%@ Page Language="C#" %>

<%@ Register Assembly="AjaxControlToolkit" Namespace="AjaxControlToolkit"
    TagPrefix="cc1" %>

<html xmlns="http://www.w3.org/1999/xhtml">
```

Listing 7-12: Using the DropShadowExtender with an Image control *(continued)*

```
<head runat="server">
    <title>DropShadowExtender Control</title>
</head>
<body>
    <form id="form1" runat="server">
    <div>
        <asp:ScriptManager ID="ScriptManager1" runat="server">
        </asp:ScriptManager>
        <cc1:DropShadowExtender ID="DropShadowExtender1" runat="server"
         TargetControlID="Image1">
        </cc1:DropShadowExtender>
        <asp:Image ID="Image1" runat="server" ImageUrl="Images/Garden.jpg" />
    </div>
    </form>
</body>
</html>
```

Here, it is as simple as using the DropShadowExtender control with a `TargetControlID` of `Image1`. With this in place, the image will appear in the browser as shown here in Figure 7-19.

Figure 7-19

As stated, in addition to images, you can use it for almost anything. Listing 7-13 shows how to use it with a Panel control.

Listing 7-13: Using the DropShadowExtender with a Panel control

```
<%@ Page Language="C#" %>

<%@ Register Assembly="AjaxControlToolkit" Namespace="AjaxControlToolkit"
```

Continued

225

Listing 7-13: Using the DropShadowExtender with a Panel control *(continued)*

```
        TagPrefix="cc1" %>

<html xmlns="http://www.w3.org/1999/xhtml">
<head runat="server">
    <title>DropShadowExtender Control</title>
</head>
<body>
    <form id="form1" runat="server">
    <div>
        <asp:ScriptManager ID="ScriptManager1" runat="server">
        </asp:ScriptManager>
        <cc1:DropShadowExtender ID="DropShadowExtender1" runat="server"
         TargetControlID="Panel1" Rounded="True">
        </cc1:DropShadowExtender>
        <asp:Panel ID="Panel1" runat="server" BackColor="Orange" Width="300"
         HorizontalAlign="Center">
            <asp:Login ID="Login1" runat="server">
            </asp:Login>
        </asp:Panel>
    </div>
    </form>
</body>
</html>
```

In this case, a Panel control with a Login control is extended with the DropShadowExtender control. The result is quite similar to that of the Image control's results. However, one addition to the DropShadowExtender control here is that the `Rounded` property is set to `true` (by default, it is set to `false`). This gives the following results as shown here in Figure 7-20.

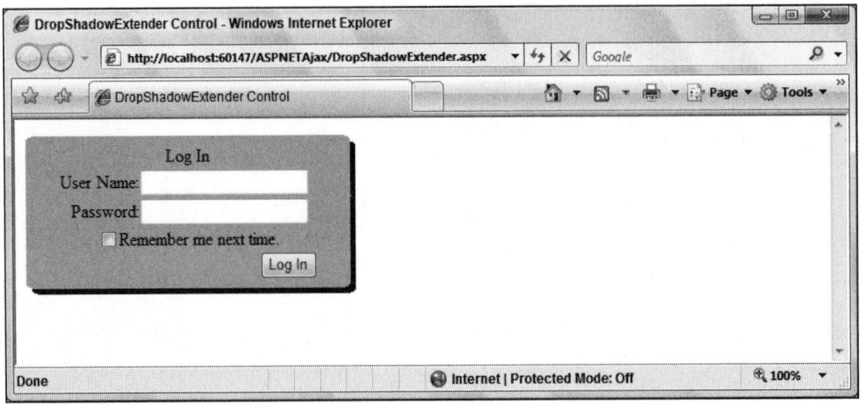

Figure 7-20

As you can see from Figure 7-20, not only are the edges of the drop shadow rounded, but also the entire Panel control has rounded edges. Other style properties that you can work with include the `Opacity` property (this controls the opacity of the drop shadow only) and the `Radius` property (this controls the radius used in rounding the edges and obviously only works if the Rounded property is set to true). By default, the Opacity setting is set at 1, which means 100% visible. To set it at, say, 50% opacity, you have to set the Opacity value to .5.

DynamicPopulateExtender

The DynamicPopulateExtender control allows you to send dynamic HTML output to a Panel control. For this to work, you will need one control or event that triggers a callback to the server to get the HTML that in turn gets pushed into the Panel control, thereby making a dynamic change on the client.

As with the AutoCompleteExtender control, you need a server-side event that returns something back to the client asynchronously. Listing 7-14 shows the code required to use this control on the .aspx page.

Listing 7-14: Using the DynamicPopulateExtender control to populate a Panel control

.ASPX

```
<%@ Page Language="C#" AutoEventWireup="true"
    CodeFile="DynamicPopulateExtender.aspx.cs"
    Inherits="DynamicPopulateExtender" %>

<%@ Register Assembly="AjaxControlToolkit"
    Namespace="AjaxControlToolkit" TagPrefix="cc1" %>

<html xmlns="http://www.w3.org/1999/xhtml">
<head runat="server">
    <title>DynamicPopulateExtender Control</title>
    <script type="text/javascript">
      function updateGrid(value) {
        var behavior = $find('DynamicPopulateExtender1');
        if (behavior) {
            behavior.populate(value);
        }
      }
    </script>
</head>
<body>
    <form id="form1" runat="server">
    <div>
        <asp:ScriptManager ID="ScriptManager1" runat="server" />
        <cc1:DynamicPopulateExtender ID="DynamicPopulateExtender1" runat="server"
            TargetControlID="Panel1" ServiceMethod="GetDynamicContent">
        </cc1:DynamicPopulateExtender>
        <div onclick="updateGrid(this.value);" value='0'>
        <asp:LinkButton ID="LinkButton1" runat="server"
         OnClientClick="return false;">Customers</asp:LinkButton></div>
        <div onclick="updateGrid(this.value);" value='1'>
        <asp:LinkButton ID="LinkButton2" runat="server"
         OnClientClick="return false;">Employees</asp:LinkButton></div>
        <div onclick="updateGrid(this.value);" value='2'>
        <asp:LinkButton ID="LinkButton3" runat="server"
         OnClientClick="return false;">Products</asp:LinkButton></div>
```

Continued

Listing 7-14: Using the DynamicPopulateExtender control to populate a Panel control *(continued)*

```
            <asp:Panel ID="Panel1" runat="server">
            </asp:Panel>
        </div>
        </form>
    </body>
    </html>
```

This `.aspx` page is doing a lot. First, there is a client-side JavaScript function called `updateGrid()`. This function calls the DynamicPopulateExtender control that is on the page. You will also find three LinkButton server controls, each of which is encased in a `<div>` element that calls the `updateGrid()` function and provides a value that is passed into the function. Since you want the `<div>` element's `onclick` event to be triggered with a click and not the LinkButton's click event, each LinkButton contains an `OnClientClick` attribute that does nothing. This is accomplished by using `return false;`.

The DynamicPopulateExtender control on the page targets the `Panel1` control as the container that will take the HTML that comes from the server on an asynchronous request. The DynamicPopulateExtender control knows where to go get the HTML, using the `ServiceMethod` attribute. The value of this attribute calls the `GetDynamicContent()` method, which is in the page's code-behind file.

Once you have the `.aspx` page in place, the next step is to create the code-behind page. This page will contain the server-side method that is called by the DynamicPopulateExtender control. This is presented in Listing 7-15.

Listing 7-15: The code-behind page of the DynamicPopulateExtender.aspx page

```
using System.Data;
using System.Data.SqlClient;
using System.IO;
using System.Web.UI;
using System.Web.UI.WebControls;

public partial class DynamicPopulateExtender : System.Web.UI.Page
{
    [System.Web.Services.WebMethodAttribute(),
     System.Web.Script.Services.ScriptMethodAttribute()]
    public static string GetDynamicContent(string contextKey)
    {
        SqlConnection conn;
        SqlCommand cmd;
        string cmdString = "Select * from Customers";

        switch (contextKey)
        {
            case ("1"):
                cmdString = "Select * from Employees";
                break;
            case ("2"):
                cmdString = "Select * from Products";
```

Listing 7-15: The code-behind page of the DynamicPopulateExtender.aspx page *(continued)*

```
            break;
    }

    conn = new
        SqlConnection(@"Data Source=.\SQLEXPRESS;
            AttachDbFilename=|DataDirectory|\NORTHWND.MDF;
            Integrated Security=True;User Instance=True");
            // Put this string on one line in your code
    cmd = new SqlCommand(cmdString, conn);
    conn.Open();

    SqlDataReader myReader;
    myReader = cmd.ExecuteReader(CommandBehavior.CloseConnection);

    DataTable dt = new DataTable();
    dt.Load(myReader);
    myReader.Close();

    GridView myGrid = new GridView();
    myGrid.ID = "GridView1";
    myGrid.DataSource = dt;
    myGrid.DataBind();

    StringWriter sw = new StringWriter();
    HtmlTextWriter htw = new HtmlTextWriter(sw);

    myGrid.RenderControl(htw);
    htw.Close();

    return sw.ToString();
    }
}
```

This code is the code-behind page for the DynamicPopulateExtender.aspx page and contains a single method that is called asynchronously. The GetDynamicContent() method takes a single parameter, contextKey, a string value that can be used to determine what link the end user clicked.

Based upon the selection, a specific command string is used to populate a DataTable object. From here, the DataTable object is used as the data source for a programmatic GridView control that is rendered and returned, as a string, to the client. The client takes the large string and uses the text to populate the Panel1 control that is on the page. The result of the clicking on one of the links is shown in Figure 7-21.

FilteredTextBoxExtender

The FilteredTextBoxExtender control works off a TextBox control to manipulate the types of characters that can be input into the control by the end user. For instance, if you want the end user to be able to enter only numbers in the textbox, then you can associate a FilteredTextBoxExtender with the TextBox control and specify such behavior. An example of this is presented in Listing 7-16.

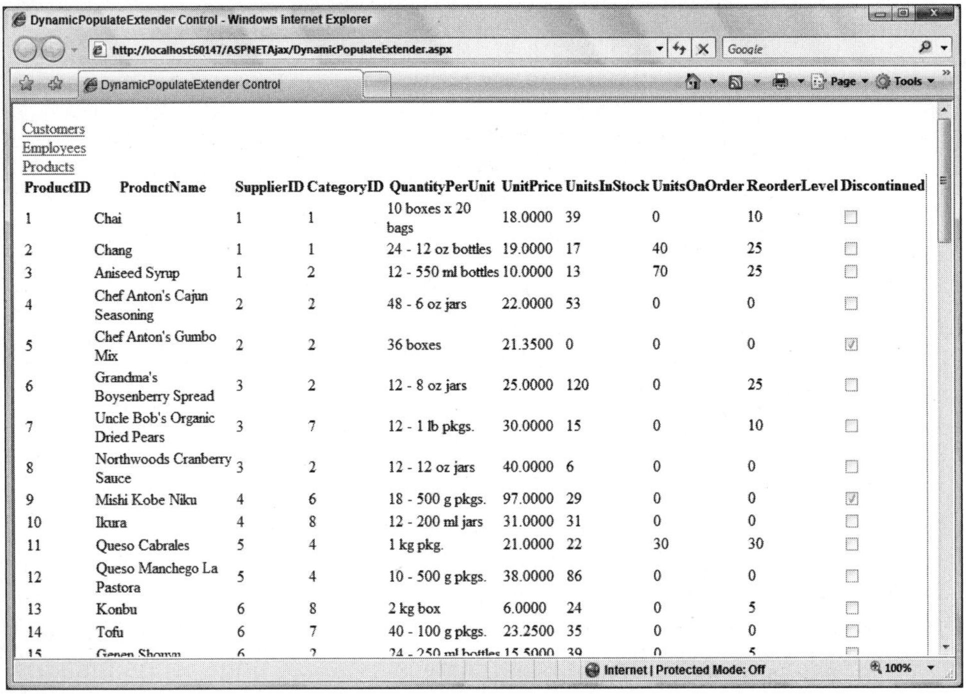

ProductID	ProductName	SupplierID	CategoryID	QuantityPerUnit	UnitPrice	UnitsInStock	UnitsOnOrder	ReorderLevel	Discontinued
1	Chai	1	1	10 boxes x 20 bags	18.0000	39	0	10	☐
2	Chang	1	1	24 - 12 oz bottles	19.0000	17	40	25	☐
3	Aniseed Syrup	1	2	12 - 550 ml bottles	10.0000	13	70	25	☐
4	Chef Anton's Cajun Seasoning	2	2	48 - 6 oz jars	22.0000	53	0	0	☐
5	Chef Anton's Gumbo Mix	2	2	36 boxes	21.3500	0	0	0	☑
6	Grandma's Boysenberry Spread	3	2	12 - 8 oz jars	25.0000	120	0	25	☐
7	Uncle Bob's Organic Dried Pears	3	7	12 - 1 lb pkgs.	30.0000	15	0	10	☐
8	Northwoods Cranberry Sauce	3	2	12 - 12 oz jars	40.0000	6	0	0	☐
9	Mishi Kobe Niku	4	6	18 - 500 g pkgs.	97.0000	29	0	0	☑
10	Ikura	4	8	12 - 200 ml jars	31.0000	31	0	0	☐
11	Queso Cabrales	5	4	1 kg pkg.	21.0000	22	30	30	☐
12	Queso Manchego La Pastora	5	4	10 - 500 g pkgs.	38.0000	86	0	0	☐
13	Konbu	6	8	2 kg box	6.0000	24	0	5	☐
14	Tofu	6	7	40 - 100 g pkgs.	23.2500	35	0	0	☐
15	Genen Shouyu	6	2	24 - 250 ml bottles	15.5000	39	0	5	☐

Figure 7-21

Listing 7-16: Filtering a textbox to use only numbers

```
<%@ Page Language="C#" %>

<%@ Register Assembly="AjaxControlToolkit" Namespace="AjaxControlToolkit"
    TagPrefix="cc1" %>

<html xmlns="http://www.w3.org/1999/xhtml">
<head runat="server">
    <title>FilteredTextBoxExtender Control</title>
</head>
<body>
    <form id="form1" runat="server">
    <div>
        <asp:ScriptManager ID="ScriptManager1" runat="server">
        </asp:ScriptManager>
        <cc1:FilteredTextBoxExtender ID="FilteredTextBoxExtender1" runat="server"
         TargetControlID="TextBox1" FilterType="Numbers">
        </cc1:FilteredTextBoxExtender>
        <asp:TextBox ID="TextBox1" runat="server"></asp:TextBox>
    </div>
    </form>
</body>
</html>
```

In this case, a FilteredTextBoxExtender control is attached to the TextBox1 control through the use of the `TargetControlID` property. The FilteredTextBoxExtender control has property called `FilterType` that has the possible values of `Custom`, `LowercaseLetters`, `Numbers`, and `UppercaseLetters`.

This example uses a `FilterType` value of `Numbers`, meaning that only numbers can be entered into the textbox. If the end user tries to enter in any other type of character, then nothing happens; it will seem to the end user as if the key doesn't even function.

Another property the FilteredTextBoxExtender control exposes is the `FilterMode` and the `InvalidChars` properties. An example of using these two properties is presented here:

```
<cc1:FilteredTextBoxExtender ID="FilteredTextBoxExtender1" runat="server"
  TargetControlID="TextBox1" InvalidChars="*" FilterMode="InvalidChars">
</cc1:FilteredTextBoxExtender>
```

The default value of the `FilterMode` property is `ValidChars`. When set to `ValidChars`, the control works from the `FilterType` property and allows only what this property defines. When set to `InvalidChars`, you then use the `InvalidChars` property and put the characters here (multiple characters just all go together with no space or item required between them).

HoverMenuExtender

The HoverMenuExtender control allows you to make a hidden control appear on the screen when the end user hovers on another control. This means that you can build either elaborate tooltips or provide extra functionality when an end user hovers somewhere in your application.

One example is to change a ListView control so that when the end user hovers over a product name, the Edit button for that row of data appears on the end user's screen. The code for the `<ItemTemplate>` in the ListView control is partially shown here in Listing 7-17.

Listing 7-17: Adding a hover button to the ListView control's ItemTemplate

```
<ItemTemplate>
    <tr style="background-color:#DCDCDC;color: #000000;">
        <td>
            <cc1:HoverMenuExtender ID="HoverMenuExtender1" runat="server"
             TargetControlID="ProductNameLabel" PopupControlID="Panel1"
             PopDelay="25" OffsetX="-50">
            </cc1:HoverMenuExtender>
            <asp:Panel ID="Panel1" runat="server" Height="50px" Width="125px">
                <asp:Button ID="EditButton" runat="server"
                 CommandName="Edit" Text="Edit" />
            </asp:Panel>
        </td>
        <td>
            <asp:Label ID="ProductIDLabel" runat="server"
             Text='<%# Eval("ProductID") %>' />
        </td>
        <td>
            <asp:Label ID="ProductNameLabel" runat="server"
```

Continued

Listing 7-17: Adding a hover button to the ListView control's ItemTemplate *(continued)*

```
            Text='<%# Eval("ProductName") %>' />
        </td>

        <!-- Code removed for clarity -->

    </tr>
</ItemTemplate>
```

Here, a HoverMenuExtender control is attached to the Label control with the ID of ProductNameLabel, which appears in each row of the ListView control. This is done using the `TargetControlID` property, while the `PopupControlID` property is used to assign the control that dynamically appears when a user hovers the mouse over the targeted control.

The HoverMenuExtender control exposes a number of different properties to control the style and behaviors of the pop-up. First, the `PopDelay` property is used in this example and provides a means to delay the pop-up from appearing (in milliseconds). The `OffsetX` and `OffsetY` properties are used to specify the location of the pop-up based upon the targeted control. In this case, the offset is set to –50 (pixels). The results of the operation are presented in Figure 7-22.

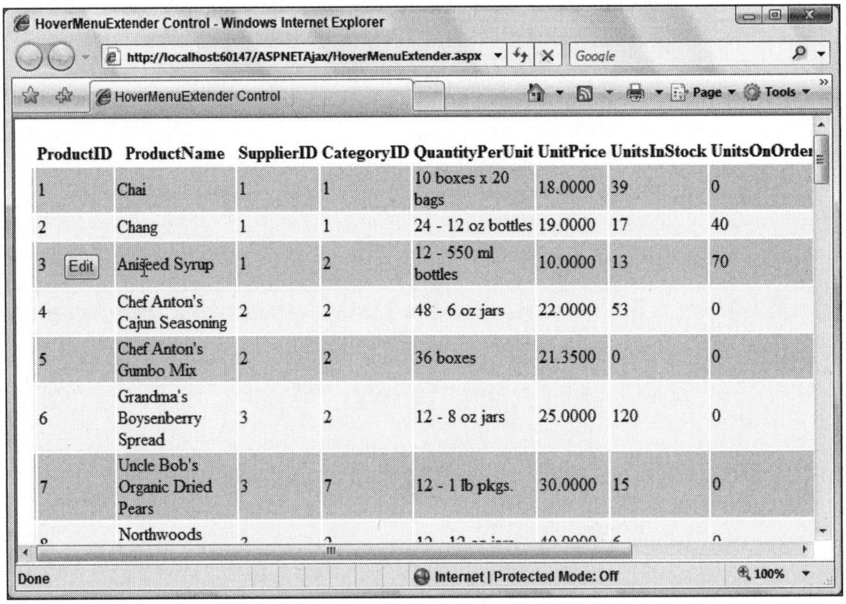

Figure 7-22

ListSearchExtender

The ListSearchExtender control extends either a ListBox or a DropDownList control. However, it does not always produce the best results in browsers such as Opera and Safari. This extender allows you to provide search capabilities over large collections that are found in either of these controls. This alleviates the need for end users to search through the collection to find the item they are looking for.

When utilized, the extender adds a search text area above the control that shows the characters the end user types for her search. Listing 7-18 shows the use of this extender.

Listing 7-18: Extending a ListBox control with the ListSearchExtender

```
<%@ Page Language="C#" %>

<%@ Register Assembly="AjaxControlToolkit" Namespace="AjaxControlToolkit"
    TagPrefix="cc1" %>

<html xmlns="http://www.w3.org/1999/xhtml">
<head runat="server">
    <title>ListSearchExtender Control</title>
</head>
<body>
    <form id="form1" runat="server">
    <div>
        <asp:ScriptManager ID="ScriptManager1" runat="server">
        </asp:ScriptManager>
        <cc1:ListSearchExtender ID="ListSearchExtender1" runat="server"
         TargetControlID="ListBox1">
        </cc1:ListSearchExtender>
        <asp:ListBox ID="ListBox1" runat="server" Width="150">
            <asp:ListItem>Aardvark</asp:ListItem>
            <asp:ListItem>Bee</asp:ListItem>
            <asp:ListItem>Camel</asp:ListItem>
            <asp:ListItem>Dog</asp:ListItem>
            <asp:ListItem>Elephant</asp:ListItem>
        </asp:ListBox>
    </div>
    </form>
</body>
</html>
```

In this case, the only property used in the ListSearchExtender control is the `TargetControlID` property, to identify which control it extends. Running this page produces the results shown in Figure 7-23.

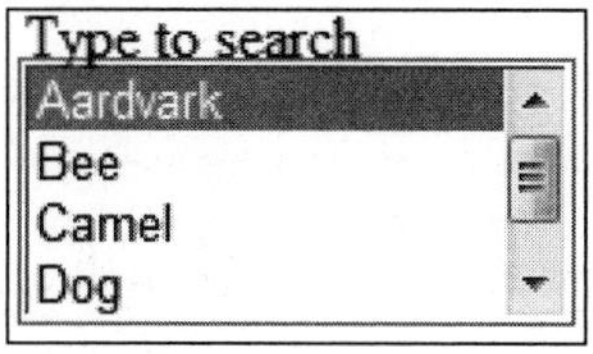

Figure 7-23

As an end user, when you start typing, you see what you are typing in the text above the control (as shown in Figure 7-24).

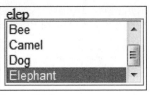

Figure 7-24

You can customize the text that appears at the top of the control through the use of the `PromptCssClass`, `PromptPosition`, and `PromptText` properties. By default, the `PromptPosition` is set to `Top` (the other possible value is `Bottom`) and the `PromptText` value is `Type to search`.

MaskedEditExtender and MaskedEditValidator

The MaskedEditExtender control is similar to the FilteredTextBoxExtender control in that it restricts the end user from entering specific text within a TextBox control. This control takes the process one-step further in that it provides the end user a template to follow within the textbox. If the end user does not follow the template, he will be unable to proceed and might get a validation warning from the control using the MaskedEditValidator control.

Listing 7-19 provides an example of using both of these controls.

Listing 7-19: Using both the MaskedEditExtender and the MaskedEditValidator controls

```
<%@ Page Language="C#" %>

<%@ Register Assembly="AjaxControlToolkit"
    Namespace="AjaxControlToolkit" TagPrefix="cc1" %>

<html xmlns="http://www.w3.org/1999/xhtml">
<head runat="server">
    <title>MaskedEditExtender Control</title>
</head>
<body>
    <form id="form1" runat="server">
    <div>
        <asp:ScriptManager ID="ScriptManager1" runat="server">
        </asp:ScriptManager>
        <cc1:MaskedEditExtender ID="MaskedEditExtender1" runat="server"
         TargetControlID="TextBox1" MaskType="Number" Mask="999">
        </cc1:MaskedEditExtender>
        <asp:TextBox ID="TextBox1" runat="server"></asp:TextBox>
        <cc1:MaskedEditValidator ID="MaskedEditValidator1" runat="server"
         ControlExtender="MaskedEditExtender1" ControlToValidate="TextBox1"
         IsValidEmpty="False" EmptyValueMessage="A three digit number is required!"
         Display="Dynamic"></cc1:MaskedEditValidator>
    </div>
    </form>
</body>
</html>
```

In this case, the MaskedEditExtender control uses the `TargetControlID` to associate itself with the `TextBox1` control. The `MaskType` property supplies the type of mask or filter to perform on the textbox. The possible values include:

❑ `None`: No validation will be performed.

❑ `Date`: A date validation will occur.

❑ `DateTime`: A date and time validation will occur.

❑ `Number`: A number validation will occur.

❑ `Time`: A time validation will occur.

Listing 7-19 uses `Number` and then specifies the mask or template the numbers need to take. This is done through the use of the `Mask` property. In this case, the `Mask` property is set to `999`. This means that all numbers can only be three digits in length.

Using `999` as a value to the `Mask` property means that when the end user enters a value in the textbox, three underscores display inside the textbox. This is the template for entering items. This is presented in Figure 7-25.

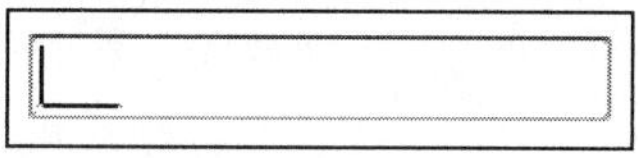

Figure 7-25

If the `Mask` property is changed to `99,999.99` as such:

```
<cc1:MaskedEditExtender ID="MaskedEditExtender1" runat="server"
 TargetControlID="TextBox1" MaskType="Number" Mask="99,999.99">
</cc1:MaskedEditExtender>
```

This change will mean that the textbox template will now appear as illustrated here in Figure 7-26.

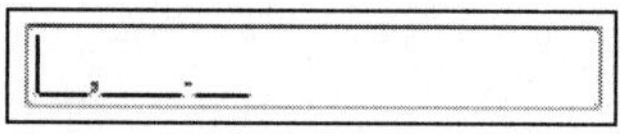

Figure 7-26

From Figure 7-26, you can see that the comma and the period are present in the template. As the end user types, he does not need to retype these values; when the first two numbers are filled in, the cursor simply moves to the next section of numbers required.

As you can see from the `Mask` property value, numbers are represented by the number 9. When working with other `MaskType` values, you also need to be aware of the other mask characters. These are provided here in the following list:

❑ `9`: Only a numeric character

❑ `L`: Only a letter

❑ `$`: Only a letter or a space

❑   C: Only a custom character (case sensitive)

❑   A: Only a letter or a custom character

❑   N: Only a numeric or custom character

❑   ?: Any character

In addition to the character specifications, the delimiters used in the template are detailed in the following list:

❑   / — Date separator

❑   : — Time separator

❑   . — Decimal separator

❑   , — Thousand separator

❑   \ — Escape character

❑   { — Initial delimiter for repetition of masks

❑   } — Final delimiter for repetition of masks

Using some of these items, you can easily change the MaskedEditExtender to deal with a DateTime value:

```
<cc1:MaskedEditExtender ID="MaskedEditExtender1" runat="server"
 TargetControlID="TextBox1" MaskType="DateTime" Mask="99/99/9999 99:99:99">
</cc1:MaskedEditExtender>
```

The template created in the textbox for this is presented in Figure 7-27.

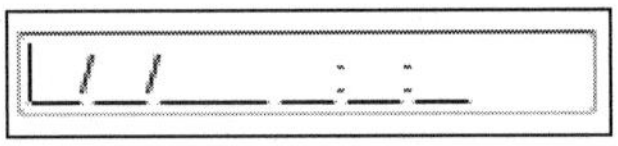

Figure 7-27

The MaskedEditExtender control has a ton of properties that control and manipulate the behavior and style of the textbox. The MaskedEditExtender control can work in conjunction with the MaskedEditValidator control, which provides validation against the TextBox controls.

From the earlier example, the validation was accomplished through an instance of the MaskedEditValidator control:

```
<cc1:MaskedEditValidator ID="MaskedEditValidator1" runat="server"
 ControlExtender="MaskedEditExtender1" ControlToValidate="TextBox1"
 IsValidEmpty="False" EmptyValueMessage="A three digit number is required!"
 Display="Dynamic"></cc1:MaskedEditValidator>
```

This control uses the ControlExtender property to associate itself with the MaskedEditExtender control and uses the ControlToValidate property to watch a specific control on the form. By default, the IsValidEmpty property is set to true, but changing it to false means that the end user will be required to enter some value in the textbox in order to pass validation and not get the error message that is presented in the EmptyValueMessage property.

Triggering the MaskedEditValidator control will give you something like what is presented here in Figure 7-28. It is important to remember that you can style the control in many ways to get the validation message appearance that you are looking for.

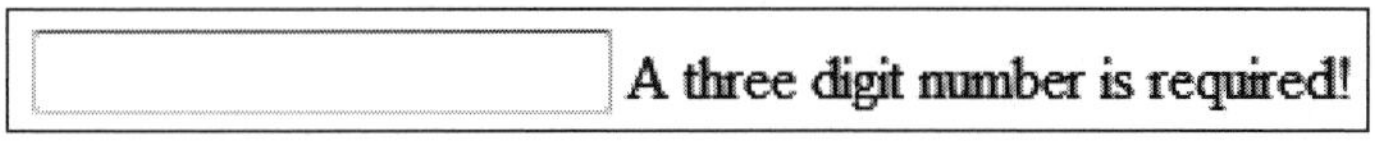

	A three digit number is required!

Figure 7-28

MutuallyExclusiveCheckBoxExtender

There are many times when you want to have a list of checkboxes that behave as if they are RadioButton controls. That is, when you have a collection of checkboxes, you want the end user to make only a single selection from the provided list of items. However, unlike using a radio button, you also want the end user to be able to deselect the item and make no selection whatsoever.

Using the MutuallyExclusiveCheckBoxExtender control, you can perform such an action. Listing 7-20 shows you how to accomplish this task.

Listing 7-20: Using the MutuallyExclusiveCheckBoxExtender control with checkboxes

```
<%@ Page Language="C#" %>

<%@ Register Assembly="AjaxControlToolkit" Namespace="AjaxControlToolkit"
    TagPrefix="cc1" %>

<html xmlns="http://www.w3.org/1999/xhtml">
<head runat="server">
    <title>MutuallyExclusiveCheckBoxExtender Control</title>
</head>
<body>
    <form id="form1" runat="server">
    <div>
        <asp:ScriptManager ID="ScriptManager1" runat="server">
        </asp:ScriptManager>
        <cc1:MutuallyExclusiveCheckBoxExtender
         ID="MutuallyExclusiveCheckBoxExtender1" runat="server"
         TargetControlID="CheckBox1" Key="MyCheckboxes" />
        <asp:CheckBox ID="CheckBox1" runat="server" Text="Blue" /><br />
        <cc1:MutuallyExclusiveCheckBoxExtender
         ID="MutuallyExclusiveCheckBoxExtender2" runat="server"
         TargetControlID="CheckBox2" Key="MyCheckboxes" />
        <asp:CheckBox ID="CheckBox2" runat="server" Text="Brown" /><br />
        <cc1:MutuallyExclusiveCheckBoxExtender
         ID="MutuallyExclusiveCheckBoxExtender3" runat="server"
         TargetControlID="CheckBox3" Key="MyCheckboxes" />
        <asp:CheckBox ID="CheckBox3" runat="server" Text="Green" /><br />
        <cc1:MutuallyExclusiveCheckBoxExtender
         ID="MutuallyExclusiveCheckBoxExtender4" runat="server"
         TargetControlID="CheckBox4" Key="MyCheckboxes" />
```

Continued

Listing 7-20: Using the MutuallyExclusiveCheckBoxExtender control with checkboxes *(continued)*

```
                <asp:CheckBox ID="CheckBox4" runat="server" Text="Orange" /><br />
        </div>
        </form>
    </body>
    </html>
```

It is impossible to associate a MutuallyExclusiveCheckBoxExtender control with a CheckBoxList control; therefore, each of the checkboxes needs to be laid out with CheckBox controls as the preceding code demonstrates. You need to have one MutuallyExclusiveCheckBoxExtender control for each CheckBox control on the page.

The way in which you form a group of CheckBox controls is through the use of the Key property. All the checkboxes that you want in one group need to have the same Key value. In the example in Listing 7-20, all the checkboxes share a Key value of MyCheckboxes.

Running this page displays a list of four checkboxes. When you select one of the checkboxes, a check will appear. Then, if you select another checkbox, the first checkbox you selected is deselected. The best part is that you can even deselect what you have selected in the group, thereby selecting nothing in the checkbox group.

NumericUpDownExtender

The NumericUpDownExtender control allows you to put some up/down indicators next to a TextBox control that enable the end user to control a selection more easily.

A simple example of this is illustrated in Listing 7-21.

Listing 7-21: Using the NumericUpDownExtender control

```
<%@ Page Language="C#" %>

<%@ Register Assembly="AjaxControlToolkit" Namespace="AjaxControlToolkit"
    TagPrefix="cc1" %>

<html xmlns="http://www.w3.org/1999/xhtml">
<head runat="server">
    <title>NumericUpDownExtender Control</title>
</head>
<body>
    <form id="form1" runat="server">
    <div>
        <asp:ScriptManager ID="ScriptManager1" runat="server">
        </asp:ScriptManager>
        <cc1:NumericUpDownExtender ID="NumericUpDownExtender1" runat="server"
         TargetControlID="TextBox1" Width="150" Maximum="10" Minimum="1">
        </cc1:NumericUpDownExtender>
```

Listing 7-21: Using the NumericUpDownExtender control *(continued)*

```
        <asp:TextBox ID="TextBox1" runat="server"></asp:TextBox>
    </div>
    </form>
</body>
</html>
```

The NumericUpDownExtender control here extends the TextBox control on the page. When using the NumericUpDownExtender control, you have to specify the width of the control with the `Width` property. Otherwise, you see only the up and down arrow keys and not the textbox area. In this case, the `Width` property is set to `150` (pixels). The `Maximum` and `Minimum` properties are used to provide the range that is used by the up and down indicators.

With a `Maximum` value setting of `10` and a `Minimum` value of `1`, the only range in the control will be 1 through 10. Running this page provides the results presented in Figure 7-29.

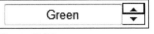

Figure 7-29

In addition to numbers as is shown with Listing 7-21, you can also use text, as illustrated in Listing 7-22.

Listing 7-22: Using characters instead of numbers with the NumericUpDownExtender

```
<cc1:NumericUpDownExtender ID="NumericUpDownExtender1" runat="server"
 TargetControlID="TextBox1" Width="150"
 RefValues="Blue;Brown;Green;Orange;Black;White">
</cc1:NumericUpDownExtender>
```

In this case, the words are defined within the `RefValues` property (all separated with a semicolon). This gives you the results presented in Figure 7-30.

Figure 7-30

PagingBulletedListExtender

The PagingBulletedListExtender control allows you to take long bulleted lists and easily apply alphabetic paging to the list. For an example of this, Listing 7-23 will work off of the `Customers` table within the Northwind database.

Listing 7-23: Paging a bulleted list from the Northwind database

```
<%@ Page Language="C#" %>

<%@ Register Assembly="AjaxControlToolkit" Namespace="AjaxControlToolkit"
    TagPrefix="cc1" %>

<html xmlns="http://www.w3.org/1999/xhtml">
<head runat="server">
    <title>PagingBulletedListExtender Control</title>
</head>
<body>
    <form id="form1" runat="server">
    <div>
        <asp:ScriptManager ID="ScriptManager1" runat="server">
        </asp:ScriptManager>
        <cc1:PagingBulletedListExtender ID="PagingBulletedListExtender1"
         runat="server" TargetControlID="BulletedList1">
        </cc1:PagingBulletedListExtender>
        <asp:SqlDataSource ID="SqlDataSource1" runat="server"
            ConnectionString="Data Source=.\SQLEXPRESS;
                AttachDbFilename=|DataDirectory|\NORTHWND.MDF;
                Integrated Security=True;User Instance=True"
            ProviderName="System.Data.SqlClient"
            SelectCommand="SELECT [CompanyName] FROM [Customers]">
        </asp:SqlDataSource>
        <asp:BulletedList ID="BulletedList1" runat="server"
            DataSourceID="SqlDataSource1" DataTextField="CompanyName"
            DataValueField="CompanyName">
        </asp:BulletedList>
    </div>
    </form>
</body>
</html>
```

This code pulls all the CompanyName values from the Customers table of the Northwind database and binds those values to the BulletList control on the page. Running this page will give you the results illustrated in Figure 7-31.

Figure 7-31

In this figure, you can see that the paging is organized alphabetically and it is sorted on the client. Only the letters for which there are values appear in the linked list of letters. Clicking any of the other letters gives you the items from the bulleted list that starts with that character.

PopupControlExtender

The PopupControlExtender control allows you to create a pop-up for any control on your page. For instance, you can completely mimic the CalendarExtender control that was presented earlier by creating a pop-up containing a Calendar control off a TextBox control. Listing 7-24 mimics this behavior.

Listing 7-24: Creating a CalendarExtender control with the PopupControlExtender

```
<%@ Page Language="C#" %>

<%@ Register Assembly="AjaxControlToolkit" Namespace="AjaxControlToolkit"
    TagPrefix="cc1" %>

<script runat="server">
    protected void Calendar1_SelectionChanged(object sender, EventArgs e)
    {
        PopupControlExtender1.Commit(Calendar1.SelectedDate.ToShortDateString());
    }
</script>
<html xmlns="http://www.w3.org/1999/xhtml">
<head runat="server">
    <title>PopupControlExtender Control</title>
</head>
<body>
    <form id="form1" runat="server">
    <div>
        <asp:ScriptManager ID="ScriptManager1" runat="server">
        </asp:ScriptManager>
        <cc1:PopupControlExtender ID="PopupControlExtender1" runat="server"
         TargetControlID="TextBox1" PopupControlID="UpdatePanel1" OffsetY="25">
        </cc1:PopupControlExtender>
        <asp:TextBox ID="TextBox1" runat="server"></asp:TextBox>
        <asp:UpdatePanel ID="UpdatePanel1" runat="server">
            <ContentTemplate>
                <asp:Calendar ID="Calendar1" runat="server" BackColor="White"
                 BorderColor="White" BorderWidth="1px" Font-Names="Verdana"
                 Font-Size="9pt" ForeColor="Black" Height="190px"
                 NextPrevFormat="FullMonth" Width="350px"
                 OnSelectionChanged="Calendar1_SelectionChanged">
                    <SelectedDayStyle BackColor="#333399" ForeColor="White" />
                    <TodayDayStyle BackColor="#CCCCCC" />
                    <OtherMonthDayStyle ForeColor="#999999" />
                    <NextPrevStyle Font-Bold="True" Font-Size="8pt"
                     ForeColor="#333333" VerticalAlign="Bottom" />
                    <DayHeaderStyle Font-Bold="True" Font-Size="8pt" />
                    <TitleStyle BackColor="White" BorderColor="Black"
                     BorderWidth="4px" Font-Bold="True" Font-Size="12pt"
                     ForeColor="#333399" />
```

Continued

241

Listing 7-24: Creating a CalendarExtender control with the PopupControlExtender *(continued)*

```
            </asp:Calendar>
          </ContentTemplate>
        </asp:UpdatePanel>
      </div>
      </form>
  </body>
  </html>
```

When you run this page, you get a single textbox on the page. Clicking within the textbox pops up a calendar that allows you to select a data that will then be populated back into the textbox (as illustrated in Figure 7-32).

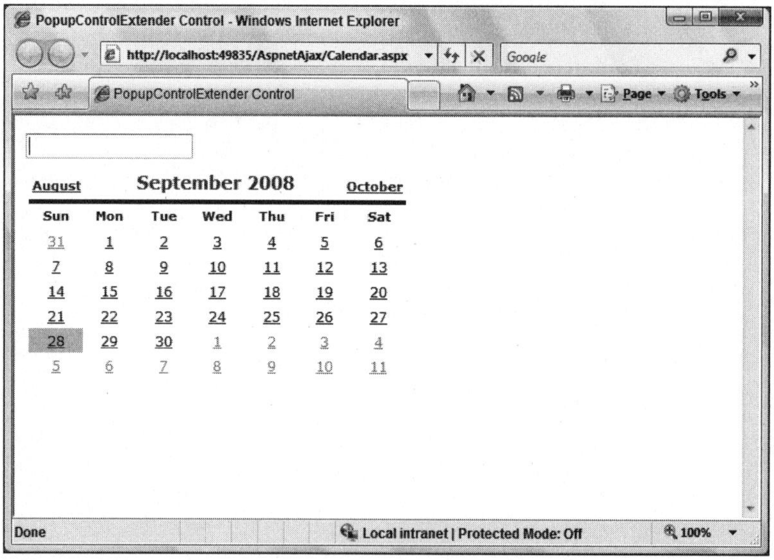

Figure 7-32

You will want to place your pop-up control within an ASP.NET AJAX UpdatePanel control and to pass the value from the pop-up control back to the target control (the `TextBox1` control), you are going to use the `Commit()` method.

```
PopupControlExtender1.Commit(Calendar1.SelectedDate.ToShortDateString())
```

ResizableControlExtender

In many situations, you may want to limit the size of an element when it is initially displayed but allow users to grow or shrink the element as they see fit. The ResizableControlExtender makes this easy. You place the ResizableControl on the page and point it to an ASP.NET Panel control, using the `TargetControlID` property.

The ResizableControlExtender control allows you to take a Panel control and give end users the ability to grab a handle and change the size of the element (smaller or bigger). Anything you put inside the Panel control changes in size according to how the end user extends the item. For this to work, you are going to have to create a handle for the end user to work from in pulling or contracting the item.

You use the `HandleCssClass` property to specify the style information about the appearance of the handle the user selects to begin resizing the panel. The `ResizableCssClass` property refers to style information shown while the panel is being altered.

The control also exposes events that are raised that you can attach code to in order to react to the panel being resized: `OnClientResizeBegin`, `OnClientResizing`, and finally `OnClientResize`. These are very useful for actions such as altering text size or retrieving additional data if the panel is grown or hiding elements if the panel is minimized. Listing 7-25 is an example of using the ResizableControlExtender with the CSS information inline in the page. The example shows you how to use the ResizableControlExtender with an image.

Listing 7-25: Using the ResizableControlExtender with an image

```
<%@ Page Language="C#" %>

<%@ Register Assembly="AjaxControlToolkit" Namespace="AjaxControlToolkit"
    TagPrefix="cc1" %>

<html xmlns="http://www.w3.org/1999/xhtml">
<head runat="server">
    <title>ResizableControlExtender Control</title>
    <style type="text/css">
        .handle
        {
        width:10px;
        height:10px;
        background-color:Black;
        }
        .resizable
        {
            border-style:solid;
            border-width:2px;
            border-color:Black;
        }
    </style>
</head>
<body>
    <form id="form1" runat="server">
    <div>
        <asp:ScriptManager ID="ScriptManager1" runat="server">
        </asp:ScriptManager>
        <cc1:ResizableControlExtender ID="ResizableControlExtender1" runat="server"
         TargetControlID="Panel1" HandleCssClass="handle"
         ResizableCssClass="resizable">
        </cc1:ResizableControlExtender>
        <asp:Panel ID="Panel1" runat="server" Width="300" Height="225">
```

Continued

Listing 7-25: Using the ResizableControlExtender with an image *(continued)*

```
            <asp:Image ID="Image1" runat="server" ImageUrl="Images/Garden.jpg"
                style="width:100%; height:100%"/>
        </asp:Panel>
    </div>
    </form>
</body>
</html>
```

In this example, the ResizableControlExtender control depends upon CSS to create the handle for the end user to grab and hold to resize the Panel control. The `TargetControlID` property points to the control to be resized.

There are two CSS references in the ResizableControlExtender control. One deals with the control as it sits on the screen with no end user interaction. This is done to show the end users that they have the ability to resize the element. This is done through the `HandleCssClass` property. The value of this property points to the CSS class `handle` contained within the same file. The second CSS reference deals with the control when the end user clicks and holds (does not let up on the mouse button). This one is done with the `ResizableCssClass` property. The value of this property points to the CSS class `resizable`.

The page generated when the code is compiled and run is presented in Figure 7-33.

Figure 7-33

From these screenshots, you can see in the image on the top how the image looks when there is no end user interaction. In this case, there is a black square (as defined by the CSS) in the lower-right corner of the image. The image on the bottom shows what happens when the end user grabs the handle and starts changing the shape of the control.

RoundedCornersExtender

The RoundedCornersExtender control allows you to put rounded corners on the elements on your page. As with the ResizableControlExtender control, you are going to want to put the element you are interested in working with inside of a Panel control. Listing 7-26 shows this done with a Login server control.

Listing 7-26: Rounding the corners of the Panel control containing a Login server control

```
<%@ Page Language="C#" %>

<%@ Register Assembly="AjaxControlToolkit" Namespace="AjaxControlToolkit"
    TagPrefix="cc1" %>

<html xmlns="http://www.w3.org/1999/xhtml">
<head runat="server">
    <title>RoundedCornersExtender Control</title>
</head>
<body>
    <form id="form1" runat="server">
    <div>
        <asp:ScriptManager ID="ScriptManager1" runat="server">
        </asp:ScriptManager>
        <cc1:RoundedCornersExtender ID="RoundedCornersExtender1" runat="server"
         TargetControlID="Panel1">
        </cc1:RoundedCornersExtender>
        <asp:Panel ID="Panel1" runat="server" Width="250px"
         HorizontalAlign="Center" BackColor="Orange">
            <asp:Login ID="Login1" runat="server">
            </asp:Login>
        </asp:Panel>
    </div>
    </form>
</body>
</html>
```

Here, the RoundedCornersExtender control simply points to the Panel control with the `TargetControlID` property. This Panel control has a background color of orange to show that the corners are indeed rounded. The result of this bit of code is shown in Figure 7-34.

Figure 7-34

You can control the degree of the rounded corners using the `Radius` property of the RoundedCornersExtender control. By default, this property is set to a value of `5`. You can even go as far as to choose which corners you want to round using the `Corners` property. The possible values of the `Corners` property include `All`, `Bottom`, `BottomLeft`, `BottomRight`, `Left`, `None`, `Right`, `Top`, `TopLeft`, and `TopRight`.

SliderExtender

The SliderExtender actually extends a TextBox control to make it look like nothing it normally does. This ASP.NET AJAX control gives you the ability to create true slider control that allows the end user to select a range of numbers using the mouse instead of having to type in the number. Listing 7-27 shows a simple example of using the slider.

Listing 7-27: Using the Slider control

```
<%@ Page Language="C#" %>

<%@ Register Assembly="AjaxControlToolkit" Namespace="AjaxControlToolkit"
    TagPrefix="cc1" %>

<html xmlns="http://www.w3.org/1999/xhtml">
<head runat="server">
    <title>SliderExtender Control</title>
</head>
<body>
    <form id="form1" runat="server">
    <div>
        <asp:ScriptManager ID="ScriptManager1" runat="server">
        </asp:ScriptManager>
        <cc1:SliderExtender ID="SliderExtender1" runat="server"
         TargetControlID="TextBox1">
        </cc1:SliderExtender>
        <asp:TextBox ID="TextBox1" runat="server"></asp:TextBox>
    </div>
    </form>
</body>
</html>
```

This little bit of code to tie a SliderExtender control to a typical TextBox control is simple and produces the result presented in Figure 7-35.

Figure 7-35

This is fine, but it is hard for end users to tell what number they are selecting. Therefore, you might find it better to give a signifier to the end user. Adding a Label control to the page (called `Label1`) and changing the SliderExtender control to include a `BoundControlID` property gives you this result. The code for this change is presented here:

```
<cc1:SliderExtender ID="SliderExtender1" runat="server" TargetControlID="TextBox1"
  BoundControlID="Label1">
</cc1:SliderExtender>
```

This small change produces the results (with the appropriate Label control on the page) presented here in Figure 7-36.

Figure 7-36

Now when the end user slides the handle on the slider, they see the number that they are working with quite easily. Some of the following properties are available to the SliderExtender control as presented here in the following list.

❑   `Decimals`: Allows you to specify the number of decimals the result should take. The more decimals you have, the more unlikely the end user will be able to pick an exact number.

❑   `HandleCssClass`: The CSS class that you are using the design the handle.

❑   `HandleImageUrl`: The image file you are using to represent the handle.

❑   `Length`: The length of the slider in pixels. The default value is `150`.

❑   `Maximum`: The maximum number represented in the slider. The default value is `100`.

❑   `Minimum`: The minimum number represented in the slider. The default value is `0`.

❑   `Orientation`: The orientation of the slider. The possible values include `Horizontal` and `Vertical`. The default value is `Horizontal`.

❑   `RailCssClass`: The CSS class that you are using to design the rail of the slider.

❑   `TooltipText`: The ToolTip when hovering on the slider. Using `{0}` within the text provides the means to show the end user the position the slider is currently in.

SlideShowExtender

The SlideShowExtender control allows you to put an image slideshow in the browser. The slideshow controls allow the end user to move to the next or previous images as well as simply playing the images as a slideshow with a defined wait between each image. Listing 7-28 shows an example that creates a slideshow.

Listing 7-28: Creating a slideshow with three images

.ASPX

```
<%@ Page Language="C#" AutoEventWireup="true" CodeFile="SlideShowExtender.aspx.cs"
    Inherits="SlideShowExtender" %>

<%@ Register Assembly="AjaxControlToolkit" Namespace="AjaxControlToolkit"
    TagPrefix="cc1" %>

<html xmlns="http://www.w3.org/1999/xhtml">
<head runat="server">
    <title>SlideShowExtender Control</title>
</head>
<body>
    <form id="form1" runat="server">
    <div>
        <asp:ScriptManager ID="ScriptManager1" runat="server">
        </asp:ScriptManager>
        <asp:Panel ID="Panel1" runat="server" Width="300px"
         HorizontalAlign="Center">
            <cc1:SlideShowExtender ID="SlideShowExtender1" runat="server"
                ImageTitleLabelID="LabelTitle" TargetControlID="Image1"
                UseContextKey="True" NextButtonID="ButtonNext"
                PlayButtonID="ButtonPlay"
                PreviousButtonID="ButtonPrevious"
                SlideShowServiceMethod="GetSlides"
                ImageDescriptionLabelID="LabelDescription">
            </cc1:SlideShowExtender>
            <asp:Label ID="LabelTitle" runat="server" Text="Label"
             Font-Bold="True"></asp:Label><br /><br />
            <asp:Image ID="Image1" runat="server"
             ImageUrl="Images/Garden.jpg" /><br />
            <asp:Label ID="LabelDescription" runat="server"
             Text="Label"></asp:Label><br /><br />
            <asp:Button ID="ButtonPrevious" runat="server" Text="Previous" />
            <asp:Button ID="ButtonNext" runat="server" Text="Next" />
            <asp:Button ID="ButtonPlay" runat="server" />
        </asp:Panel>
    </div>
    </form>
</body>
</html>
```

The SlideShowExtender control has a lot of properties available to it. You can specify the location where you are defining the image title and description using the ImageTitleLabelID and the ImageDescriptionLabelID properties. In addition to that, this page contains three Button controls. One to act as the Previous button, another for the Next button, and the final one to act as the Play button. However, it is important to note that when the Play button is clicked (to start the slideshow), it will turn into the Stop button for you.

One important property is the SlideShowServiceMethod property as this points to the server-side method that returns the images that are part of the slide show. In this case, it is referring to an image called GetSlides, which is represented here in Listing 7-29.

Listing 7-29: The GetSlides method implementation

```
public partial class SlideShowExtender : System.Web.UI.Page
{
    [System.Web.Services.WebMethodAttribute(),
     System.Web.Script.Services.ScriptMethodAttribute()]
    public static AjaxControlToolkit.Slide[] GetSlides(string contextKey)
    {
        return new AjaxControlToolkit.Slide[] {
            new AjaxControlToolkit.Slide("Images/Creek.jpg",
                "The Creek", "This is a picture of a creek."),
            new AjaxControlToolkit.Slide("Images/Dock.jpg",
                "The Dock", "This is a picture of a Dock."),
            new AjaxControlToolkit.Slide("Images/Garden.jpg",
                "The Garden", "This is a picture of a Garden.") };
    }
}
```

With the code-behind in place, the SlideShowExtender now has a server-side method to call for the photos. This method, called GetSlides(), returns an array of Slide objects which require the location of the object (the path), the title, and the description. When running this page, you get something similar to the following results illustrated in Figure 7-37.

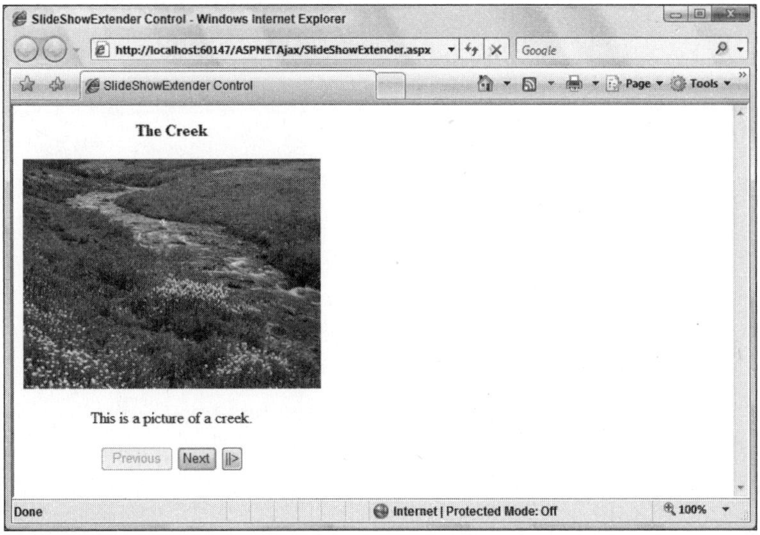

Figure 7-37

Clicking the play button on the page rotates the images until they are done. They will not repeat in a loop unless you have the SlideShowExtender control's Loop property set to true (it is set to false by default).

The other important property to pay attention to is the PlayInterval property. The value of this property is an Integer that represents the number of milliseconds that the browser will take to change to the next photo in the series of images. By default, this is set to 3000 milliseconds.

TextBoxWatermarkExtender

The TextBoxWatermarkExtender control allows you to put instructions within controls for the end users, which gives them a better understanding of what to use the control for. This can be text or even images (when using CSS). Listing 7-30 shows an example of using this control with a TextBox server control.

Listing 7-30: Using the TextBoxWatermarkExtender control with a TextBox control

```
<%@ Page Language="C#" %>

<%@ Register Assembly="AjaxControlToolkit" Namespace="AjaxControlToolkit"
    TagPrefix="cc1" %>

<html xmlns="http://www.w3.org/1999/xhtml">
<head runat="server">
    <title>TextBoxWatermarkExtender Control</title>
</head>
<body>
    <form id="form1" runat="server">
    <div>
        <asp:ScriptManager ID="ScriptManager1" runat="server">
        </asp:ScriptManager>
        <cc1:TextBoxWatermarkExtender ID="TextBoxWatermarkExtender1" runat="server"
         WatermarkText="Enter in something here!" TargetControlID="TextBox1">
        </cc1:TextBoxWatermarkExtender>
        <asp:TextBox ID="TextBox1" runat="server"></asp:TextBox>
    </div>
    </form>
</body>
</html>
```

In this case, the TextBoxWatermarkExtender control is associated with a simple TextBox control and uses the `WatermarkText` property to provide the text that will appear inside the actual TextBox control. Figure 7-38 shows the results of the code from this listing.

Enter in something here!

Figure 7-38

The text in the image from Figure 7-38 is straight text with no style inside of the TextBox control. When the end user clicks inside of the TextBox control, the text will disappear and the cursor will be properly placed at the beginning of the textbox.

To apply some style to the content that you use as a watermark, you can use the `WatermarkCssClass` property. You can change the code to include a bit of style, as shown in Listing 7-31.

Listing 7-31: Applying style to the watermark

```
<%@ Page Language="C#" %>

<%@ Register Assembly="AjaxControlToolkit" Namespace="AjaxControlToolkit"
    TagPrefix="cc1" %>

<html xmlns="http://www.w3.org/1999/xhtml">
<head runat="server">
    <title>TextBoxWatermarkExtender Control</title>
    <style type="text/css">
        .watermark
        {
         width:150px;
         font:Verdana;
         font-style:italic;
         color:GrayText;
        }

    </style>
</head>
<body>
    <form id="form1" runat="server">
    <div>
        <asp:ScriptManager ID="ScriptManager1" runat="server">
        </asp:ScriptManager>
        <cc1:TextBoxWatermarkExtender ID="TextBoxWatermarkExtender1" runat="server"
         WatermarkText="Enter in something here!" TargetControlID="TextBox1"
         WatermarkCssClass="watermark">
        </cc1:TextBoxWatermarkExtender>
        <asp:TextBox ID="TextBox1" runat="server"></asp:TextBox>
    </div>
    </form>
</body>
</html>
```

This time, the `WatermarkCssClass` property is used and points to the inline CSS class, `watermark`, which is on the page. Running this page, you see the style applied as presented in Figure 7-39.

Figure 7-39

ToggleButtonExtender

The ToggleButtonExtender control works with CheckBox controls and allows you to use an image of your own instead of the standard checkbox images that the CheckBox controls typically use. Using the ToggleButtonExtender control, you are able to specify images for checked, unchecked, and disabled statuses. Listing 7-32 shows an example using this control.

Listing 7-32: Using the ToggleButtonExtender control

```
<%@ Page Language="C#" %>

<%@ Register Assembly="AjaxControlToolkit" Namespace="AjaxControlToolkit"
    TagPrefix="cc1" %>

<html xmlns="http://www.w3.org/1999/xhtml">
<head runat="server">
    <title>ToggleButtonExtender Control</title>
</head>
<body>
    <form id="form1" runat="server">
    <div>
        <asp:ScriptManager ID="ScriptManager1" runat="server">
        </asp:ScriptManager>
        <cc1:MutuallyExclusiveCheckBoxExtender
         ID="MutuallyExclusiveCheckBoxExtender1" runat="server" Key="MyCheckBoxes"
         TargetControlID="CheckBox1">
        </cc1:MutuallyExclusiveCheckBoxExtender>
        <cc1:MutuallyExclusiveCheckBoxExtender
         ID="MutuallyExclusiveCheckBoxExtender2" runat="server" Key="MyCheckBoxes"
         TargetControlID="CheckBox2">
        </cc1:MutuallyExclusiveCheckBoxExtender>
        <cc1:ToggleButtonExtender ID="ToggleButtonExtender1" runat="server"
         TargetControlID="CheckBox1" UncheckedImageUrl="Images/Unchecked.gif"
         CheckedImageUrl="Images/Checked.gif" CheckedImageAlternateText="Checked"
         UncheckedImageAlternateText="Not Checked" ImageWidth="25"
         ImageHeight="25">
        </cc1:ToggleButtonExtender>
        <asp:CheckBox ID="CheckBox1" runat="server" Text=" Option One" />
        <cc1:ToggleButtonExtender ID="ToggleButtonExtender2" runat="server"
         TargetControlID="CheckBox2" UncheckedImageUrl="Images/Unchecked.gif"
         CheckedImageUrl="Images/Checked.gif" CheckedImageAlternateText="Checked"
         UncheckedImageAlternateText="Not Checked" ImageWidth="25"
         ImageHeight="25">
        </cc1:ToggleButtonExtender>
        <asp:CheckBox ID="CheckBox2" runat="server" Text=" Option Two" />
    </div>
    </form>
</body>
</html>
```

This page has two CheckBox controls. Each checkbox has an associated ToggleButtonExtender control, along with a MutuallyExclusiveCheckBoxExtender control to tie the two checkboxes together. The ToggleButtonExtender control uses the `CheckedImageUrl` and the `UncheckedImageUrl` properties to specify the appropriate images to use. Then, if images are disabled by the end user's browser instance, the text that is provided in the `CheckedImageAlternateText` and `UncheckedImageAlternateText` properties is used instead. You also have to specify values for the `ImageWidth` and `ImageHeight` properties for the page to run.

Running this page, you will get results similar to those presented in Figure 7-40.

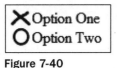

Figure 7-40

UpdatePanelAnimationExtender

Animating an UpdatePanel as its content is being refreshed is a common scenario. The UpdatePanelAnimationExtender allows you to use the broad set of animations available in the Toolkit and will automatically coordinate playing them when the specified UpdatePanel is being updated or when the update has completed.

The UpdatePanelAnimationExtender control allows you to apply an animation to a Panel control for two specific events. The first is the OnUpdating event, and the second is the OnUpdated event. You can then use the animation framework provided by ASP.NET AJAX to change the page's style based on these two events. Listing 7-33 shows an example of using the OnUpdated event when the end user clicks on a specific date within a Calendar control contained within the UpdatePanel control on the page.

Listing 7-33: Using animations on the OnUpdated event

```
<%@ Page Language="C#" %>

<%@ Register Assembly="AjaxControlToolkit" Namespace="AjaxControlToolkit"
    TagPrefix="cc1" %>

<script runat="server">
    protected void Calendar1_SelectionChanged(object sender, EventArgs e)
    {
        Label1.Text = "The date selected is " +
            Calendar1.SelectedDate.ToLongDateString();
    }
</script>
<html xmlns="http://www.w3.org/1999/xhtml">
<head runat="server">
    <title>UpdatePanelAnimationExtender Control</title>
</head>
<body>
    <form id="form1" runat="server">
    <div>
        <asp:ScriptManager ID="ScriptManager1" runat="server">
        </asp:ScriptManager>
        <cc1:UpdatePanelAnimationExtender ID="UpdatePanelAnimationExtender1"
         runat="server" TargetControlID="UpdatePanel1">
            <Animations>
                <OnUpdated>
                    <Sequence>
                        <Color PropertyKey="background" StartValue="#999966"
                        EndValue="#FFFFFF" Duration="5.0" />
                    </Sequence>
```

Continued

253

Listing 7-33: Using animations on the OnUpdated event *(continued)*

```
                </OnUpdated>
            </Animations>
        </cc1:UpdatePanelAnimationExtender>
        <asp:UpdatePanel ID="UpdatePanel1" runat="server">
            <ContentTemplate>
                <asp:Label ID="Label1" runat="server"></asp:Label><br />
                <asp:Calendar ID="Calendar1" runat="server"
                    onselectionchanged="Calendar1_SelectionChanged"></
asp:Calendar>
            </ContentTemplate>
        </asp:UpdatePanel>
    </div>
    </form>
</body>
</html>
```

With this bit of code, when you click on a date within the Calendar control, the entire background of the UpdatePanel holding the calendar changes from one color to another over a 5-second duration according to what is specified in the animation. The animations you define can get pretty complex, and building deluxe animations are beyond the scope of this chapter.

ValidatorCalloutExtender

The last extender control covered is the ValidatorCalloutExtender control. This control allows you to add a more noticeable validation message for end users working with a form. You associate this control not with the control that is being validated but instead with the validation control itself. An example of associating the ValidatorCalloutExtender control to a RegularExpressionValidator control is presented in Listing 7-34.

Listing 7-34: Creating validation callouts with the ValidationCalloutExtender

```
<%@ Page Language="C#" %>

<%@ Register Assembly="AjaxControlToolkit" Namespace="AjaxControlToolkit"
    TagPrefix="cc1" %>

<html xmlns="http://www.w3.org/1999/xhtml">
<head runat="server">
    <title>ValidatorCalloutExtender Control</title>
</head>
<body>
    <form id="form1" runat="server">
    <div>
        <asp:ScriptManager ID="ScriptManager1" runat="server">
        </asp:ScriptManager>
        <cc1:ValidatorCalloutExtender ID="ValidatorCalloutExtender1" runat="server"
            TargetControlID="RegularExpressionValidator1">
        </cc1:ValidatorCalloutExtender>
        Email Address: 
```

Listing 7-34: Creating validation callouts with the ValidationCalloutExtender *(continued)*

```
            <asp:TextBox ID="TextBox1" runat="server"></asp:TextBox>
            <asp:RegularExpressionValidator ID="RegularExpressionValidator1"
             runat="server"
             ErrorMessage="You must enter an e-mail address" Display="None"
             ControlToValidate="TextBox1"
             ValidationExpression="\w+([-+.']\w+)*@\w+([-.]\w+)*\.\w+([-.]\w+)*">
            </asp:RegularExpressionValidator><br />
            <asp:Button ID="Button1" runat="server" Text="Submit" />
        </div>
        </form>
    </body>
    </html>
```

This page has a single textbox for the form, a submit button, and a RegularExpressionValidator control. You build the RegularExpressionValidator control as you normally would, except that you make use of the `Display` property and set it to `None`. You do not want the normal ASP.NET validation control to also display its message, as it will collide with the one that will be displayed with the ValidatorCalloutExtender control. While the `Display` property is set to `None`, you still use the `ErrorMessage` property to provide the error message. Running this page produces the results presented in Figure 7-41.

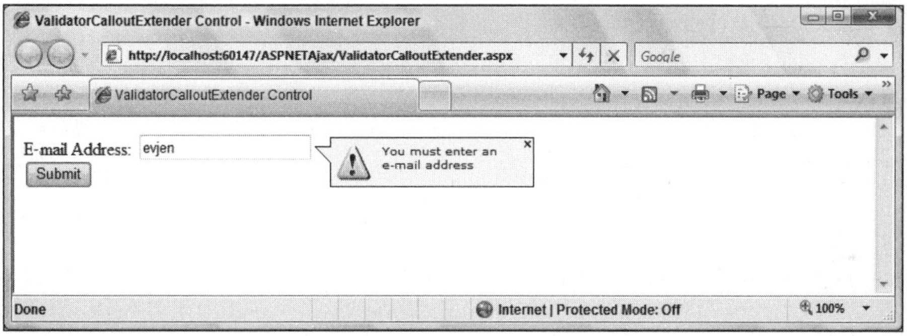

Figure 7-41

ASP.NET AJAX Control Toolkit Server Controls

The next set of ASP.NET AJAX controls actually do not always extend other ASP.NET controls, but instead, are controls themselves. The following sections details these controls.

Accordion Control

The Accordion control is used to specify a set of panes, similar to the famous menu in Microsoft Outlook. Each pane is made up of a header template and a content template. The header templates of all panes are always visible, while only one content template is visible. The user selects which pane to view by clicking the header. The content from the previously active pane is hidden from view, and the content of the newly selected pane is displayed instead.

The Accordion control can provide a fade transition when switching among active panes. You set the FadeTransitions property to true and can set the TransitionDuration and FramesPerSecond values. The default values are 250 milliseconds and 40 frames per second, respectively.

The SelectedIndex property lets you declaratively and programmatically control which pane to show. Other important properties are the AutoSize and Height properties. The AutoSize property is None by default, meaning that the size of the Accordion control changes based on the active pane. Other content on the screen may be shifted to accommodate the changing size. However, when the AutoSize property is set to Limit, the size is restricted to the Height value. The active pane displays scrollbars if the content is larger than the space available. The other possible value is Fill, which results in expanding a pane if the content is not large enough to satisfy the Height value provided. Listing 7-35 shows the Accordion control in action. The Accordion control is used with two panes.

```
<%@ Page Language="C#" %>

<%@ Register Assembly="AjaxControlToolkit" Namespace="AjaxControlToolkit"
    TagPrefix="cc1" %>

<html xmlns="http://www.w3.org/1999/xhtml">
<head runat="server">
    <title>Accordion Control</title>
    <style type="text/css">
        .titlebar
        {
         background-color:Blue;
         color:White;
         font-size:large;
         font-family:Verdana;
         border:solid 3px Black;
        }
    </style>
</head>
<body>
    <form id="form1" runat="server">
    <div>
        <asp:ScriptManager ID="ScriptManager1" runat="server">
        </asp:ScriptManager>
        <cc1:Accordion ID="Accordion1" runat="server" HeaderCssClass="titlebar"
         HeaderSelectedCssClass="titlebar"
         FadeTransitions="true"
         TransitionDuration="333"
         FramesPerSecond="30">
            <Panes>
            <cc1:AccordionPane runat="server">
                <Header>
                    This is the first pane
                </Header>
                <Content>
        Lorem ipsum dolor sit amet, consectetuer adipiscing elit.
        Donec accumsan lorem. Ut consectetuer tempus metus. Aenean tincidunt
        venenatis tellus. Suspendisse molestie cursus ipsum. Curabitur ut
        lectus. Nulla ac dolor nec elit convallis vulputate. Nullam pharetra
        pulvinar nunc. Duis orci. Phasellus a tortor at nunc mattis congue.
```

```
                    Vestibulum porta tellus eu orci. Suspendisse quis massa. Maecenas
                    varius, erat non ullamcorper nonummy, mauris erat eleifend odio, ut
                    gravida nisl neque a ipsum. Vivamus facilisis. Cras viverra. Curabitur
                    ut augue eget dolor semper posuere. Aenean at magna eu eros tempor
                    pharetra. Aenean mauris.
                        </Content>
                    </cc1:AccordionPane>
                    <cc1:AccordionPane runat="server">
                        <Header>
                            This is the second pane
                        </Header>
                        <Content>
                    Lorem ipsum dolor sit amet, consectetuer adipiscing elit.
                    Donec accumsan lorem. Ut consectetuer tempus metus. Aenean tincidunt
                    venenatis tellus. Suspendisse molestie cursus ipsum. Curabitur ut
                    lectus. Nulla ac dolor nec elit convallis vulputate. Nullam pharetra
                    pulvinar nunc. Duis orci. Phasellus a tortor at nunc mattis congue.
                    Vestibulum porta tellus eu orci. Suspendisse quis massa. Maecenas
                    varius, erat non ullamcorper nonummy, mauris erat eleifend odio, ut
                    gravida nisl neque a ipsum. Vivamus facilisis. Cras viverra. Curabitur
                    ut augue eget dolor semper posuere. Aenean at magna eu eros tempor
                    pharetra. Aenean mauris.
                        </Content>
                    </cc1:AccordionPane>
                    </Panes>
                </cc1:Accordion>
        </div>
        </form>
    </body>
    </html>
```

There is a single CSS class defined in the document and this class, titlebar, is used as the value of the HeaderCssClass and the HeaderSelectedCssClass properties. The Accordion control contains two AccordionPane controls. The sub-elements of the AccordionPane control are the <Header> and the <Content> elements. The items placed in the <Header> section will be in the clickable pane title, while the items contained within the <Content> section slide out and are presented when the associated header is selected.

You will notice that there is also a transition effect in place when the panes are switched. Running this page produces the results illustrated in Figure 7-42.

This figure shows a screenshot of each of the panes selected. Some of the more important properties are described in more detail here in the following list:

❑ AutoSize: Defines how the control deals with its size expansion and shrinkage. The possible values include None, Fill, and Limit. The default is None, and when used, items below the control may move to make room for the control expansion. A value of Fill works with the Height property, and the control will fill to the required Height. This means that some of the panes may have to grow to accommodate the space while other panes might have to shrink and include a scrollbar to handle working in less space based upon that height restriction. A value of Limit also works with the Height property and will never grow larger than this value. It is possible that the pane might be smaller than the specified height.

❑ `TransitionDuration`: The number of milliseconds it takes to transition to another pane.

❑ `FramesPerSecond`: The number of frames per second to use to transition to another pane.

❑ `RequireOpenedPane`: Specifies that at least one pane is required to be open at all times. The default setting of this property is `true`. A value of `false` means that all panes can be collapsed.

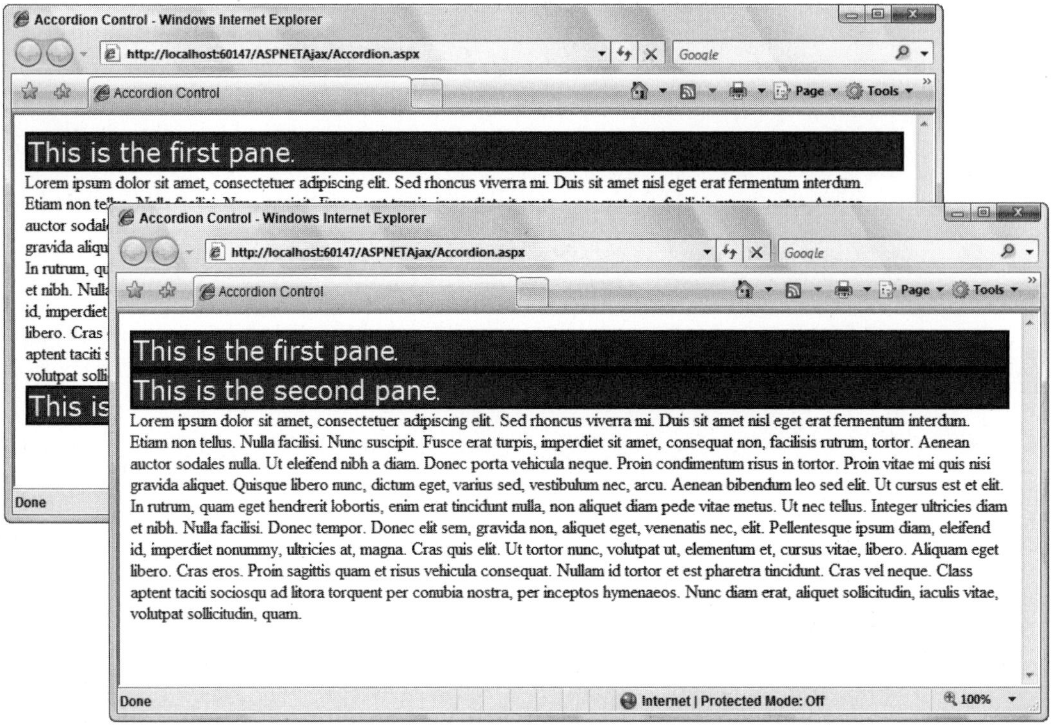

Figure 7-42

Finally, the properties of `DataSource`, `DataSourceID`, and `DataMember` allow you to bind to this control from your code.

CascadingDropDown

The available options for one DropDownList can be a function of the selection made in another DropDownList. The CascadingDropDown control makes it easy to enable this in your application. You set the `TargetControlID` to the DropDownList that should be populated by a call back to the server. You also assign a category to classify the DropDownList.

Before the DropDownList is populated, the value of the `PromptText` property is presented. Moreover, while the call to the server is underway, the value of the `LoadingText` property is displayed. You can set the `ServicePath` property to call a `ServiceMethod` on a separate Web service, or you can just set the `ServiceMethod` name to a static `ScriptMethod` located directly in the page, as is illustrated in Listing 7-36.

The first DropDownList in this example lets the user pick a state. In this example, I have included only Missouri and Oregon. Once a state is selected, a second DropDownList is populated based on the value selected by the user in the first DropDownList. The way to specify that one DropDownList is dependent on the value of another is to set the `ParentControlID` of the CascadingDropDown control.

Listing 7-36: Using the CascadingDropDown control

```csharp
<%@ Import Namespace="System.Web.Services" %>
<%@ Register Assembly="AjaxControlToolkit" Namespace="AjaxControlToolkit"
    TagPrefix="cc1" %>

<html xmlns="http://www.w3.org/1999/xhtml">
<head id="Head1" runat="server">

    <script runat="server" language="C#">

        [WebMethod]
        [System.Web.Script.Services.ScriptMethod]
        public static CascadingDropDownNameValue[]
            GetStates(string knownCategoryValues, string category)
        {
            return new[] {
        new CascadingDropDownNameValue("Missouri", "Missouri"),
        new CascadingDropDownNameValue("Oregon", "Oregon") };
        }


        [WebMethod]
        [System.Web.Script.Services.ScriptMethod]
        public static CascadingDropDownNameValue[]
            GetCounties(string knownCategoryValues, string category)
        {
            if (knownCategoryValues.Contains("Missouri"))
            {
                return new[] {
                    new CascadingDropDownNameValue("St. Charles", "St. Charles"),
                    new CascadingDropDownNameValue("St. Louis", "St. Louis"),
                    new CascadingDropDownNameValue("Jefferson", "Jefferson"),
                    new CascadingDropDownNameValue("Warren", "Warren"),
                    new CascadingDropDownNameValue("Franklin", "Franklin") };
            }
            if (knownCategoryValues.Contains("Oregon"))
            {
                return new[] {
                    new CascadingDropDownNameValue("Baker", "Baker"),
                    new CascadingDropDownNameValue("Benton", "Benton"),
                    new CascadingDropDownNameValue("Clackamas", "Clackamas"),
                    new CascadingDropDownNameValue("Clatsop", "Clatsop"),
                    new CascadingDropDownNameValue("Columbia", "Columbia") };
            }
            return null;
        }

    </script>
```

Continued

Listing 7-36: Using the CascadingDropDown control *(continued)*

```
        <title>CascadingDropDown</title>
    </head>
    <body>
        <form id="form1" runat="server">
        <asp:ScriptManager runat="server" ID="scriptManager" />
        <div>
            <asp:DropDownList runat="server" ID="ddl1" Width="200" />
            <br />
            <asp:DropDownList runat="server" ID="ddl2" Width="200" />
            <br />
            <cc1:CascadingDropDown runat="server" ID="cdd1" TargetControlID="ddl1"
                PromptText="Select a State"
                Category="state" LoadingText="[Loading States]"
                ServiceMethod="GetStates" />
            <cc1:CascadingDropDown runat="server" ID="cdd2" TargetControlID="ddl2"
                ParentControlID="ddl1"
                PromptText="Select County" Category="county"
                LoadingText="[Loading Counties]"
                ServiceMethod="GetCounties" />
        </div>
        </form>
    </body>
</html>
```

NoBot Control

The NoBot control works to control how entities interact with your forms and to help you make sure that it is actual humans who are working with your forms and not some automated code working through your application.

The NoBot control is illustrated in Listing 7-37.

Listing 7-37: Using the NoBot control to limit a login form

.ASPX

```
<%@ Page Language="C#" AutoEventWireup="true" CodeFile="NoBot.aspx.cs"
    Inherits="NoBot" %>

<%@ Register Assembly="AjaxControlToolkit" Namespace="AjaxControlToolkit"
    TagPrefix="cc1" %>

<html xmlns="http://www.w3.org/1999/xhtml">
<head runat="server">
    <title>NoBot Control</title>
</head>
<body>
    <form id="form1" runat="server">
```

Listing 7-37: Using the NoBot control to limit a login form *(continued)*

```
        <div>
            <asp:ScriptManager ID="ScriptManager1" runat="server">
            </asp:ScriptManager>
            <cc1:NoBot ID="NoBot1" runat="server" CutoffMaximumInstances="3"
                CutoffWindowSeconds="15" ResponseMinimumDelaySeconds="10"
                OnGenerateChallengeAndResponse="NoBot1_GenerateChallengeAndResponse" />
            <asp:Login ID="Login1" runat="server">
            </asp:Login>
            <asp:Label ID="Label1" runat="server"></asp:Label>
        </div>
        </form>
    </body>
    </html>
```

The NoBot control has three important properties to be aware of when controlling how your forms are submitted. These properties include the `CutoffMaximumInstances`, `CutoffWindowSeconds`, and the `ResponseMinimumDelaySeconds` properties.

The `CutoffMaximumInstances` is the number of times the end user is allowed to try to submit the form within the number of seconds that is specified in the `CutoffWindowSeconds` property. The `ResponseMinimumDelaySeconds` property defines the minimum number of seconds the end user has to submit the form. If you know the form you are working with will take some time, then setting this property to a value (even if it is 5 seconds) helps stop submissions not made by humans.

The `OnGenerateChallengeAndResponse` property allows you to define the server-side method that works with the challenge and allows you to also provide a response based on the challenge. This property is used in Listing 7-37 and will post back to the user the status of the form submission.

The code-behind for this page is represented here in Listing 7-38.

Listing 7-38: The code-behind page for the NoBot's OnGenerateChallengeAndResponse

```
using System;
using AjaxControlToolkit;

public partial class NoBot : System.Web.UI.Page
{
    protected void NoBot1_GenerateChallengeAndResponse(object sender,
        AjaxControlToolkit.NoBotEventArgs e)
    {
        NoBotState state;
        NoBot1.IsValid(out state);

        Label1.Text = state.ToString();
    }
}
```

Running this page and trying to submit the form before the 10-second minimum time results in an invalid submission. In addition, trying to submit the form more than three times within 15 seconds also results in an invalid submission.

PasswordStrength control

The PasswordStrength control allows you to check the contents of a password in a TextBox control and validate its strength. It then gives a message to the end user on whether the strength is reasonable. A simple use of the PasswordStrength control is presented in Listing 7-39.

Listing 7-39: Using the PasswordStrength control with a TextBox control

```
<%@ Page Language="C#" %>

<%@ Register Assembly="AjaxControlToolkit" Namespace="AjaxControlToolkit"
    TagPrefix="cc1" %>

<html xmlns="http://www.w3.org/1999/xhtml">
<head runat="server">
    <title>Password Strength Control</title>
</head>
<body>
    <form id="form1" runat="server">
    <div>
        <asp:ScriptManager ID="ScriptManager1" runat="server">
        </asp:ScriptManager>
        <cc1:PasswordStrength ID="PasswordStrength1" runat="server"
         TargetControlID="TextBox1">
        </cc1:PasswordStrength>
        <asp:TextBox ID="TextBox1" runat="server"></asp:TextBox>
    </div>
    </form>
</body>
</html>
```

This simple page produces a single textbox and when the end user starts typing in the textbox, they will be notified on the strength of the submission as they type. This is illustrated in Figure 7-43 in three separate requests.

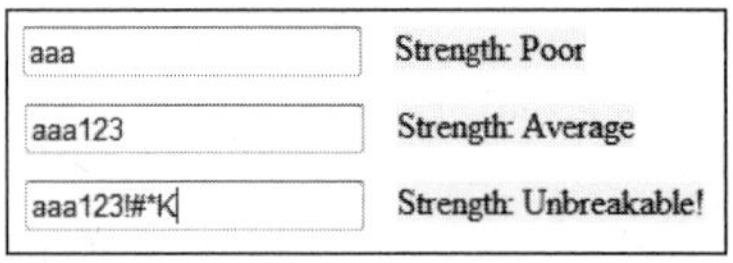

aaa	Strength: Poor
aaa123	Strength: Average
aaa123!#*K	Strength: Unbreakable!

Figure 7-43

Some of the important properties to work with here include `MinimumLowerCaseCharacters`, `MinimumNumericCharacters`, `MinimumSymbolCharacters`, `MinimumUpperCaseCharacters`, and `PreferredPasswordLength`.

Rating Control

The Rating control gives your end users the ability to view and set ratings (such as star ratings). You have control over the number of ratings, the look of the filled ratings, the look of the empty ratings, and more. Listing 7-40 shows you a page that shows a five-star rating system that gives the end users the ability to set the rating themselves.

Listing 7-40: A Rating control that the end user can manipulate

```
<%@ Page Language="C#" %>

<%@ Register Assembly="AjaxControlToolkit" Namespace="AjaxControlToolkit"
    TagPrefix="cc1" %>

<html xmlns="http://www.w3.org/1999/xhtml">
<head runat="server">
    <title>Rating Control</title>
    <style type="text/css">
        .ratingStar {
            font-size: 0pt;
            width: 13px;
            height: 12px;
            margin: 0px;
            padding: 0px;
            cursor: pointer;
            display: block;
            background-repeat: no-repeat;
        }

        .filledRatingStar {
            background-image: url(Images/FilledStar.png);
        }

        .emptyRatingStar {
            background-image: url(Images/EmptyStar.png);
        }

        .savedRatingStar {
            background-image: url(Images/SavedStar.png);
        }
    </style>
</head>
<body>
    <form id="form1" runat="server">
    <div>
        <asp:ScriptManager ID="ScriptManager1" runat="server">
        </asp:ScriptManager>
        <cc1:Rating ID="Rating1" runat="server" StarCssClass="ratingStar"
         WaitingStarCssClass="savedRatingStar"
         FilledStarCssClass="filledRatingStar" EmptyStarCssClass="emptyRatingStar">
        </cc1:Rating>
    </div>
```

Continued

Listing 7-40: A Rating control that the end user can manipulate *(continued)*

```
      </form>
  </body>
  </html>
```

Here, the Rating control uses a number of CSS classes to define its look and feel in various states. In addition to the CSS class properties (`StarCssClass`, `WaitingStarCssClass`, `FilledStarCssClass`, and `EmptyStarCssClass`), you can also specify rating alignments, the number of rating items (the default is 5), the width, the current rating, and more. The code presented in Listing 7-40 produces the following results (shown here in Figure 7-44).

Figure 7-44

TabContainer Control

The TabContainer and TabPanel controls make it easy to present the familiar tabbed UI. The user is presented with a set of tabs across the top of a single pane of content displayed for the active tab. When the user selects a different tab, the content is changed. Tabs are a great way to control a page that has a lot of content to present. The TabContainer control can contain one or more TabPanel controls that provide you with a set of tabs that show content one tab at a time.

The TabContainer allows you to attach a server event called the `ActiveTabChanged` event that is fired during a postback if the active tab has changed. You can also use the `OnClientActiveTabChanged` event to have your JavaScript event triggered in the browser when the user selects a different tab. The `ScrollBars` property lets you designate whether scrollbars should be `Horizontal`, `Vertical`, `Both`, `None`, or when set to `Auto` the control makes the determination.

The TabPanel control has a `<HeaderTemplate>` for the tab and a `<ContentTemplate>` for the body. You can forgo using the `<HeaderTemplate>` and specify the `HeaderText` property instead. It also has an event, called `OnClientClick`, that is triggered when the tab is selected. One particularly interesting aspect of the Tabs feature is the ability to disable tabs programmatically in JavaScript in the browser by setting the `Enabled` property to `false`.

Listing 7-41 shows an example of a TabContainer control with three TabPanel controls.

Listing 7-41: Showing three tabs in a TabContainer control

```
<%@ Page Language="C#" %>

<%@ Register Assembly="AjaxControlToolkit" Namespace="AjaxControlToolkit"
    TagPrefix="cc1" %>

<html xmlns="http://www.w3.org/1999/xhtml">
```

Listing 7-41: Showing three tabs in a TabContainer control *(continued)*

```
<head runat="server">
    <title>TabContainer Control</title>
</head>
<body>
    <form id="form1" runat="server">
    <div>
        <asp:ScriptManager ID="ScriptManager1" runat="server">
        </asp:ScriptManager>
        <cc1:TabContainer ID="TabContainer1" runat="server" Height="300px">
            <cc1:TabPanel runat="server">
                <HeaderTemplate>Tab 1</HeaderTemplate>
                <ContentTemplate>Here is some tab one content.</ContentTemplate>
            </cc1:TabPanel>
            <cc1:TabPanel runat="server">
                <HeaderTemplate>Tab 2</HeaderTemplate>
                <ContentTemplate>Here is some tab two content.</ContentTemplate>
            </cc1:TabPanel>
            <cc1:TabPanel runat="server">
                <HeaderTemplate>Tab 3</HeaderTemplate>
                <ContentTemplate>Here is some tab three content.</ContentTemplate>
            </cc1:TabPanel>
        </cc1:TabContainer>
    </div>
    </form>
</body>
</html>
```

The resulting simple page is presented in Figure 7-45.

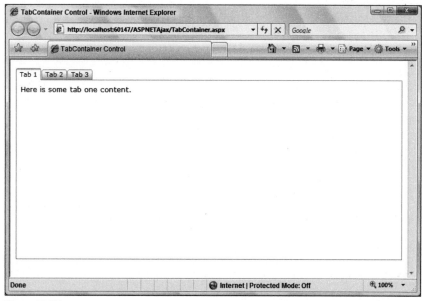

Figure 7-45

265

Summary

The ASP.NET AJAX Toolkit makes it easy to add rich animations and interactivity to a Web application. In addition to being able to use the UpdatePanel control to enable asynchronous updates of page content, you can use the UpdatePanelAnimation to show the user that background processing is occurring. The Toolkit helps blur the distinction between desktop applications and Web applications. Modal dialogs and pop-up dialogs start to push the Web application beyond what the user expects when working in the browser.

As you can see, there are a ton of new controls at your disposal. The best thing about this is that this is a community effort as well as a Microsoft one, and the list of available ASP.NET AJAX controls is going to grow over time.

This chapter took a look at the lot of the new ASP.NET AJAX controls and how to use them in your ASP.NET applications. Remember to visit the CodePlex page for these controls often and take advantage of the newest offerings out there.

8

ASP.NET AJAX
Application Services

ASP.NET provides a rich set of application services that are fundamental in building Web applications. You don't have to reinvent key aspects of the application infrastructure. Instead, you can leverage ASP.NET to take care of these details while you focus on the more unique aspects of your site. In this chapter you will see how to take advantage of ASP.NET application services in your application and how to access them from the browser with JavaScript for a better user experience.

The ASP.NET application services handle authentication, per user customization, and user membership. Forms Authentication makes it possible to easily authenticate users against virtually any backend credentials storage. The Authentication Service is built with a provider model. This architecture gives you flexibility to plug in other versions. If you don't want to use the authentication provider included with ASP.NET, you can configure it to use your own custom version. The role management service allows you to create, delete, access, or disable user accounts and track a user's membership in various roles. You can easily customize content for authenticated users based on the roles they are in. ASP.NET also includes a personalization feature for storing and retrieving profile information about specific users. This can be used for both authenticated users and anonymous users.

Before ASP.NET AJAX features were released, these services were available only from the server. You could write code in any .NET Framework language of your choosing to authenticate users, manage roles, and work with the Profile personalization data. You could also make use of a set of built-in controls for presenting the user with an interface for logging in, displaying their authentication status, creating new users, or for retrieving forgotten passwords. This can be done without writing any custom code at all by using the default service providers included with ASP.NET.

ASP.NET AJAX builds on the application services to expand their use beyond the server. By opening them up as Web services, they can be called remotely and leveraged from JavaScript code executing in the browser. The Microsoft AJAX Library includes scripts that make it easy to authenticate users, store and retrieve profile information, and manage user membership in roles defined on the server.

Authenticating Users

Some applications require you to log in, whereas others are open to the public. Others have a mixture of protected and open content. Despite several large scale efforts to provide a single login scheme that can be shared across multiple sites, nothing has really emerged yet as a de facto standard. I still seem to be forgetting logins and passwords for various applications. Until there is a universal login that everyone trusts, developers manage user accounts on their own.

ASP.NET supports several schemes for authenticating users. You can use Windows user accounts, you can use a custom authentication store, or you can leverage ASP.NET forms authentication.

Authenticating Windows Users

In the default configuration, the ASP.NET authentication mode is set to `Windows`. An object called a `WindowsPrincipal` is assigned to each request for a user authenticated against a Windows machine or domain account. The permissions of this `WindowsPrincipal` are used in checking against the operating system. File system and resource restrictions that are in effect for the user are enforced by Windows based on the `WindowsPrincipal`. The setting can be modified in the `web.config` file for the application.

```
<configuration>
    <system.web>
        <authentication mode="Windows" />
    </system.web>
</configuration>
```

When a site doesn't require any credentials, the user is referred to as the anonymous user. The anonymous user is any user that is accessing the site without authentication. There is still a `WindowsPrincipal` object assigned to the request, but it is associated with a low-privileged Windows user account.

ASP.NET doesn't do the authentication directly for Windows Authentication. It is the IIS Web server that does the authentication. IIS supports impersonation and passes the identity on to ASP.NET for each request. The default configuration for IIS is to use the built-in account without impersonating the specific user using the application. In Figure 8-1 you see the Computer Management console for IIS 7.0, where the anonymous user can be set for the site or for the application. This is where you switch from using the IUSR account to the Windows authenticated user.

A default install of Windows does not enable Windows Authentication. To enable this support, open the Control Panel and launch the Windows Features dialog from the Programs applet. The menu option is shown in Figure 8-2.

The authentication mode can also be set to `None` to skip the attachment of the `WindowsPrincipal` object to the request. This does not affect how IIS authenticates the user. IIS will still enforce the login configuration, but ASP.NET will not carry delegated credentials while executing the request. The permissions the user has for accessing Windows resources will be limited to the permissions that have been granted to the IUSR account. That is the `IdentityPrincipal` base type that will be assigned to the request.

```
<configuration>
    <system.web>
        <authentication mode="None" />
    </system.web>
</configuration>
```

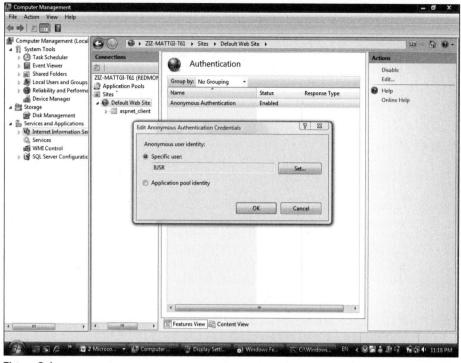

Figure 8-1

Figure 8-2

ASP.NET and IIS authentication schemes work together to provide a rich infrastructure than can carry across both static and dynamic content and be enforced by underlying Windows permissions.

Using Forms Authentication

On a corporate intranet site, the use of Windows Authentication provides seamless integration with Active Directory. But to authenticate users without requiring Windows accounts, ASP.NET provides Forms Authentication.

When using Windows Authentication, Internet Explorer negotiates for the prompting and transmission of credentials automatically. Forms Authentication can be configured to make login requirements automatic as well. Forms Authentication gets its name from the fact that the user typically provides his or her username and password in an HTML form. The form is submitted to the server where the authentication occurs. Forms Authentication allows a site to easily have thousands of users without ever requiring the overhead of managing Windows accounts within the host domain. There is a tradeoff though: you can't use Windows access control lists to restrict file and resource access, so you must be mindful of what resources you access when processing a Web request on behalf of a user. If a file is marked as restricted to members of a special Windows group the IUSR account has been granted access, Windows will not know that you want to be selective about which Forms Authentication users are able to access it.

Configure Forms Authentication

There are several steps required in configuring Forms Authentication. First, modify the web.config file of the. To enable Forms Authentication, set the mode attribute of the authentication element to Forms:

```
<configuration>
    <system.web>
        <authentication mode="Forms" />
    </system.web>
</configuration>
```

This isn't the only default value that needs to be changed. Just as IIS allows anonymous users, ASP.NET also allows anonymous access to applications. To force users to authenticate, you must also add authorization information to the web.config file to disallow anonymous users.

The web.config file shown in the following code denies access to anonymous users, while allowing all authenticated. This is done using special wildcard characters. The anonymous user is represented by the question mark, and all authenticated users are associated with the asterisk. Be careful not to confuse these symbols! And note that the class of authenticated users means all authenticated users. You will see shortly how to be more selective about which users.

```
<?xml version="1.0"?>
<configuration>
  <appSettings/>
  <connectionStrings/>
  <system.web>
    <authentication mode="Forms">
      <forms cookieless="UseCookies" />
    </authentication>
    <authorization>
```

```
            <deny users="?"/>
            <allow users="*"/>
        </authorization>
    </system.web>
</configuration>
```

It's a good practice to place the deny elements before the allow elements in your web.config. ASP.NET will stop examining these clauses when it first finds a match element. If a subsequent deny clause prevents access, it might be too late.

With this configuration, ASP.NET will now look at every request to the application, and if they have not authenticated, they will be redirected to the loginURL specified in the forms element of configuration. In this example, no loginURL is given, so the default is to use login.aspx page. Figure 8-3 shows the redirect that happens as a result of an anonymous user requesting a page called SecuredPage.aspx from the application.

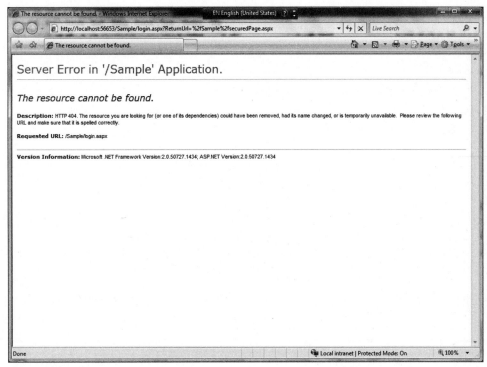

Figure 8-3

Notice that the error indicates that the requested URL was login.aspx. But the request was made for SecuredPage.aspx. Because the user was not authenticated, they were redirected to login.aspx. In the URL displayed in the browser address bar, you can see that the querystring contains a ReturnURL key-value pair, where the value is the original URL that was requested.

ASP.NET includes a control to easily display a login UI. Figure 8-4 shows a login page using just a single ASP.NET Login control.

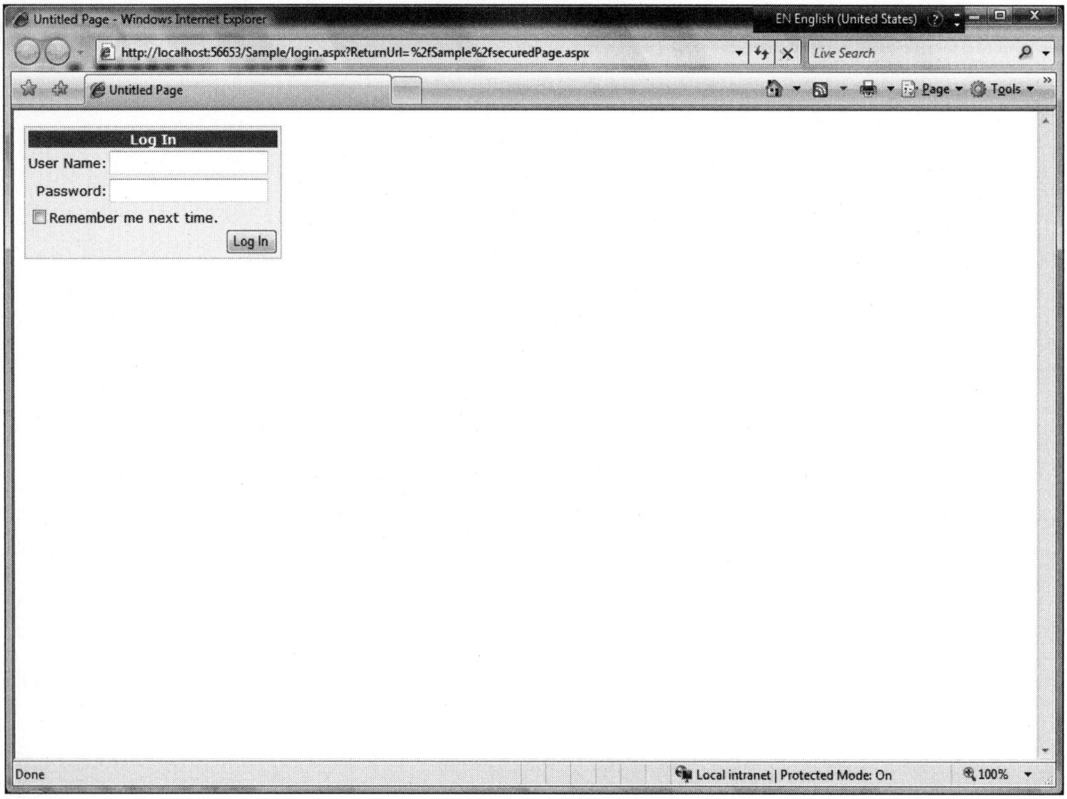

Figure 8-4

The basic styling information was provided by selecting one of the AutoFormat options for the control in Visual Studio. This can be seen in the page code in Listing 8-1. When the user submits the form, the Authenticate event is invoked. For the example, I have hardcoded a username and password. For completeness, I should remind you that hardcoding passwords is a bad practice.

Listing 8-1: Login.aspx

```
<%@ Page Language="C#" %>

<!DOCTYPE html PUBLIC "-//W3C//DTD XHTML 1.0 Transitional//EN"
"http://www.w3.org/TR/xhtml1/DTD/xhtml1-transitional.dtd">

<script runat="server">

    protected void Login1_Authenticate(object sender, AuthenticateEventArgs e)
  {
        if (("WroxUser" == Login1.UserName) && ("passw0rd" ==
Login1.Password)) {
            FormsAuthentication.RedirectFromLoginPage("WroxUser", false);
        }
```

Listing 8-1: Login.aspx *(continued)*

```
    }
</script>

<html xmlns="http://www.w3.org/1999/xhtml">
<head runat="server">
    <title>Login Page</title>
</head>
<body>
    <form id="form1" runat="server">
    <div>

        <asp:Login ID="Login1" runat="server" BackColor="#F7F7DE"
BorderColor="#CCCC99"
            BorderStyle="Solid" BorderWidth="1px" Font-Names="Verdana" Font-
Size="10pt"
            onauthenticate="Login1_Authenticate">
            <TitleTextStyle BackColor="#6B696B" Font-Bold="True"
ForeColor="#FFFFFF" />
        </asp:Login>

    </div>
    </form>
</body>
</html>
```

After the user provides credentials and is validated at the server, ASP.NET returns her to the page she was originally targeting. In addition to providing the basic login functionality in a control, ASP.NET also has controls for creating users, changing passwords, displaying the login state, and even recovering a forgotten password. The user information can be stored automatically in a database configured by running the `aspnet_regsql` tool. You can also configure your own back end for storing user information and perform custom authentication.

Custom Authentication

When authenticating users, you can leverage the built-in membership provider or provide a custom provider. The `SQLMembershipProvider` works with a published database schema against a SQL Server back end. It can even be used with the free desktop version of the database. To build a custom membership provider, you override the abstract `MembershipProvider` class and provide a custom implementation. Listing 8-2 is an excerpt from a custom membership provider (`WroxMembershipProvider.cs`). This allows you to decide what action will be taken to validate a user.

Listing 8-2: WroxMembershipProvider.cs

```
namespace Wrox.Samples {
    using System;
    using System.Web;
    using System.Configuration.Provider;
    using System.Web.Security;
    using System.Collections;
```

Continued

Listing 8-2: WroxMembershipProvider.cs *(continued)*

```csharp
using System.Collections.Specialized;

public class WroxMembershipProvider : MembershipProvider {

    public override void Initialize(string name, NameValueCollection
config) {
        base.Initialize(name, config);
    }

    public override bool ValidateUser(string username, string password) {
        return ((username == "WroxUser") && (password == "passw0rd"));
    }

    public override bool UnlockUser(string userName) {
        throw new System.NotImplementedException();
    }
}
}
```

The code in Listing 8-2 does not override all of the members of the abstract members as you would need to when providing a custom membership provider. In reality, you would want to use some better security practices than hardcoding usernames and passwords, as in the `ValidateUser` method earlier. It is a best practice to apply a one-way hash to the user's password and store that in the database instead. You can't decrypt the password and send it to the user. When a password is lost, you have to create a new replacement, but this practice minimizes the risk of someone discovering the password by compromising the storage. To use the custom provider, you add the provider and specify that you want your provider to be used by default in the `web.config` file:

```xml
<membership defaultProvider="SampleProvider">
  <providers>
    <add name="SampleProvider" type="Wrox.Samples.WroxMembershipProvider"/>
  </providers>
</membership>
```

Authenticating in JavaScript

Now that you've seen how ASP.NET provides several options for authenticating users, let's look at options for accessing these services using AJAX. Before using the Microsoft AJAX Library to authenticate users from JavaScript code running in the browser, you have to enable it. By default, the JavaScript services are not enabled. These services are off by default to keep all unneeded services disabled, which is a best practice from a security standpoint. A service can't be compromised if it is not enabled. You have to opt in to use these services.

```xml
<configuration>
  <system.web.extensions>
    <scripting>
      <webServices>
        <authenticationService enabled="true" requireSSL="false"/>
      </webServices>
```

```
        </scripting>
      </system.web.extensions>
    </configuration>
```

More information on the configuration elements can be found at www.asp.net/ajax/documentation/ live/ConfiguratingASPNETAJAX.aspx#microsoftweb. In addition to enabling the Authentication Service, you can specify whether to honor requests that are made without using SSL encryption. Similarly, other ASP.NET services are disabled for script access by default. Once enabled, the Sys.Services .AuthenticationService namespace will be available for use in the browser by all ASP.NET AJAX pages in the application that include a ScriptManager component. JavaScript code can then call back to the ASP. NET Authentication Service without requiring a full postback. You can avoid the redirect to a login page by authenticating users inline with JavaScript.

Listing 8-3 (from Membership.aspx) is a page with JavaScript code that uses the Authentication Service. It performs an out-of-band call to the login method to check the user's credentials, using the custom membership provider. The pageLoad function wires up an event handler for the Login button. The handler code then retrieves the username and password from textboxes on the page. It also declares variables for optional parameters. The isPersistent parameter is used to declare whether the authentication ticket issued should be maintained by the browser after the user closes it for use in a later session. If not set to true, the ticket will be discarded when the browser closes.

The customInfo and redirectUrl parameters are also optional. Whatever is passed in the customInfo argument will be relayed to the callback functions after the authentication is complete. redirectUrl, when provided, indicates the page that the user should be sent to when the authentication check is complete. The other two arguments to the login method are the completed and failed callback functions. You pass the name of functions that should be called when the login call completes or fails. It's important to note that the completed callback is invoked when the call to the Authentication Service completes, even if the result is a failed login attempt. The failed callback is called only if the credentials provided do not validate. Failed means the credentials were bad, not that the service call failed.

Listing 8-3: Membership.aspx

```
<!DOCTYPE html PUBLIC "-//W3C//DTD XHTML 1.0 Transitional//EN"
"http://www.w3.org/TR/xhtml1/DTD/xhtml1-transitional.dtd">
<html xmlns="http://www.w3.org/1999/xhtml" >
<head runat="server">
    <title>Membership Page</title>
</head>
<body>
    <form id="form1" runat="server">
    <div>

    <asp:scriptmanager runat="server" id="scriptmanager" />
    Username <input type="text" id="username" /><br />
    Password <input type="password" id="password" /><br />
    <input type="button" value="Login" id="login" /><br />

    </div>
    </form>
</body>
<script type="text/javascript">
```

Continued

Listing 8-3: Membership.aspx *(continued)*

```
function pageLoad() {
    $addHandler($get('login'), 'click', loginHandler);
}

function loginHandler() {
    var username = $get('username').value;
    var password = $get('password').value;
    var isPersistent = false;
    var customInfo = null;
    var redirectUrl = null;
    Sys.Services.AuthenticationService.login(
        username,
         password,
         isPersistent,
         customInfo,
         redirectUrl,
         loginCompleted,
         loginFailed);
}

function loginCompleted(result, context, methodName) {
    if(result) {
        alert("Successfuly logged in.");
    }
    else {
        alert("Failed to login.");
    }
}

function loginFailed(error, context, methodName) {
    alert(error.get_message());
}

</script>
</html>
```

ASP.NET allows you to define default handlers to be used for an event instead of specifying them with each call. This has been carried into the JavaScript support for application services as well. Once you have created the JavaScript functions you want to use as the defaults, you can make them the default for the page. The default `loginCompletedCallback`, `logoutCompletedCallback`, and `failedCallback` can all be set in the JavaScript `pageLoad` function of your page:

```
var service = Sys.Services.AuthenticationService;
service.set_defaultLoginCompletedCallback( loginCompleted );
service.set_defaultLogoutCompletedCallback( logoutCompleted );
service.set_defaultFailedCallback( authenticationFailed );
```

You still need to set the defaults on each page where the Authentication Service is going to be used, but you can standardize a set of names as shown here and have those functions defined in a script included in every page.

Accessing User Status

Of course, performing a validation check to authenticate a user is only part of what is needed in a Membership service. You also need to be able to check the current status of a user. If the user is not logged in, the option to login can be presented. And you can avoid trying to get any other data that should be available only to an authenticated user. The get_isLoggedIn function calls the Authentication Service to get the user's current status. In Listing 8-4 (Status.aspx) the user's current status is accessed and displayed as a result of clicking a button on the page.

Listing 8-4 ShowStatus.aspx

```
<!DOCTYPE html PUBLIC "-//W3C//DTD XHTML 1.0 Transitional//EN"
"http://www.w3.org/TR/xhtml1/DTD/xhtml1-transitional.dtd">
<html xmlns="http://www.w3.org/1999/xhtml" >
<head runat="server">
    <title>Membership Status Page</title>
</head>
<body>
    <form id="form1" runat="server">
    <div>
    <asp:scriptmanager runat="server" id="scriptmanager" />
    <input type="button" value="Show Status" id="status" /><br />
    </div>
    </form>
</body>
<script type="text/javascript">
function pageLoad() {
    $addHandler($get('status'), 'click', statusHandler);
}

function statusHandler() {
    var result = Sys.Services.AuthenticationService.get_isLoggedIn();
    if(result === true) {
        alert('You are logged in.');
    }
    else {
        alert('You are NOT logged in.');
    }
}

</script>
</html>
```

Logging Out

When a user chooses to log out, you may want to redirect her away from the page she is currently viewing. The logout function provides a redirectUrl parameter for this purpose. If the parameter is set, the browser navigates to the redirectUrl when the logout call completes. It is important to note that a page unload handler could interfere with the logout navigation. The unload code would need to be written knowing that logout could be called, and it must allow the redirect to happen. This unload issue is especially important if you have other developers working on the same application. Listing 8-5 (Logout.aspx) adds a button to the Status.aspx page for logging out.

Listing 8-5: Logout.aspx

```
<!DOCTYPE html PUBLIC "-//W3C//DTD XHTML 1.0 Transitional//EN"
"http://www.w3.org/TR/xhtml1/DTD/xhtml1-transitional.dtd">
<html xmlns="http://www.w3.org/1999/xhtml" >
<head runat="server">
    <title>Logout Page</title>
</head>
<body>
    <form id="form1" runat="server">
    <div>
    <asp:scriptmanager runat="server" id="scriptmanager" />
    <input type="button" value="Show Status" id="status" /><br />

    <input type="button" value="Logout" id="logout" /><br />
    </div>
    </form>
</body>
<script type="text/javascript">
function pageLoad() {
    $addHandler($get('status'), 'click', statusHandler);

    $addHandler($get('logout'), 'click', logoutHandler);
}

function statusHandler() {
    var result = Sys.Services.AuthenticationService.get_isLoggedIn();
    if(result === true) {
        alert('You are logged in.');
    }
    else {
        alert('You are NOT logged in.');
    }
}


function logoutHandler() {
    var redirectUrl = 'Logout.aspx';
    var userContext = null;
    Sys.Services.AuthenticationService.logout(redirectUrl, logoutCompletedCallback,
 logoutFailedCallback, userContext);
}

function logoutCompletedCallback(result, context, methodName) {
    alert('Logged out.')

}

function logoutFailedCallback(error, context, methodName) {
    alert(error.get_message());
}

</script>
</html>
```

The completion callbacks all have the same set of parameters. The first parameter is the result. This is the return value of the service method being called. If the method returns a Boolean, the result will be the Boolean that is returned. If it returns void, as the Logout function does, the result argument will be null.

Now you can avoid sending users through a series of redirects to log in and out. The ASP.NET AJAX Extensions make it easy to authenticate users, check their status, and log them out from any page!

User Profile Data

ASP.NET has a feature that allows you to track various kinds of data for each user easily. You can think of is a persistent version of the ASP.NET session state storage mechanism. It is often used to remember per user default or preference selections between sessions, such as the particular styling theme a user likes, or even default values for forms. The profile service can be configured to store data only for authenticated users or it can support anonymous users as well.

You define the name and types of the data that you want to store using the Profile service, using the web.config file for the application. You can then set and retrieve the specific data values from code. Although the Profile feature is similar to the Session object, it goes beyond it in several key ways. By default, the data is stored in the built-in database available to ASP.NET applications, so it is automatically persisted between user sessions. Session data is not persisted — it is stored in memory by default, but even if you choose to utilize SQL Server to hold session data, it will always be lost at the end of the user's current session.

Profile data is strongly typed, making it easier to utilize in code and avoid some common developer errors. Session data is only treated as the primitive object type and must be converted by you to the original type for each use, leading to possible runtime exceptions if the wrong type is used by mistake. ASP.NET provides the aspnet_regsql.exe tool, which can be used to configure a back-end SQL server with the tables necessary to store the profile information. The Profile information can also be made available in a server farm deployment scenario, since the database is always used as the persistence medium instead of holding values in memory.

Defining Profile Data

The first step in using the Profile feature is to establish the names and types of the data that you want to track. The following section from a web.config file declares five properties to be tracked as Profile data for each user. Note that in addition to the name and type, you can control whether the data is tracked for anonymous users. This is useful when a subset of users may authenticate themselves in parts of the application and you want to store information for only that group. You can bypass storing data for anonymous users. Conversely, maybe you have some personalization features that you specifically want to open up to anonymous users. Therefore, if the same anonymous user visits your site again, he will see that you were able to remember some facts about him, even though he didn't create a user account. Also, notice that you can define what type of serialization to utilize for storing the data as is done with the Artists.

```
<profile enabled="true" defaultProvider="SampleProvider">
  <providers>

    <add name="SampleProvider" type="Wrox.Samples.WroxProfileProvider" />
  </providers>
  <properties>
```

```
            <add name="Genre" type="System.String" allowAnonymous="true" />
            <add name="Artists" type="System.Collections.ArrayList"
allowAnonymous="true" serializeAs="Binary" />
            <add name="LastAlbumPurchased" type="Album" allowAnonymous="true"/>

            <group name="FavoriteAlbum">
              <add name="Artist" type="System.String" allowAnonymous="true" />
              <add name="Title" type="System.String" allowAnonymous="true"/>
            </group>
          </properties>
        </profile>
```

At the top level, you can have either items or groups. Groups are just a way to organize related items. A group doesn't imply any additional functionality and is used just as a coding convenience. The `Title` and `Artist` are in the `FavoriteAlbum` group. By grouping items together, you get nesting semantics, which can be especially helpful if there are a lot of Profile properties because IntelliSense can help you find the item you're looking for. If you don't use groups and the list of Profile items is long, you may have to scroll through a lot of items to find what you want. Figure 8-5 shows that the Profile items become available in the Source editor and IntelliSense helps you select the desired items and groups.

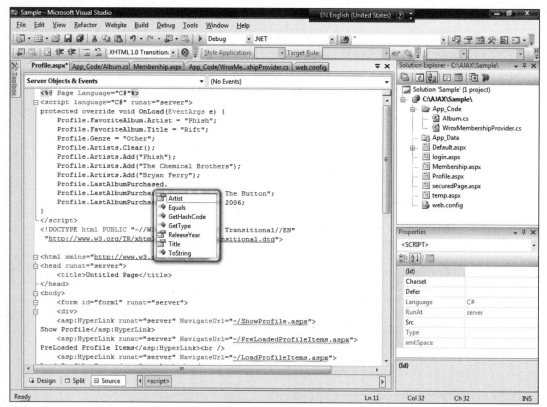

Figure 8-5

The type specified for the LastAlbumPurchased is just listed as Album, which does not exist in the .NET Framework. It is defined in a class located in the App_Code directory of the application. It is a simple class that tracks the artist, title, and year of release, as shown in Listing 8-6 (Album.cs). Because the default serialization works fine for this class and its basic types, nothing special is required to configure or use it.

Listing 8-6: Profile.aspx

```csharp
using System;

public class Album
{
    private String _artist;
    private String _title;
    private int _releaseYear;

 public Album() {
 }

    public String Artist {
        get {
            return _artist;
        }
        set {
            _artist = value;
        }
    }

    public String Title {
        get {
            return _title;
        }
        set {
            _title = value;
        }
    }

    public int ReleaseYear {
        get {
            return _releaseYear;
        }
        set {
            _releaseYear = value;
        }
    }
}
```

Accessing Profile Properties

Once the properties are defined, you can access them directly from the Profile intrinsic on any page. The Profile intrinsic is the object available in any ASP.NET page for retrieving and setting the properties for the current user that have been defined as part of the profile in the configuration. Another nice aspect of the Profile feature, as compared to using session state storage, is the strongly typed nature of the data. In this example, an integer and string are stored in `Session` state. Because `Session` state treats everything as an object, the integer and strings have to be explicitly cast to the desired type when they are read.

```
Session["count"] = 96;
Session["where"] = "anywhere";
count = (int)Session["count"];
where = (string)Session["where"];
```

If you were to declare the count and where variables are as profile properties, the code becomes much easier to read and write.

```
Profile.Count = 96;
Profile.Where = "anywhere";
int count = Profile.Count;
string where = Profile.Where;
```

Listing 8-7 (`Profile.aspx`) is a sample `.aspx` page showing profile storage in action. It links to other pages that show the current values of the profile properties by loading them from the profile storage and displaying them in the browser. There is also a page that makes updates to the profile.

Listing 8-7 Profile.aspx

```
<%@ Page Language="C#"%>
<script language="C#" runat="server">
protected override void OnLoad(EventArgs e) {
    Profile.FavoriteAlbum.Artist = "Phish";
    Profile.FavoriteAlbum.Title = "Rift";
    Profile.Genre = "Other";
    Profile.Artists.Clear();
    Profile.Artists.Add("Phish");
    Profile.Artists.Add("The Chemical Brothers");
    Profile.Artists.Add("Bryan Ferry");
    Profile.LastAlbumPurchased.Artist = "The Chemical Brothers";
    Profile.LastAlbumPurchased.Title = "Push The Button";
    Profile.LastAlbumPurchased.ReleaseYear = 2006;
}
</script>
<!DOCTYPE html PUBLIC "-//W3C//DTD XHTML 1.0 Transitional//EN"
 "http://www.w3.org/TR/xhtml1/DTD/xhtml1-transitional.dtd">

<html xmlns="http://www.w3.org/1999/xhtml" >
<head runat="server">
    <title>Untitled Page</title>
</head>
<body>
    <form id="form1" runat="server">
    <div>
    <asp:HyperLink runat="server" NavigateUrl="~/ShowProfile.aspx">
Show Profile</asp:HyperLink>
    <asp:HyperLink runat="server" NavigateUrl="~/PreLoadedProfileItems.aspx">
```

Listing 8-7 Profile.aspx *(continued)*

```
PreLoaded Profile Items</asp:HyperLink><br />
    <asp:HyperLink runat="server" NavigateUrl="~/LoadProfileItems.aspx">
Load Profile Items</asp:HyperLink><br />
    <asp:HyperLink runat="server" NavigateUrl="~/SaveProfileItems.aspx">

Save Profile Items</asp:HyperLink><br />

    </div>
    </form>
</body>
</html>
```

When this page is requested, the profile is populated with some music information, which is just hardcoded in the page's Page_Load event handler. Clicking the Show Profile link takes you to a page (ShowProfile.aspx). This page in Listing 8-8 accesses profile data and displays it. In this example, we aren't doing anything very interesting with the data, but it serves to show that the profile data is managed for you automatically that retrieves these same property values from the profile and renders them to the browser.

Listing 8-8: ShowProfile.aspx

```
<%@ Page Language="C#"%>
<script language="C#" runat="server">
protected override void OnLoad(EventArgs e) {
    string favoriteArtist = Profile.FavoriteAlbum.Artist;
    favoriteAlbumArtist.Text = artist;

    string album = Profile.FavoriteAlbum.Title;
    favoriteAlbumTitle.Text = favoriteTitle;

}
</script>
<!DOCTYPE html PUBLIC "-//W3C//DTD XHTML 1.0 Transitional//EN"
 "http://www.w3.org/TR/xhtml1/DTD/xhtml1-transitional.dtd">

<html xmlns="http://www.w3.org/1999/xhtml" >
<head id="Head1" runat="server">
    <title>Untitled Page</title>
</head>
<body>
    <form id="form1" runat="server">
    <div>
        <asp:Label ID="favoriteAlbumArtist" runat="server" /><br />
        <asp:Label ID="favoriteAlbumTitle" runat="server" /><br />
    </div>
    </form>
</body>
</html>
```

Accessing Profile Data from the Browser

So far, the examples have shown how to set up and use the Profile feature on the server. These are all tasks that can be done with ASP.NET 3.5. With ASP.NET AJAX, however, you can also access the profile information directly from JavaScript code running in the browser! The profile properties and groups have already been defined in the application's configuration file. But this alone does not make the profile data available remotely. You also have to explicitly opt in to the ability to use the Profile feature from the browser. This is done in the `system.web.extensions` section of the `web.config` file. With the authorization feature, it was only necessary to enable the service for remote access. For profile data, in addition to setting `enabled` to `true` for the `profileService` element, you need to elaborate which properties to make available. The read and write access permissions are controlled independently so that you can further control how the profile data is used. If you know that you won't need to modify profile values on the client, you should omit the `writeAccessProperties`.

```
<system.web.extensions>
  <scripting>
    <webServices>
    <profileService enabled="true"
         readAccessProperties="Genre, Artists, FavoriteAlbum.Artist,
FavoriteAlbum.Title, LastAlbumPurchased"
         writeAccessProperties="Genre, Artists, FavoriteAlbum.Artist,
FavoriteAlbum.Title, LastAlbumPurchased" />
    </webServices>
  </scripting>
</system.web.extensions>
```

ASP.NET AJAX adds a new handler for access to the Membership and Profile Services. For IIS versions earlier than 7, or for IIS7 running in the Classic mode, this setting is in the `httpHandlers` configuration section under `system.web`:

```
<system.web>
<httpHandlers>
<remove verb="*" path="*.asmx"/>
<add verb="*" path="*_AppService.axd" validate="false"
type="System.Web.Script.Services.ScriptHandlerFactory, System.Web.Extensions,
Version=1.0.61025.0, Culture=neutral, PublicKeyToken=31bf3856ad364e35"/>
</httpHandlers>
</system.web>
```

And for the IIS7 using the new Integrated mode, the setting is in the `system.webserver` section in the `handlers` element:

```
<system.webserver>
<handlers>
  <remove name="WebServiceHandlerFactory-ISAPI-2.0"/>
  <add name="ScriptHandlerFactoryAppServices" verb="*" path="*_AppService.axd"
preCondition="integratedMode"
        type="System.Web.Script.Services.ScriptHandlerFactory,
System.Web.Extensions, Version=1.0.61025.0, Culture=neutral,
PublicKeyToken=31bf3856ad364e35"/>
</handlers>
</system.webserver>
```

The configuration is now in place. You have defined a set of profile properties, enabled the service for remote access, and declared the properties to be readable and writeable. Now you need a page that accesses the Profile store from JavaScript.

Preload Profile Properties

The set of data being stored in the profile can be quite extensive. It would be wasted overhead to send all of the profile information down to the browser in the original page rendering if there's only a small chance that you'll need it all. The default is not to preload any profile properties, but this isn't ideal for the pages where you know you will need at least some profile data. The ScriptManager's `ProfileService` element has a `LoadProperties` attribute that allows you to specify what properties should be made available initially and sent down with the first page rendering.

In this example, `Genre` and `Artists` would be available in the initial page rendering. Client script could make use of them without making any calls to the server to get more data. However, access to any other profile data still requires going back to the server:

```
<asp:ScriptManager runat="server" ID="scriptManager">
    <ProfileService LoadProperties="Genre, Artists" />
</asp:ScriptManager>
```

The preloaded properties can be accessed directly from the properties object of the `ProfileService` object, which is part of the Microsoft AJAX Library:

```
var artists = Sys.Services.ProfileService.properties.Artists;
```

There is no requirement to provide callback functions or to pause and wait for an asynchronous call to the server to return the data for the preloaded properties. Listing 8-9 (`PreLoadedProfileItems.aspx`) is a page that adds a button and binds a click handler to it. The handler then shows the `Genre` and `Artists` Profile properties declared for preloading.

Listing 8-9: PreLoadProfile.aspx

```
<!DOCTYPE html PUBLIC "-//W3C//DTD XHTML 1.0 Transitional//EN"
"http://www.w3.org/TR/xhtml1/DTD/xhtml1-transitional.dtd">
<html xmlns="http://www.w3.org/1999/xhtml" >
<head runat="server">
    <title>PreLoaded Profile Items</title>
</head>
<body>
    <form id="form1" runat="server">
    <asp:ScriptManager runat="server" ID="scriptManager">
        <ProfileService LoadProperties="Genre, Artists" />
    </asp:ScriptManager>
    <div>
    <input type="button" id="showProfile" value="Show Profile" />
    </div>
    </form>
</body>
<script type="text/javascript">
```

Continued

Listing 8-9: PreLoadProfile.aspx *(continued)*

```
function pageLoad() {
    $addHandler($get('showProfile'), 'click', showProfile);
}

function showProfile() {
    var genre = "Favorite Genre : " + Sys.Services.ProfileService.properties.Genre;
    alert(genre);
    var artists = Sys.Services.ProfileService.properties.Artists;
    var message = "Favorita Artists:\r\n";
    for(var index = 0; index < artists.length; index++) {
        message += artists[index] + "\r\n";
    }
    alert(message);
}
</script>
</html>
```

Figure 8-6 shows the Artists displayed by the browser. The ArrayList on the server is translated into a JavaScript object, where the individual elements of the ArrayList are accessed through the object's indexer.

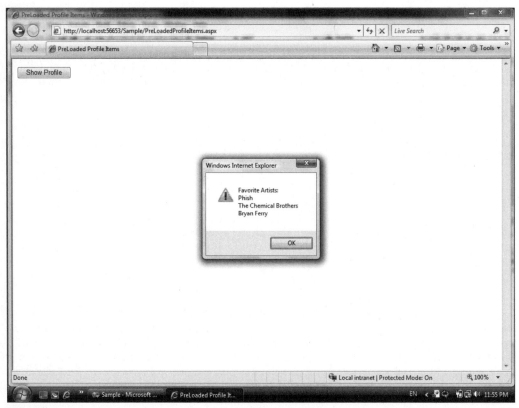

Figure 8-6

Load Profile Properties

All of the Profile properties you might want to access while the page is running do not have to be pre-loaded. As long as they are declared in the `web.config` file as accessible remotely, Profile properties can be loaded on demand at any time. However, when making a call to retrieve those properties that were not preloaded, you need to provide a callback function, since there's no way to predict how long that data-fetching operation will take. You can also make a call back to the server to refetch preloaded values, in case their value may have been changed since the page was loaded.

There are four arguments to the load method of the `ProfileService`. The first argument is an array of the names of the properties to be retrieved. The second is the callback function for completing the call. The third is the error callback. The last argument is for any user context data that should be passed to the completion events.

```
Sys.Services.ProfileService.load(
    ["FavoriteAlbum.Artist", "FavoriteAlbum.Title"],          loadCompletedCallback,
        failedCallback,
        null );
```

It is not necessary to pass anything for the `userContext` parameter unless you want to tell your callback function something extra about this particular call. In this example, I include the fourth parameter with a null that is actually redundant. JavaScript implies a null value for any parameter that you aren't required to provide. I like to be explicit about it, as doing so helps me make fewer mistakes by thinking through what is needed and what is not. It's also easier to come back to this code and add some context data in place of the null because I can see where that value should go.

The arguments to your completion callback function are the result of the call to the server method, the `userContext` that was passed to the `load` function, and the name of the method that was called. In this case, the result is the count of properties that were loaded.

```
function loadCompletedCallback(result, context, methodName) {
    alert("Retrieved " + result + " profile properties.");
}
```

The AJAX error object passed to the failed callback provides access to the type of exception that occurred and its error message. You can also get the stack trace in effect at the time the exception occurred:

```
function failedCallback(error, context, methodName) {
    var message = error.get_exceptionType() + "\r\n" +
        error.get_message() + "\r\n" +
        error.get_stackTrace();
    alert(message);
}
```

The page in Listing 8-10 (`LoadProfileItems.aspx`) has two buttons: one for loading profile data and the other for displaying it. It binds the event handlers to the button click events in the `pageLoad` method. It also adds an error handler to display more detailed information if something goes wrong. Displaying a stack trace may be helpful during development, but when the application is deployed, the end user won't be able to do anything useful with the information, so more robust and user-friendly error recovery should be added before final production deployment.

Listing 8-10: Profile.aspx

```
<!DOCTYPE html PUBLIC "-//W3C//DTD XHTML 1.0 Transitional//EN"
"http://www.w3.org/TR/xhtml1/DTD/xhtml1-transitional.dtd">
<html xmlns="http://www.w3.org/1999/xhtml" >
<head runat="server">
    <title>Load Profile Items</title>
</head>
<body>
    <form id="form1" runat="server">
    <asp:ScriptManager runat="server" ID="scriptManager">
        <ProfileService/>
    </asp:ScriptManager>

    <div>
    <input type="button" id="loadFavorite" value="Load Favorite" /><br />
    <input type="button" id="showFavorite" value="Show Favorite" />
    </div>
    </form>
</body>

<script type="text/javascript">
function pageLoad() {
    $addHandler($get('showFavorite'), 'click', showFavorite);
    $addHandler($get('loadFavorite'), 'click', loadFavorite);
}

function showFavorite() {
    alert("Favorite Album\r\n" +
        Sys.Services.ProfileService.properties.FavoriteAlbum.Title +
        " by " +
        Sys.Services.ProfileService.properties.FavoriteAlbum.Artist);
}

function loadFavorite() {
    Sys.Services.ProfileService.load(["FavoriteAlbum.Artist",
"FavoriteAlbum.Title"], loadCompletedCallback, failedCallback, null);
}

function loadCompletedCallback(result, context, methodName) {
    alert("Retrieved " + result + " profile properties.");
}

function failedCallback(error, context, methodName) {
    var message = error.get_exceptionType() + "\r\n" +
        error.get_message() + "\r\n" +
        error.get_stackTrace();
    alert(message);
}
</script>
</html>
```

Saving Profile Data

When profile data is updated in the browser, it needs to be saved back to the server to be persisted for later use. The signature of the save function is the same as that of the load function. The first argument now indicates which set of Profile properties should be saved. If you don't include a set of properties, all of the properties on the client will be sent. This can be overkill if only a few are actually in need of being updated:

```
function saveFavorite() {
    var profile = Sys.Services.ProfileService;
    profile.properties.Artists[0] = $get('favoriteArtist').value;
    profile.save(["Artists"], saveCompletedCallback, failedCallback, null);
}
```

When working with custom types, like the Album example, there are a few additional requirements to be aware of. The Profile Service counts on the custom type having a parameterless constructor and property setters for each custom type that it creates. This is a standard requirement in order to deserialize data. The Profile Service doesn't make other assumptions about how to deserialize data beyond requiring a list of name-value pairs for creating the type. To create an Album object to be saved in the profile, Artist, Title, and ReleaseYear are specified along with the values. The syntax can seem a little odd at first, but the simplicity avoids the need for any custom serialization:

```
function addLastPurchased() {
    var profile = Sys.Services.ProfileService;
    profile.properties.LastAlbumPurchased =
        { Artist: "Irina", Title: "ala riko kaavaa", ReleaseYear: "2001" };
    profile.save(
        ["LastAlbumPurchased"],
        saveCompletedCallback,
        failedCallback,
        null );
}
```

When updating the properties of a custom type that was already loaded, the name-value pair syntax is not necessary. The properties of custom objects are accessed in the same way as common .NET Framework types. You can access the property directly on the Profile property:

```
var lastArtistPurchased =
Sys.Services.ProfileService.properties.LastAlbumPurchased.Artist;
```

Or you can access the profile's version of the custom type and pass the name of the property as an indexer argument. This would be most useful if the name of the property were being extracted from a JavaScript variable.

```
var albumTitle =
Sys.Services.ProfileService.properties.LastAlbumPurchased["Title"];
```

The key thing to remember when working with custom types that are part of the profile is that in the JavaScript representation, no custom serialization or advanced type conversion occurs. Instead, the properties are reflected as simple types when sent down to the browser. And when they are sent to the server, they are treated as name-value pairs, where the name indicates the property accessor to invoke, and the value is the argument to pass to the property setter. Listing 8-11 (SaveProfileItems.aspx) is a page that displays Profile information, allows the user to modify the first element of the Artists array, and updates the last album purchased in a button's click event handler.

Listing 8-11: SaveProfileItems.aspx

```
<!DOCTYPE html PUBLIC "-//W3C//DTD XHTML 1.0 Transitional//EN"
"http://www.w3.org/TR/xhtml1/DTD/xhtml1-transitional.dtd">

<html xmlns="http://www.w3.org/1999/xhtml" >
<head runat="server">
    <title>Save Profile Items</title>
</head>
<body>
    <form id="form1" runat="server">
    <asp:ScriptManager runat="server" ID="scriptManager">
        <ProfileService LoadProperties="Artists, LastAlbumPurchased" />
    </asp:ScriptManager>
    <div><b>Favorite Artist : </b><input type="text" id="favoriteArtist" /><br />
    <input type="button" id="saveFavorite" value="Save" /><br /><br />
    <asp:Label runat="server" ID="artists" /><br /><br />
    <input type="button" id="addLast" value="Add Album"/>
    <asp:Label runat="server" ID="lastArtistPurchased" />
    </div>
    </form>
</body>
<script type="text/javascript">
var favoriteArtist = "";

function pageLoad() {
    $get('favoriteArtist').value =
Sys.Services.ProfileService.properties.Artists[0];
    $addHandler($get('saveFavorite'), 'click', saveFavorite);
    $addHandler($get('addLast'), 'click', addLastPurchased);
    updateLabel();
}

function updateLabel() {
    var theArtists = Sys.Services.ProfileService.properties.Artists;
    var theLabel = "";
    for(var i = 0; i < theArtists.length; i++) {
        theLabel += theArtists[i] + "<br />";
    }
    $get('artists').innerHTML = theLabel;
    $get('lastArtistPurchased').innerHTML =
Sys.Services.ProfileService.properties.LastAlbumPurchased["Artist"];
}

function saveFavorite() {
    var profile = Sys.Services.ProfileService;
    profile.properties.Artists[0] = $get('favoriteArtist').value;
    profile.save(["Artists"], saveCompletedCallback, failedCallback, null);
```

Listing 8-11: SaveProfileItems.aspx *(continued)*

```
    }

    function addLastPurchased() {
        var profile = Sys.Services.ProfileService;
        profile.properties.LastAlbumPurchased =
            { Artist: "Irina", Title: "ala riko kaavaa", ReleaseYear: "2001" };

        profile.save(
            ["LastAlbumPurchased"],
            saveCompletedCallback,
            failedCallback,
            null );
    }

    function saveCompletedCallback(result, context, methodName) {
        updateLabel();
        alert("Saved " + result + " profile properties.");
    }

    function failedCallback(error, context, methodName) {
        var message = error.get_exceptionType() + "\r\n" +
            error.get_message() + "\r\n" +
            error.get_stackTrace();
        alert(message);
    }

</script>
</html>
```

Profile data, whether made up of simple types or complex custom types, can now be accessed easily from JavaScript code in the browser. You can retrieve and update data on the fly without a full postback of the page.

Security Concerns about Client-side Profile Usage

You need to be aware that if you allow profile data to be read from or written to the client, a hacker might intercept the data flow in either direction. Conversely, if the profile data is accessed only from the server, there is no chance of interception. For this reason, you must be careful not to allow any sensitive data to be passed to or from the client in profile storage items. Of course, writable properties are going to be your biggest concern, since readable values will likely be rendered as viewable HTML anyway. The best usage of profile storage is to hold only user preferences, such as a favorite skin, color scheme, or default values for GUI controls, or nonsensitive user data that would not cause a problem if compromised. For example, the user's favorite background color is fine, but his or her bank account number would probably not be a good candidate for profile storage.

Managing User Roles

In addition to being able to authenticate individual users and store Profile data for them, you probably need to understand what roles they are authorized for in the application. To simplify the process of checking application rights, ASP.NET provides the Membership and Roles feature. This allows you to configure groups for a Web application that map to business roles the way that you can in the operating system itself.

Configuring Role Management

Like the other application services, Role Management must be enabled. Instead of checking against the server back-end storage on each request, role management information can be cached in a browser cookie. The `roleManager` element of the `web.config` file lets you specify how much data to cache in the cookie and how long it is cached. You can also configure the service to encrypt the data, calculate a hash value to guard against tampering, or do both:

```
<roleManager enabled="true"
cacheRolesInCookie="true"
cookieSlidingExpiration="true"
cookieProtection="All" />
```

The options for the `cookieProtection` attribute of the `roleManager` element are `All`, `Encryption`, `None`, and `Validation`. I recommend against `None` as it equates to sharing with prying eyes any roles you have defined and lets a malicious user submit request with synthetic role values.

You can create the roles using code or via the .NET Role Manager element of the IIS 7 Administration tool. Figure 8-7 shows the addition of a new Sellers role to the Sample application.

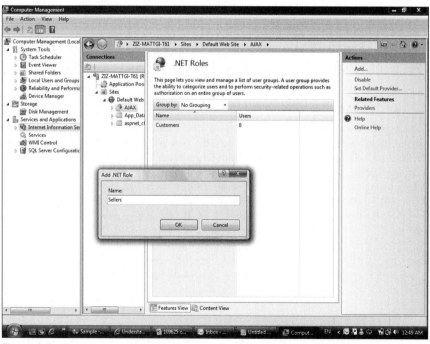

Figure 8-7

A role by itself is not very useful. It is a user's membership in the role that provides utility. Figure 8-8 shows a new user being created using the Administration tool. It includes password recovery questions and answers in addition to email, password, and username.

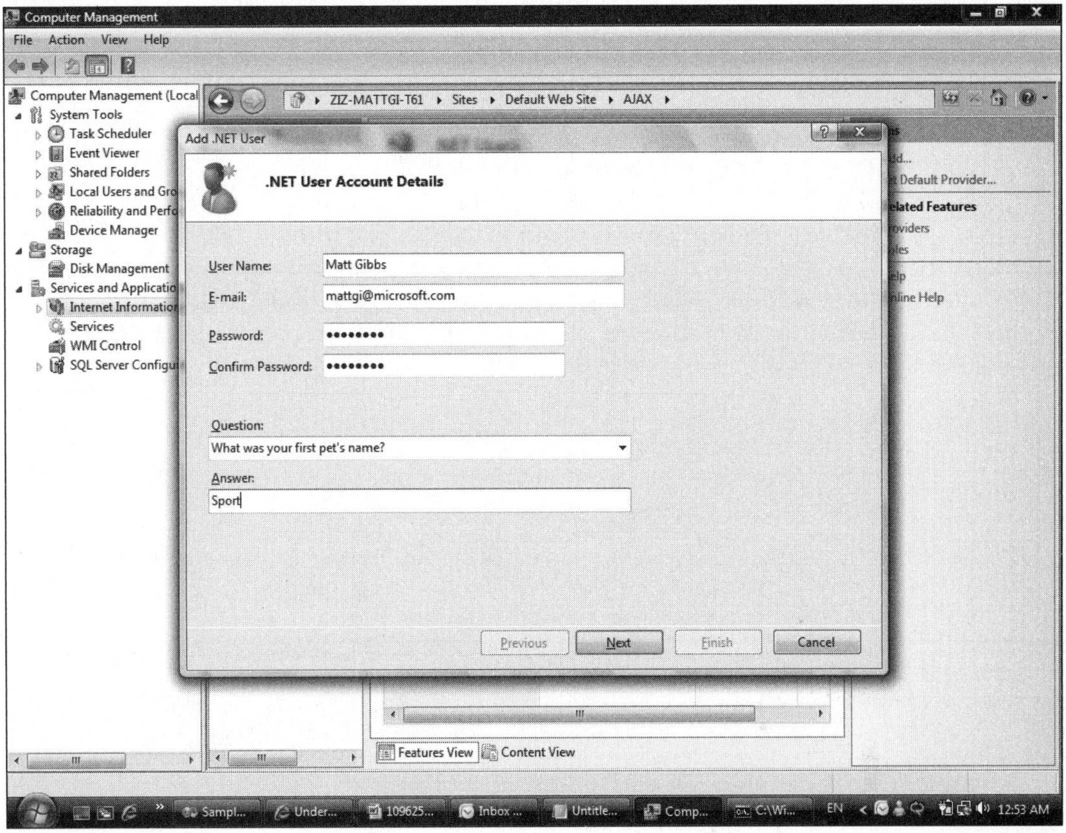

Figure 8-8

You could write code in every page to check a user's membership in a role, but ASP.NET simplifies this by allowing directories to be limited to access by specific roles. In this code snippet from a `web.config`, the `management` subdirectory of the application is configured to allow access to Managers and Administrators.

```
<configuration>
  <location path="management">
    <system.web>
      <authorization>
        <allow roles="Managers,Administrators" />
        <deny users="*" />
      </authorization>
    </system.web>
  </location>
```

Client-side Role Checks

ASP.NET AJAX allows you to validate role information from JavaScript. Like the other application services, it must be enabled for remote access in the `system.web.extensions` section of the `web.config`:

```
<system.web.extensions>
  <scripting>
    <webServices>
      <authenticationService enabled="true" requireSSL="false"/>
      <profileService enabled="true" />
      <roleService enabled="true"/>
    </webServices>
  </scripting>
</system.web.extensions>
```

The roles feature relies on the authentication feature. You can use methods of the JavaScript class to check that the current user is in a specific role, or you can load the complete set of roles for the user in a comma-delimited list.

```
function page_Load() {
    var roleList = Sys.Services.RoleService.get_roles();
    alert(roleList);
}
```

In code Listing 8-12 (`UsingRoles.aspx`), you can see the familiar pattern of calling an ASP.NET application service in an event handler in the page code and providing completion and failure callbacks.

Listing 8-12: UsingRoles.aspx

```
<!DOCTYPE html PUBLIC "-//W3C//DTD XHTML 1.0 Transitional//EN"
"http://www.w3.org/TR/xhtml1/DTD/xhtml1-transitional.dtd">
<html xmlns="http://www.w3.org/1999/xhtml" >
<head runat="server">
    <title>Using Profiles</title>
</head>
<body>
    <form id="form1" runat="server">
    <asp:ScriptManager runat="server" ID="scriptManager">
        <ProfileService/>
    </asp:ScriptManager>
    <div>
    </div>
    </form>
</body>
</html>

<script type="text/javascript">
function pageLoad() {
    Sys.Services.RoleService.load(loadCompletedCallback, failedCallback,
 null);
}

function loadCompletedCallback(result, context, methodName) {
```

Listing 8-12: UsingRoles.aspx *(continued)*

```
        if (Sys.Services.RoleService.isUserInRole("Managers")) {
            alert("Managers view enabled");
        }
    }

    function failedCallback(error, context, methodName) {
        var message = error.get_exceptionType() + "\r\n" +
            error.get_message() + "\r\n" +
            error.get_stackTrace();
        alert(message);
    }
    </script>
    </html>
```

Roles and Membership are key features for scoping the information presented to user. Using them, you can provide a unique experience for users based on their rights within the application. With ASP.NET AJAX, you have greater flexibility to dynamically check membership and reduce page refreshes and server-side content rendering.

Summary

ASP.NET AJAX makes the important application services available to JavaScript code running in the browser. It is no longer necessary to think of Forms Authentication, Roles, and Profile as server-only features. The application services simply leverage server resources for checking user credentials and for storing profile data.

You can now more easily enhance applications to gather and store data about the user, even if he or she is not authenticated, by enabling profile properties for anonymous use. And when the user returns to the site, the profile information will still be available. In addition, when a user chooses to authenticate, he can do so directly from the browser without a series of redirects to a login page and back.

Enabling the application services for AJAX is an important step in being able to write rich browser-based applications that take full advantage of the server and provide an enhanced user experience. You can make you application more dynamic and responsive for the user by reducing the need for full postbacks and content refreshes of entire pages.

9

ASP.NET AJAX Networking

At the heart of AJAX development is the ability to make asynchronous Web service calls from JavaScript code. The major Web browsers have included an `XMLHttpRequest` object for making HTTP requests. The `XMLHttpRequest` object is used to perform out-of-band communications with the server for invoking Web services, executing callbacks, and performing partial page updates. This object allows the browser to send requests to the server and to receive data from the server without requiring the entire page to be posted back to the server and subsequently refreshed in the browser.

ASP.NET AJAX provides classes for managing Web requests, processing responses, and detecting errors. It also provides support for serializing objects formatted as JavaScript Object Notation (JSON), which makes them readily usable in JavaScript in the browser. JSON is a standard serial format that is more lightweight than XML. In this chapter, you learn how to use the ASP.NET JavaScript classes to perform networking tasks such as making synchronous and asynchronous HTTP requests, serializing .NET objects to and from JavaScript, and handling errors when Web requests do not execute as expected.

The XMLHttpRequest Object

The `XMLHttpRequest` object was introduced by Microsoft as an ActiveX control for Internet Explorer 5. It was later added to Mozilla 1.0 and Safari 1.2. Internet Explorer 7 includes it as a native script object, rather than as an ActiveX control. Now, all serious browsers include support for this object. In Internet Explorer before version 7, you pass the name of the object to the `ActiveXObject` function:

```
var request = new ActiveXObject("Msxml2.XMLHTTP");
```

In Firefox and most other browsers, you can simply use the `new` keyword to create an object directly in JavaScript. In these browsers, the `XMLHttpRequest` has been added natively to the DOM.

```
var request = new XMLHttpRequest();
```

The separate implementations have some common methods, and the behavior is much the same, but ASP.NET AJAX provides objects that give you an abstraction from the differences, so you don't have to worry about browser variations. The ASP.NET AJAX Extensions JavaScript objects are also similar to those available in the .NET Framework, so the object model is more familiar to .NET developers than the native XMLHttpRequest objects.

Because ASP.NET AJAX gives you a set of standard classes to ensure consistent behavior when accessing Web resources, rather than using the browser-specific XMLHttpRequest object directly, I won't go into the details of the XMLHttpRequest object, except to point out some security and architectural issues.

XMLHttpRequest Security

The browsers all enforce a common security policy that restricts the XMLHttpRequest object from issuing cross-domain requests. This is a common-sense restriction that prevents a page from possibly sending sensitive data to a third-party site you aren't specifically addressing. Your JavaScript code can only successfully issue requests against the domain in which the page originated. In fact, the policy prohibits requests that go to a different host, use a different protocol (like HTTP instead of HTTPS), or access the server on a different port. This limits your ability to write so-called mashup applications (the term mashup means to consolidate data from different sources) that leverage a variety of different sources on the Web for a synergistic application. For example, JavaScript in a page request to http://www.wrox .com cannot use the XMLHttpRequest object to make calls to http://www.wiley.com (different domain) or to https://www.wrox.com (different protocol) or to http://www.wrox.com:81 (different port) or to http://scripts.wrox.com (different host). You are limited to using the XMLHttpRequest object only for issuing requests against the same domain, host, port, and protocol of the originating page.

Because there are many valid scenarios where you might want to allow mashups from different sites, you can take advantage of some alternate approaches for accessing remote resources. The security restriction does not guard against, including IFrame elements in a page that accesses content on different domains, because an IFrame is allowed to pull in a different page, possibly from a different site. For that reason, browsers also restrict JavaScript from communicating between frames that originate from different domains, but there are techniques to work around it. Also, a Web service on the originating site can act as a proxy and issue requests against a remote domain on behalf of your Web page. The service then returns the remote content to the browser. This involves routing additional requests to your own server, when you would prefer going directly to the servers in another domain, but it satisfies the security constraints of the browser.

Object Properties and Methods

Although there are different implementations of the XMLHttpRequest object in the standard browsers, they share some common APIs. In ASP.NET AJAX applications, you can program against the WebRequest and WebRequestManager objects to simplify your interactions with the XMLHttpRequest object, but it is also helpful to understand what is being done in the underlying object.

Some common methods allow you to initiate a request using send() and to terminate a request by calling abort(). There are also methods for setting and retrieving HTTP headers by calling setRequestHeader and getResponseHeader. The status and statusText properties yield information about the results of the call. And there are properties for retrieving the body of the response as text (responseText) or in an XML format (responseXML).

Listing 9-1 (Time.aspx) is a Web page that returns the server time to its caller. It takes no parameters and returns a string. Although it's easy to handle strings, ASP.NET makes development easier by serializing and deserializing more complex types that can be passed between Web services and JavaScript. You will see examples of this later in this chapter when Web services are used instead of invoking an ASP.NET page directly.

Listing 9-1: Time.aspx

```
<%@ Page Language="C#" %>
<script runat="server">
protected override void OnLoad(EventArgs e) {
    base.OnLoad(e);
    Response.Write(DateTime.Now.ToUniversalTime());
}
</script>
```

Listing 9-2 (CallTime.aspx) shows basic usage of the XMLHttpRequest object to call the time Web page. This is the kind of classic JavaScript code you'd find in any generic AJAX Web page. You can quickly see from this code that certain pieces of JavaScript would be repeated wherever you use XMLHttpRequest. ASP.NET AJAX abstracts much of this repetitive code to simplify and streamline your code. In this example, you first determine whether the user is browsing with a browser that supports the native XMLHttpRequest object. If not, the ActiveX object is used. Next, call the open method with parameters to perform an HTTP GET request, the service address, and a Boolean true to indicate that the request should be asynchronous. The readyStateChangedHandler function is assigned to the readyStateChange event, and then the send method is called.

Listing 9-2: CallTime.aspx

```
<!DOCTYPE html PUBLIC "-//W3C//DTD XHTML 1.0 Transitional//EN"
 "http://www.w3.org/TR/xhtml1/DTD/xhtml1-transitional.dtd">

<html xmlns="http://www.w3.org/1999/xhtml" >
<head runat="server">
    <title>Networking</title>
<script type="text/javascript">

var xmlhttp;

function pageLoad() {
    if(window.XMLHttpRequest) {
        xmlhttp = new XMLHttpRequest();
    }
    else {
        xmlhttp = new ActiveXObject("Msxml2.XMLHTTP");
    }
    xmlhttp.open("GET", "Time.aspx", true);
    xmlhttp.onreadystatechange = readyStateChangedHandler;
    xmlhttp.send("");
}
```

Continued

Listing 9-2: CallTime.aspx *(continued)*

```
function readyStateChangedHandler() {

    if(xmlhttp.readyState == 4) {
        alert(xmlhttp.responseText);
    }
}
</script>
</head>
<body>
    <form id="form1" runat="server">
    <asp:ScriptManager runat="server" ID="ScriptManager1">
    </asp:ScriptManager>
    <div>

    </div>
    </form>
</body>
</html>
```

The readyStateChange event is fired each time the state of the XMLHttpRequest object transitions to a different phase of handling the request. The states are assigned fixed numbers, and 4 happens to be the state that indicates that the request has completed. Upon finding a status of 4, you display the time in an alert dialog. The code is not overly complex but does not include any error checking or do anything with the other states of the XMLHttpRequest object. As the use of the XMLHttpRequest object increases in an application, so does the complexity of the code, and the repetition of code can lead to errors and problems with maintainability. The ASP.NET AJAX WebRequest class makes leveraging the XMLHttpRequest object easier.

Making WebRequest Calls

The WebRequest class is the central object used for managing HTTP requests in ASP.NET AJAX. It provides a cross-browser compatible object for using the different underlying XMLHttpRequest implementations. Listing 9-3 (CallTimeWebRequest.aspx) is a Web page that does the equivalent of the request and response processing shown in Listing 9-2.

Listing 9-3: CallTimeWebRequest.aspx

```
<!DOCTYPE html PUBLIC "-//W3C//DTD XHTML 1.0 Transitional//EN"
  "http://www.w3.org/TR/xhtml1/DTD/xhtml1-transitional.dtd">

<html xmlns="http://www.w3.org/1999/xhtml" >
<head runat="server">
    <title>Networking</title>
<script type="text/javascript">

var xmlhttp;

function pageLoad() {
```

Listing 9-3: CallTimeWebRequest.aspx *(continued)*

```
        var  Request = new Sys.Net.WebRequest();
        webRequest.set_url("Time.aspx");

        webRequest.add_completed(completedHandler);
        webRequest.invoke();
    }

    function completedHandler(result, eventArgs) {
        if(result.get_responseAvailable()) {
            alert(result.get_statusText());
            alert(result.get_responseData());
        }
    }
</script>
</head>
<body>
    <form id="form1" runat="server">
    <asp:ScriptManager runat="server" ID="ScriptManager1">
    </asp:ScriptManager>
    <div>
    </div>
    </form>
</body>
</html>
```

First, note that the code creates a `Sys.Net.WebRequest` object directly. You do not have to bother with checking the browser compatibility. You set the service address, add a completed callback function, and invoke the request. In the callback function, there is no need to check different integers against the status codes they represent. Instead, there is a check that the response is available, coupled with access to the data. This isn't dramatically different from what is done in Listing 9-2 when using the `XMLHttpRequest` object directly; however, it is more straightforward and avoids your having to look at each and every state change in the underlying object.

The `WebRequest` object provides abstractions for much of what is typically handled by the browser. Many of the interactions between browser and server can be controlled through the `WebRequest` object. The HTTP protocol defines a set of headers that you may want to control. You also may find that you don't want to accept the default behavior of waiting indefinitely for a server to respond once you have initiated a request.

Setting the HTTP Verb

HTTP requests include a verb for processing. Most of the time, you use either GET to query the server or POST to upload data. The HEAD verb is also used to gather information about the content type and to get caching information. The `WebRequest` object assumes a GET request unless you specify otherwise. A GET request passes values in the querystring, which many avoid from a security standpoint. Developers generally don't want their users to see the querystring, but in this case, the user doesn't see it since the request is being handled in code. A POST is more appropriate if you have a lot of data to send to the server. There are much smaller size limits for what is carried in the querystring than what can be sent in the body of a POST.

The `WebRequest` provides functions to retrieve and set the HTTP verb. In Debug mode, the class will check for a nonzero-length verb, but it has no way to verify that the verb is supported by the server, so any nonzero length value is accepted.

Listing 9-4 shows the `EchoABC.aspx` page that will receive and process a POST from the code in Listing 9-5. Note that it looks for a value by name in the request's form collection, since a POST doesn't transfer data in the querystring.

Listing 9-4: EchoABC.aspx

```
<%@ Page Language="C#" %>
<script runat="server">
protected override void OnLoad(EventArgs e)
{
    base.OnLoad(e);
    if(Request.Form["abc"] != null) {
        Response.Write(Server.HtmlEncode(Request.Form["abc"]));
    }
}
</script>
```

The page in Listing 9-5 (`SetVerb.aspx`) sets the HTTP verb to POST and sets the body to a name-value pair. The key is checked in the form collection from Listing 9-4, and its result is returned.

Listing 9-5: SetVerb.aspx

```
<!DOCTYPE html PUBLIC "-//W3C//DTD XHTML 1.0 Transitional//EN"
"http://www.w3.org/TR/xhtml1/DTD/xhtml1-transitional.dtd">

<html xmlns="http://www.w3.org/1999/xhtml" >
<head id="Head1" runat="server">
    <title>Networking</title>
<script type="text/javascript">
function pageLoad() {
    var webRequest = new Sys.Net.WebRequest();
    webRequest.set_url('EchoABC.aspx');
    webRequest.set_httpVerb('POST');
    webRequest.set_body('abc=123');
    webRequest.add_completed(completedHandler);
    webRequest.invoke();
}

function completedHandler(result, eventArgs) {
    if(result.get_responseAvailable()) {
        alert(result.get_statusText());
        alert(result.get_responseData());
    }
}
</script>
</head>
<body>
```

Listing 9-5: SetVerb.aspx *(continued)*

```
        <form id="form1" runat="server">
        <asp:ScriptManager runat="server" ID="ScriptManager1">
        </asp:ScriptManager>
        <div>
        </div>
        </form>
    </body>
    </html>
```

Establishing Timeout Limits

A call to `set_timeout` on the `WebRequest` can impose a limit on how long to you will wait for the response. The result can then be checked to find out if the call was terminated before reaching the limit. The `get_timedOut` property returns `true` if the call did not complete in time. To test your code you want to ensure that the limit is reached. You can do so by putting the thread to sleep for longer than the value of the `set_timeout` call.

```
    System.Threading.Thread.Sleep(10000);
```

Listing 9-6 (`Timeout.aspx`) adds a call to `set_timeout` for five seconds and then discovers the timeout problem in the completion callback.

Listing 9-6: Timeout.aspx

```
    <!DOCTYPE html PUBLIC "-//W3C//DTD XHTML 1.0 Transitional//EN"
     "http://www.w3.org/TR/xhtml1/DTD/xhtml1-transitional.dtd">

    <html xmlns="http://www.w3.org/1999/xhtml" >
    <head runat="server">
        <title>Networking</title>
    <script type="text/javascript">
    function pageLoad() {
        var webRequest = new Sys.Net.WebRequest();
        webRequest.set_url('Sleep.aspx');
        webRequest.set_httpVerb('POST');
        webRequest.set_body('abc=123');

        webRequest.set_timeout(5000);
        webRequest.add_completed(completedHandler);
        webRequest.invoke();
    }

    function completedHandler(result, eventArgs) {

        if(result.get_timedOut()) {
            alert('timed out');
        }
        if(result.get_responseAvailable()) {
```

Continued

Listing 9-6: Timeout.aspx *(continued)*

```
            alert(result.get_statusText());
            alert(result.get_responseData());
        }
    }
    </script>
    </head>
    <body>
        <form id="form1" runat="server">
        <asp:ScriptManager runat="server" ID="ScriptManager1">
        </asp:ScriptManager>
        <div>
        Making a WebRequest.
        </div>
        </form>
    </body>
    </html>
```

Adding Custom Headers

In addition to being able to detect timeouts, control the verb, and set the contents, you can send custom HTTP headers as part of the request. Listing 9-7 is the EchoHeaders.aspx page that simply echoes the HTTP headers that were included in a request. This server-side code creates a return page that shows exactly what is passed to it in the headers.

Listing 9-7: EchoHeaders.aspx

```
<%@ Page Language="C#" %>
<script runat="server">
protected override void OnLoad(EventArgs e)
{
    base.OnLoad(e);
    NameValueCollection headers = Request.Headers;
    foreach (string key in headers.Keys)
    {
        Response.Write(Server.HtmlEncode(key) +
            " = " +
            Server.HtmlEncode(headers[key]) +
            "<br />\r\n");
    }
}
</script>
```

Requests to the page from Internet Explorer and Firefox are shown in Figure 9-1.

The headers sent by the different browsers are not the same. Internet Explorer provides the versions of the .NET Framework that it supports in the headers, while Firefox does not. Both browsers accept gzip and deflate for encodings. The language header differs based on the selections made in the different browsers. I don't speak Japanese, but I have it in my list of preferred languages of both browsers for testing localization features.

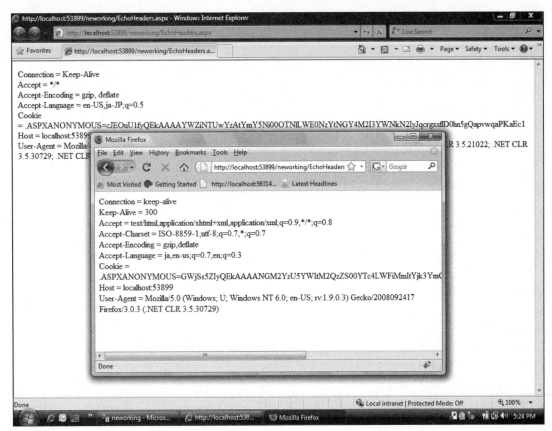

Figure 9-1

Listing 9-8 (CustomHeaders.aspx) makes a call to the EchoHeaders.aspx page, while adding a few unique headers to the request.

Listing 9-8: CustomHeaders.aspx

```
<!DOCTYPE html PUBLIC "-//W3C//DTD XHTML 1.0 Transitional//EN"
"http://www.w3.org/TR/xhtml1/DTD/xhtml1-transitional.dtd">

<html xmlns="http://www.w3.org/1999/xhtml" >
<head runat="server">
    <title>Networking</title>
<script type="text/javascript">
function pageLoad() {
    var webRequest = new Sys.Net.WebRequest();
    webRequest.set_url('EchoHeaders.aspx');

    webRequest.get_headers()["Preferred-Publisher"] = "Wrox";
    webRequest.get_headers()["Preferred-Album"] = "Rift";
```

Continued

Listing 9-8: CustomHeaders.aspx *(continued)*

```
        webRequest.get_headers()["UA-CPU"] = "Altair MIPS";
        webRequest.add_completed(completedHandler);
        webRequest.invoke();
    }

    function completedHandler(result, eventArgs) {
        if(result.get_responseAvailable()) {
            $get("placeholder").innerHTML = result.get_responseData();
        }
    }
    </script>
    </head>
    <body>
        <form id="form1" runat="server">
        <asp:ScriptManager runat="server" ID="ScriptManager1">
        </asp:ScriptManager>
        <div id="placeholder">
        </div>
        </form>
    </body>
    </html>
```

The same requests with some additional headers from Internet Explorer and Firefox now show different results than the previous request. The `Preferred-Publisher` and `Preferred-Album` headers are now reported as part of the request. Although the `preferred-publisher` and `preferred-album` are displayed, in the test with IE, the UA-CPU header is the same as it was before the request that tried to modify it. This is because IE set this header after the page set its value, since this is a standard header that IE always sets itself. The `WebRequest` object allows you to add headers, but the browser itself still has the last say about what is actually transmitted to the server. Figure 9-2 shows the result of an additional set of requests from Internet Explorer and Firefox with the requests that include new additional headers.

Passing Extra Data

The `WebRequest` class automatically passes data from the caller to the completion event handler function. Many times, you want the callback code to benefit from having more data than is typically provided in default operations. The ASP.NET AJAX `userContext` parameter provides a way to pass data from the caller to the callback without even sending it to the server, and this tells the event handler some extra context information about why or where the call was made. The framework manages this extra information and includes it as part of the callback parameters automatically, so it looks as though this information came from the server. Listing 9-9 (`UserContext.aspx`) is a page that adds `userContext` data to the call to the `EchoHeaders.aspx` page.

Listing 9-9: UserContext.aspx

```
<!DOCTYPE html PUBLIC "-//W3C//DTD XHTML 1.0 Transitional//EN"
"http://www.w3.org/TR/xhtml1/DTD/xhtml1-transitional.dtd">

<html xmlns="http://www.w3.org/1999/xhtml" >
<head runat="server">
    <title>Networking</title>
```

Listing 9-9: UserContext.aspx *(continued)*

```
<script type="text/javascript">
function pageLoad() {
    var webRequest = new Sys.Net.WebRequest();
    webRequest.set_url('EchoHeaders.aspx');

    webRequest.set_userContext('send this data to the callback');
    webRequest.add_completed(completedHandler);
    webRequest.invoke();
}

function completedHandler(result, eventArgs) {
    if(result.get_responseAvailable()) {

        var userContext = result.get_webRequest().get_userContext();
        $get('placeholder').innerHTML = userContext;
    }
}
</script>
</head>
<body>
    <form id="form1" runat="server">
    <asp:ScriptManager runat="server" ID="ScriptManager1">
    </asp:ScriptManager>
    <div id="placeholder" >
    </div>
    </form>
</body>
</html>
```

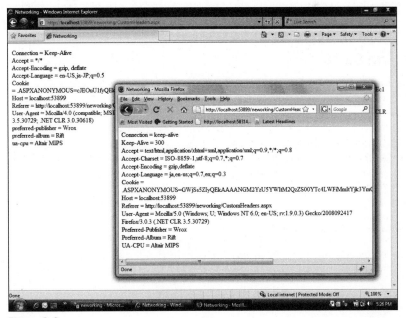

Figure 9-2

The `WebRequest` does not include the user context information in what is sent to the server. Instead, the data is stored locally and then made available during the callback. You can store complex JavaScript types without needing to worry about how they will be serialized for including in an HTTP request. This also keeps the request/response payload lighter.

Resolving the Full URL

In Web development, it is often useful to make decisions based on what part of an application the user is accessing. The `WebRequest` provides a method for retrieving the full URL of a request that is about to be made. When setting up the request, you can specify a complete address for the URL or a relative path. The `getResolvedUrl` function always yields the full path regardless of which form you provide:

```
alert(webRequest.getResolvedUrl());
```

It's important to note that you should not drive security decisions based on the resolved URL in JavaScript running in the browser. The base URL can be spoofed through script running in the JavaScript console. It's safe to assume that any JavaScript in your page might be modified by some kind of Trojan program or unauthorized process on the user's machine, so you must take care in how much trust you place in that code. You should rely on server-side validation of every aspect in the client/server interaction in cases where you have security concerns.

Managing Web Requests

The `WebRequest` object works with a static `WebRequestManager` JavaScript object to coordinate the behavior of the ASP.NET AJAX networking stack. Even though you may not reference the object directly, the individual `WebRequest` objects that you create work with it to execute requests using the `XMLHttpRequest` object. In fact, the `WebRequestManager` does not know the specifics of the `XMLHttpRequest` object. Instead, it works with the `WebRequestExecutor`, an object that abstracts some of the underlying browser-specific details. These JavaScript objects are part of the Microsoft AJAX Library. Later in this chapter, you learn how to use a `WebRequestExecutor` tailored for working with XML data instead of JSON.

Default Timeout

Listing 9-10 (`TimedSleep.aspx`) modifies the `Sleep.aspx` page to return the amount of time that has passed during request processing instead of specific form variables. The sleep of two seconds simulates a server-side process that may require two seconds to execute.

Listing 9-10: TimedSleep.aspx

```
<%@ Page Language="C#" %>
<script runat="server">
protected override void OnLoad(EventArgs e)
{
    base.OnLoad(e);
    DateTime start = DateTime.Now;
    System.Threading.Thread.Sleep(2000);
    DateTime finish = DateTime.Now;
    Response.Write(finish - start);
}
</script>
```

Listing 9-11 (`CallTimedSleep.aspx`) does not specify a timeout, so it gets the default value of 0, which indicates that the `WebRequest` should be allowed to wait indefinitely for a response from the server. This allows the two seconds of execution time to pass on the server so that the example has a reasonable value to work with instead of the near instantaneous times you would see in a development environment.

Listing 9-11: CallTimedSleep.aspx

```
<!DOCTYPE html PUBLIC "-//W3C//DTD XHTML 1.0 Transitional//EN"
 "http://www.w3.org/TR/xhtml1/DTD/xhtml1-transitional.dtd">
<html xmlns="http://www.w3.org/1999/xhtml" >
<head id="Head1" runat="server">
    <title>Networking</title>
<script type="text/javascript">

function pageLoad() {
    Sys.Net.WebRequestManager.add_completedRequest(completedHandler);
    var webRequest = new Sys.Net.WebRequest();
    webRequest.set_url('TimedSleep.aspx');
    Sys.Net.WebRequestManager.executeRequest(webRequest);

}

function completedHandler(result) {
    if(result.get_responseAvailable()) {
        $get('placeholder').innerHTML += "<br />" +
            result.get_webRequest().get_url() +
            " returned " +
            result.get_responseData();
    }
}

</script>
</head>
<body>
    <form id="form1" runat="server">
    <asp:ScriptManager runat="server" ID="ScriptManager1">
    </asp:ScriptManager>
    <div id="placeholder">processing request</div><br />
    </form>
</body>
</html>
```

The result of requesting the page using Internet Explorer is shown in Figure 9-3.

Instead of explicitly setting the timeout on each `WebRequest` object created in the page, the default timeout for all Web requests can be set on the `WebRequestManager`. Listing 9-12 (`SetDefaultTimeout.aspx`) shows the modified `pageLoad` and completion handler code to demonstrate this. The default timeout is set to one second, but the page is going to sleep for two seconds, so it will always fail. In the completion event, the timeout condition is detected and a new request is created. That request will also have the one-second timeout given to the `WebRequestManager`.

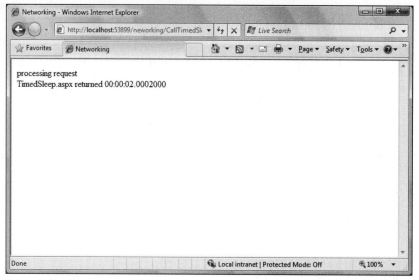

Figure 9-3

Listing 9-12: SetDefaultTimeout.aspx

```
<!DOCTYPE html PUBLIC "-//W3C//DTD XHTML 1.0 Transitional//EN"
  "http://www.w3.org/TR/xhtml1/DTD/xhtml1-transitional.dtd">
<html xmlns="http://www.w3.org/1999/xhtml" >
<head id="Head1" runat="server">
    <title>Networking</title>
<script type="text/javascript">

var numberOfTries = 0;

function pageLoad() {

    Sys.Net.WebRequestManager.set_defaultTimeout(1000);
    var webRequest = new Sys.Net.WebRequest();
    webRequest.set_url('TimedSleep.aspx');
    webRequest.add_completed(completedHandler);
    webRequest.invoke();

}

function completedHandler(result, eventArgs) {

    if(result.get_timedOut()) {
        $get('placeholder').innerText = "Timeout. Trying again after " +
numberOfTries + " times";
        numberOfTries = numberOfTries + 1;
        var anotherWebRequest = new Sys.Net.WebRequest();
        anotherWebRequest.set_url('TimedSleep.aspx');
        anotherWebRequest.add_completed(completedHandler);
```

Listing 9-12: SetDefaultTimeout.aspx *(continued)*

```
            anotherWebRequest.invoke();
        }

    if(result.get_responseAvailable()) {
        $get('placeholder').innerHTML = "time taken = " +
result.get_responseData();
        }
    }
</script>
</head>
<body>
    <form id="form1" runat="server">
    <asp:ScriptManager runat="server" ID="ScriptManager1">
    </asp:ScriptManager>
    <div id="placeholder">processing request</div><br />
    </form>
</body>
</html>
```

Global Web Request Handling

Just as you may want to set a timeout to apply to all Web requests, you may also want to provide a single function as the completion handler for all requests. In previous examples, the `add_completed` method was called on the individual `WebRequest`, but you can see that this would become repetitious when defining a set of request objects that all use the same target.

The `WebRequestManager` has the `add_completedRequest` and `remove_completedRequest` methods for attaching and detaching event handlers to be used for all requests. Listing 9-13 (`GlobalCompleted .aspx`) is a page that calls the `time.aspx` and `TimedSleep.aspx` pages and uses a single handler for both `WebRequest` instances.

Listing 9-13: GlobalCompleted.aspx

```
<!DOCTYPE html PUBLIC "-//W3C//DTD XHTML 1.0 Transitional//EN"
"http://www.w3.org/TR/xhtml1/DTD/xhtml1-transitional.dtd">
<html xmlns="http://www.w3.org/1999/xhtml" >
<head id="Head1" runat="server">
    <title>Networking</title>
<script type="text/javascript">


function pageLoad() {
    Sys.Net.WebRequestManager.add_completedRequest(completedHandler);

    var webRequest = new Sys.Net.WebRequest();
    webRequest.set_url('time.aspx');

    var webRequest2 = new Sys.Net.WebRequest();
```

Continued

Listing 9-13: GlobalCompleted.aspx *(continued)*

```
        webRequest2.set_url('TimedSleep.aspx');

        Sys.Net.WebRequestManager.executeRequest(webRequest2);
        Sys.Net.WebRequestManager.executeRequest(webRequest);

    }
```

```
    function completedHandler(executor) {
        if(executor.get_responseAvailable()) {
            $get('placeholder').innerHTML += "<br />" +
                executor.get_webRequest().get_url() +
                " returned " +
                executor.get_responseData ();
        }
    }
```

```
</script>
</head>
<body>
    <form id="form1" runat="server">
    <asp:ScriptManager runat="server" ID="ScriptManager1">
    </asp:ScriptManager>
    <div id="placeholder">processing request</div><br />
    </form>
</body>
</html>
```

Because this code just displays the results of the call, it has a single completion handler, registered with the WebRequestManager. When you call or invoke a WebRequest, it ultimately gets processed by the WebRequestManager's executeRequest method. You can also call the executeRequest method directly, as shown in Listing 9-13.

Along with the data returned from executing the Web request, the URL of the page is also displayed. The completion handler receives the WebRequestExecutor as an argument, which has a get_webRequest method. You then have access to the original WebRequest object.

The WebRequestManager also allows you to register event handlers to be called for each request as it is about to be called:

```
    Sys.Net.WebRequestManager.add_invokingRequest(invokingHandler);
```

The CancelEventArgs passed to the invokingRequest handler allows you to cancel the request before it is actually executed:

```
    function invokingHandler(sender, eventArgs) {
        if(eventArgs.get_webRequest().get_url() === 'TimedSleep.aspx') {
            eventArgs.set_cancel(true);
        }
    }
```

You can attach multiple event handlers for the invoking and completed events, and they will all be called. Even if one of the invoking event handlers cancels the request, the rest of the invoking handlers will still be called, so you have to be mindful of what handlers have been attached. And if you attach a completion handler directly to a `WebRequest` in addition to using the WebRequestManager, they will both be called.

The WebRequestExecutor

The WebRequestManager works with `WebRequest` objects to process requests using an executor object. You saw examples of using this to issue requests for `.aspx` pages and `.asmx` Web services that are only returning text. But a lot of message passing on the Web utilizes XML data for increased fidelity, flexibility, and portability. The default executor used by the WebRequestManager is `XMLHttpExecutor`. The WebRequestManager includes functions to get and set the default executor you want it to use:

```
Sys.Net.WebRequestManager.get_defaultExecutorType();
Sys.Net.WebRequestManager.set_defaultExecutorType(Sys.Net.XMLHttpExecutor);
```

In addition to the WebRequestExecutor, ASP.NET AJAX includes an `XMLHttpExecutor` that parses the XML results of a request for you. To demonstrate this process, Listing 9-14 (`XMLTime.aspx`) is a modification of the earlier page that returns the time from the server, but now the result is packaged as XML.

Listing 9-14: XMLTime.aspx

```
<%@ Page Language="C#" %>
<script runat="server">
    protected void Page_Load(object sender, EventArgs e)
    {
        Response.Write("<?xml version=\"1.0\" encoding=\"utf-8\" ?>");
        Response.Write("<time><universalTime>" +
            DateTime.Now.ToUniversalTime() +
            "</universalTime></time>");
    }

</script>
```

When the XMLHttpExecutor is used, the results are parsed as XML and the XML is available for use in the DOM. The default executor type is the XMLHttpExecutor, but I am creating it explicitly in Listing 9-15 (`XMLHttpExecutor.aspx`) to show that you can call the `executeRequest` method on it directly. Note that in Internet Explorer, running this code will show you the XML, but in Firefox you will just see "undefined." Both browsers support the XML document returned by the `get_xml()` property, Firefox simply does not support the `"xml"` field to see the raw XML as a string.

Listing 9-15: XMLHttpExecutor.aspx

```
<!DOCTYPE html PUBLIC "-//W3C//DTD XHTML 1.0 Transitional//EN"
"http://www.w3.org/TR/xhtml1/DTD/xhtml1-transitional.dtd">
<html xmlns="http://www.w3.org/1999/xhtml" >
<head id="Head1" runat="server">
    <title>Networking</title>
```

Continued

313

Listing 9-15: XMLHttpExecutor.aspx *(continued)*

```
<script type="text/javascript">
function pageLoad() {
    Sys.Net.WebRequestManager.add_completedRequest(completedHandler);
    var webRequest = new Sys.Net.WebRequest();
    webRequest.set_url('XMLTime.aspx');

    var executor = new Sys.Net.XMLHttpExecutor();
    webRequest.set_executor(executor);
    executor.executeRequest();
}

function completedHandler(executor) {
    if(executor.get_responseAvailable()) {

        alert(executor.get_xml().xml);
    }
}

</script>
</head>
<body>
    <form id="form1" runat="server">
    <asp:ScriptManager runat="server" ID="ScriptManager1">
    </asp:ScriptManager>
    </form>
</body>
</html>
```

Passing Data

The X in AJAX is for XML, and indeed many Web services today use XML for sending and receiving data. XML parsers are readily available in the browser, and classes for creating, manipulating, and serializing XML data on the server are plentiful. XML has also been the foundation for the creation of applications that leverage service-oriented architectures to produce mashup-style applications.

As developers have recognized the potential for passing data between client and server using XML, they have also recognized that XML is not always the ideal format for working with data. This section discusses JavaScript Object Notation (JSON), which is a JavaScript-friendly method of serializing data that has less overhead than XML.

Serialization

Serialization is the process of encoding data in a way that allows it to be sent over a serial connection, such as an HTTP channel, that allows it to be understood on the other side of the connection and can then be deserialized back into its original form. This is commonly used with structured types, since simple types such as strings are inherently compatible with serial channels. When objects are held in memory by a single application, there isn't a need to serialize them. It doesn't really matter how the computer represents them in memory as long as the fields, properties, and methods behave as expected. But when objects need to cross process or machine boundaries, serialization becomes essential in order for that object to be faithfully reconstructed at the other end.

The format used to serialize an object must be agreed upon by both parties that are exchanging it. If the format is not understood by both sides, the object will be corrupted after being transferred since the deserialization routine won't know how to recreate the object. For example, if I write a song, record it, and give you the file as an MP3, chances are you will have access to a device or program that can play it. My MP3 file is a serialization of the song. I could decide that I would record each instrument separately and encode it that way in the file so that I could easily modify a single instrument in a song. If I gave you the file in this custom format, you wouldn't be able to play it unless I also provided you with software that understood the serialization format I had used.

When an object is to be shared, the receiver needs to understand how the sender formats the object for transmission. There are binary formats for serialization that can't be understood when looking at the data directly. And there are formats like XML and JSON, where you can read the serialized object and make sense of it with only a little background on these formats. You don't have to know specifically how every object will be encoded as XML or JSON, because the rules of these formats are well established and easily apply to many different kinds of objects.

XML and JSON are most commonly used for exchanging data, not for exchanging programmable objects directly. In other words, functions or methods are not usually passed over a wire. You may be familiar with the remoting serialization in .NET that allows objects, including their methods and properties, to be shared across process and machine boundaries, and although you could devise a way to use JSON or XML formats to do this, it would be an atypical use of these formats.

JSON Format

The JSON format leverages a subset of the object literal notation that JavaScript supports natively. In general, the information at www.json.org classifies the notation of objects as being either unordered key-value pairs, or ordered lists of items.

Unordered key-value pairs are separated by colons and surrounded by curly braces. Ordered lists, or arrays, are separated with commas and surrounded by right and left brackets. Individual items or objects are also separated by commas. Look at the following object:

```
{
    "artist" : "Phish",
    "title" : "A Picture of Nectar",
    "releaseYear" : 1992,
    "tracks" : [
        "Llama",
        "Eliza",
        "Cavern",
        "Poor Heart",
        "Stash",
        "Manteca",
        "Guelah Papyrus",
        "Magilla",
        "The Landlady",
```

```
            "Glide",
            "Tweezer",
            "The Mango Song",
            "Chalk Dust Torture",
            "Faht",
            "Catapult",
            "Tweezer Reprise"
        ]
    }
```

This object represents an album. It has fields for the artist, title, year of release, and the array of song tracks. Individual elements can be strings, numbers, Booleans, or null. You can see that the JSON syntax is very easy to read and understand. For comparison, I have also represented the album in XML.

```xml
<?xml version="1.0" encoding="utf-8" ?>
<album>
  <artist>Phish</artist>
  <title>A Picture of Nectar</title>
  <releaseYear>1992</releaseYear>
  <tracks>
    <track>Llama</track>
    <track>Eliza</track>
    <track>Cavern</track>
    <track>Poor Heart</track>
    <track>Stash</track>
    <track>Manteca</track>
    <track>Guelah Papyrus</track>
    <track>Magilla</track>
    <track>The Landlady</track>
    <track>Glide</track>
    <track>Tweezer</track>
    <track>The Mango Song</track>
    <track>Chalk Dust Torture</track>
    <track>Faht</track>
    <track>Catapult</track>
    <track>Tweezer Reprise</track>
  </tracks>
</album>
```

The XML format is also readable and easy to understand but has a lot more overhead in terms of raw size than the equivalent JSON. Of course, you can also apply schema to XML for validation of types and apply XSLT transformations to XML more readily than with JSON, but for many applications, this additional flexibility is not needed.

Deserializing JSON-formatted types in the browser has one distinct advantage to working with XML — it is inexpensive and quick to execute. Remember that JSON leverages the object notation that is natively part of JavaScript, so accessing JSON-encoded data is as easy as using the `eval` function on it and working with the type that it produces. The `eval` function is a general constructor of objects encoded in JSON. Listing 9-16 (`Eval.aspx`) is a page that wraps the JSON string in parentheses and calls `eval` on it. The object returned has properties for the artist, title, year of release, and an array of the tracks.

Listing 9-16: Eval.aspx

```
<!DOCTYPE html PUBLIC "-//W3C//DTD XHTML 1.0 Transitional//EN"
"http://www.w3.org/TR/xhtml1/DTD/xhtml1-transitional.dtd">
<html xmlns="http://www.w3.org/1999/xhtml" >
<head id="Head1" runat="server">
    <title>Networking</title>
<script type="text/javascript">
var JSONstring = '{' +
    '"artist" : "Phish",' +
    '"title" : "A Picture of Nectar",' +
    '"releaseYear" : 1992,' +
    '"tracks" : [' +
    '    "Llama",' +
    '    "Eliza",' +
    '    "Cavern",' +
    '    "Poor Heart",' +
    '    "Stash",' +
    '    "Manteca",' +
    '    "Guelah Papyrus",' +
    '    "Magilla",' +
    '    "The Landlady",' +
    '    "Glide",' +
    '    "Tweezer",' +
    '    "The Mango Song",' +
    '    "Chalk Dust Torture",' +
    '    "Faht",' +
    '    "Catapult",' +
    '    "Tweezer Reprise"' +
    ']' +
'}';

function pageLoad() {
    var album = eval("(" + JSONstring + ")");
    var innerHTML = "artist = " + album.artist + "<br />" +
        "title = " + album.title + "<br />" +
        "releaseYear = " + album.releaseYear;
    $get('placeholder').innerHTML = innerHTML;

    var tracks = "";
    for(var i = 0; i < album.tracks.length; i++) {
        tracks += "track #" + i + " = " + album.tracks[i] + "<br />";
    }
    $get('placeholder2').innerHTML = tracks;
}

</script>
</head>

<body>
    <form id="form1" runat="server">
    <asp:ScriptManager runat="server" ID="ScriptManager1">
    </asp:ScriptManager>
    <div id='placeholder'></div>
```

Continued

Listing 9-16: Eval.aspx *(continued)*

```
        <div id='placeholder2'></div>
        </form>
    </body>
    </html>
```

Figure 9-4 shows the identical output in Internet Explorer and Firefox. Because the code is just calling the JavaScript `eval` method on the JSON-formatted object, no special processing code is required for the different browsers.

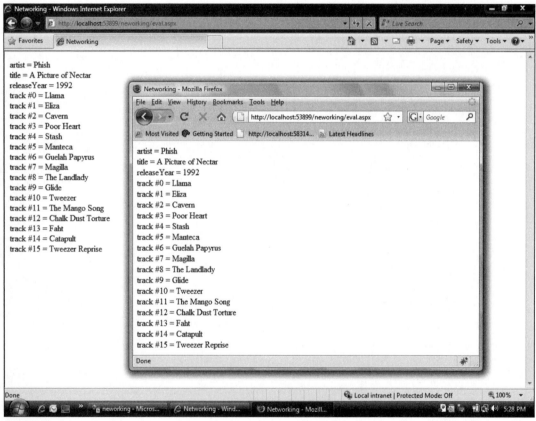

Figure 9-4

JSON Serialization

In the previous example, the JSON string was created explicitly to show the syntax and to demonstrate that calling `eval` on it results in an object. Most of the time, you aren't creating the JSON strings in JavaScript code directly. Instead, you create JavaScript objects that correspond to .NET objects created on the server.

Thus, the server might create a small .NET entity class that gets serialized into JSON and later deserialized into a JavaScript object in the browser. Thankfully, ASP.NET AJAX makes working with JSON easy. Listing 9-17 (Album.asmx) is a Web service that has the equivalent Album .NET class defined earlier in JavaScript. There are properties for title, artist, the year of release, and the album tracks.

Listing 9-17: Album.aspx

```csharp
<%@ WebService Language="C#" Class="AlbumProxy" %>

using System;
using System.Web;
using System.Web.Services;
using System.Web.Services.Protocols;
using System.Web.Script.Services;
using System.Net;
using System.Xml.Serialization;
using System.Web.Script.Serialization;

public class Album
{
    private string _artist = String.Empty;
    private string _title = String.Empty;
    private int _releaseYear;
    private string[] _tracks = new string[16];
    private DateTime _dateTime = DateTime.Now;
    private string _personalInfo = "do not show this";

    [ScriptIgnore()]
    public string PersonalInfo
    {
        get {
            return _personalInfo;
        }
        set {
            _personalInfo = value;
        }
    }


    public Album() {
    }

    public string Artist {
        get {
            return _artist;

        }
        set {
            _artist = value;
        }
    }
```

Continued

Listing 9-17: Album.aspx *(continued)*

```
    public string Title {
        get {
            return _title;
        }
        set {
            _title = value;
        }
    }

    public int ReleaseYear {
        get {
            return _releaseYear;
        }
        set {
            _releaseYear = value;
        }
    }

    public string[] Tracks {
        get {
            return _tracks;
        }
        set {
            _tracks = value;
        }
    }
}

[ScriptService]
[WebService(Namespace = "http://tempuri.org/")]
[WebServiceBinding(ConformsTo = WsiProfiles.BasicProfile1_1)]
public class AlbumProxy : System.Web.Services.WebService {

    private Album _album;

    public AlbumProxy() {
        _album = new Album();
        _album.Artist = "Phish";
        _album.Title = "A Picture of Nectar";
        _album.ReleaseYear = 1992;
        _album.Tracks.SetValue("Llama", 0);
        _album.Tracks.SetValue("Eliza", 1);
        _album.Tracks.SetValue("Cavern", 2);
        _album.Tracks.SetValue("Poor Heart", 3);
        _album.Tracks.SetValue("Stash", 4);
        _album.Tracks.SetValue("Manteca", 5);

        _album.Tracks.SetValue("Guelah Papyrus", 6);
        _album.Tracks.SetValue("Magilla", 7);
        _album.Tracks.SetValue("The Landlady", 8);
```

Listing 9-17: Album.aspx *(continued)*

```
            _album.Tracks.SetValue("Glide", 9);
            _album.Tracks.SetValue("Tweezer", 10);
            _album.Tracks.SetValue("The Mango Song", 11);
            _album.Tracks.SetValue("Chalk Dust Torture", 12);
            _album.Tracks.SetValue("Faht", 13);
            _album.Tracks.SetValue("Catapult", 14);
            _album.Tracks.SetValue("Tweezer Reprise", 15);
        }

        [WebMethod]
        [XmlInclude(typeof(Album))]
        public object GetAlbum() {
            return _album;
        }

        [WebMethod]
        [XmlInclude(typeof(Album))]
        public object GetAlbumJSON()
        {
            JavaScriptSerializer serializer = new JavaScriptSerializer();
            return serializer.Serialize(_album);
        }
    }
}
```

The Web service exposes two methods for retrieving an album instance. If you navigate your browser directly to the `Album.asmx` URL, you get options for invoking each of the methods as a SOAP service. The `GetAlbum` method returns the object directly. It is serialized using XML. The `GetAlbumJSON` method uses the `JavaScriptSerializer` class to return the album in the JSON format but when requested as a SOAP service, the JSON is still packed as the value of the XML element, so you'll see a SOAP XML wrapper around the JSON encoded object. The output from invoking both functions is shown in Figure 9-5. The XML output is shown on the left and the JSON output is shown on the right.

You can see that the data is fundamentally the same but that the JSON string is more compact, even though it has a simple XML wrapper around it. Sometimes you want the additional flexibility you can get with XML, but for many services, the JSON format is sufficient and smaller. Besides the size advantage of JSON, its use avoids the lack of a standard XML parser being available across all modern browsers.

The properties of the .NET type are serialized into fields of the JavaScript object, as you would expect. Listing 9-18 (`ScriptProxy.aspx`) includes a `ServiceReference` to the `Album.asmx` Web service. The methods can then be invoked by the proxy objects that ASP.NET AJAX generates for you. The completion function that gets the JSON string data can deserialize the result by calling the deserialize function of the `JavaScriptSerializer` object. The completion function that gets the XML data does not need to do anything to get the album object because ASP.NET AJAX manages the serialization of the return value. When it is called from the generated script proxy, ASP.NET doesn't actually return the XML as when the ASMX Service is called directly, but the JSON formatted object is returned instead.

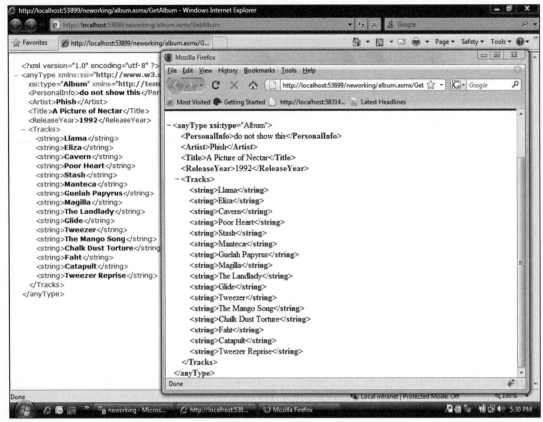

Figure 9-5

Listing 9-18: ScriptProxy.aspx

```
<%@Import Namespace="System.Web.Script.Serialization" %>
<!DOCTYPE html PUBLIC "-//W3C//DTD XHTML 1.0 Transitional//EN"
"http://www.w3.org/TR/xhtml1/DTD/xhtml1-transitional.dtd">
<html xmlns="http://www.w3.org/1999/xhtml" >
<head id="Head1" runat="server">
    <title>Networking</title>
<script type="text/javascript">

function pageLoad() {
    AlbumProxy.GetAlbumJSON(completionJSON);
    AlbumProxy.GetAlbum(completionObject);
}


function completionJSON(result) {
    var album = Sys.Serialization.JavaScriptSerializer.deserialize(result);
```

Listing 9-18: ScriptProxy.aspx *(continued)*

```
        $get('placeholder').innerHTML = album.Artist;
    }

    function completionObject(album) {
        $get('placeholder2').innerHTML = album.ReleaseYear;
    }

    </script></head>
<body>
    <form id="form1" runat="server">
    <asp:ScriptManager runat="server" ID="ScriptManager1">
    <Services>
        <asp:ServiceReference Path="Album.asmx" />
    </Services>
    </asp:ScriptManager>
    <div id='placeholder'></div><br />
    <div id='placeholder2'></div>
    </form>
</body>
</html>
```

PageMethods

You saw that a Web service class could be decorated with the `ScriptService` attribute and ASP.NET AJAX would provide JavaScript proxies to invoke it from the browser and manage the types. You can also get proxies for invoking methods contained directly in the page. The method must be a static method. You must also set the `EnablePageMethods` property of the ScriptManager to `true`. Listing 9-19 (`PageMethods .aspx`) includes the method for returning the time on the server directly in the page. The method is marked with both the `WebMethod` and `ScriptMethod` attributes. The `ScriptMethod` attribute is optional. Here it is used to change from the default POST to the GET HTTP verb. The method defined on the server is now available as a member of the `PageMethods` object on the client. On the client it is a proxy for invoking the method on the server. If it took parameters, they would be the first argument to the JavaScript method, followed by the completion callback, error callback, and user context data.

Listing 9-19: PageMethods.aspx

```
<%@ Page Language="C#" %>
<%@ Import Namespace="System.Web.Services" %>
<%@ Import Namespace="System.Web.Script.Services" %>


<!DOCTYPE html PUBLIC "-//W3C//DTD XHTML 1.0 Transitional//EN"
"http://www.w3.org/TR/xhtml1/DTD/xhtml1-transitional.dtd">


<script runat="server">
    [WebMethod]
    [ScriptMethod(UseHttpGet=true)]
```

Continued

Listing 9-19: PageMethods.aspx *(continued)*

```
      public static string ServerTime() {
           return DateTime.Now.ToUniversalTime().ToString();
      }
```

```
</script>
<script type="text/javascript">
function pageLoad() {
    $addHandler($get('timeButton'), 'click', getTime);
}

function getTime() {
    PageMethods.ServerTime(OnServerTimeComplete);
}

function OnServerTimeComplete(result, userContext, methodName) {
    alert(result);
}

</script>
```

```
<html xmlns="http://www.w3.org/1999/xhtml" >
<head runat="server">
    <title>ASP.NET AJAX PageMethod</title>
</head>
<body>
    <form id="form1" runat="server">
```

```
    <asp:ScriptManager runat="server" ID="scriptManager"
EnablePageMethods="true"></asp:ScriptManager>
    <div>
    <input type="button" value="Show Server Time" id="timeButton" />
    </div>
    </form>
</body>
</html>
```

Working with Dates

The JSON format does not natively support dates. It handles strings, numbers, Booleans, arrays, and nulls but lacks support for Date objects. If a .NET object contains a date, the JavaScriptSerializer class will encode it in a format that the AJAX script library knows how to deserialize in the browser. This is why you need to use the deserialize method of the Sys.Serialization.JavaScriptSerializer object instead of calling eval directly, so that the date will be parsed for you:

```
var objectWithDate =
Sys.Serialization.JavaScriptSerializer.deserialize(JSONstring);
var date = objectWithDate.dateProperty;
```

Bypassing Serialization

Much of the appeal for using the JSON format is due to the streamlined size of encoded objects and the speed of working with these types in JavaScript. You have seen that ASP.NET AJAX automatically turns instances of .NET objects into the JSON format so that they can be deserialized and used in the browser. But since part of the appeal is the reduced size of the JSON format, it follows that you want to be able to exert some control over the serialization behavior to reduce the number of properties you need to serialize. ASP.NET provides the `ScriptIgnore` attribute to exclude designated properties from being serialized.

Suppose that I add a .NET property that I do not want sent to the client in the `album` object:

```
private string _personalInfo = "do not show this";

public string PersonalInfo
{
    get {
        return _personalInfo;
    }
    set {
        _personalInfo = value;
    }
}
```

The default behavior of the serializer is to include all of the properties available. When looking at the data returned by invoking the object, you see that this new property is included. This is shown in Figure 9-6.

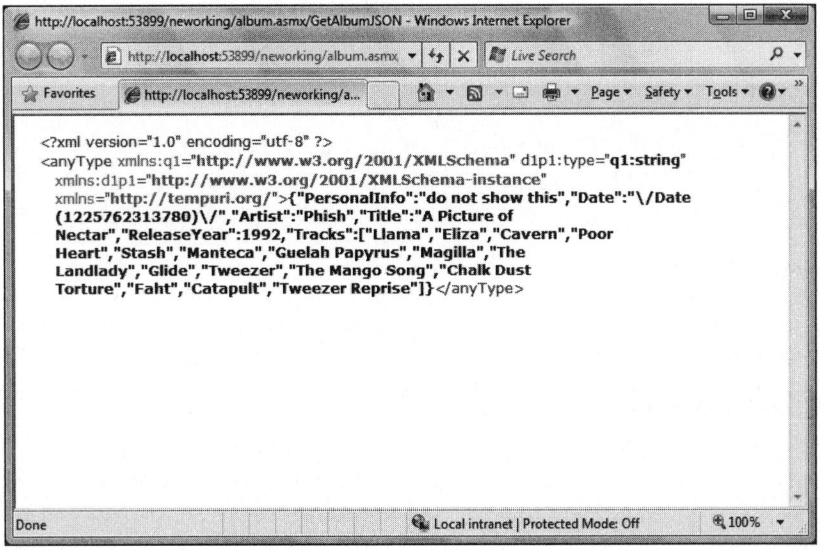

Figure 9-6

Adding the `ScriptIgnore` attribute to a property prevents the `JavaScriptSerializer` from including it in the serialized form of the object, which limits the amount of data you send to the browser:

```
[ScriptIgnore()]
public string PersonalInfo
{
    get {
        return _personalInfo;
    }
    set {
        _personalInfo = value;
    }
}
```

You could argue that the default should be to avoid serializing properties unless they are explicitly designated as being serializable for JSON, but this seemed counter to the expected use of creating simple types for passing from the server to client for manipulation in the browser. In other words, Microsoft opted for ease of use in the general case.

Configuring the JSON Serializer

The serialization examples you have seen here were pretty straightforward, but in real life, the objects you work with are often not so trivial. You rarely care what the time on the server is, and business objects are not usually limited to two or three string properties.

The ASP.NET `JavaScriptSerializer` can be configured to control its behavior. The default is to limit the depth to which objects are traversed in serializing to one hundred. There is also a limit to the length of the JSON string that is produced when serializing. If the string is longer than 2,097,152 characters, an error is produced. These limits are in place to guard against inadvertently serializing very large data structures and transmitting them to the client where the ability of the script engine to work with them will be taxed. You probably won't want to serialize an ADO.NET DataTable with half a million records!

```
<system.web.extensions>
 <scripting>
  <webServices>
    <jsonSerialization maxJsonLength="2097152" recursionLimit="100">
    </jsonSerialization>
  </webServices>
 </scripting>
</system.web.extensions>
```

Custom Serialization

The ASP.NET AJAX `JavaScriptSerializer` supports serializing the primitive types that you have seen already in this chapter. But this brute force approach doesn't scale well to complex types. In practice, you may find that the default serialization is not exactly what you are after. You can shape the server object into the structure that you want to work within the browser using a custom serialization converter.

You create the custom converter by inheriting from the `JavaScriptConverter` type in the `System` `.Web.Script.Serialization.Converters` namespace. The `JavaScriptConverter` base type has three public abstract methods to override. The `Deserialize` method allows you to take in JSON and turn it back into an instance of the supported type. You can override the `SupportedTypes` method to return the `IEnumerable` collection of types that can be handled. And the `Serialize` method is expected to return an `IDictionary` collection of name-value pairs to include in the JSON output for the object.

You can configure custom converters in the `converters` element inside the `jsonSerialization` element. If you were to define a custom converter that could convert Album objects to and from JSON format, this is how configuring it might look. With this configuration in place, Album objects will be serialized and deserialized using the converter automatically.

```
<system.web.extensions>
  <scripting>
    <webServices>
      <jsonSerialization maxJsonLength="500">

        <converters>
            <add name="AlbumConverter"
                type="MyNamespace.AlbumConverter"/>
        </converters>
      </jsonSerialization>
    </webServices>
  </scripting>
</system.web.extensions>
```

Summary

The `XMLHttpRequest` is at the heart of ASP.NET AJAX development. This object is exposed as an ActiveX control in Internet Explorer and as part of the DOM in Firefox. The `XMLHttpRequest` object allows you to communicate with the server to do partial page updates and invoke Web services.

Although the `XMLHttpRequest` object is limited to making calls back to the originating domain, proxy classes for retrieving the object and the use of embedded IFrames that talk to third-party services allow you to build mashup applications that aggregate remote applications and service providers.

JSON provides a lightweight human-readable format for serializing objects between server and client. ASP.NET AJAX makes use of the JSON format to provide easier interoperability between .NET on the server and JavaScript on the client. You can serialize between .NET objects and JavaScript objects using the `System.Web.Script.Serialization.JavaScriptSerializer` type on the server and the `Sys.Serialization.JavaScriptSerializer` object in the browser.

In addition to supporting seamless translation of compatible types between client and server, ASP.NET AJAX provides further extensibility by allowing you to write custom type converters. Any arbitrary type can be shaped to a JavaScript object through the use of a custom converter.

10

Working with Animations

By far, one of the largest features of the ASP.NET AJAX Toolkit (in terms of JavaScript code) is the animation capabilities that it provides. The ASP.NET AJAX Toolkit was covered earlier in this book in Chapter 7. It is suggested that you read this chapter prior to reading this coverage of animations.

Applying animations is a great endeavor for your Web applications that you are building today as it gives you an ability to use the Dynamic HTML (DHTML) capabilities of moving objects around on the page. I'm not saying that the old HTML <blink> tag was a good idea, but adding items like transitions, fades, and other slight movements makes your pages seem less jerky than they normally would as your end users make requests and wait for responses.

This chapter provides you with a basic overview of the animation capabilities found in the ASP.NET AJAX Toolkit and explains how to incorporate them into your pages.

Working with the Animation Control

The AnimationExtender control is part of the ASP.NET AJAX Toolkit. It is important to think of it as complete framework that can be used in your application to provide the fluidity that you are looking for rather than as simply another server control.

Using animations enables you to transition from one state to another. For instance, you can transition something on the page from one location to another. Animations aren't restricted to positioning elements, you can also use them to change other aspects of a control or series of controls in some sort of transition. For instance, you can slowly change the color of text, or fade things in and out. There is quite a bit that DHTML can do.

You can also initiate transitions based on an end user action (such as a button click). There are specific events that you can program your animations against. These events are as follows:

- ❑ OnClick
- ❑ OnHoverOver

- ❑ OnHoverOut
- ❑ OnLoad
- ❑ OnMouseOver
- ❑ OnMouseOut

For an example of this, let's work through a simple example of applying an animation to a Label control.

Animating a Single Control

In this example, a single animation is applied to a single control on the page. To work along, create a page that contains a TextBox, a Button, and a Label control. An example of this layout is presented in Figure 10-1.

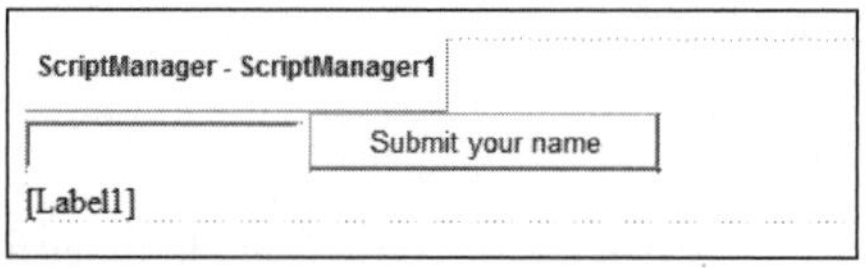

Figure 10-1

The code of the page for this example is presented in Listing 10-1.

Listing 10-1: Changing the size of the Label control

```
<%@ Page Language="C#" %>

<%@ Register Assembly="AjaxControlToolkit" Namespace="AjaxControlToolkit"
    TagPrefix="cc1" %>

<script runat="server">

    protected void Button1_Click(object sender, EventArgs e)
    {
        Label1.Text = "Hello " + TextBox1.Text;
    }

</script>

<html xmlns="http://www.w3.org/1999/xhtml">
<head runat="server">
    <title>Growing Label</title>
</head>
<body>
    <form id="form1" runat="server">
    <div>
        <asp:ScriptManager ID="ScriptManager1" runat="server" />
        <asp:TextBox ID="TextBox1" runat="server"></asp:TextBox>
         <asp:Button ID="Button1" runat="server" Text="Submit your name"
```

Listing 10-1: Changing the size of the Label control *(continued)*

```
                OnClick="Button1_Click" />
                <asp:Label ID="Label1" runat="server"></asp:Label>
                <br /><br />
                <cc1:AnimationExtender ID="Label1_AnimationExtender" runat="server"
                 Enabled="True"
                 TargetControlID="Label1">
                    <Animations>
                    <OnLoad>
                        <Sequence>
                            <Scale ScaleFactor="4" Unit="px" ScaleFont="true" FontUnit="pt"
                             Duration="2.5" Fps="50" ></Scale>
                        </Sequence>
                    </OnLoad>
                    </Animations>
                </cc1:AnimationExtender>
        </div>
        </form>
    </body>
    </html>
```

After you load this page into the browser, enter your name in the text box and click the Submit button on the page. The name you entered will be utilized in the Label control, and the text of the Label control will grow four times in size until you get something similar to what is presented in Figure 10-2 (obviously the name will be different).

Figure 10-2

I can honestly say that the image shown in Figure 10-2 doesn't do this example justice, as you can't see the animation occur. The page presented in this figure is the last stage of the image after the text has fully grown. When the page is loaded, the value of the Label control's Text property is applied the animation through the use of the AnimationExtender control on the page.

When you add an AnimationExtender control to your page, you are have to wire the control to the control that will have the animation applied to it. In the case of the example from Listing 10-1, the AnimationExtender control is wired to the Label control on the page, using the `TargetControlID` property.

```
<cc1:AnimationExtender ID="Label1_AnimationExtender" runat="server"
        Enabled="True"

            TargetControlID="Label1">

    <!-- Code removed for clarity -->

</cc1:AnimationExtender>
```

As stated earlier, you can then provide the animation using such events as `OnClick`, `OnHoverOver`, `OnHoverOut`, `OnLoad`, `OnMouseOver`, and `OnMouseOut`. This example makes use of the `OnLoad` event, through the use of the `<OnLoad>` element within the `<Animations>` element.

```
<cc1:AnimationExtender ID="Label1_AnimationExtender" runat="server"
  Enabled="True"
  TargetControlID="Label1">

    <Animations>
        <OnLoad>

        <!-- Code removed for clarity -->

        </OnLoad>
    </Animations>

</cc1:AnimationExtender>
```

Animations that you perform can run sequentially or in parallel. In this case, since there is only a single animation, it really doesn't matter which method you use.. For this example, the sequential approach is taken with the use of the `<Sequence>` element within the AnimationExtender control.

```
<cc1:AnimationExtender ID="Label1_AnimationExtender" runat="server"
  Enabled="True"
  TargetControlID="Label1">
    <Animations>
        <OnLoad>

        <Sequence>
            <Scale ScaleFactor="4" Unit="px" ScaleFont="true" FontUnit="pt"
                Duration="2.5" Fps="50" ></Scale>
        </Sequence>

        </OnLoad>
    </Animations>
</cc1:AnimationExtender>
```

In this case, there is a single transition in place `<Scale>` that will change the size of what you are working with. For this example, the font of the text within the Label control is increased by using the `ScaleFactor` property (setting it to a value of 4) in conjunction with other properties available to the `<Scale>` element.

Animation Events

Now that the first example of using an animation is done, let's turn our attention to the events that can be utilized within your pages. Here is a brief description of each of the available events:

- ❑ `OnClick` — Initiated when the end user clicks on the element to start the animation.
- ❑ `OnHoverOver` — Initiated when the end user hovers over the element with the mouse.
- ❑ `OnHoverOut` — When an end user hovers over an element, the `OnHoverOver` event is triggered. When the end user moves the mouse off the element, the `OnHoverOut` event is triggered.
- ❑ `OnLoad` — Initiated when the control is loaded onto the page.
- ❑ `OnMouseOver` — This is similar to the `OnHoverOver` trigger in that it initiates the animation when the mouse is hovered over an element.
- ❑ `OnMouseOut` — This is also very similar to the `OnHoverOut` trigger in that it will initiate the animation when the mouse is hovered off the element.

Animation Actions

In Listing 10-1, you were able to see the `<Scale>` element used as an animation to scale the size of the text from the `Label1` server control that was contained on the page. There are other types of animations besides the `<Scale>` type as defined in the previous example. The following list defines the animation actions that you can make use of in your code:

- ❑ `<Fade>` — Provides the ability to fade an element in or out of the page.
- ❑ `<FadeIn>` — Provides the ability to fade an element into the page.
- ❑ `<FadeOut>` — Provides the ability to fade an element out of the page.
- ❑ `<Pulse>` — Provides the ability to fade an element in and out in a pulsating fashion.
- ❑ `<Color>` — Provides the ability to transition the color of a element from one place in the color spectrum to another.
- ❑ `<Move>` — Provides the ability to move an element on the page.
- ❑ `<Resize>` — Provides the ability to resize an element from one size to another.
- ❑ `<Scale>` — Provides the ability to scale an element on a specific scale factor (presented earlier in Listing 10-1).

Animation Methods

Earlier you saw a demonstration of how to run an animation with the `<Sequence>` element. You really see the value of this element when running more than a single animation. Running two or more animations with the `<Sequence>` element would cause the ASP.NET AJAX animation framework to run the animations in a sequential fashion (one after the other, in the order in which they are defined). In addition to the `<Sequence>` element, here is a list of the available animation methods at your disposal:

- ❑ `<Case>` — Provides the ability to apply animations based upon a specific circumstance. You will find that this is quite similar to how a Visual Basic `Select` or a C# `switch` statement works.

❑   `<Condition>` — Provides the ability to apply an animation based upon a specific condition being present.

❑   `<Parallel>` — Provides the ability to run a group of animations in a parallel fashion.

❑   `<Sequence>` — Provides the ability to run a group of animations in a sequential fashion.

It is important to understand how these methods work with the animations on the page when working with the `<Sequence>` and `<Parallel>` options. The `<Sequence>` option allows you to define animations in a sequential flow, meaning that the second animation will not start until the previous animation has completed. When you use `<Sequence>`, each animation waits to take its turn. This workflow is presented here in Figure 10-3.

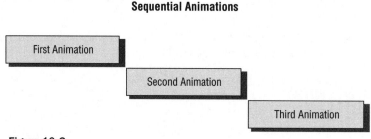

Sequential Animations

Figure 10-3

When you use the `<Parallel>` element instead of the `<Sequence>` element, items run as a group all at the same time. This approach is illustrated in Figure 10-4.

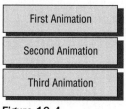

Parallel Animations

Figure 10-4

Examples of Animation Actions

Now that you have a general understanding of the framework and the tools at your disposal, this section looks at some of the actions that you can use and provides some samples of using these actions.

Using the <FadeOut> Action in a Sequence

To show an example of using the `<FadeOut>` element along with a sequence of animations, Listing 10-2 expands upon the earlier example by adding another animation to the list of sequenced animations.

Listing 10-2: Fading out text using FadeOut animation

```
<script runat="server">

<%@ Page Language="C#" %>

<%@ Register Assembly="AjaxControlToolkit" Namespace="AjaxControlToolkit"
    TagPrefix="cc1" %>

    protected void Button1_Click(object sender, EventArgs e)
    {
        Label1.Text = "Hello " + TextBox1.Text;
    }

</script>

<html xmlns="http://www.w3.org/1999/xhtml">
<head runat="server">
    <title>Growing Label</title>
</head>
<body>
    <form id="form1" runat="server">
    <div>
        <asp:ScriptManager ID="ScriptManager1" runat="server" />
        <asp:TextBox ID="TextBox1" runat="server"></asp:TextBox>
         <asp:Button ID="Button1" runat="server" Text="Submit your name"
        OnClick="Button1_Click" />
        <br /><br />
        <asp:Label ID="Label1" runat="server"></asp:Label>
        <cc1:AnimationExtender ID="Label1_AnimationExtender" runat="server"
            Enabled="True"
            TargetControlID="Label1">
            <Animations>
            <OnLoad>
                <Sequence>
                    <Scale ScaleFactor="4" Unit="px" ScaleFont="true" FontUnit="pt"
                    Duration="2.5" Fps="50" ></Scale>

                    <FadeOut Duration="5" Fps="25" />

                </Sequence>
            </OnLoad>
            </Animations>
        </cc1:AnimationExtender>
    </div>
    </form>
</body>
</html>
```

Now in this case, the sequence definition includes two animations. The first animation is the scaling of the text, and the second animation is the fading out of the text. Running this example gives you similar views to those presented in Figure 10-5.

Within the `<OnLoad>` element, a `<Sequence>` element is used to define the transition of two animations. The first is the same scaling animation, while the second is the `<FadeOut>` animation.

```
<Sequence>
    <Scale ScaleFactor="4" Unit="px" ScaleFont="true" FontUnit="pt"
    Duration="2.5" Fps="50" ></Scale>
    <FadeOut Duration="5" Fps="25" />
</Sequence>
```

Figure 10-5

The `<FadeOut>` element includes two attributes (or properties). These include the `Duration` and the `Fps` attributes. The `Duration` attribute defines the number of seconds over which the fading out transition should occur. The `Fps` attribute defines the number of frames per second in which to draw the animation. The default is 25, so there really isn't a need to define it here, as it is the same value.

Some other interesting attributes are the `MinimumOpacity` and `MaximumOpacity` properties. A value of 1 for each of these items shows the element in its full strength. This means that a value of ".5" displays the element at half strength. Try running the example from Listing 10-2 using a `<FadeOut>` element as illustrated here:

```
<FadeOut Duration="5" Fps="25" MinimumOpacity=".2" />
```

Now with this in place, the opacity will not decrease to nothing, but instead, it will decrease to 20 percent of its full value.

Using <FadeIn> and <FadeOut> Together

The <FadeIn> and <FadeOut> actions behave similarly, but in the end, they perform the opposite action. To provide an example of the two items working together, Listing 10-3 shows an <OnMouseOver> trigger along with an <OnMouseOut> trigger. This page allows end users to hover their mouse over an image and have the image fade to 20%; performing a mouseout causes the image to come back to its original state. The code for this example is presented here:

Listing 10-3: Using move the <OnMouseOver> and <OnMouseOut> triggers

```
<%@ Page Language="C#" %>

<%@ Register assembly="AjaxControlToolkit" namespace="AjaxControlToolkit"
tagprefix="cc1" %>

<html xmlns="http://www.w3.org/1999/xhtml">
<head runat="server">
    <title>FadeIn and FadeOut</title>
</head>
<body>
    <form id="form1" runat="server">
    <div>

        <asp:ScriptManager ID="ScriptManager1" runat="server">
        </asp:ScriptManager>

        <asp:Image ID="Image1" runat="server" Height="341px"
         ImageUrl="~/Sea Green Turtle.jpg"
            Width="523px" />

        <cc1:AnimationExtender ID="Image1_AnimationExtender" runat="server"
            Enabled="True" TargetControlID="Image1">
            <Animations>
            <OnMouseOver>
                <Sequence>
                    <FadeOut Duration="1" Fps="50" MinimumOpacity=".2" />
                </Sequence>
            </OnMouseOver>
            <OnMouseOut>
                <Sequence>
                    <FadeIn Duration="1" Fps="50" />
                </Sequence>
            </OnMouseOut>
            </Animations>
        </cc1:AnimationExtender>

    </div>
    </form>
</body>
</html>
```

The interesting thing with this example is that there are animations in place for more than one trigger. This means that you can perform a series of complex animations based up multiple triggers. In this case, there are two triggers in place for two distinct actions. Also, the two triggers use separately defined animations. Figure 10-6 shows an example of both states of this page.

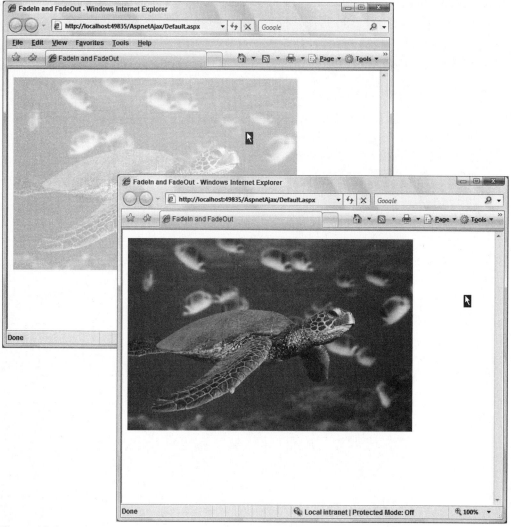

Figure 10-6

Moving and Working with a Panel

When working with the animation framework, you can easily work with everything from pop-ups to tooltips and other items held in Panel controls and `<div>` elements. This next example moves and presents a set of items contained within a `<div>` element when you click on the LinkButton server control on the page. Listing 10-4 shows an example of this.

Listing 10-4: Moving and working with a <div> using animation

```
<%@ Page Language="C#" %>

<%@ Register assembly="AjaxControlToolkit" namespace="AjaxControlToolkit"
tagprefix="cc1" %>

<html xmlns="http://www.w3.org/1999/xhtml">
<head runat="server">
    <title>Moving divs</title>
</head>
<body>
    <form id="form1" runat="server">
    <div>
        <asp:ScriptManager ID="ScriptManager1" runat="server">
        </asp:ScriptManager>
        <asp:LinkButton ID="LinkButton1" runat="server"
         OnClientClick="return false;">Vote!</asp:LinkButton><br />
        <asp:Image ID="Image1" runat="server" Height="341px"
         ImageUrl="~/Green Sea Turtle.jpg"
            Width="523px" />
        <cc1:AnimationExtender ID="LB1_AnimationExtender" runat="server"
            Enabled="True" TargetControlID="LinkButton1">
            <Animations>
            <OnClick>
                <Sequence>
                    <ScriptAction
                     script="$get('LinkButton1').style.visibility='hidden';">
                    </ScriptAction>
                    <StyleAction AnimationTarget="imageTooltip" Attribute="display"
                     Value="block"/>
                    <Parallel AnimationTarget="imageTooltip" Duration="1" Fps="25">
                        <Move Horizontal="150" Vertical="-50" />
                        <Resize Height="30" Width="350" />
                    </Parallel>
                    <FadeIn AnimationTarget="imageTooltip" Duration=".5"/>
                </Sequence>
            </OnClick>
            </Animations>
        </cc1:AnimationExtender>

        <div id="imageTooltip" style="display: none;
                                      background-color: White; border-style: solid;
                                      border-width: medium;  border-color: Black">
            <center>Vote for this image!
            <asp:Button ID="Button1" runat="server" Text="I like it!" />
            <asp:Button ID="Button2" runat="server"
             Text="I don't like it!" /></center>
        </div>
    </div>
    </form>
</body>
</html>
```

In this example, when the end user clicks the Vote button above the image, a `<div>` element below the image goes through a transition to show a set of voting buttons. The `<div>` element is presented at the bottom of the page and one important thing for this is that the style needs to be set so that the display of this element is set to none. As part of the `<Sequence>` structure, the display is reset back on using the `<StyleAction>` element.

```
<StyleAction AnimationTarget="imageTooltip" Attribute="display" Value="block"/>
```

When running this page, you get something similar to the results presented in Figure 10-7, when the Vote button is clicked.

Figure 10-7

One interesting point about the `<Sequence>` section of the document is that it also includes a `<Parallel>` element within it with its own set of animations.

Summary

This chapter took a brief look at applying animations to your ASP.NET AJAX pages, using part of the ASP.NET AJAX Control Toolkit. More specifically, this chapter looked at working with the AnimationExtender control that is part of the Toolkit.

It is important to remember that this part of the Toolkit is basically an entire framework at your disposal to provide a series of transitions to your pages based upon a series of triggers.

11

Building Custom Controls

A lot of features are packed into the ASP.NET AJAX Framework. As a result, many common tasks can be accomplished using existing controls that handle making asynchronous calls to ASP.NET pages or Web services. Many of the complexities associated with making asynchronous calls are hidden so that you can focus on building the application rather than on the message processing that happens behind the scenes. A perfect example of this is the UpdatePanel control, which makes it easy to add AJAX functionality into an ASP.NET page without writing a lot of code. Simply add an UpdatePanel to an ASP.NET page, and you have instant AJAX functionality available even if you've never made an asynchronous call before in your life.

No matter how many features are built into a framework, there will always be times when you need to build custom controls that wrap complex functionality or refactor code that may have previously been duplicated in multiple places. Writing custom ASP.NET AJAX controls is quite different from writing standard ASP.NET controls because the bulk of a control's functionality is defined in a JavaScript file as opposed to VB.NET or C# files. However, many of the same concepts apply, such as fields, properties, methods/functions, events, and event handlers.

In this chapter, you learn how to build custom ASP.NET AJAX controls capable of generating dynamic output, handling end user interactions, and connecting to Web services. Topics covered include the overall structure of client-side controls and how constructors, properties, functions, events, and event handlers can be defined and used. You'll also see how client-side scripts can be encapsulated in server controls and exposed using familiar ASP.NET server control syntax. Once this is done, you can simply drop a server control on a form and set some properties to inject client script into the response stream at runtime. Let's get started by analyzing the structure of custom client-side controls and discussing key classes provided by the ASP.NET AJAX script library.

Building Client-Side ASP.NET AJAX Controls

JavaScript files can be written using several different techniques. A great majority of scripts on the Internet consist of multiple functions thrown into one or more files used to perform client-side functionality. While these types of unstructured scripts certainly get the job done, they don't encapsulate related functions into containers for better code reuse and organization. Relatively few scripts rely on object-oriented techniques where JavaScript classes are defined using the JavaScript function and prototype design pattern.

Although JavaScript is not a true object-oriented language, it is capable of emulating several object-oriented characteristics that can be used to build new types, extend existing types, and in general create a reusable client-side object library. Building custom AJAX controls requires understanding how to leverage encapsulation features built into the JavaScript language that can be used to create classes. It also requires an understanding of how the ASP.NET AJAX script library extends JavaScript's default set of features.

Terminology between JavaScript and VB.NET or C# objects is surprisingly similar. Functionality can be grouped into classes, although JavaScript doesn't technically support the concept of a class and doesn't use the `class` keyword. However, JavaScript does support organizing related functionality into container objects much like VB.NET and C# do. Both JavaScript and .NET "classes" can expose fields, properties, and methods, although methods are typically referred to as "functions" in JavaScript, as they are defined using the `function` keyword. To keep things consistent, the remainder of this chapter uses standard .NET terminology and refers to actions a JavaScript object performs as methods rather than functions. It will also refer to variables as fields and characteristics/attributes of an object as properties.

Extending JavaScript

The ASP.NET AJAX script library extends JavaScript in several ways by allowing namespaces, classes, enumerations, and even interfaces to be defined and used on the client side. These extensions provide a familiar framework that resembles the server-side environment most ASP.NET developers are accustomed to working with and using. As a result, ASP.NET and JavaScript developers alike can create custom ASP.NET AJAX controls rather quickly once a few core concepts are understood.

One of the key classes involved in extending JavaScript's existing functionality is the ASP.NET AJAX `Type` class. The `Type` class exposes several different methods that are useful when building custom controls, as shown in the following table.

Method	Description
callBaseMethod	Returns a reference to a base class's method for the specified instance. Typically used in a control's `initialize()` method and `dispose()` method when building custom client-side controls.
implementsInterface	Determines if a type implements a specific interface. Returns a `Boolean` value.
inheritsFrom	Determines if a type inherits from a specific base type. Returns a `Boolean` value.
initializeBase	Initializes the base type of a derived type. A call to the `initialize-Base()` method is made in a control's constructor.

Method	Description
registerClass	Registers a specific type with the ASP.NET AJAX client-side framework. A base class and one or more interfaces can optionally be defined when calling registerClass().
registerInterface	Registers an interface with the ASP.NET AJAX client-side framework.
registerNamespace	Registers a namespace with the ASP.NET AJAX client-side framework.

When building a custom AJAX control, you use the Type class within client-side code to define a namespace, register a class, and possibly even an interface or enumeration with the ASP.NET AJAX framework. You'll also use the Type class when a custom control needs to inherit functionality from an existing class in the ASP.NET AJAX script library. Every client-side control used in an ASP.NET AJAX application is considered to be a "type," just as any VB.NET or C# class built using the .NET framework is considered to be a "type." As a result, methods exposed by the ASP.NET AJAX Type class are available on all AJAX controls that you create.

In addition to the Type class, the ASP.NET AJAX script library provides several different classes that can serve as the foundation for a custom control, depending upon the control's intended purpose. Three main categories of custom controls can be built, including behaviors, visual controls, and nonvisual controls. In cases where you'd like to extend an existing DOM element's behavior (to add additional style information to a button or textbox, for instance), the Sys.UI.Behavior class can be inherited from to create a custom behavior control. While controls that derive from Sys.UI.Behavior extend the overall behavior of a DOM element, they don't modify the original purpose or intent of the control. When visual controls need to be created that modify the original intent of a DOM element and extend the element's functionality, the Sys.UI.Control class can be used as the base class for the control. Nonvisual controls that don't extend the behavior of a DOM element or extend its overall functionality (a timer for example) should derive from the Sys.Component base class.

The custom control used throughout this chapter derives from the Sys.UI.Control class, as it extends the functionality of a DOM element and adds significant functionality to it. Inheriting from Sys.UI.Control provides a solid starting foundation that can be built upon, so you don't have to write the entire control from scratch. The control that you develop here is named AlbumViewer and allows users to view one or more albums, and to search through them using asynchronous calls made to a .NET Web service. Figure 11-1 shows the output generated by the AlbumViewer control.

To create the AlbumViewer control, a prescribed set of steps can be followed. These steps are fairly standard and should be followed when building ASP.NET AJAX client-side controls in general.

1. Register a namespace: Register the namespace for the control using the Type class's registerNamespace() method.

2. Create a constructor: Create the control's constructor, and pass in the DOM element that represents the container for the control as a parameter. Initialize the base class by calling the initializeBase(), method and define any fields that will be used by the control to store data.

3. Prototype properties and methods: Follow the prototype design pattern to define properties and methods exposed by the control. Properties and methods are defined using JSON notation.

4. Override `initialize()`: Within the prototype section of the control, initialize the control by overriding the `initialize()` method. Within `initialize` you can dynamically assign values to fields defined in the constructor, create delegates, handle events, plus more.

5. Override `dispose()`: Within the prototype section of the control, override the `dispose()` method to allow objects such as delegates used by the control to be cleaned up properly.

6. Register the control and inherit from a base class: Register the control with the ASP.NET AJAX client-side object model by using the `Type` class's `registerClass()` method. Pass the appropriate base class to derive from as a parameter to `registerClass()`.

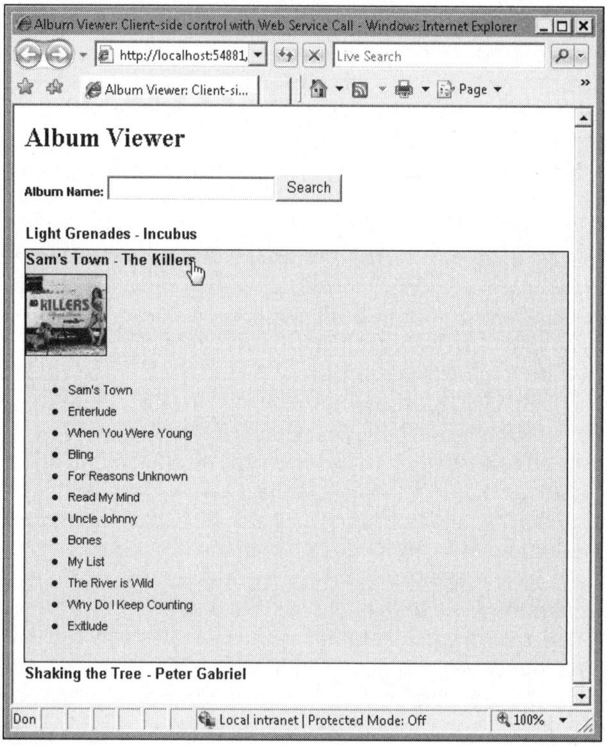

Figure 11-1

Take a look at how a custom AlbumViewer control can be created and used in an ASP.NET AJAX application.

> All of the code that follows for the AlbumViewer client-side control can be found in the `Scripts/AlbumViewerStandAlone.js` file or in the `AlbumViewer` class library project available in the code download for this book on the WROX Web site. The individual code listings that follow represent only a portion of the overall control's code and will not run on their own.

Registering a Control Namespace

When creating custom client-side controls, you'll want to define a namespace for each control to resolve any possible naming conflicts that may arise in an application. The AlbumViewer control is placed in a `Wrox.ASPAJAX.Samples` namespace and registered by using the `Type` class's `registerNamespace` method. Namespaces can contain other nested namespaces, classes, interfaces, enumerations, and even delegates and should be defined at the beginning of a control's code:

```
Type.registerNamespace("Wrox.ASPAJAX.Samples");
```

Note that no `End Namespace` keywords (as in VB.NET) or start and end brackets (as in C#) are used to define where an ASP.NET AJAX client-side namespace starts and ends. Instead, the namespace is referenced directly by a given control, as shown next.

Creating a Control Constructor

Once the namespace for a control is registered using the `Type` class, the control itself can be defined using the JavaScript `function` keyword. This is done by prefixing the control's name with the namespace that it should be placed in and defining an anonymous JavaScript function as shown in Listing 11-1.

Listing 11-1: Defining a Client-Side Class's Namespace and Constructor

```
Type.registerNamespace("Wrox.ASPJAX.Samples");
Wrox.ASPAJAX.Samples.AlbumViewer = function(element) {
    // Initialize base class
    Wrox.ASPAJAX.Samples.AlbumViewer.initializeBase(this,[element]);
    this._AlbumDivOverCssClass = null;
    this._AlbumDivOutCssClass = null;
    this._AlbumTitleCssClass = null;
    this._AlbumArtistCssClass = null;
    this._SongTitleCssClass = null;
    this._Albums = [];
    this._ServicePath = null;

    this._ServiceMethod = null;
    this._StatusLabel = null;
    this._ShowSearchBox = false;
    this._albumContainer = null;

    //Delegate definitions
    this._overHandler = null;
    this._outHandler = null;
    this._clickHandler = null;
    this._btnClickHandler = null;
    this._propertyChanged = null;
}
```

The code in Listing 11-1 associates the namespace of `Wrox.ASPAJAX.Samples` with the AlbumViewer control and creates a constructor for the control by defining a new anonymous JavaScript function.

Like VB.NET and C# constructors, JavaScript constructors can accept initialization parameters. The `AlbumViewer` constructor shown in Listing 11-1 accepts a DOM element object representing the parent container that the control will use. The AlbumViewer control uses a `div` DOM element as its parent container.

The first line of code inside of the AlbumViewer control's constructor makes a call to the `Type` class's `initializeBase()` method (recall that all controls are considered types and have access to the `Type` class's methods) to initialize the control's base class. Because the AlbumViewer control is a visual control that adds content to a `div` element, it inherits from the `Sys.UI.Control` base class provided by the ASP.NET AJAX script library. The call to `initializeBase()` instantiates the `Sys.UI.Control` class. You'll learn more about how the `AlbumViewer` class inherits from `Sys.UI.Control` later in the chapter.

The `initializeBase` method accepts two parameters. The first parameter represents the object instance to initialize the base class for (the AlbumViewer control, in this case). You'll normally use the JavaScript `this` keyword for the parameter value. The second parameter accepts an array, which is why the square brackets, `[ ]`, are used. The array can be passed to the base constructor as it initializes. Listing 11-1 passes the container element of the `AlbumViewer` control as the parameter value. Because the control uses a `div` element as its container, the `div` is passed directly to the base class's constructor.

Once the base class has been initialized, fields used by the AlbumViewer control are defined. Each field is prefixed with the `this` keyword, which represents the current class (the `this` keyword is much like the `Me` keyword that VB.NET developers use and analogous to the `this` keyword in C#). Because the fields shown in Listing 11-1 are private, their names are prefixed by the underscore character. This character isn't required and has no actual significance; it is a standard naming convention used in the ASP.NET AJAX script library for private members of a class. As a general rule, all object and array fields used by a control should be defined in the control's constructor so that the field instances are unique to all control instances and not shared across instances.

The `AlbumViewer` class defines several fields in its constructor such as `this._AlbumTitleCssClass` and `this._AlbumArtistCssClass` that are used to store the CSS class applied to various child elements within the control. It also defines an array named `this._Albums` using the shortcut [ ] JSON notation. `this._Albums` is used to store album information used by the control. Other fields such as `this._ServicePath` and `this._ServiceMethod` are used to store information about the Web service that provides album, artist, and song information to the control. The handler fields shown (`this._overHandler`, `this._outHandler`, and so on) represent delegates used by the control that route data from events to event handlers.

Using the Prototype Design Pattern with JSON

JavaScript has long supported the ability to extend objects by using the prototype property. By using it, JavaScript objects can inherit from base types and add additional properties and methods. The ASP.NET AJAX Library uses the prototype property and a pattern referred to as the "prototype design pattern" to extend existing objects and create new ones. Listing 11-2 shows how the prototype property can be used to define a `Person` object and expose two property getters and setters, as well as a method.

Listing 11-2: Defining properties using the prototype design pattern

```
function Person() {
    this._FirstName = null;
    this._LastName = null;
}

Person.prototype.get_FirstName = function() {
    return this._FirstName;
}

Person.prototype.set_FirstName = function(value) {
    this._FirstName = value;
}

Person.prototype.get_LastName = function() {
    return this._LastName;
}

Person.prototype.set_LastName = function(value) {
    this._LastName = value;
}

Person.prototype.getFullName = function() {
    return this._FirstName + " " + this._LastName;
}
```

> JavaScript doesn't officially support the concept of property getters and setters as in VB.NET or C#. However, getters and setters can be emulated by writing the corresponding methods. For example, `get_FirstName` represents the get block, while `set_FirstName` represents the set block. Both of these are officially methods in .NET terms and functions in JavaScript terms but are typically treated as properties, as they get and set the value of a field.

Usually, there is a one-to-one relationship between a prototype property and a function definition, as shown in Listing 11-2. If four methods need to be added to a custom control, the prototype property is used four times. An exception to this rule would be for objects that define their properties and methods directly in the constructor, which is not a practice followed by the ASP.NET AJAX script library. Properties and methods added directly into the constructor are duplicated each time a new object instance is created. However, by using the prototype property, properties and methods are shared across multiple object instances resulting in less bloat.

Although the code shown in Listing 11-2 is fairly standard, ASP.NET AJAX client-side controls use the prototype design pattern with JSON notation to define properties and methods rather than using the prototype property for each property or method. Listing 11-3 shows how the `Person` class shown in Listing 11-2 can be refactored using the prototype design pattern with JSON. As you look through the code, notice that all properties and methods are wrapped within a single prototype statement. Property and method names are followed by a colon that separates the name from the actual functionality. Each property and method is then separated by a comma.

Listing 11-3: Using the prototype design pattern with JSON syntax

```
function Person() {
    this._FirstName = null;
    this._LastName = null;
}

Person.prototype = {
    get_FirstName: function() {
        return this._FirstName;
    },

    set_FirstName: function(value) {
        this._FirstName = value;
    },

    get_LastName: function() {
        return this._LastName;
    },

    set_LastName: function(value) {
        this._LastName = value;
    },

    getFullName: function() {
        return this._FirstName + " " + this._LastName;
    }
}
```

The functionality for a property or method can also be defined in a separate location rather than inline, as shown in Listing 11-4. The ASP.NET AJAX script library uses this technique quite frequently to define client-side classes.

Listing 11-4: Defining properties in a separate location

```
function Person() {
    this._FirstName = null;
    this._LastName = null;
}

Person.prototype = {

    get_FirstName: Person$get_FirstName,

    set_FirstName: Person$set_FirstName,

    get_LastName: Person$get_LastName,

    set_LastName: Person$set_LastName,

    getFullName: Person$getFullName
}
```

Listing 11-4: Defining properties in a separate location *(continued)*

```
function Person$get_FirstName() {
    return this._FirstName;
}

function Person$set_FirstName(value) {
    this._FirstName = value;
}

function Person$get_LastName() {
    return this._LastName;
}

function Person$set_LastName(value) {
    this._LastName = value;
}

function Person$getFullName() {
    return this._FirstName + " " + this._LastName;
}
```

Now that you've seen the fundamentals of building constructors and using the prototype design pattern, let's take a look at some of the properties defined in the AlbumViewer control.

Defining Control Properties

Properties in client-side controls work in the same way as properties in server-side controls. However, the way properties are defined in client-side controls is quite different because JavaScript doesn't support the .NET property syntax that formally defines get and set blocks. For example, to define a getter and setter for a property named `Albums` that reads and writes to and from a private field named `this._Albums`, the following code could be written using the prototype design pattern and JSON:

```
get_Albums: function() {
    return this._Albums;
},

set_Albums: function(value) {
    this._Albums = value;
}
```

The get block normally found in VB.NET or C# classes is simulated by adding `get_` to the front of the property name, while the set block uses `set_`. Any keywords can be used, but `get_` and `set_` are used throughout the ASP.NET AJAX script library and are also used in the AlbumViewer control for the sake of consistency.

The AlbumViewer control defines several different properties used to control CSS styles, searching capabilities, and Web service calls. Each property acts as a gateway to private fields defined in the control's constructor shown in Listing 11-1. A list of properties exposed by the AlbumViewer control is shown in the following table. Keep in mind that although these properties are really JavaScript functions prefixed by `get_` and `set_` keywords, their only purpose is to get and set data, so we'll refer to them as properties to stay consistent with VB.NET and C# property definitions. However, the class consumer needs to use a function syntax when calling the getter or setter, as there is no explicit property syntax support in JavaScript.

Property Name	Description
Albums	Gets and sets an array of Albums objects.
AlbumDivOverCssClass	Gets and sets the CSS class name to use when a user hovers over an album in the control.
AlbumDivOutCssClass	Gets and sets the CSS class name to use when a user moves the mouse out of an album in the control.
AlbumTitleCssClass	Gets and sets the CSS class name to use for an individual album title.
AlbumArtistCssClass	Gets and sets the CSS class name to use for an album artist.
SongTitleCssClass	Gets and sets the CSS class name to use for album songs.
ShowSearchBox	Gets and sets a Boolean value that is used by the AlbumViewer control to determine if an album search textbox should be shown or not.
ServicePath	Gets and sets the path to the album Web service. The service is used to retrieve album data dynamically.
ServiceMethod	Gets and sets the WebMethod to call on the album Web Serviceservice.

Listing 11-5 shows how the properties in the previous table are defined and used within the AlbumViewer control's prototype definition. Each property has an associated getter and setter used to access the associated field variable defined in the control's constructor.

Listing 11-5: Defining AlbumViewer properties using the prototype design pattern

```
Wrox.ASPAJAX.Samples.AlbumViewer.prototype = {
    get_Albums: function() {
        return this._Albums;
    },

    set_Albums: function(value) {
        this._Albums = value;
    },

    get_AlbumDivOverCssClass: function() {

        return this._AlbumDivOverCssClass;
    },

    set_AlbumDivOverCssClass: function(value) {
        this._AlbumDivOverCssClass = value;
    },
```

Listing 11-5: Defining AlbumViewer properties using the prototype design pattern *(continued)*

```
get_AlbumDivOutCssClass: function() {
    return this._AlbumDivOutCssClass;
},

set_AlbumDivOutCssClass: function(value) {
    this._AlbumDivOutCssClass = value;
},

get_AlbumTitleCssClass: function() {
    return this._AlbumTitleCssClass;
},

set_AlbumTitleCssClass: function(value) {
    this._AlbumTitleCssClass = value;
},

get_AlbumArtistCssClass: function() {
    return this._AlbumArtistCssClass;
},

set_AlbumArtistCssClass: function(value) {
    this._AlbumArtistCssClass = value;
},

get_SongTitleCssClass: function() {
    return this._SongTitleCssClass;
},

set_SongTitleCssClass: function(value) {
    this._SongTitleCssClass = value;
},

get_ShowSearchBox: function() {
    return this._ShowSearchBox;
},

set_ShowSearchBox: function(value) {
    this._ShowSearchBox = value;
},

get_ServicePath : function() {
    return this._ServicePath;
},

set_ServicePath : function(value) {
    if (this._ServicePath != value) {
        this._ServicePath = value;

        this.raisePropertyChanged('ServicePath');
    }
```

Continued

Listing 11-5: Defining AlbumViewer properties using the prototype design pattern *(continued)*

```
    },

    get_ServiceMethod : function() {
        return this._ServiceMethod;
    },

    set_ServiceMethod : function(value) {
        if (this._ServiceMethod != value) {
            this._ServiceMethod = value;
            this.raisePropertyChanged('ServiceMethod');
        }
    }

    //More code follows for methods and event handlers
}
```

The majority of the properties shown in Listing 11-5 simply read and write from private fields. While the `ServicePath` and `ServiceMethod` properties follow this same pattern, the setter for each of these properties adds a call to a method named `raisePropertyChanged`. Calling this method is useful in situations where a control needs to be notified when a property changes so that it can act upon the change. This is a simple analog of the .NET event mechanism. The AlbumViewer control requires notification if the `ServicePath` or `ServiceMethod` properties are changed by the consumer of the control so that it can retrieve fresh album data.

You may wonder where the `raisePropertyChanged()` method is defined. Fortunately, it's not something you have to code manually. The AlbumViewer control derives from the `Sys.UI.Control` class, which in turn derives from the `Sys.Component` class. The `Sys.Component` class defines the `raisePropertyChanged` method as one of its members (for a complete listing of the `Control` class's properties and methods refer to the ASP.NET AJAX documentation in the MSDN Library). When `raisePropertyChanged` is called, an event is raised that can be handled by an event handler. The AlbumViewer control handles the property changed event as the `ServicePath` and `ServiceMethod` properties change and uses the two property values to call the appropriate Web service to retrieve new album data and load it into the control. Additional information about handling events such as the one raised by `raisePropertyChanged` is covered in the next section.

Initializing a Control and Handling Events

The `Sys.Component` class mentioned earlier defines an `initialize` method that's useful when a control is first initialized. When `initialize` is called, a property named `isInitialized` is set to true by `Sys.Component` through a call to `set_isInitialized`. This property is referenced by other classes in the ASP.NET AJAX script library such as `Sys.UI.Behavior` to determine if a control has been initialized or not.

Custom controls such as the AlbumViewer control can override the `initialize` method and use it to initialize a base class, initialize properties or field values, define delegates, and hook events to event handlers. The AlbumViewer control defines the `initialize` method within the prototype section of the code shown in Listing 11-6.

Listing 11-6: Creating an initialize method using the prototype design pattern

```
Wrox.ASPAJAX.Samples.AlbumViewer.prototype = {

    //Property definitions go here

    initialize : function() {
        var e = this.get_element();
        e.style.className = this.get_AlbumDivOutCssClass();

        //Initialize Delegates
        this._overHandler = Function.createDelegate(this, this._onMouseOver);
        this._outHandler = Function.createDelegate(this, this._onMouseOut);
        this._clickHandler = Function.createDelegate(this, this._onClick);
        this._btnClickHandler = Function.createDelegate(this,this._onButtonClick);
        this._propertyChanged =
          Function.createDelegate(this,this._onPropertyChanged);
        this.add_propertyChanged(this._propertyChanged);

        //Create search textbox
        if (this._ShowSearchBox) {
            var lblText = document.createElement("SPAN");
            lblText.style.cssText = "font-family:arial;font-weight:bold;" +
              "font-size:8pt;";
            lblText.innerHTML = "Album Name: ";

            var txtAlbum = document.createElement("INPUT");
            txtAlbum.setAttribute("type","text");
            txtAlbum.setAttribute("id",e.id + "_txtAlbumSearch");
            txtAlbum.style.cssText = "width:150px;";

            var btnAlbumSearch = document.createElement("INPUT");
            btnAlbumSearch.setAttribute("type","button");
            btnAlbumSearch.id = e.id + "_btnAlbumSearch";
            btnAlbumSearch.value = "Search";
            $addHandler(btnAlbumSearch,"click",this._btnClickHandler);

            e.appendChild(lblText);
            e.appendChild(txtAlbum);
            e.appendChild(btnAlbumSearch);
            e.appendChild(document.createElement("P"));
        }

        //Create div that will hold albums
        this._albumContainer = document.createElement("DIV");
        this._albumContainer.id = e.id + "_AlbumContainer";
        e.appendChild(this._albumContainer);

        Wrox.ASPAJAX.Samples.AlbumViewer.callBaseMethod(this, 'initialize');

        //Bind data if albums have been assigned
        if (this._ServicePath && this._ServiceMethod) {
            // Call the Web service
```

Continued

```
                this._invokeWebService(null);
            } else if (this._Albums != null) {
                this.set_data(this._Albums);
            }
        },

        //Additional methods go here
}
```

When the AlbumViewer control's `initialize` method is called, several tasks are performed. First, a reference to the DOM element used by the control is made by calling `get_element`. The element property is inherited from `Sys.UI.Control` and is referenced any time the `AlbumViewer` control needs to access the DOM element container. Once the DOM element is accessed, the CSS class to apply to the element is assigned by reading from the `AlbumDivOutCssClass` property. This class defines the overall style applied to the control's parent container.

Next, several delegates are created that point to various event handler methods. Delegates in ASP. NET AJAX client-side controls perform the same overall function as delegates used in VB.NET or C#: They pass data raised by an event to an event handler. Client-side delegates are created by calling the `Function` class's `createDelegate` method and passing the object context that the delegate applies to, as well as the name of the event handler method that the delegate should direct data to. The delegates created in the AlbumViewer control are used to route data when `mouseover`, `mouseout`, `click`, and `propertychanged` events are raised.

The delegate instances returned from calling `Function.createDelegate()` are assigned to private fields defined in the control's constructor because several of them are reused throughout the control and need to be globally accessible. For example, the following code creates a delegate that is responsible for routing `mouseover` event data to an event handler named `_onMouseOver`. A reference to the delegate is stored in the `this._overHandler` field.

```
this._overHandler = Function.createDelegate(this, this._onMouseOver);
```

Property changed events raised by the AlbumViewer control are routed to an event handler by calling the `add_propertyChanged` method. This method routes data raised when the `raisePropertyChanged` method discussed earlier is called to an event handler so that the change can be handled by the control. It accepts the name of the event handler method to call or a delegate instance that points to the method.

Once a delegate is created, it can be used to hook an event directly to an event handler using the ASP. NET AJAX `$addHandler` method. VB.NET developers will be quite comfortable using the `$addHandler` method, as it's similar in functionality to the VB.NET `AddHandler` keyword. `$addHandler` is a shortcut to the `Sys.UI.DomEvent` class's `addHandler` method. It accepts several parameters, including the object that raises the event, the name of the event that will be raised, and the delegate that should be used to route event data to an event handler. Listing 11-6 contains an example of using the `$addHandler` method to hook up a button control's click event to a delegate named `this._btnClickHandler`:

```
//Define Delegate
this._btnClickHandler =
  Function.createDelegate(this,this._onButtonClick);
```

```
//Hook button's click event to an event handler using the delegate
$addHandler(btnAlbumSearch,"click",this._btnClickHandler);
```

In addition to $addHandler, the ASP.NET AJAX script library provides an $addHandlers method that allows multiple event handlers to be defined for a DOM element with a single statement. For example, if you need to attach the mouseover, mouseout, and click events of a DOM element named albumDiv to event handlers, you could use $addHandlers in the following way:

```
$addHandlers(albumDiv,
    {"mouseover" : this._overHandler,
     "mouseout" : this._outHandler,
     "click" : this._clickHandler },
  this);
```

The second parameter passed to $addHandlers is a JSON object containing the different event names and related delegates that should be attached to the DOM element.

The initialize method shown in Listing 11-6 is also used to add several controls into the AlbumViewer control's parent container element. Because album data is being displayed, an end user may want to search for one or more albums based upon title. Searching is controlled by data stored in the this._ShowTextBox field of the control. When the field value is true, a span tag, textbox, and button are added to the AlbumViewer control's div container. End users can then use the controls to perform a search. Adding controls is accomplished by calling document.createElement and passing in the name of the element object that should be created. Once element objects are created, they're added to the appropriate parent container by calling its appendChild method.

The final two tasks performed by the AlbumViewer control's initialize method are calling the base Sys.UI.Control class's initialize method and binding album data to the control. The Type class's callBaseMethod method calls the initialize method of the base class. This method accepts the current object instance as well as the name of the method to call on the base class. Although not used by the AlbumViewer control, callBaseMethod returns a reference to the base class's initialize method.

Now that you've been exposed to the initialize method, let's move on to a few other methods used by the AlbumViewer control to bind data, call Web services, and perform additional functionality.

Defining Control Methods

The AlbumViewer control provides several ways for an end user to interact with the control to view albums, artists, and songs. Users can search for albums using all or part of the album name, highlight albums as they move their mouse, and click albums to view more data about an album. Each of these interactions requires event handlers to be written to handle the performed action. In addition to supporting user interactions, the AlbumViewer supports calling a Web service to retrieve album data as well as data binding. All of this functionality is handled by methods defined within the AlbumViewer control.

Methods used by the control are shown in the following table. Methods that start with an underscore are considered private, although JavaScript doesn't truly support access modifiers such as public or private.

Method Name	Description
initialize	Initializes the control as well as the base class.
dispose	Cleans up resources used by the control such as event handlers.
set_data	Binds album data supplied by the client or by a Web service to the control. Performs the bulk of the control's functionality. This method is similar in purpose to the DataBind method found on ASP.NET server controls.
_getAlbumNode	Retrieves a specific album object within the AlbumViewer control.
_invokeWebService	Calls a Web service based upon values supplied by the ServicePath and ServiceMethod properties.
_onButtonClick	Handles the search button's click event.
_onClick	Handles the click event for album divs in the control.
_onMouseOut	Handles the mouseout event for album divs in the control.
_onMouseOver	Handles the mouseover event for album divs in the control.
_onMethodComplete	Processes data returned from a Web service call and binds the data by calling set_data.
_onMethodError	Handles errors returned from calls made to a Web service.
_onPropertyChanged	Handles property changed events that occur as the ServicePath and ServiceMethod property values change.
_setStyle	Used to apply a CSS style to an album div as the user interacts with the AlbumViewer control.

The AlbumViewer control's set_data method performs the bulk of the work done by the control. It accepts a single parameter that contains the Album objects to bind to the control and display to the end user. Although Album objects aren't the focus of this chapter, it's important to note that many of the same steps followed when building a custom control are also applied to building custom client-side classes. Listing 11-7 shows a representation of the Album and Song classes consumed and bound by the set_data method. These classes are used when a client-side script creates objects and passes them to the control's set_data method. When the AlbumViewer control calls a Web service, the JSON Album objects returned from the service are used instead.

> The fields defined in the Song and Album class constructors aren't prefixed with an underscore character (to simulate a private field) so that the objects are more in line with JSON objects returned from Web service calls that have properties defined such as Title, Artist, ImageUrl, and Songs for the Album class. By matching up the Album class shown in Listing 11-7 with the objects exposed by the Web service, the AlbumViewer control can work in a flexible manner with both types of objects.

Listing 11-7: Defining album and song classes using JavaScript

```javascript
Type.registerNamespace("Wrox.ASPAJAX.Samples");

//####  Song Object ####

Wrox.ASPAJAX.Samples.Song = function(trackNumber,title)
{
    // Initialize as a base class.
    Wrox.ASPAJAX.Samples.Song.initializeBase(this);
    this.Title = title;
    this.TrackNumber = trackNumber;
}

//Define Album properties
Wrox.ASPAJAX.Samples.Song.prototype = {
    initialize: function() {
        Wrox.ASPAJAX.Samples.Song.callBaseMethod(this,"initialize");
    },

    get_Title: function() {
        /// <value type="String"></value>
        if (arguments.length !== 0) throw Error.parameterCount();
        return this.Title;
    },

    set_Title: function(value) {
        var e = Function._validateParams(arguments,
          [{name: "value", type: String}]);
        if (e) throw e;

        this.Title = value;
    },

    get_TrackNumber: function() {
        /// <value type="String"></value>
        if (arguments.length !== 0) throw Error.parameterCount();
        return this.TrackNumber;
    },

    set_TrackNumber: function(value) {
        var e = Function._validateParams(arguments,
          [{name: "value", type: String}]);
        if (e) throw e;
        this.TrackNumber = value;
    },

    dispose: function() {
        this.Title = null;
        this.TrackNumber = null;
        Wrox.ASPAJAX.Samples.Song.callBaseMethod(this, "dispose");
    }
}
```

Continued

Listing 11-7: Defining album and song classes using JavaScript *(continued)*

```
Wrox.ASPAJAX.Samples.Song.registerClass("Wrox.ASPAJAX.Samples.Song",
  Sys.Component, Sys.IDisposable);


//####  Album Object ####

Wrox.ASPAJAX.Samples.Album = function()
{
    // Initialize as a base class.
    Wrox.ASPAJAX.Samples.Album.initializeBase(this);
    this.Title;
    this.Artist;
    this.ImageUrl;
    this.Songs = [];
}

//Define Album properties
Wrox.ASPAJAX.Samples.Album.prototype = {
    initialize: function() {
        Wrox.ASPAJAX.Samples.Album.callBaseMethod(this,"initialize");
    },

    get_Title: function() {
        return this.Title;
    },

    set_Title: function(value) {
        /// <value type="String"></value>
        this.Title = value;
    },

    get_ImageUrl: function() {
        return this.ImageUrl;
    },

    set_ImageUrl: function(value) {
        /// <value type="String"></value>
        this.ImageUrl = value;
    },

    get_Artist: function() {
        return this.Artist;
    },

    set_Artist: function(value) {
        /// <value type="String"></value>
        this.Artist = value;
    },

    addSong: function(song)
    {
        /// <value type="Wrox.ASPAJAX.Samples.Song"></value>
```

Listing 11-7: Defining album and song classes using JavaScript *(continued)*

```javascript
        if (Object.getTypeName(song) != "Wrox.ASPAJAX.Samples.Song")
        {
            var e = Error.argumentType("song", Object.getType(song),
                Wrox.ASPAJAX.Samples.Song,"Wrox.ASPAJAX.Samples.Song required!");
            e.popStackFrame();
            throw e;

        }
        Array.add(this.Songs,song);
    },

    removeSong: function(song)
    {
        /// <value type="Wrox.ASPAJAX.Samples.Song"></value>
        Array.remove(this.Songs,song);
    },

    get_Songs: function()
    {
        return this.Songs;
    },

    rateSong: function(song,rating)
    {
        throw Error.notImplemented("rateSong() has not yet been implemented");
    },

    dispose: function() {
        this.Title = null;
        this.Artist = null;
        this.Songs = null;
        this.ImageUrl = null;
        Wrox.ASPAJAX.Samples.Album.callBaseMethod(this, "dispose");
    }
}

Wrox.ASPAJAX.Samples.Album.registerClass("Wrox.ASPAJAX.Samples.Album",
    Sys.Component, Sys.IDisposable);

//Added to satisfy new notifyScriptLoaded() requirement
if (typeof(Sys) !== 'undefined') Sys.Application.notifyScriptLoaded();
```

Looking through the code in Listing 11-7, you'll see that the `Album` class has several properties, including `Title`, `Artist`, `Songs`, and `ImageUrl`. These properties are used by the `AlbumViewer` control to create new `div` element objects that are used to display album data. The `AlbumViewer` control's `set_data` method is responsible for iterating through `Album` and `Song` objects passed to the control by a page or by calls made to a Web service and binding those objects to the control. It's also responsible for clearing existing albums that are displayed when a user performs a new search and assigning styles to newly created DOM element objects.

The `Album` object binding process creates new div element objects as well as several others using `document.createElement` and adds the `div` objects to the AlbumViewer control's parent `div` container. `set_data` also handles hooking up `mouseout`, `mouseover`, and `click` events for each album `div` object created to event handlers by using the `$addHandlers` method discussed earlier. Listing 11-8 shows the complete code for the `set_data` method.

Listing 11-8: Defining the set_data method

```
set_data: function(albums) {
    var e = this.get_element();
    //Clear any albums already showing
    while (this._albumContainer.childNodes.length > 0) {
        var child = this._albumContainer.childNodes[0];
        this._albumContainer.removeChild(child);
    }

    //Handle case where no albums are available to bind
    if (albums == null) {
        var noRecords = document.createElement("SPAN");
        noRecords.style.cssText = "font-weight:bold;";
        noRecords.innerHTML = "No albums found.";
        this._albumContainer.appendChild(noRecords);
        return;
    }

    //Loop through albums
    for (var i=0; i<albums.length; i++) {
        var album = albums[i];

        //Create Album Div
        var id = this.get_element().id + "_Album" + i.toString();
        var albumDiv = document.createElement("DIV");
        albumDiv.id = id;
        albumDiv.style.clear = "both";
        albumDiv.className = this._AlbumDivOutCssClass;
        this._albumContainer.appendChild(albumDiv);

        //Attach Events
        $addHandlers(albumDiv,
          {"mouseover" : this._overHandler,
           "mouseout" : this._outHandler,
           "click" : this._clickHandler },
           this);

        //Create album title
        var albumTitle = document.createElement("SPAN");
        albumTitle.className = this._AlbumTitleCssClass;
        albumTitle.innerHTML = album.Title;
        albumDiv.appendChild(albumTitle);

        //Create album artist
        var albumArtist = document.createElement("SPAN");
        albumArtist.className = this._AlbumArtistCssClass;
```

Listing 11-8: Defining the set_data method *(continued)*

```
        albumArtist.innerHTML = " - " + album.Artist;
        albumDiv.appendChild(albumArtist);

        //Create child content div
        childrenDiv = document.createElement("DIV");
        childrenDiv.id = id + "_Children";
        childrenDiv.style.display = "none";

        albumDiv.appendChild(childrenDiv);

        //Create Image div
        var albumPicDiv = document.createElement("DIV");
        var img = document.createElement("IMG");
        img.src = album.ImageUrl;
        albumPicDiv.style.paddingTop = "5px";
        albumPicDiv.appendChild(img);
        childrenDiv.appendChild(albumPicDiv);

        //Create songs div
        var albumSongsDiv = document.createElement("DIV");
        var ul = document.createElement("UL");
        albumSongsDiv.appendChild(ul);

        //Loop through songs
        var songs = album.Songs;
        for (var j=0;j<songs.length;j++) {
            var li = document.createElement("LI");
            li.className = this._SongTitleCssClass;
            li.innerHTML = songs[j].Title;
            ul.appendChild(li);
        }
        childrenDiv.appendChild(albumSongsDiv);
    }
}
```

Listing 11-9 shows how the `AlbumViewer` control's private methods are used to handle events, locate album div nodes, assign CSS styles, and call Web services. Each method is prefixed with an underscore character to convey that it's private. Several of the methods such as `_onMouseOver` and `_onMouseOut` handle style changes to album objects as the end user moves his or her mouse or clicks. Others perform more complex functionality such as calling Web services and processing results or errors.

Listing 11-9: Defining Album class private methods

```
_onMouseOver : function(evt) {
    this._setStyle(evt,this._AlbumDivOverCssClass);
},

_onMouseOut : function(evt) {
    this._setStyle(evt,this._AlbumDivOutCssClass);
},
```

Continued

Listing 11-9: Defining Album class private methods *(continued)*

```
_setStyle: function(evt,className) {
    evt.stopPropagation();
    this._getAlbumNode(evt.target).className = className;
    return true;
},

_getAlbumNode: function(node) {
    var baseID = this.get_element().id + "_Album";
    var currElem = node;

    while (!(currElem.id.startsWith(baseID) && !currElem.id.endsWith
                ("_Children")))
    {
        if (currElem.parentNode) {
            currElem = currElem.parentNode;
        } else {
            break;
        }
    }
    return currElem;
},

_onClick : function(evt) {
    var parent = this._getAlbumNode(evt.target);
    var child = $get(parent.id + "_Children");
    if (child.style.display == "block") {
        child.style.display = "none";
    } else {
        child.style.display = "block";
    }
},

_onButtonClick : function(evt) {
    var searchText = $get(this.get_element().id + "_txtAlbumSearch").value;
    this._invokeWebService(searchText);
},

_onMethodComplete : function(result, userContext, methodName) {
    //Remove status label
    this._removeStatusLabel();
    // Bind returned data
    this.set_data(result);
},

_onMethodError : function(webServiceError, userContext, methodName) {
    // Call failed
    this._removeStatusLabel();
    if (webServiceError.get_timedOut()) {
        alert("Web Service call timed out.");
    } else {
        alert("Error calling Web Service: " +
            webServiceError.get_statusCode() + " " + webServiceError.get_message());
    }
```

Listing 11-9: Defining Album class private methods *(continued)*

```
    },

    _removeStatusLabel: function() {
        if (this._StatusLabel) {
            this.get_element().removeChild(this._StatusLabel);
            this._StatusLabel = null;
        }
    },

    _invokeWebService : function(searchText) {

        //Add status label in case operation takes a while
        this._StatusLabel = document.createElement("DIV");
        this._StatusLabel.style.cssText = "font-weight:bold;color:Navy;";
        this._StatusLabel.innerHTML = "Calling Albums Web Service....";
        this.get_element().appendChild(this._StatusLabel);
        Sys.Net.WebServiceProxy.invoke(this._ServicePath, this._ServiceMethod, false,
            { prefixText:searchText, count:10 },
            Function.createDelegate(this, this._onMethodComplete),
            Function.createDelegate(this, this._onMethodError));
    },

    _onPropertyChanged : function(sender,args) {
        var propname = args.get_propertyName();
        if (propname == "ServicePath" || propname === "ServiceMethod") {
            var searchText = null;
            if (this._ShowSearchBox) {
                $get(this.get_element().id + "_txtAlbumSearch").value;
            }
            this._invokeWebService(searchText);
        }
    }
}
```

The _onPropertyChanged method, shown in Listing 11-9, handles propertychanged events raised by calling the raisePropertyChanged method discussed in the "Defining Properties" section of this chapter. Recall that _onPropertyChanged is defined as the event handler by calling the add_propertyChanged method in the AlbumViewer control's initialization phase shown in Listing 11-6.

When the ServicePath or ServiceMethod properties change, _onPropertyChanged is automatically called and used to invoke an album data Web service. This allows fresh data to be loaded into the control in cases where the consumer of the control wants to dynamically change information about the Web service. How do you actually call a Web service in a custom control when the location of the service hasn't been assigned to the ScriptManager's Services property, though? Let's take a closer look.

Calling Web Services with a Custom Control

The AlbumViewer control's set_data method can receive data from a client-side script or from a .NET Web service. Calling a Web service can be a tricky process, as different browsers that have different XmlHttp objects must be taken into account. Fortunately, the ASP.NET AJAX script library has cross-browser functionality built in that makes it straightforward to make Web service calls and retrieve data without worrying about the user agent.

The _invokeWebService method shown in Listing 11-9 calls an album viewer service for the AlbumViewer control (the album Web service is available in the download code for this chapter). The method accepts a single parameter that represents the album title the end user would like to search on. When called, _invokeWebService adds a div tag to the AlbumViewer control to notify the end user that the search has begun. Because the call is made asynchronously, this provides a nice visual clue for the user so that he or she is aware that the request is being processed. The script library's Sys.Net.WebServiceProxy class is then used to make the Web service request by calling its invoke method:

```
Sys.Net.WebServiceProxy.invoke(this._ServicePath, this._ServiceMethod,
    false, { prefixText:searchText, count:10 },
    Function.createDelegate(this, this._onMethodComplete),
    Function.createDelegate(this, this._onMethodError));
```

The invoke method works across all major browsers and creates a JavaScript proxy, calls the Web service, and processes the results. Several parameters can be passed to invoke, including the following:

❑ The path to the Web service and the name of the WebMethod to call

❑ Whether the call should be made using HttpGet

❑ The parameter data to be passed to the service (parameter data is passed using JSON)

❑ A delegate that points to the callback method that handles the response that is received (_onMethodComplete)

❑ A delegate that points to an error handler callback method (_onMethodError)

Once the Web service is called and a response is returned, _onMethodComplete is used to handle the response data. This method accepts one or more Album objects returned from the Web service, any context data associated with the call, and the name of the WebMethod that was called:

```
_onMethodComplete : function(result, userContext, methodName) {
    //Remove status label
    this._removeStatusLabel();
    // Bind returned data
    this.set_data(result);
}
```

The album data returned from the Web service is bound to the AlbumViewer control by calling the set_data method discussed earlier.

Web service calls can fail when the service is unavailable or when invalid data is passed to or from the service. Fortunately, the Sys.Net.WebServiceProxy.invoke method used to call the service allows a callback method to be specified that handles errors. The _onMethodError method handles any errors returned by the Web service or errors generated if an invalid service path or WebMethod name was used.

```
_onMethodError : function(webServiceError, userContext, methodName) {
    // Call failed
    this._removeStatusLabel();
    if (webServiceError.get_timedOut()) {
        alert("Web Service call timed out.");
    } else {
        alert("Error calling Web Service: " +
```

```
        webServiceError.get_statusCode() + " " +
        webServiceError.get_message());
    }
}
```

If an error occurs and the callback method is invoked, a Sys.Net.WebServiceError object is passed as the first parameter, along with call context data and the name of the WebMethod that was initially called. Because the AlbumViewer control can't display album data when a Web service error occurs, it displays an alert to the user that contains the status code of the error as well as the error message.

Before displaying error data, a check is made to ensure that the call didn't time out by calling get_timedOut. If the call returns true, the service was unavailable. The following table lists the properties of the Sys.Net.WebServiceError class.

Property Name	Description
exception	Gets the type of exception that occurred. A string is returned.
message	Gets the error message associated with the current error.
statusCode	Gets the status code of the current HTTP response.
stackTrace	Gets the stack trace returned by the server.
timedOut	Gets a Boolean value that indicates if the Web service call timed out.

Disposing of Control Resources

Because JavaScript is a garbage-collected language, many complexities associated with cleaning up fields, arrays, and other objects are greatly simplified and typically don't require any code to be written by a developer. However, it's important to note that specific types of resources must be explicitly cleaned up to avoid memory leaks caused by circular references. DOM event handlers used in a control, as well as processes (such as timers) that may be used internally, should be explicitly cleaned up in your custom controls.

By deriving from base classes such as Sys.Component and Sys.UI.Control, access to a method named dispose is immediately available in custom controls that can be overridden. The AlbumViewer control uses the dispose method shown in Listing 11-10 to cleanup event handlers and call its base class's dispose method.

Listing 11-10: Defining a dispose Method

```
dispose: function() {
    var e = this.get_element();
    this.remove_propertyChanged(this._propertyChanged);
    if (this._ShowSearchBox) $removeHandler($get(e.id +
      "_btnAlbumSearch"),"click",this._btnClickHandler);
    //Remove event handlers
    for (var i=0;i<e.childNodes.length;i++) {
        var albumDiv = e.childNodes[i];
        $clearHandlers(albumDiv);
    }
```

Continued

365

Listing 11-10: Defining a dispose Method *(continued)*

```
            this._overHandler = null;
            this._outHandler = null;
            this._clickHandler = null;
            this._btnClickHandler = null;
            this._propertyChanged = null;
            Wrox.ASPAJAX.Samples.AlbumViewer.callBaseMethod(this, "dispose");
    }
```

When all event handlers attached to a given DOM element need to be removed, you can call the ASP.NET AJAX script library's $clearHandlers method. When a specific event handler needs to be removed the $removeHandler method can be called. Property changed event handlers can be removed by calling the remove_propertyChanged method.

After dispose is called and event handlers are cleaned up, a call is made to the base Sys.UI.Control class's dispose method via callBaseMethod, which raises a disposing event and unregisters the control from the application. Removal occurs as a result of the following calls made in the Sys.Component class's dispose method:

```
    Sys.Application.unregisterDisposableObject(this);
    Sys.Application.removeComponent(this);
```

While you don't have to override the dispose() method on every client-side object or control used in an ASP.NET AJAX application, it's important to override it in cases where event handlers or processes are used by a control and need to be cleaned up to prevent memory issues.

Registering a Custom Control Class

Now that you've seen how to create a custom control's constructor, properties, and methods, let's examine how the control can inherit from a base class and register itself with the ASP.NET AJAX framework. Although you can't use the VB.NET Inherits keyword or the C# colon character to handle inheritance, you can call the registerClass method available to all ASP.NET AJAX types through the Type class.

The registerClass method accepts three parameters. The first parameter is a string containing the fully qualified name of the class to register with the framework. The parameter value should include the namespace and class name. The second parameter represents the base class that the control should inherit from. The third parameter specifies one or more interfaces that the control implements. This parameter is optional. Following is an example of using registerClass to register the AlbumViewer control. Notice that the control derives from Sys.UI.Control.

```
    Wrox.ASPAJAX.Samples.AlbumViewer.registerClass(
        "Wrox.ASPAJAX.Samples.AlbumViewer", Sys.UI.Control);
```

As with any client-side script used by the ASP.NET AJAX framework, the AlbumViewer control adds the following line of code at the bottom the script file to notify the framework when the entire script has been loaded and is ready to be used:

```
    if (typeof(Sys) !== 'undefined') Sys.Application.notifyScriptLoaded();
```

Creating a Client-Side Control Instance

Once a custom client-side control has been written, it needs to be instantiated by an application. To do this, the control's script must be referenced by the page either by using the standard script tag or by declaring it in the `ScriptManager`'s `Scripts` property. Once the control script is available for use in a page, the control can be instantiated by using the ASP.NET AJAX script library's `$create` method. `$create` is an alias for the `Sys.Component` class's `create` method.

The `$create` method accepts several different parameters as shown in the following table.

Parameter	Description
type	The type of component or control that should be created.
properties	A JSON object containing properties and values that should be passed to the control. This parameter is optional.
events	A JSON object containing events and associated handlers defined through delegates. This parameter is optional.
references	A JSON object containing references to other control properties.
element	The DOM element that the control uses as its parent container. Output rendered by the control will be placed in this element. This parameter is optional.

Listing 11-11 (`AlbumViewerClientBinding.aspx` in the sample code) shows how the `$create` method can be used to instantiate a new instance of the AlbumViewer control and hook it to a `div` container. When the `pageLoad` event handler is called, two new `Album` objects are created and added to an array. The `$create` method is then used to instantiate the AlbumViewer control and attach it to a `div` element named `divAlbums`. Initial CSS property values used by the control, as well as the `Album` objects to bind, are passed into `$create` using a JSON object. Because the control's `initialize` method calls `set_data`, the two albums are iterated through and added into the parent container automatically as the control initializes and loads.

Listing 11-11: AlbumViewerClientBinding.aspx

```
<%@ Page Language="C#" %>
<!DOCTYPE html PUBLIC "-//W3C//DTD XHTML 1.0 Transitional//EN"
  "http://www.w3.org/TR/xhtml1/DTD/xhtml1-transitional.dtd">
<html xmlns="http://www.w3.org/1999/xhtml" >
<head runat="server">
    <title>Album Viewer: Client-side Control</title>
    <link href="Style/Styles.css" rel="stylesheet" type="text/css" />

    <script type="text/javascript">
        function pageLoad()
        {
            //Create albums
            var album = new Wrox.ASPAJAX.Samples.Album();
```

Continued

Listing 11-11: AlbumViewerClientBinding.aspx *(continued)*

```
album.set_Artist("Incubus");
album.set_Title("Light Grenades");
album.set_ImageUrl("Images/Incubus_Light_Grenades.jpg");
album.addSong(new Wrox.ASPAJAX.Samples.Song(1,"QuickSand"));
album.addSong(new Wrox.ASPAJAX.Samples.Song(2,
  "A Kiss to Send Us Off"));
album.addSong(new Wrox.ASPAJAX.Samples.Song(3,"Dig"));
album.addSong(new Wrox.ASPAJAX.Samples.Song(4,"Anna Molly"));
album.addSong(new Wrox.ASPAJAX.Samples.Song(5,"Love Hurts"));

album.addSong(new Wrox.ASPAJAX.Samples.Song(6,"Light Grenades"));
album.addSong(new Wrox.ASPAJAX.Samples.Song(7,"Earth to Bella Pt 1"));
album.addSong(new Wrox.ASPAJAX.Samples.Song(8,"Oil and Water"));
album.addSong(new Wrox.ASPAJAX.Samples.Song(9,"Diamonds and Coal"));
album.addSong(new Wrox.ASPAJAX.Samples.Song(10,"Rogues"));
album.addSong(new Wrox.ASPAJAX.Samples.Song(11,"Paper Shoes"));
album.addSong(new Wrox.ASPAJAX.Samples.Song(12,"Earth to Bella Pt 1"));
album.addSong(new Wrox.ASPAJAX.Samples.Song(13,"Pendulous Threads"));

var album2 = new Wrox.ASPAJAX.Samples.Album();
album2.set_Artist("The Killers");
album2.set_Title("Sam's Town");
album2.set_ImageUrl("Images/The_Killers_Sams_Town.jpg");
album2.addSong(new Wrox.ASPAJAX.Samples.Song(1,"Sam's Town"));
album2.addSong(new Wrox.ASPAJAX.Samples.Song(2,"Enterlude"));
album2.addSong(new Wrox.ASPAJAX.Samples.Song(3,"When You Were Young"));
album2.addSong(new Wrox.ASPAJAX.Samples.Song(4,"Bling"));
album2.addSong(new Wrox.ASPAJAX.Samples.Song(5,"For Reasons Unknown"));
album2.addSong(new Wrox.ASPAJAX.Samples.Song(6,"Read My Mind"));
album2.addSong(new Wrox.ASPAJAX.Samples.Song(7,"Uncle Johnny"));
album2.addSong(new Wrox.ASPAJAX.Samples.Song(8,"Bones"));
album2.addSong(new Wrox.ASPAJAX.Samples.Song(9,"My List"));
album2.addSong(new Wrox.ASPAJAX.Samples.Song(10,"The River is Wild"));
album2.addSong(new Wrox.ASPAJAX.Samples.Song(11,
  "Why Do I Keep Counting"));
album2.addSong(new Wrox.ASPAJAX.Samples.Song(12,"Exitlude"));

var albums = [];
Array.add(albums,album);
Array.add(albums,album2);

//Create AlbumViewer object and pass in albums
$create(Wrox.ASPAJAX.Samples.AlbumViewer,
    {Albums: albums,AlbumDivOverCssClass: "AlbumDivOver",
     AlbumDivOutCssClass: "AlbumDivOut",
     AlbumTitleCssClass: "AlbumTitle",
     AlbumArtistCssClass: "AlbumArtist",
     SongTitleCssClass: "SongTitle"},
    null, //Events and handlers
    null, //References to other control properties
    $get("divAlbums"));  //parent container DOM element
```

```
            }
        </script>
    </head>
    <body>
        <form id="form1" runat="server">
        <asp:ScriptManager id="smgr" runat="Server">
            <Scripts>
                <asp:ScriptReference Path="~/Scripts/Album.js" />
                <asp:ScriptReference Path="~/Scripts/AlbumViewerStandAlone.js" />

            </Scripts>
        </asp:ScriptManager>
        <h2>Album Viewer</h2>
        <div id="divAlbums" style="width:500px;">
        </div>
        </form>
    </body>
    </html>
```

A Web service can also automatically be called when an AlbumViewer control is created to retrieve album data, rather than creating the album objects in the page as in Listing 11-11. This is done by passing the path to the Web service along with the name of the WebMethod to call in the JSON object that contains properties and values. An example of using the $create method to pass ServicePath and ServiceMethod property values to the control is shown in Listing 11-12 (AlbumViewerWSBinding.aspx in the sample code). The ShowSearchBox property is also set to a value of true so that the album search textbox and button controls are created and shown. The output generated by the control is shown in Figure 11-1.

Listing 11-12: AlbumViewerWSBinding.aspx

```
function pageLoad()
{
    $create(Wrox.ASPAJAX.Samples.AlbumViewer,
        {ShowSearchBox: true,AlbumDivOverCssClass: "AlbumDivOver",
         AlbumDivOutCssClass: "AlbumDivOut",AlbumTitleCssClass: "AlbumTitle",
         AlbumArtistCssClass: "AlbumArtist",SongTitleCssClass: "SongTitle",
         ServicePath: "AlbumService.asmx",ServiceMethod: "GetAlbums"},
        null,
        null,
        $get("divAlbums"));
}
```

Building a Server-Side ASP.NET AJAX Control

Creating custom ASP.NET AJAX client-side controls is a fairly intensive exercise in JavaScript. Calling control methods, handling events, and even instantiating the control itself requires JavaScript code to be written. While some ASP.NET developers understand how to write JavaScript code, others may not have a complete understanding of the language and may prefer to work with server-side objects that can be manipulated using VB.NET or C#. They may prefer to be shielded from JavaScript code whenever possible.

Because server-side controls can output both HTML and JavaScript, they're good candidates for use with ASP.NET AJAX client-side controls. Developers familiar with defining and interacting with server-side controls can use an AJAX-enabled server-side control without having to worry about the client-side complexities. A nice "feature" of ASP.NET AJAX server-side controls is that once you have created the client-side script that handles all of the HTML output and event handling (as with the AlbumViewer control shown in this chapter), going a little further to create a server-side control is fairly straightforward and requires very little VB.NET or C# code. After all, most of the control's functionality is performed by the client-side script.

There are a few different paths to creating an ASP.NET AJAX server control. To choose the correct path, you need to decide what type of control you want to create. Will the control be visual, or is it something that runs in the background like a timer? Will the control extend functionality of another control? The answer to these questions determines how the server-side control is built. For example, if you want to extend an existing control's functionality by adding AJAX capabilities to it, you'll want to derive from the `System.Web.UI.ExtenderControl` class. If you're writing a visual control from scratch that generates HTML and JavaScript, you'll want to derive from `System.Web.UI.ScriptControl` derives from `System.Web.UI.WebControl`.

The AlbumViewer server-control, discussed next, derives from `ScriptControl` and leverages the AlbumViewer client-side control script discussed earlier in this chapter. It lives in an ASP.NET control library project within Visual Studio 2008. Before getting into specifics about the server-side control, let's examine how to embed a client-side control script into a server-side control assembly.

Embedding Scripts in Server-Side Controls

ASP.NET AJAX server-side controls perform two main functions. First, they output a client-side control script to the browser that handles the bulk of the functionality required by the control. This includes interaction with the end user, event handling, data binding, calls to remote data source, and more. Second, they define properties that can be set on the server-side and passed to the client-side script.

his allows ASP.NET developers to define properties using standard ASP.NET control syntax without worrying about writing custom JavaScript code or even using the ASP.NET AJAX script library's `$create` method to instantiate the control.

Client-side ASP.NET AJAX control scripts can be embedded directly in ASP.NET server control assemblies by marking the scripts as an embedded resource. First, add a script file to an ASP.NET server control project (officially called a Class Library project in Visual Studio 2008) and add all of the client-side functionality to it. Next, right-click the created script file in the Visual Studio 2008 Solution Explorer, select Properties and set the Build Action property to a value of Embedded Resource. This causes the compiler to embed the script file directly in the control's assembly. Figure 11-2 shows the Properties window for the embedded script file.

To make the script accessible, add the following assembly attribute immediately above the server control's namespace definition in code file (C# is shown here):

```
[assembly: System.Web.UI.WebResource("AlbumViewer.AlbumViewer.js",
  "text/javascript")]
```

Figure 11-2

This makes the script accessible through an `HttpHandler` built into ASP.NET AJAX called `ScriptResource.axd` and avoids the need to deploy the physical script file along with the server control assembly, which can greatly simplify deployment and maintenance. The `WebResource` attribute's constructor accepts the name of the resource followed by the content-type of the resource. The name given to the resource is the assembly name followed by the name of the script (`AlbumViewer.AlbumViewer.js`, in this case). Although JavaScript is used in this example, images can also be embedded in custom server controls using the same technique. One disadvantage of embedding scripts or images into assemblies is that they can't be modified on the Web server; you would have to rebuild the assembly with the modified objects and redeploy it to the Web server.

Creating a Control Class

The AlbumViewer ASP.NET AJAX server-side control allows a developer to set properties on the control using familiar ASP.NET server control syntax. After property values are set, the control handles outputting the client-side control script that's embedded as a resource and creates a new instance of the control using the `$create` method. Property values set on the server side are passed to the `$create` method through a JSON object that is passed as a parameter to `$create`.

Because the `AlbumViewer` server-side control doesn't extend an existing control it derives from `System.Web.UI.ScriptControl`. Had the control extended an existing control, such as a TextBox, it would inherit from `System.Web.UI.ExtenderControl` located in the `System.Web.Extensions.dll` assembly that's installed with the ASP.NET AJAX framework. The `ScriptControl` class contains two key methods, shown in the following table.

Method	Description
`GetScriptDescriptors`	Gets a collection of script descriptors that represent JavaScript components on the client. This method is used to map server-side control properties to client-side control properties.
`GetScriptReferences`	Gets a collection of `ScriptReference` objects that define script resources required by the control. This method is used to identify one or more embedded script resources in a control assembly and output them to the client.

Listing 11-13 shows the shell for the AlbumViewer server-side control. Notice that it derives from `ScriptControl`.

Listing 11-13: Creating an AlbumView server-side control

```
using System;
using System.Configuration;
using System.Collections.Generic;
using System.Web;
using System.Web.UI;
using System.Web.UI.WebControls;
using System.Web.UI.HtmlControls;

//Client-side script file embedded in assembly
[assembly: System.Web.UI.WebResource("AlbumViewer.AlbumViewer.js",
  "text/javascript")]
namespace Wrox.ASPAJAX.Samples
{
    public class AlbumViewer : ScriptControl
    {

        protected override IEnumerable<ScriptReference> GetScriptReferences()
        {
            return GetControlScriptReferences();
        }

        protected override IEnumerable<ScriptDescriptor> GetScriptDescriptors()
        {
            return GetControlScriptDescriptors();
        }


    }
}
```

The two overridden methods shown in Listing 11-13 delegate processing to two custom methods included in the class named `GetControlScriptReferences` and `GetControlScriptDescriptors`. These two methods are shown in Listing 11-14.

Listing 11-14: Mapping server-side properties to client-side properties and defining script references

```
protected virtual IEnumerable<ScriptDescriptor> GetControlScriptDescriptors()
{
    ScriptControlDescriptor descriptor =
      new ScriptControlDescriptor("Wrox.ASPAJAX.Samples.AlbumViewer",
      this.ClientID);
    descriptor.AddProperty("AlbumDivOverCssClass", this.AlbumDivOverCssClass);
    descriptor.AddProperty("AlbumDivOutCssClass", this.AlbumDivOutCssClass);
    descriptor.AddProperty("AlbumTitleCssClass", this.AlbumTitleCssClass);
    descriptor.AddProperty("AlbumArtistCssClass", this.AlbumArtistCssClass);
    descriptor.AddProperty("SongTitleCssClass", this.SongTitleCssClass);
```

Listing 11-14: Mapping server-side properties to client-side properties and defining script references *(continued)*

```
        descriptor.AddProperty("ServicePath", this.ServicePath);
        descriptor.AddProperty("ServiceMethod", this.ServiceMethod);
        descriptor.AddProperty("ShowSearchBox", this.ShowSearchBox);
        //could also use: yield return descriptor;

        return new ScriptDescriptor[] { descriptor };
    }

    protected virtual IEnumerable<ScriptReference> GetControlScriptReferences()
    {
        ScriptReference r = new ScriptReference();
        r.Assembly = "AlbumViewer";
        r.Name = "AlbumViewer.AlbumViewer.js";
        //could also use:  yield return r;
        return new ScriptReference[] { r };
    }
```

The `GetControlScriptReferences` method shown in Listing 11-14 creates a `ScriptReference` object and identifies the script resource that the server control needs to send to the client (`AlbumViewer .AlbumViewer.js`, in this case). The `GetControlScriptDescriptors` method creates a new `ScriptControlDescriptor` object that maps server-side control properties to client-side control properties. This is necessary so that the property values set on the control by a developer can be passed to the `$create` method used to instantiate the client-side control. The properties defined in the `AlbumViewer` server-side control are the same ones discussed earlier in the chapter for the client-side control (`AlbumDivOverCssClass`, `AlbumDivOutCssClass`, and so on).

Listing 11-15 shows the complete code for the `AlbumViewer` server-side control.

Listing 11-15: The completed AlbumViewer control

```
using System;
using System.Configuration;
using System.Collections.Generic;
using System.Web;
using System.Web.UI;
using System.Web.UI.WebControls;
using System.Web.UI.HtmlControls;

//Client-side script file embedded in assembly
[assembly: System.Web.UI.WebResource("AlbumViewer.AlbumViewer.js",
  "text/javascript")]
namespace Wrox.ASPAJAX.Samples
{
    public class AlbumViewer : ScriptControl
    {
        string _AlbumDivOverCssClass;
        string _AlbumDivOutCssClass;
        string _AlbumTitleCssClass;
```

Continued

373

Listing 11-15: The completed AlbumViewer control *(continued)*

```csharp
        string _AlbumArtistCssClass;
        string _SongTitleCssClass;
        string _ServicePath;
        string _ServiceMethod;
        bool _ShowSearchBox;

        #region Properties

        public string AlbumDivOverCssClass

        {
            get { return _AlbumDivOverCssClass; }
            set { _AlbumDivOverCssClass = value; }
        }

        public string AlbumDivOutCssClass
        {
            get { return _AlbumDivOutCssClass; }
            set { _AlbumDivOutCssClass = value; }
        }

        public string AlbumTitleCssClass
        {
            get { return _AlbumTitleCssClass; }
            set { _AlbumTitleCssClass = value; }
        }

        public string AlbumArtistCssClass
        {
            get { return _AlbumArtistCssClass; }
            set { _AlbumArtistCssClass = value; }
        }

        public string SongTitleCssClass
        {
            get { return _SongTitleCssClass; }
            set { _SongTitleCssClass = value; }
        }

        public string ServicePath
        {
            get { return _ServicePath; }
            set { _ServicePath = value; }
        }

        public string ServiceMethod
        {
            get { return _ServiceMethod; }
            set { _ServiceMethod = value; }
        }

        public bool ShowSearchBox
        {
```

Listing 11-15: The completed AlbumViewer control *(continued)*

```
        get { return _ShowSearchBox; }
        set { _ShowSearchBox = value; }
    }

    #endregion

    public AlbumViewer() {}

    protected virtual IEnumerable<ScriptDescriptor>
      GetControlScriptDescriptors()
    {
        ScriptControlDescriptor descriptor =
          new ScriptControlDescriptor("Wrox.ASPAJAX.Samples.AlbumViewer",
          this.ClientID);
        descriptor.AddProperty("AlbumDivOverCssClass",
          this.AlbumDivOverCssClass);
        descriptor.AddProperty("AlbumDivOutCssClass",
          this.AlbumDivOutCssClass);
        descriptor.AddProperty("AlbumTitleCssClass", this.AlbumTitleCssClass);
        descriptor.AddProperty("AlbumArtistCssClass",
          this.AlbumArtistCssClass);
        descriptor.AddProperty("SongTitleCssClass", this.SongTitleCssClass);
        descriptor.AddProperty("ServicePath", this.ServicePath);
        descriptor.AddProperty("ServiceMethod", this.ServiceMethod);
        descriptor.AddProperty("ShowSearchBox", this.ShowSearchBox);
        //could also use: yield return descriptor;
        return new ScriptDescriptor[] { descriptor };
    }

    protected virtual IEnumerable<ScriptReference> GetControlScriptReferences()
    {
        ScriptReference r = new ScriptReference();
        //Use following when client-side script isn't
        //embedded in custom control:
        //reference.Path = this.ResolveClientUrl("~/Scripts/AlbumViewer.js");
        r.Assembly = "AlbumViewer";
        r.Name = "AlbumViewer.AlbumViewer.js";
        //could also use:  yield return r;
        return new ScriptReference[] { r };
    }

    protected override IEnumerable<ScriptReference> GetScriptReferences()
    {
        return GetControlScriptReferences();
    }

    protected override IEnumerable<ScriptDescriptor> GetScriptDescriptors()
    {
        return GetControlScriptDescriptors();
    }
    }
}
```

Now that you've seen the steps required to build a custom ASP.NET AJAX server control, let's examine how to use one in an ASP.NET page.

Using a Custom ASP.NET AJAX Control in an ASP.NET Page

Once the AlbumViewer server-side control project is compiled and the generated assembly is referenced by an ASP.NET Web site project, the control can be registered in an ASP.NET page by using the `Register` directive:

```
<%@ Register Assembly="AlbumViewer" Namespace="Wrox.ASPAJAX.Samples"
    TagPrefix="ajax" %>
```

This directive references the assembly name (`AlbumViewer`), the namespace that the control resides in (`Wrox.ASPAJAX.Samples`), as well as the tag prefix that should be used to define the control in the ASP.NET page (`ajax`). Once registered, this control can be used in the page just the same as any other ASP.NET server control. You simply need to define the tag prefix and class name followed by all of the necessary properties in the `Register` directive. An example of adding the AlbumViewer control into a page is shown here:

```
<ajax:AlbumViewer ID="divAlbums" runat="server" ShowSearchBox="true"
    AlbumDivOverCssClass="AlbumDivOver"
    AlbumDivOutCssClass="AlbumDivOut" AlbumTitleCssClass="AlbumTitle"
    AlbumArtistCssClass="AlbumArtist" SongTitleCssClass="SongTitle"
    ServicePath="AlbumService.asmx" ServiceMethod="GetAlbums" />
```

After the page is called by an end user through a browser, the necessary client-side script code used by the AlbumViewer control will automatically be added to the rendered output by the ScriptManager control. A portion of the output generated by ScriptManager that instantiates the AlbumViewer control is shown in Listing 11-16.

Listing 11-16: $create client-side code output by the AlbumViewer control

```
<script type="text/javascript">
<!--
    Sys.Application.initialize();
    Sys.Application.add_init(function() {

        $create(Wrox.ASPAJAX.Samples.AlbumViewer,
            {"AlbumArtistCssClass":"AlbumArtist",
             "AlbumDivOutCssClass":"AlbumDivOut",
             "AlbumDivOverCssClass":"AlbumDivOver",
             "AlbumTitleCssClass":"AlbumTitle",
             "ServiceMethod":"GetAlbums",
             "ServicePath":"AlbumService.asmx",
             "ShowSearchBox":true,
             "SongTitleCssClass":"SongTitle"},
            null, null,
            $get("divAlbums"));
        });
// -->
</script>
```

The `AlbumViewer.js` script embedded in the control is automatically referenced through a `script` tag embedded into the page. The `script` tag's `src` attribute points to a `ScriptResource.axd` `HttpHandler` that will extract the script from the server-side assembly where it was embedded and send it down to the browser:

```
<script
  src="/Chapter11/ScriptResource.axd?d=eyWA0k6p8cJT5ZxERTSqjh74z_7LL-
      XVOadc8XgiZ-JKa85A2IV0dD9FkMF5UiS40&amp;t=633048513771318000"
  type="text/javascript">
</script>
```

Creating a Control Extender using the ASP.NET AJAX Control Toolkit

Functionality of existing ASP.NET controls such as TextBox and GridView can be extended by using the `System.Web.UI.ExtenderControl` class included in the `System.Web.Extensions` assembly or the `AjaxToolkit.ExtenderControlBase` class provided by the ASP.NET AJAX Control Toolkit's `AjaxControlToolkit` assembly (additional details on using the toolkit were provided in Chapter 7). Both classes allow existing controls to be extended with client-side behaviors. For example, a filter could be added to a TextBox control to only allow specific characters to be entered or a GridView control's header could be frozen so that it stays fixed as a user scrolls through rows.

Although both classes ultimately lead to the same end result, the `ExtenderControlBase` class and related classes available in the AJAX Control Toolkit can simplify the process of mapping server-side properties to client-side properties and minimize the amount of code you have to write to extend and existing control. This section outlines key steps you can follow to build a custom AJAX control using ASP.NET AJAX Control Toolkit classes.

Creating a Client-Side Extender Class

To get started building a custom extender control, you need to create a Class Library project in Visual Studio and place the `AjaxControlToolkit.dll` assembly in the project's bin folder (download the toolkit and related assembly from `www.codeplex.com/AjaxControlToolkit`). When the toolkit assembly is in the bin folder you can create the client-side functionality that will be applied to an existing control to extend it. To do this, add a JavaScript file into the project, right-click it in the Solution Explorer and select Properties from the menu. Change the file's Build Action property to a value of Embedded Resource.

Figure 11-3 shows an example of how a client-side extender control can be applied to a GridView control at runtime. The extender freezes the header row as users scroll through rows of data so that it remains at a fixed position. Listing 11-17 shows the code for the client-side extender class.

> **The code in Listing 11-17 is provided for demonstration purposes and is designed to work with Firefox and Internet Explorer only. Additional testing and functionality may be needed if you plan to use it in a production environment or with other browsers.**

Figure 11-3

Listing 11-17: Defining the GridViewHeaderBehavior client-side class

```
Type.registerNamespace('Wrox.ASPAJAX.Samples');

Wrox.ASPAJAX.Samples.GridViewHeaderBehavior = function(element) {
    /// <summary>
    /// The GridViewHeaderBehavior is used to fix a GridView control header and
    /// make the control scrollable
    /// </summary>
    /// <param name="element" type="Sys.UI.DomElement">
    /// The GridView element this behavior is associated with
    /// </param>
    Wrox.ASPAJAX.Samples.GridViewHeaderBehavior.initializeBase(this, [element]);
    this._WrapperDivCssClass = null;
}

Wrox.ASPAJAX.Samples.GridViewHeaderBehavior.prototype = {
    initialize : function() {
        /// <summary>
        /// Initialize the behavior
        /// </summary>
        Wrox.ASPAJAX.Samples.GridViewHeaderBehavior.callBaseMethod(this,
          'initialize');
        var element = this.get_element();
```

Listing 11-17: Defining the GridViewHeaderBehavior client-side class *(continued)*

```
            this._FreezeGridViewHeader();
        },

        dispose : function() {
            /// <summary>
            /// Dispose the behavior
            /// </summary>
            var element = this.get_element();
            Wrox.ASPAJAX.Samples.GridViewHeaderBehavior.callBaseMethod(this,
             'dispose');
        },

        _FreezeGridViewHeader : function () {
            var grid = this.get_element();
            if (grid != 'undefined')
            {
                grid.style.visibility = 'hidden';
                var div = null;
                if (grid.parentNode != 'undefined')
                {
                    div = grid.parentNode;
                    if (div.tagName == 'DIV')
                    {
                        div.className = this._WrapperDivCssClass;
                        div.style.overflow = 'auto';
                    }
                }
                var tags = grid.getElementsByTagName('TBODY');
                if (tags != 'undefined')
                {
                    var tbody = tags[0];
                    var trs = tbody.getElementsByTagName('TR');
                    var headerHeight = 8;
                    if (trs != 'undefined')
                    {
                        headerHeight += trs[0].offsetHeight;
                        var headTR = tbody.removeChild(trs[0]);
                        var head = document.createElement('THEAD');
                        head.appendChild(headTR);
                        grid.insertBefore(head, grid.firstChild);
                    }
                    tbody.style.height = (div.offsetHeight -  headerHeight) + 'px';
                    tbody.style.overflowX = 'hidden';
                    tbody.overflow = 'auto';
                    tbody.overflowX = 'hidden';
                }
                grid.style.visibility = 'visible';
            }
        },

        get_WrapperDivCssClass : function() {
            return this._WrapperDivCssClass;
```

Continued

Listing 11-17: Defining the GridViewHeaderBehavior client-side class *(continued)*

```
        },

        set_WrapperDivCssClass : function(value) {
            this._WrapperDivCssClass = value;
            this.raisePropertyChanged('WrapperDivCssClass');
        }
    }
}

Wrox.ASPAJAX.Samples.GridViewHeaderBehavior.registerClass(
    'Wrox.ASPAJAX.Samples.GridViewHeaderBehavior', AjaxControlToolkit.BehaviorBase);
```

The code in Listing 11-17 follows the standard prototype design pattern discussed earlier and relies on the ASP.NET AJAX script library's `Type` class to register a namespace and derive the `Wrox.ASPAJAX` `.Samples.GridViewHeaderBehavior` custom client-side extender class from a base class named `AjaxControlToolkit.BehaviorBase`. As the namespace infers, `BehaviorBase` is provided by the ASP.NET AJAX Control Toolkit.

Creating a Server-Side Extender Class

Once you have a client-side extender class available to use, add a reference to the `AjaxControlToolkit` assembly located in the bin folder. Then add a new C# or VB.NET class into the project (the class discussed here is named `GridViewHeaderExtender`). The class must import the `AjaxControlToolkit` namespace and derive from `ExtenderControlBase` which is located in the `AjaxControlToolkit` namespace.

The `GridViewHeaderExtender` server-side extender control needs to automatically output the script shown earlier in Listing 11-17 to the client. This can be accomplished by using the `WebResource` attribute along with the Toolkit's `ClientScriptResource` attribute, as shown in Listing 11-18.

Listing 11-18: Defining the GridViewHeaderDemo server-side class

```
using System;
using System.Web.UI.WebControls;
using System.Web.UI.HtmlControls;
using System.Web.UI;
using System.ComponentModel;
using System.ComponentModel.Design;
using AjaxControlToolkit;

[assembly: WebResource("GridViewHeaderDemo.GridViewHeaderBehavior.js",
           "text/javascript")]

namespace GridViewHeaderDemo
{

    [TargetControlType(typeof(GridView))]
    [ClientScriptResource("Wrox.ASPAJAX.Samples.GridViewHeaderBehavior",
      "GridViewHeaderDemo.GridViewHeaderBehavior.js")]
    [ToolboxItem("System.Web.UI.Design.WebControlToolboxItem, System.Design,
      Version=2.0.0.0, Culture=neutral, PublicKeyToken=b03f5f7f11d50a3a")]
```

Listing 11-18: Defining the GridViewHeaderDemo server-side class *(continued)*

```csharp
public class GridViewHeaderExtender : ExtenderControlBase
{
    [DefaultValue("")]
    [Description("CSS class to apply to the GridView wrapper div element.
      Example of a wrapper div style: .WrapperDiv
      {width:800px;height:400px;border: 1px solid black;}")]
    [ExtenderControlProperty]
    [ClientPropertyName("WrapperDivCssClass")]
    public string WrapperDivCssClass
    {
        get { return GetPropertyValue<string>("WrapperDivCssClass",
          string.Empty); }
        set { SetPropertyValue<string>("WrapperDivCssClass", value); }
    }

    protected override void OnPreRender(EventArgs e)
    {
        base.OnPreRender(e);

        if (String.IsNullOrEmpty(this.WrapperDivCssClass))
        {
            throw new ApplicationException("WrapperDivCssClass property " +
              "value must be defined for the GridViewHeaderExtender " +
              "control. Here's an example of a wrapper div style that " +
              "should be defined in the page and referenced with the" +
              "WrapperDivCssClass property: .WrapperDiv " +
              "{width:800px;height:400px;border: 1px solid black;}");
        }

        if (this.Enabled && !this.Page.Items.Contains("GridViewHeaderStyles"))
        {
            this.Page.Items["GridViewHeaderStyles"] = true;
            this.Page.Header.StyleSheet.CreateStyleRule(
              new GridViewThCssClass(), null, "." +
                this.WrapperDivCssClass + " TH");
            this.Page.Header.StyleSheet.CreateStyleRule(
              new GridViewTrCssClass(), null, "." +
                this.WrapperDivCssClass + " TR");
        }
    }

    private class GridViewTrCssClass : Style
    {
        protected override void FillStyleAttributes(
          CssStyleCollection attributes, IUrlResolutionService urlResolver)
        {
            base.FillStyleAttributes(attributes, urlResolver);
            attributes[HtmlTextWriterStyle.Height] = "0px";
        }
    }

    private class GridViewThCssClass : Style
```

Continued

Listing 11-18: Defining the GridViewHeaderDemo server-side class *(continued)*

```
    {
        protected override void FillStyleAttributes(
          CssStyleCollection attributes, IUrlResolutionService urlResolver)
        {
            base.FillStyleAttributes(attributes, urlResolver);
            attributes[HtmlTextWriterStyle.Position] = "relative";
        }
    }
  }
}
```

Looking through the code in Listing 11-18 you'll see that the GridViewHeaderExtender class targets a GridView control by using the TargetControlType attribute. It also exposes a single property named WrapperDivCssClass that represents the CSS class that will be applied to the div that wraps the GridView control that will be extended. The extender class's WrapperDivCssClass property is mapped to the corresponding client-side property by using the Toolkit's ExtenderControlProperty and ClientPropertyName attributes. These two attributes greatly simplify the property mapping process especially compared to what is typically required when you use the ScriptControl and ScriptControlDescriptor classes discussed earlier in the chapter.

In addition to specifying which script should be output and mapping server-side properties to client-side properties, the GridViewHeaderExtender class also overrides OnPreRender to dynamically output two CSS classes into the page that are needed to help freeze the GridView header row so that it doesn't move when a user scrolls through rows. This is done by calling the CreateStyleRule method, which leverages two nested style classes embedded in the GridViewHeaderExtender class to generate the necessary CSS data.

Using an Extender Class in a Web Page

Once you've created an ASP.NET AJAX Control Toolkit extender class you can use it to extend controls in your Web applications. To extend a GridView control using the GridViewHeaderExtender class, create a new Web site in Visual Studio 2008 and reference the extender control project using Add Reference. Once the project is referenced, you can add a Register directive into the page to use the control as shown next:

```
<%@ Register  Assembly="GridViewHeaderDemo" Namespace="GridViewHeaderDemo"
    TagPrefix="toolkit" %>
```

Once the GridViewHeaderExtender control has been referenced, you'll need to define the CSS class that will be used to wrap the target GridView control (add borders around it if desired, set the height and width, plus more) in the page or in an external CSS stylesheet:

```
<style type="text/css">
    .WrapperDiv {
        width:800px;height:400px;border: 1px solid black;
    }
</style>
```

Finally, the GridViewHeaderExtender control can be added into the page. The GridView control that it targets can be assigned by using the `TargetControlID` property, and the CSS class that should be applied to the grid can be assigned by using the `WrapperDivCssClass`. Running the page will result in a `$create` method call being automatically output in the page; this is used to invoke the client-side `Wrox.ASPAJAX` `.Samples.GridViewHeaderBehavior` extender and freeze the `GridView`'s header row.

```
<toolkit:GridViewHeaderExtender ID="gvExtender" runat="server"
 TargetControlID="GridView1" WrapperDivCssClass="WrapperDiv"/>
```

Summary

Custom ASP.NET AJAX controls allow you to add specialized functionality to an application that can be reused over and over. In this chapter, you've seen how to create a client-side ASP.NET AJAX control capable of generating custom output. Core steps that should be followed when creating controls were discussed, including making a constructor, using the prototype design pattern, initializing controls, and disposing of control resources. You've also seen how control events can be hooked up to event handlers and how controls can be created and used in an application.

This chapter also discussed how to create custom server-side ASP.NET AJAX controls. Server-side controls can be created to extend existing controls, or new controls can be built from the ground up that add unique features and functionality. You've seen how the `System.Web.UI.ScriptControl` and `AjaxControlToolkit.ExtenderControlBase` classes can be used to build custom server-side ASP.NET AJAX classes and how scripts and properties used by a client-side script can be referenced and mapped. Finally, you've seen how a custom server-side control and extender control can be defined and used in a page.

12

Web Parts

Some of the Web sites that we deal with on the Internet are quite rigid in their presentation and present the same view to all users that come to the site. On the other hand, sometimes you are going to want to provide your end users with a site that allows for a high degree of customization by the end user. In some cases, you are going to want to provide the end users with a design surface or canvas so that they can design their own view of the information or service that you are providing.

The concept of a page component or Web Part has been around for some time. Web Parts are something that you can build with ASP.NET 3.5 applications (ever since ASP.NET 2.0), and it is something that is a part of the Microsoft SharePoint world. With Web Parts available to put together your pages, the next question is how you can incorporate AJAX and the capabilities the ASP.NET AJAX Library provides into the Web Parts that you build. This chapter will take a look at the possibilities.

Introducing Web Parts

To make it easier to retain the page customization settings that your end users apply to your page, Microsoft includes Web Parts in ASP.NET. Web Parts, as components of the larger Portal Framework, provide an outstanding way to build a modular Web site that can be customized with dynamically reapplied settings on a per user basis. Web Parts are objects in the Portal Framework, which the end user can open, close, minimize, maximize, or move from one part of the page to another.

The Portal Framework enables you to build pages that contain multiple Web Parts, which are part of the ASP.NET server control framework and are used like any other ASP.NET server controls. This means that you can also extend Web Parts if necessary.

The components of the Portal Framework provide the means to build a truly dynamic Web site, whether that site is a traditional Internet site, an intranet site, a browser-based application, or any other typical portal.

When you first look at Web Parts in ASP.NET 3.5, it may remind you of Microsoft's SharePoint offering. Be forewarned, however, that these two technologies are not the same. Web Parts, and the resulting Portal Framework, besides being offered in ASP.NET, are also used by the Windows SharePoint Services (WSS). Microsoft, as it often does, is simply creating a technology that can be used by other Microsoft offerings. In this process, Microsoft is trying to reach the Holy Grail of computing — *code reuse!*

The modular and customizable sites that you can build with the Portal Framework enable you to place the Web page in view into several possible modes for the end user. The following list describes the available modes and what each means to the end user viewing the page:

❑ **Browse mode**: Puts the page in a normal state, which means that the end user cannot edit or move sections of the page. This is the mode used for standard page viewing.

❑ **Edit mode**: Enables end users to select particular sections on the page for editing. The selected section allows all types of editing capabilities from changing the part's title, changing the part's color, or even setting custom properties — such as allowing the end user to specify his zip code to pull up a customized weather report.

❑ **Design mode**: Enables end users to rearrange the order of the page's modular components. The end user can bring items higher or lower within a zone, delete items from a zone, or move items from one page zone to another.

❑ **Catalog mode**: Displays a list of available sections (Web Parts) that can be placed in the page. Catalog mode also allows the end user to select in which zone on the page the items should appear.

Figure 12-1 shows a screenshot of a sample portal utilizing the Portal Framework with the Edit mode enabled.

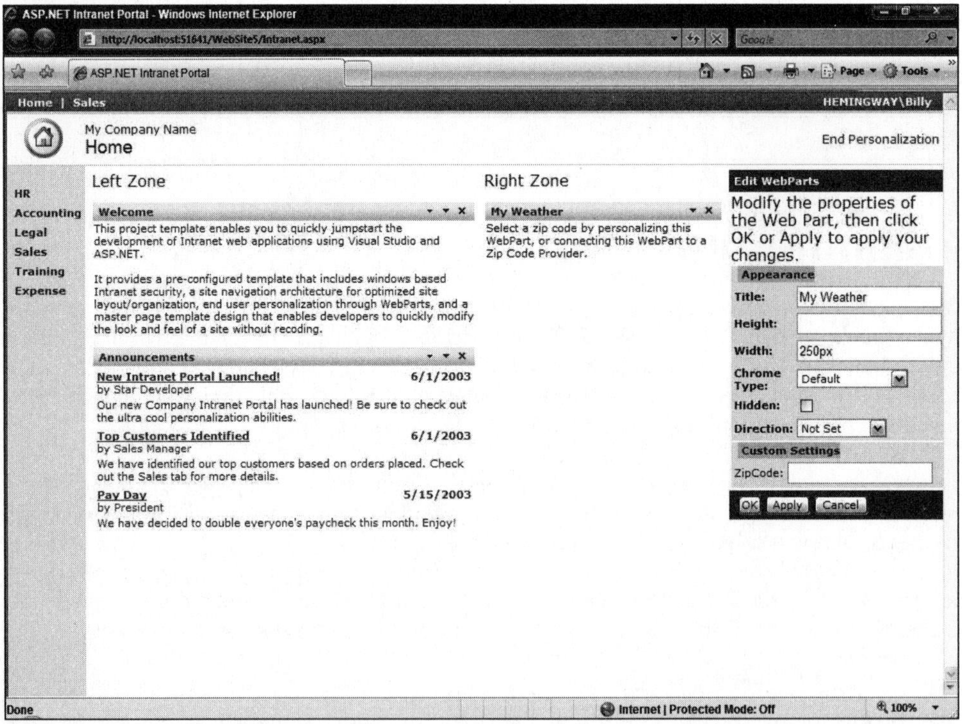

Figure 12-1

The Portal Framework is a comprehensive and well-thought-out framework that enables you to incorporate everything you would normally include in your ASP.NET applications. You can apply security using either Windows Authentication or Forms Authentication, just as you can with a standard ASP. NET page. This framework also enables you to leverage the other aspects of ASP.NET 3.5, such as applying role management, personalization, and membership features to any portal that you build.

Before getting into working with Web Parts and ASP.NET AJAX together, this chapter starts with a page that makes use of the Portal Framework without AJAX to see how it behaves.

Building a Web Parts Page without AJAX

As you begin using the Portal Framework to build Web sites, note that the framework defines everything in *zones*. There are zones for laying out as well as for editing content. The zones that a page might incorporate are managed by a Portal Framework manager. The Portal Framework manager performs the management on your behalf, meaning that you do not have to manage them yourself in any fashion. This makes working with the Portal Framework a breeze.

This framework contains a lot of moving parts, and these multiple pieces that are heavily dependent upon each other. For this reason, this section starts by examining a simple page built with a couple of Web Parts. This page is presented in Listing 12-1.

Listing 12-1: A simple page using Web Parts without AJAX

```
<%@ Page Language="C#" %>
<%@ Import Namespace="System.Web.UI.WebControls.WebParts"%>
<%@ Register src="HelloUser.ascx" tagname="HelloUser" tagprefix="uc1" %>

<script runat="server">

    protected void Page_Load(object sender, EventArgs e)
    {
        if(!Page.IsPostBack)
        {
            WebPartManager1.DisplayMode = WebPartManager.BrowseDisplayMode;
        }
    }

    protected void Calendar1_SelectionChanged(object sender, EventArgs e)
    {
        Label1.Text = "You selected " + Calendar1.SelectedDate.ToShortDateString();
    }

    protected void LinkButtonBrowse_Click(object sender, EventArgs e)
    {
        WebPartManager1.DisplayMode = WebPartManager.BrowseDisplayMode;
    }

    protected void LinkButtonDesign_Click(object sender, EventArgs e)
```

Continued

Listing 12-1: A simple page using Web Parts without AJAX *(continued)*

```
        {
            WebPartManager1.DisplayMode = WebPartManager.DesignDisplayMode;
        }

</script>

<html xmlns="http://www.w3.org/1999/xhtml">
<head runat="server">
    <title>Basic Web Parts</title>
</head>
<body>
    <form id="form1" runat="server">
    <div>
        <asp:WebPartManager ID="WebPartManager1" runat="server">
        </asp:WebPartManager>
        <asp:LinkButton ID="LinkButtonBrowse" runat="server"
            onclick="LinkButtonBrowse_Click">Browse</asp:LinkButton>  
        <asp:LinkButton ID="LinkButtonDesign" runat="server"
            onclick="LinkButtonDesign_Click">Design</asp:LinkButton>
        <table>
            <tr valign="top">
                <td colspan="2"><h1>Bill Evjen's Web Page</h1></td>
            </tr>
            <tr valign="top">
                <td>
                    <asp:WebPartZone ID="WebPartZone1" runat="server">
                        <ZoneTemplate>
                            <asp:Calendar ID="Calendar1" runat="server"
                             Title="Select a date"
                             OnSelectionChanged="Calendar1_SelectionChanged">
                            </asp:Calendar>
                            <asp:Label ID="Label1" runat="server"
                             Title="Selected Date:"></asp:Label>
                        </ZoneTemplate>
                    </asp:WebPartZone>
                </td>
                <td>
                    <asp:WebPartZone ID="WebPartZone2" runat="server">
                        <ZoneTemplate>
                            <uc1:HelloUser ID="HelloUser1" runat="server"
                             Title="Entry Form" />
                        </ZoneTemplate>
                    </asp:WebPartZone>
                </td>
            </tr>
        </table>
    </div>
    </form>
</body>
</html>
```

The WebPartManager Server Control

There are some important pieces to this page of code. The first and foremost thing to understand is the WebPartManager control that is on the page. The WebPartManager control is an ASP.NET server control that completely manages the state of the zones and the content placed in these zones on a per user basis. This control, which has no visual aspect, can add and delete items contained within each zone of the page. The WebPartManager control can also manage the communications sometimes required between different elements contained in the zones. For example, you can pass a specific name-value pair from one item to another item within the same zone, or between items contained in separate zones. The WebPartManager control provides the capabilities to make this communication happen.

The WebPartManager control must be in place on every page in your application that works with the Portal Framework. A single WebPartManager control does not manage an entire application; instead, it manages on a per page basis.

> *You can also place a WebPartManager server control on the master page (if you are using one) to avoid having to place one on each and every content page.*

WebPartZone Server Controls

After you place the WebPartManager control on the page, the next step is to create zones from which you can utilize the Portal Framework. You should give this step some thought because it contributes directly to the usability of the page you are creating. Web pages are constructed in a linear fashion — either horizontally or vertically. Web pages are managed in square boxes — sometimes using tables that organize the columns and rows in which items appear on the page.

First, the page from Listing 12-1 includes the `<asp:WebPartManager>` control that manages the items contained in the two zones on this page. Within the table, the `<asp:WebPartZone>` server control specifies two Web zones. You can declare each Web zone in one of two ways. You can use the `<asp:WebPartZone>` element directly in the code, or you can create the zones within the table by dragging and dropping WebPartZone controls onto the design surface at appropriate places within the table. Figure 12-2 shows what the sample from Listing 12-1 looks like in the Design view of Visual Studio 2008.

When using Visual Studio 2008, note that by default this IDE creates a Microsoft SQL Server Express Edition file called `ASPNETDB.MDF` and stores it in the `App_Data` folder of your Web project. This database file is where the Portal Framework stores all the customization points. Although, Visual Studio 2008 uses SQL Server Express by default, you can also code this page to work from the full version of SQL Server 2008, 2005, 2000, or even 7.0.

Now that you have seen the use of WebPartZone controls, which are managed by the WebPartManager control, the next section takes a closer look at the WebPartZone server control itself.

Understanding the WebPartZone Control

The WebPartZone control defines an area of items, or Web Parts, that can be moved, minimized, maximized, deleted, or added based on programmatic code or user preferences. When you drag and drop WebPartZone controls onto the design surface using Visual Studio 2008, the WebPartZone control is drawn at the top of the zone, along with a visual representation of any of the items contained within the zone.

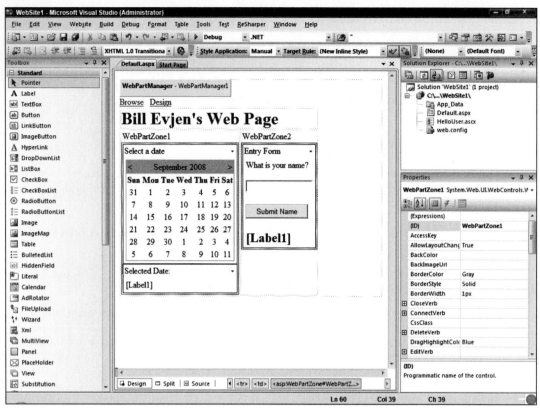

Figure 12-2

You can place almost anything in one of the Web zones. For example, you can include the following:

- ❑ HTML elements (when putting a `runat="server"` on the element)
- ❑ HTML server controls
- ❑ Web server controls
- ❑ User controls
- ❑ Custom controls

As you can see from Listing 12-1, WebPartZone controls are declared like this:

```
<asp:WebPartZone ID="WebPartZone1" runat="server"></asp:WebPartZone>
```

The items that are placed in the WebPartZone controls from this listing are standard controls, such as the Calendar and the Label controls. There is also a user control in this page. To build the same user control, add a user control (`.ascx`) to your project and name the control `HelloUser.ascx`. The code for this user control is defined here in Listing 12-2.

Listing 12-2: The user control to use and place within the WebPartZone control

```
<%@ Control Language="C#" ClassName="HelloUser" %>

<script runat="server">

    protected void Button1_Click(object sender, EventArgs e)
    {
        if (TextBox1 != null)
        {
            Label1.Text = "Hello " + TextBox1.Text;
        }
    }

</script>

<p>What is your name?</p>
<p>
    <asp:TextBox ID="TextBox1" runat="server"></asp:TextBox>
</p>
<p>
    <asp:Button ID="Button1" runat="server" onclick="Button1_Click"
        Text="Submit Name" />
</p>
<p>
    <asp:Label ID="Label1" runat="server" Font-Bold="True"
     Font-Size="Large"></asp:Label>
</p>
```

As page demonstrates, this is a pretty simple user control that performs a postback operation when the button on the page is clicked.

Allowing Users to Change the Page Mode

By working with the WebPartManager class either directly or through the use of the WebPartManager server control, you can enable your users to change the page's mode. Changing the mode of the page being viewed allows the user to add, move, or change the pages they are working with. The nice thing about the Web Part capabilities of ASP.NET is that these changes are then recorded to the ASPNETDB.MDF database file and are, therefore, recreated the next time the user visits the page.

The page from Listing 12-1 allows the end user to work with two page modes: Browse and Design. The Browse mode is a view that allows the end users only to view the page; they are unable to make any page adjustments. However, when the end users switch to the Design mode, they can move the parts or controls of the page around to completely customize the page's appearance (although not all browsers successfully support this feature). The mode is set to Browse when the page is first generated:

```
protected void Page_Load(object sender, EventArgs e)
{
 if(!Page.IsPostBack)
 {
```

```
                WebPartManager1.DisplayMode = WebPartManager.BrowseDisplayMode;
        }
    }
```

To change the mode of the page, the end user has only to click one of the LinkButton controls that are at the top of the page. Clicking on one of the controls changes the `DisplayMode` property of the WebPartManager control:

```
    protected void LinkButtonBrowse_Click(object sender, EventArgs e)
    {
        WebPartManager1.DisplayMode = WebPartManager.BrowseDisplayMode;
    }

    protected void LinkButtonDesign_Click(object sender, EventArgs e)
    {
        WebPartManager1.DisplayMode = WebPartManager.DesignDisplayMode;
    }
```

Understanding Postbacks with Web Parts

When you are working with Web Parts in ASP.NET, it is important to understand how much traffic goes back and forth across the wire. To watch the traffic directly, download Fiddler at `www.fiddlertool.com` and have this tool open when you build and run the page from Listing 12-1.

At first, you will notice that none of the traffic of your page is showing up in the Fiddler tool (use with IE). This is due to the fact that you are working locally using `localhost`. To correct this, add a period directly after the `localhost` (or `127.0.0.1`) so that your URL is similar to the following:

```
    http://localhost.:3405/WebSite1/Default.aspx
```

Obviously, the port number you are working with (mine is 3405) will be different. Once you add the period, click refresh in the browser to start seeing the traffic being monitored. Figure 12-3 provides a sample of what a recoded page in Fiddler looks like.

Now when you take any action on the page, as you would expect, these actions cause a postback and the entire page is once again returned to the browser. You will also notice that there is the dramatic page flicker going on because of the postback. This request and response is presented here in Figure 12-4 as viewed in Fiddler.

When you click the Design mode link, the page changes to allow you to move Web Parts around the page. Even changing modes causes the entire page to be reposted. When in the Design mode, you can change the order of the parts as they appear in each of the WebPartZone areas. Not only can you change the order in which Web Parts appear in a zone, but you can also move Web Parts from one zone to another. If you add the capability to enter the Design mode through the drop-down list that you can put on your page, you can easily provide the end user with the same ability to move Web parts around. Simply entering Design mode allows this type of movement.

The Design option changes the page so that the user can see the zones defined on the page, as illustrated in Figure 12-5.

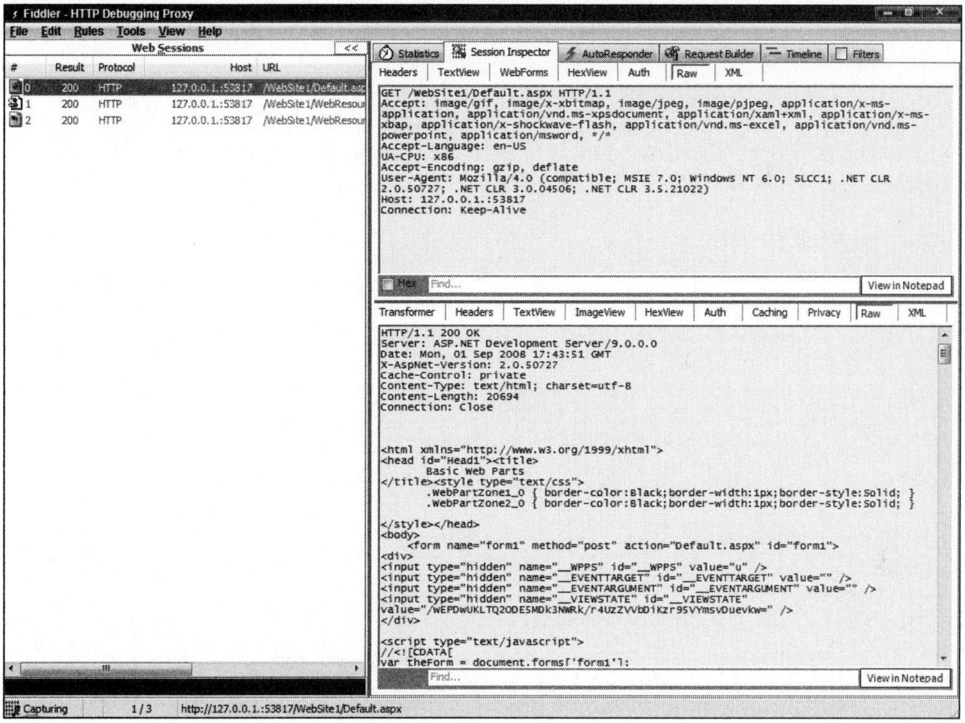

Figure 12-3

Figure 12-4

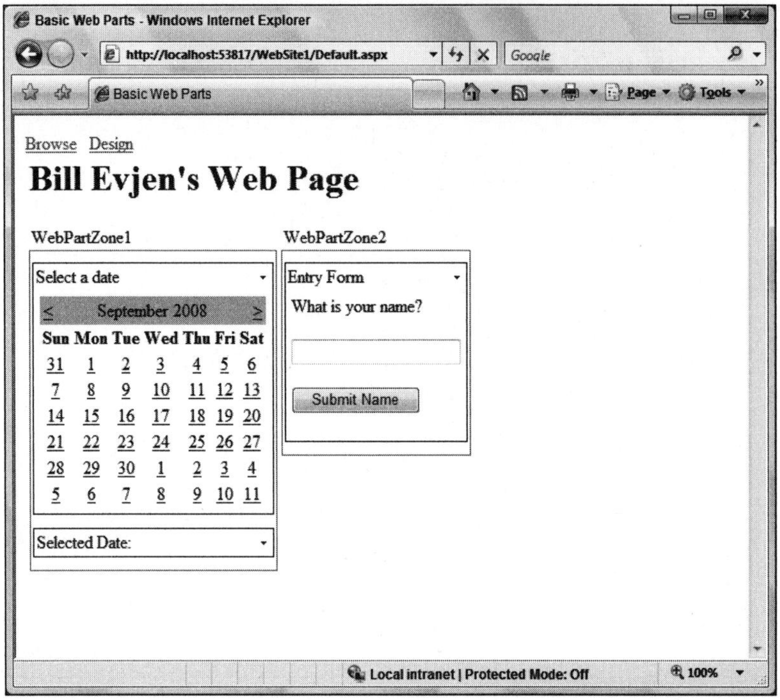

Figure 12-5

From this figure, you can see the two zones (WebPartZone1, and WebPartZone2). At this point, the end user can select one of the Web Parts contained in one of these zones and either change its order in the zone or move it to an entirely different zone on the page. To grab one of the Web Parts, the user simply clicks and holds the left mouse button on the title of the Web Part. When done correctly, the crosshairs, which appear when the end user hovers over the Web Part's title, turn into an arrow. This means that the user has grabbed hold of the Web Part and can drag it to another part of the page.

While the user drags the Web Part around the page, a visual representation of the item appears (see Figure 12-6). In this state, the Web Part is a bit transparent and its location in the state of the page is defined with a blue line (the darker line shown at the top of WebPartZone2). Releasing the left mouse button drops the Web Part at the blue line's location.

After the end user places all the items where he wants them, the locations of the items on the page are saved for later use. When he reopens the browser, everything is then drawn in the last state in which he left the page. This is done on a per user basis, so any other users browsing to the same page see either their own modified results or the default view if it is a first visit to the page. The user can then leave the Design view by clicking the Browse button on the page.

Even when Web Parts are moved from one location on the page to another, this information about how the end user wants to personalize the page is stored in the database and another request is sent to the server.

This is where AJAX can make the story a lot better than it is, as presented here.

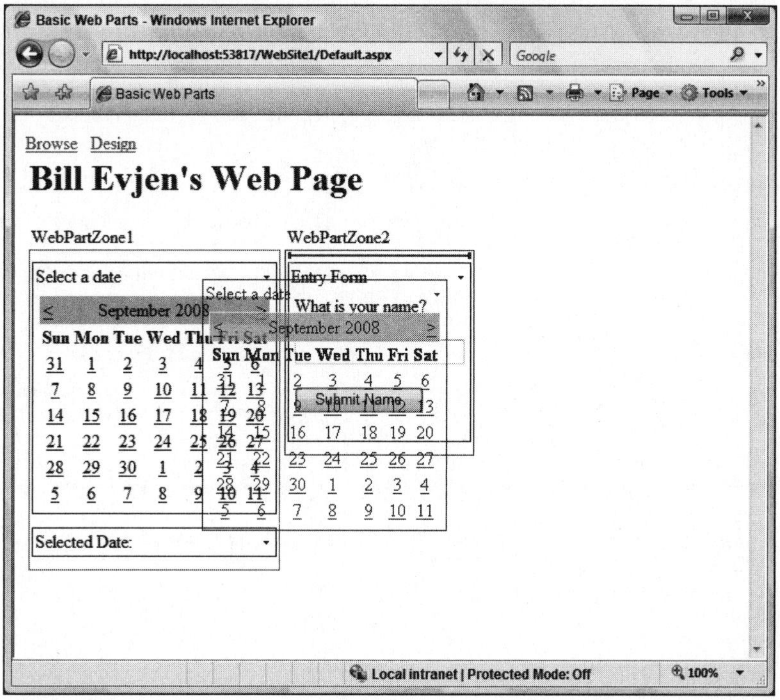

Figure 12-6

Adding AJAX to the Web Parts Page

The next step will be to add AJAX capabilities to the page that was just built. This example lessens the amount of data going back and forth between the client and the server, it will also remove the flicker that happens with pages that are not using AJAX capabilities.

The first step is to add your ScriptManager server control to the page and then encapsulate much of the Web Part capabilities inside of the UpdatePanel control. This approach is illustrated in Listing 12-3.

Listing 12-3: Incorporating AJAX capabilities into a page with Web Parts

```
<%@ Page Language="C#" %>

<%@ Import Namespace="System.Web.UI.WebControls.WebParts" %>
<%@ Register Src="HelloUser.ascx" TagName="HelloUser" TagPrefix="uc1" %>

<script runat="server">

    protected void Page_Load(object sender, EventArgs e)
    {
        if (!Page.IsPostBack)
```

Continued

Listing 12-3: Incorporating AJAX capabilities into a page with Web Parts *(continued)*

```
        {
            WebPartManager1.DisplayMode = WebPartManager.BrowseDisplayMode;
        }
    }

    protected void Calendar1_SelectionChanged(object sender, EventArgs e)
    {
        Label1.Text = "You selected " + Calendar1.SelectedDate.ToShortDateString();
    }

    protected void LinkButtonBrowse_Click(object sender, EventArgs e)
    {
        WebPartManager1.DisplayMode = WebPartManager.BrowseDisplayMode;
    }

    protected void LinkButtonDesign_Click(object sender, EventArgs e)
    {
        WebPartManager1.DisplayMode = WebPartManager.DesignDisplayMode;
    }

</script>

<html xmlns="http://www.w3.org/1999/xhtml">
<head runat="server">
    <title>Web Parts with AJAX</title>
</head>
<body>
    <form id="form1" runat="server">
    <div>
        <asp:ScriptManager ID="ScriptManager1" runat="server">
        </asp:ScriptManager>
        <asp:UpdatePanel ID="UpdatePanel1" runat="server">
            <ContentTemplate>
                <asp:WebPartManager ID="WebPartManager1" runat="server">
                </asp:WebPartManager>
                <asp:LinkButton ID="LinkButtonBrowse" runat="server"
                 OnClick="LinkButtonBrowse_Click">
                 Browse</asp:LinkButton>  
                <asp:LinkButton ID="LinkButtonDesign" runat="server"
                 OnClick="LinkButtonDesign_Click">
                 Design</asp:LinkButton>
                <table>
                    <tr valign="top">
                        <td colspan="2">
                            <h1>Bill Evjen's Web Page</h1>
                        </td>
                    </tr>
                    <tr valign="top">
                        <td>
                            <asp:WebPartZone ID="WebPartZone1" runat="server">
                                <ZoneTemplate>
                                  <asp:Calendar ID="Calendar1" runat="server"
```

Listing 12-3: Incorporating AJAX capabilities into a page with Web Parts *(continued)*

```
                                  Title="Select a date"
                                  OnSelectionChanged="Calendar1_SelectionChanged">
                                </asp:Calendar>
                                <asp:Label ID="Label1" runat="server"
                                  Title="Selected Date:"></asp:Label>
                            </ZoneTemplate>
                        </asp:WebPartZone>
                    </td>
                    <td>
                        <asp:WebPartZone ID="WebPartZone2" runat="server">
                            <ZoneTemplate>
                                <uc1:HelloUser ID="HelloUser1" runat="server"
                                  Title="Entry Form" />
                            </ZoneTemplate>
                        </asp:WebPartZone>
                    </td>
                </tr>
            </table>
        </ContentTemplate>
    </asp:UpdatePanel>
  </div>
  </form>
</body>
</html>
```

When looking over the code from Listing 12-3, you can see that there are now two managers. There is a manager for the AJAX capabilities on the page (the ScriptManager control) and then there is a manager for the Web Parts capabilities (the WebPartManager control).

It is important that the WebPartManager server control is contained within the ScriptManager control. The WebPartManager manages the movement of the Web Parts and the WebPartZone controls as well. If you do not put the WebPartManager control directly inside an UpdatePanel server control, you won't be able to move parts when in the Design mode.

With the code from Listing 12-3 in place, when the page is first loaded, there are scripts called for AJAX in addition to the other calls. This is illustrated here in Figure 12-7.

				Web Sessions	<<
#	**Result**	**Protocol**	**Host**	**URL**	**Body**
0	200	HTTP	127.0.0.1:53817	/WebSite1/Default.aspx	23,065
1	200	HTTP	127.0.0.1:53817	/WebSite1/WebResource.axd?d=...	20,931
2	200	HTTP	127.0.0.1:53817	/WebSite1/ScriptResource.axd?d...	5,518
3	200	HTTP	127.0.0.1:53817	/WebSite1/ScriptResource.axd?d...	66,717
4	200	HTTP	127.0.0.1:53817	/WebSite1/ScriptResource.axd?d...	21,141

Figure 12-7

With the AJAX capabilities built into the page, you will now be able to work with the Web Parts and to move them around the page with very few annoyances from an end user perspective. There is no flicker for the page as the entire page contents is encased within that UpdatePanel control.

Building a Custom Web Part with AJAX

When adding items to a page that utilizes the Portal Framework, you add the preexisting ASP.NET Web server controls, user controls, or custom controls. In addition to these items, you can also build and incorporate custom Web Parts. Using the `WebParts` class, you can create your own custom Web Parts. Although similar to ASP.NET custom server control development, the creation of custom Web Parts provides some additional capabilities. Creating a class that inherits from the `WebPart` class instead of the `Control` class enables your control to use the new personalization features and to work with the larger Portal Framework, thereby allowing for the control to be closed, maximized, minimized, and more.

To create a custom Web Part control, the first step is to create a project in Visual Studio 2008. From Visual Studio, choose File ➪ New Project. This pops open the New Project dialog. In this dialog, select ASP.NET Server Control. Name the project **MyStateListBox**, and click OK to create the project. You are presented with a class that contains the basic framework for a typical ASP.NET server control. Ignore this framework; you are going to change it so that your class creates a custom Web Parts control instead of an ASP.NET custom server control. Listing 12-4 details the creation of a custom Web Part control that incorporates the use of AJAX.

Listing 12-4: Building a Web Part that makes use of AJAX

```
using System;
using System.Web.UI;
using System.Web.UI.WebControls;
using System.Web.UI.WebControls.WebParts;

namespace Wrox
{
    public class StateListBox : WebPart
    {
        private String _LabelStartText = " Enter State Name: ";
        readonly TextBox StateInput = new TextBox();
        readonly ListBox StateContents = new ListBox();

        public StateListBox()
        {
            AllowClose = false;
        }

        [Personalizable, WebBrowsable]
        public String LabelStartText
        {
            get { return _LabelStartText; }
            set { _LabelStartText = value; }
        }

        protected override void CreateChildControls()
        {
            Controls.Clear();

            UpdatePanel updatePanel = new UpdatePanel();
            ScriptManager scriptManager = new ScriptManager();

            Label InstructionText = new Label();
```

Listing 12-4: Building a Web Part that makes use of AJAX *(continued)*

```
            InstructionText.BackColor = System.Drawing.Color.LightGray;
            InstructionText.Font.Name = "Verdana";
            InstructionText.Font.Size = 10;
            InstructionText.Font.Bold = true;
            InstructionText.Text = LabelStartText;

            scriptManager.ID = "scriptHandler";
            updatePanel.ID = "refreshName";
            updatePanel.UpdateMode = UpdatePanelUpdateMode.Conditional;
            updatePanel.ChildrenAsTriggers = true;

            Literal LineBreak = new Literal();
            LineBreak.Text = "<br />";

            Button InputButton = new Button();
            InputButton.Text = "Input State";
            InputButton.Click += Button1_Click;

            Literal Spacer = new Literal();
            Spacer.Text = "<p>";

            updatePanel.ContentTemplateContainer.Controls.Add(InstructionText);
            updatePanel.ContentTemplateContainer.Controls.Add(LineBreak);
            updatePanel.ContentTemplateContainer.Controls.Add(StateInput);
            updatePanel.ContentTemplateContainer.Controls.Add(InputButton);
            updatePanel.ContentTemplateContainer.Controls.Add(Spacer);
            updatePanel.ContentTemplateContainer.Controls.Add(StateContents);

            Controls.Add(scriptManager);
            Controls.Add(updatePanel);

            ChildControlsCreated = true;
        }

        private void Button1_Click(object sender, EventArgs e)
        {
            StateContents.Items.Add(StateInput.Text);
            StateInput.Text = String.Empty;
            StateInput.Focus();
        }
    }
}
```

To review, you first import the `System.Web.UI.WebControls.WebParts` namespace. The important step in the creation of this custom control is to make sure that it inherits from the `WebPart` class instead of the customary `WebControl` class. As stated earlier, this gives the control access to the advanced functionality of the Portal Framework that a typical custom control would not have.

```
public class StateListBox : WebPart
{

}
```

You are also going to have to make a reference to the System.Web.Extensions DLL in your project so that you can later instantiate the AJAX pieces that you are going to need for the control.

After the class structure is in place, a few properties are defined, and the constructor is defined as well. The constructor directly uses some of the capabilities that the WebPart class provides. These capabilities will not be available if this custom control has the WebControl class as its base class and is making use of the WebPart.AllowClose property.

```
public StateListBox()
{
    AllowClose = false;
}
```

This constructor creates a control that explicitly sets the control's AllowClose property to false — meaning that the Web Part will not have a Close link associated with it when generated in the page. When you use the WebPart class instead of the Control class, in addition to the an AllowClose property, you have access to other WebPart class properties such as AllowEdit, AllowHide, AllowMinimize, AllowZoneChange, and more.

In the example shown in Listing 12-4, you see a custom-defined property: LabelStartText. This property allows you to change the instruction text displayed at the top of the control. The big difference with this custom property is that it is preceded by the Personalizable and the WebBrowsable attributes.

The Personalizable attribute enables the property to be personalized, and the WebBrowsable attribute specifies whether or not the property should be displayed in the Properties window in Visual Studio. The Personalizable attribute can be defined further, using a PersonalizationScope enumeration. The only two possible enumerations — Shared and User — can be defined in the following ways:

```
[Personalizable(PersonalizationScope.Shared), WebBrowsable]
public String LabelStartText
{
    get { return _LabelStartText; }
    set { _LabelStartText = value; }
}
```

A PersonalizationScope of User means that any modifications are done on a per user basis. This is the default setting and means that if a user makes modifications to the property, the changes are seen only by that particular user and not by the other users that browse the page. If the PersonalizationScope is set to Shared, changes made by one user will be viewed by others requesting the page.

After you have the properties in place, the next step is to define what is rendered to the page by overriding the CreateChildControls method. In the example in Listing 12-4, the CreateChildControls method renders Label, Literal, TextBox, Button, and ListBox controls.

The CreatChildControls method also includes the AJAX pieces of the control that you must to include to make this work. In the code for this method, you can see that an UpdatePanel and a ScriptManager instance are created. You create the control instances of the Label, Literal, TextBox,

Button, and ListBox controls programmatically and then place them inside the UpdatePanel instance through the following code:

```
updatePanel.ContentTemplateContainer.Controls.Add(InstructionText);
updatePanel.ContentTemplateContainer.Controls.Add(LineBreak);
updatePanel.ContentTemplateContainer.Controls.Add(StateInput);
updatePanel.ContentTemplateContainer.Controls.Add(InputButton);
updatePanel.ContentTemplateContainer.Controls.Add(Spacer);
updatePanel.ContentTemplateContainer.Controls.Add(StateContents);
```

Once these items are in place within the UpdatePanel instance, the next step is to add everything to the overall control. However, before this occurs, you must add in the ScriptManager control before adding in the controls.

```
Controls.Add(scriptManager);
Controls.Add(updatePanel);
```

In addition to defining the properties of some of these controls, a single event is associated with the Button control (`Button1_Click`) that is also defined in this class.

Now that the custom Web Part control is in place, build the project so that a DLL is created. The next step is to open up the ASP.NET Web project where you want to utilize this new control and, from the Visual Studio Toolbox, add the new control. You can quickly accomplish this task by right-clicking in the Toolbox on the tab where you want the new control to be placed. After right-clicking the appropriate tab, select Choose Items. Click the Browse button and point to the new `MyStateListBox.dll` that you just created. After this is done, the StateListBox control is highlighted and checked in the Choose Toolbox Items dialog, as illustrated in Figure 12-8.

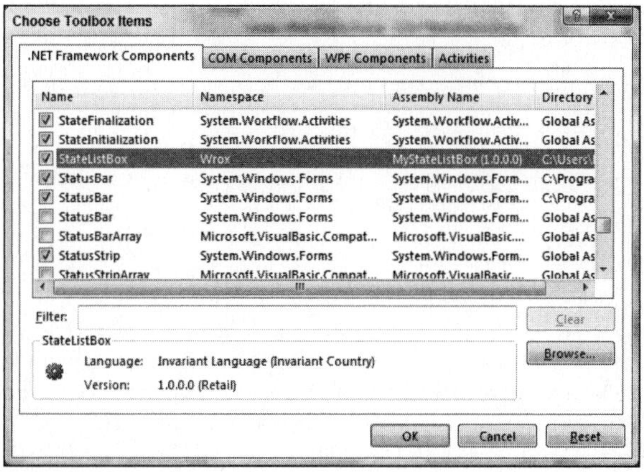

Figure 12-8

Click OK to add the control to your Toolbox. Now you are ready to use this new control as a Web Part control. To do this, simply drag and drop the control into one of your Web Part Zone areas. This does a couple of things. First, it registers the control on the page using the Register directive:

```
<%@ Register TagPrefix="cc1" Namespace="MyStateListBox.Wrox"
    Assembly="MyStateListBox" %>
```

Once registered, the control can be used on the page. If you drag it and drop it onto the page's design surface, you get a control in the following construct:

```
<cc1:StateListBox Runat="server" ID="StateListBox1"
 LabelStartText=" Enter State Name: " AllowClose="False" />
```

The two important things to notice with this construct are that the custom property, `LabelStartText`, is present and has the default value in place, and the `AllowClose` attribute is included. The `AllowClose` attribute is present only because earlier you made the control's inherited class `WebPart` and not `Control`. Because `WebPart` is set as the inherited class, you have access to these Web Part–specific properties. When you draw the StateListBox control on the page, you can see that, indeed, it is part of the larger Portal Framework and allows for things such as minimization and editing. End users can use this custom Web Part control as if it were any other type of Web Part control. As you can see, you have a lot of power when you create your own Web Part controls.

In addition, because `LabelStartText` uses the `WebBrowsable` attribute, you can use the PropertyGridEditorPart control to allow end users to edit this directly in the browser. With this in place, end users will be able to edit the text of the control themselves.

After you run this page and it is generated in the browser, all additions to the ListBox are added using AJAX, as demonstrated with this example request and response:

Request

```
POST /AspnetAjax/Default1.aspx HTTP/1.1
Accept: */*
Accept-Language: en-us
Referer: http://localhost.:3405/AspnetAjax/Default1.aspx
x-microsoftajax: Delta=true
Content-Type: application/x-www-form-urlencoded; charset=utf-8
Cache-Control: no-cache
UA-CPU: x86
Accept-Encoding: gzip, deflate
User-Agent: Mozilla/4.0 (compatible; MSIE 7.0; Windows NT 5.1; .NET CLR 2.0.50727;
Zune 2.5; .NET CLR 3.0.04506.648; .NET CLR 3.5.21022; .NET CLR 3.0.4506.2152; .NET
CLR 3.5.30729)
Host: localhost.:3405
Content-Length: 454
Connection: Keep-Alive
Pragma: no-cache

WebPartManager1%24StateListBox1%24scriptHandler=WebPartManager1%24StateListBox1%24
refreshName%7CWebPartManager1%24StateListBox1%24ctl04&__WPPS=u&__EVENTTARGET=
&__EVENTARGUMENT=&__VIEWSTATE=%2FwEPDwUKMTk5OTg1OTg1MGRkMlOfVbp1YNYdar89Ds3HJ8m0q
Ds%3D&__EVENTVALIDATION=%2FwEWBAKqu%2FqgBAKRmJmrDAKJlqqyBgLurIydDHmBcWT5yw1PMvS%2
Bp90wfPZzfB2z&WebPartManager1%24StateListBox1%24ctl03=Missouri&__ASYNCPOST=true&
WebPartManager1%24StateListBox1%24ctl04=Input%20State
```

Response

```
HTTP/1.1 200 OK
Server: ASP.NET Development Server/9.0.0.0
Date: Mon, 01 Sep 2008 17:13:46 GMT
```

```
X-AspNet-Version: 2.0.50727
Cache-Control: private
Content-Type: text/plain; charset=utf-8
Content-Length: 1320
Connection: Close
```

```
438|updatePanel|WebPartManager1_StateListBox1_refreshName|<span
style="background-color:LightGrey;font-family:Verdana;font-size:10pt;
font-weight:bold;"> Enter State Name: </span><br />
<input name="WebPartManager1$StateListBox1$ctl03" type="text"
id="WebPartManager1_StateListBox1_ctl03" /><input type="submit"
name="WebPartManager1$StateListBox1$ctl04" value="Input State" /><p>
<select size="4" name="WebPartManager1$StateListBox1$ctl06">
<option value="Missouri">Missouri</option>

</select>|0|hiddenField|__LASTFOCUS||0|hiddenField|__EVENTTARGET||0|hiddenField|
__EVENTARGUMENT|||160|hiddenField|__VIEWSTATE|/wEPDwUKMTk5OTg1OTg1MA9kFgICBA9kFgICAQ
9kFgIFDVN0YXRlTGlzdEJveDEPZBYCAgEPZBYCZg9kFgICBQ8QZA8WAWYWARAFCE1pc3NvdXJpBQhNaXNzb
3VyaWdkZGR2AxtIM7SS2C0P9hDKGQH009IShQ==|72|hiddenField|__EVENTVALIDATION|/wEWBQLd7d
R0AomWqrIGAu6sjJ0MAt+YhIUKApGYmasMsdxVBNBabBH6tER6OxIqDz18/eA=|0|
asyncPostBackControlIDs|||0|postBackControlIDs|||42|updatePanelIDs||
tWebPartManager1$StateListBox1$refreshName|0|childUpdatePanelIDs|||41|
panelsToRefreshIDs||WebPartManager1$StateListBox1$refreshName|2|
asyncPostBackTimeout||90|13|formAction||Default1.aspx|109|scriptBlock|ScriptPath|
/AspnetAjax/ScriptResource.axd?d=SJ68zay-cFtXy0ZMZpeiURz5pPNxfk17Mof7BD
sGU963y7AcpfHT87QK701rjloY0&t=38f3a940|35|focus||
WebPartManager1_StateListBox1_ctl03|
```

Summary

This chapter introduced you to the WebPartManager, WebPartZone, and WebPart controls. These controls allow for easy customization of the look and feel of either the Web Parts or the zones in which they are located.

This chapter also showed you how to create your own custom Web Part controls and how to incorporate AJAX into these controls. The capability to create your own controls was always one of the benefits provided by ASP.NET, and this benefit has been taken one step further with the capability to create Web Part controls. Web Part controls enable you to take advantage of some of the complex features that you do not get with custom ASP.NET server controls.

You may find the Portal Framework to be one of the more exciting features of ASP.NET 3.5; you may like the idea of creating modular and customizable Web pages. End users like this feature, and it is quite easy for you to implement.

13

Localization

Often developers approach the building and deployment of their Web applications in their native language and then, as the audience for the application expands, they realize they need to globalize the application. Of course, the ideal is to build the Web application to handle an international audience right from the start — but, in many cases, this may not be possible because of the extra work it requires.

It is good to note that with the ASP.NET 3.5 Framework, a considerable effort has been made to address the internationalization of Web applications. You quickly realize that changes to the API, the addition of capabilities to the server controls, and even Visual Studio itself equip you to do the extra work required to bring your application to an international audience more easily.

As an ASP.NET developer, you might be well aware of the ways in which you can work with localization in the applications that you develop, but before the introduction of ASP.NET AJAX, all your localization was focused on what you could do on the server side of your application. AJAX introduces complexity with localization in that you now have to be concerned with how the JavaScript on your page changes the end application that also works with the localization of the application you desire.

This chapter looks at some of the important items to consider when building your Web applications on the server side and the client side, starting off with an introduction on what it takes to localize your applications overall.

What Is Localization?

The first thing to work through is in what localization actually means to you and how it will be implemented in your application. What are you going to localize for your end users? Most developers think it is simply a matter of changing the text on the screen so that it is translated for the end user. This means that if you are offering your site in U.S. English, that you also offer it in another language such as Finnish or French based upon an end user preference.

It is true that text translation is one example of localizing a site, but there really is more to the picture than this. In addition to translating text, you also can change and work with the formatting of items such as date/time values, how numbers are represented, and how items sort within collections. In addition to this, you might also change images on the screen based upon a cultural setting.

For instance, in the financial services world, most cultures associate the color green as a good thing and the color red as a bad thing. When showing the up and down movements of a stock on the market, you will see green arrows for stocks that are moving up in value and red arrows for stocks that are moving down. These colors are actually specific to certain cultures.

For instance, in Japan, the opposite is true. In Japan, the color green is used to signify a negative trend, while the color red is used to signify a positive trend. In this case, the localization of the application that you might build would have to be localized to include the correct color indicators for stock movements. This point is important in that it is vital to remember that localization is not only about changing text but instead can be anything else as well. You will also need to take images, colors, and even features into account when localizing applications.

Cultures and Regions

The ASP.NET page that is pulled up in an end user's browser runs under a specific culture and region setting. When building an ASP.NET application or page, the defined culture in which it runs is dependent upon a culture and region settings coming from the server in which the application is run or from a setting applied by the end user (the client). By default, ASP.NET runs under a culture setting defined by the server.

The world is made up of a multitude of cultures, each of which has a language and a set of defined ways in which it views and consumes numbers, uses currencies, sorts alphabetically, and so on. The .NET Framework defines cultures and regions using the Request for Comments 1766 standard definition (Tags for Identification, and Languages) that specifies a language and region using two-letter codes separated by a dash. The following table provides examples of some culture definitions.

Culture Code	Description
en-US	English language; United States
en-GB	English language; United Kingdom (Great Britain)
en-AU	English language; Australia
en-CA	English language; Canada

This table defines four distinct cultures that have some similarities and some differences. All four cultures speak the same language (English). For this reason, the language code of en is used in each culture setting. After the language setting comes the region setting. Even though these cultures speak the same language, it is important to distinguish them further by setting their region (such as US for the United States, GB for the United Kingdom, AU for Australia, and CA for Canada). As you are probably well aware, the English language in the United States is slightly different from the English language that is used in the United Kingdom, and so forth. Beyond language, differences exist in the way dates and numerical values are represented. This is why a culture's language and region are presented together.

The differences do not break down by the country only. Many times, countries contain more than a single language and each area has its own preference for notation of dates and other items. For example, en-CA specifies English speakers in Canada. Because Canada is not only an English-speaking country, it also includes the culture setting of fr-CA for French-speaking Canadians.

Understanding Culture Types

The culture definition you have just seen is called a specific culture definition. This definition is as detailed as you can possibly get — defining both the language and the region. The other type of culture definition is a neutral culture definition. Each specific culture is associated with a specified neutral culture. For instance, the English language cultures shown in the previous table are separate, but they also all belong to one neutral culture EN (English). The diagram presented in Figure 13-1 illustrates how these culture types relate to one another.

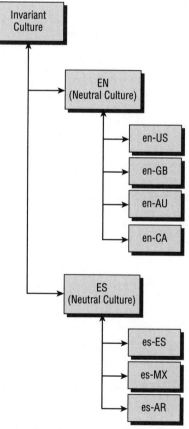

Figure 13-1

From this diagram, you can see that many specific cultures belong to a neutral culture. Higher in the hierarchy than the neutral culture is an invariant culture, which is an agnostic culture setting that should be utilized when passing items (such as dates and numbers) around a network. When performing these kinds of operations, make your back-end data flows devoid of user-specific culture settings. Instead, apply these settings in the business and presentation layers of your applications.

Also, pay attention to the neutral culture when working with your applications. Invariably, you are going to build applications with views that are more dependent on a neutral culture rather than on a specific culture. For instance, if you have a Spanish version of your application, you probably make this version available to all Spanish speakers regardless of their regions. In many applications, it will not matter if the Spanish speaker is from Spain, Mexico, or Argentina. In a case where it does make a difference, use the specific culture settings.

Understanding ASP.NET Culture

When the end user requests an ASP.NET page, this Web page is executed on a thread from the thread pool. The thread has a culture associated with it. You can get information about the culture of the thread programmatically and then check for particular details about that culture. You can view information about the thread in which it runs by printing out some information from the server. This is illustrated in Listing 13-1.

Listing 13-1: Viewing the thread's culture in ASP.NET

```
<%@ Page Language="C#" %>
<%@ Import Namespace="System.Globalization"%>

<script runat="server">

    protected void Page_Load(object sender, EventArgs e)
    {
        CultureInfo ci = System.Threading.Thread.CurrentThread.CurrentCulture;
        Response.Write("<b><u>CURRENT CULTURE'S INFO</u></b>");
        Response.Write("<p><b>Culture's Name:</b> " + ci.Name + "<br>");
        Response.Write("<b>Culture's Parent Name:</b> " + ci.Parent.Name +
            "<br>");
        Response.Write("<b>Culture's Display Name:</b> " + ci.DisplayName +
            "<br>");
        Response.Write("<b>Culture's English Name:</b> " + ci.EnglishName +
            "<br>");
        Response.Write("<b>Culture's Native Name:</b> " + ci.NativeName +
            "<br>");
        Response.Write("<b>Culture's Three Letter ISO Name:</b> " +
            ci.Parent.ThreeLetterISOLanguageName + "<br>");
        Response.Write("<b>Calendar Type:</b> " + ci.Calendar + "</p >");
    }
</script>

<html xmlns="http://www.w3.org/1999/xhtml">
<head runat="server">
    <title>Viewing the thread's culture</title>
</head>
<body>
    <form id="form1" runat="server">
    <div>

    </div>
    </form>
</body>
</html>
```

Running this page shows the details of the culture in the thread in which ASP.NET is running. This bit of code in the `Page_Load()` event checks the `CurrentCulture` property. You can place the result of this value in a `CultureInfo` object. To get at this object, you import the `System.Globalization` namespace in your code. The `CultureInfo` object contains a number of properties that provides you with specific culture information. The following items, which are displayed in a series of simple `Response.Write()` statements, are only a small sampling of what is actually available. Running this page produces results similar to what is shown in Figure 13-2.

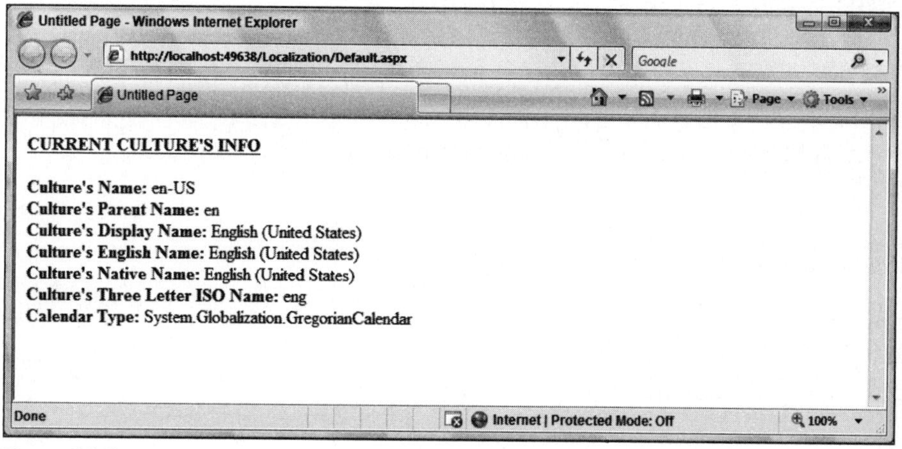

Figure 13-2

From this figure, you can see that the en-US culture is the default setting in which the ASP.NET thread executes. In addition to this, you can use the `CultureInfo` object to get at a lot of other descriptive information about the culture.

If you are interested in controlling the culture of the thread yourself, there are a number of ways to accomplish this task. One way to do this is to programmatically change the thread's culture using the `CultureInfo` object. This is shown here in Listing 13-2.

Listing 13-2: Changing the thread culture programmatically

```
protected void Page_Load(object sender, EventArgs e)
{

    // Now I am defining the culture to Thai
    System.Threading.Thread.CurrentThread.CurrentCulture = new CultureInfo("th-TH");

    CultureInfo ci = System.Threading.Thread.CurrentThread.CurrentCulture;
    Response.Write("<b><u>CURRENT CULTURE'S INFO</u></b>");
    Response.Write("<p><b>Culture's Name:</b> " + ci.Name + "<br>");
    Response.Write("<b>Culture's Parent Name:</b> " + ci.Parent.Name +
        "<br>");
    Response.Write("<b>Culture's Display Name:</b> " + ci.DisplayName +
        "<br>");
    Response.Write("<b>Culture's English Name:</b> " + ci.EnglishName +
```

Continued

Listing 13-2: Changing the thread culture programmatically *(continued)*

```
        "<br>");
    Response.Write("<b>Culture's Native Name:</b> " + ci.NativeName +
        "<br>");
    Response.Write("<b>Culture's Three Letter ISO Name:</b> " +
        ci.Parent.ThreeLetterISOLanguageName + "<br>");
    Response.Write("<b>Calendar Type:</b> " + ci.Calendar + "</p>");
    }
```

In this case, only a single line of code is added to assign a new instance of the `CultureInfo` object to the `CurrentCulture` property of the thread being executed by ASP.NET. The culture setting enables the `CultureInfo` object to define the culture you want to utilize. In this case, the Thai language of Thailand is assigned, and the results produced in the browser are illustrated in Figure 13-3.

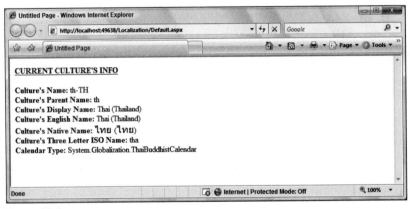

Figure 13-3

From this figure, you can see that the .NET Framework goes so far as to provide the native name of the language used even if it is not a Latin-based letter style. In this case, the results are presented for the Thai language in Thailand, and some of the properties that are associated with this culture (such as an entirely different calendar than the one used in Western Europe and the United States). Remember that you reference `System.Globalization` to get at the `CultureInfo` object.

Server-Side versus Client-Side Localization

So far, the culture has been defined completely on the server side and has not been changed for any reason (most important being changing the culture based upon what the end user's culture is set to). This next section looks at how to set culture on the server side and bring localization down to the client as well.

Server-Side Culture Declarations

ASP.NET enables you to define the culture used by your entire ASP.NET application or by a specific page within your application. You can specify the culture for any of your ASP.NET applications by means of the appropriate configuration files. In the default install of ASP.NET, no culture is specified as is evident when you look at the global `web.config.comments` file (meant for documentation purposes) found in the ASP.NET 2.0 CONFIG folder (`C:\WINDOWS\Microsoft.NET\Framework\v2.0.50727\CONFIG`). Remember that ASP.NET 3.5 is built on top of ASP.NET 2.0 and uses the same configuration files. In the `web.config.comments` file, you find a `<globalization>` section of the configuration document. This section is presented in Listing 13-3.

Listing 13-3: The <globalization> section in the web.config.comments file

```
<globalization requestEncoding="utf-8" responseEncoding="utf-8" fileEncoding=""
  culture="" uiCulture="" enableClientBasedCulture="false"
  responseHeaderEncoding="utf-8" resourceProviderFactoryType=""
  enableBestFitResponseEncoding="false" />
```

Note the two attributes represented in bold — `culture` and `uiCulture`. The `culture` attribute enables you to define the culture to use for processing incoming requests, whereas the `uiCulture` attribute enables you define the default culture needed to process any resource files in the application. (The use of these attributes is covered later in this chapter.)

As you look at the configuration declaration in Listing 13-3, you can see that nothing is specified for the culture settings. One option you have when specifying a culture on the server is to define this culture in the server version of the `web.config` file found in the CONFIG folder. This causes every ASP.NET 3.5 application on this server to adopt this particular culture setting. The other option is to specify these settings in the `web.config` file of the application, as illustrated in Listing 13-4.

Listing 13-4: Defining the <globalization> section in the web.config file

```
<configuration>
    <system.web>

        <globalization culture="ru-RU" uiCulture="ru-RU" />

    </system.web>
</configuration>
```

In this case, the culture established for just this ASP.NET application is the Russian language in the country of Russia. In addition to setting the culture at either the server-wide or the application-wide level, another option is to set the culture at the page level. This is illustrated in Listing 13-5.

Listing 13-5: Defining the culture at the page level using the @Page directive

```
<%@ Page Language="C#" UICulture="ru-RU" Culture="ru-RU" %>
```

This example determines that the Russian language and culture settings are used for everything on the page. You can see this in action by using this `@Page` directive and a simple Calendar control on the page. Figure 13-4 shows the output.

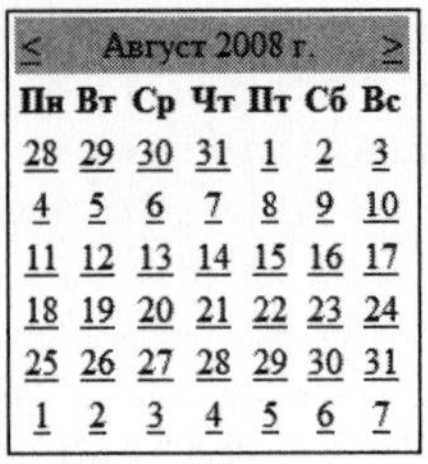

Figure 13-4

How End Users Choose the Culture on the Client

In addition to using server-side settings to define the culture for your ASP.NET pages, you also have the option of defining the culture based on the client's browser preference settings.

When end users install Microsoft's Internet Explorer and some of the other browsers, they have the option to select their preferred cultures in a particular order (if they have selected more than a single culture preference). To see this in action in IE, select Tools ➪ Internet Options from the IE menu bar. On the first tab exposed (General), you see a Languages button at the bottom of the dialog. Select this button and you are provided with the Language Preference dialog shown in Figure 13-5.

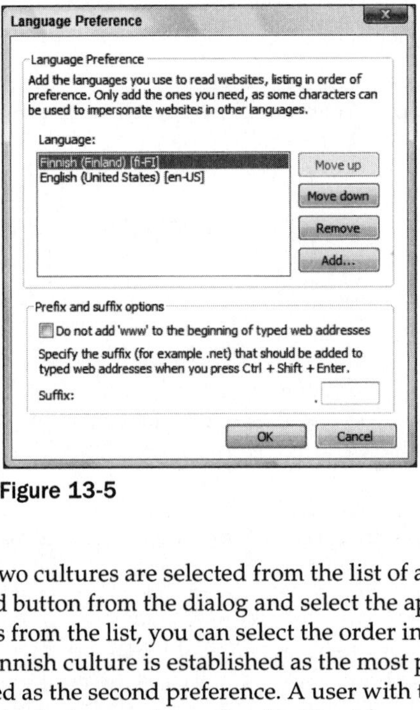

Figure 13-5

In this figure, you can see that two cultures are selected from the list of available cultures. To add more cultures to the list, click the Add button from the dialog and select the appropriate culture from the list. After you have selected cultures from the list, you can select the order in which you prefer to use them. In the case of Figure 13-5, the Finnish culture is established as the most preferred culture, whereas the U.S. version of English is selected as the second preference. A user with this setting gets the Finnish language version of the application before anything else; if a Finnish version is not available, a U.S. English version is presented.

After the end user's selection is enumerated, you can use the auto feature provided in ASP.NET 3.5. Instead of specifying a distinct culture in any of the configuration files or from the @Page directive, you can also state that ASP.NET should automatically select the culture provided by the end user requesting the page. This is done using the auto keyword, as illustrated in Listing 13-6.

Listing 13-6: Changing the culture to the end user's selection

```
<%@ Page Language="C#" UICulture="auto" Culture="auto" %>
```

With this construction in your page, the dates, calendars, and numbers now appear in the preferred culture of the requestor. What happens, however, if you have translated resources in resource files (shown later in the chapter) that depend on a culture specification? What if you have only specific translations and cannot handle every possible culture that might be returned to your ASP.NET page? In this case, you can specify the auto option with an additional fallback option if ASP.NET cannot find the culture settings of the user (such as culture-specific resource files). This usage is illustrated in Listing 13-7.

Listing 13-7: Providing a fallback culture from the auto option

```
<%@ Page Language="C#" UICulture="auto:en-US" Culture="auto:en-US" %>
```

In this case, the automatic detection is utilized, but if the culture the end user prefers is not present, then en-US is used.

Client-Side Culture Details

When working with culture on the client side, the culture that is used is the culture that is defined on the server. Therefore, if you have the culture set to en-US on your server, this is the default that is utilized on the client-side operations as well. Consider the example presented in Listing 13-8.

Listing 13-8: Viewing dates with a culture setting as set on the server

```
<%@ Page Language="C#" %>
<%@ Import Namespace="System.Globalization"%>

<script runat="server">

    protected void Page_Load(object sender, EventArgs e)
    {
        Response.Write("Date from the server before setting culture: " +
            DateTime.Now + "<br />");
        System.Threading.Thread.CurrentThread.CurrentCulture =
            new CultureInfo("ru-RU");
        Response.Write("Date from the server after setting culture: " +
            DateTime.Now);
    }
```

Continued

```
</script>

<html xmlns="http://www.w3.org/1999/xhtml">
<head runat="server">
    <title></title>
    <script type="text/javascript">

        function pageLoad() {

            var date = new Date();
            $get('Label1').innerHTML = "Date after setting culture on the client: "
              + date.localeFormat("D");
            alert(String.localeFormat("{0:dddd, dd MMMM yyyy hh:mm:ss tt}",
              new Date()));

        }

    </script>
</head>
<body>
    <form id="form1" runat="server">
    <div>
        <asp:ScriptManager ID="ScriptManager1" runat="server"
         EnableScriptGlobalization="true" />
        <span id="Label1"></span>
    </div>
    </form>
</body>
</html>
```

First off, to work with setting the culture on the server, you need to import the `System.Globalization` namespace. The first thing that the page does from Listing 13-8 is write out the server's date and time to the page using a simple `Response.Write()` statement. After this, the culture is changed from the server default to a new culture of `ru-RU` (this is the Russian culture) and then the date and time is again written to the page using the same `Response.Write()` statement.

Now that the culture of the page has been set to `ru-RU`, even though it started as `en-US` (in this case), `ru-RU` will be the culture that is utilized on the client. This page contains a JavaScript function called `pageLoad()`, and in this function the `Label1` control is populated with the date and for good measure, an alert is thrown with the date and time again.

You will notice that the JavaScript output are also done in Russian using the `ru-RU` culture as it is set on the server. The result of this is presented here in Figure 13-6.

The only way to make this work is to enable globalization on the client, and this is done through the `EnableScriptGlobalization` attribute of the ScriptManager server control. In this case, you set the values of both of these attributes to `true`.

```
<asp:ScriptManager ID="ScriptManager1" runat="server"
 EnableScriptGlobalization="true" />
```

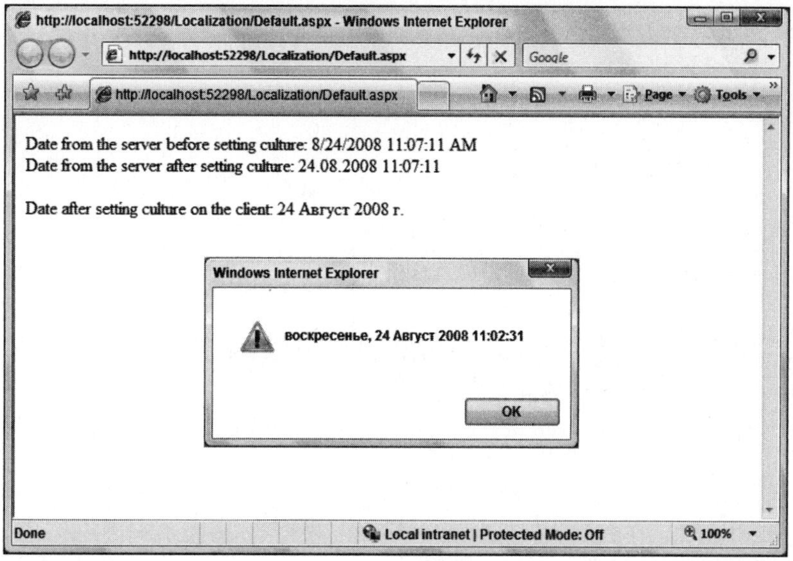

Figure 13-6

However, how do you set the culture on the client to what the end user expects? For instance, suppose that the culture on the client is set to fi-FI as is shown earlier in Figure 13-5. It is one thing to set it to a specific culture as shown in the previous example (e.g. ru-RU), and it is possible to provide end users with a drop-down list for setting their language and culture preferences when working with your application. Nevertheless, what if you wanted to grab the culture of the end user without asking them to make any selections? In this case, you use the Request.UserLanguages[] option.

When a request is made to your Web application, the culture options of the requestor are found in the HTTP header. For instance, here is an example HTTP header:

```
GET /WebSite1/Default.aspx HTTP/1.1
Accept: */*
```

```
Accept-Language: fi-FI,en-us;q=0.5
```

```
UA-CPU: x86
Accept-Encoding: gzip, deflate
User-Agent: Mozilla/4.0 (compatible; MSIE 7.0; Windows NT 5.1; .NET CLR 2.0.50727;
    Zune 2.5; .NET CLR 3.0.04506.648; .NET CLR 3.5.21022; .NET CLR 3.0.4506.2152;
    .NET CLR 3.5.30729)
Host: localhost.:2972
Connection: Keep-Alive
Pragma: no-cache
```

You will notice that the highlighted line in this header is an ordered list of specific cultures that the end user has configured on their machine. In this case, there are two cultures set. The first one is fi-FI (for Finnish as spoken in Finland), and the second one is en-US (for English as spoken in the United States).

From this, you are able to take first setting in the ordered list and set that as the page's culture. An example of this is presented in Listing 13-9.

Listing 13-9: Setting the culture to the client's culture

```
<%@ Page Language="C#" %>
<%@ Import Namespace="System.Globalization"%>

<script runat="server">

    protected void Page_Load(object sender, EventArgs e)
    {
        Response.Write("Date from the server before setting culture: " +
            DateTime.Now + "<br />");

        System.Threading.Thread.CurrentThread.CurrentCulture =
            new CultureInfo(Request.UserLanguages[0]);

        Response.Write("Date from the server after setting culture: " +
            DateTime.Now);
    }
</script>

<html xmlns="http://www.w3.org/1999/xhtml">
<head runat="server">
    <title></title>
    <script type="text/javascript">

        function pageLoad() {

            var date = new Date();
            $get('Label1').innerHTML = "Date after setting culture on the client: "
                + date.localeFormat("D");
            alert(String.localeFormat("{0:dddd, dd MMMM yyyy hh:mm:ss tt}",
                new Date()));

        }

    </script>
</head>
<body>
    <form id="form1" runat="server">
    <div>
        <asp:ScriptManager ID="ScriptManager1" runat="server"
        EnableScriptGlobalization="true" />
        <span id="Label1"></span>
    </div>
    </form>
</body>
</html>
```

In this case, the culture is set to the client's culture as is passed in by the HTTP header. If the previous header example is utilized, then the end result of this request is presented in Figure 13-7 (in my case, my culture is set to en-US).

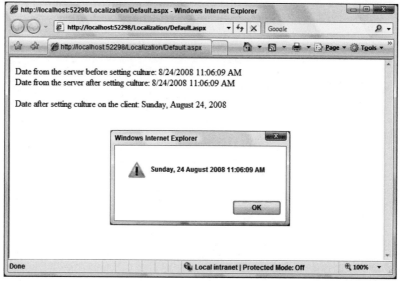

Figure 13-7

ASP.NET 3.5 Resource Files

When you work with ASP.NET 3.5, all resources are handled by a resource file. A resource file is an XML-based file that has a .resx extension. You can have Visual Studio 2008 help you construct this file. Resource files provide a set of items that are utilized by a specified culture. In your ASP.NET 3.5 applications, you store resource files as either local or global resources. The following sections look at how to use each type of resource.

Making Use of Local Resources

You would be surprised how easily you can build an ASP.NET page so that it can be localized into other languages. Really, the only thing you need to do is build the ASP.NET page as you normally would and then use some built-in capabilities from Visual Studio 2008 to convert the page to a format that allows you to plug in other languages easily.

To see this in action, build a simple ASP.NET page as presented in Listing 13-10.

Listing 13-10: Building the basic ASP.NET page to localize

```
<%@ Page Language="C#" %>

<script runat="server">

    protected void Button1_Click(object sender, EventArgs e)
    {
```

Continued

417

Listing 13-10: Building the basic ASP.NET page to localize *(continued)*

```
            Label2.Text = TextBox1.Text;
        }

</script>

<html xmlns="http://www.w3.org/1999/xhtml">
<head runat="server">
    <title>Sample Page</title>
</head>
<body>
    <form id="form1" runat="server">
    <div>
        <asp:Label ID="Label1" runat="server"
         Text="What is your name?"></asp:Label><br />
        <br />
        <asp:TextBox ID="TextBox1" runat="server"></asp:TextBox> 
        <asp:Button ID="Button1" runat="server" Text="Submit Name"
            onclick="Button1_Click" /><br />
        <br />
        <asp:Label ID="Label2" runat="server"></asp:Label>
    </div>
    </form>
</body>
</html>
```

As you can see, there is not much to this page. It is composed of a couple of Label controls, as well as TextBox and Button controls. The end user enters her name into the textbox, and then the Label2 server control is populated with the inputted name and a simple greeting.

The next step is what makes Visual Studio so great. To change the construction of this page so that it can be localized easily from resource files, open the page in Visual Studio and select Tools ➪ Generate Local Resource from the Visual Studio menu. Note that you can select this tool only when you are in the Design view of your page. It will not work in the Split view or the Code view of the page.

Selecting the Generate Local Resource from the Tool menu option causes Visual Studio to create an App_LocalResouces folder in your project if you already do not have one. A .resx file based upon this ASP.NET page is then placed in the folder. For instance, if you are working with the Default.aspx page, the resource file is named Default.aspx.resx. These changes are shown in Figure 13-8.

Figure 13-8

Right-click on the .resx file and select View Code; notice that the .resx file is nothing more than an XML file with an associated schema at the beginning of the document. The resource file that is generated for you takes every possible property of every translatable control on the page and gives each item a key value that can be referenced in your ASP.NET page. If you look at the code of the page, notice that all the text values that you placed in the page have been left in the page, but they have also been placed inside the resource file. You can see how Visual Studio changed the code of the Default.aspx page in Listing 13-11.

Listing 13-11: Looking at how Visual Studio altered the page code

```
<%@ Page Language="C#" meta:resourcekey="PageResource1" %>

<script runat="server">

    protected void Button1_Click(object sender, EventArgs e)
    {
        Label2.Text = TextBox1.Text;
    }

</script>

<html xmlns="http://www.w3.org/1999/xhtml">
<head runat="server">
    <title>Sample Page</title>
</head>
<body>
    <form id="form1" runat="server">
    <div>
        <asp:ScriptManager ID="ScriptManager1" runat="server">
        </asp:ScriptManager>
        <asp:Label ID="Label1" runat="server" Text="What is your name?"
         meta:resourcekey="Label1Resource1"></asp:Label><br />
        <br />
        <asp:UpdatePanel ID="UpdatePanel1" runat="server">
            <ContentTemplate>
                <asp:TextBox ID="TextBox1" runat="server"
                 meta:resourcekey="TextBox1Resource1"></asp:TextBox> 
                <asp:Button ID="Button1" runat="server" Text="Submit Name"
                 OnClick="Button1_Click"
                    meta:resourcekey="Button1Resource1" /><br />
                <br />
                <asp:Label ID="Label2" runat="server"
                 meta:resourcekey="Label2Resource1"></asp:Label>
            </ContentTemplate>
        </asp:UpdatePanel>
    </div>
    </form>
</body>
</html>
```

From this bit of code, you can see that the attribute meta:resourcekey has been added to each of the controls along with an associated value. This is the key from the .resx file that was created on your behalf. Double-clicking on the Default.aspx.resx file opens the resource file in the Resource Editor, which you will find is built into Visual Studio. This editor is presented in Figure 13-9.

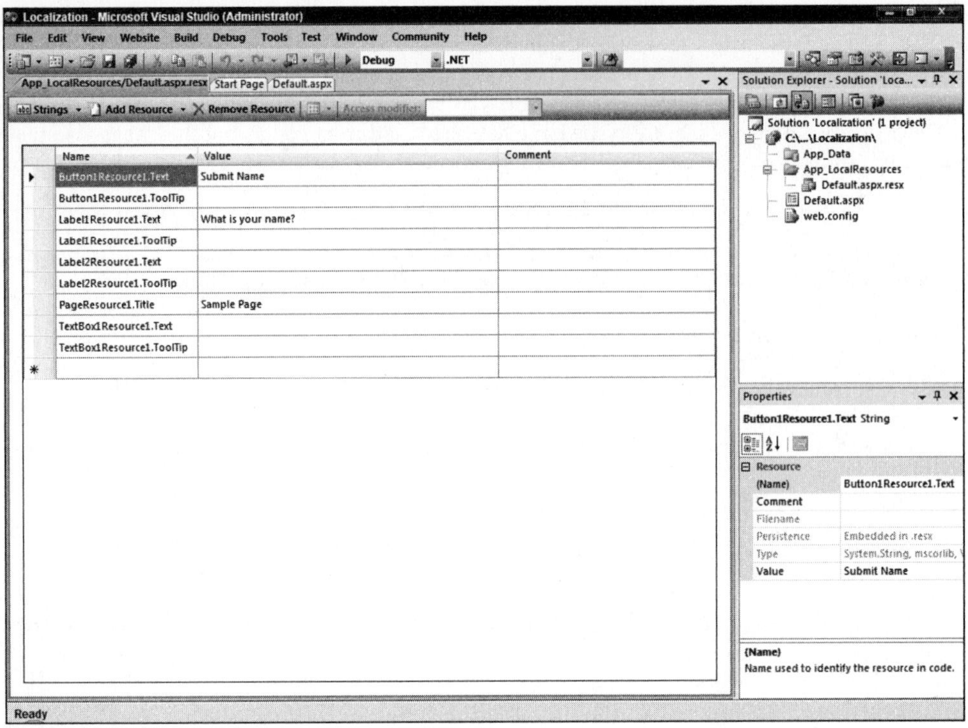

Figure 13-9

In the figure, note that a couple of properties from each of the server controls have been defined in the resource file. For instance, the Button server control has its `Text` and `ToolTip` properties exposed in this resource file, and the Visual Studio localization tool has pulled the default `Text` property value from the control based on what you placed there. Looking more closely at the Button server control constructions in this file, you can see that both the `Text` and `ToolTip` properties have a defining `Button1Resource1` value preceding the property name. This key is used in the Button server control you saw earlier.

```
<asp:Button ID="Button1"
 runat="server" Text="Submit Name"
 meta:resourcekey="Button1Resource1" />
```

You can see that a `meta:resourcekey` attribute has been added and, in this case, it references `Button1Resource1`. All the properties using this key in the resource file (for example, the `Text` and `ToolTip` properties) are applied to this Button server control at runtime.

Adding Another Language Resource File

Now that the `Default.aspx.resx` file is in place, this is a file for an invariant culture. No culture is assigned to this resource file. If no culture can be determined, this resource file is then utilized. To add another resource file for the `Default.aspx` page that handles another language altogether, you copy and paste the `Default.aspx.resx` file into the same `App_LocalResources` folder and rename the newly copied file. If you use `Default.aspx.fi-FI.resx`, you give the following keys the following values to make a Finnish language resource file:

```
Button1Resource1.Text    Lähetä Nimi
Label1Resource1.Text     Mikä sinun nimi on?
PageResource1.Title      Näytesivu
```

You want to create a custom resource in both resource files, using the key `Label2Answer`. The `Default.aspx.resx` file should have the following new key:

```
Label2Answer     Hello
```

Now you can add the key `Label2Answer` to the `Default.aspx.fi-FI.resx` file, as shown here:

```
Label2Answer     Hei
```

You now have resources for specific controls and a resource that you can access later programmatically.

Finalizing the Building of the Default.aspx Page

To finalize the `Default.aspx` page, you want to work with the `Button1_Click()` event so that when the end user enters a name into the textbox and clicks the Submit Name button, the `Label2` server control provides a greeting to him or her that is pulled from the local resource files. When all is said and done, you should have a `Default.aspx` page that resembles the one in Listing 13-12.

Listing 13-12: The final Default.aspx page

```
<%@ Page Language="C#" meta:resourcekey="PageResource1" %>

<script runat="server">

    protected void Button1_Click(object sender, EventArgs e)
    {

        Label2.Text = GetLocalResourceObject("Label2Answer") + " " +
            TextBox1.Text;

    }

</script>

<html xmlns="http://www.w3.org/1999/xhtml">
<head runat="server">
    <title>Sample Page</title>
</head>
<body>
    <form id="form1" runat="server">
    <div>
        <asp:ScriptManager ID="ScriptManager1" runat="server">
        </asp:ScriptManager>
        <asp:Label ID="Label1" runat="server" Text="What is your name?"
         meta:resourcekey="Label1Resource1"></asp:Label><br />
```

Continued

Listing 13-12: The final Default.aspx page *(continued)*

```
                <br />
                <asp:UpdatePanel ID="UpdatePanel1" runat="server">
                    <ContentTemplate>
                        <asp:TextBox ID="TextBox1" runat="server"
                         meta:resourcekey="TextBox1Resource1"></asp:TextBox> 
                        <asp:Button ID="Button1" runat="server" Text="Submit Name"
                         OnClick="Button1_Click"
                            meta:resourcekey="Button1Resource1" /><br />
                        <br />
                        <asp:Label ID="Label2" runat="server"
                         meta:resourcekey="Label2Resource1"></asp:Label>
                    </ContentTemplate>
                </asp:UpdatePanel>
        </div>
        </form>
    </body>
    </html>
```

In addition to pulling local resources using the `meta:resourcekey` attribute in the server controls on the page to get at the exposed attributes, you can also get at any property value contained in the local resource file by using `GetLocalResourceObject()`. When using `GetLocalResourceObject()`, you simply use the name of the key as a parameter, as shown here:

```
GetLocalResourceObject("Label2Answer")
```

You could just as easily get at any of the controls property values from the resource file programmatically, using the same construct:

```
GetLocalResourceObject("Button1Resource1.Text")
```

With the code from Listing 13-12 in place and the resource files completed, you can run the page, entering a name in the textbox and then clicking the button to get a response, as illustrated in Figure 13-10.

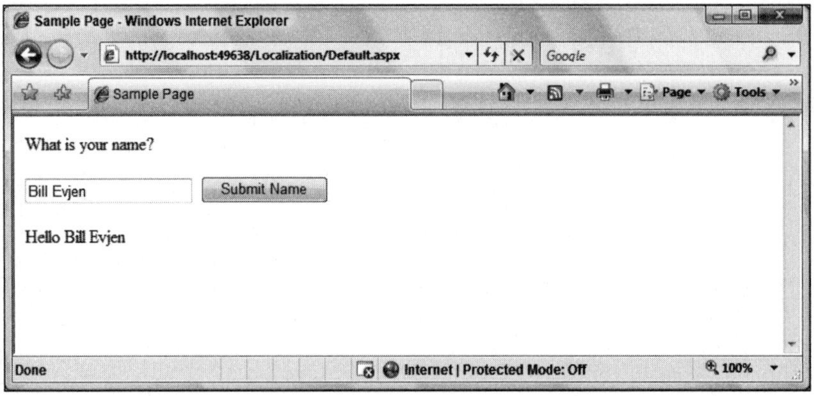

Figure 13-10

What happened behind the scenes that caused this page to be constructed in this manner? First, only two resource files, `Default.aspx.resx` and `Default.aspx.fi-FI.resx`, are available. The `Default.aspx.resx` resource file is the invariant culture resource file, whereas the `Default.aspx.fi-FI.resx` resource file is for a specific culture (`fi-FI`). Because I requested the `Default.aspx` page and my browser is set to `en-US` as my preferred culture, ASP.NET found the local resources for the `Default.aspx` page. From there, ASP.NET made a check for an `en-US`–specific version of the `Default.aspx` page. Because there is not a specific page for the `en-US` culture, ASP.NET made a check for an `EN` (neutral culture) specific page. Not finding a page for the `EN` neutral culture, ASP.NET was then forced to use the invariant culture resource file of `Default.aspx.resx`, producing the page presented in Figure 13-10.

Now, if you set your IE language preference as `fi-FI` and rerun the `Default.aspx` page, you see a Finnish version of the page, as illustrated in Figure 13-11.

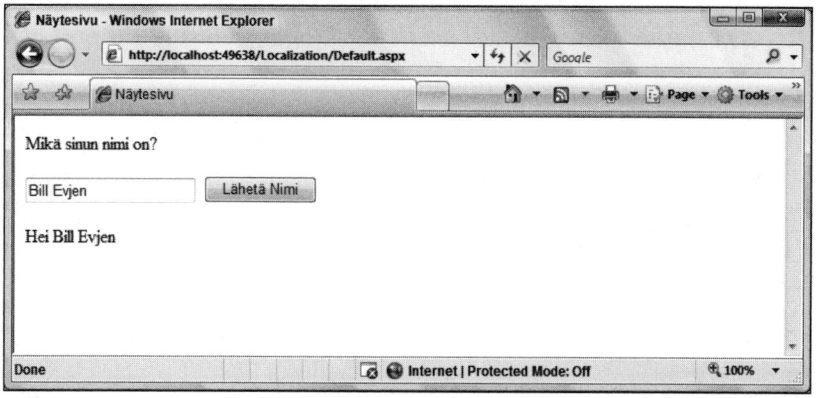

Figure 13-11

In this case, having set my IE language preference to fi-FI, I am presented with this culture's page instead of the invariant culture page that was presented earlier. ASP.NET found this specific culture through use of the `Default.aspx.fi-FI.resx` resource file.

You can see that all the control properties that were translated and placed within the resource file are utilized automatically by ASP.NET, including the page title presented in the title bar of IE.

Neutral Cultures Are Generally More Preferred

When you are working with the resource files from this example, note that one of the resources is for a *specific culture*. The `Default.aspx.fi-FI.resx` file is for a specific culture — the Finnish language as spoken in Finland. Another option would be to make this file work not for a specific culture but instead for a neutral culture. To accomplish this task, you simply name the file `Default.aspx.FI.resx` instead. In this example, it really does not make that much difference because no other countries speak Finnish. It would make sense for languages such as German, Spanish, or French. These languages are spoken in multiple countries. For instance, if you are going to have a Spanish version of the `Default.aspx` page, you could definitely build it for a specific culture, such as `Default.aspx.es-MX.resx`. This construction is for the Spanish language as spoken in Mexico. With this in place, if someone requests the `Default.aspx` page with the language setting of `es-MX`, that user is provided with the contents of this resource file. However, what if the requestor has a setting of `es-ES`? He will not get the `Default.aspx.es-MX.resx` resource file; instead he will get the invariant culture resource file, `Default.aspx.resx`. If you are going to make only a single translation into German, Spanish, or another language for your site or any of your pages, you want to construct the resource files to be for neutral cultures rather than for specific cultures.

If you have the resource file `Default.aspx.ES.resx`, then it won't matter if the end user's preferred setting is set to `es-MX`, `es-ES`, or even `es-AR` — the user will get the appropriate ES neutral culture version of the page.

Making Use of Global Resources

Besides using only local resources that specifically deal with a particular page in your ASP.NET application, you also have the option of creating *global* resources that can be used across multiple pages. To create a resource file that can be utilized across the entire application, right-click on the project in the Solution Explorer of Visual Studio and select Add New Item. In the Add New Item dialog, select Resource file.

Selecting this option provides you with a `Resource.resx` file. Visual Studio places this file in a new folder called `App_GlobalResources`. Again, this first file is the invariant culture resource file. Add a single string resource, giving it the key of `PrivacyStatement` and a value of some kind (a long string).

After you have the invariant culture resource file completed, the next step is to add another resource file, but this time name it `Resource.fi-FI.resx`. Again, give this resource file a string key of `PrivacyStatement` and a different value altogether from the one you used in the other resource file.

The idea of a global resource file is that you have access to these resources across your entire application. You can gain access to the values that you place in these files in several ways. One way is to work the value directly into any of your server control declarations. For instance, you can place this privacy statement in a Label server control, as presented in Listing 13-13.

Listing 13-13: Using a global resource directly in a server control

```
<asp:Label ID="Label1" runat="server"
 Text='<%$ Resources: Resource, PrivacyStatement %>'></asp:Label>
```

With this construction in place, you can now grab the appropriate value of the `PrivacyStatement` global resource, according to the language preference of the end user requesting the page. To make this work, you use the keyword `Resources` followed by a colon. Next, you specify the name of the resource file class. In this case, the name of the resource file is `Resource` because this statement goes to the `Resource.resx` and `Resource.fi-FI.resx` files in order to find what it needs. After the particular resource file to use, the next item in the statement is the key — in this case, `PrivacyStatement`.

Another way of achieving the same result is to use some built-in dialogs within Visual Studio. To accomplish this task, highlight the server control you want in Visual Studio from Design view so that the control appears within the Properties window. For my example, I highlighted a Label server control. From the Properties window, you click the button within the Expressions property. This launches the Expressions dialog and enables you to bind the `PrivacyStatement` value to the `Text` property of the control. This is illustrated in Figure 13-12.

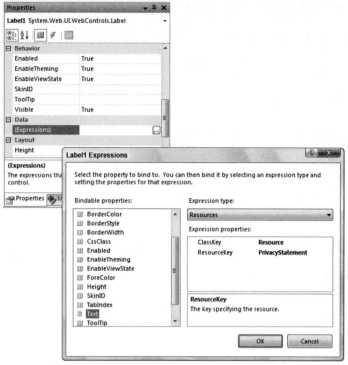

Figure 13-12

To make this work, highlight the Text property in the Bindable properties list. You then select an expression type from a drop-down list on the right-hand side of the dialog. Your options include AppSettings, ConnectionStrings, and Resources. Select the Resources option, and you are asked for the ClassKey and ResourceKey property values. The ClassKey is the name of the file that should be utilized. In this example, the name of the file is Resource.resx. Therefore, use the Resource keyword as a value. You are provided with a drop-down list in the ResourceKey property section with all the keys available in this file. Because only a single key exists at this point, you find only the PrivacyStatement key in this list. Make this selection and click the OK button. The Label server control changes and appears as shown earlier in Listing 13-13.

One nice feature is that the resources provided via global resources are available in a strongly typed manner. For instance, you can programmatically get at a global resource value by using the construction presented in Listing 13-14.

Listing 13-14: Programmatically getting at global resources

```
Label1.Text = Resources.Resource.PrivacyStatement;
```

In Figure 13-13, you can see that you have full IntelliSense for these resource values.

Figure 13-13

Looking at the Resource Editor

Visual Studio 2008 provides an editor for working with resource files. You have already seen some of the views available from this editor. Resources are categorized visually by the data type of the resource. So far, this chapter has dealt only with the handling of strings, but other categories exist (as well as images, icons, audio files, miscellaneous files, and other items). These options are illustrated in Figure 13-14.

Figure 13-14

Script Localization with Static Files

When working with the localization of your ASP.NET AJAX applications, another important aspect of localization is in how the scripts themselves are localized. For instance, if alerts and other items in your scripts require localization, you can perform localization to make a script for each language or culture that you are working with to get your ASP.NET page to work with the correct script based upon the end user's culture setting.

To show an example of this in action, Listing 13-15 provides a simple ASP.NET application that makes use of server-side JavaScript files.

Listing 13-15: Localizing client-side JavaScript files

```
<%@ Page Language="C#" %>

<html xmlns="http://www.w3.org/1999/xhtml">
<head runat="server">
    <title>Script Localization</title>

    <script type="text/javascript">

        function pageLoad() {
            populateItems();
        }

    </script>
</head>
<body>
    <form id="form1" runat="server">
    <div>
        <asp:ScriptManager ID="ScriptManager1" runat="server"
          EnableScriptLocalization="true">
            <Scripts>
                <asp:ScriptReference Path="~/Scripts/ScriptLocalization.js"
                  ResourceUICultures="fi-FI" />
            </Scripts>
        </asp:ScriptManager>
        <span id="Label1"></span><br />
        <span id="Label2"></span>
    </div>
    </form>
</body>
</html>
```

This page is quite simple in that only two <span> elements are populated by a script (shown shortly) that contains the function populateItems(). Since you are going to want your application to be localized based on the end user's culture setting in their browser, you are going to need to extend upon the ScriptManager control.

The first step is to set the `EnableScriptLocalization` attribute to `true` within the ScriptManager control. The ScriptManager section can take a `<Scripts>` section and within this, you are able to reference script files directly using the `<ScriptReference>` control.

The reference is to the default script that you are going to use. In this case, it is the `ScriptLocalization.js` file. Through the `ResourceUICultures` attribute, you can specify the cultures you are going to work with directly.

This example has only two resource files. Create a new folder called Scripts within your project and add two script files — `ScriptLocalization.js` and `ScriptLocalization.fi-FI.js`. Your solution will look as presented here in Figure 13-15.

Figure 13-15

First, take a look at what is contained in the `ScriptLocalization.js` file. This is presented here in Listing 13-16.

Listing 13-16: ScriptLocalization.js

```
function populateItems() {
    $get('Label1').innerText = PageItems.Greeting;
    $get('Label2').innerText = PageItems.Question;
}

PageItems = {
    'Greeting': 'Hello World',
    'Question': 'How are you today?'
}
```

This script simply populates the `Label1` and `Label2` controls found on the ASP.NET page. Now to create the Finnish version of the script, you have to include everything that is included in this English version of the script, and change the string items to the correct Finnish equivalents (obviously). The Finnish version of the script file is presented here in Listing 13-17.

Listing 13-17: ScriptLocalization.fi-FI.js

```
function populateItems() {
    $get('Label1').innerText = PageItems.Greeting;
    $get('Label2').innerText = PageItems.Question;
}

PageItems = {
    'Greeting': 'Hei Maailma',
    'Question': 'Mitä sinulle kuuluu?'
}
```

Not only is much the same here, but it is important to notice the name of the file. The name of the file uses a specific culture value of `fi-FI`. It would have also been possible to use a neutral culture value in the name instead if you wished. If you chose this route, the name of the file would have been `ScriptLocalization.fi.js`.

Now let's go back to the ScriptManager control:

```
<asp:ScriptManager ID="ScriptManager1" runat="server"
 EnableScriptLocalization="true">
    <Scripts>
        <asp:ScriptReference Path="~/Scripts/ScriptLocalization.js"
         ResourceUICultures="fi-FI" />
    </Scripts>
</asp:ScriptManager>
```

One of the important settings here is the `ResourceUICultures` setting. This points the cultures of the files that you are going to work with. It expects to find the files for the other cultures in the exact same spot that you have the default file located in. In this case, the value of the `ResourceUICultures` setting is `fi-FI`. If you are working with multiple cultures, separate them with a comma.

```
<asp:ScriptManager ID="ScriptManager1" runat="server"
 EnableScriptLocalization="true">
    <Scripts>
        <asp:ScriptReference Path="~/Scripts/ScriptLocalization.js"
         ResourceUICultures="fi-FI, ru-RU" />
    </Scripts>
</asp:ScriptManager>
```

Running this page with your browser culture set at en-US and then again at fi-FI will produce the following results presented in Figure 13-16. Remember that for this all to work, you have to have the `Culture` and `UICulture` set to `auto` in either the `@Page` directive or within the `<globalization>` element of the `web.config` file.

Looking at the page source, you will notice that the correct `<script>` tag is added to the file based upon the culture setting used. If the user used something other than en-US or fi-FI, then the default `ScriptLocalization.js` file would be used.

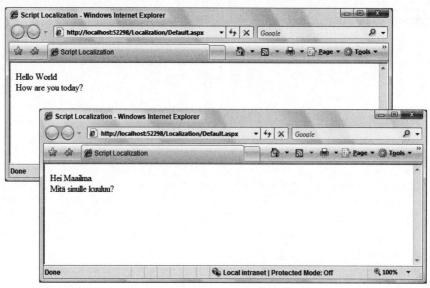

Figure 13-16

Embedding JavaScript Files

Another option for localizing your JavaScript files is to embed the files directly into the assembly. This approach is a bit different, but it also shows you how to achieve results similar to those just presented.

For this example, create an ASP.NET Web Application Project by selecting File ⇨ New ⇨ Project rather than File ⇨ New ⇨ Web Site. Instead of creating multiple scripts for each of the languages that you are going to want to work with, you store the language differences in resource files.

First, create a resource file called `PageItems.resx`. As before, this file contains two items only: Greeting and Question. Enter the same values you entered before. The other file to create is another resource file called `PageItems.fi-FI.resx` with the same keys as the other file. Figure 13-17 shows how both of these files should appear in the resource editor in Visual Studio 2008.

Once you have the resource files created in your project, the next step is to create a JavaScript file called `ScriptLocalization.js` that will use either of the resource files that you created. This resource file is presented here in Listing 13-18.

Listing 13-18: A JavaScript file that will work from resource files

```
function populateItems() {
    $get('Label1').innerText = PageItems.Greeting;
    $get('Label2').innerText = PageItems.Question;
}
```

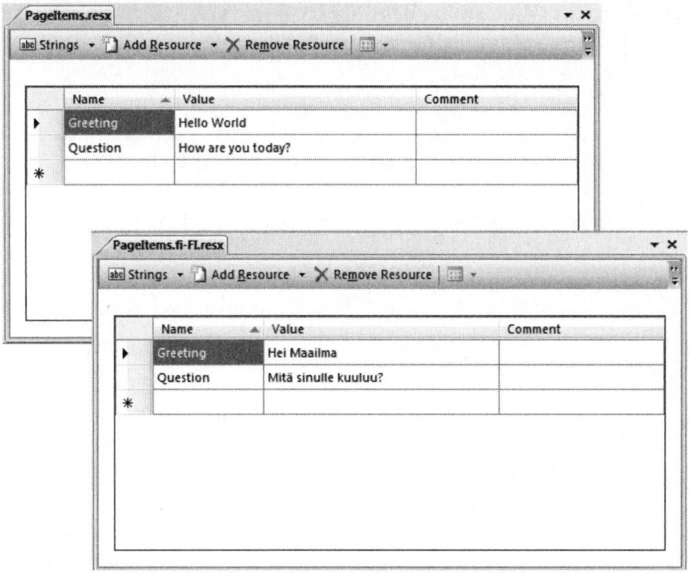

Figure 13-17

Again, the idea is that the page contains two `<span>` elements that will be populated with values from this script file. Remember that unlike the static script file approach shown earlier, in this case, there is only a single script file and it is using one of the appropriate resource files to finish how it is completed.

ASP.NET will find the appropriate items from the resource files through the namespace, `PageItems`, which is defined later in this example. Using this namespace, the `Greeting` and `Question` keys from the resource files can be accessed as is done in this example.

The last change you need to make to the `ScriptLocalization.js` file is to make the file an embedded resource. Meaning that it will be embedded into the application's DLL when the application is compiled. To accomplish this task, highlight the JavaScript file in the Visual Studio Solution Explorer and change the Build Action property (found in the Properties dialog) from Content to Embedded Resource, as shown here in Figure 13-18.

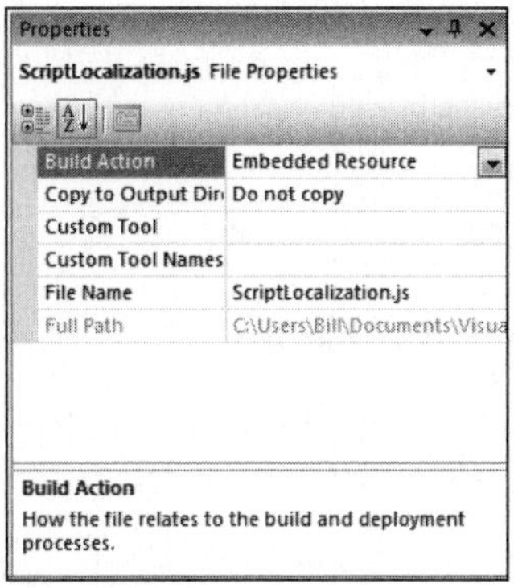

Figure 13-18

Next, expand the Properties folder in the Solution Explorer and find the `AssemblyInfo.cs` file. Open this file and add some references to the items that you just created. At the bottom of the file, add the two lines that are presented in Listing 13-19.

Listing 13-19: Adding references to the AssemblyInfo.cs file

```
[assembly: WebResource("WebApplication1.ScriptLocalization.js",
    "application/x-javascript")]
[assembly: ScriptResource("WebApplication1.ScriptLocalization.js",
    "WebApplication1.PageItems", "PageItems")]
```

The first thing to add is a `WebResource` value. You also need to reference the `System.Web.UI` namespace for this to work. The first parameter of this is the fully qualified script. In this case, it is the name of your solution (in my case, `WebApplication1`), followed by the script file itself.

```
WebApplication1.ScriptLocalization.js
```

My qualification looks like this because my `ScriptLocalization.js` file is located in the root folder of my Web solution. If I kept my scripts in a folder called Scripts, then I would have to include the folder in the qualification as well.

```
WebApplication1.Scripts.ScriptLocalization.js
```

The second parameter used in the `WebResource` declaration is the MIME type of the file. In this case, it is `application/x-javascript`.

The next assembly declaration is the `ScriptResource` line. In this part, again you fully qualify the script you are working with and follow that with the link to the resource files that you are associating to this script file. Since the script files that you are working with start with the word `PageItems`, this is what you use in the specification.

```
WebApplication1.PageItems
```

In this association to the resource files, you do not include the culture part of the names nor the `.resx` file extension. The last parameter of this line is the single word `PageItems`. This is the keyword that you are using in the JavaScript file to associate as the namespace in working with the keys from the file. For example, in the script file there is use of the `PageItems.Greeting` object. The `PageItems` part of this statement comes from this declaration.

The last part of this example puts it all together in the Web page that you are working with. Listing 13-20 shows an example of this page.

Listing 13-20: Putting everything together in the WebForm1.aspx page

```
<%@ Page Language="C#" AutoEventWireup="true" CodeBehind="WebForm1.aspx.cs"
    Inherits="WebApplication1.WebForm1" Culture="auto" UICulture="auto" %>

<html xmlns="http://www.w3.org/1999/xhtml">
<head id="Head1" runat="server">
```

Listing 13-20: Putting everything together in the WebForm1.aspx page *(continued)*

```
            <title>Script Localization</title>

            <script type="text/javascript">

                function pageLoad() {
                    populateItems();
                }

            </script>
        </head>
        <body>
            <form id="form1" runat="server">
            <div>
                <asp:ScriptManager ID="ScriptManager1" runat="server"
                 EnableScriptLocalization="true">
                  <Scripts>
                     <asp:ScriptReference Assembly="WebApplication1"
                      Name="WebApplication1.ScriptLocalization.js" />
                  </Scripts>

                </asp:ScriptManager>
                <span id="Label1"></span><br />
                <span id="Label2"></span>
            </div>
            </form>
        </body>
        </html>
```

There are a few things to notice here. First, you will need to set the `Culture` and `UICulture` to a value of `auto` in either the file (as is done here), or in the `web.config` file within the `<globalization>` element.

The `pageLoad()` function calls the `ScriptLocalization.js` file's `populateItems()` function. This script is found through the script reference done with the ScriptReference control within the ScriptManager control.

```
    <asp:ScriptManager ID="ScriptManager1" runat="server"
     EnableScriptLocalization="true">
       <Scripts>
          <asp:ScriptReference Assembly="WebApplication1"
           Name="WebApplication1.ScriptLocalization.js" />
       </Scripts>
    </asp:ScriptManager>
```

It is important that the ScriptManager has the `EnableScriptLocalization` property set to `true` for this all to work. The ScriptReference control points to the embedded resource through the `Assembly` property and this is set to the name of the Solution followed by a `Name` property value of the file that is used. Again, this is the fully qualified reference to the file.

Compiling this solution, you will find that everything is embedded and you will find the alternate resource files (such as the fi-FI resource file that you created) is also embedded into the solution (as illustrated in this view of the Solution Explorer from Figure 13-19). Click on the Show All Files button if you do not see the bin folder in your solution.

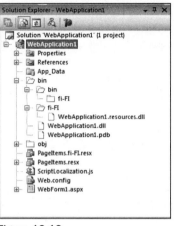

Figure 13-19

Running this page, produces the simple results presented in Figure 13-20.

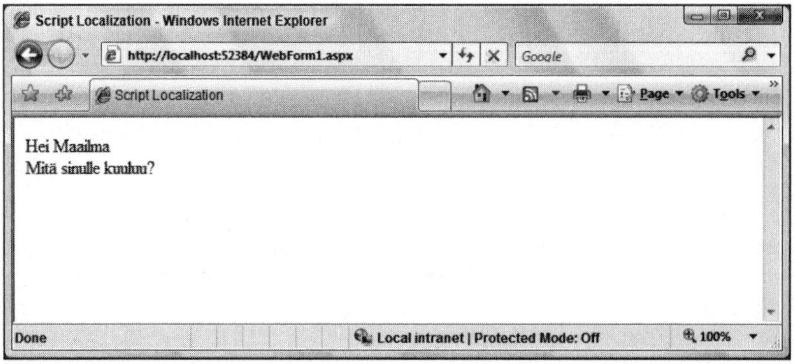

Figure 13-20

Summary

There is tremendous value in building your application to display what the end user is expecting to see when working with the pages. It is quite possible that your end users are from different places in the world and are expecting the page to adapt to the format they defined in their browser's operating system's culture settings.

This chapter looked at some of the issues you face when localizing your ASP.NET AJAX applications and some of the built-in tools provided via both Visual Studio and the .NET Framework to make this process easier for you.

This chapter took a look at not only how to localize your ASP.NET pages but also how to localize the scripts that also change items on the page.

14

State Management

Simply put — building ASP.NET applications is more difficult than other types of applications, such as building a Windows Forms application, mainly because Web applications are a stateless type of application.

The Internet is *stateless* by nature. You are simply making requests and responses (generally over HTTP). The server receives an HTTP request for a particular page and sends the caller the requested page (the response). The server that is sending the response does not keep track of who made the request. Every request is equal in the server's eyes.

When the same calling application makes a second request, the server gives it the second piece of information but still does not house any information about this calling application. The server does not know that this application is the same one that just recently requested the first piece of logic.

This creates a problem if you want your Web application to remember information about the calling application. Remembering the calling application and being able to make a distinction between requests allows end users to work through an application in a continuous manner. You may want your application to retain certain information: who the users are, their preferences, or any other pertinent information about them as they makes multiple requests. You do this by using varying techniques that you can apply throughout your Web application's code.

One of the common techniques of the past and present is to use the `Session` object, but by simply using ASP.NET, you have so much more at your disposal. ASP.NET offers a wide variety of features and techniques to apply when working with state management. You might have used many of these techniques with Web applications that you developed in the past.

Caching on the other hand, although also focused on storing information, is a means to provide a better experience for your end users by making the application load and perform faster than otherwise. This chapter takes a look at both using state management and caching with your ASP.NET AJAX pages.

Understanding State in .NET

If you are working with state management in your Web application, it is important to understand state as it works within .NET as a whole. The .NET Framework and ASP.NET provide a plethora of options in dealing with state. Some of your server-side options are described in the following table.

Session Type	Description
Application	Using the `Application` object, you can store state that is applicable to all users. You are unable to use this for providing different state options to different users.
Cache	Using the `Cache` object, you are able to also store state for every user of the application. This object supports the ability to expire the cache and it also provides the ability to set dependencies on how the cache is expired.
Database-driven `Session`	A means of using the `Session` object and having all the state stored safely on a SQL server.
Session	Using the `Session` object, you are able to store state on the server on a per user basis. The `Session` object allows you to store the state in-proc (in the same process as the application), out-of-proc (in a different process), or even using the aforementioned database approach.

If it were all about the server-side options, it would not be that long of a story to tell. ASP.NET also includes a good list of client-side state management techniques that make the process of storing state rather easy. The following table defines your client-side options.

Session Type	Description
ControlState	A means of providing state to controls (for the control developer) that is quite similar to ViewState.
Cookie	A means of storing state directly in the file system of the client. Cookies can be rejected by clients.
Hidden Field	Using hidden fields, you can store state for a user directly in the code of the page to use on subsequent requests that are posted back to the server.
Querystring	Using the querystring capabilities provided, you are able to store state within the actual URL on a per user basis.
ViewState	Provides the ability to use encoded state within the page code.

As you can see, there are a number of ways to work with state (not even all of them are listed). It is important to understand that there isn't a right or wrong way to work with state. It really has a lot to do with what you are trying to achieve and work with in your application. Next, this chapter will look at some of these options.

Understanding Sessions

Sessions within an ASP.NET application enable users to easily maintain application state. Sessions will remain with the user as he works through repeated calls to an application for a defined period.

Sessions are easily created, and it is just as easy to retrieve information from them. Use the following code to create a session for the user or calling application that can be accessed later in the application or to assign a value to an already established session.

```
Session["EmployeeID"] = Value1;
```

This will assign what was being held in the variable `Value1` to the `EmployeeID Session` object. To retrieve this information from the session and then use it in your code, do the following:

```
Value2 = Session["EmployeeID"];
```

In ASP.NET, session timeout is similar to what it was in classic ASP — a session would timeout on the user after 20 minutes. If the user opened a page within a Web application (thereby creating a session) and then walked away for a cup of coffee, when the user came back to the page 40 minutes later, the session would not be there for them. You could get around this by going into the server and changing the time allotted to the session timeout property, but this was cumbersome and required that you stop the server and then start it again for the changes to take effect. In addition, because sessions are resource intensive, you would not want to store too many sessions for too long.

With ASP.NET it is now possible to change the session timeout property quite easily. On the application level, it is now stored in the `web.config` file. The `machine.config` file stores the default timeout setting for the entire server. By changing the setting in the `web.config` file, you can effectively change the timeout property of sessions within the application. The great thing about changing this property within this XML application file is that the server does not have to be stopped and started for the changes to take effect. After the `web.config` file is saved with its changes, the changes take effect immediately.

The part of the `web.config` file that deals with session state management is the `<sessionState>` node as presented in Listing 14-1.

Listing 14-1: Reviewing the <sessionState> element in the web.config file

```
<sessionState
    mode="InProc"
    stateConnectionString="tcpip=127.0.0.1:42424"
    sqlConnectionString="data source=127.0.0.1;user id=sa;password="
    cookieless="false"
    timeout="20" />
```

The `<sessionState>` node of the `web.config` file is where session state is managed. The property that you are concerned with now is the `timeout` property.

The `timeout` property is set to 20 (the default setting). This setting represents minutes of time. Therefore, if you want the users' sessions to last for one hour, you set the `timeout` property to 60.

Running Sessions In-Process

Presently, the default setting for sessions in ASP.NET stores the sessions in the in-process mode. Running sessions in-process means that the sessions are stored in the same process as the ASP. NET worker process. Therefore, if IIS is shut down and then brought back up again, all sessions are destroyed and unavailable to users. On mission-critical Web applications, this can be a nightmare.

In order to run the sessions in-process, set the mode property in the `<sessionState>` node to `InProc`. Running sessions in-process provides the application with the best possible performance.

The following table describes all the session modes available.

Mode	Description
InProc	Session state is in-process with the ASP.NET worker process. Running sessions InProc is the default setting.
Off	Session state is not available.
StateServer	Session state is using an out-of-process server to store state.
SQLServer	Session state is using an out-of-process SQL Server to store state.

Running Sessions Out of Process

It is possible to run sessions out of process. Running a session out of process allows IIS to be stopped and then restarted, while maintaining the user's sessions.

Along with the .NET Framework is a Windows service called ASPState. This service enables you to run sessions out of process, but it has to be started in order to use it to manage sessions.

To start the ASPState service, open the Command Prompt (Start ➪ Programs ➪ Accessories ➪ Command Prompt). On the Command Prompt line type the following command:

```
CD \WINDOWS\Microsoft.NET\Framework\v2.0.50727
```

Next, press Enter. This changes the directory of the command prompt. After typing that line in the command prompt, type:

```
net start aspnet_state
```

This turns on the session out-of-process capabilities, as shown in Figure 14-1.

The path shown is for Windows XP Professional. If you are on a different operating system, the path could be different. Also, look at the path within Windows Explorer and view the version of the .NET Framework that you are running. Since you are working with the .NET Framework 3.0 or 3.5, then you will find this file in the 2.0 version of the framework, as shown in the previous example.

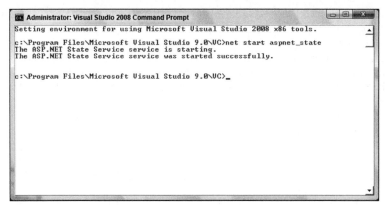

Figure 14-1

It is also possible to turn on the ASP.NET State Service through the Services console. In Windows XP, open the console by selecting Start ⇨ Control Panel ⇨ Performance and Maintenance ⇨ Administrative Tools ⇨ Services. You are then presented with a list of services available on the server. In Windows XP, you can start or stop the ASP.NET State Service by clicking the appropriate link. In Windows Vista you will find the Services option in the Administrator Tools section. The Services application is presented in Figure 14-2.

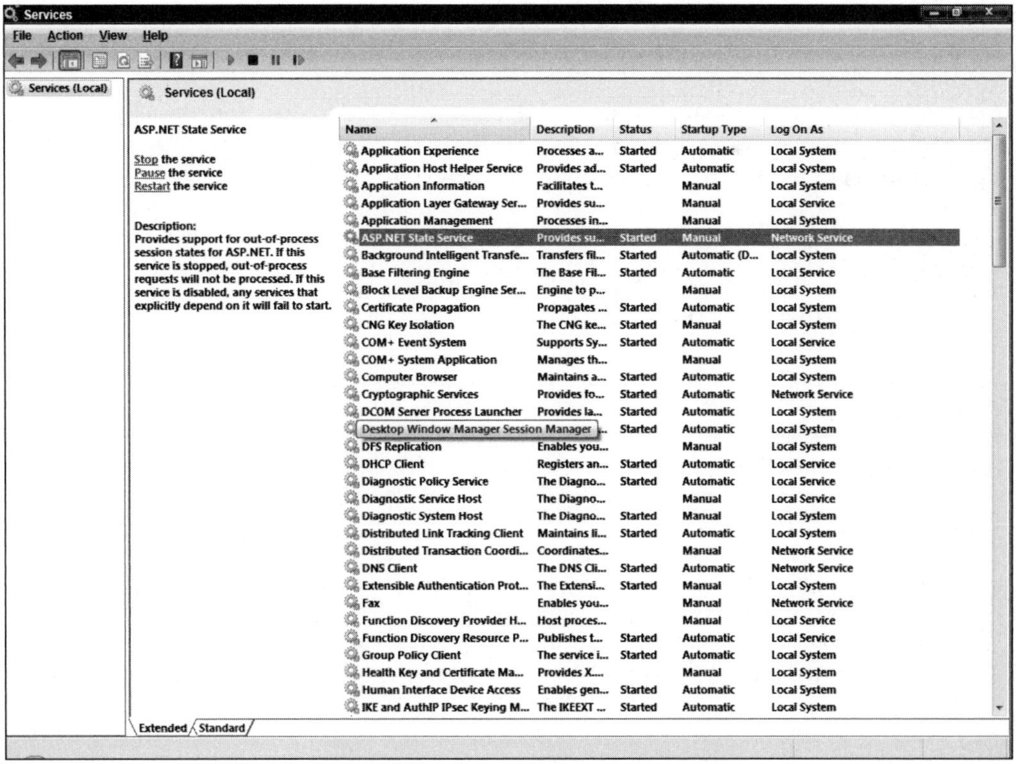

Figure 14-2

Once the out-of-process mode is enabled, you can change the settings in the `<sessionState>` node of the `web.config` file so that all the users sessions are run in this manner. You do this by setting the mode to `StateServer`, as illustrated in Listing 14-2.

Listing 14-2: Setting the Session object to use the StateServer option

```
<sessionState
    mode="StateServer"
    stateConnectionString="tcpip=127.0.0.1:42424"
    sqlConnectionString="data source=127.0.0.1;user id=sa;password="
    cookieless="false"
    timeout="20" />
```

Now the user can turn IIS off and then on again and her sessions will remain intact, although doing this is a little more resource-intensive than running the sessions in-process.

If the mode is set to `StateServer`, the server looks to the `stateConnectionString` property to assign the sessions to a specified server and port. In this case, which is the default setting, it is set to the local server. You can easily change this so that the sessions are stored on a completely separate server.

Running sessions out of process is a great advantage with ASP.NET. This is a great tool when running Web applications in a Web farm where you are unsure which server the user will navigate to. This gives you the ability to move users from one server to another and yet maintain their state.

Maintaining Sessions on SQL Server

Another option to run sessions out of process is to employ SQL Server to store the user sessions. Storing sessions in SQL Server also enables users to move from one server to another and maintain their state. It is the same as the `StateServer` mode but instead stores the sessions in SQL Server.

If you installed the .NET Framework, you also installed a mini-version of SQL Server on your computer. This SQL Server–lite version enables you to store your sessions to use for state management. It is recommended, however, that you use a full-blown version of SQL Server, such as SQL Server 2008. This is a more dependable solution.

The first thing to do in order to use SQL Server as a repository of your sessions is to create the database within SQL that ASP.NET can use. Included in the version folder of ASP.NET (found at `C:\WINDOWS\Microsoft.NET\Framework\v2.0.50727`) are two scripts that work with SQL Server session management. The first is the install script, `InstallSqlState.sql`. This script instructs SQL Server which database tables and procedures to create. You can look at the script instructions, which are quite readable, by opening the script in Notepad.

If you ever wish to remove these tables and stored procedures from SQL Server, use the uninstall script, `UninstallSqlState.sql`.

If you wish to use SQL Server to manage your sessions, run the install script. To do this, open up the command prompt again and navigate to the version folder of ASP.NET that you are running. On the command line, type:

```
OSQL -S localhost -U sa -P <InstallSqlState.sql
```

The OSQL utility enables you to enter Transact-SQL statements, system procedures, and script files. This utility uses ODBC to communicate with the server. Running this command creates the tables and procedures needed to run the SQL Server session management option. The notation –S in the command line is specifying the location of the server that is to be used. In this case, you are using localhost, meaning your local server.

The notation -U refers to the SQL server's assigned username to gain access. In this case, it is just the typical sa.

The notation -P is for the SQL server's password, if required. In this case, it is not required. Therefore, you leave it blank.

Following the SQL server's setting specifications, you then specify the script that you wish to install, InstallSqlState.sql. This installs what is necessary to run SQL Server session management.

After you have created the tables and procedures necessary, change the <sessionState> node of the web.config file, as shown in Listing 14-3.

Listing 14-3: Using SQL Server as a state server

```
<sessionState
   mode="SQLServer"
   stateConnectionString="tcpip=127.0.0.1:42424"
   sqlConnectionString="data source=127.0.0.1;user id=sa;password="
   cookieless="false"
   timeout="20" />
```

To use SQL Server to manage sessions, the mode of the <sessionState> node needs to be set to SQLServer. After the mode is set to SQLServer, ASP.NET then looks to the sqlConnectionString property to find the SQL server to connect to when storing state. The value of this property should be set so that the data source is the server where the SQL and any needed login information are located.

Deciding on the State of Sessions

The mode you choose for running sessions within your Web application makes a considerable difference in the performance, functionality, and reliability of your Web application.

Which mode should you choose? The following list summarizes the best conditions for each option:

❑ InProc: The session is run in the same process as the ASP.NET worker process. Therefore, this option should be used when maintaining sessions is not mission critical to the application. This option has the best performance possible out of all the choices.

❑ StateServer: This Windows Service option runs the sessions out of process and is, therefore, best when used on multiple servers or when sessions need to be maintained if IIS is stopped and then restarted. This option provides better performance than the other out-of-process option, SQLServer.

❑ SQLServer: This out-of-process option is the most reliable choice because the sessions are stored directly in SQL Server. Even though this is the most reliable choice, this option ranks worst in performance.

Cookieless Session State

All the options mentioned so far also allow you to set the sessions so that they employ a cookieless option. This is for visitors to your site who choose to have cookies disabled in their browsers. You enable the cookieless-session-state environment by setting the `cookieless` property in the `<sessionState>` node of the `web.config` file to `true`, as shown here in Listing 14-4.

Listing 14-4: Providing a cookieless session state

```
<sessionState
   mode="StateServer"
   stateConnectionString="tcpip=127.0.0.1:42424"
   sqlConnectionString="data source=127.0.0.1;user id=sa;password="
   cookieless="true"
   timeout="20" />
```

ASP.NET embeds the user's session directly into the URL. When a user calls an ASP.NET page with a URL, the URL is rendered to contain the user's session ID in the middle of the URL itself.

For an example of this, use the same session counter method that you used earlier in this chapter and change the `web.config` file so that the `cookieless` property is set to `True`. Figure 14-3 shows an example of running the same Web application with this setting in place.

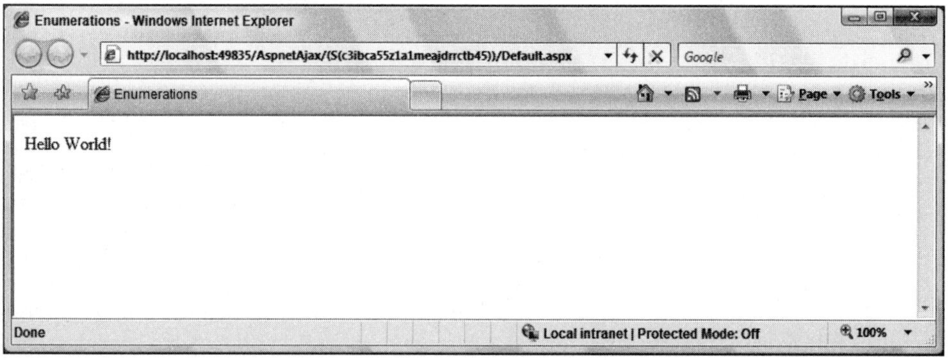

Figure 14-3

The URL in the browser's address box now contains the session ID right in the middle:

```
http://localhost/AspnetAjax/(S(c3ibca55z1a1meajdrrctb45))/Default.aspx
```

Because you set the `web.config` file to perform cookieless sessions, it gave the user a session ID of (`z5wjrf452csfky55cny15y3e`). ASP.NET uses this to identify the user on any subsequent Web requests. The drawback is that the user could change the contents of his session, thus destroying the session.

Using the Application Object

Just as you can use the Session object, you are able to use the Application object within your ASP. NET applications. The Application object is a shared container for managing state within your applications. This object enables you to store variables or object references that are available to all the visitors to the Web site for the life of the application. Unlike the Session object, the Application object can only run in-process, meaning that it can only run in the same process as ASP.NET. This means that if the ASP.NET is shut down for any reason, all Application data is lost.

Even though there are some limitations when compared to Session objects, you will find many benefits to using Application objects within your ASP.NET applications. Next, this chapter takes a quick look at how to use an Application objects within your code.

Very much like working with sessions, working with an Application object is easy. First, to create an Application instance, you just assign a value to the Application object as shown here:

```
Application["City"] = "Helsinki";
```

It is also just as easy to assign a variable the value of the Application object as shown in the following code:

```
string ProgramCity = Application["City"];
```

You probably noticed that this syntax is the same as the syntax you use with sessions. There is, however, a big difference between the two that you should always be aware of. Because the Application object is an application-wide object that is accessible by all users of your Web application, two users could simultaneously attempt to update the same Application object. To resolve such possible conflicts, ASP.NET has provided two methods — Lock() and UnLock().

The idea is to lock down the Application object while the first user is updating it. This prevents a second user from changing any information before the first user has had the chance to make his changes. After the first user is finished making the update to the Application object, the Application object is unlocked, thereby allowing the second user to make his own changes. See how this is done in Listing 14-5.

To show the differences between Session and Application, build an ASP.NET page that uses both to keep track of the number of times that the page is accessed. Keep in mind that the Session is per user and that the Application is for the Web application as a whole and will continue to keep on counting the numbers of hits regardless of the number of different users or applications that are hitting the page.

Listing 14-5: Working with the Application object

```
<%@ Page Language="C#" %>

<script runat="server">

    protected void Page_Load(object sender, EventArgs e)
    {
        int appHits = ApplicationHits();
        int userHits = SessionHits();
```

Continued

Listing 14-5: Working with the Application object *(continued)*

```
            Label1.Text = userHits.ToString();
            Label2.Text = appHits.ToString();
        }

        public int ApplicationHits()
        {
            if (Application["ApplicationHitsCount"] == null)
            {
                Application.Lock();
                Application["ApplicationHitsCount"] = 1;
                Application.UnLock();
            }
            else
            {
                Application.Lock();
                Application["ApplicationHitsCount"] =
            ((int)Application["ApplicationHitsCount"]) + 1;
                Application.UnLock();
            }
            return (int)Application["ApplicationHitsCount"];
        }

        public int SessionHits()
        {
            if (Session["SessionHitsCount"] == null)
            {
                Session["SessionHitsCount"] = 1;
            }
            else
            {
                Session["SessionHitsCount"] =
                ((int)Session["SessionHitsCount"]) + 1;
            }
            return (int)Session["SessionHitsCount"];
        }

    </script>

    <html xmlns="http://www.w3.org/1999/xhtml">
    <head runat="server">
        <title>Working with the Application Object</title>
    </head>
    <body>
        <form id="form1" runat="server">
        <div>
            Session object count:
            <asp:Label ID="Label1" runat="server"></asp:Label><br /><br />
            Application object count:
            <asp:Label ID="Label2" runat="server"></asp:Label>
        </div>
        </form>
    </body>
    </html>
```

After you have you typed all the code, press F5 to build and start your Web application, it will invoke the two available methods. The first is the `SessionHits()` method. This method is counting the number of times that you, as a user, have accessed this method.

Now it is time to construct the other method, `ApplicationHits()`, counts the number of times that you, as a generic user, has accessed the page. If you keep hitting the refresh button both numbers will increment together as presented here in Figure 14-4.

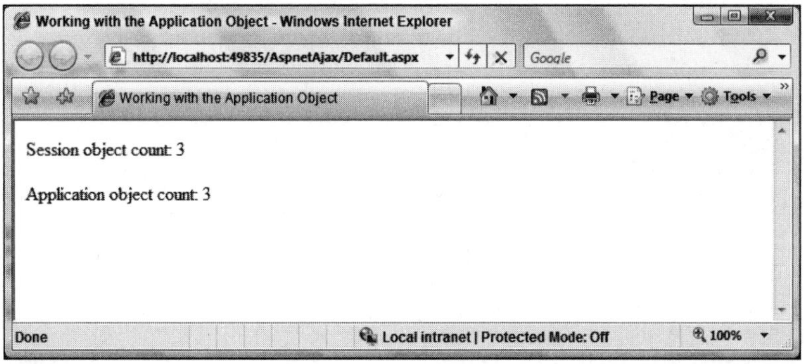

Figure 14-4

To see the differences between `Application` and `Session` objects, close the browser instance that is opened and, within Visual Studio 2008, deploy the Web application again by pressing F5 a second time. This time you are a second user, according to ASP.NET.

Now the `ApplicationHits()` and the `SessionHits()` methods are invoked again. This time notice that you are given the number 1 in the `Session` object because this is the first time that you have accessed this method as this particular user.

Now you will also notice that you will get a higher count through the `Application` object. This object has kept record of the total number of hits to the method regardless of the user (as shown here in Figure 14-5). It is a global variable that is saved for any user who can access it and saved for the lifetime of the Web application.

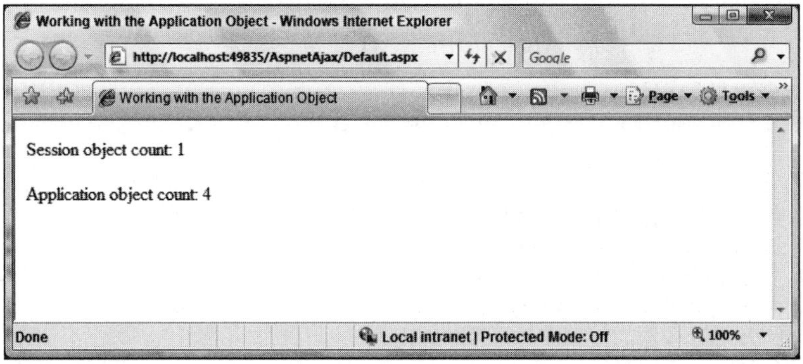

Figure 14-5

Now, change something in the `web.config` and recompile or refresh your page. This causes the old Web application to be killed and a new one to be put into its place, thereby creating a new Web application. If you go back to the page, you will notice that the count has once again started at the beginning.

One thing to note is that you should lock your `Application` object before you make a change to it to avoid concurrency issues. You do this with the `Lock()` method that is available with the `Application` object. After you are done making the necessary changes, you use the `UnLock()` method to open it up to any other users. If you do not use the `UnLock()` method, the .NET Framework does the unlock for you when the request completes, when the request times out, or when an unhandled error occurs during request execution and causes the request to fail. This automatic unlocking prevents the application from deadlocking.

Using Cookies

Cookies are key-value pairs that are stored on the client computer. Using cookies to persist information is a simple and easy option in ASP.NET if you need to maintain state when working with Web applications. Cookies are passed along with the HTTP request to the server and are used to identify the user upon receipt.

Advantages to Using Cookies

There are advantages to using cookies within your ASP.NET Web applications to store simple data. First, cookies do not require server resources because none of the cookies are stored on the server. Second, you can set cookies to expire when the browser is shut down or at any date in the future. Therefore, it is possible for the application to remember the user if he returns weeks or months later.

Disadvantages to Using Cookies

There are also some negatives to using cookies. One negative is that cookies need to be small. You cannot send large amounts of data to the clients to store on their machines. Generally, there is a 4,096-byte limit to the size of a cookie, limiting the types of data that you can store. For some applications, cookies can cause some serious security risks. It is easy for knowledgeable users to change cookies. This can be a major problem if you are using cookies to help users gain access to private information.

I know of a financial institution that was storing each user's account number as a cookie on the client's machine. The application that displayed information about the users' accounts used this cookie to give a user access to his account. You can see the problem here. All you had to do was change the numbers in the cookie and you were in someone else's account.

Listing 14-6 provides an example working with cookies.

Listing 14-6: Working with cookies

```
<%@ Page Language="C#" %>

<script runat="server">

    protected void Page_Load(object sender, EventArgs e)
    {
        HttpCookie MyCookie1 = Request.Cookies["CalcAccess"];
```

Listing 14-6: Working with cookies *(continued)*

```
        if (MyCookie1 != null)
        {
            Label1.Visible = true;
            Label1.Text = "You last accessed this calculator on: " +
                        MyCookie1["LastAccessed"];
        }
    }

    protected void Button1_Click(object sender, EventArgs e)
    {
        HttpCookie MyCookie = new HttpCookie("CalcAccess");

        Label2.Text = ((Int32.Parse(TextBox1.Text) +
                        Int32.Parse(TextBox2.Text)).ToString());

        MyCookie.Values.Add("LastAccessed", (DateTime.Now).ToString());
        Response.AppendCookie(MyCookie);
    }

</script>

<html xmlns="http://www.w3.org/1999/xhtml">
<head runat="server">
    <title>Working with Cookies</title>
</head>
<body>
    <form id="form1" runat="server">
    <div>
        <asp:ScriptManager ID="ScriptManager1" runat="server">
        </asp:ScriptManager>
        <p>
            <font face="Verdana" size="2"><strong>
             Enter two numbers and press the Add button.</strong></font></p>
        <p>
            <asp:TextBox ID="TextBox1" runat="server"></asp:TextBox></p>
        <p>
            <asp:TextBox ID="TextBox2" runat="server"></asp:TextBox></p>
        <asp:UpdatePanel ID="UpdatePanel1" runat="server">
            <ContentTemplate>
                <p>
                    <asp:Button ID="Button1" runat="server" Text="Add"
                     OnClick="Button1_Click"></asp:Button></p>
                <p>
                    <asp:Label ID="Label1" runat="server"
                     Visible="False"></asp:Label></p>
                <p>
                    <asp:Label ID="Label2" runat="server"></asp:Label></p>
            </ContentTemplate>
        </asp:UpdatePanel>
    </div>
    </form>
</body>
</html>
```

In this example, you placed a cookie on the client's machine whenever he accessed the button click event. Therefore, the second time the client clicked the Web application, he was posted a message indicating the last time he accessed the page. You will find that using cookies along with the consumption of Web applications is a good and easy way to maintain state in your applications.

Using ViewState

ViewState is another ASP.NET feature that allows you to easily maintain the state of your controls between roundtrips to the server. As the page makes this trip to the server and back, it remembers the state of each control, including the controls to which you bind data to, and it populates each control's status back into the control as the page is redrawn. It does this by including a hidden form field element within your form page. If you look at the source of your .aspx page, notice that there is a ViewState model right at the beginning of the form. Listing 14-7 displays the beginning of an ASP.NET page.

Listing 14-7: The top of the ASP.NET page

```
<!DOCTYPE html PUBLIC "-//W3C//DTD XHTML 1.0 Transitional//EN"
 "http://www.w3.org/TR/xhtml1/DTD/xhtml1-transitional.dtd">

<html xmlns="http://www.w3.org/1999/xhtml">
<head><title>
 Working with Cookies
</title></head>
<body>
    <form name="form1" method="post" action="Default6.aspx" id="form1">
<div>
<input type="hidden" name="__EVENTTARGET" id="__EVENTTARGET" value="" />
<input type="hidden" name="__EVENTARGUMENT" id="__EVENTARGUMENT" value="" />
<input type="hidden" name="__VIEWSTATE" id="__VIEWSTATE"
 value="/wEPDwUKLTg1OTgwNDQzOWRkMd6LzIcVw3I5z+i7jJ4zbUMFgQg=" />
```

This unreadable mess within the hidden form field shows the state of all the controls on the Web page. Instead of listing the state of the controls directly, this information is put into a format that is not readable by you and me, but is readable by the ASP.NET parser. The parser takes this data and repopulates that page's controls.

Toggling ViewState on and Off

Keeping the ViewState functionality on is not always a priority with every Web page you create. For this reason, you can turn off the ViewState, thus saving server resources and increasing the speed of your application. You can turn off this functionality in two ways. The first is to disable ViewState on the page level, and the other is to disable it on the control level. To disable ViewState for the entire page, turn off this functionality within the page directive.

To turn off the ViewState functionality for the entire page, just add the following attribute to the page directive at the top of the page:

```
<%@ Page EnableViewState="False" %>
```

It is also possible to disable ViewState on the control level. If maintaining a control's state is not an important feature of that control, turn it off. This mildly increases the performance of the page overall. To turn off ViewState for a control, add the `EnableViewState` attribute to the control, use the following:

```
<asp:Label id="Label1" Runat="server" EnableViewState="False" />
```

Paying attention to which pages and controls are ViewState-enabled leads to better overall application performance.

Extending ViewState

There are times when you might want to include user-specific information in your Web pages that needs to be carried across server roundtrips but is beyond the state of the control. In this case, it is possible to piggyback onto the ViewState functionality. In a sense, you are adding your own set of name-value pairs to ViewState. This bit of code shows a simple example of using this functionality to incorporate a page-count function.

```
ViewState["count"] = 1;
```

State Management and ASP.NET AJAX

The nice thing with ASP.NET AJAX is that you now have the ability to record state back to the server in a quick and little request. Before AJAX, you would have to make an entire post of the page and send back the entire page in the response just to write something to a `Session` object or some other aspect of recording state.

To provide an example of this, Listing 14-8 shows an ASP.NET AJAX page that is working with a `Session` object on the server and changing aspects of the page using an UpdatePanel server control.

Listing 14-8: Working with a Session object from an ASP.NET AJAX page

```
<%@ Page Language="C#" %>

<script runat="server">

    protected void Button1_Click(object sender, EventArgs e)
    {
        int resultCount = int.Parse(Session["count"].ToString());
        resultCount += 1;
        Session["count"] = resultCount.ToString();
        Label1.Text = "Hello " + TextBox1.Text;
        Label2.Text = "You have put in your name " + Session["count"] + " times.";
    }

    protected void Page_Load(object sender, EventArgs e)
    {
        if (!Page.IsPostBack)
        {
```

Continued

```
                Session["count"] = 0;
            }
        }
</script>

<html xmlns="http://www.w3.org/1999/xhtml">
<head runat="server">
    <title>Working with Sessions</title>
</head>
<body>
    <form id="form1" runat="server">
    <div>
        <asp:ScriptManager ID="ScriptManager1" runat="server" />
        <asp:TextBox ID="TextBox1" runat="server"></asp:TextBox>
        <asp:UpdatePanel ID="UpdatePanel1" runat="server">
            <ContentTemplate>
                <asp:Button ID="Button1" runat="server"
                 Text="Submit your name numerous times" OnClick="Button1_Click" />
                <br /><br />
                <asp:Label ID="Label1" runat="server"></asp:Label>
                <br />
                <asp:Label ID="Label2" runat="server"></asp:Label>
            </ContentTemplate>
        </asp:UpdatePanel>
    </div>
    </form>
</body>
</html>
```

For this example, type you name in the TextBox server control and then click the page's button a number of times. Each time you click on the button the page count is counted up. This number is being stored up on the server in a `Session` object (even though you could have just as easily worked on the value from the client).

The request from this page (as captured using Fiddler) is presented here in Listing 14-9.

Listing 14-9: The request after clicking the button

```
POST /WebSite1/Default.aspx HTTP/1.1
Accept: */*
Accept-Language: en-us
Referer: http://localhost.:2972/WebSite1/Default.aspx
x-microsoftajax: Delta=true
Content-Type: application/x-www-form-urlencoded; charset=utf-8
Cache-Control: no-cache
UA-CPU: x86
Accept-Encoding: gzip, deflate
User-Agent: Mozilla/4.0 (compatible; MSIE 7.0; Windows NT 5.1; .NET CLR 2.0.50727;
```

Listing 14-9: The request after clicking the button *(continued)*

```
    .NET CLR 3.0.04506.648; .NET CLR 3.5.21022; .NET CLR 3.0.4506.2142;
    .NET CLR 3.5.30729; Zune 3.0)
Host: localhost.:2972
Content-Length: 304
Connection: Keep-Alive
Pragma: no-cache
Cookie: ASP.NET_SessionId=fm140145nufe3355auhpig45

ScriptManager1=UpdatePanel1%7CButton1&__EVENTTARGET=&__EVENTARGUMENT=&__VIEWSTATE=%
2FwEPDwUKLTI2NTM4Mzg2OGRkmCUF3vkmxzkjgRzR4MjeLNLBYZU%3D&__EVENTVALIDATION=%2FwEWAwL
2iLTMCALs0bLrBgKM54rGBlaCxawV0gCxB8d%2FaZ6tfsVDTHbN&TextBox1=Bill%20Evjen&
__ASYNCPOST=true&Button1=Submit%20your%20name%20numerous%20times
```

The response in this case is smaller than returning the entire page as the labels you are working with are encapsulated within the UpdatePanel server control. The response is presented here in Listing 14-10.

Listing 14-10: The AJAX response

```
HTTP/1.1 200 OK
Server: ASP.NET Development Server/9.0.0.0
Date: Sat, 20 Sep 2008 17:43:38 GMT
X-AspNet-Version: 2.0.50727
Cache-Control: private
Content-Type: text/plain; charset=utf-8
Content-Length: 882
Connection: Close

313|updatePanel|UpdatePanel1|
                <input type="submit" name="Button1" value="Submit your name
                 numerous times" id="Button1" />
                <br /><br />
                <span id="Label1">Hello Bill Evjen</span>
                <br />
                <span id="Label2">You have put in your name 1 times.</span>

|184|hiddenField|__VIEWSTATE|/wEPDwUKLTI2NTM4Mzg2OA9kFgICBA9kFgICBQ9kFgJmD2QWBAIDDw
8WAh4EVGV4dAUQSGVsbG8gQmlsbCBFdmplbmRkAgUPDxYCHwAFFIllvdSBoYXZlIHB1dCBpbiB5b3VyIG5hb
WUgMSB0aW1lcy5kZGSh1ltQhlo4FNr+uUq79Ib9uA1Yaw==|56|hiddenField|__EVENTVALIDATION|/w
EWAwKfgM6jAwKM54rGBgLs0bLrBsdqWqQTIx9avehV7hvlmI1t0ilI|0|asyncPostBackControlIDs|||
0|postBackControlIDs|||13|updatePanelIDs||tUpdatePanel1|0|childUpdatePanelIDs|||12|
panelsToRefreshIDs||UpdatePanel1|2|asyncPostBackTimeout||90|13|formAction||
Default.aspx|21|pageTitle||Working with Sessions|
```

Instead of working with Sessions, you could have also just as easily used ViewState as a means to maintain state. Changing all the `Session` objects to ViewState would have produced a response as presented here in Listing 14-11.

Listing 14-11: The response using ViewState

```
HTTP/1.1 200 OK
Server: ASP.NET Development Server/9.0.0.0
Date: Sat, 20 Sep 2008 17:50:10 GMT
X-AspNet-Version: 2.0.50727
Cache-Control: private
Content-Type: text/plain; charset=utf-8
Content-Length: 894
Connection: Close


313|updatePanel|UpdatePanel1|
                <input type="submit" name="Button1" value="Submit your name
                 numerous times" id="Button1" />
                <br /><br />
                <span id="Label1">Hello Bill Evjen</span>
                <br />
                <span id="Label2">You have put in your name 1 times.</span>

|196|hiddenField|__VIEWSTATE|/wEPDwUKLTI2NTM4Mzg2OA8WAh4FY291bnQFATEWAgIED2QWAgIFD2
QWAmYPZBYEAgMPDxYCHgRUZXh0BRBIZWxsbyBCaWxsIEV2amVuZGQCBQ8PFgIfAQUiWW91IGhhdmUgcHV0I
GluIHlvdXIgbmFtZSAxIHRpbWVzLmRkZAH9HdFUrhSDLax5cvGNjRHGAA1+|56|hiddenField|
__EVENTVALIDATION|/wEWAwK2wPbTAgKM54rGBgLsObLrBp11MhefZsuvFEU1uX7sQsrglEM5|0|
asyncPostBackControlIDs|||0|postBackControlIDs|||13|updatePanelIDs||tUpdatePanel1|0
|childUpdatePanelIDs|||12|panelsToRefreshIDs||UpdatePanel1|2|asyncPostBackTimeout||
90|13|formAction||Default.aspx|21|pageTitle||Working with Sessions|
```

In this case, the ViewState in the response is a bit longer, as this is where the count value is stored.

Summary

The Internet has produced some great applications, but it has also made the development of these applications difficult. Because the Internet is a disconnected environment, (meaning that the only real time that you are connected to an application or remote server is when you are making a request or getting a response), it is quite difficult at times to maintain state on it. However, ASP.NET has answered this difficulty with a number of solutions that, if used properly, can quickly make you forget about the disconnected world in which you work and play.

In this chapter, you took a look at how state works in your Web applications. You took a look at the Session object, the Application object, as well as cookies and ViewState.

15

Testing and Debugging ASP.NET AJAX Applications

Microsoft's ASP.NET AJAX Framework provides a solid foundation for building efficient and high-performance Web-based applications that can enhance the overall end user experience. No matter how good a development platform is, however, bugs and other issues can be introduced by developers and triggered by end users. Knowing how to quickly debug ASP.NET AJAX applications can greatly increase your productivity as a developer and reduce the amount of frustration experienced while tracking down issues.

In this chapter you'll be introduced to debug functionality available in the ASP.NET AJAX script library that can be used to make assertions and perform tracing operations. You'll also learn about several different debugging techniques available in Visual Studio 2008, Internet Explorer, and Firefox that can simplify the process of debugging ASP.NET AJAX applications. Finally, you'll learn how to use different tools to intercept and view request and response messages, to more easily track down data issues and monitor AJAX request and response message sizes.

Debug and Release Scripts

ASP.NET 3.5 ships with debug and release versions of client script files that drive functionality in AJAX-enabled pages. The scripts are embedded in the System.Web.Extensions.dll assembly (which is installed in the Global Assembly Cache) as resources. Figure 15-1 shows what the script resources look like when viewed in Reflector (download Reflector from www.red-gate.com/products/reflector/index.htm).

Understanding how to switch between debug and release scripts can simplify the process of debugging ASP.NET AJAX applications and make it easier to step through Microsoft's client-side script files as well as any custom script files you may write.

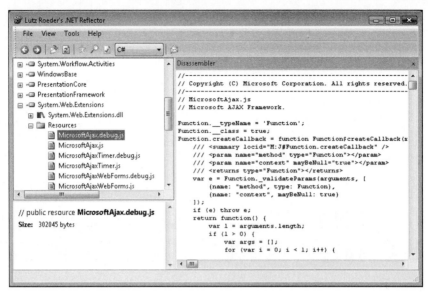

Figure 15-1

To tell the ASP.NET AJAX framework which version of the library scripts you want to use, you have to set the ScriptManager's `ScriptMode` property to one of four values defined in a `ScriptMode` enumeration, as shown in the following table.

Member	Description
Auto	The client script files to use are determined at runtime based upon configuration settings in `web.config` and `machine.config`. If the deployment element's `retail` attribute is set to `false` (the default) and the page element's `debug` attribute is set to `true`, debug scripts are used. Otherwise, release scripts are used.
Inherit	When applied directly to the ScriptManager control, it is the same as using `Auto`. When applied to a `ScriptReference` object (nested in a ScriptManager control), the settings are inherited from the ScriptManager control's `ScriptMode` property.
Debug	Debug versions of the client script files are loaded into an AJAX-enabled page and used by the framework. This setting is overridden if the deployment element's `retail` attribute is set to `true` in `machine.config`, in which case release scripts are used.
Release	Release versions of the client script files are loaded into an AJAX-enabled page and used by the framework.

If you don't specify a value for the ScriptManager's `ScriptMode` property, it defaults to `Auto`. In this case, the control looks at the `compilation` element's `debug` attribute value in `web.config` as well as the `deployment` element's `retail` attribute value in `machine.config`. The following example shows how to define the `compilation` element and associated `debug` attribute in `web.config`.

```
<system.web>
    <!-- Debug scripts will be used when ScriptMode is Auto -->
    <compilation debug="true" />
</system.web>
```

> The deployment element is optional and can be defined in `machine.config`. Its `retail` attribute has a default value of `false`. The `retail` attribute can be set to `true` to indicate that this is a production server. The purpose of this attribute is to ensure that you won't use the Debug mode in production by mistake. A common problem is that many people forget to disable debugging in `web.config` when making a production deployment, so this setting will override `web.config`. Once the `retail` attribute is set to `true`, trace output, custom error, and debug configuration settings are disabled on the server, but runtime performance is increased. The discussion that follows assumes that the `retail` attribute is set to the default value of `false`.

By letting the ScriptManager controls within a Web site default to `Auto`, you can easily control which client scripts are loaded by simply changing the `debug` attribute in `web.config`. When the `ScriptMode` property is set to `Auto` and the `debug` attribute in `web.config` is set to `true`, debug versions of client scripts will be loaded and used. When debug is set to `false`, release versions of the client script files will be loaded and used.

You can force release scripts to be loaded even when the debug attribute is set to true in `web.config` by changing the `ScriptMode` to `Release`, as shown in Listing 15-1.

Listing 15-1: Using the ScriptMode property to load release scripts

```
<asp:ScriptManager ID="ScriptManager1" runat="server" ScriptMode="Release">
    <scripts>
        <asp:ScriptReference Path="~/Scripts/Album.js" />
    </scripts>
</asp:ScriptManager>
```

Conversely, debug scripts can be loaded regardless of the debug value in `web.config` by setting the `ScriptMode` to `Debug`, as shown in Listing 15-2.

Listing 15-2: Using the ScriptMode property to load debug scripts

```
<asp:ScriptManager ID="ScriptManager1" runat="server" ScriptMode="Debug">
    <scripts>
        <asp:ScriptReference Path="~/Scripts/Album.js" />
    </scripts>
</asp:ScriptManager>
```

Because the ASP.NET AJAX debug scripts have nicely formatted code that is easy to read and step through, you'll want to set the ScriptMode to Debug (or Auto and change the debug attribute in web.config to true) while working through application problems. Although you can use the release client scripts during development, they have all formatting stripped out and are more difficult to use for debugging purposes.

In addition to loading ASP.NET AJAX client script files, the ScriptManager control can be used to load custom script files. This is done using the ScriptManager's Scripts property, as shown in Listing 15-3. Custom scripts are loaded by adding a ScriptReference component within a Scripts tag inside of the ScriptManager control. ScriptReference defines the path to the script as well as the ScriptMode. One key advantage of loading script code this way is to let you load different scripts depending on whether the application is running in Debug mode or not.

Listing 15-3: Using the ScriptMode property to load the debug version of a custom script

```
<asp:ScriptManager ID="ScriptManager1" runat="server">
    <Scripts>
        <asp:ScriptReference Path="~/Scripts/Album.js" ScriptMode="Debug" />
    </Scripts>
</asp:ScriptManager>
```

If you're loading custom scripts using the ScriptReference component, you must notify the ScriptManager when the script has finished loading by adding the following code at the bottom of the script:

```
if (typeof(Sys) !== 'undefined') Sys.Application.notifyScriptLoaded ();
```

Because the ScriptMode attribute is set to a value of Debug in Listing 15-3, the ScriptManager control will automatically look for a file named Album.debug.js instead of Album.js. If the file is not found, an error will be raised.

Having both release and debug versions of a script can be useful in some situations. For example, the release version of the script may have all whitespace stripped out of it to minimize its size, while the debug script may be formatted nicely to make it easy to step through; plus, it may contain additional debugging statements to help you isolate problems. Microsoft follows this practice with the client scripts used in the ASP.NET AJAX Library.

> **Several different tools can be used to compress JavaScript files by removing whitespace and comments and sometimes even shortening variable names. Some examples of JavaScript compressors can be found at** http://dynamic-tools.net/toolbox/javascript_compressor **and** www.xmlforasp.net/JSCompressor.aspx.

When the ScriptMode property is set to Inherit on the ScriptReference component, the correct version of the custom script to load (debug or release) will be determined by the value defined on the ScriptManager's ScriptMode property. In other words, the ScriptReference's ScriptMode value will be inherited from the ScriptManager's ScriptMode. Listing 15-4 shows how ScriptMode settings can be inherited from the ScriptManager.

Listing 15-4: Using the ScriptMode property's Inherit member

```
<asp:ScriptManager ID="ScriptManager1" runat="server" ScriptMode="Debug">
    <Scripts>
        <asp:ScriptReference Path="~/Scripts/Album.js" ScriptMode="Inherit" />
    </Scripts>
</asp:ScriptManager>
```

Now that you've seen how debug and release client scripts can be loaded, let's examine the ASP.NET AJAX Library classes that can be used in various debugging situations.

Using the Error Class

The ASP.NET AJAX Script Library includes several useful classes with respect to debugging and testing, including the `Error` and `Sys.Debug` classes. The `Error` class extends the native JavaScript `Error` object and allows more specific error objects and messages to be created for a given error. It is used extensively throughout the ASP.NET AJAX Library debug scripts to test that the correct number of parameters are passed to functions, passed parameter types match up with the expected types, types aren't undefined, functions are fully implemented, and much more. The `Error` class is used sparingly in the release version of the ASP.NET AJAX Library scripts so that file sizes are minimized as much as possible.

The `Error` class has several different functions that can be used to create specific types of errors. The majority of the functions that can be called to create error objects relate specifically to function parameters, but others exist that are used by classes such as the `PageRequestManager` class. All of the `Error` class's available functions are shown in the following table.

Function Name	Description
`argument(paramName, message)`	Used to create a `Sys.ArgumentException` object with the name of the function parameter that caused the exception, as well as the specified error message.
`argumentNull(paramName, message)`	Used to create a `Sys.ArgumentNullException` object with the name of the function parameter that caused the exception, as well as the specified error message.
`argumentOutOfRange(paramName, actualValue, message)`	Used to create a `Sys.OutOfRangeArgumentException` object. It accepts three parameters, including the parameter name, the actual value the parameter, and the error message.
`argumentType(paramName, actualType, expectedType, message)`	Used to create a `Sys.ArgumentTypeException` object. Can be used when a parameter passed to a function is not the proper type. It accepts four parameters, including the parameter name, actual type passed for the parameter, the expected type of the parameter, and the error message.

Continued

Function Name	Description
`argumentUndefined(paramName, message)`	Used to create a `Sys.ArgumentUndefinedException` object with the name of the function parameter that caused the exception as well as the specified error message.

`create(message, errorInfo)`	Used to create a new instance of an `Error` object with the specified message and extended information about the error. The `errorInfo` object passed must contain a name field containing a string that identifies the error.
	An example of creating an `errorInfo` parameter is:
	`Error.create(a,`
	`{name:"Sys.ArgumentTypeException",`
	
	`paramName:d,actualType:c,expectedType:b})`

`invalidOperation(message)`	Used to create a `Sys.InvalidOperationException` with the specified error message.
`format(message)`	Used to raise a `Sys.FormatException` exception when the format of an argument does not meet the parameter specifications of the invoked method.
`notImplemented(message)`	Used to create a `Sys.NotImplementedException` object with the specified error message.
`parameterCount(message)`	Used to create a `Sys.ParameterCountException` object with the specified error message. Used to validate the number of parameters passed to a function.
`popStackFrame()`	Used to update the `fileName` and `lineNumber` fields of the `Error` object instance to indicate where the `Error` was thrown. This solves problems in browsers that assign values to the `fileName` and `lineNumber` fields based upon where the `Error` object was created rather than where it was thrown.

You can use the `Error` object to raise specific types of errors when invalid parameters are passed to a function, when calls are made to functions that aren't fully implemented, or when you need to ensure that the correct line number and filename show up when errors are raised.

Listing 15-5 shows an example of using the Error object's `argumentType`, `popStackFrame`, and `notImplemented` functions with a custom script that defines an `Album` class.

Listing 15-5: Using the Error object

```
Wrox.ASPAJAX.Samples.Album.prototype = {

    //Additional code removed for brevity

    addSong: function(song)
```

Listing 15-5: Using the Error object *(continued)*

```
{
    /// <value type="Wrox.ASPAJAX.Samples.Song"></value>
    if (Object.getTypeName(song) != 'Wrox.ASPAJAX.Samples.Song')
    {
        var e = Error.argumentType('song', Object.getType(song),
            Wrox.ASPAJAX.Samples.Song,"Wrox.ASPAJAX.Samples.Song required!");
        e.popStackFrame();
        throw e;
    }
    Array.add(this._songs,song);
},
rateSong: function(song,rating)
{
    throw Error.notImplemented("rateSong() has not yet been implemented");
}

//Additional code removed for brevity

}
```

The first use of the `Error` object is in the definition for the `addSong` function in Listing 15-5. This function accepts a `Wrox.ASPAJAX.Samples.Song` object as a parameter. If a `Song` parameter type is not passed, a call is made to the `Error.argumentType` function to create a `Sys.ArgumentTypeException` error object. This function accepts the name of the parameter in error (song in this example), the actual parameter type passed, the expected parameter type, and the error message that should be shown to the caller. Once the `Error` object is created, a call is made to `popStackFrame` to ensure that the line number and filename are properly reported to the caller. In some browsers, the line number is reported at the location that the error was created rather than the location where it was actually thrown. The `popStackFrame` function remedies this problem and ensures that the line number and filename are reported correctly.

The `Error` object is also used in the definition for the `rateSong` function in Listing 15-5. Because this function is not yet implemented, a call is made to the `Error.notImplemented` function, and the error message that the caller should see is passed as a parameter. Listing 15-6 shows calls to the `Album` class's `addSong` and `rateSong` methods and demonstrates how to catch returned errors.

Listing 15-6: Catching Error object instances

```
function RateSong()
{
    var album = new Wrox.ASPAJAX.Samples.Album();
    var song = new Wrox.ASPAJAX.Samples.Song(3,$get("txtSong"));
    try
    {
        //Should pass song object here but demonstrate using Error object in Album
        //to verify proper parameter type is passed
        album.addSong(album);
    }
    catch(e)
    {
```

Continued

Listing 15-6: Catching Error object instances *(continued)*

```
            alert(e.message);
        }
        try
        {
            //rateSong() not implemented
            album.rateSong(song,$get("txtSongRating"));
            alert("Song rated!");
        }
        catch(e)
        {
            alert(e.message);
        }
    }
```

Now that you've seen how the ASP.NET AJAX Script Library's `Error` class can be used, let's take a look at the `Sys.Debug` class and see how it can be used to write error messages and identify the reason they occurred.

Using the Sys.Debug Class

The ASP.NET AJAX Library includes a helper class named `Sys.Debug` that can be used on the client side to write to trace logs, perform assert statements, and trigger a debug session in Visual Studio. Knowing how to use the `Sys.Debug` class can help simplify the process of ensuring that client-side functionality is performing properly and allow you to more easily view data passed from function to function in an application.

The `Sys.Debug` class is included in the release and debug versions of the `MicrosoftAjax.js` client-side script file shipped with ASP.NET AJAX. It defines several different functions that can be called to perform assertions, tracing, and debugging. The following table shows the different functions available on the `Sys.Debug` class.

Function Name	Description
`assert(condition, message, displayCaller)`	Asserts that the `condition` parameter is `true`. If the condition being tested is `false`, a message box will be used to display the `message` parameter value. If the `displayCaller` parameter is `true`, the method also displays information about the caller.
`clearTrace()`	Erases statements output from tracing operations.
`fail(message)`	Causes the program to stop execution and break into the debugger. The `message` parameter can be used to provide a reason for the failure.
`trace(message)`	Writes the `message` parameter to the trace output.
`traceDump(object, name)`	Outputs an object's data in a readable format. The `name` parameter can be used to provide a label for the trace dump. Any subobjects within the object being dumped will be written out by default.

Performing Trace Operations

If you've used ASP.NET's built-in trace functionality, you'll feel right at home with the `Sys.Debug` class's tracing capabilities. It can be used to write client-side trace messages that can be used to track the flow of an ASP.NET AJAX application. An example of using the `Sys.Debug` class to write to the client-side trace output is shown in Listing 15-7. Figure 15-2 shows what the trace log looks like when rendered to the page.

Listing 15-7: Using the Sys.Debug.trace function

```
var album = new Wrox.ASPAJAX.Samples.Album();
album.set_title("Sam's Town");
album.set_artist("The Killers");

Sys.Debug.trace("Set album title and artist properties");

$get("lblTitle").innerHTML = album.get_title();
$get("lblArtist").innerHTML = album.get_artist();

Sys.Debug.trace("Album properties written out to page");
```

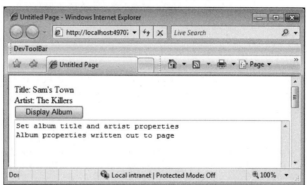

Figure 15-2

Adding `Sys.Debug.trace` statements into existing JavaScript code doesn't automatically cause the trace messages to be written to the page. In fact, at first glance you'll wonder if any type of tracing operation was performed at all when viewing a page that contains one or more trace statements. To view trace output in the page, you'll need to add a `TextArea` tag into the page and give it an ID of `TraceConsole`. The trace function looks for the `TraceConsole` id defined on a `TextArea` tag as it writes out trace messages. Listing 15-8 shows code from the ASP.NET AJAX Library that handles writing trace statements.

Listing 15-8: ASP.NET AJAX Script Library's Sys$_Debug$_appendTrace function

```
function Sys$_Debug$_appendTrace(text) {
    var traceElement = document.getElementById('TraceConsole');
    if (traceElement && (traceElement.tagName.toUpperCase() === 'TEXTAREA')) {
```

Continued

461

Listing 15-8: ASP.NET AJAX Script Library's Sys$_Debug$_appendTrace function *(continued)*

```
            traceElement.value += text + '\n';
        }
    }
```

Here's an example of defining a `TextArea` tag to capture and display trace information:

```
<textarea id="TraceConsole" rows="25" cols="60"></textarea>
```

You may look at this and wonder if there is a better way to view trace output. After all, once an application is ready to move to production, it would be time-consuming (and error prone) to locate all of the pages that have `TextArea` tags used to display trace statements and then remove them. Fortunately, Visual Studio can also be used to view trace output using the Output window, as shown in Figure 15-3. This won't require you to use a `TraceConsole TextArea` on your page.

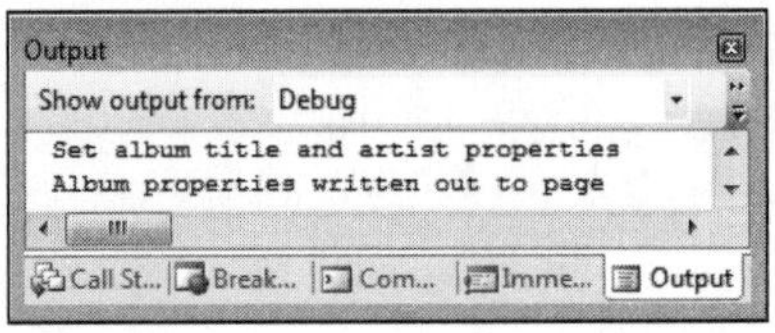

Figure 15-3

Additional information about using Visual Studio to debug ASP.NET AJAX applications and view other useful information is covered later in this chapter.

In addition to allowing custom trace data to be written to the page, the `Sys.Debug` class's `traceDump` function can be used to convert JSON objects into a more readable format to easily inspect the data within an object. This will show all the properties of the object without requiring you to specify them individually. The `traceDump` function accepts the object to display as a parameter along with a label to associate with the trace dump to make it easier to identify. Listing 15-9 shows an example of using the `traceDump` function to write the values contained within an `Album` object. Figure 15-4 shows the output.

Listing 15-9: Using the Sys.Debug.traceDump function

```
var album = new Wrox.ASPAJAX.Samples.Album();
album.set_title("Sam's Town");
album.set_artist("The Killers");
Sys.Debug.trace("Set album title and artist properties");

$get("lblTitle").innerHTML = album.get_title();
$get("lblArtist").innerHTML = album.get_artist();

Sys.Debug.trace("Album properties written out to page");

//Dump the album object to the trace output console
Sys.Debug.traceDump(album,"Album Details:");
```

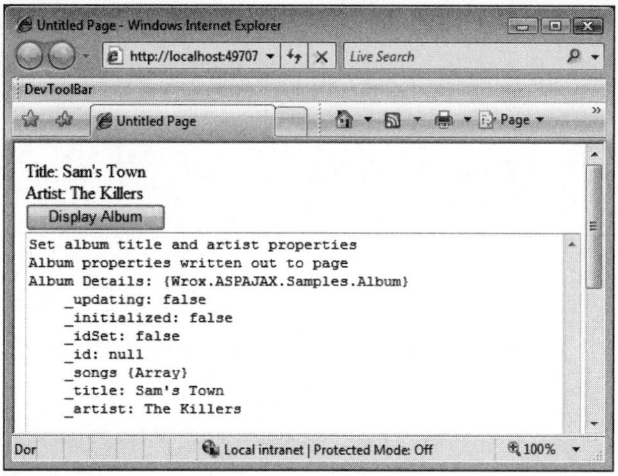

Figure 15-4

The `Sys.Debug.traceDump` function also handles writing nested subobjects automatically. For example, Listing 15-10 shows how an `Album` object containing an array of nested `Song` objects is written to the page. Looking at the output generated from this call (see Figure 15-5), you'll see that it is fairly verbose. In cases where you would like to clear the current trace log so that other trace statements are easier to find in the trace console area, you can use the `Sys.Debug.clearTrace` function.

Listing 15-10: Using Sys.Debug.traceDump to View Object Data in the Trace Console

```
var album = new Wrox.ASPAJAX.Samples.Album();
album.set_title("Sam's Town");
album.set_artist("The Killers");

//Add Song objects into Album's song array
album.addSong(new Wrox.ASPAJAX.Samples.Song(3,"When you were young"));
album.addSong(new Wrox.ASPAJAX.Samples.Song(7,"Uncle Johnny"));

$get("lblTitle").innerHTML = album.get_title();
$get("lblArtist").innerHTML = album.get_artist();
Sys.Debug.trace("Album properties written out to page");

//Write out Album and nested Song objects
Sys.Debug.traceDump(album,"Album and Song Details:");
```

Performing Assert Operations

The `Sys.Debug` class can also be used to assert that a condition is true in order to check that objects are available to call or that an action has occurred as expected. In cases where the condition fails, a message box will be displayed. The `assert` function accepts three parameters, including the condition to check, the message to display if the assertion fails, and whether or not the caller's information should be displayed.

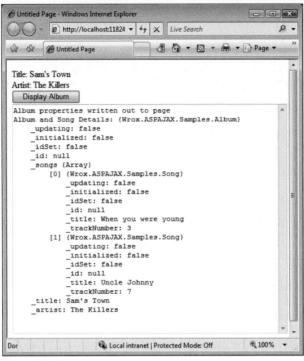

Figure 15-5

Using the assert function makes it straightforward to test a specific condition within JavaScript code and alert you when it doesn't evaluate to true. It's a nice feature, as it doesn't require you to add conditional statements (if or switch statements) to an application.

An example of using the Sys.Debug.assert function to check that an Album contains songs is shown in Listing 15-11, while an example of the output is shown in Figure 15-6.

Listing 15-11: Using the Sys.Debug.assert function

```
var album = new Wrox.ASPAJAX.Samples.Album();
album.set_title("Sam's Town");
album.set_artist("The Killers");

//Assert that the songs.length condition is true or not
Sys.Debug.assert(album.get_songs.length > 0,"No songs for album");
```

Figure 15-6

You can also obtain additional details about the condition being evaluated by passing a third `Boolean` parameter named `displayCaller` to the assert function as shown next:

```
debug.assert(album.get_songs.length > 0,"No songs for album",true);
```

Figure 15-7 shows what the assert message box looks like when the `displayCaller` parameter is set to `true`.

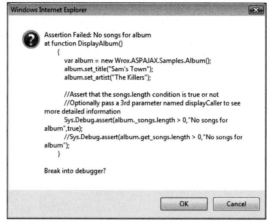

Figure 15-7

When an assertion fails, you are given the option to break into a debugger to more thoroughly evaluate the condition and step through the code. A debug session can also be started by calling the `Sys.Debug.fail` function within JavaScript code. For debugging to start and work properly, however, specific settings within Internet Explorer must be enabled. In the next section, you'll see how to enable Internet Explorer for debugging and work with Visual Studio.

Enabling Internet Explorer for Debugging

Debugging JavaScript has proven to be somewhat of a challenge and has resulted in many developers resorting to "alert-style" debugging to better understand how an application is working. Fortunately, Internet Explorer 6 or higher includes integrated debugging functionality that can be used to start a debug session and step through ASP.NET AJAX code with a debugging tool such as Visual Studio 2008. Learning how to leverage Internet Explorer debugging features can enhance your productivity and significantly minimize the amount of time you spend hunting down bugs and other issues.

The debug capabilities in Internet Explorer 6 or higher are disabled by default but can be turned on by going to Tools ➪ Internet Options ➪ Advanced. The Advanced tab defines two items that need to be unchecked (a check means you can't debug):

- ❏ Disable script debugging (Internet Explorer)
- ❏ Disable script debugging (Other)

Also, check the Display a notification about every script error checkbox below these items so that you're notified as errors occur in a page. If this box isn't checked, an icon appears in the lower-left corner of the browser; unless you click it, you may miss noting that a client-side error occurred. A side effect of checking this checkbox is that you'll find that many other Web sites have errors as you browse to them, so you may want to leave it unchecked when you're not debugging your own applications.

Figure 15-8 shows what the Internet Explorer 7 Advanced settings should look like to enable debugging.

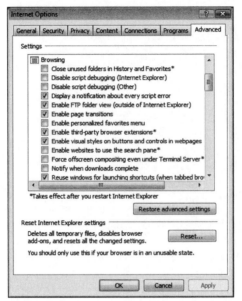

Figure 15-8

Once debugging is enabled in Internet Explorer, an ASP.NET AJAX page can be debugged using Visual Studio 2008.

Debugging with Internet Explorer and Visual Studio 2008

You can start a debug session several different ways. One of the easiest ways is to use the built-in script debugging capabilities of Internet Explorer. To start a debug session for an ASP.NET AJAX page, navigate to the page that you'd like to debug and select View ➪ Script Debugger from the Internet Explorer menu (see Figure 15-9). For this to work, you must enable Internet Explorer for debugging as described in the previous section.

You'll be presented with two different options, Open and Break at Next Statement, as shown in Figure 15-9. If you select Open, you'll be prompted to start using Visual Studio as the debugger, as shown in Figure 15-10. If Visual Studio is already open, you can begin debugging, or you can choose to start a new instance of Visual Studio 2008 to use for debugging. If you select Break at Next Statement, nothing happens until an action is performed that causes script within the page (or script referenced by the page) to execute. Once script code is executed in Internet Explorer, you'll be prompted to use the Visual Studio Just-In-Time debugger.

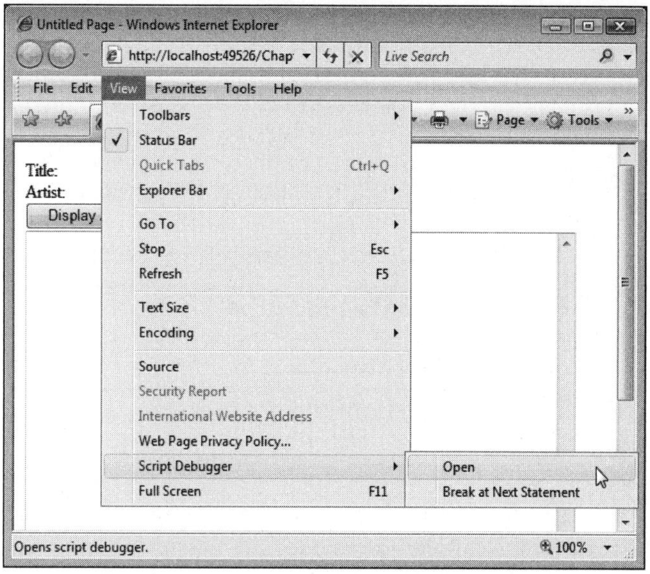

Figure 15-9

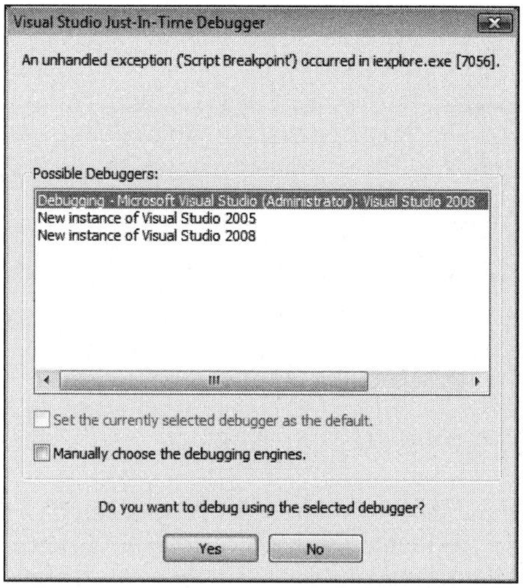

Figure 15-10

Once Visual Studio 2008 is open and loaded you can set a breakpoint in the page on the line where you'd like to start debugging. Visual Studio 2008 allows breakpoints to be set directly within JavaScript code embedded inline within a page, which is a nice feature previously unavailable in Visual Studio 2005.

In addition to manually setting breakpoints in the code editor, you can also trigger one or more breakpoints using different techniques. The first technique requires that you add the JavaScript `debugger` statement directly into the code where you'd like to start a debug session. This will force a breakpoint to occur at runtime at that location of the `debugger` statement in the code. While this technique works, ASP.NET AJAX's `Sys.Debug` class (discussed in the previous section) is designed for this purpose and is a more appropriate choice for debugging AJAX applications. You can call the `Sys.Debug` class's `fail` function to trigger the debugger when a specific line of code is hit.

The `Sys.Debug.fail` function accepts only one parameter that represents the reason for the failure. Listing 15-12 shows an example of using the `Sys.Debug.fail` function to break into a debug session right before songs are added into an `Album` object.

Listing 15-12: Using the Sys.Debug.fail function

```
var album = new Wrox.ASPAJAX.Samples.Album();
album.set_title("Sam's Town");
album.set_artist("The Killers");

//Force the debugger to appear
Sys.Debug.fail("Debug song additions");

album.addSong(new Wrox.ASPAJAX.Samples.Song(3,"When you were young"));
album.addSong(new Wrox.ASPAJAX.Samples.Song(7,"Uncle Johnny"));
$get("lblTitle").innerHTML = album.get_title();
$get("lblArtist").innerHTML = album.get_artist();
```

It's helpful to call `Sys.Debug.fail` to trigger a debug session when a line of JavaScript code is executed, but you must remember to remove all these calls before moving an application to a production environment, because it will always trigger the debugger when debugging is enabled in Internet Explorer. You can have two versions of your script (Microsoft does this with its debug and release scripts) and set the appropriate `ScriptMode` on the `ScriptManager` to determine which script is loaded at runtime, as discussed at the beginning of this chapter. Although this means that your code is duplicated, the release script can have all whitespace characters stripped out of it to minimize its size, while the debug script can provide an easy-to-read script that contains the necessary calls to the `Sys.Debug` class for debugging, tracing, assertions and other operations.

In addition to supporting breakpoints within inline scripts, Visual Studio 2008 also allows breakpoints to be set in external `.js` files. Figure 15-11 shows an example of JavaScript in a file named `Listing15-12.js` that has a breakpoint successfully set.

As you begin debugging a script and step into other scripts you'll notice that Visual Studio 2008 automatically loads the necessary scripts for you so that you can step into and out script files with ease. This is made possible by Visual Studio 2008's Script Documents window. Script Documents can be used to load dynamic scripts in the editor (including ASP.NET AJAX Library scripts) so that you can step into them easily using the debugger. Figure 15-12 shows an example of the Script Documents window and the script files used in an ASP.NET AJAX-enabled page named `Listing15-12WithScriptFile.aspx`. The Script Documents window appears at the top of the Solution Explorer during a Visual Studio 2008 debug session.

Figure 15-11

Figure 15-12

In addition to starting a debug session using Internet Explorer, you can also start a debug session directly in Visual Studio 2008 much as you would when debugging VB.NET or C# code. First, right-click the page you'd like to debug in the Solution Explorer and select Set As Start Page from the menu. Then press F5 or click the green play button (the button with the green arrow on it) on the debug tool-bar to start Internet Explorer (assuming that it is set as your default browser) and display the page. Set your breakpoints in the separate script files, and then trigger the breakpoints by performing the action you'd like to debug in the browser.

> **If debugging hasn't been enabled in Internet Explorer, you'll be prompted to enable it before debugging a script.**

As you step through code, you have full access to standard debugging windows such as the Autos, Locals, Watch, and Immediate as shown in Figure 15-13. By using these windows, you can quickly access variable data and drill down into your applications to see what is happening internally.

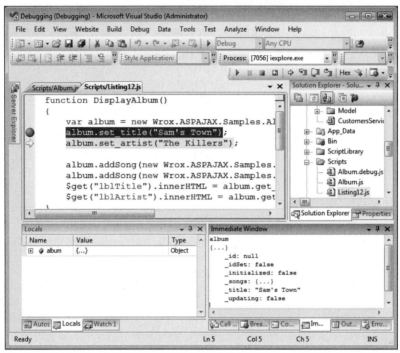

Figure 15-13

Although this section focuses on debugging features in Visual Studio 2008, Visual Web Developer 2008 Express also has integrated debugging features that can be used to debug ASP.NET AJAX applications.

Debugging with Firefox and Firebug

Although Internet Explorer is still the most widely used browser according to statistics available at the time this chapter is being written, Mozilla Firefox has made significant inroads and is being used by more and more people. As a result, you'll likely need to debug your ASP.NET AJAX applications in Firefox as well as Internet Explorer. Firefox doesn't offer any direct integration with Visual Studio 2008, unfortunately, but it does have extensions that can be downloaded and installed that make it rather straightforward to debug ASP.NET AJAX applications.

One of the most popular debugging extensions available for Firefox is Firebug. You can download Firebug from `http://getfirebug.com`. Once installed, Firebug allows you to view the Document Object Model (DOM) of a page, view CSS details, and perform various debugging operations.

You can view a page directly in Firefox from Visual Studio by right-clicking the page in the Solution Explorer and selecting Browse With from the menu. The Browse With dialog box appears. Click the Add button to view the Add Program dialog box, as shown in Figure 15-14, and locate where `firefox.exe` was installed on your computer. Once the program is added to the list of available browsers, you can select it and press the Browse button to view any page directly in Firefox instead of in Internet Explorer.

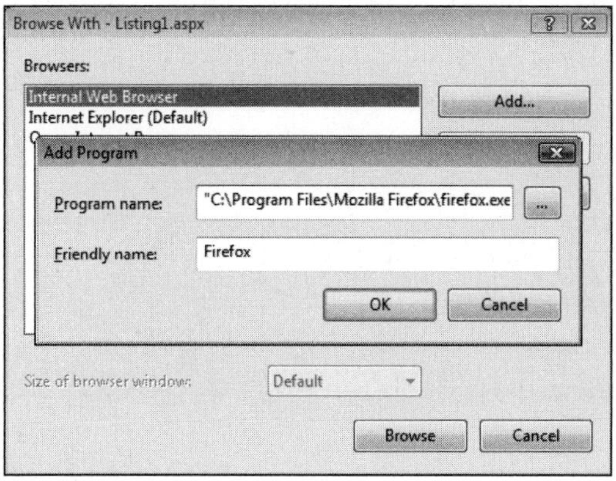

Figure 15-14

Once a page is loaded in Firefox, you can access Firebug functionality in several ways. First, you can go to Firefox's Tools menu and select Firebug ⇨ Open Firebug from the menu (or use the Ctrl+Shift+L hotkey). You can also add a call to `Sys.Debug.fail` in your JavaScript code. When the fail function is called, Firebug automatically appears at the bottom of the browser and allows you to step through the code line by line. Figure 15-15 shows what Firebug looks like. You'll notice that it has several different tabs that allow access to scripts, HTML, DOM elements, and CSS.

It's quick and easy to get started with Firebug. All scripts loaded in a page are easily accessible without additional effort. When a script is needed by Firebug, its source code automatically appears in the Script window. Variables within client-side script files are accessible through the Console window (which acts much like Visual Studio's Command window) and in the Script window. HTML code, styles, and other DOM features can be accessed in their respective windows.

Figure 15-16 shows an example of the Script window during a debug session. Notice that several buttons located in the top of the Firebug toolbar are available for stepping into, stepping over, and stepping out of code. Breakpoints can be set by clicking in the gray tray area where the line numbers are shown. As code is being debugged, the value of the variables currently in scope are displayed to the right of the Script window, allowing you to easily access properties and their associated values. For example, Figure 15-16 shows information for a variable named `album`.

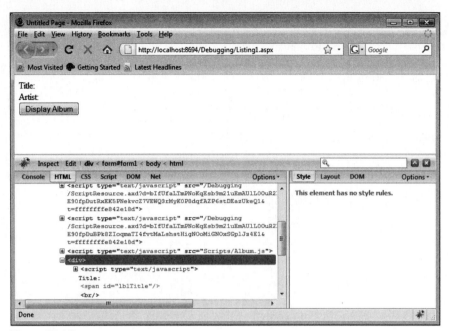

Figure 15-15

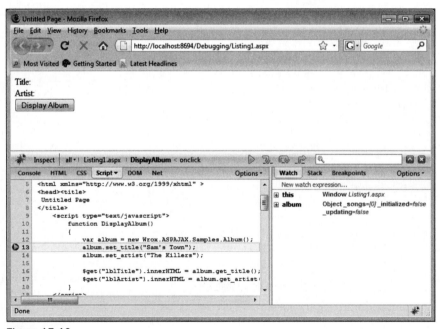

Figure 15-16

Firebug makes it easy to walk through client scripts and is also useful for inspecting HTML code. It can also come in handy when you need to look at how CSS styles are being applied to different elements in a page.

Viewing ASP.NET AJAX Request and Response Messages

Once you've ironed out all of the bugs in an ASP.NET AJAX Application, you'll probably want to perform other types of tests to ensure that the application performs as expected. It's difficult to know how an application truly performs unless you take the time to look at some of the request and response messages being sent from the client to the server. By looking at the raw message data, you may discover ways to minimize the size of the messages and speed up the request/response mechanism. It's also important to see the actual request and response because this is a 100-percent authoritative view of what communication is actually taking place between the browser and Web server; if this appears different from what you intended, it can alert you to bugs.

Several free and easy-to-use tools exist for inspecting request and response messages. The next sections introduce several such tools, including Fiddler and the Web Development Helper.

Using Fiddler to Inspect Messages

Fiddler is an excellent tool created by Microsoft's Eric Lawrence that can be used to inspect AJAX messages exchanged between the client and server. It can be downloaded from www.fiddlertool.com and is free to use. It provides a simple and effective way to view many different details about messages, including request and response headers, raw message data, message sizes, and other useful information.

After Fiddler is installed, it can be accessed directly from the Internet Explorer Tools menu or loaded from the Windows Start ➪ Programs menu. During installation, Fiddler registers itself with Internet Explorer by setting itself up as a proxy. Requests for 127.0.0.1 (localhost) are automatically routed to port 8888, which Fiddler listens on. All requests made from the browser will automatically show up in the Fiddler HTTP Sessions list, as shown in Figure 15-17.

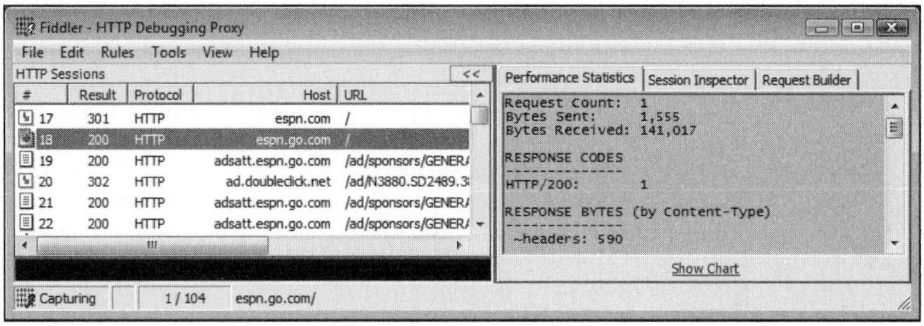

Figure 15-17

Fiddler can be useful when you want to see the overhead involved with using automated versus manual AJAX updates, such as the difference between using an UpdatePanel and using pure JavaScript or XML Script calls. While the UpdatePanel is easier to use, it typically has a larger message payload than equivalent calls made with JavaScript or XML Script. For example, the code shown in Listing 15-13 uses the UpdatePanel to load customer data into a GridView control based upon a country or a customer ID that the end user types into textboxes. Using Fiddler, it's easy to see exactly what data is passed to the server as well as what data is passed back in the response message.

Listing 15-13: Using the UpdatePanel with Fiddler

```
<asp:UpdatePanel ID="udPanel" runat="server">
  <ContentTemplate>
    <asp:GridView ID="gvCustomers" runat="Server" Width="96%"
      GridLines="none" ShowHeader="false" AutoGenerateColumns="false">
        <RowStyle HorizontalAlign="left" />
        <Columns>
            <asp:BoundField ItemStyle-Width="25%" DataField="CustomerID" />
            <asp:BoundField ItemStyle-Width="25%" DataField="ContactName" />
            <asp:BoundField ItemStyle-Width="25%" DataField="CompanyName" />
            <asp:BoundField ItemStyle-Width="25%" DataField="Country" />
        </Columns>
    </asp:GridView>
    <asp:HiddenField ID="hidField" runat="server" />
  </ContentTemplate>
  <Triggers>
    <asp:AsyncPostBackTrigger ControlID="btnSubmit" EventName="Click" />
    <asp:AsyncPostBackTrigger ControlID="btnSubmit2" EventName="Click" />
  </Triggers>
</asp:UpdatePanel>
```

Using Fiddler, you can inspect the messages being sent as the UpdatePanel is triggered and refreshed. Figure 15-18 shows what the different messages look like in Fiddler using the Session Inspector tab.

The top pane in the figure shows the request message, while the bottom pane shows the response message. Although the request message is fairly small, you can see that the response message is relatively large. It contains all of the data that will be updated in the GridView control as well as ViewState information and other details. If ViewState is not needed, it can be turned off, which will significantly reduce the size of the UpdatePanel's response message. In this example, the response message size can be reduced from 4,908 characters to 3,106 by turning off ViewState on the GridView control.

If you try to view Listing15-13.aspx *using Visual Studio 2008's built-in Web server, you may notice that the request and response messages do not show up in Fiddler. To see the request and response messages in Fiddler, add a period (.) character immediately after* localhost *(but before the colon and port number) in the browser. For example, the following URL will show up in Fiddler properly (notice the "." after localhost):* http://localhost.:49526/Chapter15/Listing15-13.aspx. *If you happen to get a network exception after doing this go to Fiddler's Tools ➪ Fiddler Options menu and uncheck the Enable IPv6 (if available) checkbox.*

There's much more to Fiddler than can be discussed in this chapter. However, you've seen the fundamentals on how it can be used to view request and response messages so that you can locate data errors and compare techniques of sending request and response messages.

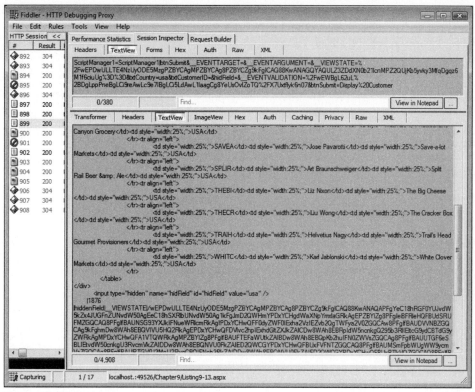

Figure 15-18

Using Web Development Helper to Inspect Messages

Fiddler isn't the only tool that can be used to view ASP.NET AJAX request and response messages. Another great tool is the Web Development Helper. Web Development Helper is written by Nikhil Kothari, one of the key ASP.NET architects at Microsoft. It's an excellent tool that can perform a variety of tasks such as viewing HTTP requests and responses, debugging scripts, and viewing the DOM of a page. You can download the tool at `http://projects.nikhilk.net/WebDevHelper/Default.aspx`.

Once installed, the tool is accessible directly in Internet Explorer by selecting Tools ⇨ Web Development Helper from the menu. The tool loads directly into Internet Explorer, which makes it easy to access and use. Figure 15-19 shows what the Web Development Helper tool looks like while running within Internet Explorer.

To inspect request and response messages, you can click the Enable Logging checkbox on the Web Development Helper toolbar. All messages sent or received using localhost will automatically be logged, along with the status code and response message size. Double-clicking a logged message allows you to see the request and response headers as well as all of the content within the individual messages. Figure 15-20 shows an example of using the Web Development Helper to view an UpdatePanel request and response. Response messages can be viewed in Partial Rendering mode (shown in Figure 15-20), in raw text mode, or in a Hex mode. Partial Rendering mode is especially useful because it parses the raw response message and makes it easy to view controls that trigger asynchronous postbacks, child UpdatePanel IDs, hidden-Fields (ViewState and so on), as well as UpdatePanel response data.

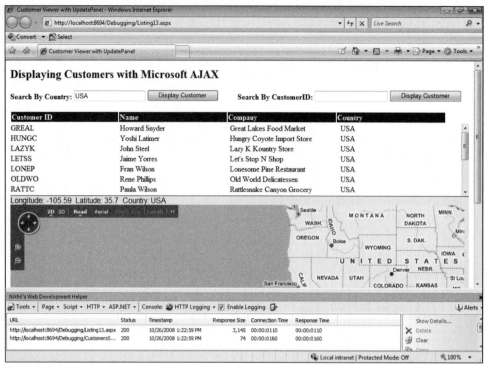

Figure 15-19

Figure 15-20

Web Development Helper allows you to apply filters to limit the types of HTTP requests it monitors. You can access the filtering options by going to Tools ⇨ Options ⇨ HTTP Logging on the Web Development Helper toolbar. If you'd only like to monitor requests made to `.aspx` and `.asmx` files, you can type `.aspx, .asmx` into the Logging Filter text box to filter out all other types of requests.

Summary

Understanding the options for debugging ASP.NET AJAX applications is an important part of enhancing an application's overall performance and stability as well as maximizing developer productivity. In this chapter, you've seen how debug and release client-side script versions can be loaded using the `ScriptMode` property of the ScriptManager control. You've also seen how to use ASP.NET AJAX Library classes such as `Error` and `Sys.Debug`. The `Error` class allows you to create specific types of `Error` objects, while the `Sys.Debug` class allows for tracing, JSON object viewing, assertions, and debugging.

Several options exist for debugging ASP.NET AJAX applications running in Internet Explorer and Firefox. Those running Visual Studio 2008 (or Visual Web Developer Express) will find the debugger to be very functional. Those without access to Visual Studio 2008 can leverage the Firebug debugger with Firefox.

Testing ASP.NET AJAX applications may involve inspecting request and response messages to see if their size can be minimized by reducing ViewState or other data. Several tools exist for viewing request and response messages, such as Fiddler and the Web Development Helper. By using these tools, you can quickly see what data is being sent across the wire.

16

Deploying ASP.NET AJAX Applications

When you think of deploying a Web application, you may just think of the process necessary to move the application from a development machine or a test environment on to the production machine. But of course, there is more to it than just copying files across the network. In this chapter, you will see that there are really three distinct phases to deployment: preparing for deployment, the process of deployment itself, and the final stage: monitoring and tuning and application.

Once the application is developed and tested, as discussed in the previous chapter, you need to prepare it for deployment. You can think of this as the predeployment phase with a checklist to utilize to ensure the best results possible. There is a common set of pitfalls that can be avoided by checking and then double-checking some settings before proceeding to deployment that will save you time in the long run. And a key part of the checklist is ensuring that the production servers have the necessary bits (the code, images, and Web pages) duplicated from the development environment to handle the deployment without error. People often talk about "the bits" being moved when they are referring to the settings, code, and binaries involved in an application.

The development environment and the production environment are usually different. They have different hardware, distinct database back ends, unique connection strings, and separate network topologies. The Web Deployment projects of Visual Studio provide an environment for automating the process of deploying your application from a development environment into a test environment and ultimately into production.

And once the application is in production, you need to know how it is behaving. You will want to examine the load and potentially find ways to optimize for better performance. This chapter offers some options for tuning ASP.NET AJAX for maximum throughput and resilience. By leveraging client and server caches intelligently, an application can yield better response times and minimize server processes. This makes an application appear faster to the user and can significantly reduce processing power requirements.

Installing the Bits

There are several distinct parts that make up the functionality of ASP.NET AJAX. The core ASP.NET AJAX release was originally shown as part of a CTP. A CTP is a Community Technology Preview released before the product is ready for final consumption in order to share progress and gather early feedback. It was then released in supported form as an add-on to version 2.0 of the .NET Framework. It was subsequently incorporated into the .NET Framework 3.5 update.

The ASP.NET team continues to explore new feature investments and provides tech previews to gather input and share the work being done. The APIs and features in the previews will evolve over time as the work progresses towards a fully supported release. Bertrand LeRoy has provided some insight in his AJAX Roadmap document available at `www.codeplex.com/aspnet/Release/ProjectReleases .aspx?ReleaseId=14924`.

The ASP.NET AJAX Toolkit is a set of shared source behaviors and control extenders that are central to writing richer Web applications. These elements build on top of the core ASP.NET AJAX platform pieces to provide the key pieces necessary to push Web development further. Many developers view the Toolkit as a fundamental part of ASP.NET AJAX although they continue to be distinct installs.

ASP.NET AJAX

ASP.NET AJAX is the core platform for building richer Web applications using ASP.NET and the bulk of what this book is about. The object-oriented type system built in JavaScript is transmitted to the browser and cached by the client. All subsequent requests for the JavaScript library are satisfied by the browser cache. To configure the Web servers to support ASP.NET AJAX applications, they must have the server components installed. The Microsoft naming convention for the releases has not made it easy to follow what is required. Version 2.0 of the .NET Framework did not contain the AJAX libraries. Version 3.0 was built on top of version 2.0 and is an addition to the core 2.0 release. It is not required for ASP.NET AJAX development. ASP.NET AJAX was then released as a standalone install that would also go on top of .NET Framework 2.0. This was independent of the 3.0 release. All of this functionality was then incorporated into the .NET Framework 3.5 update. And the .NET Framework 3.5 has now been updated with a service pack. The latest supported release should be installed on servers to ensure that security fixes, functionality and performance improvements are in place for everyday use.

In early preview builds, it wasn't necessary for the ASP.NET AJAX assemblies to be installed in the Global Assembly Cache (GAC), but as features were added and refined, it became necessary to assert full trust in order to provide the complete functionality across trust levels. Assemblies in the GAC are considered trusted because they must be installed by someone with administrator credentials. This allows ASP.NET AJAX to get access to global configuration data and use .NET Framework reflection, both of which are necessary for full trust across trust levels. If you are using a Web server managed by a third party, you must ensure that .NET Framework 3.5 has been installed on their servers. It is available as a backwards compatible update for version 2.0. To download the latest release of ASP.NET with Service Pack 1, visit `www.asp.net/downloads/3.5-SP1/default.aspx`.

One key thing to note is that Microsoft has now made the source code for the .NET Framework, including the ASP.NET AJAX pieces available for download. You can actually set a breakpoint and step from your code right into the ASP.NET AJAX platform code and back out again. This is a great improvement over using various tools to look at the IL (Intermediate Language) code and try to interpolate what is happening when an application is not behaving as you would expect. Now you can trace through the code execution from beginning to end. The previous chapter has more detailed information about debugging ASP.NET applications. Symbols can be referenced online or downloaded from the Reference Source Code Center at `http://referencesource.microsoft.com/Default.aspx`.

When you deploy an ASP.NET AJAX application, there is no automatic check to verify that ASP.NET AJAX is installed. When deploying it to a hosted environment on the Web, check to see that the host has the latest service release for the .NET Framework. In most cases, there will be no change to the functionality, as service releases strive to maintain backward compatibility, but it is a recommended practice to ensure that servers are up to date with the latest servicing release.

The ASP.NET AJAX Control Toolkit

The ASP.NET AJAX Control Toolkit builds on ASP.NET AJAX and can be found here: `www.codeplex.com/AjaxControlToolkit/Release/ProjectReleases.aspx?ReleaseId=16488`.

The Toolkit contains a set of controls and control extenders with an impressive set of rich behaviors. For example, the ModalPopup control dims the page content except for a new layer that displays the pop-up content. This effect is shown in Figure 16-1.

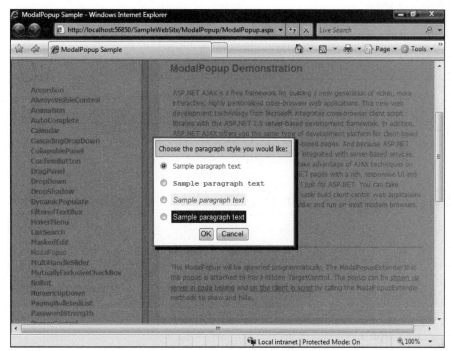

Figure 16-1

This is just one example out of a long list of controls and control extenders. The effects are key to providing a rich user interface that works in multiple browsers. There are a wide range of effects available, ranging from drag-and-drop support, to animations, to an autocomplete textbox, as well as rounded corners and drop shadow effects. Many of the UI elements familiar to desktop application developers are included in the Toolkit.

The Toolkit does not require installation into the GAC. Instead, you deploy it by simply copying the `AjaxControlToolkit.dll` into the `bin` directory of your Web application. The controls work in partial trust environments and can be used in hosted environments where permissions are limited. You don't need to provide Adminstrator credentials to leverage the Toolkit.

ASP.NET Futures CTP

There have been several different "Future" releases from Microsoft related to ASP.NET over the past couple of years. There are multiple feature teams focused on different aspects of ASP.NET and their progress is at varying stages. The work has been brought together for unified public preview releases at various points. Now the team is providing several different downloads of various features rather than waiting to coalesce them into a single build. While this provides a benefit in getting access to the work more rapidly, it can be taxing to keep track of all the pieces.

The current and previous preview releases are available at www.codeplex.com/aspnet and include both server and client source code access. Developers have a chance to shape the features as they do development, by trying out the preview releases and providing feedback to the team. Be aware, however, that the earliest previews come with no guarantee that the APIs won't change in the next release or that pieces won't be dropped altogether based on feedback. The degree of churn is reduced quickly as the designs are completed and integrated with other new feature work.

A key distinction between the ASP.NET AJAX releases and the preview releases is that the preview assemblies are not typically get installed in the GAC. Instead, they are placed in the /bin directory of your application. Any feature that needs full trust must get it by virtue of your application being run in full trust. From time to time, a feature in the preview release will have limited functionality because of the need for full trust. This is something to check for in the release notes if you are deploying an early build to a hosted environment where things run under partial trust.

Preparing for Web Farm Deployment

In many situations, there is no need to deploy an application across multiple servers. The anticipated load is not sufficient to warrant the extra investment. However, if the load increases and performance tuning can't yield enough improvement, you may find that it is necessary to scale your Web application beyond a single server. A Web farm is a cluster of servers that work together to service requests for a single application. The ASP.NET platform scales well from a single server into a full Web farm environment, but you do need to take a few extra steps in preparation and deployment.

Setting the MachineKey

The primary concerns related to deploying an application to a cluster of servers are not unique to AJAX. The ViewState data transmitted with a page is hashed by a hashing routine that is tied to the MachineKey of that server. The hash validation on subsequent requests can detect if anyone has modified the data. Problems arise when one server handles a request, but the subsequent request goes to a different server in the Web farm. If the MachineKey values are unique, as they would be by default, then you can't successfully balance the requests of an individual user across multiple machines.

To setup a Web farm for ASP.NET, you must synchronize the MachineKey values for all servers that are part of the Web farm cluster. If the MachineKey values are not identical, ViewState created by one server will be treated as invalid when it is posted to another server. This isn't because of any action by the user. The Web farm will simply be balancing requests across multiple machines. You take a random alphanumeric string and put it in the .config section for MachineKey in place of the default value of AutoGenerate, which would provide a key for you but not persist it in the configuration data. When the MachineKey values are coordinated, the ViewState hashed by one server will be validated by another that has the same key.

Handling Session State

Session state storage is another concern in Web farm environments. The default for session state is to store the data in-memory. Requests that get handled by another server will not have access to the correct session data. To ensure the fastest performance, ASP.NET prefers to use in-memory session state to avoid the need to go to another process or require setup and maintenance of a back-end database.

To support Web farms, however, ASP.NET also provides an out-of-process session state server that can be referenced by multiple servers. This is a Windows service that must run on one of the servers in the cluster, and then all the Web servers must point to it as the repository of all session state data. The configuration data you use is a value to indicate that the mode is StateServer instead of InProc. The server running the state service and the port and protocol are also specified.

```
<configuration>
  <system.web>
    <sessionState mode="StateServer"
        stateConnectionString="tcpip=dataserver:42424"
        cookieless="false"
        timeout="20"/>
    </sessionState>
  </system.web>
</configuration>
```

The state server allows you to start sharing sessions across multiple machines but doesn't scale as well as a back-end database. Although leveraging a database as a state server is slower than using the Windows Service running on the same box, it can eliminate a single-point-of-failure risk if you have a robust clustered database. In ASP.NET 1.0, a SQL server could be configured as the storage point for session information. In ASP.NET 2.0 and after, the provider architecture allows for any back-end data service to be plugged in for storing and retrieving session data.

```
<configuration>
  <system.web>
    <sessionState mode="Custom" customProvider="SampleProvider">
      <providers>
        <add name="SampleProvider" type="SampleProvider" />
      </providers>
    </sessionState>
  </system.web>
</configuration>
```

In addition to making the state server pluggable, Microsoft has released the sources for the SQL session state provider. This is a great resource for developing your own session state provider if you have an environment where one of the released providers is not a good match. Additionally, some members of the community have offered up custom provider implementations for other data storage solutions. You can learn more at www.asp.net.

Using a Different Platform

The Microsoft AJAX Library is available in a standalone zip file. It includes the scripts that are sent down to the browser to enable AJAX functionality. You can deploy these files to any Web server on any platform. As already discussed, script files are not versioned like a binary file is, so the zip file includes a path with version information. If you follow this convention when deploying the files, you can easily migrate to a new version of the AJAX Library when it becomes available. The versions are backward compatible, so you can also run one version of scripts alongside a newer version if some new behavior or change requires updating code. This versioning is helpful in making it easy to switch between versions after validating functionality and features. This is particularly useful in ensuring a smooth transition when updating an existing application with features found in a new release.

When it comes to deployment, if you aren't using any of the server features of ASP.NET AJAX, you could just put the Microsoft AJAX Library JavaScript files on the server and have them downloaded to the browser.

The three library files all come in release and debug versions:

❑   MicrosoftAjax.debug.js

❑   MicrosoftAjax.js

❑   MicrosoftAjaxTimer.debug.js

❑   MicrosoftAjaxTimer.js

❑   MicrosoftAjaxWebForms.debug.js

❑   MicrosoftAjaxWebForms.js

The release also includes a large set of files in a Globalization subdirectory for greater reach. Localized versions of error messages and warnings are included to facilitate better and more accurate feedback for the user. In the first version of ASP.NET AJAX, there was also a pid.txt file, which included licensing information you were required to provide if you called in to Microsoft support with a question. After that release, the features were incorporated directly into the .NET Framework, and the separate pid.txt file was no longer necessary.

The ASP.NET team has validated the functionality on Internet Explorer, Firefox, Safari, and Opera browsers. The team is usually testing against the latest released versions and working on the beta versions.

Avoiding Common Configuration Problems

Now, that you've ensured that the requisite packages are installed on your production machine, you should guard against some common pitfalls before proceeding directly to application deployment. This is a key part of the predeployment checklist. Many of the problems in deployment turn out to be errors in the configuration files. Much of the behavior of ASP.NET can be adjusted in the `machine.config` and `web.config` files. One change to the root machine-level configuration can have a negative impact on all of the applications running on the server. If you change a setting in these files to gather information during development and forget to return it to the default before rolling out to production, you may face performance or security problems.

Disable Debugging

When developing a Web application, you often want to be able to step through code as it is running in order to find problems. When launching a Web application for debugging, Visual Studio will remind you, as shown in Figure 16-2 that Internet Explorer needs to have script debugging enabled. Leaving it enabled may affect your experience with other applications when script errors are encountered, but it won't have any adverse impact on your application itself.

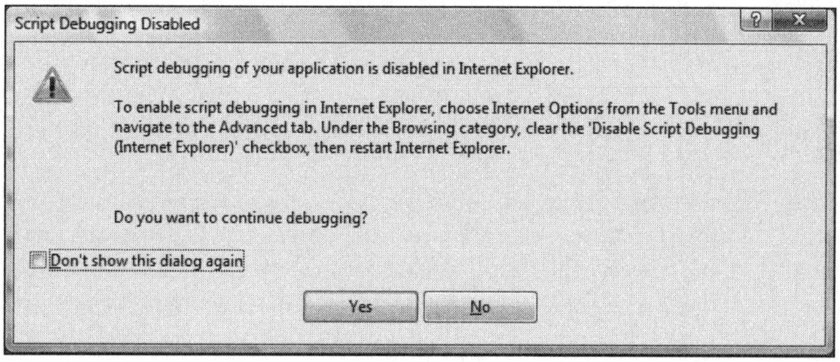

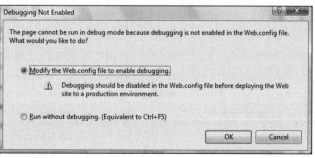

Figure 16-2

Visual Studio will even offer to automatically modify the `web.config` file to enable debugging. This is shown in Figure 16-3. This is the source of a common production problem. The dialog warns that debugging should be disabled in production, but it's easy to forget. Visual Studio can't yet tell when you've decided things are ready to go and to remind you to switch this setting back.

Figure 16-3

The comment that Visual Studio puts in the `web.config` file is also a reminder to disable it for deployment:

```
<system.web>
    <!--
      Set compilation debug="true" to insert debugging
```

```
        symbols into the compiled page. Because this
        affects performance, set this value to true only
        during development.
    -->
    <compilation debug="true"/>
```

In production, the primary manifestation of this problem is very slow request throughput. Instead of having multiple threads trying to serve many requests simultaneously, ASP.NET will use a single synchronized thread to run pages. Essentially, all requests must get in line to wait their turn while only one request is processed at a time. This, of course, greatly reduces efficiency, and requests will start to queue up waiting for their turn or when the queue is long enough, they may even be rejected outright. This can go undetected if you aren't monitoring the site carefully (see "Performance Monitoring," later in this chapter).

Enable Custom Errors

When an error occurs during the processing of a page, the stack trace information can be very useful in figuring out what is going wrong. But you don't want this sort of information to be shown to the end user. What to show in error conditions is controlled by the customErrors configuration section.

The default setting for custom errors is remoteOnly. This means that when browsing to localhost on a machine, you get detailed error reporting, but when viewing the application from another machine, custom error messages are shown instead. The custom error page is normally a user-friendly error page that hides the technical details of what went wrong. This default setting is designed to allow you to get good information during development on the local machine but to avoid showing potentially sensitive data to the end user. In many development environments, multiple developers are working together on a single application, so they want additional error information when browsing remotely. You can turn off custom errors by setting the mode to off so that you get the same information whether you are browsing locally or not.

```
    <system.web>
        The <customErrors> section enables configuration
        of what to do if/when an unhandled error occurs
        during the execution of a request. Specifically,
        it enables developers to configure html error pages
        to be displayed in place of a error stack trace.

    <customErrors mode="RemoteOnly" defaultRedirect="GenericErrorPage.htm">
        <error statusCode="403" redirect="NoAccess.htm" />
        <error statusCode="404" redirect="FileNotFound.htm" />
    </customErrors>
```

After the error is found and fixed, it is easy to forget to change the custom errors mode back to RemoteOnly or On instead of Off. And you probably won't notice it until some problem arises in the production environment and you discover that error pages are showing customers stack traces instead of something more friendly. Stack traces can give hints about the source code organization beyond what you'd like to show the general public. There are people out there looking for vulnerabilities to exploit and giving them any extra hints is not your goal, so hide error stacks from end users.

Another new feature has been added to custom errors based on user feedback. By default, when an error is encountered, the browser is redirected to the custom error and the URL is changed to correspond to the error handler. By changing the RedirectMode of the customErrors section to ResponseRewrite, you change the behavior from redirecting to keeping the same request URL while executing the targeted error page for output.

Disable Tracing

Information leakage is a big concern in running a Web application. The Tracing feature, while extremely helpful, can lead to sharing more information about your server than you intend. Tracing allows you to automatically gather information about the requests being processed. You can then access the trace .axd handler to view the information locally or remotely. This handler is requested from a browser just as though it were a physical page. Remember that the trace information is available from the local server only if localOnly is true.

```
<system.web>
  <trace enabled="true" localOnly="true"/>
```

The top-level tracing output, shown in Figure 16-4, is a listing of the most recent requests. Selecting one of the View Details links from the list takes you to output like that shown in Figure 16-5. These are the details for a single request. It includes information about the most recent request, including the ASP.NET session identifier; the time to complete each phase of the page lifecycle; the control hierarchy of the page; and markup size rendered. The page also includes a listing of various server variables, which is probably more information than you want to share with users!

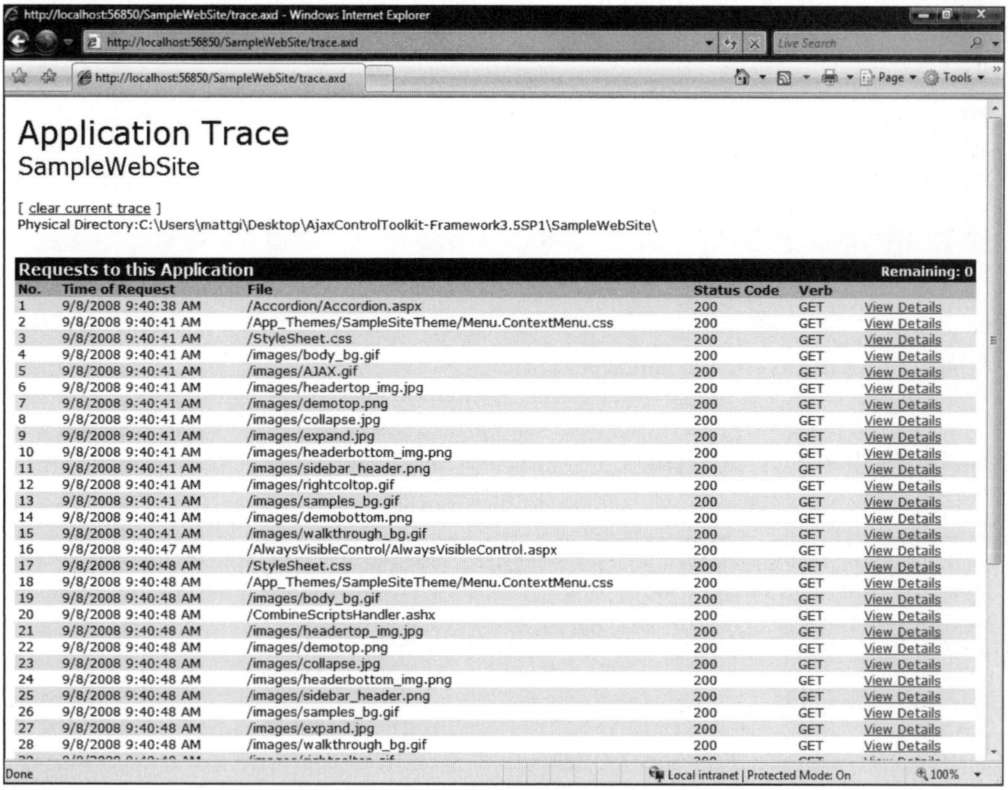

Figure 16-4

The tracing feature is not enabled by default. But if you enable it, remember to disable it again for production Web sites. Not only is there the possibility that you are sharing information that you don't want to, but there is some overhead associated with tracing. If you aren't using it, there's no need to tax the performance of your site needlessly and expose the information to prying eyes.

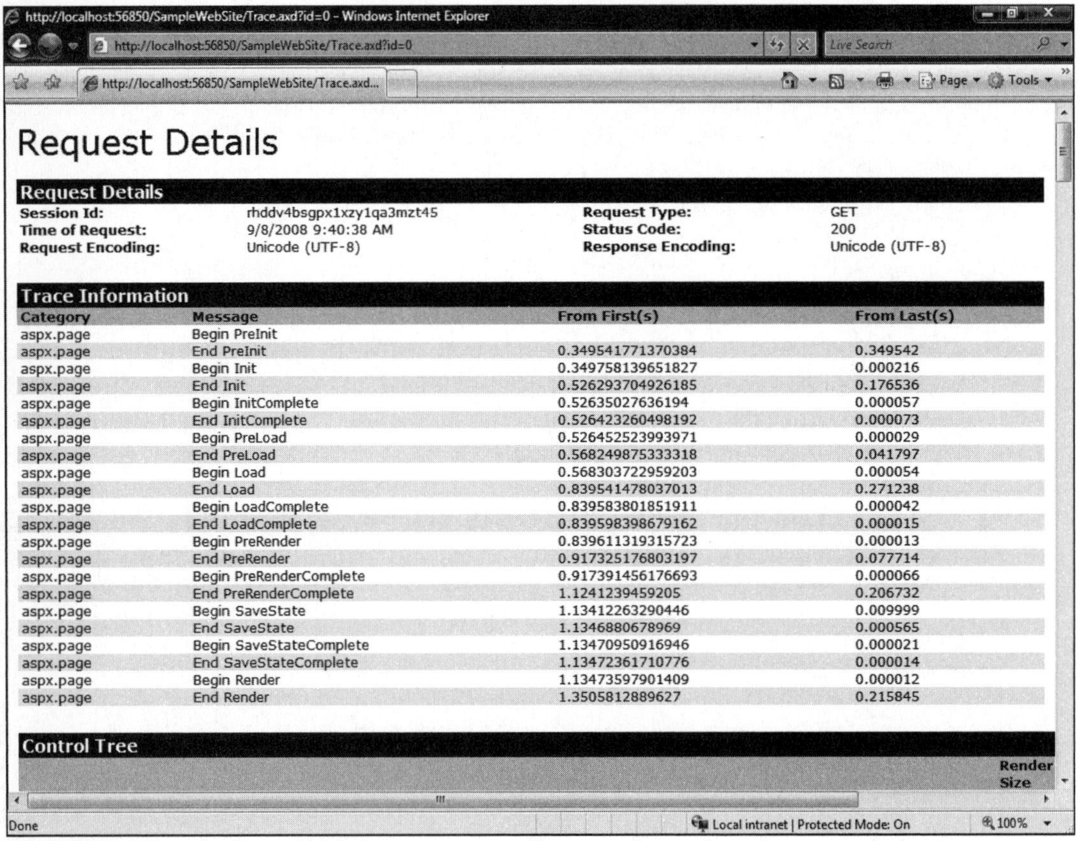

Category	Message	From First(s)	From Last(s)
aspx.page	Begin PreInit		
aspx.page	End PreInit	0.349541771370384	0.349542
aspx.page	Begin Init	0.349758139651827	0.000216
aspx.page	End Init	0.526293704926185	0.176536
aspx.page	Begin InitComplete	0.52635027636194	0.000057
aspx.page	End InitComplete	0.526423260498192	0.000073
aspx.page	Begin PreLoad	0.526452523993971	0.000029
aspx.page	End PreLoad	0.568249875333318	0.041797
aspx.page	Begin Load	0.568303722959203	0.000054
aspx.page	End Load	0.839541478037013	0.271238
aspx.page	Begin LoadComplete	0.839583801851911	0.000042
aspx.page	End LoadComplete	0.839598398679162	0.000015
aspx.page	Begin PreRender	0.839611319315723	0.000013
aspx.page	End PreRender	0.917325176803197	0.077714
aspx.page	Begin PreRenderComplete	0.917391456176693	0.000066
aspx.page	End PreRenderComplete	1.1241239459205	0.206732
aspx.page	Begin SaveState	1.13412263290446	0.009999
aspx.page	End SaveState	1.1346880678969	0.000565
aspx.page	Begin SaveStateComplete	1.13470950916946	0.000021
aspx.page	End SaveStateComplete	1.13472361710776	0.000014
aspx.page	Begin Render	1.13473597901409	0.000012
aspx.page	End Render	1.3505812889627	0.215845

Figure 16-5

Set Deployment Mode

There are a number of configuration settings that have the potential to impact production environments negatively. And because it is easy to forget to change a setting when moving from the development environment, there is a global configuration setting that overrides the other settings. The deployment section has the retail attribute for this purpose. When set to `true`, the configuration, tracing, and debug section settings are overridden to more production-friendly values:

```
<system.web>
  <deployment retail="true"/>
```

The deployment setting can only be used at the machine level in the `machine.config` file and affects all Web applications on the server. You can't enable it for just a single application. This setting should always be used on production Web servers, so if anyone forgets to modify their `web.config` on one particular application, this setting will trump the specific application setting. It's nice to have a big switch to help you avoid some common mistakes! Be aware, however, that it can also cause confusion when you start toggling one of the other configuration settings and see no effect. Of course, you don't usually want to be doing debugging on a production server anyway. In rare cases where you might need to trace a problem in production that can't be easily duplicated in a development or test environment, the extra config change would be necessary to get things set up.

Creating Web Deployment Projects

Many of the problems that arise when deploying an application stem from differences between the development environment and the production environment. The deployed application may need to use a different database back end. Directory permissions may be different between the test and production systems. Web service calls may need to be redirected to a live server instead of test infrastructure. To help with these problems, there is an add-in available for Visual Web Developer for a project type focused on the deployment process itself, called a Web Setup project.

```
http://go.microsoft.com/fwlink/?linkid=55111
```

The Web Deployment project leverages the aspnet_merge tool. This tool can take the individual DLLs of a precompiled Web application and combine them into a single DLL. With default settings, aspnet_merge will compile the entire application, including code from the App_Code directory as well as the generated code from the `.aspx` pages, and combine them into a single DLL for deployment. This not only simplifies the job of deployment but also minimizes the overhead time that would happen to compile specific pages on demand. There will still be a JIT (just-in-time) compilation needed at runtime to covert the IL code to native code. aspnet_merge and the Web Deployment project are not a replacement for the native code generation services provided by the CLR (Common Language Runtime). The main complication that results from using aspnet_merge is that you won't be able to modify a single page and redeploy it individually unless you use the partial precompilation method discussed later.

You create the Web Deployment project in an existing Web site or Web application by selecting Add Web Deployment Project from the Build menu (see Figure 16-6).

The default behavior for the Web Deployment project is to reuse the existing project name with a suffix that ends in _deploy, but you can change this naming as shown in Figure 16-7. It is important to note that although you have the option to change the location of the deployment project, you cannot select the same root folder as the main project.

Figure 16-8 shows the compilation options. If you check the Allow this precompiled site to be updatable box, it will cause your `.aspx` files to be deployed verbatim without being precompiled and merged with the other files. This is only a partial precompilation, which allows you to modify an individual page later and deploy only that page. If you uncheck that box, however, your `.aspx` files will be fully precompiled and replaced with files of the same name containing the text "This is a marker file generated by the precompilation tool, and should not be deleted!"

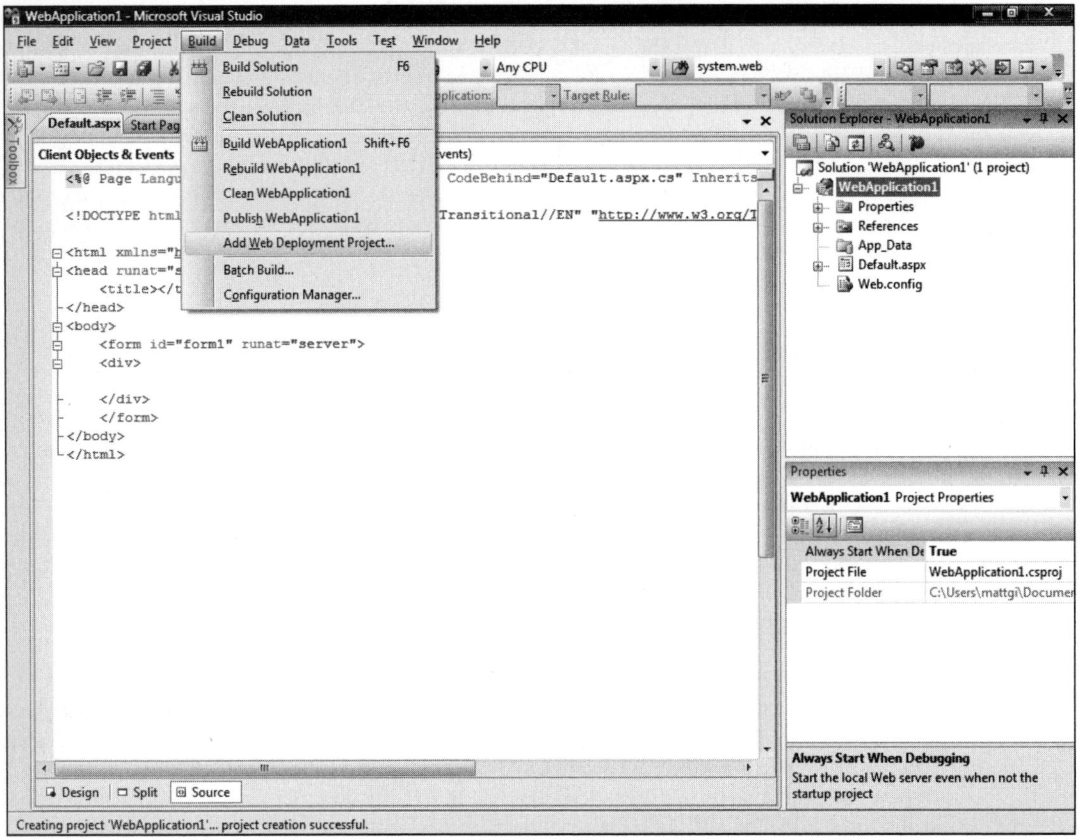

Figure 16-6

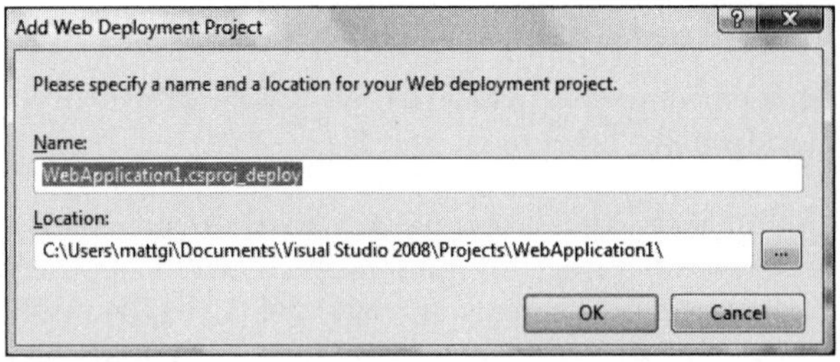

Figure 16-7

In Figure 16-9, you see the options for the assembly outputs. You can opt to have a single assembly, an assembly per directory, or even a separate assembly for each page. There is some additional runtime memory cost for extra assemblies, but unless the site contains a very large quantity of individual pages, this overhead should be negligible.

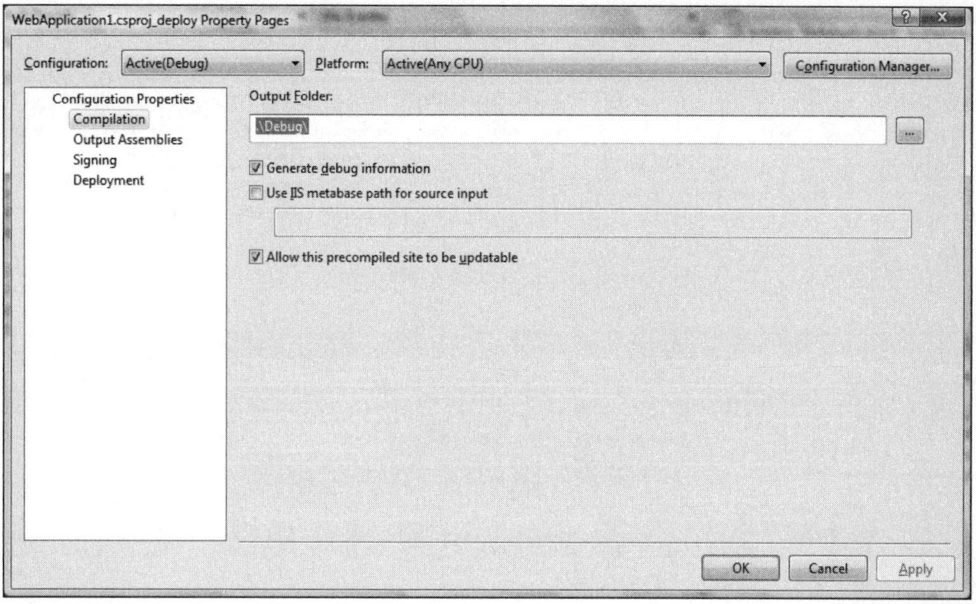

Figure 16-8

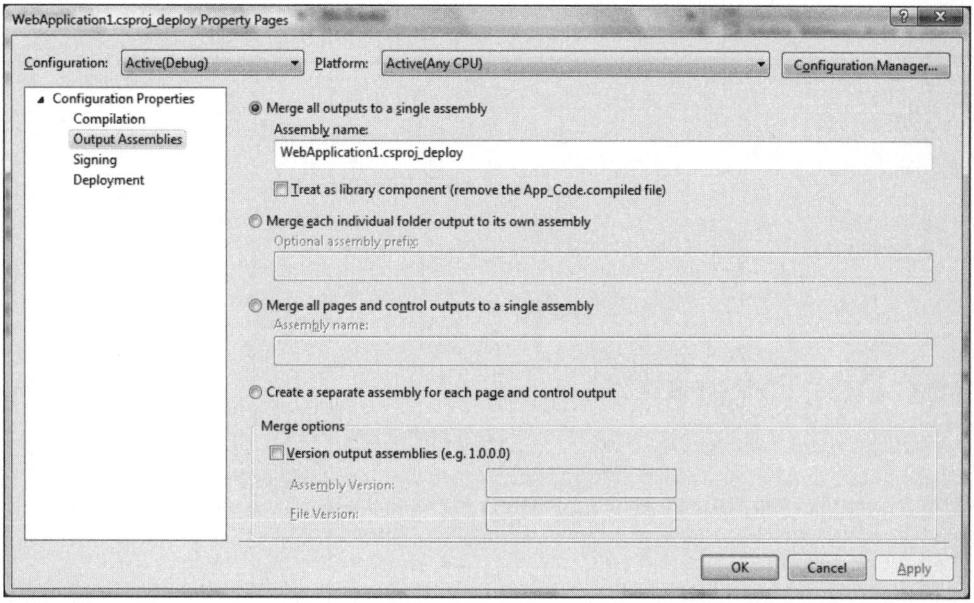

Figure 16-9

That gives you greater control over compiled outputs, which is nice but doesn't solve the problem of needing different sets of configuration data when deploying the code. You can manage that on the

Deployment property page, shown in Figure 16-10, where you can specify configuration sections that should be swapped out for updated versions. Check the Enable Web.config file section replacement box and provide the section name and the name of a file that contains the updated section. The file must not have any other sections in it. It must be a direct replacement for the original section. The Web deployment project simply parses the `.config` file as XML and swaps the old section with the contents of the specified file. There is no context for configuration inheritance or validation of attribute values. Here is an example where the section we want to replace is `connectionStrings` and the file that will provide the new section is `deploymentConnectionStrings.config`:

```
connectionStrings=deploymentConnectionStrings.config
```

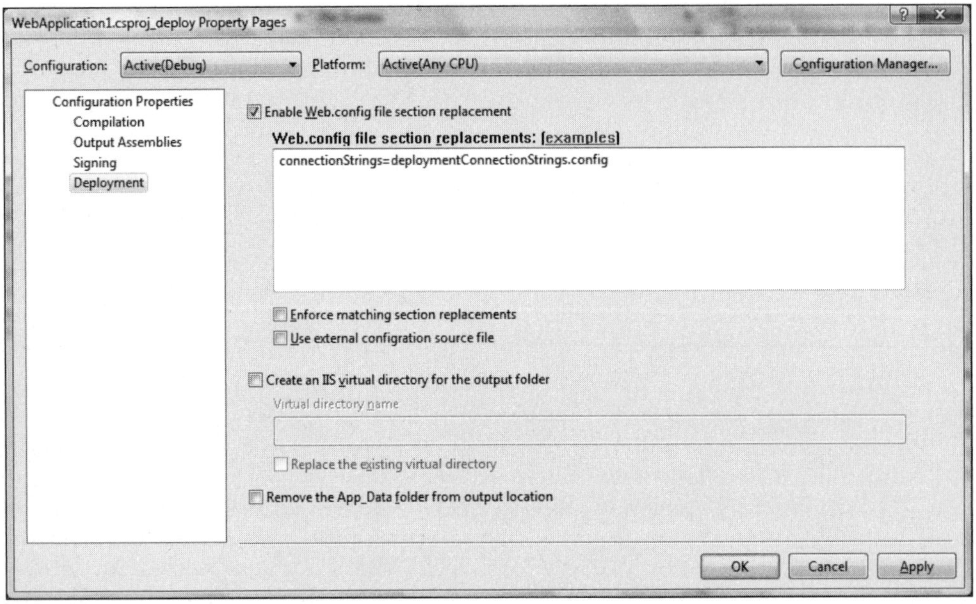

Figure 16-10

After Deployment

The application has been developed and tested, the predeployment checklist has been satisfied, and deployment is completed. Now it's time to keep an eye on things and consider what changes might be necessary with the application running in the real world. You will need to monitor performance counters and consider other configuration changes to satisfy production demands.

Performance Monitoring

As you monitor the performance of a deployed ASP.NET application, it is key to understand that performance is really a complex balancing act. Incoming requests can be handled very quickly if the content is cached. However, caching content increases the memory consumption and can put additional pressure on the system to page memory to disk. And caching implies that the output sent for any single request is only as accurate or up to date as when it went into the cache. Some content that is customized based on unique user input may not be cacheable and may truly require that dynamic results be produced. This becomes even more complex when you add that the application is running in a garbage-collected environment that is periodically preempting other work in order to clean up unused memory and add and remove worker threads in a self-tuning effort.

You can gather some data from Windows performance counters on the server in order to monitor how it is running, using the Perfmon tool that comes with Windows. Don't focus entirely on a single performance metric. In a balancing act, different components must be considered. You can find an excellent article, "ASP.NET Performance Monitoring, and When to Alert Administrators," by Thomas Marquardt of the ASP.NET team on the MSDN site at `http://msdn2.microsoft.com/en-us/library/ms972959.aspx`. Marquardt recommends a specific set of performance counters as the minimum set to watch. Among other counters, his list includes:

❑ `Processor(_Total)\% Processor Time` and `Process(aspnet_wp)\% Processor Time`: If the total processor time is consistently high and the ASP.NET worker process isn't responsible, the Web application may be getting starved for processing power because of other things happening on the machine. If the worker process time is consistently high, it may indicate that you are hitting the limit of the load the machine can handle.

❑ `Process(aspnet_wp)\Private Bytes`: The private bytes counter indicates how much memory the process has committed. A steady increase is a good indicator that something in the application is allocating resources that aren't being returned to the system. This will lead to problems of process recycling and should be investigated.

❑ `Process(aspnet_wp)\Virtual Bytes`: The virtual bytes correspond to the virtual address space the process has consumed. As this approaches the limit of 2GB (or optionally 3GB in 64-bit environments when it is enabled), it indicates that the address space is becoming fragmented. Items held in a cache may still be pinned, while other memory used transiently is been returned. Just as defragmenting your hard drive can improve performance, so can defragmenting the address space of the worker process. However, there isn't a great way to do this now, so the solution is to recycle the worker process. ASP.NET will do this for you automatically. The threshold at which this happens is configured as the Maximum Virtual Memory setting, found in the Internet Services Manager on the Recycling tab for the Application Pool.

❑ `ASP.NET\Application Restarts`: Application restarts incur a cost of compilation checks and starting from scratch in populating the cache. Keep an eye out for excessive application restarts that can be caused by tools touching key files such as `machine.config` or `web.config`. This problem is known to be a side effect of some virus-scanning tools.

❑ `ASP.NET\Requests Rejected`: Rejected requests are bad. The server refused to deliver a page to someone trying to access the Web application. When requests queued and requests executing exceed a limit, ASP.NET will start rejecting requests in order to catch up.

Monitoring this small set of performance counters can give you insight into how healthy the application is after it has been deployed and can alert you to problems. Several commercial tools are available that will monitor performance counters and can be configured to send mail, page you, or even call you when thresholds are exceeded. The sophistication of monitoring suites continues to improve as the approaches to making the most of the ASP.NET runtime are refined.

Controlling AJAX Features

The `system.web.extensions` section itself is essentially all commented out except for the structure definition. When deploying an application, it is important to understand what default behaviors are controlled by configuration and ensure that the actual values correspond to your intentions.

By default, the JSON serializer of ASP.NET limits the length of JSON strings that it will consume. If the incoming data exceeds the limit, an exception is thrown. This is done to guard against wasting processing power on excessively long strings that may be created by someone to attack a server. The `jsonSerialization` section lets you customize the limit on JSON strings that will be processed. It can also accept a definition of custom converters for serializing and deserializing additional types:

```
<system.web.extensions>
 <scripting>
  <webServices>
<!-- Uncomment this line to customize maxJsonLength and add a custom converter --
>
  <!--
  <jsonSerialization maxJsonLength="102400">
   <converters>
    <add name="ConvertMe" type="Acme.SubAcme.ConvertMeTypeConverter"/>
   </converters>
  </jsonSerialization>
  -->
```

Script access to the ASP.NET application services is not enabled by default; you must turn them on explicitly. The authentication service can be configured to reject requests that aren't using SSL for security. The profile service must be enabled if you want to use it. You also have to define what properties are available for reading or writing remotely from script:

```
<!--
  <authenticationService enabled="true" requireSSL = "true|false"/>
  -->
<!--
  <profileService enabled="true"
          readAccessProperties="propertyname1,propertyname2"
          writeAccessProperties="propertyname1,propertyname2" />
  -->
  </webServices>
```

The Roles Service was not available in the original ASP.NET AJAX release and is not available now unless it is explicitly enabled:

```
<!--
  <roleService enabled="true" />
  -->
```

In the `scriptResourceHandler` section, you control whether requests for dynamic script are compressed or cached; normally, you want these features:

```
<!--
  <scriptResourceHandler enableCompression="true" enableCaching="true" />
  -->
```

```
  </scripting>
 </system.web.extensions>
```

With script compression enabled, your server pays a small upfront price to do the compression, but text compresses well, and with caching enabled the amortized cost across multiple requests is almost nonexistent.

Configuring IIS7

IIS7 also introduces a new configuration section for your `web.config` file: `system.webServer`. IIS7 supports two modes: Classic and Integrated. Classic mode preserves backward compatibility in the way that ISAPI filters and extensions are called. In integrated mode, the old model is replaced by a new pipeline in which the two separate lifecycles of IIS and ASP.NET are merged into one for greater efficiency. The `ScriptModule` is added to the integrated mode pipeline. The `httpHandler` modifications made in the `system.web` section are duplicated in the `handlers` section of the new section.

This change isn't specific to ASP.NET AJAX, but you should be aware of the validation element, as it can cause confusion. The `validateIntegratedModeConfiguration` option is set to `false`. Setting this value to `false` means that it is not an error to have duplicate entries in the `handler` and `httpHandlers` sections and the `modules` and `httpModules` sections:

```
<system.webServer>
 <validation validateIntegratedModeConfiguration="false"/>
 <modules>
  <add name="ScriptModule" preCondition="integratedMode"
type="System.Web.Handlers.ScriptModule, System.Web.Extensions, Version=3.5.0.0,
Culture=neutral, PublicKeyToken=31bf3856ad364e35"/>
 </modules>
 <handlers>
  <remove name="WebServiceHandlerFactory-Integrated" />
  <add name="ScriptHandlerFactory" verb="*" path="*.asmx"
preCondition="integratedMode"
     type="System.Web.Script.Services.ScriptHandlerFactory,
System.Web.Extensions, Version=3.5.0.0, Culture=neutral,
PublicKeyToken=31bf3856ad364e35"/>
  <add name="ScriptHandlerFactoryAppServices" verb="*"
 path="*_AppService.axd" preCondition="integratedMode"
     type="System.Web.Script.Services.ScriptHandlerFactory,
System.Web.Extensions, Version=3.5.0.0, Culture=neutral,
PublicKeyToken=31bf3856ad364e35"/>
  <add name="ScriptResource" preCondition="integratedMode" verb="GET,HEAD"
path="ScriptResource.axd" type="System.Web.Handlers.ScriptResourceHandler,
System.Web.Extensions, Version=3.5.0.0, Culture=neutral,
PublicKeyToken=31bf3856ad364e35" />
 </handlers>
</system.webServer>
```

The `web.config` template is larger than it used to be as a starting point but has everything necessary to get started and works across several versions of the Web server. One common symptom of a configuration error with the `ScriptResource` handler is an error message in the browser stating that objects in the `Sys` namespace are not defined. When running in debug mode, the error message is more explicit in its explanation that the AJAX Library did not load. This wouldn't typically be associated with deployment, but given the separate definitions for different versions of IIS, it is something to be aware of when moving from test to production environments.

Using Compression for Scripts

Modern browsers have the ability to decompress files, so you can reduce the time needed to download files to the browser by sending them in a compressed format. Text files compress very well. For example, the `MicrosoftAjax.js` file is more than 100K originally, but when compressed, it is reduced to about one third that size. It requires some extra CPU usage on the server to do the compression, but the compressed scripts can be cached on the server, so the processing overhead shouldn't matter much. The client will decompress the file once and then cache it as well, so the impact is minimal and the overall effect can be a benefit to the server and to the client.

Compression of Dynamic Scripts

Scripts embedded as a resource within a dll and extracted by ASP.NET on demand are referred to as dynamic scripts. ASP.NET AJAX supports compressing those scripts as they are extracted from the DLL. Custom controls that use the ScriptManager to access their dynamic scripts also get the benefit of having their JavaScript compressed and cached.

The compression of dynamic scripts is controlled in the `web.config` file. The `enableCompression` and `enableCaching` attributes should be set to `true`:

```
<system.web.extensions>
 <scripting>
  <scriptResourceHandler enableCompression="true" enableCaching="true" />
 </scripting>
</system.web.extensions>
```

Note that there are some tradeoffs in using compression and caching. Using compression without caching will make the server perform the compression work for every request. This can increase the load significantly on the server. However, caching the scripts can increase the memory used by the ASP.NET worker process, putting pressure on the cache and affecting the overall throughput as a result.

On the other hand, the compressed scripts are smaller and thus transmitted more quickly to the browser, freeing up a connection and thread more quickly. Most environments will benefit from allowing the Script Resource Handler to compress and cache scripts, but busy servers need to be monitored to watch out for possible negative impacts to memory or processor usage.

Compression of Static Scripts

IIS can compress static scripts to get the same benefit. In IIS7, JavaScript files are compressed by default. In IIS6, this is not the default. Instead, it has to be enabled, and there are several steps necessary to set it up.

First, use the Internet Services Manager to go to the Property pages for the Web site. On the Services tab, check the Compress static files check box, and specify a directory for the server to use in caching the compressed output. This saves the overhead of recompressing the content after a process restart.

The MMC snap-in does not expose one key setting that should be changed to enable compression of the `.js` files for both standard compression types that are supported. You have to make the change in the IIS6 metabase directly. You can use the `adsutil.vbs` file installed in `\WINNT\System32\Inetpub\AdminScripts`.

To enable IIS to use deflate and gzip compression on .js files, use the following command lines:

```
cscript.exe adsutil.vbs set w3svc/Filters/Compression/DEFLATE/HcFileExtensions "js"
cscript.exe adsutil.vbs set w3svc/Filters/Compression/GZIP/HcFileExtensions "js"
```

Now, IIS will compress static JavaScript files and cache them to disk. However, there is still one other change needed for IIS6. To avoid having compressed scripts cached by proxy servers and gateways and returned to browsers that don't support compression, the cache expiration header is set to a date in the past. When IIS6 was released, the level of support for compression in browsers was still lacking, but now it's safer to assume that the browsers accessing a site have such support. If you leave a backdated expiration date, the browser will request that the AJAX scripts on every page have access to an AJAX-enabled page. I'd rather send 100K of uncompressed script to the browser once and have it cached than send 30K of compressed script on every page request. You can view the parameters being used for compression by using the adsutil script and then modify them to a date you are comfortable with by using a set parameter instead of enum:

```
cscript.exe adsutil.vbs enum w3svc/filters/compression/parameters
```

You should look at the output and consider your application variables before setting a new expiration to ensure that you are picking an appropriate expiration date for your environment.

Consider Using Shared Scripts

High-volume applications make use of edge servers to maximize the use of their hardware. They move lots of static content to a separate server in order to partition the load. The Web server can deliver a lot of static content very fast and with low CPU impact. Multiple applications that all make use of the same set of resources gain an advantage when you corral them in a single place referenced by all applications. This also applies to a lot of ASP.NET AJAX applications on the same server, all serving up the same set of JavaScript files.

The ScriptManager control has a ScriptPath property that can be set to an absolute path to make use of a copy of the scripts shared by multiple applications and directories. This can avoid the impact of many different applications consuming additional memory to cache the scripts and bypasses the need to compress them again.

The ScriptManager uses the ScriptPath as the root location to search for scripts and takes into account the assembly name and version. If you want to cache the scripts in a folder under the root of the Web site, you thus need to copy them from their default location. In earlier releases, they would have been located under C:\Program Files\Microsoft ASP.NET. But in the latest release, they are not installed by default and instead must be downloaded separately from www.asp.net. For example, you could set ScriptPath="/scripts" and then copy the files into C:\InetPub\wwwroot\scripts\System.Web .Extensions\3.5.2121022.8\, assuming your Web root folder is C:\InetPub\wwwroot. In previous releases, the path did not contain a version number for the scripts, but this has been updated to better accommodate any incremental version updates that may occur. This would allow you to keep using a previous version while validating behavior of a service release.

The ScriptManager also includes a new feature in Service Pack 1 that allows for scripts to be combined to minimize overhead. By default, browsers will only open two simultaneous requests back to the original server. When a page contains multiple separate script files, the access to them must be queued to use the two connections..

Don't Change Version Paths

The `ScriptPath` setting of the ScriptManager applies to all of the `ScriptReferences` that it contains. However, the `ScriptReference` has a `Path` property that can override that setting. You may be tempted to override the path directly to put the AJAX scripts in a simpler path without the version, but I recommend against it. The use of the version number identifies the scripts so that servicing and subsequent releases will use a different folder to avoid problems.

If you switch from the dynamic scripts to the static versions, you also need to be aware of a servicing concern. If the ASP.NET team releases an updated version of the scripts, you will need to update your deployed copy in order to get the fix. It will no longer be sufficient to just install the updated `System.Web.Extensions.dll` in the GAC.

> *If you install a new version of* `System.Web.Extensions.dll` *in the GAC and create a new version-coded folder to hold the scripts, you may also want to keep the old dll in the GAC and keep the old scripts in place to service older applications that haven't been updated yet.*

Summary

Deploying ASP.NET AJAX applications is not considered to be overly complex, but there are some pitfalls to be avoided. This is made worse by the fact that development environments are typically different from the final production environment. Configuration changes are typically a necessary part of deployment. Attention to detail and being deliberate about avoiding problems can go a long way in ensuring that the performance and behavior of an application lives up to your expectation.

The Web Deployment project add-in for Visual Web Developer can help in automating a reusable process for moving from development into production. It allows for extensive customization for your unique environment and makes it easy to establish an environment where designers and developers collaborate to produce the application and the automated processes that are employed to move it into production reliably.

The increased use of JavaScript in developing rich Web applications brings some potentially interesting challenges. High-volume applications will need to be monitored and tuned for the absolute best performance. Coalescing script use to a single location for multiple applications can provide a performance benefit. Another potential win is to use the new ScriptManager feature for automatically coalescing several strips into a single client download.

For single applications that deploy to a cluster of Web servers, there are additional configuration concerns. Machine keys need to be synchronized, and you may need to use a back-end database to store session state. ASP.NET doesn't have a native understanding of Web farm environments, but utilizes a provider model that allows data services like session and profile features to be leveraged across servers.

Outside of an ASP.NET application, it is still possible to use the Microsoft AJAX Library. This allows you to use the rich object-oriented approach to writing JavaScript in various environments and to avoid another context switch for the developer, using multiple libraries to produce rich Internet applications.

ASP.NET AJAX Resources

Microsoft ASP.NET AJAX official page: www.asp.net/ajax

ASP.NET AJAX Control Toolkit: www.asp.net/ajax/ajaxcontroltoolkit

ASP.NET AJAX Control Toolkit Samples: www.asp.net/ajax/ajaxcontroltoolkit/samples

ASP.NET AJAX Documentation: www.asp.net/AJAX/Documentation

ASP.NET AJAX Forums: http://forums.asp.net/default.aspx?GroupID=34

MIX Videos: http://sessions.visitmix.com

Author Blogs

Bill Evjen: www.geekswithblogs.net/evjen

Matt Gibbs: http://blogs.msdn.com/mattgi

Dan Wahlin: http://weblogs.asp.net/dwahlin

Dave Reed: http://weblogs.asp.net/infinitiesloop

Index

H

N

Name, 157
namespaces
  AJAX Library, 109–112
  controls, 345
  DLL, 109
  .NET Framework, 109
  scope, 111–112
name-value pairs, 289
Navigate, 189
.NET, 93
  AJAX, 11
  Booleans, 78
  client-side, 71–74
  JavaScript, 349
  state management, 436
.NET Framework, 19
  AJAX Library, 107
  CodeDOM, 99
  namespaces, 109
  numbers, 127
  strings, 127
.NET Reflector, 206
Netscape, 8
networking, AJAX, 297–327
new, 297
NoBot control, 260–262
nonImplemented (message), 458
NotImplementedException, 62
null, 85–86
  redirectUrl, 166
null value, 287
  variables, 9
num, 95
Numbers, 231
numbers
  adding, 80
  AJAX Library, 127–129

  JavaScript, 8, 77
  .NET Framework, 127
numeric characters, 235
NumericUpDownExtender, 238–239

O

object-oriented programming (OOP), 107, 109
objects, 10
ODBC, 441
Off, 438
OffsetX, 232
OffsetY, 232
OkcontrolID, 220
_onButtonClick, 356
OnCancelScript, 220
OnClick, 210, 329, 332, 333
_onClick, 356
OnClick, **211**
OnClientActiveTabChanged, 264
OnClientClick, 228
OnClientClick ( ), 219
OnClientResize, 243
OnClientResizeBegin, 243
OnClientResizing, 243
OnGenerateChallengeAndResponse, 261
OnHoverOut, 210, 330, 332, 333
OnHoverOver, 210, 329, 332, 333
OnLoad, 210, 330, 332, 333
OnLoad, **332**
_onMethodComplete, 356
_onMethodError, 356, 364–365
OnMouseOut, 210, 330, 332, 333
_onMouseOut, 356, 361
OnMouseOut, **337**
OnMouseOver, 210, 330, 332, 333
_onMouseOver, 353, 356, 361
OnMouseOver, **336**
OnOkScript, 220